Windows NT™ Messages

Microsoft®

WINDOWS NT RESOURCE KIT

Microsoft PRESS®

For Windows NT Workstation and Windows NT Server Version 3.5

PUBLISHED BY
Microsoft Press
A Division of Microsoft Corporation
One Microsoft Way
Redmond, Washington 98052-6399

Library of Congress Cataloging-in-Publication Data
Windows NT messages / by Microsoft Corporation. -- 2nd ed.
p. cm. -- (Microsoft Windows NT resource kit for Windows NT workstation and Windows NT server version 3.5 ; 3)
Includes index.
ISBN 1-55615-654-5 (v. 3)
1. Operating systems (Computers) 2. Microsoft Windows NT.
I. Microsoft Corporation. II. Series.
QA76.76.O63M52455 1995 vol. 3
005.4'469--dc20 94-42919
CIP
r95

Printed and bound in the United States of America.

3 4 5 6 7 8 9 QMQM 0 9 8 7 6 5

Distributed to the book trade in Canada by Macmillan of Canada, a division of Canada Publishing Corporation.

A CIP catalogue record for this book is available from the British Library.

Microsoft Press books are available through booksellers and distributors worldwide. For further information about international editions, contact your local Microsoft Corporation office. Or contact Microsoft Press International directly at fax (206) 936-7329.

This book is dedicated to the Windows NT developers who gave so generously of their time, despite imminent beta and final deadlines, to work with us, and our own imminent deadlines, to improve the clarity and usefulness of the messages for both technical support people and individual users. And all this before the product shipped!

Contributors to this book include the following:

Technical Writers:
Sharon Carroll, Peggy Etchevers, Eric Hough, Sharon Kay, Mark Williams, and Stephen Wood

Database Designer and System Administrator:
Cary E. Reinstein

Team Manager:
Chris Kagen

Technical Editors:
Karin Carter, Sonia Marie Moore, and Sharon Tighe

Production Team:
Karye Cattrell, Yong Ok Chung, Evelyn Jarosz, and Lori Robinson

Graphic Designer:
Sue Wyble

Graphic Artists:
Gwen Grey, Elizabeth Read, and Stephen Winard

Contents

Welcome

Welcome to *Microsoft Windows NT Resource Kit Volume 3: Windows NT Messages* for the Microsoft® Windows NT™ Workstation and Microsoft Windows NT Server operating system, a guide to error and system-information messages.

This introductory section covers the following topics:

- A description of the information provided in this book
- How to set up, start, and quit the Messages database
- How to maintain the Messages database

About This Book

This is the printed guide to most of the error and system-information messages generated by the Windows NT operating system. Some messages generated by applications or device drivers have also been included. An online database with additional messages is also provided and includes a run-time version of Microsoft Access® with a customized graphical user interface.

This book and its accompanying database are not intended as an exclusive reference. You may find other sources, such as online Help, more immediately helpful for network error messages. If, for example, you encounter one in the command prompt window, you can find help for the network problem by typing **net helpmsg** and the message identification number.

Context-sensitive as well as procedural Help is provided on using the database and its graphical user interface. If you have any questions about an option or command, select the item and then press F1 to display Help information. A glossary of common terms used in messages, and some possible user actions, are included in Help as well as in this book.

Chapter 1, "Common Message Terms and User Actions," provides in-depth discussions, including both definitions and examples, of many technical terms that you may encounter in messages. The printed book also contains some additional reference information that is not available online. For example, Chapter 2, "Windows NT Executive Messages," discusses in detail the various types of messages generated by the Windows NT Executive, and categorizes them by their type and severity and also by possible user action. It also includes basic information on how to set up and use the Windows NT debugger program. Chapter 3, "Network Reference Tables," contains two numerically ordered lists of network error messages.

Chapter 4, "Message Reference," contains the error and system-information messages, which have been organized as follows:

- Messages are presented in alphabetical order. However, messages that begin with a replaceable parameter are alphabetized at the beginning of the list by the variable name used to replace that parameter. For a complete list of the variable names used in the Messages database, see the following section, "Variable Names List."
- Variable names appear between arrow brackets in the online Messages database and in italics in the printed book. Otherwise, the text is formatted the same in the book as in the online Messages database, which reflects the formatting used in the on-screen messages.
- Messages are normally followed by a description of the circumstances that might generate the message and, if appropriate or needed, by a suggested user action.
- Some self-explanatory or simple messages are available only in the online Messages database and not in the book. Most status messages that require no user action are not documented.
- Where possible, each message is associated with one or more components of the operating system, such as Notepad or File Manager.
- Network messages are included in the alphabetical list along with their network message ID number. Two numerically ordered lists of network messages are also provided in Chapter 3, "Network Reference Tables."

Variable Names List

If you cannot find the message that appears on your screen in Chapter 4, "Message Reference," check at the beginning of the list. The message may begin with a replaceable parameter. Variable names, which are placeholders for the specific word or number that appears in the message, are used as substitutes for replaceable parameters. They appear in italics in the printed book and, when a message starts with one, you will find it alphabetized separately at the beginning of the list. For example, if the book says, "*Time* is not a valid specification for minutes," the message that appears on your screen will contain the actual time in minutes.

The following is a list of all the variable names used in the Messages database as substitutes for replaceable parameters:

address	*date*	*name*	*text*
application	*drive letter*	*number*	*time*
code	*file system*	*parameter*	*user name*
command	*filename*	*path*	
computer name	*group*	*systemroot*	

Product Support Suggestions

Sometimes, the only suggested user action is to obtain help from your own or another technical support group. In that case, we suggest you collect the following information before contacting technical support:

- The type of hardware that you are using, including networking hardware, if applicable
- The exact content of the message that appears on the screen
- A description of what happened and what you were doing when the problem occurred

Microsoft offers a variety of support options to help you get the most from your Microsoft product. For information on these options, please refer to the "Microsoft Support Services" section in the "Welcome" chapter of your *Installation Guide*.

Setting Up, Starting, and Quitting the Messages Database

Use the Setup program (SETUP.EXE) located on the *Windows NT Resource Kit* compact disc (CD) to install the Microsoft Windows NT Messages database on your own computer for individual use or on a network server for shared use. If you want to wait and install it at a later time, you may use a separate Messages database Setup program that is located under the \WINNTMSG directory.

▶ To set up the Messages database

1. Start Windows NT.

   If you want to share the Messages database with other users, be sure to log on as the Administrator before installing the database.

2. Insert the Windows NT Resource Kit compact disc in the CD-ROM drive.
3. In Program Manager, choose Run from the File menu.

   The Run dialog box appears.

4. Type *CD-ROM drive letter*:**\winntmsg\setup** in the Command Line box.
5. Choose the OK button.
6. Follow the instructions on screen to complete Setup.

   If you want to share the Messages database with other users, specify a path to a network server when Setup asks where you want to install it.

   When it asks if you want to join an existing workgroup, choose the No button unless you have already set one up on the network. You can use the Change WorkGroup icon to do that later.

After installing the files you need, the Setup program creates a Microsoft Windows NT Messages program group and puts the following icons in the program group: Microsoft Windows NT Messages, Compact Database, Change WorkGroup, and Readme.

Note If you have installed the Messages database on a Windows NT file system (NTFS) partition, use the File Manager Security menu to ensure that all users have Change (RWXD) permission for the directory and its contents.

▶ To start the Messages database from Program Manager

1. In Program Manager, open the Microsoft Windows NT Messages program group.
2. Double-click the Microsoft Windows NT Messages icon.

   The Messages startup screen appears within the Microsoft Access main application window.

▶ **To start the Messages database from the Windows NT command line**

1. In Program Manager, open the Main program group.
2. Double-click the Command Prompt icon.
3. At the command line, change to the directory containing the database, which could be either on your own computer or on a network server.
4. Type **msarn110 winntmsg.mdb**

   The Messages startup screen appears within the Microsoft Access main application window.

▶ **To quit the Messages database**

- From the Microsoft Access File menu, choose Exit to quit the Messages database and Microsoft Access.

Note If you are running the Messages database with the full Microsoft Access program, rather than the run-time version supplied with Windows NT, you can choose Close to close only the database form. You can then use any feature of the full Microsoft Access program to work with your Messages data.

Running the Database Under Windows NT

Detailed procedures on how to use the Find, Notes, and Print buttons on the Messages form to work in the database are provided in the online Help files that accompany this database. They include information on the following topics:

- Searching for information in the Messages database
- Using a variable as a search criterion
- Initiating a new search
- Adding and removing notes to the Messages database
- Setting up to print
- Printing a database report

Running the Database Under MS-DOS with Windows

To use the Messages database on a computer that has MS-DOS® with Microsoft Windows™ 3.1 or later, you need the following:

- IBM-compatible personal computer with an 80386 or higher processor (including 80386sx)
- Hard disk with 4.5 to 5 megabytes (MB) of free space
- Microsoft Mouse or other compatible pointing device (optional)
- VGA or higher, or compatible display
- MS-DOS version 5 or later

You can use the same *Windows NT Resource Kit* CD to set up and run the Messages database on MS-DOS with Windows as you did to run it under Windows NT.

Maintaining the Database

Microsoft Windows NT Messages provides functionality for maintaining your database and the Messages table. You can perform regular backups of both the database and the Messages table. You can also compact the database whenever you notice a marked increase in the file size, as displayed in File Manager, after adding notes or running search queries.

Backing Up the Database

Backups protect you against the loss of your data and the information that describes your data. If you make unwanted, irreversible changes to a database, you can always return to the most recent backup copy.

Important When backing up your database, you should also create a backup of the system database file, SYSTEM.MDA, which stores the default user options and security account information. If your SYSTEM.MDA file is lost or damaged, you will not be able to start the Messages database. If you do not have a backup of that file, you can copy the SYSTEM.MDA file from the *Windows NT Resource Kit* CD to your Messages directory.

▶ To back up the entire Messages database

1. Close the Messages database and Microsoft Access by choosing Exit from the Microsoft Access File menu.

   In a multiuser environment, make sure that all other users have also closed the database. You can check to see who is connected to your computer by using the Server option in Control Panel.

2. Using the backup method of your choice (such as File Manager, backup software, or the **copy** command), copy the WINNTMSG.MDB file to another file, such as WINNTBAK.MDB, on a backup medium such as tape, floppy disk, or another network drive.

▶ To restore the Messages database from a backup copy

- Copy the backup version of the WINNTMSG.MDB file (WINNTBAK.MDB) to your database directory.

  In a multiuser environment, first make sure that all other users have closed the database. You can check to see who is connected to your computer by using the Server option in Control Panel.

After having backed up the entire database at least once to a WINNTBAK.MDB file, you now have the option of just backing up the Messages table while the Messages database is still open.

▶ To back up and restore just the Messages table

1. If you do not want to close the Messages database, choose the Backup button on the Messages form (or the Backup command under the Microsoft Access File menu) to back up only the messages data, including notes, to a previously created WINNTBAK.MDB file.

2. To restore the Messages table data, choose the Restore command on the Microsoft Access File menu.

Compacting the Database

Because the database adds your notes and also keeps a temporary record of your search queries, it can gradually increase in size. Periodically, you should compact your database to make the file smaller.

When you compact a database, the data and security permission settings from your original file are copied to a temporary file and then copied back over the original one, WINNTMSG.MDB. Before compacting, you should make sure that you have enough storage space on your disk (at least an additional 4 MB of free space) for both the original and the temporary compacted version of the database. The compacting operation will fail if you do not have enough storage space.

▶ **To compact the Messages database**

1. Close the Messages database.

   In a multiuser environment, make sure that all other users have also closed the database. You can check to see who is connected to your computer by using the Server option in Control Panel.

2. In the Microsoft Windows NT Messages program group, double-click the Compact Database icon.

CHAPTER 1

Common Message Terms and User Actions

This chapter goes beyond providing simple definitions of terms, and includes in-depth information and many suggested user actions or examples wherever appropriate. The terms are also defined with regard to how they relate to Windows NT messages. Many of these terms are very technical and do not appear in the *Windows NT Workstation System Guide* or *Windows NT Server System Guide.* Those terms that do may be slightly altered here to provide more information for understanding how they are used in messages.

Reading the information presented here should make subsequent technical discussions more understandable, both in reading this book and talking with technical support people.

access control entry (ACE)
An entry in an access control list (ACL). Each access control entry defines the protection or auditing to be applied to a file or other object for a specific user or group of users.

access control list (ACL)
The part of a security descriptor that enumerates both the protections to accessing and the auditing of that accessing that are applied to an object. The owner of an object has discretionary access control of the object and can change the object's ACL to allow or disallow others access to the object. Access control lists are ordered lists of access control entries (ACEs).

access right
A permission granted to a process to manipulate a particular object in a particular way (for example, by calling a service). Different object types support different access rights, which are stored in an object's access control list (ACL).

access token, or security token

An object that uniquely identifies a user who has logged on. An access token is attached to all the user's processes and contains the user's security ID (SID), the SIDs of any groups to which the user belongs, any privileges that the user owns, the default owner of any objects that the user's processes create, and the default access control list (ACL) to be applied to any objects that the user's processes create. *See also* privilege.

access violation

An attempt to carry out a memory operation that is not allowed by Windows NT memory management. An access violation has nothing to do with the Security Manager's checking of User-mode access rights to objects.

There are four basic kinds of actions that can cause access violations:

- Attempting an invalid operation, such as writing to a read-only buffer
- Attempting to access memory beyond the limit of the current program's address space (also known as a "length violation")
- Attempting to access a page to which the system forbids access. (For example, code is not allowed to run in the low-order 64K of the Windows NT User-mode address.)
- Attempting to access a page that is currently resident but dedicated to the use of an Executive component. (For example, User-mode code is not allowed access to a page that the Kernel is using.)

address space, or virtual address space

The set of addresses available for a process's threads to use. In Windows NT, every process has a unique address space of 4 GB.

algorithm

In its most general sense, an algorithm is any set of instructions that can be followed to carry out a particular task. In computer usage, an algorithm is a set of instructions within a program. If, for example, in the Network option in Control Panel, you encounter a message that says that "A binding algorithm failed," this means that the program was unable to execute a set of instructions designed to bind together elements necessary for a functional network configuration.

allocation units

See clusters.

anonymous-level security token

The type of security token used when a server impersonates a client. If, when the client calls the server, the client specifies an anonymous impersonation mode, the server cannot access any of the client's identification information, such as its security identifier (SID) or privileges. The server will have to use an anonymous-level security token when representing the client in successive operations. *See also* access token.

application programming interface (API)

A set of routines that an application program uses to request and carry out lower-level services performed by the operating system.

For example, programming code is built using a series of function calls or routines that perform certain actions. Suppose that every workday you got up at 7 A.M., showered, dressed, fixed and ate breakfast, brushed your teeth, and then drove to work. If you were really a computer and never deviated from this pattern, a programmer could write a program for you called DAILY_ROUTINE that would perform these actions automatically. So, instead of having to specify each action, the programmer could just write DAILY_ROUTINE in the code, and the actions would be carried out. Thus, in this example, DAILY_ROUTINE would constitute an API.

authentication package

A subsystem that verifies that the logon information that a user supplies matches the information stored in a security database.

AUTOEXEC.NT and CONFIG.NT files

Windows NT configures the MS-DOS environment by reading the AUTOEXEC.BAT file when you log on, and by reading the AUTOEXEC.NT and CONFIG.NT files when you start an application in a new command window. The AUTOEXEC.NT and CONFIG.NT files are the Windows NT versions of AUTOEXEC.BAT and CONFIG.SYS.

When you log on to Windows NT, the path and environment variables stored in the AUTOEXEC.BAT file are appended to the Windows NT path and environment settings. Because this portion of the operating environment is established at logon, the values set for the path and environment variables are available to each application you use. If you change these values, you must log off from and then log on to Windows NT again so that the changes take effect.

When you start an MS-DOS-based or a 16-bit Windows-based application in a new command window, Windows NT reads the CONFIG.NT and AUTOEXEC.NT files to configure the environment for the application. If, for example, you change an application's driver in the CONFIG.NT file, restarting the application puts the change into effect. You can edit these files just as you would CONFIG.SYS and AUTOEXEC.BAT. The files are located in the C:*systemroot*\\SYSTEM32 directory.

bad-sector mapping

A technique used by the NTFS file system to handle write errors. When an error is detected, the file system takes a free block, writes the data to that block instead of to the bad block, and updates a bad-block map. A copy of this map is written to disk.

binding

A series of bound paths from the upper-layer network services and protocols to the lowest layer of adapter card device drivers. Each network component can be bound to one or more network components above it or below it to make the component's services available to any component that can benefit from them.

boot partition

The boot partition for Windows NT is the volume, formatted for either a Windows NT file system (NTFS), file allocation table (FAT), or high-performance file system (HPFS), that has the Windows NT operating system and its support files. The boot partition can be (but does not have to be) the same as the system partition. It cannot be part of a stripe set or volume set, but it can be part of a mirror set. *See also* system partition.

circular dependency

A dependency in which an action that appears later in a chain is contingent upon an earlier action. For example, three services (A, B, and C) are linked. A is dependent upon B to start. B is dependent upon C to start. A circular dependency results when C is dependent upon A to start. *See also* dependency.

clusters, or allocation units

In data storage, a cluster is a disk-storage unit consisting of a fixed number of sectors (storage segments on the disk) that the operating system uses to read or write information to; typically, a cluster consists of two to eight sectors, each of which holds a certain number of bytes (characters).

A formatted disk is divided into sectors, and a cluster is a set of contiguous sectors allocated to files as a single unit. This clustering of sectors reduces disk fragmentation but may result in wasted space within the cluster.

Under both the NTFS and FAT file systems, the size of a cluster is based upon the size of the partition. However, with NTFS, you can override this with a switch, which forces a smaller (or larger) cluster size. Under FAT, the size of a cluster cannot be changed; the larger the partition, the more sectors you will have per cluster. Therefore, under FAT, you can have 1, 2, 4, 8, 16, 32, and 64 sectors per cluster.

CONFIG.NT files

See AUTOEXEC.NT and CONFIG.NT files.

control set

All Windows NT startup-related data that is not computed during startup is saved in one of the Registry hives. This startup data is organized into control sets, each of which contains a complete set of parameters for starting up devices and services. The Registry always contains at least two control sets, each of which contains information about all the configurable options for the computer: the current control set and the LastKnownGood control set. *See also* LastKnownGood (LKG) control set.

corrupted data

Data in memory or on disk that has been unintentionally changed, thereby altering or obliterating its meaning.

current control set

The control set that was used most recently to start the computer and that contains any changes made to the startup information during the current session. *See also* LastKnownGood (LKG) control set.

cyclic redundancy check (CRC)

A procedure used on disk drives to ensure that the data written to a sector is read correctly later.

This procedure is also used in checking for errors in data transmission. The procedure is known as a redundancy check because each data transmission includes not only data but extra (redundant) error-checking values. The sending device generates a number based on the data to be transmitted and sends its result along with the data to the receiving device. The receiving device repeats the same calculation after transmission. If both devices obtain the same result, it is assumed that the transmission is error-free.

deadlock condition

A run-time error condition that occurs when two threads of execution are blocked, each waiting to acquire a resource that the other holds, and both unable to continue running.

debugger breakpoints

Set by the user of the Kernel debugger (KD) before running the Windows NT Executive, a breakpoint is put into the Executive code at an instruction. Then, when the Executive is run, if and when that instruction is executed, execution is stopped, and the current values of registers and flags are displayed. KD breakpoints are "sticky" in the sense that they remain in the program until explicitly removed. It is possible for code to have breakpoints in it that are never explicitly removed. *See also* Kernel debugger.

dependency

A situation in which one action must take place before another can happen. For example, if action A does not occur, then action D cannot occur.

Some Windows NT drivers have dependencies on other drivers or groups of drivers. For example, driver A will not load unless some driver from the G group loads first. *See also* circular dependency.

domain

For Windows NT Server, a collection of computers that share a common accounts database and security policy. Each domain has a unique name.

A set of servers and workstations grouped together for efficiency and security, and the basic administrative unit in Windows NT Server. A network can be divided, for example, into domains by department, workgroup, or building floor.

Domains keep large networks manageable. For example, users displaying a list of servers will see only the servers for their domain. But they can still access resources on servers in any domain if they have been granted the necessary rights.

domain controller

For a Windows NT Server domain, this refers to the server that maintains the security policy and the master database for a domain and, along with backup domain controllers, authenticates domain logons.

down level

A term that refers to earlier operating systems, such as Windows for Workgroups or LAN Manager, that can still interoperate with Windows NT Workstation or Windows NT Server.

dynamic-link library (DLL)

A library of routines that User-mode applications access through ordinary procedure calls. The operating system automatically modifies the user's executable image to point to DLL procedures at run time. That way, the code for the procedures does not have to be included in the user's executable image.

enumeration operation

The counting, accessing, or listing of an entire set of similar objects. When the last object in the set has been counted, accessed, or listed, the enumeration operation is complete.

error logging

The process by which errors that cannot readily be corrected by the majority of end users are written to a file instead of being displayed on the screen. System administrators, support technicians, and users can use this log file to monitor the condition of the hardware in a Windows NT computer, to tune the configuration of the computer for better performance, and to debug problems as they occur.

exception

A synchronous error condition resulting from the execution of a particular computer instruction. Exceptions can be either hardware-detected errors, such as division by zero, or software-detected errors, such as a guard-page violation.

Executive

The Executive is the part of the Windows NT operating system that runs in Kernel mode. *Kernel mode* is a privileged processor mode in which a thread has access to system memory and to hardware. (In contrast, *User mode* is a nonprivileged processor mode in which a thread can only access system resources by calling system services.) The Windows NT Executive provides process structure, thread scheduling, interprocess communication, memory management, object management, object security, interrupt processing, I/O capabilities, and networking.

The Windows NT Kernel is the part of the Windows NT Executive that manages the processor. It performs thread scheduling and dispatching, interrupt and exception handling, and multiprocessor synchronization. It also provides primitive objects to the Windows NT Executive, which uses them to create User-mode objects.

Executive messages

Two types of character-mode messages occur when the Windows NT Kernel detects an inconsistent condition from which it cannot recover: STOP messages and hardware-malfunction messages.

Character-mode STOP messages are always displayed on a full character-mode screen rather than in a Windows-mode message box. They are also uniquely identified by a hexadecimal number and a symbolic string, as in the following example:

```
*** STOP: 0x00000001
APC_INDEX_MISMATCH
```

The content of the symbolic string may suggest, to a trained technician, the part of the Kernel that detected the condition from which there was no recourse but to stop. However, keep in mind that the cause may actually be in another part of the system.

Character-mode hardware-malfunction messages are caused by a hardware condition detected by the processor. The first one or two lines of a hardware-malfunction message may differ depending on which company manufactured the computer. However, these lines always convey the same idea, as shown in the following example for an x86-based computer:

```
Hardware malfunction.
Call your hardware vendor for support.
```

The additional lines in each manufacturer's message screen also differ in format and content.

The Executive displays a Windows-mode STATUS message box when it detects conditions within a process (generally, an application) that you should know about. STATUS messages can be divided into three types:

- System-information messages. All you need to do is read the information in the message box and choose the OK button. The Kernel will continue running the process or thread.
- Warning messages. Some advise you to take an action that will enable the Kernel to keep running the process or thread. Others warn you that, although the process or thread will continue running, the results may not be correct.
- Application-termination messages. These warn you that the Kernel is about to terminate either a process or a thread.

For an in-depth discussion of the these messages, see Chapter 2, "Windows NT Executive Messages."

extended attribute
Windows NT FAT files have four basic parts: the data, the file system attributes (such as creation time and date, and FAT attributes), the security descriptors, and the extended attributes (EAs). EAs make up the set of extended information about a file, and are structured as name/value pairs. Typical Windows NT system uses of EAs are actions such as storing the icon of an executable image or indicating that the file is a symbolic link.

extended partition
This is created from free space on a hard disk and can be subpartitioned into zero or more logical drives. The free space in an extended partition can also be used to create volume sets or other kinds of volumes for fault-tolerance purposes. Only one of the four partitions allowed per physical disk can be an extended partition, and no primary partition needs to be present to create an extended partition.

file control block (FCB)
In MS-DOS, a 36-byte block of memory that contains all the information MS-DOS needs to know about an open file, such as the filename, what drive it is on, current file size, and date and time of creation.

globally unique identifier (GUID)
See universally unique identifier (UUID).

guard-page protection
The Windows NT Virtual Memory Manager can put a guard page at the end of a data structure, such as a dynamic array, and generate a warning message when a User-mode thread accesses the guard-page memory. The User-mode process can respond appropriately, for example, by extending the array.

handle

In general, a unique identifier (often an integer) by which a client refers to an object in the Windows NT operating system. Clients call servers to get a handle to an object on which the client wants to operate. Then the client sends requests for operations to the object, referring to the object by its handle. The server actually does the operation. This ensures that the client does not operate on the object directly.

In the Registry, each of the first-level key names begins with HKEY_ to indicate to software developers that this is a handle that can be read by a program. A handle is a value used to provide a unique identifier for a resource so that a program can access it.

hexadecimal

A base-16 number system that consists of the digits 0 through 9 and the uppercase and lowercase letters A (equivalent to decimal 10) through F (equivalent to decimal 15).

high memory area (HMA)

A 64K memory block located just above the 1 MB address in a Virtual DOS Machine (VDM). This memory becomes visible when the A20 address line is turned on, enabling 21-bit addressing in the VDM.

hive

The Registry is divided into parts called hives, so named as an analogy to the cellular structure of a beehive. A hive is a part of the Registry that maps to a file on your hard disk. Each user profile is a separate hive, which means that it is also a separate file. Therefore, an administrator can copy a user profile as a file, and view, repair, or copy entries using Registry Editor on another computer.

hot key

In a user interface, hot keys provide an alternative to the mouse for manipulating interface objects. For example, instead of using the mouse, you can press the key combination ALT+F to open the File menu on the menu bar. ALT+F is a hot key.

impersonation

The ability of a thread in one process to take on the security identity of a thread in another process and to perform operations on the other thread's behalf. Impersonation is used by the Windows NT environment subsystems and network services to access remote resources on behalf of client applications.

.INF file

One of a set of files used by the Setup program, either during Windows NT installation or during maintenance Setup, or both. An .INF file generally contains a script for Setup to follow, along with configuration data that ends up in the Registry.

input/output control (IOCTL)

An IOCTL command enables a program to communicate directly with a device driver. This is done, for example, by sending a string of control information recognized by the driver. None of the information passed from the program to the device driver is sent to the device itself (in other words, the control string sent to a printer driver is not displayed on the printer).

installable file system (IFS)

A file system that can be loaded into the operating system dynamically. Windows NT can support multiple installable file systems at one time, including the file allocation table (FAT) file system, the high-performance file system (HPFS), the Windows NT file system (NTFS), and the CD-ROM file system (CDFS). Windows NT automatically determines the format of a storage medium, and reads and writes files in the correct format.

interrupt

An asynchronous operating system condition that disrupts normal execution and transfers control to an interrupt handler. Interrupts can be issued by both software and hardware devices requiring service from the processor. When software issues an interrupt, it calls an interrupt service routine (ISR). When hardware issues an interrupt, it signals an interrupt request (IRQ) line.

interrupt request level (IRQL)

A ranking of interrupts by priority. A processor has an interrupt request level (IRQL) setting that threads can raise or lower. Interrupts that occur at or below the processor's IRQL setting are masked, whereas interrupts that occur above the processor's IRQL setting are not. Software interrupts are almost always lower priority than hardware interrupts.

I/O bus

A hardware path inside a computer that is used for transferring information to and from the processor and various input and output devices.

Kernel

The Windows NT Kernel is the part of the Windows NT Executive that manages the processor. It performs thread scheduling and dispatching, interrupt and exception handling, and multiprocessor synchronization. It also provides primitive objects to the Windows NT Executive, which uses them to create User-mode objects.

Kernel debugger

The Windows NT Kernel debugger (KD) is a 32-bit application that is used to debug the Kernel and device drivers, and to log the events leading up to a Windows NT Executive STOP, STATUS, or hardware-malfunction message.

The Kernel debugger runs on another Windows NT host computer that is connected to your Windows NT target computer. The two computers send debugging (troubleshooting) information back and forth through a communications port that must be running at the same baud rate on each computer. *See also* debugger breakpoints; system debugger, and WINDBG.EXE.

Kernel mode

See Executive.

keyword

A special type of command parameter that includes a value. The syntax of the "width" keyword illustrates this: width=40.

LastKnownGood (LKG) control set

The most recent control set that correctly started the system and resulted in a successful startup. The control set is saved as the LKG control set when you have a successful logon.

A copy of the control set used to start the system is also stored as the Clone subkey in the Registry. At startup time, the Service Control Manager copies the Clone subkey to the LastKnownGood control set before any new changes are made to the control set. This helps to ensure that the computer always contains a working control set. *See also* current control set.

local security authority (LSA)

A component of the Windows NT security system that maintains all aspects of local security on a system. This collection of information is known as the local security policy. The local security policy identifies, among other things, the following: domains trusted to authenticate logon attempts, who may access the system, how they may access it (locally, from the network, or as a service), who is assigned privileges, and what security auditing is to be performed.

mapped I/O, or mapped file I/O

This is file I/O that is performed by reading and writing to virtual memory that is backed by a file.

memory control block (MCB)

MS-DOS organizes available memory as a pool of blocks that are maintained as a chain (or linked list). The memory control block (MCB) occupies the bottom 16 bytes of each memory block and, among other things, points to the next memory block in the chain. If a memory control block is corrupted, MS-DOS cannot find the next block in the chain and does not know which memory blocks have been allocated and which have not.

mounting a volume

Finding a file system that recognizes the format of a volume, and associating the file system with the volume. Windows NT does this automatically the first time a program accesses a volume (or, for other forms of removable media such as floppy disks or CD-ROMs, each time the user reinserts the floppy disk or CD into a drive and performs I/O on it). A volume must be mounted before I/O operations can be done on it.

named pipe

An interprocess communication mechanism that enables one process to send data to another local or remote process. *See also* pipe.

network control block (NCB)

A block of sequential data of fixed length. This data includes an operation code that indicates the operation to be performed, and elements that indicate the status of the operation. *See also* opcode.

network transport

This can be either a particular layer of the OSI reference model between the Network Layer and the Session Layer, or a communications protocol between two different computers on a network.

object

A single run-time instance of a Windows NT-defined object type. It contains data that can be manipulated only by using a set of services provided for objects of its type.

In Windows NT Performance Monitor, an object is a standard mechanism for identifying and using a system resource. Objects are created to represent individual processes, sections of shared memory, and physical devices. Performance Monitor groups counters by object type. Each object type can also have several instances. For example, the Processor object type will have multiple instances if a system has multiple processors. The Physical Disk object type has two instances if a system has two disks. Some object types (such as Memory and Server) do not have instances.

opcode

Operation code; a code, usually a number, that specifies an operation to be performed. An opcode is often the first component in a contiguous block of data; it indicates how other data in the block should be interpreted. *See also* network control block.

paging file, or swap file

A system file that contains the contents of virtual pages that have been temporarily removed from physical memory by the Virtual Memory Manager.

With virtual memory under Windows NT, some of the program code and other information are kept in RAM, while other information is temporarily swapped to a virtual-memory paging file. When that information is required again, Windows NT pulls it back into RAM and, if necessary, swaps other information to virtual memory. This activity is invisible, although you might notice that your hard disk is working. The resulting benefit is that you can run more programs at one time than your system's RAM would usually allow. *See also* virtual memory.

parameter

Parameters are used in commands entered at the Windows NT command prompt to customize that particular use of the command. For example, the MS-DOS **copy** command has two parameters: the path to the file to copy and the path to where the copy will be put. These two parameter values could be any valid path; by changing these each time you use the **copy** command, you are customizing the command.

partition

A portion of a physical disk that functions as though it were a physically separate unit. You can use a partitioning program, such as FDISK for the MS-DOS and OS/2® operating systems and Disk Administrator for Windows NT, to create these unformatted units. You must then use the **format** command (either from the command prompt or from within Disk Administrator) to format them for use with a specific file system. A partition is usually referred to as either a primary or an extended partition. *See also* volume.

partition table

A structure on a disk that the operating system uses to divide a disk into logical divisions called partitions, which can then be formatted to a specific file system. Primary partitions are defined by a data entry in the main partition table of a hard disk. Extended partitions are defined by a nondata entry in the main partition table.

permission

A rule associated with an object (usually a directory, file, or printer) in the form of a discretionary access control list (DACL) that is used to regulate which users or groups can have access to the object and in what manner. You can set file and directory permissions only on drives formatted to use the Windows NT File System (NTFS). *See also* right.

pipe

An interprocess communication mechanism. Writing to and reading from a pipe is much like writing to and reading from a file, except that the two processes are actually using a shared memory segment to communicate data. *See also* named pipe.

primary partition

A portion of a physical disk that can be marked as active for use by an operating system. Active means that the POST (power-on self-test) routine can locate a boot sector on the partition. There can be up to four primary partitions (or up to three if there is already an extended partition) per physical disk. A primary partition cannot be subpartitioned.

privilege

The representation of most user rights in access tokens. An example of one is the backup privilege. Holders of that privilege are allowed to bypass file-system security. In a secure system, not all users will have that privilege. *See also* access token.

privileged instruction

Processor-privileged instructions have access to system memory and the hardware.

process

A logical division of labor in an operating system.

A Windows NT process is created when a program runs. A process can be either an application (such as Microsoft Word or Corel® Draw), a service (such as Event Log or Computer Browser), or a subsystem (such as POSIX). In Windows NT, it comprises a virtual address space, an executable program, one or more threads of execution, some portion of the user's resource quotas, and the system resources that the operating system has allocated to the process's threads. A process is implemented as an object. *See also* object.

Registry

A secure, unified database that stores application configuration data, hardware configuration data (such as device-driver configuration data, and network protocol and adapter card settings), and user data in a hierarchical form for a Windows NT Workstation or Windows NT Server computer.

Registry key

The configuration data in the Registry is stored in a hierarchical form, and keys are the building blocks of this hierarchy. In the Registry, there are four top-level keys that contain per-computer and per-user databases. Each key can contain data items, called value entries, and can also contain additional subkeys. In the Registry structure, keys are analogous to directories, and the value entries are analogous to files. *See also* value entries.

remote procedure call (RPC)

A message-passing facility that enables a distributed application to call services available on various computers in a network without regard to their locations. Remote network operations are handled automatically. RPC provides a procedural, rather than a transport-centered, view of networked operations.

remote procedure call (RPC) binding

A logical connection between the client and server, or the process by which the client establishes a logical connection to the server.

remote procedure call (RPC) connection

A transport-level virtual circuit between the client and server. The RPC run time establishes the circuit when the client binds to the server interface instance. Connections are not visible to the client. A client may have more than one connection to the server.

remote procedure call (RPC) endpoint

An endpoint identifies a specific server instance (or address space) on a host. The format of the endpoint depends on the transport protocol used. There are well-known endpoints and dynamic endpoints. Well-known endpoints are registered in the name service database. Dynamic endpoints are assigned to server instances at run time.

remote procedure call (RPC) protocol sequence

A character string that identifies the network protocols used to establish a relationship between a client and a server. The protocol sequence contains a set of options that the RPC run time must know about to establish a binding. These options include the RPC protocol, the format of the network address, and the transport protocol. For example, a protocol sequence string might be as follows:

```
ncacn_ip_tcp
```

remote procedure call (RPC) server

The program or computer that processes remote procedure calls from a client.

revision level

A revision level is built into many Windows NT data structures, such as security descriptors and access control lists (ACLs). This enables the structure to be passed between systems or stored on disk even though it is expected to change in the future.

right

A right authorizes a user to perform certain actions on the system. In most situations, rights should be provided to a user by adding that user's account to one of the built-in groups that already possesses the needed rights, rather than by administering the user rights policy. Rights apply to the system as a whole, and are different from permissions, which apply to specific objects. *See also* permission.

root directory

In a file system structured as a hierarchy of directories on a partition or volume, the root directory is the parent of all the other directories. The root directory name in FAT, HPFS, and NTFS is a backslash (\).

secrets

Encrypted pieces of information.

security accounts manager (SAM)

A Windows NT-protected subsystem that maintains the security accounts database.

security descriptor

A data structure that houses all the security information related to an object. It contains a discretionary access control list (DACL), a system access control list (SACL) that controls auditing on the object, an owner, and a primary group of the object.

security ID (SID)

A number that identifies a user, a global group of users, a local group of users, or a domain within Windows NT.

security token

See access token.

semaphore

Generally, semaphores are signaling devices or mechanisms. However, in Windows NT, system semaphores are objects used to synchronize activities on an interprocess level. For example, when two or more processes share a common resource such as a printer, video screen, or memory segment, semaphores are used to control access to those resources so that only one process can alter them at any particular time.

server message block (SMB)

A block of data that contains a work request from a workstation to a server, or that contains the response from the server to the workstation. SMBs are used for all communications that go through the server or workstation service, such as file I/O, creating and removing remote connections, or performing any other network function that the redirector needs to carry out.

Microsoft network redirectors use this structure to send remote requests or information over the network to a remote computer, which can be either a Windows NT Workstation or Windows NT Server computer.

single system image (SSI)

A domain that has the Logon service running and that propagates its user accounts database throughout the domain.

stand-alone

A workstation or server that is not currently a member of a domain. Or, a workstation or server at which logon requests are not validated by a logon server.

swap file

See paging file.

switch

A special type of command parameter that is denoted by a leading slash (/) or leading dash (-). Switches are normally used for parameters that are simple toggles (on/off switches). For example, in the **chkdsk** command, an optional parameter is the **/f** switch. If it is used, **chkdsk** attempts to fix any problems it finds on a disk. If it is not used, **chkdsk** only reports the problems and does not attempt to fix them.

syntax

The rules governing the structure and content of commands entered into the computer. For example, when you enter commands at the Windows NT command prompt, if the structure and content of a command violate the syntax rules, the Windows NT command processor cannot interpret the command and generates a syntax error message.

system debugger

The Windows NT system debugger (NTSD) is a 32-bit application that supports the debugging of User-mode applications and dynamic-link libraries (DLLs). NTSD can also read and write paged and nonpaged memory, and supports multiple-thread debugging and multiprocess debugging.

NTSD enables you to display and execute program code, set breakpoints that stop the execution of your program, and examine and change values in memory. NTSD also enables you to refer to data and instructions by name rather than by address. It can access program locations through addresses, global symbols, or line-number references, making it easy to locate and debug specific sections of code. You can debug C programs at the source-file level as well as at the machine-code level. You can also display the source statements of a program, the disassembled machine code of the program, or a combination of source statements and disassembled machine code.

In contrast to NTSD, the Windows NT Kernel debugger (KD) supports the debugging of Kernel-mode code. It cannot be used to set breakpoints in User-mode nor to read or write paged-out memory. KD also does not provide support for threads. However, it does support multiprocess debugging.

You would, therefore, use NTSD for debugging User-mode programs and KD for debugging the Kernel and device drivers. *See also* Kernel debugger and WINDBG.EXE.

system files

Files that are used by either the operating system or the file system to store special system data. NTFS uses them to store special data on the file system.

Operating systems use these files to store information and programs that are used to start the computer and load the operating system. MS-DOS system files include IO.SYS, MSDOS.SYS, and COMMAND.COM. Windows NT system files include NTLDR, NTDETECT.COM, BOOT.INI, and several of the files in the *systemroot*\SYSTEM32 directory.

system partition

The system partition for Windows NT is the volume that has the hardware-specific files needed to load Windows NT. On x86-based computers, it must be a primary partition that has been marked as active for startup purposes and must be located on the disk that the computer accesses when starting up the system. There can be only one active system partition at a time, which is denoted on the screen by an asterisk. If you want to use another operating system, you must first mark its system partition as active before restarting the computer.

Partitions on a RISC-based computer are not marked active. Instead, they are configured by a hardware configuration program supplied by the manufacturer. On RISC-based computers, the system partition must be formatted for the FAT file system. On either type of computer, the system partition can never be part of a stripe set or volume set, but it can be part of a mirror set. *See also* boot partition.

terminated process

In Windows NT, a process object is a program invocation, including the address space and resources required to run the program. When the Windows NT Executive terminates a process, it quits running the program and returns the address space and resources to the system. From the user's point of view, the application is no longer running.

thread

An executable entity that belongs to one (and only one) process. It comprises a program counter, a User-mode stack, a Kernel-mode stack, and a set of register values. All threads in a process have equal access to the process's address space, object handles, and other resources.

In Windows NT Performance Monitor, threads are objects within processes that execute program instructions. They allow concurrent operations within a process and enable one process to execute different parts of its program on different processors simultaneously. Each thread running on a system shows up as an instance for the Thread object type and is identified by association with its parent process. For example, if Print Manager has two active threads, Performance Monitor identifies them as Thread object instances Printman ==> 0 and Printman ==> 1.

transport driver interface (TDI)

A Windows NT interface for network redirectors and servers to use in sending network-bound requests to network transport drivers. This interface provides transport independence by abstracting transport-specific information.

trap

A processor's mechanism for capturing an executing thread when an unusual event (such as an exception or interrupt) occurs, and then transferring control to a fixed location in memory where the handler code resides. The trap handler determines the type of condition and transfers control to an appropriate handling routine.

trust relationship

Trust relationships are links between domains that enable pass-through authentication, in which a user has only one user account in one domain, yet can access the entire network. User accounts and global groups defined in a trusted domain can be given rights and resource permissions in a trusting domain, even though those accounts don't exist in the trusting domain's database. A trusting domain honors the logon authentications of a trusted domain.

universal naming convention (UNC) name

A name given to a device, computer, or resource to enable other users and applications to establish an explicit connection and access the resources over the network. Also known as the uniform naming convention. The following example shows the syntax of a UNC name:

\\<*computername*>\<*sharename*>\<*filename*>

universally unique identifier (UUID)

A unique identification string associated with the remote procedure call interface. Also known as a globally unique identifier (GUID).

These identifiers consist of eight hexadecimal digits followed first by a hyphen, then by three groups of four hexadecimal digits with each group followed by a hyphen, and finally by twelve hexadecimal digits. For example, 12345678-1234-1234-1234-123456789ABC is a syntactically correct identifier. The identifiers on the client and server must match for the client and server to bind.

User mode

See Executive.

value entries

The value for a specific entry under a key or subkey in the Registry. Value entries appear as a string with three components: a name, a type, and the value. *See also* Registry key.

virtual address space

See address space.

virtual DOS machine (VDM)

Provides a complete MS-DOS environment and a character-based window in which to run an MS-DOS–based application. Any number of VDMs can run simultaneously.

virtual memory

A logical view of memory that does not necessarily correspond to the memory's physical structure.

Normally, virtual memory is the space on your hard disk that Windows NT uses as if it were actually memory. Windows NT does this through the use of the paging file. However, virtual memory can also be unused address space that is allocated to a process but not yet in use. In this case, the memory will not physically exist anywhere until it is actually used (that is, until data or code is loaded into it).

The benefit of using virtual memory is that you can run more applications at one time than your system's physical memory would otherwise allow. The drawbacks are the disk space required for the virtual-memory paging file and the decreased execution speed when swapping is required. *See also* paging file.

volume

A file-based medium that has been initialized with a file system structure (for example, a floppy disk, a hard disk, a tape reel, or a particular partition on a hard disk). A disk partition or collection of partitions that have been formatted for use by a file system and that can also be used as volume sets, stripe sets, and mirror sets. *See also* partition.

WINDBG.EXE

The Windows NT debugger (WINDBG.EXE) is a 32-bit application that, along with a collection of DLLs, is used for debugging the Kernel, device drivers, and applications. The same application can also be used on all hardware platforms, although there is a different build of it for each platform. It can be used for either remote or local debugging and can also be used in conjunction with the System Recovery option in Control Panel.

working set

The set of virtual pages that are in physical memory at any moment for a particular process. In a virtual memory system like Windows NT, a memory management system provides a large address space to each process by mapping the processes' virtual addresses into physical addresses as the processes' threads use them. When physical memory becomes full, the memory management system swaps selected memory contents to disk, reloading them from disk on demand.

CHAPTER 2

Windows NT Executive Messages

The Executive is the part of the Windows NT operating system that runs in Kernel mode. *Kernel mode* is a privileged processor mode in which a thread has access to system memory and to hardware. (In contrast, *User mode* is a nonprivileged processor mode in which a thread can only access system resources by calling system services.) The Windows NT Executive provides process structure, thread scheduling, interprocess communication, memory management, object management, object security, interrupt processing, I/O capabilities, and networking.

The Windows NT Kernel is the part of the Windows NT Executive that manages the processor. It performs thread scheduling and dispatching, interrupt and exception handling, and multiprocessor synchronization. It also provides primitive objects to the Windows NT Executive, which uses them to create User-mode objects.

There are three types of Windows NT Executive messages:

- Character-mode STOP messages
- Character-mode hardware-malfunction messages
- Windows-mode STATUS messages

Many of these messages were created to cover everything else that could possibly happen, so you may never see them. For example, one of the STOP messages is "Unhandled Kernel exception." This message is only displayed after the Kernel exception dispatcher has exhausted its search of the Kernel call stack for exception-handling code. Similarly, a STATUS message announces the termination of a thread only after the Executive has searched the entire user call stack and the subsystem associated with the application for exception-handling code.

For help with hardware-malfunction messages, you should first contact a technician within your own organization to run hardware diagnostics on your computer. If you then need to find help outside your organization, contact the hardware vendor for your specific brand of computer, adapter, or peripheral device.

Most users will also need to ask for help with the STOP messages from a technical support person who has been trained to support Windows NT. Information on what you can do to help that trained technician use the Windows NT debugger application (WINDBG.EXE) appears in the "Windows NT Debugger" section at the end of this chapter.

Character-Mode Messages

Two types of character-mode messages occur when the Windows NT Kernel detects an inconsistent condition from which it cannot recover: STOP messages and hardware-malfunction messages. You can organize these messages into the following groups:

- STOP messages that could happen only during the relatively short Windows NT startup period, which is Phase 4 of the Windows NT boot sequence
- STOP messages that can be traced back to a software condition detected by the processor
- Hardware-malfunction messages that can be traced back to a hardware condition detected by the processor
- All the rest of the STOP messages

The STOP Message Screen

Character-mode STOP messages are always displayed on a full character-mode screen rather than in a Windows-mode message box. They are also uniquely identified by a hexadecimal number and a symbolic string, as in the following example:

```
*** STOP: 0x00000001
APC_INDEX_MISMATCH
```

The content of the symbolic string may suggest, to a trained technician, the part of the Kernel that detected the condition from which there was no recourse but to stop. However, keep in mind that the cause may actually be in another part of the system.

The following is an example of a complete STOP message screen generated by the Windows NT Kernel.

```
*** STOP: 0x0000001E (0x80000003,0x80106fc0,0x8025ea21,0xfd6829e8)
Unhandled Kernel exception c0000047 from fa8418b4 (8025ea21,fd6829e8)


Dll Base  Date Stamp - Name            Dll Base  Date Stamp - Name
80100000  2be154c9   - ntoskrnl.exe    80400000  2bc153b0   - hal.dll
80258000  2bd49628   - ncrc710.sys     8025c000  2bd49688   - SCSIPORT.SYS
80267000  2bd49683   - scsidisk.sys    802a6000  2bd496b9   - Fastfat.sys
fa800000  2bd49666   - Floppy.SYS      fa810000  2bd496db   - Hpfs_Rec.SYS
fa820000  2bd49676   - Null.SYS        fa830000  2bd4965a   - Beep.SYS
fa840000  2bdaab00   - i8042prt.SYS    fa850000  2bd5a020   - SERMOUSE.SYS
fa860000  2bd4966f   - kbdclass.SYS    fa870000  2bd49671   - MOUCLASS.SYS
fa880000  2bd9c0be   - Videoprt.SYS    fa890000  2bd49638   - NCR77C22.SYS
fa8a0000  2bd4a4ce   - Vga.SYS         fa8b0000  2bd496d0   - Msfs.SYS
fa8c0000  2bd496c3   - Npfs.SYS        fa8e0000  2bd496c9   - Ntfs.SYS
fa940000  2bd496df   - NDIS.SYS        fa930000  2bd49707   - wdlan.sys
fa970000  2bd49712   - TDI.SYS         fa950000  2bd5a7fb   - nbf.sys
fa980000  2bd72406   - streams.sys     fa9b0000  2bd4975f   - ubnb.sys
fa9c0000  2bd5bfd7   - mcsxns.sys      fa9d0000  2bd4971d   - netbios.sys
fa9e0000  2bd49678   - Parallel.sys    fa9f0000  2bd4969f   - serial.SYS
faa00000  2bd49739   - mup.sys         faa40000  2bd4971f   - SMBTRSUP.SYS
faa10000  2bd6f2a2   - srv.sys         faa50000  2bd4971a   - afd.sys
faa60000  2bd6fd80   - rdr.sys         faaa0000  2bd49735   - bowser.sys

Address  dword dump                                    Dll Base - Name
801afc20 80106fc0 80106fc0 00000000 00000000 80149905 : fa840000 - i8042prt.SYS
801afc24 80149905 80149905 ff8e6b8c 80129c2c ff8e6b94 : 8025c000 - SCSIPORT.SYS
801afc2c 80129c2c 80129c2c ff8e6b94 00000000 ff8e6b94 : 80100000 - ntoskrnl.exe
801afc34 801240f2 80124f02 ff8e6df4 ff8e6f60 ff8e6c58 : 80100000 - ntoskrnl.exe
801afc54 80124f16 80124f16 ff8e6f60 ff8e6c3c 8015ac7e : 80100000 - ntoskrnl.exe
801afc64 8015ac7e 8015ac7e ff8e6df4 ff8e6f60 ff8e6c58 : 80100000 - ntoskrnl.exe
801afc70 80129bda 80129bda 00000000 80088000 80106fc0 : 80100000 - ntoskrnl.exe

Kernel Debugger Using: COM2 (Port 0x2f8, Baud Rate 19200)
Restart and set the recovery options in the system control panel or the
/CRASHDEBUG system start option. If this message reappears, contact
your system administrator or technical support group.
```

As shown in the preceding example, STOP messages are presented in four parts:

- The first part contains the most important error diagnostic information. In the preceding example, that diagnostic information is contained in the first two lines. These lines contain the STOP error code, its four parameters, and the text of the STOP error message.

  You should always record, at least, those first few lines before trying to restart your computer. While those lines are important and a knowledgeable technician can often diagnose the source of a STOP condition with that information alone, they can be used best when combined with the information in the rest of the STOP screen.

  Note Under some conditions, the Kernel will be able to display only the top line of the STOP message. The services it needs to display the rest of the information may not be available.

- The second part is a two-column display of the names of all the drivers loaded on the computer at the time the STOP message occurred, along with their base addresses in memory and a date-stamp that indicates the driver's file date. This section is important because many STOP messages contain in their parameter list the address of the instruction that caused the error. If the address falls within the base address of one of the drivers on this list, then that driver may be the cause of this error.
- The third part is a dump of some of the calls on the stack that led up to the STOP message. Sometimes, the first few lines can tell an experienced support technician what component or driver caused the error. However, the last calls on the stack are not always the cause of the problem.
- The fourth part provides confirmation of the communications parameters used by the Kernel debugger on the target computer, if enabled, and the following standard user response to a STOP message:

  ```
  Restart and set the recovery options in the system control panel or
  the/CRASHDEBUG system start option. If this message reappears,
  contact your system administrator or technical support group.
  ```

The user response in the fourth part of the STOP message implies the following:

- If you restart your computer, the STOP condition may not happen again. If the error does persist, you need to enable the Kernel debugger in either DEBUG or CRASHDEBUG mode on this computer. Instructions on configuring the computer for debugging can be found in the "Windows NT Debugger" section at the end of this chapter.
- In general, debugging requires a trained technician, who will need all the information displayed in the STOP message to determine the cause of the error. The technician may also have to connect to the computer either locally or remotely using a modem to resolve the STOP condition.
- Trained technicians are often available within one's own organization. Even if they cannot diagnose the condition, they are probably the people best able to talk with a technical support group about the contents of the STOP message.

Sample STOP Messages

The following two messages are typical examples of STOP messages.

Message ID	Text string
0x0000000A	Memory at *<address>* was referenced at IRQL *<number>* for *<number>* access from *<address>*
0x0000001E	Unhandled Kernel exception *<code>* from *<address>* (*<parameter>*, *<parameter>*)

The top two lines of the STOP message screen might look like the following ones for the STOP message uniquely identified by the hexadecimal number 0x0A.

```
*** STOP: 0x0000000A (0x0019524C,0x00000002,0x00000000,0x801122E5)
Memory at 19524c was referenced at IRQL 2 for 0 access from 801122e5.
```

The four most important pieces of diagnostic information are shown here twice: once as a parameter list on the top line, and then again embedded in the message text on the second line. The second and third parameters in this STOP message give the IRQL level (in this case, 2) and the access mode (where 0 = Read, and 1 = Write).

The fourth parameter, from *address*, identifies the location in memory of the instruction that caused the STOP error. This address can be used to identify the program module that was running at the time of the error. In the example of a complete STOP message given in the preceding section, the module I8042PRT.SYS has a base address at FA840000, which is the closest base address to FA8418B4.

The top two lines of the STOP message screen might look like the following ones for the STOP message uniquely identified by the hexadecimal number 0x1E.

```
*** STOP: 0x0000001E (0x80000003,0x80106FD0,0x00000000,0x00000000)
Unhandled Kernel exception 80000003 from 80106fd0 (0,0).
```

In this case, the second parameter identifies the module that was running at the time of the error.

The third and fourth parameters may be zero or nonzero. In the preceding example, they are both zero. The content of these two parameters is specific to the exception code generated. In other words, the value of the first parameter determines the values of the third and fourth parameters. Also, the third and fourth parameter values can only be interpreted in the context of the first parameter value.

STOP Messages That Occur Only at Executive Initialization

There is a group of STOP messages that happen only during the relatively short Windows NT startup period, which is Phase 4 of the Windows NT boot sequence. Executive initialization is one step during Phase 4. That step can be further broken down into two phases: Phase 0 and Phase 1. During Phase 0 initialization, interrupts are disabled and only a few Executive components, such as the hardware abstraction layer (HAL), are initialized. During Phase 1 initialization, the system is fully operational, and the Windows NT subcomponents do a full initialization.

If you get one of the following Phase 0 initialization STOP messages, run the hardware diagnostics. If no hardware problems are found, reinstall Windows NT and try to initialize it again. If you get the same message again, contact a trained technician.

Table 2.1 Phase 0 Initialization STOP Messages

Message ID	Symbolic name
0x0031	PHASE0_INITIALIZATION_FAILED
0x005C	HAL_INITIALIZATION_FAILED
0x005D	HEAP_INITIALIZATION_FAILED
0x005E	OBJECT_INITIALIZATION_FAILED
0x005F	SECURITY_INITIALIZATION_FAILED
0x0060	PROCESS_INITIALIZATION_FAILED

If you get one of the following Phase 1 initialization STOP messages, reinstall Windows NT and try to initialize it again. If you still get the same message, contact a trained technician.

Table 2.2 Phase 1 Initialization STOP Messages

Message ID	Symbolic name
0x0032	PHASE1_INITIALIZATION_FAILED
0x0061	HAL1_INITIALIZATION_FAILED
0x0062	OBJECT1_INITIALIZATION_FAILED
0x0063	SECURITY1_INITIALIZATION_FAILED
0x0064	SYMBOLIC_INITIALIZATION_FAILED
0x0065	MEMORY1_INITIALIZATION_FAILED
0x0066	CACHE_INITIALIZATION_FAILED
0x0067	CONFIG_INITIALIZATION_FAILED
0x0068	FILE_INITIALIZATION_FAILED
0x0069	IO1_INITIALIZATION_FAILED
0x006A	LPC_INITIALIZATION_FAILED
0x006B	PROCESS1_INITIALIZATION_FAILED
0x006C	REFMON_INITIALIZATION_FAILED
0x006D	SESSION1_INITIALIZATION_FAILED
0x006E	SESSION2_INITIALIZATION_FAILED
0x006F	SESSION3_INITIALIZATION_FAILED
0x0070	SESSION4_INITIALIZATION_FAILED
0x0071	SESSION5_INITIALIZATION_FAILED

STOP Messages Caused by a Software Trap

Another group of STOP messages is caused by a software condition detected by the processor. This condition, called a software trap, happens when a processor detects a problem in an executing instruction from which the processor will not continue. For instance, a processor will not carry out an instruction that contains invalid operands.

When you get a STOP message that is caused by a software trap, follow the steps given in "Remaining STOP Messages," later in this chapter.

The following is an example of the first line of the STOP message that is displayed for all software traps:

```
*** STOP: 0x0000007F (0x0000000n, 00000000, 00000000, 00000000)
UNEXPECTED_KERNEL_MODE_TRAP
```

The first parameter (shown as 0x0000000*n* in the example) in the message parameter list indicates which of twelve possible traps has occurred. For instance, in the case of an instruction that contains invalid operands, the message will appear as follows:

```
*** STOP: 0x0000007F (0x00000006, 00000000, 00000000, 00000000)
UNEXPECTED_KERNEL_MODE_TRAP
```

The following table shows the possible values and their meanings for that first parameter.

Parameter	Processor detected
0x00000000	An attempt to divide by zero.
0x00000001	A system-debugger call.
0x00000003	A debugger breakpoint.
0x00000004	An arithmetic operation overflow.
0x00000005	An array index that exceeds the array bounds.
0x00000006	Invalid operands in an instruction or an attempt to execute a protected-mode instruction while running in real mode.
0x00000007	A hardware coprocessor instruction, with no coprocessor present.
0x00000008	An error while processing an error (also known as a "double fault").
0x0000000A	A corrupt Task State Segment.
0x0000000B	An access to a memory segment that was not present.
0x0000000C	An access to memory beyond the limits of a stack.
0x0000000D	An exception not covered by some other exception (also known as a "general protection fault").

Hardware-Malfunction Messages

Hardware-malfunction messages are caused by a hardware condition detected by the processor. The first one or two lines of a hardware-malfunction message may differ depending on which company manufactured the computer. However, these lines always convey the same idea, as shown in the following example for an x86-based computer:

```
Hardware malfunction.
Call your hardware vendor for support.
```

The additional lines in each manufacturer's message screen also differ in format and content. Therefore, before doing what the sample message recommends, contact a technician within your own organization to run hardware diagnostics on your computer. The information provided below the first two lines will help your technician decide which hardware diagnostics to run. For example, for x86-based ISA bus computers, information is displayed that indicates whether this is a memory-parity error or a bus-data error. On x86-based EISA computers, if the hardware problem is in an adapter, the adapter slot number on the system board is displayed.

If you then still need to find help from outside your organization to interpret the information on the screen, contact the hardware vendor for your specific brand of computer, adapter, or peripheral device.

Remaining STOP Messages

A typical user will not be able to diagnose the cause of any of the remaining STOP messages. When you get one of these messages, first record the top few lines of the STOP message and then restart the computer. If the STOP message occurs again, you have four options for diagnosing the STOP condition, all of which should be handled by a trained technician at your own site:

- Diagnose the problem using the information displayed in the STOP message and any pertinent information from the Windows NT forum on CompuServe®, where Microsoft maintains an up-to-date list of causes for these STOP messages.
- Use the Windows NT debugger to get more information about the problem.

  If you use this option or the next one, be sure to switch Windows NT to debug mode before you restart your computer. See "Windows NT Debugger," later in this chapter, for information on how to prepare your computer for debugging.

- Contact your own or another technical support group for assistance in using the Windows NT debugger remotely.
- Contact your own or another technical support group to discuss the information in the STOP message. They may see a familiar pattern in the information and save everyone time.

The following list provides the ranges of unique hexadecimal numbers for the STOP messages that are least likely to happen. However, if one does occur, it will be after Windows NT Executive startup is complete and will not be caused by hardware or software traps in a processor. If you want more information about these messages, you can refer to the alphabetical list provided in Chapter 4, "Message Reference." However, most trained technicians will only need the unique hexadecimal number.

```
0x00000001 through 0x00000009
0x0000000B through 0x0000001D
0x0000001F through 0x00000030
0x00000033 through 0x0000005B
0x00000072 through 0x0000007B
```

Windows-Mode STATUS Messages

The Executive displays a Windows-mode STATUS message box when it detects conditions within a process (generally, an application) that you should know about. STATUS messages can be divided into three types:

- System-information messages. All you can do is read the information in the message box and choose the OK button. The Kernel will continue running the process or thread.
- Warning messages. Some advise you to take an action that will enable the Kernel to keep running the process or thread. Others warn you that, although the process or thread will continue running, the results may not be correct.
- Application-termination messages. These warn you that the Kernel is about to terminate either a process or a thread.

System-Information Messages

System-information messages from the Executive provide status information on conditions within a process that should be noted but that will not stop the application from running. All that you can do with these messages is read the information and choose the OK button. If one of the following messages appears frequently while you are working in the same application, contact either the supplier of the application or your system administrator to adjust the configuration of your Windows NT computer.

Expedited Data Received
Image Relocated
Invalid Current Directory
Local Session Key
Object Exists
Partial Data Received
Partial Expedited Data Received
Password Too Complex
Redundant Read
Redundant Write
Registry Recovery
Segment Load
Serial IOCTL Complete
Serial IOCTL Timeout
TDI Event Done
TDI Event Pending
Thread Suspended
Working Set Range Error

Warning Messages

Warning messages from the Executive provide status information on more serious conditions within a process that could potentially stop the application or cause damage to your data. Some warning messages will prompt you indirectly for a user action, as in the following example:

```
Out of Paper:  The printer is out of paper.
```

If one of the following messages appears frequently while you are working in the same application, contact either the supplier of the application or your system administrator to adjust the configuration of your Windows NT computer.

Alignment Fault
Breakpoint
Buffer Overflow
Device Busy
Device Offline
Device Power Is Off
End of Media
Filemark Found
Guard Page Exception
GUID Substitution
Handles Closed
Illegal EA
Inconsistent EA List
Invalid EA Flag
I/O Bus Reset
Kernel Debugger Awakened
Media Changed
No more EAs
No More Entries
No More Files
Non-Inheritable ACL
Out of Paper
Page Locked
Page Unlocked
Partial Copy
Single Step
Too Much Information
Verifying Disk

Application-Termination Messages

Application-termination messages from the Executive appear when the Kernel is about to terminate either the process in which an application is running or the thread of an application. Some of these messages will advise you to perform an action before restarting the application, as in the following example:

```
The application or DLL <filename> is not a valid Windows NT image.
Please check this against your installation disk.
```

In other cases, the user action is strongly implied, as in the following example:

```
The dynamic link library <filename> could not be found in the specific
path <path>
```

This example implies that you should make sure that the DLL is in the path before you restart the application.

In yet other cases, you can only restart the application. If one of the following messages reappears, contact the supplier of the application.

Message box title	Message text
Access Denied	A process has requested access to an object, but has not been granted those access rights.
Already Committed	The specified address range is already committed.
Application Error	The exception *name* (*number*) occurred in the application at location *address*.
Application Error	The application failed to initialize properly (*number*). Click on OK to terminate the application.
Application Exit by CTRL+C	The application terminated as a result of a CTRL+C.
Bad CRC	A cyclic redundancy check (CRC) checksum error occurred.
Bad File	The attributes of the specified mapping file for a section of memory cannot be read.
Bad Image	The application or DLL *filename* is not a valid Windows NT image. Please check this against your installation diskette.
Buffer Too Small	The buffer is too small to contain the entry. No information has been written to the buffer.
Cancel Timeout	The driver *name* failed to complete a canceled I/O request in the allotted time.
Cannot Continue	Windows NT cannot continue from this exception.

Message box title	Message text *(continued)*
Conflicting Address Range	The specified address range conflicts with the address space.
Corrupt Disk	The file system structure on the disk is corrupt and unusable.
	Please run the Chkdsk utility on the volume *name*.
Corrupt File	The file or directory *filename* is corrupt and unreadable.
	Please run the Chkdsk utility.
Data Error	An error in reading or writing data occurred.
Data Late	A data late error occurred.
Data Not Accepted	The TDI client could not handle the data received during an indication.
Data Overrun	A data overrun error occurred.
Device Timeout	The specified I/O operation on *name* was not completed before the time-out period expired.
DLL Initialization Failed	Initialization of the dynamic link library *filename* failed. The process is terminating abnormally.
Drive Not Ready	The drive is not ready for use; its door may be open.
	Please check drive *drive letter* and make sure that a disk is inserted and that the drive door is closed.
Entry Point Not Found	The procedure entry point *name* could not be located in the dynamic link library *filename*.
EXCEPTION	A real-mode application issued a floating-point instruction and floating-point hardware is not present.
EXCEPTION	Array bounds exceeded.
EXCEPTION	Floating-point denormal operand.
EXCEPTION	Floating-point division by zero.
EXCEPTION	Floating-point inexact result.
EXCEPTION	Floating-point invalid operation.
EXCEPTION	Floating-point overflow.
EXCEPTION	Floating-point stack check.
EXCEPTION	Floating-point underflow.
EXCEPTION	Integer division by zero.
EXCEPTION	Integer overflow.
EXCEPTION	Privileged instruction.
EXCEPTION	Possible deadlock condition.
Fatal System Error	The *name* system process terminated unexpectedly with a status of *address*. The system has been shutdown.

Message box title	Message text *(continued)*
File Not Found	The file *filename* does not exist.
Floppy Disk Error	While accessing a floppy disk, the track address from the sector ID field was found to be different than the track address maintained by the controller.
Floppy Disk Error	While accessing a floppy disk, an ID address mark was not found.
Floppy Disk Error	The floppy disk controller reported an error that is not recognized by the floppy disk driver.
Floppy Disk Error	While accessing a floppy-disk, the controller returned inconsistent results via its registers.
Hard Disk Error	While accessing the hard disk, a recalibrate operation failed, even after retries.
Hard Disk Error	While accessing the hard disk, a disk operation failed even after retries.
Hard Disk Error	While accessing the hard disk, a disk controller reset was needed, but even that failed.
Illegal Instruction	An attempt was made to execute an illegal instruction.
Incorrect Network Resource Type	The specified device type (LPT, for example) conflicts with the actual device type on the remote resource.
Incorrect Password to LAN Manager Server	You specified an incorrect password to a LAN Manager 2.x or MS-NET server.
Incorrect System Call Level	An invalid level was passed into the specified system call.
Incorrect Volume	The target file of a rename request is located on a different device than the source of the rename request.
Invalid Lock Sequence	An attempt was made to execute an invalid lock sequence.
Invalid Mapping	An attempt was made to create a view for a section which is bigger than the section.
Invalid Parameter	The specified information class is not a valid information class for the specified object.
Missing System File	The required system file *filename* is bad or missing.
Network Name Not Found	The specified share name cannot be found on the remote server.
Network Request Timeout	The session with a remote server has been disconnected because the time-out interval for a request has expired.
No Disk	There is no disk in the drive. Please insert a disk into drive *drive letter*.
No Paging File Specified	No paging file was specified in the system configuration.
Not Enough Quota	Not enough virtual memory or paging file quota is available to complete the specified operation.

Message box title	Message text *(continued)*
Not Implemented	The requested operation is not implemented.
Operation Failed	The requested operation was unsuccessful.
Ordinal Not Found	The ordinal *number* could not be located in the dynamic link library *filename*.
Out of Virtual Memory	Your system is running low on virtual memory. Please close some applications. You can then start the System option in the Control Panel and choose the Virtual Memory button to create an additional paging file or to increase the size of your current paging file.
Path Not Found	The path *path* does not exist.
Privilege Failed	The I/O permissions for the process could not be changed.
Registry File Failure	The registry cannot load the hive (file): *name* or its log or alternate. It is corrupt, absent, or not writable.
Section Too Large	The specified section is too big to map the file.
Sector Not Found	The specified sector does not exist.
Still Busy	The specified I/O request packet (IRP) cannot be disposed of because the I/O operation is not complete.
The Registry Is Corrupt	The structure of one of the files that contains Registry data is corrupt, or the image of the file in memory is corrupt, or the file could not be recovered because the alternate copy or log was absent or corrupt.
Unable to Create Paging File	The creation of the paging file *filename* failed (*number*). The requested size was *number*.
Unable To Locate DLL	The dynamic link library *filename* could not be found in the specified path *path*.
Unable to retrieve browser server list	The list of servers for this workgroup is not currently available.
Unexpected Failure in DebugActiveProcess	An unexpected failure occurred while processing a DebugActiveProcess API request. You may choose OK to terminate the process, or Cancel to ignore the error.
Unknown Disk Format	The disk in drive *drive letter* is not formatted properly. Please check the disk, and reformat if necessary.
Write Protect Error	The disk cannot be written to because it is write protected. Please remove the write protection from the volume *name* in drive *drive letter*.

Message box title	Message text *(continued)*
Wrong Type	There is a mismatch between the type of object required by the requested operation and the type of object that is specified in the request.
Wrong Volume	The wrong volume is in the drive. Please insert volume *name* into drive *drive letter*.

Windows NT Debugger

The Windows NT debugger (WinDbg) is a 32-bit application that, along with a collection of DLLs, is used for debugging the Kernel, device drivers, and applications. This section, however, will only discuss how to use WinDbg for Kernel debugging. The same application can be used on all hardware platforms, although there is a different build of it for each platform. It is provided on the Windows NT CD-ROM under the \SUPPORT\DEBUG directory.

It can be used for either remote or local Kernel debugging and can also be used in conjunction with the Recovery option located under the System option in Control Panel. Both remote and local Kernel debugging require that WinDbg run on another Windows NT host computer that is connected to your Windows NT target computer. The two computers send debugging (troubleshooting) information back and forth through communications ports that must be running at the same baud rate on each computer.

With local Kernel debugging, the host computer is located within a few feet of the target computer, and the two computers communicate through a null-modem serial cable. With remote Kernel debugging, the host computer can be any distance from the target computer, since communication takes place through modems.

Using the Recovery option allows you to configure the target computer to write debugging information to a log file when a STOP error occurs. This file preserves the state of the computer at the time of the STOP error, and the log file can be used later by WinDbg to troubleshoot the problem. By using this option, you can run WinDbg on any computer after loading the log file, including the computer on which the STOP error occurred.

When you get a Windows NT Executive STOP or STATUS message on a Windows NT Workstation computer, you should restart the computer after recording the important information in the message. (On a Windows NT Server computer, the computer restarts by default after writing an event to the system log, alerting administrators, and dumping system memory to the log file called MEMORY.DMP. Therefore, to preserve log files, you should copy them to a new filename each time a STOP error occurs.) You may then want to continue running Windows NT until the message is redisplayed.

When that happens, you need to decide whether to debug the STOP error locally or remotely and then configure your system appropriately. If a trained technician is available, you could also ask him or her to do one of the preparatory procedures given in this section to set up your computer to run WinDbg remotely. Or you could call your technical support group and request assistance with the debugging.

Configuring a System for Debugging

Ordinarily, you will run Windows NT Workstation or Windows NT Server with the debug mode turned off, which is the default when Windows NT Setup installs the system. In that mode, an Executive STOP or STATUS message will not enable the debugger. To switch Windows NT into debug mode, you have to edit the Windows NT startup file, BOOT.INI, and include one of the two debug-mode switches: **/crashdebug** or **/debug**. If you include the **/crashdebug** switch in the BOOT.INI file, the debugger is loaded when you start but remains inactive unless a Kernel error occurs. This mode is useful if you are experiencing random, unpredictable Kernel errors. When you include the **/debug** switch, the debugger is loaded when you start and can be activated at any time by a debugger connected to the computer. This is the standard mode used when debugging problems that are regularly reproducible.

You can also change the default communications port and baud rate by editing the BOOT.INI file. Since the code that enables remote Kernel debugging resides in the hardware abstraction layer (HAL), the defaults for the communications port and baud rate may vary from one computer to another. On x86-based computers, if you have more than one communications port, the default debug port is set to COM2. However, if you have a serial mouse attached to COM2, the default debug port is set to COM1. If you do not set the baud rate, the default baud rate is 9600 if a modem is attached. If necessary, you can verify later what baud rate has been set. On RISC-based computers, the default debug port is set to COM1.

When you are finished debugging the computer, you should turn the debug mode off again. To do this, repeat the process of editing the BOOT.INI file or the OSLOADOPTIONS environmental variable, and delete any values you set to enable debugging. On a RISC-based computer, this may mean the OSLOADOPTIONS variable has no values, which is acceptable.

To specify settings, you can use the following procedure, which will prepare your computer for either remote or local Kernel debugging.

▶ To prepare an x86-based target computer for remote or local debugging

1. For remote debugging, connect a modem to the communications port, turn the power on, and set the modem to auto-answer. This could also be done on a second computer and then the modem could be moved to the target computer after a Kernel error occurs.

   For local debugging, connect the null-modem serial cable to any available communications port.

2. Restart the computer under MS-DOS or Windows NT.

   If you can restart under Windows NT, double-click the Command Prompt icon in the Main group to access the command line.

3. To turn off the system, hidden, and read-only attributes of the BOOT.INI file, type:

   attrib -s -h -r boot.ini

   The BOOT.INI file is usually located in the root directory of the partition from which the Windows NT NTLDR program was loaded, which is ordinarily C:\.

4. To use MS-DOS Editor to change the BOOT.INI file, type:

   edit boot.ini

   The BOOT.INI file appears within the MS-DOS Editor window and normally looks something like the following example:

   ```
   [boot loader]
   timeout=30
   default=multi(0)disk(0)rdisk(0)partition(1)\WINDOWS
   [operating systems]
   multi(0)disk(0)rdisk(0)partition(1)\WINDOWS="Windows NT" Version 3.5"
   multi(0)disk(0)rdisk(0)partition(1)\WINDOWS="Windows NT" Version 3.5
   [VGA mode]" /BASEVIDEO
   C:\="MS-DOS"
   ```

   Each entry in the [operating systems] section should correspond to the options listed in the boot menu during a normal system startup.

5. Select the startup option that you normally use and add either the **/debug** or **/crashdebug** switch at the end of the line.

   An alternative to using the **/debug** switch is to add switches at the end of the line that explicitly set the communications port and baud rate your computer will use to send debugging information.

6. To specify the communications port, add the switch **/debugport=com***x*, where *x* is the communications port that you want to use.

7. To specify the baud rate, add the switch **/baudrate=<*baudrate*>**.

   Valid speeds for the baud rate range from 75 to 115,200 baud. The hardware will determine the speed chosen. 9600 baud is the normal rate for remote debugging over a modem. Local debugging over a serial cable can run as fast as 57,600 baud or higher if both computers can support the speed.

   The following is an example of a startup-option line specifying the communications port and baud rate:

   ```
   multi(0)disk(0)rdisk(0)partition(1)\WINDOWS="Windows NT" Version 3.5"
   /debugport=com1 /baudrate=9600
   ```

8. Save the file and quit MS-DOS Editor.
9. Restart the computer to run under Windows NT.

   You may now contact your technical support group or a trained technician and have them call the modem to establish a remote debugging session.

Preparing a RISC-based computer for remote or local Kernel debugging also involves editing one line in a startup file, but you access that file in a different manner.

▶ **To prepare a RISC-based target computer for remote or local debugging**

1. For remote debugging, connect a modem to the communications port, turn the power on, and set the modem to auto-answer. This could also be done on a second computer and then the modem could be moved to the target computer after a Kernel error occurs.

   For local debugging, connect the null-modem serial cable to any available communications port.

2. Restart the computer.

   The ARC System screen appears, displaying the main menu from which you can select an action.

3. On a MIPS RISC-based system, choose Run Setup to display the Setup menu and then choose Manage Startup to display a menu of the boot options.

   On a Digital Alpha AXP RISC-based system, choose Supplementary Menu, Set Up the System, and Manage Boot Selection Menu to display a menu of the boot options.

4. Choose Change a Boot Selection to display a list of the operating systems that are installed on this computer.

5. Choose the Windows NT operating system. If you have more than one version of Windows NT installed, select the one that you want to debug.

   A two-part screen appears for changing the current settings of the environment variables used to start the RISC-based computer. The environment variable that controls whether or not the RISC-based computer starts up in debug mode is the OSLOADOPTIONS variable.

6. To edit the value for the OSLOADOPTIONS variable, use the arrow keys to select it from the list of variables.

   Once selected, it appears in the Name box at the top of the screen.

7. Press ENTER to display the Value box.

8. Type **debug** or **crashdebug** in the Value box and press ENTER to save it and turn the debug mode on.

   You may also add a value that explicitly sets the communications port, as in the following example:

   ```
   OSLOADOPTIONS  debug  debugport=com2
   ```

   If you do not specify the debug port, the default debug port is set to COM1. Since RISC-based computers allow only a default baud rate of 19200, you do not need to specify the baud rate.

9. Press ESC to stop editing.

10. On a MIPS RISC-based system, choose Return To Main Menu and then Exit to return to the ARC System screen.

    On a Digital Alpha AXP RISC-based system, choose Supplementary Menu, save your changes, and then choose Boot Menu to return to the ARC System screen.

    If this is the first time that you have debugged a Digital Alpha AXP RISC-based system, after connecting the local host computer, you now need to do the following:

    - Shut down both computers
    - Restart the host (debugger) computer
    - Run WinDbg in Kernel-debug mode
    - Restart the target (Digital Alpha AXP RISC-based) computer while WinDbg is running on the host computer to set up configuration information on the target computer and prepare it for either local or remote debugging.

11. Restart the computer to run under Windows NT.

    You may now contact your technical support group or a trained technician and have them call the modem to establish a remote debugging session.

Using WinDbg for Local Kernel Debugging

The WinDbg host computer can also be local to the target Windows NT computer. WinDbg runs on the Windows NT host computer and communicates through an industry-standard null-modem serial cable with the target Windows NT computer. For local Kernel debugging, the target computer has to be prepared in the same way as it is for remote Kernel debugging.

Setting Up a System for Local Kernel Debugging

To debug Windows NT Executive messages using a local debugging system, you need to prepare the host and target computers and then connect the two computers with an industry-standard null-modem serial cable. Be sure to start the host computer before restarting the target computer.

A standard, commercially available null-modem serial cable has the following configuration:

- Transmit Data connected to Receive Data
- Receive Data connected to Transmit Data
- Ground connected to Ground

For 9-pin and 25-pin D-subminiature connectors, the cable connects as follows:

- Pin 2 to pin 3
- Pin 3 to pin 2
- Pin 7 to pin 7

The WinDbg logic does not depend on any control pins (such as Data Terminal Ready, Data Set Ready, Request To Send, or Clear To Send). However, in the connectors on both ends of the cable, you may have to put a jumper from Data Terminal Ready to Data Set Ready and from Request To Send to Clear To Send.

- On a db9 connector, this would be a jumper from pin 4 to pin 6 and a jumper from pin 7 to pin 8.
- On a db25 connector, this would be a jumper from pin 20 to pin 6 and from pin 4 to pin 5.

Preparing the target computer for local Kernel debugging is the same as for remote Kernel debugging. The only difference is that instead of connecting a modem to one of the target computer's communications ports, you connect a null-modem serial cable. See "Configuring a System for Debugging," earlier in this chapter, for detailed procedures.

Which port you use (COM1 or COM2) depends on what you did to prepare your target and host computers. The default connection is from COM1 of the host computer to COM2 of the target computer. However, you may change that by editing the boot configuration on the target computer or by changing the command line parameters used when you start WinDbg.

The Windows NT Setup program does not install WinDbg as part of the Windows NT installation process. However, you can easily copy the WinDbg program directly onto the hard disk of the host computer. It is distributed on the Windows NT CD-ROM in an uncompressed format under the \SUPPORT\DEBUG directory.

Note If you do not have a CD-ROM drive, the WinDbg program is also available from Microsoft Support Network. You can request that they send you the software on a floppy disk, or ask for instructions on how to download it from CompuServe.

▶ To copy and start WinDbg on the host computer

1. Connect the null-modem serial cable to the communications port defined in the BOOT.INI file of the host computer.

   Notice that the communications port can be different for the host and target computers.

2. Create a subdirectory called \SYMBOLS on the host computer's hard disk under the directory in which you have installed Windows NT.

3. Copy the debugging symbols from the \SUPPORT\DEBUG\\<*platform*>\SYMBOLS directory on the CD-ROM to the \SYMBOLS directory on the host computer. *Platform* refers to the hardware platform of the host computer.

4. Copy all the files from the \SUPPORT\DEBUG\\<*platform*> directory on the CD-ROM to the \SYSTEM32 directory on the host computer. This can be done with the **xcopy** or **copy** command. Make sure that the following files are copied to the host computer:

EECXXALP.DLL	IMAGEHLP.DLL	TLLOC.DLL
EECXXMIP.DLL	KDEXTALP.DLL	TLPIPE.DLL
EECXXX86.DLL	KDEXTMIP.DLL	TLSER.DLL
EMALP.DLL	KDEXTX86.DLL	WINDBG.EXE
EMMIP.DLL	SHCV.DLL	WINDBG.HLP
EMX86.DLL	SYMCVT.DLL	WINDBGRM.EXE

5. To start WinDbg in Kernel-debug mode from either the command line or the File Run dialog box in Program Manager, type:

   <*path*> **windbg -k** <*target platform*> <*com port*> <*speed*> **-y** <*symbol path*> **-v**

   where:

   Path is the path to the WINDBG.EXE file.

   -k invokes the Kernel-debug mode.

   Target platform refers to the hardware platform of the target computer and corresponds to the name of the directory from which you obtained the WinDbg files, such as I386, MIPS, or ALPHA.

   Com port is the port to which you have connected the null-modem serial cable.

   Speed is the baud rate.

   -y indicates that the next parameter is the symbol path.

   Symbol path is the path to the \SYMBOLS directory created in step 2.

   The following is an example of such a command:

   ```
   c:\ windbg -k i386 com1 19200 -y c:\windows\symbols
   ```

6. To create a log of the debugging session, from the Options menu, choose Debug.
7. In the Logfile section of the Debugger Options dialog box, you can:
   - Select the Open Automatically check box to have WinDbg open a log file whenever it starts. If you want to specify a path and name for the log file, type one in the Name text box.
   - Select the Append check box to append new data to an existing log file. Otherwise, the file will be overwritten.

   For more information on WinDbg settings, see the online Help file.

Running a Local Debugging Session

Once you have prepared the two computers and connected them, you can start a debugging session. There can be many objectives for a debugging session; this chapter discusses the objective of collecting information (in the debug-session log file on the host computer) about the events leading up to a particular Windows NT Executive message on the target computer.

Note Once you are in the Kernel-debug mode of WinDbg, you can display a list of commands by typing **help** or **?** at the KD command prompt on the host computer. The Kernel-debug character-mode command-line interface has a vocabulary of about four dozen commands, plus it supports advanced debugging features such as watches and breakpoints. For more information on the commands and advanced features, see the online Help file.

Quitting a Local Debugging Session

Quitting WinDbg on the host computer at the end of a local debugging session will also save the debug-session log file.

▶ **To quit WinDbg and save the log file on the host computer**

1. From the Run menu, choose Stop Debugging.
2. From the File menu, choose Exit.
3. Restart the target computer.

Using WinDbg with the Recovery Option

If you do not want to or are unable to do local or remote debugging, you can use the Recovery option located under the System option in Control Panel. Whenever a Windows NT Executive STOP error occurs, Windows NT can save the state of the computer system to a log file on the boot partition. This file contains all the information needed by WinDbg to troubleshoot the STOP error as if you were connected to a live computer experiencing the problem. In addition, all the WinDbg commands that work during a local or remote debugging session also work in this mode.

This enables you to examine the error at any time and immediately restart the computer that failed instead of keeping it down during the debug session. The only drawback to this method is that, to contain all the necessary information for a debug session, you must have sufficient space on your hard disk for the resulting log file, which will be as large as your RAM memory. Therefore, whenever a STOP error occurs, a computer with 32 MB of RAM will produce a 32-MB log file.

To configure Windows NT to save STOP information to a log file

1. In Control Panel, choose the System option.
2. In the System dialog box, choose the Recovery button.
3. In the Recovery dialog box, select the Write Debugging Information To check box, and either accept the default path and filename (C:*systemroot*\\MEMORY.DMP) or type your own in the text box.

   To have this log file overwrite any file of the same name, select the Overwrite Any Existing File check box. If you clear this check box, Windows NT will not write a log file if there is already a file by that name.

To debug a log file using WinDbg

1. Create a subdirectory called \SYMBOLS on the host computer's hard disk under the directory in which you have installed Windows NT.
2. Copy the debugging symbols, corresponding to the target computer that produced the log file, from the \SUPPORT\DEBUG\\<*platform*>\SYMBOLS directory on the CD-ROM to the \SYMBOLS directory on the host computer.

   Platform refers to the hardware platform of the host computer.
3. Copy all the files from the \SUPPORT\DEBUG\\<*platform*> directory on the CD-ROM to the \SYSTEM32 directory on the host computer.

   This can be done with the **xcopy** or **copy** command.
4. To start WinDbg in Kernel-debug mode from either the command line or the File Run dialog box in Program Manager, type:

   <*path*> **windbg -z** <*filename*> **-y** <*symbol path*>

   Where:

   Path is the path to the WINDBG.EXE file.

   -z invokes the Kernel-debug mode using the MEMORY.DMP file.

   Filename is the path and name of the log file that you want to debug.

   -y indicates that the next parameter is the symbol path.

   Symbol path is the path to the \SYMBOLS directory.

   The following is an example of such a command:

   ```
   c:\ windbg -z c:\windows\memory.dmp -y c:\windows\symbols
   ```

5. To create a log of the debugging session, from the Options menu, choose Debug.
6. In the Logfile section of the Debugger Options dialog box, you can:
   - Select the Open Automatically check box to have WinDbg open a log file whenever it starts. If you want to specify a path and name for the log file, type one in the Name text box.
   - Select the Append check box to append new data to an existing log file. Otherwise, the file will be overwritten.

For more information on WinDbg settings, see the online Help file.

CHAPTER 3

Network Reference Tables

There should always be more than one way to look up information. Normally, references provide information that is organized in alphabetical order. However, the network messages also have a unique identification number that can be used for sorting these messages.

This chapter provides two numerically organized lists of the network messages: network message ID numbers and down-level network message ID numbers.

Network Message ID Numbers

Network messages have an error code or message identification number associated with them and can be seen by typing **net helpmsg** *message number* at the command prompt. They can also be divided into two groups: Windows NT Workstation/Windows NT Server Network Messages and Down-level Network Messages.

In Chapter 4, "Message Reference," the network messages are presented alphabetically and interspersed with the other system messages. In the following table, they have been arranged numerically. Missing or skipped numbers could be related to simple messages, such as "Password expires," that were not included in the printed version, or they may be in the Down-level Network Message ID Numbers table, which is provided in the second section of this chapter.

ID	Message text
2102	The workstation driver is not installed.
2104	An internal error occurred. The network cannot access a shared memory segment.
2105	A network resource shortage occurred.
2106	This operation is not supported on workstations.
2114	The Server service is not started.
2115	The queue is empty.
2116	The device or directory does not exist.
2118	The name has already been shared.
2119	The server is currently out of the requested resource.
2121	Requested addition of items exceeds the maximum allowed.
2123	The API return buffer is too small.
2136	A general network error occurred.
2137	The Workstation service is in an inconsistent state. Restart the computer before restarting the Workstation service.
2138	The Workstation service has not been started.
2140	An internal Windows NT error occurred.
2141	The server is not configured for transactions.
2142	The requested API is not supported on the remote server.
2144	The computer name already exists on the network. Change it and restart the computer.
2146	The specified component could not be found in the configuration information.
2147	The specified parameter could not be found in the configuration information.
2150	The printer does not exist.

ID	Message text *(continued)*
2151	The print job does not exist.
2180	The service does not respond to control actions.
2182	The requested service has already been started.
2184	The service has not been started.
2185	The service name is invalid.
2186	The service is not responding to the control function.
2187	The service control is busy.
2189	The service could not be controlled in its present state.
2191	The requested pause or stop is not valid for this service.
2194	A thread for the new service could not be created.
2202	The user name or group name parameter is invalid.
2203	The password parameter is invalid.
2211	The server is configured without a valid user path.
2219	The security database could not be found.
2220	The group name could not be found.
2221	The user name could not be found.
2222	The resource name could not be found.
2223	The group already exists.
2224	The user account already exists.
2226	This operation is only allowed on the primary domain controller of the domain.
2227	The security database has not been started.
2229	A disk I/O failure occurred.
2233	Unable to add to the user accounts database session cache segment.
2234	This operation is not allowed on this special group.
2236	The user already belongs to this group.
2237	The user does not belong to this group.
2239	This user account has expired.
2240	The user is not allowed to log on from this workstation.
2241	The user is not allowed to log on at this time.
2242	The password of this user has expired.
2245	The password is shorter than required.
2246	The password of this user is too recent to change.
2247	The security database is corrupted.
2249	This replicant database is outdated; synchronization is required.
2250	The network connection could not be found.

ID	**Message text** *(continued)*
2251	This asg_type is invalid.
2270	The computer name could not be added as a message alias. The name may already exist on the network.
2273	This message alias could not be found on the network.
2276	This message alias already exists locally.
2277	The maximum number of added message aliases has been exceeded.
2278	The computer name could not be deleted.
2280	An error occurred in the domain message processor.
2281	The message was sent, but the recipient has paused the Messenger service.
2282	The message was sent but not received.
2283	The message alias is currently in use. Try again later.
2285	The name is not on the local computer.
2289	The broadcast message was truncated.
2294	This is an invalid device name.
2297	A duplicate message alias exists on the network.
2298	This message alias will be deleted later.
2299	The message alias was not successfully deleted from all networks.
2310	This shared resource does not exist.
2311	This device is not shared.
2312	A session does not exist with that computer name.
2351	This computer name is invalid.
2357	Could not determine the type of input.
2362	The buffer for types is not big enough.
2378	This log file has changed between reads.
2401	There are open files on the connection.
2403	This share name or password is invalid.
2404	The device is being accessed by an active process.
2432	An invalid or nonexistent alert name was raised.
2453	Could not find the domain controller for this domain.
2457	This server's clock is not synchronized with the domain controller's clock.
2470	Try down-level (remote admin protocol) version of API instead.
2481	The UPS service is not configured correctly.
2482	The UPS service could not access the specified Comm Port.
2483	The UPS indicated a line fail or low battery situation. Service not started.
2484	The UPS service failed to perform a system shutdown.

ID	Message text *(continued)*
2550	The browser service was configured with MaintainServerList=No.
3020	A power failure was detected at *name*. The server has been paused.
3021	Power has been restored at *name*. The server is no longer paused.
3022	The UPS service is starting shutdown at *name* due to low battery.
3023	There is a problem with a configuration of user specified shutdown command file. The UPS service started anyway.
3030	The server cannot export directory *name*, to client *name*. It is exported from another server.
3031	The replication server could not update directory *name* from the source on *name* due to error *code*.
3032	Master *name* did not send an update notice for directory *name* at the expected time.
3034	The domain controller for domain *name* failed.
3035	Failed to authenticate with *name*, a Windows NT Server for domain *name*.
3038	Replicator could not access *name* on *name* due to system error *code*.
3039	Replicator limit for files in a directory has been exceeded.
3040	Replicator limit for tree depth has been exceeded.
3041	The replicator cannot update directory *name*. It has tree integrity and is the current directory for some process.
3042	Network error *code* occurred.
3045	System error *code* occurred.
3047	IMPORT path *path* cannot be found.
3049	Replicated data has changed in directory *name*.
3051	The Registry or the information you just typed includes an illegal value for *text*.
3054	A request for resource could not be satisfied.
3056	A system error has occurred.
3057	An internal consistency error has occurred.
3060	The service did not respond to control and was stopped with the DosKillProc function.
3061	An error occurred when attempting to run the service program.
3062	The sub-service failed to start.
3064	There is a problem with the file.
3095	This Windows NT computer is configured as a member of a workgroup, not as a member of a domain. The Netlogon service does not need to run in this configuration.
3096	The Windows NT primary domain controller for this domain could not be located.

ID	Message text *(continued)*
3100	The operation failed because a network software error occurred.
3106	An unexpected network control block (NCB) was received. The NCB is the data.
3112	An illegal server message block (SMB) was received. The SMB is the data.
3113	Initialization failed because the requested service *name* could not be started.
3140	The service has stopped due to repeated consecutive occurrences of a network control block (NCB) error. The last bad NCB follows in raw data.
3152	An illegal server message block (SMB) was received. The SMB is the data.
3170	The Alerter service had a problem creating the list of alert recipients. The error code is *code*.
3172	There was an error sending *name* the alert message - *text*. The error code is *code*.
3173	There was an error in creating or reading the alerter mailslot. The error code is *code*.
3206	The replicator cannot update directory *name*. It has tree integrity and is the current directory for some process.
3207	The server cannot export directory *name* to client *name*. It is exported from another server.
3208	The replication server could not update directory *name* from the source on *name* due to error *code*.
3209	Master *name* did not send an update notice for directory *name* at the expected time.
3210	Failed to authenticate with *name*, a Windows NT Server for domain *name*.
3212	Network error *code* occurred.
3215	Unrecognized message received in mailslot.
3216	System error *code* occurred.
3218	IMPORT path *path* cannot be found.
3222	Replicator could not access *filename* on *name* due to *code* system error.
3223	The primary domain controller for domain *name* has apparently failed.
3224	An error occurred while changing this computer's password.
3226	An error occurred while synchronizing with primary domain controller *name*.
3230	A power failure was detected at the server.
3231	The UPS service performed server shutdown.
3232	The UPS service did not complete execution of the user specified shutdown command file.
3236	The UPS service failed to execute a user specified shutdown command file *filename*. The error code is the data.
3257	The system returned an unexpected error code. The error code is the data.
3408	The program cannot be used with this operating system.

ID	**Message text** *(continued)*
3501	You used an invalid option.
3502	System error *code* has occurred.
3503	The command contains an invalid number of arguments.
3504	The command completed with one or more errors.
3505	You used an option with an invalid value.
3506	The option *name* is unknown.
3507	Option *name* is ambiguous.
3510	A command was used with conflicting switches.
3511	Could not find subprogram *name*.
3513	More data is available than can be returned by Windows NT.
3515	This command can be used only on a Windows NT Server system.
3521	The *name* service is not started.
3523	The *name* service could not be started.
3527	The *name* service is stopping.
3528	The *name* service could not be stopped.
3533	The service is starting or stopping. Please try again later.
3534	The service did not report an error.
3538	The *name* service failed to resume.
3539	The *name* service failed to pause.
3540	The *name* service continue is pending. *text*
3541	The *name* service pause is pending. *text*
3544	The *name* service has been started by another process and is pending. *text*
3547	A service-specific error occurred: *code*.
3679	An error occurred while reading your profile.
3689	The Workstation service is already running. Windows NT will ignore command options for the workstation.
3691	There are open files and/or incomplete directory searches pending on the connection to *name*.
3710	An error occurred while opening the Help file.
3711	The Help file is empty.
3712	The Help file is corrupted.
3713	Could not find a primary domain controller for domain *name*.
3716	The device type is unknown.
3719	A matching share could not be found so nothing was deleted.
3721	The password is invalid for *name*.
3722	An error occurred while sending a message to *name*.

ID	Message text *(continued)*
3723	The password or user name is invalid for *name*.
3725	An error occurred when the share was deleted.
3726	The user name is invalid.
3727	The password is invalid.
3728	The passwords do not match.
3729	Your persistent connections were not all restored.
3730	This is not a valid computer name or domain name.
3732	Default permissions cannot be set for that resource.
3734	A valid password was not entered.
3735	A valid name was not entered.
3736	The resource named cannot be shared.
3737	The permissions string contains invalid permissions.
3738	You can only perform this operation on printers and communication devices.
3742	*Name* is an invalid user or group name.
3743	The server is not configured for remote administration.
3753	User *user name* is not a member of group *name*.
3754	User *user name* is already a member of group *name*.
3755	There is no such user: *user name*.
3756	This is an invalid response.
3757	No valid response was provided.
3760	*Date* is not a recognized day of the week.
3761	The time range specified ends before it starts.
3762	*Number* is not a recognized hour.
3763	*Number* is not a valid specification for minutes.
3764	Time supplied is not exactly on the hour.
3765	12 and 24 hour time formats may not be mixed.
3766	*Text* is not a valid 12-hour suffix.
3767	An illegal date format has been supplied.
3768	An illegal day range has been supplied.
3769	An illegal time range has been supplied.
3770	Arguments to NET USER are invalid. Check the minimum password length and/or arguments supplied.
3771	The value for ENABLESCRIPT must be YES.
3773	An illegal country code has been supplied.
3774	The user was successfully created but could not be added to the USERS local group.

ID	Message text *(continued)*
3775	The user context supplied is invalid.
3776	The dynamic-link library *name* could not be loaded, or an error occurred while trying to use it.
3777	Sending files is no longer supported.
3778	You may not specify paths for ADMIN$ and IPC$ shares.
3779	User or group *name* is already a member of local group *name*.
3780	There is no such user or group: *name*.
3781	There is no such computer: *computer name*.
3782	The computer *computer name* already exists.
3790	The system could not find message: *text*.
3802	This schedule date is invalid.
3805	The Server service has not been started.
3806	The AT job ID does not exist.
3809	The command line cannot exceed 259 characters.
3813	The AT schedule file was deleted.
3815	The AT command has timed-out. Please try again later.
3816	The minimum password age for user accounts cannot be greater than the maximum password age.
3817	You have specified a value that is incompatible with servers with down-level software. Please specify a lower value.
3870	*Computer name* is not a valid computer name.
3871	*Code* is not a valid Windows NT message number.
3912	Could not locate a time-server.
3913	Could not find the primary domain controller for domain *name*.
3915	The user's home directory could not be determined.
3916	The user's home directory has not been specified.
3917	The name specified for the user's home directory *name* is not a universal naming convention (UNC) name.
3932	*Name* is not a valid domain or workgroup name.
3951	You specified too many values for the *name* option.
3952	You entered an invalid value for the *name* option.
3953	The syntax is incorrect.
3960	You specified an invalid file number.
3961	You specified an invalid print job number.
3963	The user or group account specified cannot be found.

ID	Message text *(continued)*
4738	The share name entered is not accessible from an MS-DOS workstation. Are you sure you want to use this share name? *name*:
5022	Printing errors occurred.
5305	A network control block (NCB) command timed-out. The session may have terminated abnormally. The NCB is the data.
5309	No resource was available in the network adapter. The network control block (NCB) request was refused. The NCB is the data.
5317	The local session table is full. The network control block (NCB) request was refused. The NCB is the data.
5334	There are too many network control block (NCB) commands outstanding. The NCB request was refused. The NCB is the data.
5508	The security database full synchronization has been initiated by the server *name*.
5509	Windows NT could not be started as configured. A previous working configuration was used instead.
5510	The exception 0x*number* occurred in the application *application* at location 0x*number*.
5511	The server *name* claims to be a primary domain controller for the *name* domain. However, the security identifier on the server *name* in that domain and on the primary domain controller *name* don't match. One of the servers should be removed from the domain.
5512	The server *name* and *name* both claim to be the primary domain controller for the *name* domain. One of the servers should be demoted or removed from the domain.
5513	The computer *computer name* connected to server *name* using the trust relationship to the *name* domain. However, the computer doesn't properly know the security identifier (SID) for the domain. Reestablish the trust relationship.
5601	The password for this computer is not found in the local security database.
5602	An internal error occurred while accessing the computer's local or network security database.
5700	The Netlogon service could not initialize the replication data structures successfully. The service is terminated.
5701	The Netlogon service failed to update the domain trust list.
5702	The Netlogon service could not add the RPC interface. The service is terminated.
5703	The Netlogon service could not read a mailslot message from *name*.
5704	The Netlogon service failed to register the service with the service controller. The service is terminated.
5705	The change log cache maintained by the Netlogon service for database changes is corrupted. The Netlogon service is resetting the change log.
5706	The Netlogon service could not create server share *name*.

ID	**Message text** *(continued)*
5707	The down-level logon request for the user *user name* from *name* failed.
5708	The down-level logoff request for the user *user name* from *name* failed.
5709	The Windows NT *network* logon request for the user *name* from *computer name* (via *name*) failed.
5710	The Windows NT *network* logoff request for the user *name* from *computer name* failed.
5711	The partial synchronization request from the server *name* completed successfully. *Number* change(s) has (have) been returned to the caller.
5712	The partial synchronization request from the server *name* failed.
5715	The partial synchronization replication of the *name* database from the primary domain controller *name* completed successfully. *Number* change(s) is (are) applied to the database.
5716	The partial synchronization replication of the *name* database from the primary domain controller *name* failed.
5717	The full synchronization replication of the *name* database from the primary domain controller *name* completed successfully.
5718	The full synchronization of the *name* database from the primary domain controller *name* failed.
5719	No Windows NT Server for the domain *name* is available.
5720	The session setup to the Windows NT Server *name* for the domain *name* failed because the computer *computer name* does not have a local security database account.
5721	The session setup to the Windows NT Server *name* for the domain *name* failed because the Windows NT Server does not have an account for the computer *computer name*.
5722	The session setup from the computer *computer name* failed to authenticate. The name of the account referenced in the security database is *user name*.
5723	The session setup from the computer *computer name* failed because there is no trust account in the security database for this computer. The name of the account referenced in the security database is *user name*.
5724	Could not register control handler with service controller *name*.
5725	Could not set service status with service controller *name*.

Down-level Network Message ID Numbers

This table contains the messages that can be returned to a Windows NT Workstation or Windows NT Server system from an earlier operating system (such as Windows for Workgroups or LAN Manager), which is called, for convenience, a down-level system.

In Chapter 4, "Message Reference," the network messages are presented alphabetically and interspersed with the other system messages. In the following table, they have been arranged numerically. Missing or skipped numbers could be related to simple messages, such as "Password expires," that were not included in the printed version, or they may be in the Windows NT Workstation/Windows NT Server Network Message ID Numbers table, which is provided in the preceding section of this chapter.

ID	Message text
2103	The server could not be located.
2107	The device is not connected.
2117	The operation is invalid on a redirected resource.
2122	The Peer service supports only two simultaneous users.
2127	A remote API error occurred.
2131	An error occurred when opening or reading the configuration file.
2139	The requested information is not available.
2143	The event name is invalid.
2149	A line in the configuration file is too long.
2152	The printer destination cannot be found.
2153	The printer destination already exists.
2154	The printer queue already exists.
2155	No more printers can be added.
2156	No more print jobs can be added.
2157	No more printer destinations can be added.
2158	This printer destination is idle and cannot accept control operations.
2159	This printer destination request contains an invalid control function.
2160	The print processor is not responding.
2161	The spooler is not running.
2162	This operation cannot be performed on the print destination in its current state.
2163	This operation cannot be performed on the printer queue in its current state.
2164	This operation cannot be performed on the print job in its current state.
2165	A spooler memory allocation failure occurred.
2166	The device driver does not exist.

ID	**Message text** *(continued)*
2167	The data type is not supported by the print processor.
2168	The print processor is not installed.
2181	The service table is full.
2183	The service does not respond to control actions.
2188	The configuration file contains an invalid service program name.
2190	The service ended abnormally.
2192	The service control dispatcher could not find the service name in the dispatch table.
2193	The service control dispatcher pipe read failed.
2200	This workstation is already logged on to the local-area network.
2201	The workstation is not logged on to the local-area network.
2204	The logon processor did not add the message alias.
2205	The logon processor did not add the message alias.
2206	The logoff processor did not delete the message alias.
2207	The logoff processor did not delete the message alias.
2209	Network logons are paused.
2210	A centralized logon-server conflict occurred.
2212	An error occurred while loading or running the logon script.
2214	The logon server was not specified. Your computer will be logged on as STANDALONE.
2215	The logon server could not be found.
2216	There is already a logon domain for this computer.
2217	The logon server could not validate the logon.
2225	The resource permission list already exists.
2228	There are too many names in the user accounts database.
2230	The limit of 64 entries per resource was exceeded.
2231	Deleting a user with a session is not allowed.
2232	The parent directory could not be located.
2235	This user is not cached in the user accounts database session cache.
2238	This user account is undefined.
2243	The password of this user cannot change.
2244	This password cannot be used now.
2248	No updates are necessary to this replicant network/local security database.
2252	This device is currently being shared.
2271	The Messenger service is already started.
2272	The Messenger service failed to start.

ID	**Message text** *(continued)*
2275	This message alias has been added but is still forwarded.
2279	Messages cannot be forwarded back to the same workstation.
2284	The Messenger service has not been started.
2286	The forwarded message alias could not be found on the network.
2287	The message alias table on the remote station is full.
2288	Messages for this alias are not currently being forwarded.
2295	A write fault occurred.
2300	This operation is not supported on computers with multiple networks.
2314	There is not an open file with that identification number.
2315	A failure occurred when executing a remote administration command.
2316	A failure occurred when opening a remote temporary file.
2318	This device cannot be shared as both a spooled and a non-spooled resource.
2319	The information in the list of servers may be incorrect.
2320	The computer is not active in this domain.
2331	The operation is invalid for this device.
2332	This device cannot be shared.
2333	This device was not open.
2334	This device name list is invalid.
2335	The queue priority is invalid.
2337	There are no shared communication devices.
2338	The queue you specified does not exist.
2340	This list of devices is invalid.
2341	The requested device is invalid.
2342	This device is already in use by the spooler.
2343	This device is already in use as a communication device.
2354	The string and prefix specified are too long.
2356	This path component is invalid.
2370	Profile files cannot exceed 64K.
2371	The start offset is out of range.
2372	The system cannot delete current connections to network resources.
2373	The system was unable to parse the command line in this file.
2374	An error occurred while loading the profile file.
2375	Errors occurred while saving the profile file. The profile was partially saved.
2377	Log file *filename* is full.
2380	The source path cannot be a directory.

ID	Message text *(continued)*
2381	The source path is illegal.
2382	The destination path is illegal.
2383	The source and destination paths are on different servers.
2385	The Run server you requested is paused.
2389	An error occurred when communicating with a Run server.
2391	An error occurred when starting a background process.
2392	The shared resource you are connected to could not be found.
2400	The LAN adapter number is invalid.
2402	Active connections still exist.
2405	The drive letter is in use locally.
2430	The specified client is already registered for the specified event.
2431	The alert table is full.
2433	The alert recipient is invalid.
2434	A user's session with this server has been deleted because the user's logon hours are no longer valid.
2440	The log file does not contain the requested record number.
2450	The user accounts database is not configured correctly.
2451	This operation is not permitted when the Netlogon service is running.
2452	This operation is not allowed on the last administrative account.
2454	Could not set logon information for this user.
2455	The Netlogon service has not been started.
2456	Unable to add to the user accounts database.
2458	A password mismatch has been detected.
2460	The server identification does not specify a valid server.
2461	The session identification does not specify a valid session.
2462	The connection identification does not specify a valid connection.
2463	There is no space for another entry in the table of available servers.
2464	The server has reached the maximum number of sessions it supports.
2465	The server has reached the maximum number of connections it supports.
2466	The server cannot open more files because it has reached its maximum number.
2467	There are no alternate servers registered on this server.
2480	The UPS driver could not be accessed by the UPS service.
3000	Drive *name* is nearly full. *Number* bytes are available. Please warn users and delete unneeded files.
3001	*Number* errors were logged in the last *number* minutes. Please review the server's error log.

ID	**Message text** *(continued)*
3002	*Number* network errors occurred in the last *number* minutes. Please review the server's error log. The server and/or network hardware may need service.
3003	There were *number* bad password attempts in the last *number* minutes. Please review the server's audit trail.
3004	There were *number* access-denied errors in the last *number* minutes. Please review the server's audit trail.
3006	The error log is full. No errors will be logged until the file is cleared or the limit is raised.
3007	The error log is 80% full.
3008	The audit log is full. No audit entries will be logged until the file is cleared or the limit is raised.
3009	The audit log is 80% full.
3010	An error occurred closing file *filename*. Please check the file to make sure it is not corrupted.
3011	The administrator has closed *filename*.
3012	There were *number* access-denied errors in the last *number* minutes.
3025	A defective sector on drive *drive letter* has been replaced (hotfixed). No data was lost. You should run CHKDSK soon to restore full performance and replenish the volume's spare sector pool. The hotfix occurred while processing a remote request.
3026	A disk error occurred on the HPFS volume in drive *drive letter*. The error occurred while processing a remote request.
3027	The user accounts database (NET.ACC) is corrupted. The local security system is replacing the corrupted NET.ACC with the backup made on *date* at *time*. Any updates made to the database after this time are lost.
3028	The user accounts database (NET.ACC) is missing. The local security system is restoring the backup database made on *date* at *time*. Any updates made to the database after this time are lost.
3029	Local security could not be started because the user accounts database (NET.ACC) was missing or corrupted, and no usable backup database was present. THE SYSTEM IS NOT SECURE.
3033	User *user name* has exceeded the account limitation *text* on server *name*.
3036	The replicator attempted to log on at *computer name* as *user name* and failed.
3046	Cannot log on. User is currently logged on and argument TRYUSER is set to NO.
3048	EXPORT path *path* cannot be found.
3050	Replicator failed to update signal file in directory *name* due to *code* system error.
3052	The required parameter was not provided on the command line or in the configuration file.

ID	Message text *(continued)*
3053	LAN Manager does not recognize *name* as a valid option.
3055	A problem exists with the system configuration.
3058	The configuration file or the command line has an ambiguous option.
3059	The configuration file or the command line has a duplicate parameter.
3063	There is a conflict in the value or use of these options: *name*.
3075	Bad or missing LAN Manager root directory.
3076	The network software is not installed.
3077	The server is not started.
3078	The server cannot access the user accounts database (NET.ACC).
3079	Incompatible files are installed in the LANMAN tree.
3080	The LANMAN\LOGS directory is invalid.
3081	The domain specified could not be used.
3082	The computer name is being used as a message alias on another computer.
3083	The announcement of the server name failed.
3084	The user accounts database is not configured correctly.
3085	The server is not running with user-level security.
3087	The workstation is not configured properly.
3088	View your error log for details.
3089	Unable to write to this file.
3090	ADDPAK file is corrupted. Delete LANMAN\NETPROG\ADDPAK.SER and reapply all ADDPAKs.
3091	The LM386 server cannot be started because CACHE.EXE is not running.
3092	There is no account for this computer in the security database.
3093	This computer is not a member of the group SERVERS.
3094	The group SERVERS is not present in the local security database.
3098	The service failed to authenticate with the primary domain controller.
3099	There is a problem with the security database creation date or serial number.
3101	The system ran out of a resource controlled by the *name* option.
3102	The service failed to obtain a long-term lock on the segment for network control blocks (NCBs). The error code is the data.
3103	The service failed to release the long-term lock on the segment for network control blocks (NCBs). The error code is the data.
3104	There was an error stopping service *name*. The error code from NetServiceControl is the data.
3105	Initialization failed because of a system execution failure on path *path*. The system error code is the data.

ID	Message text *(continued)*
3107	The network is not started.
3108	A DosDevIoctl or DosFsCtl to NETWKSTA.SYS failed. The data shown is in this format: DWORD approx CS:IP of call to ioctl or fsctl; WORD error code; WORD ioctl or fsctl number
3109	Unable to create or open system semaphore *name*. The error code is the data.
3110	Initialization failed because of an open/create error on the file *filename*. The system error code is the data.
3111	An unexpected NetBIOS error occurred. The error code is the data.
3114	Some entries in the error log were lost because of a buffer overflow.
3120	Initialization parameters controlling resource usage other than net buffers are sized so that too much memory is needed.
3121	The server cannot increase the size of a memory segment.
3122	Initialization failed because account file *filename* is either incorrect or not present.
3123	Initialization failed because network *name* was not started.
3124	The server failed to start. Either all three chdev parameters must be zero or all three must be nonzero.
3125	A remote API request was halted due to the following invalid description string: *text*.
3126	The network *name* ran out of network control blocks (NCBs). You may need to increase NCBs for this network. The following information includes the number of NCBs submitted by the server when this error occurred: *text*.
3127	The server cannot create the *name* mailslot needed to send the ReleaseMemory alert message. The error received is: *code*.
3128	The server failed to register for the ReleaseMemory alert, with recipient *computer name*. The error code from NetAlertStart is the data.
3129	The server cannot update the AT schedule file. The file is corrupted.
3130	The server encountered an error when calling NetIMakeLMFileName. The error code is the data.
3131	Initialization failed because of a system execution failure on path *path*. There is not enough memory to start the process. The system error code is the data.
3132	Longterm lock of the server buffers failed. Check the swap disk's free space and restart the system to start the server.
3141	The Message server has stopped due to a lock on the Message server shared data segment.
3150	A file system error occurred while opening or writing to the system message log file *filename*. Message logging has been switched off due to the error. The error code is the data.
3160	The workstation information segment is bigger than 64K. The size follows, in DWORD format: *text*.

ID	Message text *(continued)*
3161	The workstation was unable to get the name-number of the computer.
3162	The workstation could not initialize the Async NetBIOS Thread. The error code is the data.
3163	The workstation could not open the initial shared segment. The error code is the data.
3164	The workstation host table is full.
3165	A bad mailslot server message block (SMB) was received. The SMB is the data.
3166	The workstation encountered an error while trying to start the user accounts database. The error code is the data.
3167	The workstation encountered an error while responding to an SSI revalidation request. The function code and the error codes are the data.
3171	There was an error expanding *name* as a group name. Try splitting the group into two or more smaller groups.
3174	The server could not read the AT schedule file.
3175	The server found an invalid AT schedule record.
3176	The server could not find an AT schedule file so it created one.
3177	The server could not access the *name* network with NetBiosOpen.
3178	The AT command processor could not run *application*.
3180	WARNING: Because of a lazy-write error, drive *drive letter* now contains some corrupted data. The cache is stopped.
3181	A defective sector on drive *drive letter* has been replaced (hotfixed). No data was lost. You should run CHKDSK soon to restore full performance and replenish the volume's spare sector pool. The hotfix occurred while processing a remote request.
3182	A disk error occurred on the HPFS volume in drive *drive letter*. The error occurred while processing a remote request.
3183	The user accounts database (NET.ACC) is corrupted. The local security system is replacing the corrupted NET.ACC with the backup made at *date*. Any updates made to the database after this time are lost.
3184	The user accounts database (NET.ACC) is missing. The local security system is restoring the backup database made at *date*. Any updates made to the database after this time are lost.
3185	Local security could not be started because the user accounts database (NET.ACC) was missing or corrupted, and no usable backup database was present. THE SYSTEM IS NOT SECURE.
3186	Local security could not be started because an error occurred during initialization. The error code returned is *code*. THE SYSTEM IS NOT SECURE.
3190	A NetWksta internal error has occurred: *code*.

ID	Message text *(continued)*
3191	The redirector is out of a resource: *name*.
3192	A server message block (SMB) error occurred on the connection to *name*. The SMB header is the data.
3193	A virtual circuit error occurred on the session to *name*. The network control block (NCB) command and return code is the data.
3194	Hanging up a stuck session to *name*.
3195	A network control block (NCB) error occurred *code*. The NCB is the data.
3196	A write operation to *filename* failed. Data may have been lost.
3197	Reset of driver *name* failed to complete the network control block (NCB). The NCB is the data.
3198	The amount of resource *name* requested was more than the maximum. The maximum amount was allocated.
3204	The server could not create a thread. The THREADS parameter in the CONFIG.SYS file should be increased.
3205	The server could not close *filename*. The file is probably corrupted.
3211	The replicator attempted to log on at *computer name* as *user name* and failed.
3213	Replicator limit for files in a directory has been exceeded.
3214	Replicator limit for tree depth has been exceeded.
3217	Cannot log on. User is currently logged on and argument TRYUSER is set to NO.
3219	EXPORT path *path* cannot be found.
3220	Replicator failed to update the signal file in directory *name* due to *code* system error.
3221	Disk Fault Tolerance Error *code*.
3225	An error occurred while updating the logon or logoff information for *user name*.
3233	The UPS driver could not be opened. The error code is the data.
3250	Initialization failed because of an invalid or missing parameter in the configuration file *filename*.
3251	Initialization failed because of an invalid line in the configuration file *filename*. The invalid line is the data.
3252	Initialization failed because of an error in the configuration file *filename*.
3253	The file *filename* has been changed after initialization. The boot-block loading was temporarily terminated.
3254	The files do not fit to the boot-block configuration file *filename*. Change the BASE and ORG definitions or the order of the files.
3255	Initialization failed because the dynamic-link library *name* returned an incorrect version number.
3256	There was an unrecoverable error in the dynamic-link library of the service.

ID	**Message text** *(continued)*
3258	The fault-tolerance error log file, LANROOT\LOGS\FT.LOG, is more than 64K.
3259	The fault-tolerance error log file, LANROOT\LOGS \FT.LOG, had the update in progress bit set upon opening, which means that the system crashed while working on the error log.
3304	A network error occurred.
3400	There is not enough memory to start the Workstation service.
3401	An error occurred when reading the NETWORKS entry in the LANMAN.INI file.
3402	This is an invalid argument: *name*.
3403	The *text* NETWORKS entry in the LANMAN.INI file has a syntax error and will be ignored.
3404	There are too many NETWORKS entries in the LANMAN.INI file.
3406	An error occurred when opening network device driver *name* = *name*.
3407	Device driver *name* sent a bad BiosLinkage response.
3409	The redirector is already installed.
3411	There was an error installing NETWKSTA.SYS. Press ENTER to continue.
3412	Resolver linkage problem.
3512	The software requires a newer version of the operating system.
3526	The workstation has open files.
3535	An error occurred controlling the device.
3675	The session from *computer name* has open files.
3677	New connections will not be remembered.
3678	An error occurred while saving your profile. The state of your remembered connections has not changed.
3680	An error occurred while restoring the connection to *name*.
3694	The shared queue cannot be deleted while a print job is being spooled to the queue.
3714	This operation is privileged on systems with earlier versions of the software.
3717	The log file has been corrupted.
3718	Program filenames must end with .EXE.
3720	A bad value is in the units-per-week field of the user record.
3758	The destination list provided does not match the destination list of the printer queue.
3759	Your password cannot be changed until *date*.
3803	The LANMAN root directory is unavailable.
3804	The SCHED.LOG file could not be opened.

ID	**Message text** *(continued)*
3807	The AT schedule file is corrupted.
3808	The delete failed due to a problem with the AT schedule file.
3810	The AT schedule file could not be updated because the disk is full.
3812	The AT schedule file is invalid. Please delete the file and create a new one.
5170	The workstation must be started with the Net Start command.
5281	*Drive letter* has a remembered connection to *name*. Do you want to overwrite the remembered connection? *path*
5301	Illegal network control block (NCB) buffer length on SEND DATAGRAM, SEND BROADCAST, ADAPTER STATUS, or SESSION STATUS. The NCB is the data.
5302	The data descriptor array specified in the network control block (NCB) is invalid. The NCB is the data.
5303	The command specified in the network control block (NCB) is illegal. The NCB is the data.
5304	The message correlator specified in the network control block (NCB) is invalid. The NCB is the data.
5306	An incomplete network control block (NCB) message was received. The NCB is the data.
5307	The buffer address specified in the network control block (NCB) is illegal. The NCB is the data.
5308	The session number specified in the network control block (NCB) is not active. The NCB is the data.
5310	The session specified in the network control block (NCB) was closed. The NCB is the data.
5311	The network control block (NCB) command was canceled. The NCB is the data.
5312	The message segment specified in the network control block (NCB) is illogical. The NCB is the data.
5313	The name already exists in the local adapter name table. The network control block (NCB) request was refused. The NCB is the data.
5314	The network adapter name table is full. The network control block (NCB) request was refused. The NCB is the data.
5315	The network name has active sessions and is now de-registered. The network control block (NCB) command completed. The NCB is the data.
5316	A previously issued Receive Lookahead command is active for this session. The network control block (NCB) command was rejected. The NCB is the data.
5318	A network control block (NCB) session open was rejected. No LISTEN is outstanding on the remote computer. The NCB is the data.
5319	The name number specified in the network control block (NCB) is illegal. The NCB is the data.

ID	Message text *(continued)*
5320	The call name specified in the network control block (NCB) cannot be found or did not answer. The NCB is the data.
5321	The name specified in the network control block (NCB) was not found. Cannot put '*' or 00h in the NCB name. The NCB is the data.
5322	The name specified in the network control block (NCB) is in use on a remote adapter. The NCB is the data.
5323	The name specified in the network control block (NCB) has been deleted. The NCB is the data.
5324	The session specified in the network control block (NCB) ended abnormally. The NCB is the data.
5325	The network protocol has detected two or more identical names on the network. The network control block (NCB) is the data.
5326	An unexpected protocol packet was received. There may be an incompatible remote device. The network control block (NCB) is the data.
5333	The NetBIOS interface is busy. The network control block (NCB) request was refused. The NCB is the data.
5335	The adapter number specified in the network control block (NCB) is illegal. The NCB is the data.
5336	The network control block (NCB) command completed while a cancel was occurring. The NCB is the data.
5337	The name specified in the network control block (NCB) is reserved. The NCB is the data.
5338	The network control block (NCB) command is not valid to cancel. The NCB is the data.
5351	There are multiple network control block (NCB) requests for the same session. The NCB request was refused. The NCB is the data.
5352	There has been a network adapter error. The only NetBIOS command that may be issued is an NCB RESET. The network control block (NCB) is the data.
5354	The maximum number of applications was exceeded. The network control block (NCB) request was refused. The NCB is the data.
5356	The requested resources are not available. The network control block (NCB) request was refused. The NCB is the data.
5364	A system error has occurred. The network control block (NCB) request was refused. The NCB is the data.
5365	A ROM checksum failure has occurred. The network control block (NCB) request was refused. The NCB is the data.
5366	A RAM test failure has occurred. The network control block (NCB) request was refused. The NCB is the data.
5367	A digital loopback failure has occurred. The network control block (NCB) request was refused. The NCB is the data.

ID	**Message text** *(continued)*
5368	An analog loopback failure has occurred. The network control block (NCB) request was refused. The NCB is the data.
5369	An interface failure has occurred. The network control block (NCB) request was refused. The NCB is the data.
5370	An unrecognized network control block (NCB) return code was received. The NCB is the data.
5380	A network adapter malfunction has occurred. The network control block (NCB) request was refused. The NCB is the data.
5381	The network control block (NCB) command is still pending. The NCB is the data.
5500	The update log on *name* is over 80% capacity. The primary domain controller *name* is not retrieving the updates.
5501	The update log on *name* is full, and no further updates can be added until the primary domain controller *name* retrieves the updates.
5502	The time difference with the primary domain controller *name* exceeds the maximum allowed skew of *number* seconds.
5503	The account of user *user name* has been locked out on *name* due to *number* bad password attempts.
5504	The *filename* log file cannot be opened.
5505	The *filename* log file is corrupted and will be cleared.
5506	The Application log file could not be opened. *Filename* will be used as the default log file.
5507	The *filename* log file is full.
5600	Could not share the User or Script path.
5713	The full synchronization request from the server *name* completed successfully. *Number* object(s) has (have) been returned to the caller.
5714	The full synchronization request from the server *name* failed.

CHAPTER 4

Message Reference

This chapter contains an alphabetical listing of error and system-information messages generated by the Windows NT operating system. The Messages database provides an online version of this chapter plus some additional online-only messages.

Messages beginning with a replaceable parameter are alphabetized at the beginning of the list by the variable name used to replace that parameter. For a list of the variable names used in the Messages database, see the "Welcome" chapter at the beginning of this book.

"*name*" **node does not speak any of our protocols**

[Dynamic Data Exchange]

No communication can take place with the specified node because that node is not using any of the protocols used by NetDDE.

Load one of the protocols that NetDDE supports on the specified node.

"*name*" **node selected an invalid protocol:** *name*

[Dynamic Data Exchange]

The computer at the specified node tried to use a protocol that is not supported by NetDDE.

Account Deleted

[Services for Macintosh (SFM)]

The security ID (SID) on the permissions for a Macintosh directory belongs to a user or group account that was deleted through User Manager.

Use the MacFile menu in File Manager to assign a new user or group to the directory.

Account Invalid

[Services for Macintosh (SFM)]

The security ID (SID) on the permissions for a Macintosh directory belongs to a user or group account that was deleted through User Manager.

Use the MacFile menu in File Manager to assign a new user or group to the directory.

Account Unknown

[Services for Macintosh (SFM)]

If the security ID (SID) for user or group permissions for a Macintosh directory are left over from a previous installation of Windows NT Advanced Server, this message is displayed.

Use the MacFile Permissions menu in File Manager to reassign the owner or group permissions to a new account.

address **is not a valid default gateway. The service could not be started.**

[Netevent]

The IP address specified for the default gateway is invalid.

Use the Network option in Control Panel to correct the default gateway parameter for the TCP/IP protocol. Select TCP/IP protocol and then choose Configure. Restart the computer once you have reconfigured the protocol.

application - **OS/2 Subsystem Bound Application Load Failure**

[OS/2 Subsystem]

You cannot run this application under the OS/2 subsystem, because it uses an OS/2 API that is not supported by the subsystem. However, you might be able to run it using Forcedos.

After the application terminates, try again using Forcedos.

application **: '** *name* **' is a directory!**

[TFTP]

When you use the Tftp command to transfer files from a remote computer to your computer, you cannot specify the directory name as the destination on your local computer. You must use a filename.

Retype the Tftp command, specifying a filename for the local destination instead of a directory.

application **: Argument missing after /** *text*

[FINDSTR]

In the Findstr command line, if you specify the c:/, f:/, or /g: switches, they must be followed immediately by some text (a literal string, text pattern, or filename, depending on the switch).

Correct your usage of these switches in the Findstr command line and retry the command. To see what item of text to follow these switches with, type HELP followed by the command line (in this case, Findstr).

application **: bad argument** *text*

[TCP/IP]

You specified an invalid Internet (IP) address in the Route command.

Make sure the Internet address arguments are typed correctly, and then retry the Route command.

application **: Bad command line**

[FINDSTR]

You have entered a bad command. For instance, you may not have specified any strings to search for in the Findstr command line.

To see the correct syntax for the command line, type HELP followed by the command name (in this case, Findstr).

application **: bad gateway address** *address*

[TCP/IP]

If you used a network name or alias for the destination parameter in the Route command and you get this message, then the Route command was unable to find the name or alias in the HOSTS file on the local computer (the path to the HOSTS file is \systemroot\system32\drivers\etc). If you used an IP address, you specified an invalid format. For example, you may not have used a dotted decimal form, such as 11.1.12.17.

Make sure the gateway is physically attached to the network adapter that is in your computer (is part of the same subnet). Then retry the Route command, using a valid gateway address.

application **: bad port number--** *number*

[FTP Server]

The port number parameter you used in an Ftp command is not valid.

Retry the command using a different port number.

application **: can't establish connection**

[TCP/IP]

The TCP/IP utility named at the beginning of the message could not establish a connection with the remote host, either because there is no networking software on the remote computer, the corresponding server is not running on the remote computer, or no route can be found between your computer and the remote computer.

Make sure you are using the right remote host. If so, wait, and then retry the remote command. If you still get this message, ask your network administrator to check the condition of the remote computer and the routers between the two computers.

application **: can't establish stderr**

[TCP/IP]

The TCP/IP utility cannot establish a stderr connection with a remote host. There may be no networking software on the remote computer, the corresponding server may not be running on the remote computer, or no route can be found between your computer and the remote computer.

Make sure you are trying to use the right remote host. If you are, wait, and then retry the remote command. If you still get this message, ask your network administrator to check the condition of the remote computer and the routers between the two computers.

application **: can't open local file '** *filename* **' unable to open file for read** *text.*

[TFTP]

The TCP/IP utility, Tftp, was transferring a file from your computer to a remote computer, but was unable to open the file on your computer.

Make sure you specified the correct path to the file in the Tftp command, and that you did not mistype it. Also, check that you have permission to read the file. Then, retry the Tftp command.

application **: can't read from local file '** *filename* **'**

[TFTP]

You specified a file to transfer to a remote computer, but you do not have read access to that particular file.

Ask your system administrator to give you the needed access.

application **: Cannot read file list from** *filename*

[FINDSTR]

The Findstr utility was unable to open the file that contains the list of files to search.

Check the Findstr command line and make sure that you specified the correct path and that there are no misspellings. You may need to use File Manager to search for the file. Also, check that you have access rights to the file.

application **: Cannot read strings from** *filename*

[FINDSTR]

The Findstr utility was unable to open the file that contains the search strings.

Check the Findstr command line and make sure that you specified the correct path and that there are no misspellings. You may need to use File Manager to search for the file. Also, check that you have access rights to the file.

application **: don't know host '** *name* **'**

[TFTP]

Your computer cannot resolve the host name you used as a parameter in the Tftp command into a remote network hardware address.

Make sure you typed the parameter correctly in the Tftp command. If you did, there may be several reasons why your computer cannot resolve the remote computer name. Contact your network administrator to sort out the problem.

application : **Error reading file** *filename*.

[FINDSTR]

There are probably bad sectors in this file.

Restore the file from a backup copy. Then try again.

Application - **FROZEN**

[Virtual DOS Machine (VDM)]

This is a status message. For instance, NTVDM might display this message in the title bar of the Command Prompt window when the user minimizes an application while it is displaying a full-screen graphic display. This message reminds the user that as long as the application is minimized, it is not running.

application : **No search strings**

[FINDSTR]

Probably, in using the Findstr command, you specified a file that is to contain the string(s) to search for, but that file is empty. Or you may not have specified strings to search for in the Findstr command line.

Retry the Findstr command, but this time specify the strings to search for.

application : **not a plain file.** *filename*

[FTP Server]

Using the Ftp command, you attempted to retrieve the file named in the message, but the file is either a directory or a special device.

Verify the name of the file you want to retrieve and retry the Ftp command, using that name.

application : **Out of memory**

[FINDSTR]

The Findstr utility has run out of memory.

Quit some unneeded applications, then retry the Findstr command.

application : **Read file failed. (Cannot create file mapping.)**

[FINDSTR]

You do not have enough Windows NT quota right now to carry out the Findstr command, which uses memory-mapped files.

This is a dynamic situation. Either wait a few seconds and retry the Findstr command, or quit some unneeded applications which may be using up some of your quota. If you still get this message, you may have to ask your system administrator to increase your quota.

application **: remote terminal session not supported**

[TCP/IP]

You must specify a command parameter with the Rsh command. Initiating a remote login session by using the Rsh command with no parameter is not supported by Windows NT.

Use the TCP/IP utility, Telnet, to initiate a remote login session. Or, if you just forgot to use the command parameter with the Rsh command, retry the Rsh command.

application **:** *text* **ignored**

[FINDSTR]

You used a switch in the Findstr command line that is not recognized by the Findstr utility. The utility ignored the parameter and went ahead with its task. This can happen if you forget the colon (:) suffix required of some Findstr switches.

To avoid this message in the future, stop using the parameter named in the message. To see which switches are recognized by the Findstr utility, and which ones require the trailing colon, type HELP followed by the command name (in this case, Findstr).

application **: tftp/udp: unknown service**

[TFTP]

To transfer files to or from a remote computer using the TCP/IP Tftp command, the remote computer must have Ftp server running. It does not.

If you can transfer the files to a different computer, try using it. Similarly, if the files you are getting from the remote computer also reside on another computer, try using it. Otherwise, you will have to contact someone at the remote computer, or your network administrator, to get the Ftp server running on the remote computer.

application **: transfer aborted**

[TFTP]

The process receiving the file transfer has ended before the file transfer was completed.

Retry the file transfer. If you still get this message, contact your network administrator.

application **: unexpected M_PROTO type:** *code*

[TCP/IP]

The Netstat utility was gathering statistics about a protocol (TCP, UDP, or IP) and received a reply that had the wrong format (a format not consistent with the protocol).

No direct user action is necessary. The Netstat utility will continue executing. If you get this message often, ask your network administrator to interpret the protocol type code that is displayed at the end of the message, and take appropriate action.

application **: Write error**

[FINDSTR]

You may have tried to redirect the output of the Findstr command to a file (from the console) and the disk the file is on is full.

If you must redirect the output of the Findstr command to a disk file, either first delete some unneeded files from the disk or use a different disk when you retry the Findstr command.

application **:TLI Error** *code*

[FTP Server] [TCP/IP]

The TCP/IP utility named at the start of the message had a data connection fail due to an unexpected TLI error.

Retry the operation. If you get this message again, contact your network administrator to interpret the meaning of the TLI error code displayed at the end of the message and take corrective action.

application **:TLOOK returned** *code*

[FTP Server] [TCP/IP]

The TCP/IP utility named at the start of the message had a data connection fail due to an unexpected event.

Retry the operation. If you still get this message, contact your network administrator to interpret the meaning of the event number that is displayed at the end of the message and take corrective action.

application **could not copy all files to the Emergency Repair Disk. One or more configuration file was not found.**

[Repair Disk]

The Rdisk utility could not find one or more necessary files in your \<systemroot>\repair directory and therefore could not copy the files to your Emergency Repair Disk. If the SETUP.LOG file is missing, the Emergency Repair Disk is unusable. If any other file is missing, the Emergency Repair Disk might be partially usable.

If SETUP.LOG, DEFAULT.*, SECURITY.*, or SAM.* are missing, reinstall Windows NT because the Rdisk utility cannot recreate these files. If the missing files are SYSTEM.* and/or SOFTWARE.*, run Rdisk to update the repair information and recreate the missing files. Then create the Emergency Repair Disk again.

application **could not copy all files to the Emergency Repair Disk. The Emergency Repair Disk is full. The configuration files were saved in your hard disk.**

[Repair Disk]

The repair disk might not be usable. During the repair process, use the repair information on the hard disk rather than the repair information on the Emergency Repair Disk.

application **could not save all configuration files.**

[Repair Disk]

Some of the repair information in your \<systemroot>\repair directory could not be saved to an Emergency Repair disk. A repair disk created after you see this message might not be usable unless you are attempting to repair system files.

application **is unable to get configuration information for the selected floppy disk drive.**

[Repair Disk]

A hardware problem might be preventing the repair disk from detecting the type of floppy drive on your computer.

Check the Hardware Compatibility List to verify that your floppy drive is compatible with Windows NT. If so, contact the hardware manufacturer. You might also want to contact technical support.

application **was unable to format the disk.**

[Repair Disk]

The disk is probably bad.

Try again, using a different disk.

application **was unable to load required floppy disk operation support.**

[Repair Disk]

The dynamic link library that operates on the floppy drive could not be loaded. The system may be corrupted.

Run Setup to repair the system files.

code **is not a valid Windows NT network message number.**

[Network] Net Message ID: 3871

The specified message number does not represent a Windows NT message.

Check that you typed the correct message number. To see more information about system messages, type NET HELPMSG <message>#, where <message># is the message number or error code.

command **: bad destination address** *address*

[TCP/IP]

If you used a network name or alias for the destination parameter in the Route command and you get this message, then the Route command was unable to find the name or alias in the NETWORKS file on the local computer (the path to the NETWORKS file is \systemroot\system32\drivers\etc). If you used an IP address, you specified an invalid format. For example, you may not have used a dotted decimal format, such as 127, 284.122.107, or 284.122.108).

Retry the Route command, specifying a valid destination.

command **: internal error - unknown remote command service**

[TCP/IP]

Retry the remote command. If you still get this message, contact your technical support group.

computer name **is a domain controller of domain** *name*. **Focus will be set to domain** *name*.

[User Manager]

You specified a domain controller rather than a domain in the Domain text box of the Select Domain dialog. The domain for which that computer is a controller will be selected.

Choose OK.

computer name **is not a valid computer name.**

[Network] Net Message ID: 3870

The computer name you specified is invalid.

Check the spelling of the computer name.

computer name **received an ICMP error packet on a nonexistent connection. Type** *text*, **Code** *code*, **Source** *address*, **Destination** *address*.

[Netevent]

An endpoint that no longer exists received an ICMP error packet.

No action is needed.

day **is not a recognized day of the week.**

[Network] Net Message ID: 3760

The day you specified is invalid. Valid days are Monday, Tuesday, Wednesday, Thursday, Friday, Saturday, and Sunday. Valid abbreviations are M, T, W, Th, F, Sa, and Su.

Retype the command using valid names or abbreviations.

drive letter **does not contain a tape.**

[Backup]

You attempted to back up files to a backup drive that does not contain a tape.

Insert a tape in the specified backup drive, then choose OK.

drive letter **has a remembered connection to** *name*. **Do you want to overwrite the remembered connection?** *name* **:** *text*

[Network]

You have attempted to assign a remote resource to a drive letter or port name that has been used for a different remote resource. The remote resource usually assigned to this driver letter or port name is not currently connected, but there would normally be an attempt to connect to it the next time you log on.

If you want to change the remote resource assigned to this drive letter or port name, choose Yes. To keep the old assignment, choose No, and then assign the new resource to a different drive letter or port name.

drive letter : text **failed, error =** *number*

[CD Player]

An internal software error has occurred.

Exit and restart CD Player. If the problem persists, contact your system administrator.

drive letter : text **: General Failure!**

[CD Player]

A general failure has occurred in CD Player.

Attempt to restart the application. If this message reappears, contact technical support.

drive letter : **Device I/O Error!**

[CD Player]

An error occurred when CD Player sent a command to the CD-ROM.

Attempt to repeat the operation that you were performing when the message appeared. If the message reappears, restart CD Player.

drive letter : **Device Not Ready!**

[CD Player]

Your CD-ROM device is not ready.

Make sure that there is a disc in the drive, and that the drive door is closed.

drive letter : **Invalid Device Request!**

[CD Player]

CD Player does not support your drive. Or CD Player does support the drive, but the CDAUDIO.SYS needs to be enabled. The following are the drives that CD Player supports: NEC®, Denon®, Pioneer®, and Hitachi®.

If your drive is a supported drive, use the Services option in Control Panel to enable CDAUDIO.SYS.

drive letter : **No Media in Drive!**

[CD Player]

You attempted to use CD Player to read an empty drive.

Insert a valid disc.

drive letter : **Sector Not Found!**

[CD Player]

CD Player attempted to play something that does not exist on the disc that is currently in the CD-ROM. For example, if you remove a disc, its titles may still appear in the CD Player window. If you insert another disc, then select a title from the first disc and choose Play, CD Player will generate this message.

Exit and restart CD Player.

drive letter : **Unrecognized Media!**

[CD Player]

You attempted to use CD Player to read a drive that is empty, or that contains damaged disc, or a disk that is not an audio disk.

Insert a valid audio disc, then try again.

file system **is not a valid file system**

[Convert]

The Convert utility does not support the target file system you specified in the second parameter of the Convert command. In version 1.0 of Windows NT, the only valid target file system for the Convert utility is NTFS.

If you want to convert the drive to the NTFS file system, retype the Convert command and specify NTFS as the target file system. To check the syntax of the Convert command, type HELP CONVERT at the command prompt.

file system **is not available for** *drive letter* **drives.**

[Utilities]

For example, the HPFS file system is not available on floppy disk drives.

Use a different file system.

filename *filename* **Could not expand second filename so as to match first**

[File Compare]

The Fc command expanded the wild cards in the second file you specified, but was unable to find a file on the path you specified to use. In other words, no filenames on the path satisfied the wild cards. Therefore, the Fc command did not compare any files.

Retry the command, either using a different path or a different set of wild cards in the second file specification parameter.

filename **Invalid time stamp.**

[Chkdsk]

The file allocation table stores the time as year, month, day, hour, minute, and second. The minute and second must be less than 60. The hour must be less than 34. The day must be less than 32. And the month must be less than 13.

Contact technical support.

filename **Is cross linked on allocation unit** *number*

[Chkdsk]

Two files (or directories) attempted to access the same disk space.

Run the Chkdsk command with the /f switch to fix the problem.

filename **: Read file failed. (Cannot map view of file.)**

[FINDSTR]

You must be searching for strings in a huge file.

Split the file you are searching into two parts and use the Findstr command separately on each file.

filename **Another file already exists by this name. Use a different file name.**

[Paintbrush]

You have attempted to save a file under the name of a file that has been previously saved.

Assign a name to the file that has not already been used.

filename **Cannot access this file. Check security privileges over the network drive.**

[Common Dialog]

You have specified a file that you do not have access to.

Check the privileges on this file and on the directory in which it resides, or ask the administrator to check it for you. The administrator might need to change the permissions on the file or directory so that you have access to it.

filename **Cannot access this file. Please verify security privileges on the network drive.**

[Common Dialog]

You cannot access this file, probably because you do not have the necessary permissions on the shared directory in which it resides.

Ask the network administrator to make sure you have the necessary permissions on the shared directory that you have assigned this drive letter to. When that is done, try again.

filename **Cannot find this file. Either something has happened to the network or possibly the file has been renamed or moved. Do you want to try again?**

[Write]

You attempted to open or to save a file that cannot currently be located.

If this message reappears when you try again, make sure that you have specified the correct location and filename for the file. If the file is located on a network share, and the network connection has gone down, wait until the connection is restored, then try again.

filename **Cannot find this file. Make sure that the correct path and file name are given.**

[Paintbrush]

You attempted to open a file that does not exist in the path that you have specified.

Specify a valid path to the file and a valid filename.

filename **Cannot find this file. Please verify that the correct path and filename are given.**

[Common Dialog]

Check that the path is correct and complete, and that you have the right filename. Then try again, making sure the path and filename are typed correctly.

filename **Cannot read this file. Either something has happened to the network or possibly the file has been renamed or moved.**

[Write]

You have attempted an operation on a file that Write can no longer locate.

Make sure that you have specified the correct location and filename. If the file is located on a network share, and the network connection has gone down, wait, then try again.

filename **Cannot rename this file. Either something has happened to the network or possibly the file has been renamed or moved.**

[Write]

You attempted to rename a file that cannot currently be located.

Make sure that you have specified the correct location and filename. If the file is located on a network share, and the network connection has gone down, wait, then try again.

filename **Cannot save this file.**

[Cardfile]

You have attempted to save a file that is read-only protected. Or, if MS-DOS is still on your computer, the temporary file setting in your AUTOEXEC.BAT file may be incorrect.

Use the Properties option in File Manager to determine if the file is read-only. If the file is read-only protected, save the current file under a different name. If the file is not read-only protected, exit File Manager, open MS-DOS, and ensure that your AUTOEXEC.BAT file contains both a TEMP and a TMP setting.

filename **does not contain file version information.**

No action is needed.

filename **exists. You can either replace the existing version or use the Save Contents command to save to a different filename. Do you want to replace the existing version?**

In Object Packager, you attempted to assign to a package a name that you have already assigned to a package in the current directory.

Assign a unique filename to the package. Or assign the same filename, but save the package to a different directory.

filename **File not found. Please verify that the correct path and filename are given.**

[Write]

You directed Write to open a file that does not exist in the path that you have specified.

Specify a valid path to the file.

filename **File not found. Please verify the correct file name was given.**

[Common Dialog]

You specified a file that does not exist. This could be a result of mistyping the filename, or you might have the wrong name for the file, or the file might have been deleted.

Make sure that you have the correct filename and that the file exists. Then try again, making sure you type the name correctly.

filename **has been changed. Save this file before closing?**

[Backup]

When you change a file, and then attempt to exit the application, Backup presents you with this message.

If you want to save the changed file, choose Yes. If not, choose No.

filename **is an invalid font file**

[Program Manager]

You must remove the old version of this font before you can install the new version.

Reinstall the font from the disk supplied by the vendor.

filename **is an invalid font file.**

[Program Manager]

The file you specified does not contain fonts. The file is missing or corrupt.

filename **is an invalid TrueType font file**

[Program Manager]

You must remove the old version of this font before you can install the new version.

Reinstall the font from the disk supplied by the vendor.

filename **is not a program and cannot be associated with a file extension.**

[File Manager]

Choose the filename of an application. It will have a file type of .exe, .pif, .com, or .bat.

filename **Not able to open this file because the format is not recognized. Create a new file or open a valid bitmap image file.**

[Paintbrush]

Paintbrush supports the following formats: PCX, BMP, Monochrome, 16-color, 256-color, and 24-bit. The bitmap that you have attempted to open in Paintbrush is in a format that Paintbrush does not support.

Follow the action specified in the message.

filename **Not able to open this file. Make sure that the correct path and file name are given.**

[Paintbrush]

You have attempted to open a file that does not exist in the path that you have indicated.

Specify a valid path to the file and a valid filename.

filename **Not able to open this file. Make sure that the path and file name are correct.**

[Paintbrush]

You have attempted to open a file that does not exist in the path that you have indicated.

Specify a valid path to the file and a valid filename.

filename **Not able to save this file. Close one or more files in other applications, and then try again.**

[Paintbrush]

There is not enough disk space to save this file.

Delete some files from the disk and try again. Or, save the file to a different disk.

filename **Paintbrush cannot load this file because it was created using a version of Windows earlier than 3.0.**

[Paintbrush]

Some applications were designed for previous versions of Windows and do not work correctly with Windows 3.0 and later. In addition, files created in these older applications may not perform reliably or at all in Windows 3.1 or Windows NT.

No action is needed.

filename **The above file name is invalid.**

[Common Dialog]

The filename does not meet the criteria for a valid filename.

Try again, using a valid filename. Filenames can contain any uppercase or lowercase characters except the following: ? " / \ < > * | :

filename **The image has changed. Do you want to save current changes?**

[Paintbrush]

You have changed a Paintbrush image, and have attempted to exit the Paintbrush file before saving it.

If you want to save your changes to the Paintbrush file, select Yes. If not, select No. If you want to return to the Paintbrush image, select Cancel.

filename **This document has changed. Save current changes?**

[Write]

Any time that you change a Write file, Write displays this confirmation message.

If you want to save the current file, choose Yes. If not, choose No. To return to the document, choose Cancel.

filename **This file exists and is read-only. Use a different filename.**

[Common Dialog]

Saving the file with this filename would overwrite the existing file. However, since the file has Read Only permissions, you cannot overwrite it.

Try again, specifying a different filename.

filename **This file exists with Read Only attributes. Please use a different file name.**

[Common Dialog]

Saving the file with this filename would overwrite the existing file. However, since the file has Read Only permissions, you cannot overwrite it.

Try again, specifying a different filename.

filename **This file is already in use. Select a new name or close the file in use by another application.**

[Common Dialog]

Go to the window that was used to open the file, and close the file from there. Then try again.

filename **This file is already in use. Use a new filename or close the file in use by another application.**

[Common Dialog]

Go to the window that was used to open the file, and close the file from there. Then try again.

filename **This file is in use. Use a new filename or close the file in use by another application.**

[Write]

You have attempted to save a Write file that is being used by another application.

Close the application that is using the file, then try again to save the file. Or save the file to a new filename.

filename **This file is not in the correct format for use with Paintbrush. Create a new file or open a valid bitmap image file.**

[Paintbrush]

The file was created by a different application, or the file is corrupt. It might be that the file was simply renamed to have a .BMP extension, but was not converted to a bitmap image file.

If the file was created by a different application, use that application to work with the file. You might be able to save the file as a bitmap image file from within that application.

filename **This file is on a network drive with create but no modify privileges. Ask the administrator of this network to change this condition.**

[Common Dialog]

In order to make any changes to files in this shared directory, you must have Change or Full Control permission on the directory. You do not have such permissions on this shared directory.

Ask the administrator to set the permissions to allow you to modify this file.

filename **This file name is not valid.**

[Paintbrush]

When saving a file to a FAT volume, you are permitted to assign to Paintbrush images filenames no longer than eight characters. In addition, you can only assign a Paintbrush image a .BMP or a .PCX extension.

Double-check the name that you have assigned your Paintbrush image. If the filename is longer than eight letters, shorten it or change it altogether. If the extension is not .BMP or .PCX, assign one of these extensions to it.

filename **This filename is not valid.**

[Write]

If you are saving a file to a FAT volume, filenames must be no longer than eight characters long with a three character extension. The filename that you typed does not follow these specifications. Or you have typed a filename that contains a space or illegal characters.

Type a valid filename that contains only alphanumeric characters.

filename **This filename is not valid.**

[Common Dialog]

The filename does not meet the criteria for a valid filename.

Try again, using a valid filename. Filenames can contain any uppercase or lowercase characters except the following: ? " / \ < > * | :

filename.**EXE - No Disk**

[OS/2 Subsystem]

There is no disk in the drive.

Insert a disk in the drive and try again.

filename.**EXE - Write Protect Error**

[OS/2 Subsystem]

The disk cannot be written to because it is write protected.

Remove the right protection from the disk and try again.

group **is a global group. Global groups cannot be created or edited in Low Speed Connection mode.**

[User Manager]

Clear Low Speed Connection in the Options menu and try again. If the physical connection to this computer does not support a high speed connection, you might need to go to that computer to create the global group. Or, edit the individual user accounts to add users to or remove users from this group.

name **Directory has non-zero file size.**

[Chkdsk]

The specified directory entry is corrupt. The entry claims to be a directory, but has a non-zero file size. This state is not valid for a FAT directory entry.

No action is needed.

name **Unrecognized EA handle.**

[Chkdsk]

The extended attribute handle in the directory entry is invalid and will be zeroed out.

No action is needed.

name **: A required parameter is missing from the Registry.**

[Netevent]

The driver parameters are invalid.

Reinstall the driver using the Network option in Control Panel.

name **: Could not allocate the resources necessary for operation.**

[Netevent]

The network driver could not allocate the necessary resources, usually memory, for operation.

Remove some memory-intensive adapters or install more memory.

name **: Could not connect to the interrupt number supplied.**

[Netevent]

The network driver tried to connect to an interrupt that is in use by another device or adapter card.

Use Network in Control Panel to change the jumpers of your adapter card or run the configuration utility that was supplied with the adapter. See your system administrator if you need assistance.

name **: Could not find an adapter.**

[Netevent]

The network driver could not find the adapter.

Contact your system administrator. Check the configuration of the adapter card by selecting Network in Control Panel. Make sure the adapter card is configured according to the manufacturer's specifications and that the adapter card's configuration does not conflict with the configurations of other hardware.

name **: Does not support the configuration supplied.**

[Netevent]

The parameters given to the driver are invalid.

Use Network in Control Panel to remove and then reinstall the driver. If you continue to see this error message, contact technical support.

name **: Has determined that the adapter is not functioning properly.**

[Netevent]

The network driver received an invalid response from the adapter.

No action is needed. However, if you see this message frequently, ask your system administrator to make sure that the adapter card is configured properly and that its configuration does not conflict with the configurations of other hardware.

name **: Has encountered a conflict in resources and could not load.**

[Netevent]

The network driver failed to initialize due to an apparent conflict between the adapter card and some other hardware.

Contact your system administrator. Check the configuration of the adapter card by selecting Network in Control Panel. Make sure the adapter card is configured according to the manufacturer's specifications and that the configuration does not conflict with the configurations of other hardware.

name **: Has encountered an internal error and has failed.**

[Netevent]

The network driver encountered a fatal error and terminated.

Contact your system administrator. Your administrator should verify that the adapter is configured properly and that the adapter card's configuration does not conflict with the configurations of other hardware. Your administrator may want to replace your adapter card if this error message occurs frequently.

name **: Has encountered an invalid network address.**

[Netevent]

The network address for the adapter card is not configured properly.

Ask your system administrator to reconfigure your card.

name **: The adapter has returned an invalid value to the driver.**

[Netevent]

The adapter responded incorrectly to the driver.

Check the configuration of the adapter. If you see this message frequently, the adapter card may need to be replaced.

name **: The adapter is configured such that the receive space is smaller than the maximum packet size. Some packets may be lost.**

[Netevent]

Due to the space limitations of the adapter, your computer cannot use the full capabilities of the network.

If possible, your system administrator may reconfigure the adapter card either to use more memory or to use memory more effectively. Otherwise, no action is needed.

name **: The adapter is disabled. The driver cannot open the adapter.**

[Netevent]

The adapter is not enabled.

Contact your system administrator to run the adapter's configuration utility and then enable the adapter. Contact the vendor of the adapter if this does not correct the problem.

name **: The I/O base address supplied does not match the jumpers on the adapter.**

[Netevent]

The base address supplied in the Network option of Control Panel does not match the adapter card settings.

Contact your system administrator. Your administrator should verify that the adapter card is configured properly and that the card's configuration does not conflict with the configurations of other hardware. Your administrator may want to replace your adapter card if this error message occurs frequently.

name **: The version number is incorrect for this driver.**

[Netevent]

The network driver version number is incompatible with this operating system.

Contact the vendor to replace the network driver.

name **: There is a interrupt conflict at interrupt number** *number***.**

[Netevent]

The network driver tried to connect to the specified interrupt which is in use by another device or adapter.

Use the Network option in Control Panel to change the jumpers of your adapter card or to run the configuration utility that was supplied with the adapter. See your system administrator if you need assistance.

name : **There is a memory conflict at address 0x** ***address*.**

[Netevent]

Both the adapter and another device are using the address specified. Each device should have a unique address.

Contact your system administrator. Check the configuration of the adapter card by selecting Network in Control Panel. Make sure the adapter card is configured according to the manufacturer's specifications and that the card's configuration does not conflict with the configurations of other hardware.

name : **There is a resource conflict at DMA channel** ***number*.**

[Netevent]

The adapter and another device are trying to use the specified DMA channel.

Contact your system administrator. Check the configuration of the adapter card by selecting Network in Control Panel. Make sure the adapter card is configured according to the manufacturer's specifications and that the configuration does not conflict with the configurations of other hardware.

name : **There is an I/O port conflict.**

[Netevent]

The adapter card and another device are configured to use the same I/O port.

Contact your system administrator. Check the configuration of the adapter card by selecting Network in Control Panel. Make sure the adapter card is configured according to the manufacturer's specifications and that the configuration does not conflict with the configurations of other hardware.

name : **There is an I/O port or DMA channel conflict.**

[Netevent]

The adapter card and another device are configured to use the same I/O port or DMA channel.

Contact your system administrator. Check the configuration of the adapter card by selecting Network in Control Panel. Make sure the adapter card is configured according to the manufacturer's specifications and that the card's configuration does not conflict with the configurations of other hardware.

name : **Timed out during an operation.**

[Netevent]

The adapter card did not respond to a command.

No action is needed. However, if this occurs frequently, ask your system administrator to check the adapter settings and/or replace the adapter card.

name : **Unknown host.**

[FTP Server]

You specified a host name in the Ftp command that does not have an entry in the HOSTS file (which is located in \\systemroot\\system32\\drivers\\etc).

Either try again with a different host name, or create an entry for the host name in the HOSTS file. You might need to ask your network administrator to do this for you.

name **:TLI Error** *number*

[TCP/IP]

The TCP/IP utility named at the start of the message had a data connection fail due to an unexpected TLI error.

Retry the operation. If you get this message again, contact your network administrator to interpret the meaning of the TLI error code displayed at the end of the message and take corrective action.

name **:TLOOK returned** *number text*

[TCP/IP]

The TCP/IP utility named at the start of the message had a data connection fail due to an unexpected event.

Retry the operation. If you still get this message, contact your network administrator to interpret the meaning of the event number that is displayed at the end of the message and take corrective action.

name **could not allocate a resource of type** *number* **due to a specifically configured limit of** *number***.**

[Netevent]

One of the Registry parameters, MaxLinks or MaxConnections, has been changed. The default for these parameters is unlimited.

Ask your system administrator to increase the MaxLinks or MaxConnections parameter in the Registry.

name **could not allocate a resource of type** *number* **due to its configured size of** *number***.**

[Netevent]

Your server has reached the configured limit for NetBIOS.

Ask your system administrator to increase the configured size of the protocol if it is not already configured to its maximum limit. The protocol's size can be changed by choosing Server in Network in Control Panel.

name **could not allocate a resource of type** *number* **due to system resource problems.**

[Netevent]

The resource pool is not available because the server is busy.

Ask your system administrator to restart the server, or you can wait a few minutes and then try the operation again. If you see this message frequently, your system administrator may need to increase the server's memory.

name **could not create a link to a remote computer. Your computer has exceeded the number of connections it can make to that remote computer.**

[Netevent]

Your computer created too many connections to the network.

Wait a few minutes, then retry the operation.

name **could not find adapter** *name***.**

[Netevent]

Ask your system administrator to verify that the NDIS driver loaded correctly.

name **could not transfer a packet from the adapter. The packet was dropped.**

[Netevent]

A hardware problem has occurred.

Check the event log in Event Viewer for related errors that may indicate the hardware problem. If the related errors are serious, you should contact technical support.

name **discarded a read IOCTL ACK/NAK message of unknown type** *text***.**

[Netevent]

A lower layer of the protocol stack issued an invalid ACK/NAK message.

Contact technical support.

name **discarded a read IOCTL message of unknown type** *text***.**

[Netevent]

A user-level application generated an invalid read IOCTL message. The application attempted to perform an operation that the protocol does not recognize.

Ask your system administrator to identify the application. The event log in Event Viewer may contain information about related errors which could help to identify the application so the problem can be corrected. Also, contact the vendor of the application.

name **discarded a read message of unknown type** *text***.**

[Netevent]

An upper or lower layer of the protocol stack issued an invalid read message. This can occur during development of a streams-based transport.

Contact technical support.

name **discarded a read PROTO message of unknown type** *text***.**

[Netevent]

An upper or lower layer of the protocol stack issued an invalid read PROTO message. This can occur during development of a streams-based transport.

Contact technical support.

name **discarded a write IOCTL message of unknown type** *text***.**

[Netevent]

A user-level application generated an invalid write IOCTL message. The application attempted to perform an operation that the protocol does not recognize.

Ask your system administrator to identify the application. The event log in Event Viewer may contain information about related errors which could help to identify the application so the problem can be corrected. Also, contact the vendor of the application.

name **discarded a write message of unknown type** *text.*

[Netevent]

An upper or lower layer of the protocol stack issued an invalid write message. This can occur during development of a streams-based transport.

Contact technical support.

name **discarded a write PROTO message of unknown type** *text.*

[Netevent]

An upper or lower layer of the protocol stack issued an invalid write PROTO message. This can occur during development of a streams-based transport.

Contact technical support.

name **failed to bind to adapter** *name.*

[Netevent]

The specified adapter did not load, is out of memory, or is not configured properly.

Ask your system administrator to verify that the NDIS driver loaded correctly. Check the event log with Event Viewer for related errors.

name **failed to register itself with the NDIS wrapper.**

[Netevent]

The specified device is not the correct version for the NDIS wrapper.

Ask your system administrator to reinstall the correct version of the device from the Setup disks.

name **failed while querying OID** *number* **on adapter** *name.*

[Netevent]

There is either a hardware or driver problem with the NDIS driver.

Check the event log with Event Viewer for related errors.

name **failed while setting OID** *number* **on adapter** *name.*

[Netevent]

The NDIS driver has either a hardware or driver problem.

Check the event log with Event Viewer for related errors.

name **has received** *number* **ICMP error packets on nonexistent connections.**

[Netevent]

Multiple ICMP orphans have been received. This message gives the history of the error packets.

No action is needed.

name **is already installed. Remove this font and re-install.**

[Program Manager]

You must remove the old version of this font before you can install the new version.

name **is already installed. Remove this font and re-install.**

[Program Manager]

You must remove the old version of this font before you can install the new version.

name **is an invalid user or group name.**

[Network] Net Message ID: 3742

You typed an invalid user name or group name.

Check the spelling of the user or group name. To see a list of existing users, type NET USER. To see a list of existing local groups, type NET LOCALGROUP. To see a list of existing global groups, type NET GROUP, if you are running Windows NT Advanced Server. If you are running Windows NT, type NET GROUP /domain. The Windows NT workstation must be a member of a domain that is running Windows NT Advanced Server. Otherwise, you will see a message that tells you that NET GROUP is a Windows NT Advanced Server command only.

name **is not a user account or group.**

[User Manager]

The word you typed is not the name of a user account or group. It might have been mistyped.

Make sure you have the correct name. Then try again, making sure the name is typed correctly.

name **is not a user account. Only users can be renamed.**

[User Manager]

You cannot rename groups.

No action is needed. If you want, you can create a new group with the different name.

name **is not a valid domain or workgroup name.**

[Network] Net Message ID: 3932

The name you specified is not a valid domain or workgroup name.

Check the spelling of the name. Retype the command with a valid domain or workgroup name.

name **is not a valid workstation name. You must either specify valid workstation names or leave the fields blank.**

[User Manager]

The workstation name you entered does not follow the naming conventions for workstation names. The name can be up to 15 characters long and cannot include any of the following special characters: bullet (ALT+ 0149) currency sign (ALT+ 0164) broken vertical bar (ALT+ 0166) section sign (ALT+ 0167) paragraph sign (ALT+ 0182)

Try again, making sure to enter a valid workstation name. Or leave the fields blank.

name **received an ICMP error packet of type** *text*, **code** *code*.**The packet that caused the error was sent from source** *address* **to destination** *address*.

[Netevent]

Your local subnet received an invalid ICMP packet.

Ask your system administrator to correct the packets generated by the computer at the specified source IP address.

name **received an unexpected** *text* **packet from a remote computer.**

[Netevent]

Your network is experiencing hardware problems or the software versions on the two computers may conflict.

Contact technical support.

name text **: name too long.**

[TCP/IP]

This is an internal error in the Rpc utility.

Retry the operation. If you still get this message, contact your technical support group.

name **was unable to extract the value of parameter** *name* **from the Registry. Setting to the default value of** *text*.

[Netevent]

The device could not find the specified configurable parameter in the Registry so the default value was used.

No action is needed.

name **was unexpected at this time.**

[Command Prompt]

While processing a batch file, command prompt encountered an unexpected command.

Correct the batch file, then try running it again.

name **was unexpected at this time.**

[Command]

While processing a batch file, command prompt encountered an unexpected command.

Correct the batch file, then try running it again.

name: *command*/**tcp: unknown service**

[TCP/IP]

The service required to process the command named at the beginning of the message is not running on the remote host. The required service is named in the message.

Either run the command on a different server, or ask your network administrator to get the required service running on the remote host. You may need to contact the administrator of the remote host to do this.

number **ARP requests received from other networks.**

[Netevent]

Several invalid ARP requests were received from other networks and were discarded.

No action is needed.

number **corrupt file was backed up.**

[Backup]

One of the files that was backed up was corrupt.

No action is needed.

number **corrupt files were backed up.**

[Backup]

Some of the files that were backed up were corrupt.

No action is needed.

number **directories were not found.**

[Backup]

Some directories that were in the backup set's catalog were not found while verifying files.

No action is needed. If the verify was done after a backup, the directory may have been removed between the backup and verify operations. If the verify was done after a restore, the restore of the directory could have failed.

number **directory was not found.**

[Backup]

One directory that was in the backup set's catalog was not found while verifying files.

No action is needed. If the verify was done after a backup, the directory may have been removed between the backup and verify operations. If the verify was done after a restore, the restore of the directory could have failed.

number **errors were logged in the last** *number* **minutes. Please review the server's error log.**

[Network] Net Message ID: 3001

This message should occur only on a down-level computer. Any action to correct the problem should be performed on that computer. The server and/or network hardware may need service.

Contact your network administrator.

number **file was different.**

[Backup]

One file was different in the target directory than on the backup tape. No differences were detected in the other files.

No action is needed.

number **file was in use.**

[Backup]

One file could not be backed up because it was in use.

No action is needed.

number **file was skipped.**

[Backup]

One file was not restored. It may have been open on the target disk, or the backup copy may have been corrupt.

No action is needed.

number **files were different.**

[Backup]

The specified number of files were different in the target directory than on the backup tape. No differences were detected in the other files.

No action is needed.

number **files were in use.**

[Backup]

Some files could not be backed up because they were in use.

No action is needed.

number **files were not found.**

[Backup]

The specified number of files were found on the backup tape but not in the target directory.

No action is needed. However you might want to restore the missed files in a separate operation. The missed files are listed in the summary box, and also in the log file for this operation.

number **files were skipped.**

[Backup]

The specified number of files were not restored. They may have been open on the target disk, or the backup copies may have been corrupt.

No action is needed.

number **in-use file was restored.**

[Backup]

One file was in use when the backup version of that file was restored. The backup version was restored anyway.

No action is needed.

number **in-use files were restored.**

[Backup]

Some files were in use when the backup version of those files were restored. The backup versions were restored anyway.

No action is needed.

number **is not a recognized hour.**

[Network] Net Message ID: 3762

You specified an hour in a format that could not be recognized. The hour can be a number from 0 to 12 in 12-hour format or 0 to 24 in 24-hour format. If you use the 12-hour format, you must specify either AM or PM for each time.

Retype the command with the correct hour format.

number **is not a valid entry. Please specify a value between** *number* **and** *number* **for this field.**

[Control Panel]

The value for this entry must be in the range specified; no other values can be used.

Enter a value in the specified range.

number **is not a valid specification for minutes.**

[Network] Net Message ID: 3763

You specified the minutes in a format that could not be recognized. Typing the minutes is optional, but if included, the format must be :00 (a colon and two zeros).

Retype the command, either omitting the minutes or using the correct format, :00.

number **lost allocation units found in** *number* **chains.**

[Chkdsk]

This is an informational message displayed by Chkdsk. These lost allocation units could be converted to files or to free space.

No action is needed.

number **message allocations have failed since initialization.**

[Netevent]

No action is needed unless you see this message frequently. Then add more memory.

number **network errors occurred in the last** *number* **minutes. Please review the server's error log. The server and/or network hardware may need service.**

[Network] Net Message ID: 3002

This message should occur only on a down-level computer. Any action to correct the problem should be performed on that computer.

Contact your network administrator.

number **security difference was found.**

[Backup]

The data may have been in use when the backup was done or there may have been a problem with the backup or restore operation.

Use the Security menu in File Manager to view the security information on both versions of the data. If the information is not different, try backing up or restoring the data again.

number **security differences were found.**

[Backup]

The data may have been in use when the backup was done or there may have been a problem with the backup or restore operation.

Use the Security menu in File Manager to view the security information on both versions of the data. If the information is not different, try backing up or restoring the data again.

path **Entry has a bad link**

[Chkdsk]

The directory specified in the message has an entry with a bad link (the file allocation table chain has been broken).

Run the Chkdsk command with the /f switch to fix the problem.

path **Entry has a bad size**

[Chkdsk]

The directory specified in the message has an entry with a bad file size.

Run the Chkdsk command with the /f switch to fix the problem.

path **has a remembered connection to** *drive letter***.**

[Network]

The indicated remote resource is usually assigned to the indicated driver letter or port name. It is not currently connected, but there would normally be an attempt to connect to it the next time you log on.

No action is needed.

path **is an invalid path name. Please enter a valid path name.**

[User Manager]

In the User Environment Profile dialog box, you specified a command path in the Home Directory or Profile Path option that does not exist in the location that you have specified.

Choose OK, then specify a valid Home Directory or Profile Path.

path **is an invalid relative path name. Please enter a valid relative path name.**

[User Manager]

In the User Environment Profile dialog box, you specified a command path in the Logon Script Name option that does not meet the criteria for a relative path.

Choose OK, then re-enter the pathname. Make sure to use a backslash (\) between the directory name and filename.

path **is not a full path name.**

[Utilities]

Enter a fully-qualified path (for example, d:\\winnt\\system32 is a fully-qualified path because it includes the drive letter and all sub directories leading to the target directory).

path **Path does not exist. Please verify that the correct path is given.**

[Common Dialog]

Check that the path is correct and complete. Then try again, making sure the path is typed correctly.

path **Path does not exist. Please verify the correct path was given.**

[Common Dialog]

You specified a path that does not exist. This could be a result of mistyping the path, or you might have the wrong name for the path, or some directories in this path might have been deleted.

Make sure that you have the correct path and that the path exists. Then try again, making sure you type the name correctly.

text **First allocation unit is invalid, entry truncated**

[Chkdsk]

The first allocation unit for the specified directory entry is invalid--since allocation in the FAT is chain-based, this means that the directory entry is useless.

No action is needed.

text **: bad argument:** *text*

The command cannot be carried out with this argument.

Try again, making sure to type the command correctly and use only the arguments that are valid for this command.

text **: Cannot open** *filename*

[FINDSTR]

The Findstr utility cannot open the file named in the message.

Check the Findstr command line and make sure that you specified the correct path and that there are no misspellings. You may need to use File Manager to search for the file. Also, check that you have access rights to the file.

text **: No such device (CdRom** *number* **)!**

[CD Player]

An error occurred when CD Player attempted to read configuration information from the Registry.

Quit and restart CD Player. Or, in the Registry, make sure that the SCSI ID's are correct.

text **: not rerouted**

[Utilities]

This is an informational message to notify you that LPTn: is not rerouted.

No action is needed.

text **: unknown mode**

[FTP Server]

The file transfer mode specified in an Ftp command is invalid or not supported. ASCII and binary/image are the supported modes.

Retry the Ftp command, specifying either ASCII or binary/image as the file transfer mode.

text **Contains** *number* **non-contiguous blocks.**

[Chkdsk]

This is an informational message.

No action is needed.

text **FORMAT does not support user selected allocation unit sizes.**

[Format]

The /a parameter was used when formatting a volume to a file system which does not support user selected allocation unit sizes. Only NTFS supports the /a parameter.

Do not use the /a parameter when formatting a volume to FAT or HPFS.

text **is an invalid Trap Destination.**

[TCP/IP]

Trap destinations are the names or IP addresses of hosts to which you want the SNMP service to send traps with the selected community name.

In the Host Name or IP Address text box, enter the name or IP address of a computer in the community you have selected. Then choose Add.

text **is not a valid 12-hour suffix.**

[Network] Net Message ID: 3766

You tried to use the 12-hour format, but the time was followed by text that was neither AM nor PM. If you use the 12-hour format, you must follow each time with either AM, A.M., PM, or P.M.

Retype the command with the correct forms of AM and PM.

user name **has open files. Disconnecting** *user name* **may result in loss of data. Are you sure you want to disconnect this user from the Macintosh-Accessible volume** *name* **?**

[Services for Macintosh (SFM)]

Use Server Manager or File Manager to send a disconnect message to the specified user. In using either manager, select the MacFile menu. In Server Manager, select Send Message. In File Manager, select View/Modify Volumes and then select Send Message.

username **has a Logon Hours setting which is not specified as days-per-week or hours-per-week. You may edit this setting, but it will be initially reset. Do you wish to reset and edit the Logon Hours setting for** *username***?**

[User Manager]

You changed a user's logon hours setting directly through the API.

If you wish to reset and edit the logon hours setting, choose OK.

username **has a Logon Hours setting which is specified as days-per-week. Is it OK to convert** *username***'s setting to hours-per-week?**

[User Manager]

You changed a user's logon hours setting directly through the API.

If you wish to convert the logon hours setting, choose OK.

' *name* **' is an invalid port name.**

[Print Manager]

You attempted to configure a port, and specified the name of a file that does not exist or a network resource to which you are not currently connected. Or you typed a name that contains invalid characters.

Specify a valid port name.

',' expected

[Help]

This error is from the Macro Language Editor for on-line help, and should not appear while using the Help file. Report this error to the provider of the Help file.

(Error occurred in environment variable)

[Command]

The error displayed with this message occurred in the DIRCMD environment variable, rather than on the command line.

Use the Set command to view the current settings for the DIRCMD environment variable. Then type HELP DIR at the command prompt to see the correct syntax for the command.

(Setup is unable to access this disk.) *name*

[Setup]

The disk might not be accessible through the network. It might be off line. Setup cannot install Windows NT on the disk. This message is part of a larger message that contains more information about the error.

Install Windows NT on another disk.

***** NAME TOO LONG! *****

[PORTUAS]

Try again, using a shorter name.

****** Aborting ... Completing backup of file ******

[Backup]

The backup process will be stopped as soon as the application finishes backing up the file it is copying now.

No action is needed.

****** Aborting ... Completing restore of file ******

[Backup]

The restore process will be stopped as soon as the application finishes restoring the file it is copying now.

No action is needed.

****** Process Aborted ******

[Backup]

Either the process was canceled or it encountered an error that would not let it continue.

No action is needed. You can start restoring files again.

-- Error in conversion.

[Convert]

This access control entry could not be converted.

Apply permissions manually.

-- superfluous Access Control Entry dropped.

[Convert]

A LAN Manager access control entry which grants no permissions to a group has no effect, which is why the entry is superfluous. Such access control entries are dropped during conversion.

-- User or group ID not found.

[Convert]

This access control entry was not converted because the referenced user or group ID does not exist in this Windows NT system.

Create the appropriate user or group and manually apply the permissions.

Computer name **is a member of domain** *name*. **Focus will be set to domain** *name*.

[User Manager]

You are focusing User Manager on an Advanced Server that is not the domain controller.

No action is needed.

NetDDE Agent **Not enough memory.**

[Dynamic Data Exchange]

Close some applications and try again.

?Ambiguous command

[FTP Server]

During either a Telnet or Ftp session, you used a shortened version of a command that has more than one interpretation. For instance, at the ftp> prompt, you could type “qu,” but that would be an ambiguous command because both “quit” and “quote” are valid commands in an Ftp session.

Retry the command, using a longer version, for example, spelling the command name all the way out. To see a list of all the valid commands in a Telnet or Ftp session, type “?” or “HELP” at the session command prompt.

?Ambiguous help command *command*

[FTP Server]

During either a Telnet or Ftp session, you used a shortened version of a command in a Help request, and that shortened version has more than one interpretation. For instance, at the ftp> prompt, you could type “help c,” but that would be an ambiguous request for help because “connect,” “close,” and “crmod” are all valid commands in a Telnet session.

Change the form of the Help command to clear up the ambiguity, and retry the command.

?Invalid command

[FTP Server]

During either a Telnet or Ftp session, you used a command that is invalid in that session. For instance, "frammis" is not a valid command in either a Telnet or Ftp session.

During either a Telnet or Ftp session, you can display a list of valid commands by entering "?" or "HELP."

?Invalid help command *command*

[FTP Server]

During either a Telnet or Ftp session, you requested Help on a command for which there is no Help. The command you used in the help request is probably not a valid command in the session.

During either a Telnet or Ftp session, you requested Help on a command for which there is no Help. The command you used in the help request is probably not a valid command in the session.

[XOFF] (Press Ctrl-Break to reset.)

[Terminal]

The Xon/Xoff in the Communications dialog box dictates that a file transfer automatically pauses when the buffer is full. This setting is now activated, the buffer is full, and the file transfer in progress has paused.

No action is needed.

{Access Denied}A process has requested access to an object, but has not been granted those access rights.

[Kernel]

This is a Windows NT Executive STATUS error message. Choose an option from the message box. Retry the operation. If this message reappears, contact your system administrator to change your privilege level.

{Already Committed}The specified address range is already committed.

[Kernel]

This is a Windows NT Executive STATUS error message. Choose an option from the message box. Retry the operation. If this message reappears, contact your system administrator or your technical support group.

{Application Error}The application failed to initialize properly (0x*code*1x). Click on OK to terminate the application.

[Kernel]

This is a Windows NT Executive STATUS error message. After you terminate the application, try running it again. If this message reappears, contact the supplier of the application.

{Application Error}The exception *code* (0x*code*8lx) occurred in the application at location 0x*code*8lx.

[Kernel]

This is a Windows NT Executive STATUS error message. Choose an option from the message box and then try running the application again. If this message reappears, contact the supplier of the application.

{Application Exit by CTRL+C}The application terminated as a result of a CTRL+C.

[Kernel]

This is a Windows NT Executive STATUS error message. Choose an option from the message box. Then restart the application if you need to.

{Bad CRC}A cyclic redundancy check (CRC) checksum error occurred.

[Kernel]

This is a Windows NT Executive STATUS error message. Choose an option from the message box.

{Bad File}The attributes of the specified mapping file for a section of memory cannot be read.

[Kernel]

This is a Windows NT Executive STATUS error message. Choose an option from the message box. Retry the operation. If this message reappears, contact your system administrator or your technical support group.

{Bad Image Checksum}The image *name* is possibly corrupt. The header checksum does not match the computed checksum.

[Kernel]

This is a Windows NT Executive STATUS error message. Choose one of the options from the message box. Then try running the application again. If this message reappears, contact the supplier of the executable file.

{Bad Image}The application or DLL *name* is not a valid Windows NT image. Please check this against your installation diskette.

[Kernel]

This is a Windows NT Executive STATUS error message. Correct the condition, as suggested in the message box, and restart the application (or .DLL). If this message reappears, contact your system administrator or the supplier of the executable file.

{Buffer Overflow}The data was too large to fit into the specified buffer.

[Kernel]

This Windows NT Executive STATUS message is a warning. Choose one of the options from the message box. You may want to check the results from the running application.

{Buffer Too Small}The buffer is too small to contain the entry. No information has been written to the buffer.

[Kernel]

This is a Windows NT Executive STATUS error message. Choose an option from the message box. Retry the operation. If this message reappears, contact your system administrator or your technical support group.

{Cancel Timeout}The driver *name* failed to complete a canceled I/O request in the allotted time.

[Kernel]

This is a Windows NT Executive STATUS error message. Choose one of the options from the message box and retry the operation. If this message reappears, contact your system administrator, your technical support group, or the I/O device supplier.

{Conflicting Address Range}The specified address range conflicts with the address space.

[Kernel]

This is a Windows NT Executive STATUS error message. Choose an option from the message box. Retry the operation. If this message reappears, contact your system administrator or your technical support group.

{Corrupt Disk}The file system structure on the disk is corrupt and unusable. Please run the Chkdsk utility on the volume *name*.

[Kernel]

This is a Windows NT Executive STATUS error message. Correct the condition, as suggested in the message box, and restart the application. If this message reappears, contact your system administrator or your technical support group.

{Corrupt File}The file or directory *name* is corrupt and unreadable. Please run the Chkdsk utility.

[Kernel]

This is a Windows NT Executive STATUS error message. Choose one of the options from the message box and then run the Chkdsk utility.

{Data Error}An error in reading or writing data occurred.

[Kernel]

This is a Windows NT Executive STATUS error message. Choose an option from the message box. You may need to contact your technical support group.

{Data Late}A data late error occurred.

[Kernel]

This is a Windows NT Executive STATUS error message. Choose an option from the message box. You may need to contact your technical support group.

{Data Not Accepted}The TDI client could not handle the data received during an indication.

[Kernel]

This is a Windows NT Executive STATUS error message. Choose one of the options from the message box and retry the operation. If this message reappears, contact your system administrator or your technical support group.

{Data Overrun}A data overrun error occurred.

[Kernel]

This is a Windows NT Executive STATUS error message. Choose an option from the message box. Retry the operation. If this message reappears, run hardware diagnostics on your disk drives and controllers. You may have to contact the vendor of the device, and you may have to replace the controller, the disk drive, or both.

{Device Busy}The device is currently busy.

[Kernel]

This Windows NT Executive STATUS message is a warning. Choose one of the options from the message box (you may want to wait until the device may no longer be busy).

{Device Offline}The printer has been taken offline.

[Kernel]

This Windows NT Executive STATUS message is a warning. Choose one of the options from the message box (you may want to correct the situation first).

{Device Power Is Off}The printer power has been turned off.

[Kernel]

This Windows NT Executive STATUS message is a warning. Choose one of the options from the message box (you may want to correct the situation first).

{Device Timeout}The specified I/O operation on *computer name* **was not completed before the time-out period expired.**

[Kernel]

This is a Windows NT Executive STATUS error message. Choose an option from the message box.

{DLL Initialization Failed}Initialization of the dynamic link library *name* **failed. The process is terminating abnormally.**

[Kernel]

This is a Windows NT Executive STATUS error message. Note the filename of the dynamic-link library and choose OK. Try reinstalling the .DLL from its distribution media and then retry the operation. If this message reappears, contact the supplier of the dynamic-link library.

{Drive Not Ready}The drive is not ready for use; its door may be open. Please check drive *drive letter* and make sure that a disk is inserted and that the drive door is closed.

[Kernel]

This is a Windows NT Executive STATUS error message. Check the drive and then choose one of the options from the message box.

{End of Media}The end of the media was encountered.

[Kernel]

This Windows NT Executive STATUS message is a warning. Choose one of the options from the message box.

{Entry Point Not Found}The procedure entry point *text* could not be located in the dynamic link library *name*.

[Kernel]

This is a Windows NT Executive STATUS error message. Choose one of the options from the message box. You may have to reinstall the dynamic-link library or contact its supplier.

{EXCEPTION}A real-mode application issued a floating-point instruction and floating-point hardware is not present.

[Kernel]

This is a Windows NT Executive STATUS error message. Choose one of the options from the message box.

{EXCEPTION}Alignment FaultA datatype misalignment was detected in a load or store instruction.

[Kernel]

This Windows NT Executive STATUS message is a warning. Choose one of the options from the message box.

{EXCEPTION}Array bounds exceeded.

[Kernel]

This is a Windows NT Executive STATUS error message. Choose an option from the message box. Then contact your technical support group.

{EXCEPTION}BreakpointA breakpoint has been reached.

[Kernel]

This Windows NT Executive STATUS message is a warning. Choose one of the options from the message box. If you are running the application in an end-user environment, rather than in a development environment, contact the supplier of the running application about this message. This should not happen when a finished program is running.

{EXCEPTION}Cannot Continue Windows NT cannot continue from this exception.

[Kernel]

This is a Windows NT Executive STATUS error message. Choose an option from the message box. Then contact your technical support group.

{EXCEPTION}Floating-point denormal operand.

[Kernel]

This is a Windows NT Executive STATUS error message. Choose an option from the message box. Then contact your technical support group.

{EXCEPTION}Floating-point division by zero.

[Kernel]

This is a Windows NT Executive STATUS error message. Choose an option from the message box. Then contact your technical support group.

{EXCEPTION}Floating-point inexact result.

[Kernel]

This is a Windows NT Executive STATUS error message. Choose an option from the message box. Then contact your technical support group.

{EXCEPTION}Floating-point invalid operation.

[Kernel]

This is a Windows NT Executive STATUS error message. Choose an option from the message box. Then contact your technical support group.

{EXCEPTION}Floating-point overflow.

[Kernel]

This is a Windows NT Executive STATUS error message. Choose an option from the message box. Then contact your technical support group.

{EXCEPTION}Floating-point stack check.

[Kernel]

This is a Windows NT Executive STATUS error message. Choose an option from the message box. Then contact your technical support group.

{EXCEPTION}Floating-point underflow.

[Kernel]

This is a Windows NT Executive STATUS error message. Choose an option from the message box. Then contact your technical support group.

{EXCEPTION}Guard Page ExceptionA page of memory that marks the end of a data structure, such as a stack or an array, has been accessed.

[Kernel]

This Windows NT Executive STATUS message is a warning. Choose one of the options from the message box.

{EXCEPTION}Integer division by zero.

[Kernel]

This is a Windows NT Executive STATUS error message. Choose an option from the message box. Then contact your technical support group.

{EXCEPTION}Integer overflow.

[Kernel]

This is a Windows NT Executive STATUS error message. Choose an option from the message box. Then contact your technical support group.

{EXCEPTION}Possible deadlock condition.

[Kernel]

This is a Windows NT Executive STATUS error message. Choose an option from the message box. Then contact your technical support group.

{EXCEPTION}Privileged instruction.

[Kernel]

This is a Windows NT Executive STATUS error message. Choose an option from the message box. Then contact your technical support group.

{EXCEPTION}Single StepA single step or trace operation has just been completed.

[Kernel]

This Windows NT Executive STATUS message is a warning. Choose one of the options from the message box. If you are running the application in an end-user environment, rather than in a development environment, contact the supplier of the running application about this message. This should not happen when a finished program is running.

{Fatal System Error}The *name* **system process terminated unexpectedly with a status of 0x***code***8x. The system has been shutdown.**

[Kernel]

This is a Windows NT Executive STATUS error message. Write down any information you can about the shutdown event and restart your computer. If this message reappears, contact your system administrator or your technical support group.

{File Not Found}The file *filename* **does not exist.**

[Kernel]

This is a Windows NT Executive STATUS error message. Choose one of the options from the message box. Then use File Manager to search for the file. You may have to move the file, or install it, to avoid this message in the future.

{Filemark Found}A filemark was detected.

[Kernel]

This Windows NT Executive STATUS message is a warning. Choose one of the options from the message box. No other action is needed.

{Floppy Disk Error}The floppy disk controller reported an error that is not recognized by the floppy disk driver.

[Kernel]

This is a Windows NT Executive STATUS error message. Choose one of the options from the message box. Retry the operation, using a different floppy disk or a floppy disk with a different density. If this message reappears, contact the hardware supplier or the floppy disk driver software supplier.

{Floppy Disk Error}While accessing a floppy disk, an ID address mark was not found.

[Kernel]

This is a Windows NT Executive STATUS error message. Try running the application again. If this message reappears, contact the supplier of the application.

{Floppy Disk Error}While accessing a floppy disk, the track address from the sector ID field was found to be different than the track address maintained by the controller.

[Kernel]

This is a Windows NT Executive STATUS error message. Choose one of the options from the message box. Retry the operation, using a different floppy disk or a floppy disk with a different density. If this message reappears, contact the hardware supplier or the floppy disk driver software supplier.

{Floppy Disk Error}While accessing a floppy-disk, the controller returned inconsistent results via its registers.

[Kernel]

This is a Windows NT Executive STATUS error message. Choose one of the options from the message box. This is either a hardware problem or a device driver problem. Check the hardware first. If this message reappears, contact the supplier of the floppy disk driver software and report your computer configuration.

{GUID Substitution}During the translation of an HPFS global identifier (GUID) to a Windows NT security ID (SID), no administratively-defined GUID prefix was found. A substitute prefix was used, which will not compromise system security. However, this may provide a more restrictive access than intended.

[Kernel]

This may provide a more restrictive access than intended, so this warning message is displayed.

This Windows NT Executive STATUS message is a warning. Choose one of the options from the message box.

{Handles Closed}Handles to objects have been automatically closed as a result of the requested operation.

[Kernel]

This Windows NT Executive STATUS message is a warning. Choose one of the options from the message box. You may want to check the results from the running application.

{Hard Disk Error}While accessing the hard disk, a disk controller reset was needed, but even that failed.

[Kernel]

This is a Windows NT Executive STATUS error message. Choose one of the options from the message box. Then contact the hard disk vendor and/or disk controller vendor.

{Hard Disk Error}While accessing the hard disk, a disk operation failed even after retries.

[Kernel]

This is a Windows NT Executive STATUS error message. Choose one of the options from the message box. Then run the Chkdsk utility, with the /r option, on the hard disk. After that, if this message reappears, run hardware diagnostics on the disk drive and its controller. If the diagnostics do not detect a problem, contact the hardware and/or driver software suppliers. Before you contact the suppliers, note the information about the event that is in the Event Log. Information in both the Description and Data areas of the Event Detail window will be relevant to this problem.

{Hard Disk Error}While accessing the hard disk, a recalibrate operation failed, even after retries.

[Kernel]

This is a Windows NT Executive STATUS error message. Choose one of the options from the message box. Run the Chkdsk utility, with the /r option, on the hard disk. After that, if this message reappears, run hardware diagnostics on the disk drive and its controller. If the diagnostics do not detect a problem, contact the hardware and/or driver software suppliers. Before you contact the suppliers, note the information about the event that is in the Event Log. Information in both the Description and Data areas of the Event Detail window will be relevant to this problem.

{Illegal EA}The specified extended attribute (EA) name contains at least one illegal character.

[Kernel]

This Windows NT Executive STATUS message is a warning. Choose one of the options from the message box.

{Image Relocated}An image file could not be mapped at the address specified in the image file. Local fixups must be performed on this image.

[Kernel]

This Windows NT Executive STATUS message is for your information. Choose OK to continue.

{Inconsistent EA List}The extended attribute (EA) list is inconsistent.

[Kernel]

This Windows NT Executive STATUS message is a warning. Choose one of the options from the message box.

{Incorrect Network Resource Type}The specified device type (LPT, for example) conflicts with the actual device type on the remote resource.

[Kernel]

This is a Windows NT Executive STATUS error message. Choose one of the options from the message box. Then contact your network administrator.

{Incorrect Password to LAN Manager Server}You specified an incorrect password to a LAN Manager 2.x or MS-NET server.

[Kernel]

This is a Windows NT Executive STATUS error message. Choose one of the options from the message box. Then try a different password.

{Incorrect System Call Level}An invalid level was passed into the specified system call.

[Kernel]

This is a Windows NT Executive STATUS error message. Choose one of the options from the message box and retry the operation. If this message reappears, contact your system administrator or your technical support group.

{Incorrect Volume}The target file of a rename request is located on a different device than the source of the rename request.

[Kernel]

This is a Windows NT Executive STATUS error message. Choose one of the options from the message box. If you can, rename the file by copying it, or specify the same drive for both the original and changed file names.

{Insufficient Resources on Remote Computer}The remote computer has insufficient resources to complete the network request. For instance, there may not be enough memory available on the remote computer to carry out the request at this time.

[Kernel]

Wait a few seconds, then retry the operation. If this message reappears, ask your network administrator to check the remote computer.

{Invalid Current Directory}The process cannot switch to the startup current directory *name*. Select OK to set current directory to *name*, or select CANCEL to exit.

[Kernel]

This Windows NT Executive STATUS message is for your information. Choose an option from the message box.

{Invalid EA Flag}An invalid extended attribute (EA) flag was set.

[Kernel]

There is a problem with disk I/O.

This Windows NT Executive STATUS message is a warning. Choose one of the options from the message box.

{Invalid Lock Sequence}An attempt was made to execute an invalid lock sequence.

[Kernel]

This is a Windows NT Executive STATUS error message. Choose an option from the message box. Retry the operation. If this message reappears, contact your system administrator or your technical support group.

{Invalid Mapping}An attempt was made to create a view for a section which is bigger than the section.

[Kernel]

This is a Windows NT Executive STATUS error message. Choose an option from the message box. If you can, retry the operation. If this message reappears, contact your system administrator or your technical support group.

{Invalid Parameter}The specified information class is not a valid information class for the specified object.

[Kernel]

This is a Windows NT Executive STATUS error message. Choose an option from the message box. Retry the operation. If this message reappears, contact your system administrator or your technical support group.

{Kernel Debugger Awakened}the system debugger was awakened by an interrupt.

[Kernel]

This Windows NT Executive STATUS message is a warning. Choose one of the options from the message box.

{Local Session Key}A user session key was requested for a local RPC connection. The session key returned is a constant value and not unique to this connection.

[Kernel]

This Windows NT Executive STATUS message is for your information. Choose OK to continue. No other action is needed.

{Lost Delayed-Write Data}The system was attempting to transfer file data from buffers to *filename*. The write operation failed, and only some of the data may have been written to the file.

[Kernel]

There may have been a loss of data. Decide if the missing data is important enough to restore the file from backup and redo the file operations that led up to the message.

{Mapped View Alignment Incorrect}An attempt was made to map a view of a file, but either the specified base address or the offset into the file were not aligned on the proper allocation granularity.

[Kernel]

This is a Windows NT Executive STATUS error message. Choose one of the options from the message box and retry the operation. If this message reappears, contact your system administrator or your technical support group.

{Missing System File}The required system file *filename* is bad or missing.

[Kernel]

This is a Windows NT Executive STATUS error message. Note the filename in the message and choose one of the options from the message box. Then reinstall the Windows NT system file named in the message.

{Network Name Not Found}The specified share name cannot be found on the remote server.

[Kernel]

This is a Windows NT Executive STATUS error message. Choose one of the options from the message box. You might want to contact your network administrator.

{Network Request Timeout}The session with a remote server has been disconnected because the time-out interval for a request has expired.

[Kernel]

This is a Windows NT Executive STATUS error message. Choose one of the options from the message box. You may want to try to reestablish the connection with the server.

{No Disk}There is no disk in the drive. Please insert a disk into drive *drive letter*.

[Kernel]

This is a Windows NT Executive STATUS error message. You may want to insert a disk in the drive. Then choose the appropriate option from the message box.

{No Media}There is no media in the drive. Please insert media into drive *drive letter*.

[Kernel]

This is a Windows NT Executive STATUS error message. You may want to insert media into the drive named in the message. Then choose the appropriate option from the message box.

{No More EAs}No more extended attributes (EAs) were found for the file.

[Kernel]

This Windows NT Executive STATUS message is a warning. Choose one of the options from the message box. No other action is needed.

{No More Entries}No more entries are available from an enumeration operation.

[Kernel]

This Windows NT Executive STATUS message is a warning. Choose one of the options from the message box. No other action is needed.

{No More Files}No more files were found which match the file specification.

[Kernel]

This Windows NT Executive STATUS message is a warning. Choose one of the options from the message box. No other action is needed.

{No Paging File Specified}No paging file was specified in the system configuration.

[Kernel]

This is a Windows NT Executive STATUS error message. Choose one of the options from the message box. Then contact your system administrator to change the system configuration.

{No Quotas}No system quota limits are specifically set for this account.

[Kernel]

This Windows NT Executive STATUS message is supplemental information about a successful logon. Choose OK to continue. No other action is needed.

{Non-Inheritable ACL}An access control list (ACL) contains no components that can be inherited.

[Kernel]

This Windows NT Executive STATUS message is a warning. Choose one of the options from the message box. No other action is needed.

{Not Enough Quota}Not enough virtual memory or paging file quota is available to complete the specified operation.

[Kernel]

This is a Windows NT Executive STATUS error message. Try running the application again. If this message reappears, contact your system administrator to adjust your paging file size or your quota.

{Not Implemented}The requested operation is not implemented.

[Kernel]

This is a Windows NT Executive STATUS error message. Choose an option from the message box. If you retry the operation and this message reappears, contact your system administrator or your technical support group.

{Object Exists}An attempt was made to create an object and the object name already existed.

[Kernel]

This Windows NT Executive STATUS message is for your information. Choose OK to continue. No other action is needed.

{Operation Failed}The requested operation was unsuccessful.

[Kernel]

This is a Windows NT Executive STATUS error message. Choose an option from the message box. If you choose Retry and this message reappears, contact your system administrator or your technical support group.

{Ordinal Not Found}The ordinal *text* could not be located in the dynamic link library *name*.

[Kernel]

This is a Windows NT Executive STATUS error message. Choose one of the options from the message box. You may have to reinstall the dynamic-link library or contact its supplier.

{Out of Paper}The printer is out of paper.

[Kernel]

This Windows NT Executive STATUS message is a warning. Choose one of the options from the message box (you may want to correct the situation first).

{Out of Virtual Memory}Your system is running low on virtual memory. Please close some applications. You can then start the System option in the Control Panel and choose the Virtual Memory button to create an additional paging file or to increase the size of your current paging file.

[Kernel]

This is a Windows NT Executive STATUS error message. Choose one of the options from the message box and then close some unneeded applications. Later, you may want to create another paging file or increase the size of your current paging file.

{Page Locked}One of the pages to lock was already locked.

[Kernel]

This Windows NT Executive STATUS message is a warning. Choose one of the options from the message box. No other action is needed.

{Page Unlocked}The page protection of a locked page was changed to 'No Access' and the page was unlocked from memory and from the process.

[Kernel]

This Windows NT Executive STATUS message is a warning. Choose one of the options from the message box. No other action is needed.

{Partial Copy}Due to protection conflicts not all the requested bytes could be copied.

[Kernel]

This Windows NT Executive STATUS message is a warning. Choose one of the options from the message box. You may want to check the results from the running application.

{Password Too Complex}The NT password is too complex to be converted to a LAN Manager password. The LAN Manager password returned is a NULL string.

[Kernel]

This Windows NT Executive STATUS message is for your information. Choose OK to continue. No other action is needed.

{Path Not Found}The path *path* does not exist.

[Kernel]

This is a Windows NT Executive STATUS error message. Check the path displayed in the message. You may have to create a directory or, if you enter a path through the application user interface, specify a different path. Try running the application again. If this message reappears, contact your system administrator or your technical support group.

{Privilege Failed}The I/O permissions for the process could not be changed.

[Kernel]

This is a Windows NT Executive STATUS error message. Choose one of the options from the message box. Then contact your system administrator about changing privilege levels.

{Redundant Read}To satisfy a read request, the NT fault-tolerant file system successfully read the requested data from a redundant copy. This was done because the file system encountered a failure on a member of the fault-tolerant volume, but was unable to reassign the failing area of the device.

[Kernel]

This Windows NT Executive STATUS message is for your information. Choose OK to continue. No other action is needed.

{Redundant Write}To satisfy a write request, the NT fault-tolerant file system successfully wrote a redundant copy of the information. This was done because the file system encountered a failure on a member of the fault-tolerant volume, but was not able to reassign the failing area of the device.

[Kernel]

This Windows NT Executive STATUS message is for your information. Choose OK to continue. No other action is needed.

{Registry File Failure}The registry cannot load the hive (file):*filename* or its log or alternate. It is corrupt, absent, or not writeable.

[Kernel]

This is a Windows NT Executive STATUS error message. Contact your system administrator right away about this computer configuration (Registry) problem.

{Registry Recovery}One of the files containing the system's Registry data had to be recovered by use of a log or alternate copy. The recovery was successful.

[Kernel]

This Windows NT Executive STATUS message is for your information. Choose OK to continue. No other action is needed.

{Reply Message Mismatch}An attempt was made to reply to an LPC message, but the thread specified by the client Id in the message was not waiting on that message.

[Kernel]

This is a Windows NT Executive STATUS error message. Choose one of the options from the message box. If you retry the operation and this message reappears, contact your system administrator or your technical support group.

{Section Too Large}The specified section is too big to map the file.

[Kernel]

This is a Windows NT Executive STATUS error message. Choose an option from the message box. If you choose Retry and this message reappears, contact your technical support group.

{Sector Not Found}The specified sector does not exist.

[Kernel]

There is a problem with disk I/O.

This is a Windows NT Executive STATUS error message. Choose an option from the message box. If you choose Retry and this message reappears, contact your system administrator, your technical support group, or your hardware supplier.

{Segment Load}A virtual DOS machine (VDM) is loading, unloading, or moving an MS-DOS or Win16 program segment image. An exception is raised so a debugger can load, unload or track symbols and breakpoints within these 16-bit segments.

[Kernel]

This Windows NT Executive STATUS message is for your information. Choose OK to continue.

{Serial IOCTL Complete}A serial I/O operation was completed by another write to a serial port.(The IOCTL_SERIAL_XOFF_COUNTER reached zero.)

[Kernel]

This Windows NT Executive STATUS message is for your information. Choose OK to continue. No other action is needed.

{Serial IOCTL Timeout}A serial I/O operation completed because the time-out period expired.(The IOCTL_SERIAL_XOFF_COUNTER had not reached zero.)

[Kernel]

This Windows NT Executive STATUS message is for your information. Choose OK to continue. No other action is needed.

{Still Busy}The specified I/O request packet (IRP) cannot be disposed of because the I/O operation is not complete.

[Kernel]

This is a Windows NT Executive STATUS error message. If you have a chance to continue the application, wait a while and then continue. Otherwise, try running the application again. If this message reappears, contact your system administrator.

{The Registry Is Corrupt}The structure of one of the files that contains Registry data is corrupt, or the image of the file in memory is corrupt, or the file could not be recovered because the alternate copy or log was absent or corrupt.

[Kernel]

This is a Windows NT Executive STATUS error message. Choose one of the options from the message box. Then contact your system administrator right away about this computer configuration Registry problem.

{Thread Suspended}A thread termination occurred while the thread was suspended. The thread was resumed, and termination proceeded.

[Kernel]

This Windows NT executive STATUS message is for your information. Choose OK to continue. No other action is needed.

{Too Much Information}The specified access control list (ACL) contained more information than was expected.

[Kernel]

This Windows NT Executive STATUS message is a warning. Choose one of the options from the message box. You may need to contact your system administrator to look at, and possibly edit, the access control list.

{Unable to Create Paging File}The creation of the paging file *filename* **failed (***code***x). The requested size was** *number***.**

[Kernel]

This is a Windows NT Executive STATUS error message. Choose one of the options from the message box. Then try creating a smaller paging file, or use a different disk partition for the paging file.

{Unable To Locate DLL}The dynamic link library *name* **could not be found in the specified path** *path***.**

[Kernel]

This is a Windows NT Executive STATUS error message. Note the filename and path listed in the message box and then choose an option. Use File Manager to locate a path to the DLL on your computer. You will either have to change the path, move the dynamic-link library, or install the dynamic-link library.

{Unable to Retrieve Browser Server List}The list of servers for this workgroup is not currently available.

[Kernel]

This is a Windows NT Executive STATUS error message. Choose one of the options from the message box and retry the operation. If this message reappears, contact your system administrator.

{Unexpected Failure in DebugActiveProcess}An unexpected failure occurred while processing a DebugActiveProcess APIrequest. You may choose OK to terminate the process, or Cancel to ignore the error.

[Kernel]

This is a Windows NT Executive STATUS error message. Choose an option from the message box.

{Unknown Disk Format}The disk in drive *drive letter* **is not formatted properly. Please check the disk, and reformat if necessary.**

[Kernel]

This is a Windows NT Executive STATUS error message. Choose an option from the message box and check the disk as suggested in the message. After that, if this message reappears, contact your disk hardware vendor.

{Verifying Disk}The media has changed and a verify operation is in progress so no reads or writes may be performed to the device, except those used in the verify operation.

[Kernel]

This Windows NT Executive STATUS message is a warning. Choose one of the options from the message box. Wait and retry the operation.

{Virtual Circuit Closed}An existing connection (virtual circuit) has been broken at the remote computer. There is probably something wrong with the network software protocol or the network hardware on the remote computer.

[Kernel]

Try the operation again. If this message reappears, ask your network administrator to check the network adapter and wiring connections on the remote computer. Also, the remote computer may have the wrong version of the network protocol installed.

{Virtual Circuit Closed}The network transport on a remote computer has closed a network connection. There may or may not be I/O requests outstanding.

[Kernel]

If you expected this message, no other action is needed. If the message is unexpected, you may want to check the results of the application that was disconnected. If this message often occurs unexpectedly, contact your network administrator.

{Virtual Circuit Closed}The network transport on your computer has closed a network connection because it had to wait too long for a response from the remote computer.

[Kernel]

Try the operation again. If this message reappears, ask your network administrator to check the status of the remote computer.

{Virtual Circuit Closed}The network transport on your computer has closed a network connection. There may or may not be I/O requests outstanding.

[Kernel]

If you expected this message, no other action is needed. If the message is unexpected, you may want to check the results of the application that was disconnected. If this message often occurs unexpectedly, contact your network administrator.

{Working Set Range Error}An attempt was made to set the working set minimum or maximum to values which are outside of the allowable range.

[Kernel]

This Windows NT Executive STATUS message is for your information. Choose OK to continue. No other action is needed.

{Write Protect Error}The disk cannot be written to because it is write protected. Please remove the write protection from the volume *name* **in drive** *drive letter***.**

[Kernel]

This is a Windows NT Executive STATUS error message. Correct the condition and either continue running the application or restart the application. If this message reappears, contact the supplier of the application.

{Wrong Type}There is a mismatch between the type of object required by the requested operation and the type of object that is specified in the request.

[Kernel]

This is a Windows NT Executive STATUS error message. Choose an option from the message box. If you Retry and this message reappears, contact your system administrator or your technical support group.

0.0.0.0 is an invalid Default Gateway address.

[TCP/IP]

At least one of the numbers in the Default Gateway address must be non-zero. This is the IP address of the default gateway used to forward packets to other networks or subnets. If this parameter is not provided, IP functionality will be limited to the local subnet unless a route is specified with the ROUTE command.

Ask your network administrator for the correct Default Gateway address.

10 Mismatches - ending compare

[File Compare]

The Comp command has found enough differences between the two files it is comparing to conclude that the files are indeed different. Doing any more compares would be a waste of time.

12 and 24 hour time formats may not be mixed.

[Network] Net Message ID: 3765

You mixed 12- and 24-hour formats in your time specification. If you use the 12-hour format (with AM and PM), the hours must be from 0 to 12. If you use 24-hour format, the hours must be from 0 to 24.

Retype the command with either the 12- or 24-hour format.

A adapter name specified was greater than the maximum length allowed for adapter "*name* ".

[Services for Macintosh (SFM)]

Adapter names are limited to 32 characters.

In the Registry, change the value of key, HKEY_LOCAL_MACHINE\SYSTEM\CurrentControlSet\AppleTalk\Adapters\<adapter name>\PortName, to be less than 32 characters.

A bad mailslot server message block (SMB) was received. The SMB is the data.

[Network] Net Message ID: 3165

This message should occur only on a down-level computer. Any action to correct the problem should be performed on that computer. A software error occurred.

Contact technical support.

A bad value is in the units-per-week field of the user record.

[Network] Net Message ID: 3720

This message should occur only on a down-level computer. Any action to correct the problem should be performed on that computer. The internal record of this user is invalid.

Contact technical support.

A call to a system service failed unexpectedly. The data is the error.

[FTP Server]

A critical system call failed so the FTP service could not be initialized. The service could not register with the service controller.

Contact technical support.

A centralized logon-server conflict occurred.

[Network] Net Message ID: 2210

You can't start the Netlogon service on this server because a server in the domain with an earlier version of the software is running the Netlogon service.

Before you can start the Netlogon service on this server, you must stop the Netlogon service on all servers in the domain running earlier versions of the software.

A child window failed to initialize! App will exit.

[CD Player]

Either you are low on system resources, or an internal software error has occurred.

No action is needed.

A command or response in the device .INF file section refers to an undefined macro.

[Remote Access Service]

One of the Remote Access configuration files probably contains invalid information.

The easiest way to resolve this problem is to reinstall Remote Access. Use the Network option in Control Panel to remove and then reinstall RAS. If you are using a modem that is not supported by Remote Access, switch to a supported modem, or see "Modem Script File" in the Remote Access Service online Help for information about modifying the modem script file for your modem. The Remote Access script files (PAD.INF, MODEM.INF, and SWITCH.INF) are in the \SYSTEM32\RAS subdirectory of your Windows NT directory.

A command was used with conflicting switches.

[Network] Net Message ID: 3510

You typed a command with two options that conflict, such as /YES and /NO.

Retype the command without contradictory options.

A comment must be provided for the scope.

[DHCP]

Enter a descriptive comment in the Comment text box.

A conflict has been detected between two drivers which claimed equivalent IRQs. Driver *name*, with device *name*, claimed an interrupt with Level in data address0x28, vector in data address 0x2c and Affinity in data address 0x30.

Two drivers are requesting exclusive use of the same interrupt (IRQ). The second driver cannot be loaded, and functionality dependent on this driver will not be available.

Change the IRQ value for the specified driver. Or, if you know which driver is competing for this IRQ, change the IRQ value for that driver.

A conflict has been detected between two drivers which claimed two overlapping IO port regions. Driver *name*, with device *name*, claimed an IO port range with starting address in data address 0x28 and 0x2c, and length in data address 0x30.

Two drivers are requesting exclusive use of the same I/O ports. The second driver cannot be loaded, and functionality dependent on this driver will not be available

Change the set of I/O ports for the specified driver. Or, if you know which driver is competing for this range of I/O ports, change them for that driver.

A connection could not be established to the specified computer.

[Clipboard]

You attempted unsuccessfully to connect to a remote computer. The computer may not be started.

Wait and try again.

A continuous RESET state has been entered.

[Virtual DOS Machine (VDM)]

The virtual DOS keyboard is in a continuous reset state and is unusable.

Terminate the application, then restart it. If you still get this message, contact your technical support group or the supplier of the application.

A corrupt extension "*path* " was detected in the registry. This value was ignored.

[Services for Macintosh (SFM)]

The corrupt extension may not have any characters or it may have more than three characters.

Use the Registry editor to correct the corrupt extension. Delete the invalid extension in the \\HKEY_LOCAL_MACHINE\System\CurrentControlSet\Services\MacFile\Parameters\Extensions Registry key.

A corrupt type/creator pair with type "*text*" and creator "*text*" was detected in the registry. This value was ignored.

[Services for Macintosh (SFM)]

Use the Registry Editor to change the corrupt value in the Registry. The value is located in the \\HKEY_LOCAL_MACHINE\System\CurrentControlSet\Services\MacFile\Parameters\Type_Creators key.

A cross-encrypted password is necessary to change this user password.

[Kernel32]

Contact the supplier of the running application.

A defective sector on drive *drive letter* has been replaced (hotfixed). No data was lost. You should run CHKDSK soon to restore full performance and replenish the volume's spare sector pool. The hotfix occurred while processing a remote request.

[Network] Net Message ID: 3181

This message should occur only on a down-level computer. Any action to correct the problem should be performed on that computer. The fault-tolerant system found a bad disk sector and rerouted data to a good sector (this is called hotfixing).

Run CHKDSK soon to ensure that enough good disk sectors are available for hotfixing.

A device attached to the system is not functioning.

[Kernel32]

An attached device is not working for one of these reasons: (1) it is switched off, or connected improperly; (2) the floppy disk and drive types are incompatible; (3) the floppy disk is not properly inserted in the drive; (4) the drive door is open; or (5) the floppy disk is not properly formatted.

Correct the problem and retry the command.

A different disk is expected in drive *drive letter* **:.Please insert the appropriate disk.**

[Common Dialog]

Remove the disk that is in the indicated drive, and insert the disk required by the program.

A directory change notification was missed on volume "*name* **".**

[Services for Macintosh (SFM)]

A change was made to a directory but the Services for Macintosh File Server could not be notified of the change. The change may have been that a file was created or deleted or renamed. The size or date on a file might have changed also. The view of the disk seen by a Macintosh client may not be consistent with the actual state of the disk. The notification could have been missed because the server may be running out of memory.

Use the Services option in Control Panel to stop and restart the File Server for Macintosh service.

A disk fault tolerance set member listed in the configuration information was missing.

[Disk Administrator]

This can only happen at system startup. Check the cables to your disk drives. Then restart your computer. If you still get this message, contact technical support or your disk vendor to run hardware diagnostics on your disk drives.

A disk I/O failure occurred.

[Network] Net Message ID: 2229

A software error occurred while Windows NT tried to access the down-level security database file.

Type the command again. If the error persists, use a backup copy of the security database from a server and try the command again. If the error persists, your disk drive may have hardware problems.

A domain controller for your domain could not be contacted. You have been logged on using cached account information. Changes made to your profile since you last logged on may not be available.

[Workstation-Logon]

Possibly, your domain controller is temporarily malfunctioning. When you log on to a domain, the logon information is saved, but changes made to your profile may not be.

You can still log on, but you may wish to wait until the domain controller can be contacted.

A DosDevIoctl or DosFsCtl to NETWKSTA.SYS failed. The data shown is in this format:DWORD approx CS:IP of call to ioctl or fsctlWORD error codeWORD ioctl or fsctl number

[Network] Net Message ID: 3108

This message should occur only on a down-level computer. Any action to correct the problem should be performed on that computer. A software error occurred.

Contact technical support.

A drive error was detected.

[Backup]

The tape drive did not initialize properly.

Messages that preceded this one provided more information about the error.

A driver packet received from the I/O subsystem was invalid. The data is the packet.

[Netevent]

The driver is functioning properly but is logging incorrectly formatted packets in the event log.

Examine the data in the event log in Event Viewer for the Unicode version of the driver's name and replace the packets or contact the supplier of the driver.

A duplicate file name exists, or the file cannot be found.

[Command]

Command Prompt cannot find the file that you want to rename, or there is another file in the directory using the new name.

Make sure you typed the correct filename and path. If a file with that name already exists, rename it, delete it, or specify a different filename for the file that you want to rename.

A duplicate file name exists, or the file cannot be found.

[Command Prompt]

Command Prompt cannot find the file that you want to rename, or there is another file in the directory using the new name.

Make sure you typed the correct filename and path. If a file with that name already exists, rename it, delete it, or specify a different filename for the file that you want to rename.

A duplicate message alias exists on the network.

[Network] Net Message ID: 2297

The name you specified is already in use as a message alias on the network.

Use a different name.

A duplicate name exists on the network.

[Kernel32]

Another computer or user on the network is already using this name. Your computer name must be unique on the network.

Choose another name for your computer, then retry the command.

A dynamic link library (DLL) initialization routine failed.

[Kernel32]

Contact the supplier of the dynamic-link library (DLL).

A failure occurred when executing a remote administration command.

[Network] Net Message ID: 2315

This message should occur only on a down-level computer. Any action to correct the problem should be performed on that computer. The command cannot run on the remote server, probably because of a problem with the server's operating system configuration.

Have your network administrator check the configuration of the server's operating system.

A failure occurred when opening a remote temporary file.

[Network] Net Message ID: 2316

This message should occur only on a down-level computer. Any action to correct the problem should be performed on that computer. The command could not be completed because it could not open a temporary file on the server.

See your network administrator. If you need further help, contact technical support.

A fatal error occurred while initialize a helper thread.

[Services for Macintosh (SFM)]

Restart your computer. If you see this message again, contact technical support.

A fatal internal error was detected in the AppleTalk stack.

[Services for Macintosh (SFM)]

Contact technical support.

A file contains extended attributes, but the extended attribute file was not found.

[Convert]

During a FAT to NTFS file conversion, the Convert utility could not find the extended attribute file associated with a FAT file.

The FAT volume is corrupted. Run the Chkdsk utility with the /f option and then retry the conversion.

A file or directory by this name already exists. Within a directory, file and directory names must be unique.

[File Manager]

Using the Rename option, you attempted to assign a file a name that already exists in the current directory.

Follow the user action specified in the message.

A file system error occurred while opening or writing to the system message log file *filename*. Message logging has been switched off due to the error. The error code is the data.

[Network] Net Message ID: 3150

This message should occur only on a down-level computer. Any action to correct the problem should be performed on that computer. An error occurred when the Messenger service tried to access the message log, so message logging has stopped. The error may have been caused by a full disk, a disk error, the file being locked by another process, or any other situation that would cause an error while writing to a file.

If the disk is full, free space on it by deleting unnecessary files and directories. Then check that the message log file is accessible, and start message logging by typing NET LOG /ON.

A floating-point operation at the RPC server caused a division by zero.

[Kernel32]

In a distributed (RPC) application, a server attempted a floating-point divide by zero operation.

Contact the supplier of the running application.

A floating-point overflow occurred at the RPC server.

[Kernel32]

In a distributed (RPC) application, a floating-point overflow occurred at the server.

Contact the supplier of the running application.

A floating-point underflow occurred at the RPC server.

[Kernel32]

In a distributed (RPC) application, a floating-point underflow occurred at the server.

Contact the supplier of the running application.

A general error occurred while trying to decompress the file *filename*.

[Setup]

The Windows NT Setup program cannot copy a distribution file for some non-specific reason.

Select the Retry option. If you still get this message, select Exit Setup and retry the Setup operation from the beginning. You may have to get another copy of the distribution medium.

A general error occurred while trying to decompress the file *filename*.

[Repair Disk]

The Windows NT Setup program cannot copy a distribution file for some non-specific reason.

Select the Retry option. If you still get this message, select Exit Setup and retry the Setup operation from the beginning. You may have to get another copy of the distribution medium.

A general network error occurred.

[Network] Net Message ID: 2136

A general failure occurred in the network hardware. This problem may be due to a hardware conflict and could have been generated by any number of other Server service commands (for example, Replicator).

See your network administrator. The problem could have occurred because of the hardware or software installed on your computer.

A key could not be created/opened

[WINS Service]

The WINS configuration is stored in the Registry, under Current Control Set\Software\WINS key. One of the keys in this section could not be created (or opened).

Ask the administrator to check that the entry is correct, or reinstall WINS.

A line in the configuration file is too long.

[Network] Net Message ID: 2149

This message should occur only on a down-level computer. Any action to correct the problem should be performed on that computer.

Edit the configuration file.

A list variable in the .INF file *filename* is not terminated.

[Setup]

Setup loaded an .INF file and began interpreting it. It could not be interpreted.

Select Retry to retry the operation. If you get the same message, select Exit Setup. Then restore the .INF file from the distribution medium (you will have to decompress the file). Retry the Setup operation from the beginning. If you get this same message, contact your technical support group.

A list variable in the .INF file *filename* is not terminated.

[Repair Disk]

Setup loaded an .INF file and began interpreting it. It could not be interpreted.

Select Retry to retry the operation. If you get the same message, select Exit Setup. Then restore the .INF file from the distribution medium (you will have to decompress the file). Retry the Setup operation from the beginning. If you get this same message, contact your technical support group.

A lock request was not outstanding for the supplied cancel region.

[Kernel32]

Contact the supplier of the running application.

A logon request contained an invalid logon type value.

[Kernel32]

Three logon types are recognized by Windows NT: interactive, network, and service.

Contact the supplier of the running application.

A machine account for ***user name*** **already exists.**

[Server Manager]

You cannot create an account for this computer name because there is already one on the domain. You cannot add a new computer with this name unless the old computer name is removed from the domain.

Make sure you typed the computer name correctly. If this is the computer name you wanted to add, no action is needed.

A Macintosh workstation submitted a job with Adobe Document Structuring Convention comments that could not be processed. The job from ***computer name*** **was canceled.**

[Services for Macintosh (SFM)]

Switch to a driver that uses a more recent version. Adobe LaserWriter GX is not supported.

A macro required by the device was not found in the device .INF file section.

[Remote Access Service]

One of the Remote Access configuration files probably contains invalid information.

The easiest way to resolve this problem is to reinstall Remote Access. Use the Network option in Control Panel to remove and reinstall RAS. If you are using a modem that is not supported by Remote Access, switch to a supported modem, or see "Modem Script File" in the Remote Access Service online Help for information about modifying the modem script file for your modem. The Remote Access script files (PAD.INF, MODEM.INF, and SWITCH.INF) are in the \SYSTEM32\RAS subdirectory of your Windows NT directory.

A matching share could not be found so nothing was deleted.

[Network] Net Message ID: 3719

Windows NT could not find the resource you wanted to stop sharing.

Check the spelling of the share name. To see a list of the resources the server is sharing, type NET SHARE.

A message was received on an association. The association is in a bad state. This indicates a bug in WINS code.

[WINS Service]

Contact Microsoft Product Support.

A MIDI map was not found. There may be a problem with the driver, or the MIDIMAP.CFG file may be corrupt or missing.

Restore your MIDIMAP.CFG file from a backup copy, and try again.

A name release request was received for a record *number* **that didn't have the same address as the requester. The request has been ignored.**

[WINS Service]

A multihomed client released a name that had not yet been marked as multihomed in the WINS database. This can happen when only one registration for a name has reached the WINS server; the other names might have gone to another WINS server and not been replicated yet.

No action is needed.

A name release request was received for a record that didn't match the unique/group type indicated in the request. The request has been ignored.

[WINS Service]

One computer registered a name (unique or group) and then powered off. A second computer then registered the same name as a the other type (unique or group), and then released it. This second registration went to a backup WINS server, but the release went to the primary WINS server. The primary had not yet received the replica from the backup, and so the type specified in the release is not the same as the type specified in the registration it has.

No action is needed.

A NetBIOS error has occurred.

[Remote Access Service]

Your modem may not have negotiated the connection correctly, or the line may be noisy.

Set the modem to a lower initial speed (bps), and dial again. For more information see "Setting Modem Features" and "Modem Idiosyncrasies" in the Remote Access Service online Help. Please record the Fail Code (a NetBIOS error code), and make it available to your technical support staff if you call for help.

A NetWksta internal error has occurred: *code*

[Network] Net Message ID: 3190

This message should occur only on a down-level computer. Any action to correct the problem should be performed on that computer. A software error occurred.

Contact technical support.

A network adapter at the server failed.

[Remote Access Service]

Contact your system administrator and report this error.

A network adapter hardware error occurred.

[Kernel32]

The hardware that connects your computer to the local area network is experiencing a problem.

Make sure the cable on the back of your computer is properly connected, then retry the command. If you continue to have problems, contact your network administrator or the manufacturer of the network hardware.

A network resource shortage occurred.

[Network] Net Message ID: 2105

The network hardware could not access the resources it needed. This may have occurred because too many sessions are operating or the server is out of memory.

Try the command again later.

A new member could not be added to a local group because the member does not exist.

[Kernel32]

Contact the supplier of the running application.

A new member could not be added to a local group because the member has the wrong account type.

[Kernel32]

Contact the supplier of the running application.

A newer version of Help is needed to read this Help file.

[Help]

You tried to view a Help file that was written for a more recent version of the Help engine than is installed on your computer.

Install the latest version of Windows NT.

A non-existent section was referenced in a Setup Script command in section:

[Setup]

Setup was unable to interpret the .INF file. It is probably corrupted.

Select OK to exit Setup. Then restore the .INF file from the distribution medium (you will have to decompress the file). Retry the Setup operation. If you get this same message, contact your technical support group.

A non-existent section was referenced in a Setup Script command in section:

[Repair Disk]

Setup was unable to interpret the .INF file. It is probably corrupted.

Select OK to exit Setup. Then restore the .INF file from the distribution medium (you will have to decompress the file). Retry the Setup operation. If you get this same message, contact your technical support group.

A non-recoverable error occurred. The process ended.

[Command Prompt]

A system error has ended the current process, and the specific nature of the error cannot be determined.

If possible, reinitiate the process.

A non-recoverable error occurred. The process ended.

[Command]

A system error has ended the current process, and the specific nature of the error cannot be determined.

If possible, reinitiate the process.

A null context handle was passed from the client to the host during a remote procedure call.

[Kernel32]

Contact the supplier of the running distributed application.

A null reference pointer was passed to the stub.

[Kernel32]

This happened during a remote procedure call (RPC).

Contact the supplier of the running distributed application.

A parity error was detected on *name*.

Check the hardware cabling for the named device. After that, if this message reappears, contact the vendor of the named device.

A password mismatch has been detected.

[Network] Net Message ID: 2458

This message should occur only on a down-level computer. Any action to correct the problem should be performed on that computer. You have recently changed your password and the server does not recognize it.

Log off from the network, and then log on again. This changes the user accounts database and allows the server to recognize the password.

A person answered instead of a modem.

[Remote Access Service]

A modem did not pick up the phone.

Please check the number and dial again.

A power failure has occurred at *computer name***. Please terminate all activity with this server.**

[Network]

The server is about to shut down due to a power failure. Any files that you have open on the server when it shuts down could be corrupted.

Immediately close all files and applications that are on or are using this server.

A power failure was detected at *name***. The server has been paused.**

[Network]

No connections can be made to the server while it is paused.

Because servers are usually paused before they are shut down, you should close any files or applications that you have open on this server.

A power failure was detected at the server.

[Network] Net Message ID: 3230

The server had a power failure.

The UPS service is shutting down the server. Stop applications that are running on the server and have users disconnect from the server.

A primary domain controller is already running in this domain.

[Network]

The Primary Domain Controller (PDC) was temporarily removed from the network and a Backup Domain Controller (BDC) was promoted. This error appears when the original PDC is reconnected.

Demote one of the PDCs, using Server Manager.

A problem exists with the Emergency Repair Information File on the disk you have provided or the Windows NT installation you specified: *text* **Setup cannot repair the file. \a To skip this file, press ENTER. The file will not be repaired. To exit Setup, press F3.**

[Setup]

Let Setup search your hard disk for a Windows NT installation to repair.

A problem exists with the Emergency Repair Information File on the disk you have provided or the Windows NT installation you specified: *filename* **Setup cannot use the file to repair the selected Windows NT installation. \a To provide a different Emergency Repair Disk or to specify a different Windows NT installation, press ENTER. To exit Setup, press F3.**

[Setup]

Let Setup search your hard disk for a Windows NT installation to repair.

A problem exists with the system configuration.

[Network] Net Message ID: 3055

This message should occur only on a down-level computer. Any action to correct the problem should be performed on that computer. The system is not configured correctly.

Contact your network administrator.

A Problem occurred while initializing CD Player. App will be terminated.

[CD Player]

Either you are low on system resources, or an internal software error has occurred.

If you have a number of applications running, close some of them, and then try again to initialize CD Player. If this message reappears, shut down and restart Windows NT.

A read-only file cannot be changed and saved. If you want to save this version of the file, use the Save As command to save the file to a different file name or use the Properties command in File Manager to change the file attributes.

[Paintbrush]

You attempted to save changes to a read-only file.

If the file belongs to you, follow the action specified in the message. If the file does not belong to you, you should copy it and save it under a different name.

A record could not be registered because it already existed. However, the same record then could not be found. The database might be corrupt.

[WINS Service]

Stop and restart the WINS service. If this error occurs often, call Microsoft Product Support.

A remote API error occurred.

[Network] Net Message ID: 2127

This message should occur only on a down-level computer. Any action to correct the problem should be performed on that computer. The program or command you were running on a server could not be completed. There may be communication problems on the network, or the remote server may be short of resources.

Contact your network administrator. Your administrator should make sure that the server is configured with enough resources. Specifically, the NUMBIGBUF entry in the server's configuration file may need to be increased. Tell your network administrator that a remote API error occurred.

A remote API request was halted due to the following invalid description string: *text.*

[Network] Net Message ID: 3125

This message should occur only on a down-level computer. Any action to correct the problem should be performed on that computer. The server received an invalid request to run a command. The request may have been damaged by the network.

No action is needed. If this error occurs frequently, contact technical support. Tell technical support that a remote API request was halted due to an invalid description string.

A remote procedure call (RPC) protocol error occurred.

[Kernel32]

The server and workstation configurations may be incompatible.

Contact your network administrator to check the compatibility of your workstation and the server on the network. If they are compatible, and this message reappears, you will have to contact the supplier of the running distributed application.

A replica clashed with a static record in the database. The replica was rejected.

[WINS Service]

An address has been dynamically assigned by one computer that was already statically assigned by another computer.

Check the WINS databases of other WINS servers and eliminate duplication of this address. Check the static record; you might choose to delete it.

A request for resource could not be satisfied.

[Network] Net Message ID: 3054

The service required more of the listed resource than was available.

Increase the amount of this resource. Stopping other services or applications may free some resources, such as memory. Also, check the disk where your pagefile(s) are located. If this disk is full, delete unnecessary files and directories from it to clear space.

A request has been submitted to promote the computer to backup when it is already a master browser.

[Netevent]

The computer is already at the highest level that it can reach. In the browser, computers are either client, potential, backup, or master, with client computers having the least power and master browsers having the most power. When a browser comes online, it announces itself to the master browser. The master browser asks a fraction of these browsers to become backup browsers. The master browser itself has received one of these requests.

Contact your network administrator to verify that there is only one master browser and that browsing is functioning properly.

A required privilege is not held by the client.

[Kernel32]

An application has requested a service that it does not have the privilege to perform. Most, but not all, system services check the client's privileges before performing a requested service. For example, no privilege is required to get the system time, but a privilege is required to set the system time.

Ask your system administrator for the privilege to use the service.

A response keyname in the device .INF file is not in the expected format.

[Remote Access Service]

One of the Remote Access configuration files probably contains invalid information.

The easiest way to resolve this problem is to reinstall Remote Access. Use the Network option in Control Panel to remove and reinstall RAS. If you are using a modem that is not supported by Remote Access, switch to a supported modem, or see "Modem Script File" in the Remote Access Service online Help for information about modifying the modem script file for your modem. The Remote Access script files (PAD.INF, MODEM.INF, and SWITCH.INF) are in the \SYSTEM32\RAS subdirectory of your Windows NT directory.

A retry was successful on *name*.

A retry succeeded on the named device.

You can ignore this message. It is for informational purposes only.

A SCSI tape device has been detected, but the tape driver has either not been installed, or failed to start. Make sure that the appropriate driver has been installed using the Add/Remove Tape Devices option in the Options menu of Windows NT Setup.

[Backup]

To run Backup, you must install the appropriate device driver.

Follow the action specified in the message.

A sector failure occurred on accesses to both copies of the data.

[Disk Administrator]

An I/O operation failed for both the primary and the redundant copy of the data. It is unlikely that bad spots have appeared at the same offset on both disks.

Make sure the drives are on-line and are functioning properly. Check for Eventlog entries close to this one that indicate a hardware problem with one or both drives.

A security descriptor is not in the right format (absolute or self-relative).

[Kernel32]

Contact the supplier of the running application.

A seeding adapter had no network range specified for adapter "*name* ".

[Services for Macintosh (SFM)]

The seeding adapter setting was deleted by directly accessing the Registry instead of using the Network option in Control Panel.

Use the Network option in Control Panel to correct the configuration of the seeding adapter. Select Services for Macintosh and then choose Configure. Check the Enable Routing check box and then choose Advanced. Check the Seed this Network check box.

A seeding adapter had no zone list specified on adapter "*name* ".

[Services for Macintosh (SFM)]

The seeding adapter setting was deleted by directly accessing the Registry instead of using the Network option in Control Panel.

Use the Network option in Control Panel to specify a zone list for the adapter. Select Services for Macintosh and then choose Configure. Check the Enable Routing check box and then choose Advanced. Check the Seed this Network check box.

A seeding adapter had too many zones specified on adapter "*name* ". The limit on zones is 255.

[Services for Macintosh (SFM)]

The seeding adapter setting was changed by directly accessing the Registry instead of using the Network option in Control Panel.

Use the Network option in Control Panel to remove zone from the adapter. Select Services for Macintosh and then choose Configure. Check the Enable Routing check box and then choose Advanced. Check the Seed this Network check box.

A server message block (SMB) error occurred on the connection to *computer name*.The SMB header is the data.

[Network] Net Message ID: 3192

This message should occur only on a down-level computer. Any action to correct the problem should be performed on that computer. An error occurred on a request that was sent to the specified server. The workstation may have been connected to a resource that is no longer shared.

Ask a network administrator to reshare the resource so that you can use it. If this solution fails, contact technical support.

A service specific error occurred: *code*.

[Network] Net Message ID: 3547

A service-specific error occurred.

Refer to the Help or documentation for that service to determine the problem.

A session does not exist with that computer name.

[Network] Net Message ID: 2312

The specified computer does not have a session with the server.

Check the spelling of the computer name. To display a list of workstations and users that have sessions with the server, type NET SESSION.

A signal is already pending.

[Kernel32]

This signal could not be posted because the process has another signal to process.

Try again at a later time.

A specified authentication package is unknown.

[Kernel32]

Contact the supplier of the running application.

A specified privilege does not exist.

[Kernel32]

Contact the supplier of the currently running application.

A spooler memory allocation failure occurred.

[Network] Net Message ID: 2165

This message should occur only on a down-level computer. Any action to correct the problem should be performed on that computer. The spooler ran out of memory.

To free memory for the spooler, delete one or more printer queues or print jobs, or remove one or more printers from all print queues on the server.

A stop control has been sent to a service which other running services are dependent on.

[Kernel32]

The service stop control sent by a custom service management user interface program was ignored.

Stop the dependent services first, then retry the stop request.

A stripe set or volume set member listed in the configuration information was missing.

[Disk Administrator]

Check the cables to your disk drives. Then restart your computer. If you still get this message, contact technical support or your disk vendor to run hardware diagnostics on your disk drives.

A subdirectory or file *name* already exists.

[Command]

At the command prompt, you used the Md command to attempt to create a directory that already exists on the current drive.

Use the Md command and after the command, specify a unique directory name.

A subdirectory or file *name* already exists.

[Command Prompt]

At the command prompt, you used the Md command to attempt to create a directory that already exists on the current drive.

Use the Md command and after the command, specify a unique directory name.

A system error has occurred.

[Network] Net Message ID: 3056

The system error may be an internal LAN Manager or Windows NT error.

If the error code is Error 52, you need to delete the duplicate domain name in the [othdomains] section of your configuration file. If an error code beginning with NET is displayed, you can use the Helpmsg command to see more information about the error as follows: NET HELPMSG <message>#, where <message># is the actual error number. If no error number was displayed, contact technical support.

A tape access reached a filemark.

[Kernel32]

Contact the supplier of the running application.

A tape access reached the end of a set of files.

[Kernel32]

No user action is possible. If the application does not continue to run, contact the supplier of the application.

A tape device has been detected, and the tape driver started. However, the tape device is not responding. Check that tape device power is on and cables are properly connected.

[Backup]

Backup is not functioning properly.

Follow the action specified in the message.

A thread could not be created.

[WINS Service]

The WINS server is low on resources.

Reboot the WINS server. Also, check available disk space on that computer, and delete some files if necessary.

A thread could not be created for the service.

[Kernel32]

An application tried to start a service which requires a thread, but no threads were available. The service did not start.

Stop running some nonessential programs, then try to start the service again. You may need to get more memory for you computer.

A thread for the new service could not be created.

[Network] Net Message ID: 2194

The system temporarily could not access the resources it needed.

Try the command again later.

A transport driver received a frame which violated the protocol.

Check the device cabling, particularly the SCSI termination. After that, if you still get this message, run hardware diagnostics. You may have to contact the vendor of the device, and you may have to replace the controller, the disk drive, or both.

A TrueImage Interpreter error occurred for which no error string is defined.(Document Name: *name* **), Error Code:** *code*

[Services for Macintosh (SFM)]

Contact technical support.

A TrueImage Interpreter frame buffer memory allocation failed.(Document Name: *name* **)**

[Services for Macintosh (SFM)]

The server may be running out of memory or resources.

Try stopping other running applications. You might also need to remove unused files and applications from the server's disk.

A user's session with this server has been deleted because the user's logon hours are no longer valid.

[Network] Net Message ID: 2434

This message should occur only on a down-level computer. Any action to correct the problem should be performed on that computer. LAN Manager ended a user's session with this server because the user's logon time expired.

No action is needed. To define the times during which a user can access the server, type NET USER <user name> /TIMES:<times>.

A valid name was not entered.

[Network] Net Message ID: 3735

You typed an invalid name.

Type a valid name.

A valid password was not entered.

[Network] Net Message ID: 3734

You typed an invalid password.

Type a valid password.

A WINS RPC thread encountered an exception.

[WINS Service]

Other activity on the computer has affected the activity of the specified thread. WINS will try to recover from the exception automatically.

No action is needed. If this error occurs often, stop and restart the WINS service.

A WINS thread could not reset a handle.

[WINS Service]

Other activity on the computer has affected the activity of the thread. WINS will try to recover from the exception automatically.

No action is needed. If this error occurs more than once, reboot the computer.

A WINS thread could not signal a handle.

[WINS Service]

No action is needed. If this error occurs more than once, reboot the computer.

A WINS thread could not signal the main thread after closing its session. This would be the last thread in WINS closing the database.

[WINS Service]

An error occurred that affects the successful closing of the database. This could result in a corrupt database.

Stop and restart WINS. You may need to restore the database from a backup.

A WINS worker thread encountered an exception.

[WINS Service]

Other activity on the computer has affected the activity of the specified thread. WINS will try to recover from the exception automatically.

No action is needed. If this error occurs often, stop and restart the WINS service.

A word is expected *text* the operator *text*. Your query was missing this word or used a word which isn't in the Search word list.

[Disk Administrator]

The command is not complete as you typed it and cannot be carried out without further information.

A worker thread could not be created.

[WINS Service]

The WINS server is running out of resources (probably disk space or memory).

Close some applications to free memory. Check available disk space and delete some files if necessary. Then stop and restart the WINS service.

A Worker thread is shutting down due to some error condition.

[WINS Service]

The WINS database might be corrupt.

Stop and restart the WINS service. If this message appears again, restore the WINS database from a backup copy.

A write fault occurred on the network.

[Kernel32]

An error occurred while data was being written to disk. Data might have been lost.

Ensure that the disk that you want to write to has enough space available, and that you have permission to write to the target file. Then retry the command.

A write fault occurred.

[Network] Net Message ID: 2295

This message should occur only on a down-level computer. Any action to correct the problem should be performed on that computer. LAN Manager found an error when writing to the message log file.

Contact your network administrator.

A write operation to ***filename*** **failed. Data may have been lost.**

[Network] Net Message ID: 3196

This message should occur only on a down-level computer. Any action to correct the problem should be performed on that computer. An attempt to write data to a file failed.

See if the specified disk is full. Also be sure that you have write permission for the target file.

A write-behind operation has failed to the remote server *computer name***. The data contains the amount requested to write and the amount actually written.**

[Netevent]

Data may have been lost. Retry the command or action.

About to revert to the last known good configuration because the *name* **service failed to start.**

[Netevent]

A critical service or driver failed to start; therefore the system will revert to the last saved configuration.

Ask your system administrator to check the event log with Event Viewer for details about the service or driver errors that preceded this one.

Access Denied

[Registry Editor]

You attempted to access an object in Registry Editor without sufficient permission.

Use the Owner option to determine who owns the object, then see the owner to get permission to access it. If you are the owner, log onto a user account under which you have permission to access the object.

Access denied - *filename*

[Attrib]

You tried to write to a read-only file, or the file is already being used by another program or person on a network, or you don't have writing privileges for this file on a network.

Use the Attrib command to see if the file is read-only. If it is read-only and you want to write to this file, use the Attrib command with the -r switch to remove the read-only attribute. Otherwise, make sure another program isn't using this file. If you are on a network and you do have privileges for this file, another person may be using this file. Wait a while and then try again.

Access denied - *filename*

[Replace]

You tried to write to a read-only file, or the file is already being used by another program or person on a network, or you don't have writing privileges for this file on a network.

Use the Attrib command to see if the file is read-only. If it is read-only and you want to write to this file, use the Attrib command with the -r switch to remove the read-only attribute. Otherwise, make sure another program isn't using this file. If you are on a network and you do have privileges for this file, another person may be using this file. Wait a while and then try again.

Access denied - *filename*

[Xcopy]

You tried to write to a read-only file, or the file is already being used by another program or person on a network, or you don't have writing privileges for this file on a network.

Use the Attrib command to see if the file is read-only. If it is read-only and you want to write to this file, use the Attrib command with the -r switch to remove the read-only attribute. Otherwise, make sure another program isn't using this file. If you are on a network and you do have privileges for this file, another person may be using this file. Wait a while and then try again.

Access denied - *filename*

[Utilities]

You tried to write to a read-only file, or the file is already being used by another program or person on a network, or you don't have writing privileges for this file on a network.

Use the Attrib command to see if the file is read-only. If it is read-only and you want to write to this file, use the Attrib command with the -r switch to remove the read-only attribute. Otherwise, make sure another program isn't using this file. If you are on a network and you do have privileges for this file, another person may be using this file. Wait a while and then try again.

Access denied because username and/or password is invalid on the domain.

[Remote Access Service]

Type your username, password, and domain. If you are unsure of this information, ask your system administrator. If you do not specify a domain, the Remote Access server attempts to verify your username and password on the domain of which it is a member.

Access Denied.

[Backup]

You do not have permission to view the contents of the tape.

Access denied.

[File Manager]

You have attempted to access a file that you do not have permission to access.

Contact your system administrator or the owner of the file or directory. If you are the owner of the file, log on under the user account that you used to assign permissions on the file.

Access denied.

[Xcopy]

The volume is already being used by another program, or you don't have privileges to open the volume.

Make sure another program isn't using this volume, and that you have privileges to open the volume.

Access denied.

[Utilities]

The volume is already being used by another program, or you don't have privileges to open the volume.

Make sure another program isn't using this volume, and that you have privileges to open the volume.

Access Denied. Granted access = ***text*****, Error code:** *code*

[Dynamic Data Exchange]

You have only the access permissions indicated. This is not sufficient for the access you tried to perform.

You can ask that your permissions be changed to allow the desired access.

Access is denied

[Dynamic Data Exchange]

You do not have the necessary permissions to access the desired resource.

You can ask that your permissions be changed to allow the desired access.

Access is denied.

[Kernel32]

One of the following has occurred: (1) the file is marked read-only; (2) the resource, such as a file or subdirectory, that you tried to access is in use, or the named pipe, queue, or semaphore is a shared resource in use; (3) you tried to access a resource or to perform an action for which you do not have sufficient privilege; (4) the filename is incorrect.

Do one of the following, then retry the command: (1) use the Attrib command to change the read-only attribute; (2) try to access the resource again later; (3) log on with sufficient privilege (if you do not have sufficient privilege, request it from the administrator who controls access); or (4) correct the filename.

Access is denied. You must be logged on with Administrative privilege to run Disk Administrator.

[Disk Administrator]

If there are no hard disks attached to the system, there exists on the system no entity for Disk Administrator to administer.

Beyond that specified in the message itself, no action is needed.

Access to the extended attribute was denied.

[Kernel32]

Check your access rights with your system administrator. You may need to contact the supplier of the running application.

Access to the specified device, path or file is denied.

You attempted to access an Object Packager object that you do not have the right to access.

Contact your system administrator. Or contact the owner of the package.

Access to the specified device, path or file is denied.

[Task Manager]

Ask the network administrator to set the permissions on this device or file, or on the directories in the path to the device or file, to allow you access.

Access to the specified device, path, or file is denied.

The 16-bit compatibility subsystem tried to load an application, but access was denied. Access may have been denied to the file, or to the directory or device that contains the file.

Ask your system administrator for permission to access the device, path, or file.

Accessing Registry DDE Share information failed

[Dynamic Data Exchange]

DDE Share information could not be found in the Registry. You might not have permission to access a key in the registry. The key involved is either HKEY_LOCAL_MACHINE\Software\Microsoft\NetDDE or HKEY_CURRENT_USER\Software\Microsoft\NetDDE.

An experienced user of Regedit32 should check the permissions on these keys. Or, that person can delete the key and then run Setup to re-configure these keys.

Account *name* was not found.

[User Manager]

Make sure you have the correct user account name. Then try again, making sure to type the name correctly.

Account Deleted

[User Manager]

You tried to change the file or directory permissions for an account, but the account has been marked for deletion.

No action is needed.

Account Unknown

[Network]

There is no user account by this name in this group. In some cases this message will appear if the account has been deleted or if no primary or backup domain controller can be reached on the user's domain.

Check that you have the correct name. Then try again, taking care to type the name correctly.

Account Unknown

[User Manager]

Permissions have been associated with Security ID number, but no other account information could be found for that number. The account might be on a domain that is no longer trusted, or on a domain that cannot be reached at the moment. Or the account might have been deleted.

No action is needed.

ACLCONV cannot determine the file system on target volume.

[Aclconv]

Aclconv can only convert permissions for an NTFS volume. Since it cannot determine whether this is an NTFS volume, it did not convert permissions.

Make sure that the specified drive name is valid and that you have permission to access it.

ACLCONV cannot restore permissions onto drive *drive letter*

[Aclconv]

Aclconv could not find the drive specified.

Make sure that the drive name is valid.

Active connections still exist.

[Network] Net Message ID: 2402

This message should occur only on a down-level computer. Any action to correct the problem should be performed on that computer. You tried to delete a network connection that has an active process, or you tried to log off while you have an active process.

Be sure that the processes running on a server are completed before you break the connection to that server, and that processes on all remote servers are completed before you log off.

Add list box item failed.

[Remote Access Service]

There was a problem allocating memory.

Adjusting instance tags to prevent rollover on file *filename***.**

[Chkdsk]

CHKDSK is adjusting an internal file system structure for greater reliability. Each attribute record in an NTFS file record segment (FRS) has a unique tag ID. If the counter used to assign tag IDs for a particular FRS rolls over, duplicate tags would be created for different attribute records. This would mean that a routine that fetches attribute records could get the wrong record which could result in a loss of data.

No action is needed.

AFP information on "*filename* **" was corrupted.**

[Services for Macintosh (SFM)]

The file information is corrupted.

The defaults were set so no action is needed.

After starting, the service hung in a start-pending state.

[Kernel32]

Contact the supplier of the running application.

All AppleTalk routing configuration information for this computer will be lost. Are you sure you want to disable routing?

[Services for Macintosh (SFM)]

If you select Yes, all seeding information that you have specified will be lost. The AppleTalk® protocol routing will be according to the configuration of the network.

All available drive letters are already assigned. You will not be able to access the *name* from Windows NT unless you rearrange drive letter usage. Do you wish to continue and create the *name* anyway?

[Disk Administrator]

You can assign only 24 drive letters for accessing the volumes that you create (drives A and B are reserved for floppy disk drives). You have used up these 24 letters.

Either delete some drives, or remove the letter from one of your existing drives and assign it to the one that you want to create.

All COM ports are being used. Remove a device connected to one of the ports and try again.

[Terminal]

You attempted to configure a COM port for a device, and all of the available COM ports are being used.

When you have removed a device, return to the Communications dialog box and select None. This selection will cause Terminal to check the ports until it reaches the one that is available.

All copies of first block of bad block list bad on tape, cannot use this tape. From device: *name*

[QIC117]

This tape is corrupt.

Use a different tape.

All data in the mirror will be lost! Are you sure you want to break the selected mirror and delete its component partitions?

[Disk Administrator]

When you choose to break a mirror, Disk Administrator presents you with this standard confirmation message.

If you want to break the mirror, choose Yes. If not, choose No to return to the Disk Administrator window.

All data in the partition or logical drive will be lost! Are you sure you want to delete the chosen partition or logical drive?

[Disk Administrator]

When you choose to delete a partition or a logical drive, Disk Administrator presents you with this standard confirmation message.

If you want to delete the partition or drive, choose Yes. If not, choose No to return to the Disk Administrator window.

All data in the stripe set will be lost! Are you sure you want to delete the selected stripe set?

[Disk Administrator]

When you choose to delete a stripe set, Disk Administrator presents you with this standard confirmation message.

If you still want to delete the selected stripe set, choose Yes. If not, choose No to return to the Disk Administrator window.

All data in the volume set will be lost! Are you sure you want to delete the selected volume set?

[Disk Administrator]

When you choose to delete a volume set in Disk Administrator, you are presented with this standard confirmation message.

If you want to delete the volume set, choose Yes. If not, choose No to return to the Disk Administrator window.

All drive letters are already assigned.

[Disk Administrator]

Disk Administrator allows you to assign only 24 drive letters, and all of these are assigned.

Remove a drive letter from one of the existing volumes, and assign the letter to the volume that you want to create.

All handles to windows in a multiple-window position structure must have the same parent.

[Kernel32]

Contact the supplier of the running application.

All NTFS boot sectors are unreadable. Cannot continue.

[NTFS]

When both boot sectors on an NTFS disk partition are unreadable, the entire partition is inaccessible.

This is extremely unlikely to happen. But if it does, a work-around is to repartition the disk so at least one boot sector is on a readable portion of the disk. You may want to contact the hardware supplier.

All NTFS boot sectors are unwriteable. Cannot continue.

[NTFS]

Neither boot sector could be written to the NTFS partition. The disk may be in an inconsistent state.

Contact the disk hardware supplier.

All pipe instances are busy.

[Kernel32]

The pipe cannot be accessed because another process is using it.

Try the operation again later.

All system timers are currently being used by other applications. Quit one or more applications, and then try again.

[Terminal]

You attempted to activate the Timer Mode option from the Settings menu when other applications are using all system timers.

Follow the user action specified in the message.

All user accounts in a domain belong to its Domain Users global group. This membership list cannot be displayed.

[Network]

This group is never displayed because it is usually too large to display successfully.

No action is needed.

All zones in the zone list will be removed. Do you want to continue?

[Services for Macintosh (SFM)]

If you select Yes, you will be unable to seed the network. Seeding requires that a default zone be specified. You will be unable to specify a default zone if you remove the entire zone list.

Leave at least one zone in the list.

Already connected to *name*, **use disconnect first.**

[FTP Server]

While running the Ftp command, Ftp attempted to connect to a host it was already connected to

Disconnect from the remote host named in the message, and then retry the Ftp command.

Amount of data in received packet does not match the size specified in the header. Source *address*, **Destination** *address*, **Protocol** *name*,**Specified size** *number*, **Actual size** *number*.

[Netevent]

The network received an invalid packet and discarded it.

Ask your system administrator to correct the packets generated by the computer at the specified source IP address.

An AARP packet could not be sent on adapter "*name* ".

[Services for Macintosh (SFM)]

An AppleTalk Address Resolution Protocol packet could not be sent due to insufficient resources.

The packet will be resent subsequently. However, if you see this message frequently, increase the server's memory.

An AARP packet was not completely available in the look ahead data from NDIS on adapter "*name* ".

[Services for Macintosh (SFM)]

The adapter is not working properly. The AppleTalk Address Resolution Protocol may not be able to communicate with some computers.

Check the Event Log in Event Viewer for messages related to this one. Try a different adapter if the specified adapter cannot communicate with a computer on the network and you see this message frequently.

An abnormal error was encountered during WINS initialization.

[WINS Service]

While WINS was trying to start, it encountered an error that it does not normally encounter at that time. The error prevented WINS from starting.

Check the Event log to find out what error WINS encountered. Then take the appropriate action for that error.

An addressing error occurred in the RPC server.

[Kernel32]

In a distributed (RPC) application, a memory addressing error occurred at a server.

Contact the supplier of the running application.

An Alert condition has occurred on Computer: *computer name* **; Object:** *name* **; Counter:** *name* **; Instance:** *number* **; Parent:** *name* **; Value:** *number* **; Trigger:** *name*

[Performance Monitor]

Performance Monitor has been set to generate an alert when these conditions occur.

Take the appropriate action for these conditions. If you want, use Performance Monitor to view the alert log or to change the criteria for alerts.

An application has attempted to allocate Expanded Memory, which cannot be supported. This may cause the application to function incorrectly.

[Virtual DOS Machine (VDM)]

Try to ignore this message. If you are able to continue, you might want to check the results of the running application. Otherwise, contact the supplier of the running application.

An application has attempted to directly access the hard disk, which cannot be supported. This may cause the application to function incorrectly.

[Virtual DOS Machine (VDM)]

Choose to ignore the message. The particular application you are running might retain all the functionality you need after the functionality that depends on direct access to the hard disk is taken away. In the case of other applications, you will have to run them directly under MS-DOS or Windows 3.1.

An application has attempted to load a 16-bit MS-DOS device driver, which cannot be supported. This may cause the application to function incorrectly.

[Virtual DOS Machine (VDM)]

Block-mode device drivers, such as RAM disk drivers, are not supported. To find out which driver is not supported in your case, insert an Echoconfig command in your CONFIG.NT file and restart the virtual DOS machine. As each CONFIG.NT file command is executed, it will be echoed on the screen.

The particular application you are running may be able to run without this driver.

An application has attempted to perform an unknown internal 'BOP' opcode, which cannot be supported. This may cause the application to function incorrectly.

[Virtual DOS Machine (VDM)]

Try to ignore this message. If you are able to continue, you might want to check the results of the running application. Otherwise, terminate the application, then restart it. If you still get this message, contact your technical support group or the supplier of the running application.

An application has attempted to use a third-party mouse driver, which cannot be supported. This may cause the application to function incorrectly.

[Virtual DOS Machine (VDM)]

Contact the supplier of the third-party mouse driver and check whether it has been rewritten to run under Windows NT. If not, delete any reference to it in your CONFIG.SYS and/or CONFIG.NT files.

An ARP request was received for IP address *address* on network *name*.

[Netevent]

The network received an ARP request that specifies an invalid address.

Ask your system administrator to correct the packets generated by the computer at the specified source IP address.

An asynchronous request is pending.

[Remote Access Service]

This error should not occur under normal circumstances.

Restart your computer to make sure that all recent configuration changes have taken effect. If the error persists, consult the Windows NT event log for detailed warnings or errors.

An attempt by RASSER.DLL to get an async media access control handle failed.

[Remote Access Service]

The async media access control handle driver either is not loaded or cannot be opened.

Restart your system. If the problem persists, remove and reinstall the Remove Access Service using the Network option in Control Panel.

An attempt has been made to operate on an impersonation token by a thread that is not currently impersonating a client.

[Kernel32]

Only impersonation threads can call a service to create a new object without supplying a security token.

Contact the supplier of the running application.

An attempt to connect to the remote WINS server with address *address* returned with an error. Check to see that the remote WINS server is running and available, and that WINS is running on that server.

[WINS Service]

Make sure the remote WINS server is on the network and running WINS.

An attempt was made to establish a session to a network server, but there are already too many sessions established to that server.

[Kernel32]

There may be multiple logon sessions established on a LAN Manager server, but there is a limit to the number and that limit has been reached on the server you are attempting to logon to.

Wait for a session to end, and try again.

An attempt was made to exceed the limit on the number of domains per server.

[Kernel32]

Contact the supplier of the running application.

An attempt was made to logon, but the network logon service was not started.

[Kernel32]

Use the Services icon in Control Panel to check the status of the Net Logon service on your local computer. If it is not started, start it and retry the operation. If the service was started on your computer, the source of this message will be a remote computer. Contact the network administrator to start the Net Logon service on remote computers you are trying to use.

An attempt was made to move the file pointer before the beginning of the file.

[Kernel32]

Contact the supplier of the running application.

An attempt was made to reference a token that does not exist.

[Kernel32]

Contact the supplier of the running application.

An attempt was made to remember a device that had previously been remembered.

[Kernel32]

The connection request was rejected because the local device already has a remembered connection to a different network resource.

Either attempt to make the connection again, without having the computer remember it, or delete the existing remembered connection information.

An error has occurred from which WINS will try to recover. If recovery fails, check previous Event log entries to determine what went wrong, and take appropriate action on that error.

[WINS Service]

If WINS is unable to recover from the error, check previous entries in the Event log and take appropriate action on the error or errors preceding this message.

An error has occurred in the registry. The Program Manager's settings and groups can not be accessed.

[Program Manager]

An error in the Registry makes it impossible for Program Manager to read a program group's settings.

Restart your system. If Program Manager's settings and groups still cannot be accessed, contact technical support.

An error has occurred while printing. Make sure the printer is properly configured and selected.

[File Manager]

To check the configuration of your printer, exit or minimize File Manager, then use Print Manager to properly configure your printer.

An error has occurred. ClipBook Viewer cannot complete this procedure.

[Clipboard]

An internal software error has occurred.

Try restarting Windows NT, and then try again. If this message reappears, contact technical support.

An error has prevented wins from updating the database. the database may be corrupt.

[WINS Service]

Restore the database from a backup copy, and then pull data from the WINS server's push partner.

An error occurred trying to find a mark in the INF file.

[Remote Access Service]

RAS has three .INF files, MODEM.INF, PAD.INF, and SWITCH.INF. One of these files may be corrupted which is why the mark or line location cannot be found in the file. RAS cannot be configured.

Compare the RAS .INF files in your \<systemroot>\system32\ras directory with the distributed RAS .INF files.

An error occurred while reading your profile.

[Network] Net Message ID: 3679

Ask your system administrator to check your user profile.

An error occurred while saving the changes. Some changes will not be remembered.

[Program Manager]

The new settings could not be saved to the Registry, probably due to very low memory.

If some of the changes you made don't appear, use the Control Panel to make the changes again. If the problem persists, close some applications and try again.

An error occurred while saving the changes. Some changes will not be remembered.

[Program Manager]

If some of the changes you made don't appear the next time you log on, make the changes again.

An error occurred while setting a mark on a section in the INF file.

[Remote Access Service]

The server is running out of memory.

Try stopping other running applications and services. Also try removing and reinstalling RAS and restarting the server. If you continue to see this message, contact technical support.

An error occurred closing file *filename*. Please check the file to make sure it is not corrupted.

[Network]

Try to open the file using the appropriate application, and examine it to make sure no part of the file is missing or garbled.

An error occurred during construction of a control. The system may be low on resources or memory.

[WINS Service]

You will probably be unable to use the dialog box

Close some applications and try again.

An error occurred during translation of data to or from the tape in *drive letter*.

[Backup]

There was some problem with the data returned by the tape drive. The data on the tape or the tape drive may be lost.

Check the tape drive's cabling connections. If you continue to receive this message, contact the supplier of the tape drive.

An error occurred in sending the command to the application.

[File Manager]

Attempt to perform the action again. If this message reappears, quit and restart File Manager.

An error occurred in the domain message processor.

[Network] Net Message ID: 2280

An error occurred when the workstation was receiving or processing a domain-wide message.

Check the workstation's Event log by selecting System from the Log menu using Event Viewer. Stop and restart the Messenger service. If the problem persists, contact technical support.

An error occurred reading from or writing to the disk. The disk is unusable.

[Repair Disk]

Try again with a different disk.

An error occurred sending the command to the application.

[Program Manager] [Task Manager]

Program Manager is unable to start the application.

Try again. If this does not work, close the applications that you have running, and restart your system.

An error occurred when attempting to run the service program.

[Network] Net Message ID: 3061

The service you specified could not start.

In the [services] section of your configuration file, find the name of the program file for this service. Be sure this file exists and is an executable file with a filename extension of .EXE or .COM. If the program file exists, it may be damaged. If possible, restore the file from a backup version. Otherwise, contact technical support.

An error occurred when communicating with a Run server.

[Network] Net Message ID: 2389

This message should occur only on a down-level computer. Any action to correct the problem should be performed on that computer. LAN Manager found a problem while trying to complete the task.

Type the command again in a few minutes. If you continue to receive this message, see your network administrator.

An error occurred when opening network device driver *name* **=** *name***.**

[Network] Net Message ID: 3406

This message should occur only on a down-level computer. Any action to correct the problem should be performed on that computer. The listed device driver could not be installed.

Check that the listed entry in the [networks] section of the LANMAN.INI file is valid. In the CONFIG.SYS file, check the DEVICE entry that loads this device driver--the parameters of that entry may not be correct. Also check that the DEVICE entry specifies the correct path of the device driver.

An error occurred when opening or reading the configuration file.

[Network] Net Message ID: 2131

This message should occur only on a down-level computer. Any action to correct the problem should be performed on that computer. The configuration file is missing or contains invalid information.

Ask your network administrator to review the contents of the configuration file.

An error occurred when reading the NETWORKS entry in the LANMAN.INI file.

[Network] Net Message ID: 3401

This message should occur only on a down-level computer. Any action to correct the problem should be performed on that computer. LAN Manager could not read the entries in the [networks] section of the LANMAN.INI file.

Be sure that the LANMAN.INI file exists (in the LANMAN directory). Check the format of the entries in the [networks] section.

An error occurred when starting a background process.

[Network] Net Message ID: 2391

This message should occur only on a down-level computer. Any action to correct the problem should be performed on that computer. LAN Manager found a problem while trying to complete the task.

Type the command again in a few minutes. If you continue to receive this message, see your network administrator.

An error occurred when the share was deleted.

[Network] Net Message ID: 3725

An error occurred when Windows NT tried to stop sharing the resource.

Try again to stop sharing the resource. If no more information about this error is displayed, use Event Viewer to read the system log. If no information appears in Event Viewer and the problem persists, contact technical support.

An error occurred while attempting to recover data from the fault tolerance set containing *text*.

[Disk Administrator]

There is a bad sector on one of the disks on one side of the mirror set. Your data security is at some risk. There is still a good sector on the other side of the mirror set, and the probability that the same sector number will go bad on both sides of the mirror is quite low.

To regain complete data security, do the following: (1) examine the event logs to identify which drive has the bad sector; (2) back up all data on that drive; (3) reformat the drive using the verify switch to map out the bad sector; and (4) restore the backed up data.

An error occurred while loading or running the logon script.

[Network] Net Message ID: 2212

This message should occur only on a down-level computer. Any action to correct the problem should be performed on that computer. The logon script for your account may contain unrecognized commands or commands that could not run.

Ask your network administrator to review your logon script.

An error occurred while loading the profile file.

[Network] Net Message ID: 2374

This message should occur only on a down-level computer. Any action to correct the problem should be performed on that computer. The system could not open the profile.

The profile file may be damaged. Create a new profile. If you need assistance, contact your network administrator.

An error occurred while opening the Help file.

[Network] Net Message ID: 3710

Windows NT could not find a file of Help information.

Be sure the NET.HLP file is in the same directory as NET.EXE, which is usually in your system directory. This directory should also be on your search path (specified by the Path command). If you cannot find the Help file on your computer, contact your network administrator. Your administrator should copy the Help file from the Windows NT distribution disks to your computer.

An error occurred while processing the logon hours for user ***user name*****.**

[PORTUAS]

The time zone for the Windows NT system must be the same as the time zone in the down-level system.

Contact technical support.

An error occurred while processing the workstation list for user ***user name*****.**

[PORTUAS]

When PORTUAS was translating the list of workstations from the user accounts database to the Windows NT security database, the system ran out of memory or one of the workstations has an invalid name. Workstation or computer names must have between 1 to 15 characters, must not begin or end with a blank space, and must not contain any control characters. The names also must not contain any forward or backslashes (\\ /), double backslashes (\\\), brackets ([ ]), angle brackets (< >), colons (:), semicolons (;), quotation marks ("), pluses (+), or equal signs (=), question marks (?), wildcards (*), or vertical bars (|).

Verify that the workstation names from the down-level user accounts database are valid.

An error occurred while restoring the connection to ***name*****.**

[Network] Net Message ID: 3680

This message should occur only on a down-level computer. Any action to correct the problem should be performed on that computer. A persistent connection could not be restored. This usually occurs because the specified server is not available.

If you do not wish to maintain this persistent connection, type NET LOGON again and type NO when asked whether you want to attempt accessing this resource in the future. If you want to use the resource, attempt to connect when it becomes available, or type NET LOGON to log on again.

An error occurred while running format.

[Utilities]

Try another disk or another file system.

An error occurred while sending a message to ***user name*****.**

[Network] Net Message ID: 3722

An error occurred when a message was sent to the alias you selected. An additional error message should follow this one. It will tell you what action to take to correct the error.

Follow the recommended action in the second error message.

An error occurred while synchronizing with primary domain controller *computer name*

[Network] Net Message ID: 3226

The local copy of the security database may be out of synchronization with that of the domain controller because an error occurred while the database was being updated.

Use the Synchronize With Domain option in Server Manager to synchronize the security databases.

An error occurred while updating disk configuration. Drive letter and fault tolerance information may be lost and/or some partitions may be inaccessible.

[Disk Administrator]

Windows NT tried to write to the partition table and could not.

Attempt to update your disk configuration again. Or contact your technical support group.

An error occurred while updating the logon or logoff information for *user name***.**

[Network] Net Message ID: 3225

This message should occur only on a down-level computer. Any action to correct the problem should be performed on that computer. The current logon statistics may not be accurate because an error occurred while the logon and logoff information was being updated.

No action is needed.

An error was encountered during an operation on the static data file *filename***.**

[WINS Service]

Make sure the specified file exists and has Read privileges set for the user who started WINS. If the file is present and readable, open and examine it to make sure it is not corrupt.

An error was encountered during configuration or reconfiguration of WINS.

[WINS Service]

Take the action recommended by the message that accompanied this one. Then try again.

An error was encountered in the database. You might need to restore the database from a backup.

[WINS Service]

Restore the database from a backup copy. If this message appears often, call Microsoft Product Support.

An error was reported while attempting to initialize the monitor with the list of port information from the registry. The information is located in theSYSTEM\\CurrentControlSet\\Control\\Print\\Monitors\AppleTalk Printing Deviceskey. The data is the error code.

[Services for Macintosh (SFM)]

If you can, verify the port information in the Registry. If so, contact technical support.

An event could not be created

[WINS Service]

The WINS server is out of resources, probably disk space.

Delete some files and then reboot the computer.

An exception occurred in the service when handling the control request.

[Kernel32]

While handling a control request, the service attempted to access an illegal address.

Contact your technical support group.

An exception was encountered while trying send a push trigger notification to a remote WINS.

[WINS Service]

Something happened that kept this WINS server from sending a push trigger to its push partner. The failure might be due to a communications failure.

No action is needed. Another request will be sent to the push partner after the usual time interval has elapsed. If you want to, you can send a push trigger now, using the Replication Partners dialog box.

An exception was encountered while trying service a pull range request from a remote WINS.

[WINS Service]

A remote WINS server asked this server for a range of database records, but the local server was unable to process the request.

Check the Event log to find out what error preceded this message. Then take the appropriate action for that error. If you find nothing in the Event log that could prompt this error, call Microsoft Product Support.

An exception was encountered while trying to inform a remote WINS to update the version number.

[WINS Service]

Something happened that kept this WINS server from sending update information to another WINS server. The failure might be due to a communications failure.

Make sure that the other WINS server is running and that the router is running.

An extended error has occurred.

[Kernel32]

An application has returned a network-specific error code.

You will have to look at the documentation from the network provider to find the meaning of this network-specific error code.

An extended partition already exists on the disk.

[Disk Administrator]

You have attempted to create an extended partition on a disk on which an extended partition already exists.

Choose OK, then create an extended partition on another disk.

An extensible counter has closed the Event Log for RASCTRS.DLL

[Remote Access Service]

This message is for your information. It indicates the Event Log is being closed during the shutdown of the application.

No action is needed.

An extensible counter has opened the Event Log for RASCTRS.DLL

[Remote Access Service]

This message is only for your information. It indicates that the specified dynamic library initialized.

No action is needed.

An I/O failure occurred on *name*.

[Disk Administrator]

The specified name is a fault tolerance set member name; it refers to a fault tolerance partition.

Retry the operation. If you still get this message, contact technical support.

An I/O operation initiated by the Registry failed unrecoverably. The Registry could not read in, or write out, or flush, one of the files that contain the system's image of the Registry.

[Kernel32]

The system could not read in, write out, or flush one of the files that contain the system's image of the Registry, because of an unrecoverable I/O error.

Restart the system. You may have to use the Emergency Repair Disk to restore the system configuration information.

An illegal country code has been supplied.

[Network] Net Message ID: 3773

You typed an invalid country code.

Specify a valid country code

An illegal date format has been supplied.

[Network] Net Message ID: 3767

You used an illegal date format.

Retype the command with a correct date format. Dates should be typed in the form <mm/dd/yy> or <dd/mm/yy>, depending on the user's country code. Months can be represented by a number, spelled out, or abbreviated to exactly 3 letters. Use commas or slashes to separate the parts of the date--do not use spaces. If you do not specify the year, Windows NT assumes it to be the next occurrence of the date.

An illegal day range has been supplied.

[Network] Net Message ID: 3768

You specified an illegal range of days. You must also type a hyphen between the first and last days of each range.

When specifying days, use only the complete names of the days or valid Windows NT abbreviations. Valid abbreviations are M, T, W, Th, F, Sa, Su. Use a hyphen to separate the beginning and end of each range of days.

An illegal server message block (SMB) was received. The SMB is the data.

[Network] Net Message ID: 3112

A software error occurred.

Contact technical support.

An illegal time range has been supplied.

[Network] Net Message ID: 3769

You typed an invalid time range.

Retype the command with a valid time range. Use either the 12-hour format, with the numbers 0-12 and AM and PM, or the 24-hour format, with the numbers 0-24. Use a hyphen to separate the beginning and end of a time range, as in 9AM-4PM.

An inconsistency was encountered on the tape in *drive letter.*

[Backup]

There was some problem with the data returned by the tape drive.

Check the tape drive's cabling connections. If you continue to receive this message, contact the supplier of the tape drive.

An inconsistency was encountered on the tape in *drive letter.* **Do not append to this tape.**

[Backup]

When Backup detects a format inconsistency in a tape, it warns you against jumping to the end of the tape so that you will not risk losing data. You may be using a tape that Backup does not support.

Try a different tape.

An incorrect parameter was entered for the command.

[Command]

You specified a parameter that is not valid for this command.

To find out which parameters are valid for this command, type the Help command at the command prompt, followed by the name of the command on which you want help.

An incorrect parameter was entered for the command.

[Command Prompt]

You specified a parameter that is not valid for this command.

To find out which parameters are valid for this command, type the Help command at the command prompt, followed by the name of the command on which you want help.

An incorrect volume label was entered for this drive.

[Format]

As an added protection for hard drives, Format requires that you enter the drive's current volume label to make sure that Format is formatting the correct volume.

Check the current drive letter assignment to the drives and then specify the correct volume label. You can get this information from Disk Administrator.

An installable Virtual Device Driver failed DLL initialization.

[Virtual DOS Machine (VDM)]

Ask your system administrator to double-check the installation of the Virtual Device Driver on your computer. You may have to reinstall the dynamic-link library. After that, if you still get this message, contact the supplier of the dynamic-link library.

An installation file required by NTVDM is missing, execution must terminate.

[Virtual DOS Machine (VDM)]

The virtual DOS machine cannot start up because it is either unable to locate or to read the NTIO.SYS file.

Reinstall the NTIO.SYS file from your Windows NT distribution media (you will have to decompress the file). The file should be put in the Windows NT \systemroot\system32 directory.

An instance of the service is already running.

[Kernel32]

An application tried to start a service that is not in a stopped state. No more than one instance of a service may be running at a time on a computer.

There is no need to start a second instance of a running service.

An internal consistency error has occurred.

[Network] Net Message ID: 3057

A software error occurred.

Contact technical support.

An internal error -6002 occurred.

[Services for Macintosh (SFM)]

Error 6002 indicates that an invalid ID has been supplied by a component of Services for Macintosh.

Contact technical support.

An internal error -6003 occurred.

[Services for Macintosh (SFM)]

Services for Macintosh specified invalid parameters.

Contact technical support.

An internal error -6004 occurred.

[Services for Macintosh (SFM)]

An invalid code page value for the MACCP key is in the Registry.

Use the Network option in Control Panel to remove and reinstall Services for Macintosh. Otherwise, contact technical support.

An internal error -6008 occurred.

[Services for Macintosh (SFM)]

The Macintosh volume is read only.

Contact technical support.

An internal error -6011 occurred.

[Services for Macintosh (SFM)]

The buffer size may be too small.

Contact technical support.

An internal error -6015 occurred.

[Services for Macintosh (SFM)]

The server is in an invalid state.

Try restarting the server. If you continue to see this message, contact technical support.

An internal error -6024 occurred.

[Services for Macintosh (SFM)]

Too many Creator/Type extension mappings have occurred.

Contact technical support.

An internal error has occurred. Try configuring again.

[Services for Macintosh (SFM)]

A memory allocation failure occurred or Registry entries were removed when configuring the system.

Reconfigure Services for Macintosh using the Network option in Control Panel. Also try restarting the system.

An internal error occurred in a remote procedure call (RPC).

[Kernel32]

There is a programming error in the distributed RPC application. The error could have occurred on either the client side or the server side.

Contact the supplier of the running application.

An internal error occurred while accessing the computer's local or network security database.

[Network] Net Message ID: 5602

Either Windows NT did not install properly or the local or network security database is corrupted.

If you receive this message after your initial installation of the operating system, reinstall Windows NT. Otherwise, contact your network administrator.

An internal error occurred. The network cannot access a shared memory segment.

[Network] Net Message ID: 2104

An internal error occurred.

Contact technical support.

An internal Windows NT error occurred.

[Network] Net Message ID: 2140

A software error occurred.

Contact technical support.

An invalid AARP packet was received on adapter "*name* ".

[Services for Macintosh (SFM)]

An invalid AppleTalk Address Resolution Protocol packet was received on the network. The computer is malfunctioning.

Contact your network administrator to investigate.

An invalid adapter is configured to be the default adapter "*name* ". Localtalk adapters cannot be a default adapter in a routing configuration.

[Services for Macintosh (SFM)]

When routing is enabled on Services for Macintosh, only non-LocalTalk adapters can be set as the default adapter.

Use the Network option in Control Panel to set a non-LocalTalk adapter as the default adapter.

An invalid or nonexistent alert name was raised.

[Network] Net Message ID: 2432

A software error occurred.

Be sure the Alerter service is started. If this error occurs while the Alerter service is started, contact technical support.

An invalid request was sent to the admin support thread for the Remote Access Service, possibly from a down-level admin tool. The request was not processed.

[Remote Access Service]

Restart your computer. If the problem persists, check your system's configuration, quotas, and resources. For further information, consult your Windows NT documentation.

An invalid zone name specified in the zone list for adapter "*name* ".

[Services for Macintosh (SFM)]

Zone names are invalid if they are greater than 32 characters. The zone name was incorrectly changed by directly accessing the Registry instead of using the Network option in Control Panel.

Use the Network option in Control Panel to specify a correct zone name for the adapter. Then, restart the computer for the changes to take effect.

An IO error has occurred.

[File Manager]

You tried to format or write to a disk that is not valid for writing.

Make sure that the disk is not read-only or write-protected. Then try again.

An operation failed while attempting to format the volume.

[Disk Administrator]

The volume was not formatted.

Check the event log for errors that occurred at about the same time as this one and that involved this volume or drive. Take the appropriate action on those errors, and try again.

An operation is pending.

[Remote Access Service]

This error should not occur under normal circumstances.

Restart your computer to make sure that all recent configuration changes have taken effect. If the error persists, consult the Windows NT event log for detailed warnings or errors.

An overrun occurred on *name*.

The named device continued to send data to a buffer, even though the buffer was full.

Retry the operation. If you still get this message, run hardware diagnostics on the disk drive named in the message, and on its controller. You may have to contact the vendor of the device, and you may have to replace the controller, the disk drive, or both.

An unexpected NetBIOS error occurred. The error code is the data.

[Network] Net Message ID: 3111

This message should occur only on a down-level computer. Any action to correct the problem should be performed on that computer. A software error occurred.

Contact technical support.

An unexpected network error has occurred on the virtual circuit to *name*.

[Netevent]

Wait a few minutes, then retry the command.

An unexpected network error occurred.

[Kernel32]

Your computer received an error from the network that was not expected in this situation.

Retry the operation. If you continue to have problems, contact your network administrator.

An unknown error has occurred reading from or writing to the disk. The disk is possibly unusable.

[Repair Disk]

Try again with a different disk. If you continue to see this message, there might be a hardware problem with your disk.

An unknown error occurred.

[Network]

Reinstall the component you were using when this error occurred.

An unknown error occurred.

[Services for Macintosh (SFM)]

Contact technical support.

Annotations are damaged; please exit WinHelp, delete *filename* and recreate annotations.

[Help]

When you annotate a Help topic, Help saves these annotations to a .ANN file. The file that is used to save these annotations is damaged and needs to be deleted.

Use the Annotate option on the Edit menu to recreate your annotations.

Another driver on the system, which did not report its resources, has already claimed the interrupt used by *name*.

A third party device driver has been installed that is taking the resource without informing the system that it has done so.

Remove the device. Notify the vendor of the device driver, and Microsoft, of this problem.

Another instance of Setup may already be running.

[Setup]

When you select OK, Setup will automatically exit. Then retry the Setup operation.

Another instance of Setup may already be running.

[Repair Disk]

When you select OK, Setup will automatically exit. Then retry the Setup operation.

AppleTalk is not bound to the adapter "*name* ". Request for the adapter ignored.

[Services for Macintosh (SFM)]

Choose the Network option in Control Panel to bind the protocol to the adapter. Select Services for Macintosh and then choose the Bindings button.

Are you sure you want to allow all users access to the System Partition?

[Disk Administrator]

To allow users to examine or copy system configuration files, some administrators prefer to permit a larger variety of users to access the System partition.

Are you sure you want to clear statistics?

[WINS Service]

You attempted to clear the statistics. This message allows you to change your mind if you want to.

If you are sure you want to clear the statistics, answer Yes. Otherwise, answer No.

Are you sure you want to close all file forks on *computer name* **?**

[Services for Macintosh (SFM)]

Users could lose any unsaved data.

Use Server Manager or File Manager to send a disconnect message to users. In using either manager, select the MacFile menu. In Server Manager, select Send Message. In File Manager, select View/Modify Volumes and then select Send Message.

Are you sure you want to close the current connection?

[WINS Service]

You attempted to close a network connection. This message allows you to change your mind if you want to.

If you are sure you want to close this connection, answer Yes. Otherwise, answer No.

Are you sure you want to delete group ' *group* **'?**

[Program Manager]

You chose to delete a program group in Program Manager, and this is a standard confirmation message.

If you are sure that you want to delete the currently selected program group, choose Yes. If not, choose No to return to Program Manager.

Are you sure you want to delete item ' *name* **'?**

[Program Manager]

You chose to delete a program item in Program Manager, and this is a standard confirmation message.

If you are sure that you want to delete the currently selected program item, choose Yes. If not, choose No to return to Program Manager.

Are you sure you want to disconnect *computer name* **from all connected resources?**

[Server Manager]

You directed Server Manager to disconnect a user from the target server, and this is a standard confirmation message.

If you are certain that you want to disconnect the specified user from all connected resources, choose Yes. If not, choose No to return to the Shared Resources dialog box.

Are you sure you want to disconnect *user name* **from all connected volumes?**

[Services for Macintosh (SFM)]

The user could lose any unsaved data.

Use Server Manager or File Manager to send a disconnect message to the specified user. In using either manager, select the MacFile menu. In Server Manager, select Send Message. In File Manager, select View/Modify Volumes and then select Send Message.

Are you sure you want to disconnect all connected users?

[FTP Server]

If the connected user is disconnected from a computer on which he or she has files open, those files could be corrupted.

If you are sure you want to disconnect all connected users, choose Yes. You might want to choose No, advice all connected users to close files and disconnect, and then try again.

Are you sure you want to disconnect all users connected to the *name* **share from all connected resources?**

[Server Manager]

You chose to disconnect all users from a shared resource, and this is a standard confirmation message.

If you are sure you want to disconnect all users from the specified resource, choose Yes. If not, choose No.

Are you sure you want to disconnect all users connected to the Macintosh-Accessible volume *name* **?**

[Services for Macintosh (SFM)]

Use Server Manager or File Manager to send a disconnect message to users. In using either manager, select the MacFile menu. In Server Manager, select Send Message. In File Manager, select View/Modify Volumes and then select Send Message.

Are you sure you want to disconnect all users from all connected resources?

[Server Manager]

You chose to disconnect all users from a all resources, and this is a standard confirmation message.

If you are sure you want to disconnect all users from all resources, choose Yes. If not, choose No.

Are you sure you want to disconnect all users from all connected volumes?

[Services for Macintosh (SFM)]

Disconnecting the users might cause them to lose unsaved data.

Are you sure you want to disconnect the user *user name* **connected to the Macintosh-Accessible volume** *name* **?**

[Services for Macintosh (SFM)]

The user could lose any unsaved data.

Use Server Manager or File Manager to send a disconnect message to the specified user. In using either manager, select the MacFile menu. In Server Manager, select Send Message. In File Manager, select View/Modify Volumes and then select Send Message.

Are you sure you want to erase the tape in the drive ?

[Backup]

When you select the Erase Tape command on the Operations menu, Backup presents you with this confirmation message.

If you want to erase the tape, choose Yes. If not, choose No to return to the Backup window.

Are you sure you want to force *user name* **to close** *name* **?**

[Services for Macintosh (SFM)]

The specified user could lose any unsaved data if forced to close the specified file.

Use Server Manager or File Manager to send a disconnect message to the specified user. In using either manager, select the MacFile menu. In Server Manager, select Send Message. In File Manager, select View/Modify Volumes and then select Send Message.

Are you sure you want to move the selected files or directories to *name***?**

[File Manager]

Using the mouse, you attempted to move a file/directory, and this is a confirmation message. Or you attempted to move a file/directory to a different drive.

If you wish to complete the procedure, choose Yes. If not, choose No. If you don't want to see this message in the future, deselect the options in the Confirmation dialog box.

Are you sure you want to overwrite the *filename* file?

[Terminal]

You attempted to save the current settings file under a filename that already exists.

If you want to replace the previously existing file with the current file of the same name, select Yes. If not, select No. To return to Terminal, select Cancel.

Are you sure you want to pause the *name* service?

[Server Manager]

You directed Server Manager to pause a service on a computer, and this is a confirmation message. Be aware that if you choose Yes, no new user will be allowed to connect to the service. Currently connected users, however, will not be affected.

If you want to pause the specified service, choose Yes.

Are you sure you want to remove *computer name* from the list of domains and computers from which to import files?

[Server Manager]

You chose to remove a computer or domain from the list of domains and computers from which to import files, and this is a standard confirmation message.

If you are certain that you want to complete this operation, choose Yes. If not, choose No to return to the Directory Replication dialog box.

Are you sure you want to remove *computer name* from the list of domains and computers to which to export files?

[Server Manager]

You chose to remove a name from the list of domains and computers to which to export files, and this is a standard confirmation message.

If you are sure that you want to complete this operation, choose Yes. If not, choose No to return to the Directory Replication dialog box.

Are you sure you want to remove the subdirectory *name* from the list of subdirectories which are exported from this computer?

[Server Manager]

You chose to remove a subdirectory from the list of subdirectories that are exported from a server, and this is a standard confirmation message.

If you are sure that you want to remove the selected subdirectory, choose Yes. If not, choose No to return to the Manage Exported Directories dialog box.

Are you sure you want to remove the subdirectory *name* from the list of subdirectories which are imported to this computer?

[Server Manager]

You chose to remove a subdirectory from the list of subdirectories that are imported to a computer, and this is a standard confirmation message.

If you are sure that you want to complete this operation, choose Yes. If not, choose No to return to the Manage Imported Directories dialog box.

Are you sure you want to restrict access to the System Partition to System Administrators?

[Disk Administrator]

To prevent accidental or unauthorized changes to the system configuration, some administrators prefer to restrict access to the System partition.

Are you sure you want to start *name* using *filename* as the initial file?

[File Manager]

When you drag a text file onto a program file, Windows NT presents you with this confirmation message.

If you want to start the designated program file using the designated text file as the initial file, choose Yes. If not, choose No.

Are you sure you want to stop the *name* service?

[Server Manager]

In the Services dialog box, you chose to stop a service on a target computer, and this is a standard confirmation message.

If you are sure that you want to stop the service, choose Yes. If not, choose No to return to the Services dialog box.

Are you sure you wish to delete *name* ?

[Print Manager]

You chose to delete a printer, and this is a standard confirmation message.

Are you sure you wish to delete your connection to *name* ?

[Print Manager]

You chose to delete a connection to a printer, and this is a standard confirmation message.

Arg list too long *text*

Try again, using fewer arguments to the command.

Arguments to NET USER are invalid. Check the minimum password length and/or arguments supplied.

[Network] Net Message ID: 3770

You typed invalid options or variables with the command.

Retype the command using valid options and variables. When you add a user account, the password you set for the user must conform to your system's guidelines for password length.

Arithmetic result exceeded 32 bits.

[Kernel32]

Contact the supplier of the running application.

ARP cannot link to DataLink interface version *number***.**

[Netevent]

TCP/IP and STREAMS versions do not match.

Ask your system administrator to load compatible versions of TCPIP.SYS and STREAMS.SYS.

ARP-datalink registration failed. Unable to allocate a *number* **byte message.**

[Netevent]

ARP could not initialize because of insufficient memory.

Stop other applications from running and retry the operation in few minutes. If the problem persists, your system administrator may need to add more memory to your system.

At initialization, WINS creates a security object and attaches an ACL to it. This security object is then used to authenticate RPC calls made to WINS. WINS could not create the above security object. In short, WINS could not initialize with the security subsystem properly.

[WINS Service]

The WINS service could not start.

Reboot the WINS server.

At least one of your network adapters has automatic DHCP configuration enabled. In order to correctly install the DHCP Server, setup will disable automatic DHCP configuration. Are you sure you want to install the DHCP Server?

[TCP/IP]

Only DHCP clients can be configured automatically. If you configure this computer as a DHCP Server, the configuration must be explicitly assigned.

Choose Yes to install DHCP Server, or choose No to cancel the operation.

Attempt to access invalid address.

[Kernel32]

Contact the supplier of the running application.

Attempt to change computer name failed; error was *code*

[Control Panel]

In the Network option in Control Panel, you attempted to change the name of your computer, and this attempt failed.

Consult the event log in Event Viewer for details. Then contact your system administrator.

Attempt to determine the number of Lanas failed.

[Dynamic Data Exchange]

The Network Dynamic Data Exchange utility was unable to find out how many Local Area Network adapters (LANAs) there are on this computer. It cannot be used to communicate over the network until it has this information.

Make sure you have at least one adapter card installed in this computer.

Attempt to leave old primary domain incomplete; error was *code*

[Control Panel]

In the Network option, you tried to leave your old primary domain, and this attempt failed.

Consult the event log in Event Viewer for details. Then contact your system administrator.

Attempt to move past end of tape

[Backup]

Backup attempted to move to a position on the tape that does not exist.

Check the Hardware Compatibility List for a compatible version of the tape drive. You might also want to contact technical support. Be sure to record any messages and information you see for them.

Attempt to release mutex not owned by caller.

[Kernel32]

You must be the current owner of a mutex semaphore in order to release it.

Request ownership of the mutex semaphore; then retry the command. You may have to contact the supplier of the running application.

Attempt to use a file handle to an open disk partition for an operation other than raw disk I/O.

[Kernel32]

Contact the supplier of the running application.

Attempted to add nonunicast IP address *address* **to the ARP cache.**

[Netevent]

ARP caches cannot receive broadcast messages.

Contact your system administrator or consult the ARP documentation.

Attempted to set a macro not listed in device .INF file section.

[Remote Access Service]

One of the Remote Access configuration files probably contains invalid information.

The easiest way to resolve this problem is to reinstall Remote Access. Use the Network option in Control Panel to remove and reinstall RAS. If you are using a modem that is not supported by Remote Access, switch to a supported modem, or see "Modem Script File" in the Remote Access Service online Help for information about modifying the modem script file for your modem. The Remote Access script files (PAD.INF, MODEM.INF, and SWITCH.INF) are in the \SYSTEM32\RAS subdirectory of your Windows NT directory.

Audit attempt has failed.

This is a Windows NT Executive character-mode STOP message.

Restart and set the Recovery options in the System Control Panel or the /CRASHDEBUG system start option. If this message reappears, contact your system administrator or technical support group.

AutoRefresh is not available for remote registries; Registry Editor will disable AutoRefresh mode.

[Registry Editor]

This message appears when you attempt to select the Auto Refresh option while displaying windows from a remote Registry in Registry Editor. You cannot set Auto Refresh on a remote Registry.

No action is needed.

Bad 'Escape' operator.

[Fonts (CP)]

There is a problem with the font.

Contact the vendor of the font and report this message.

Bad arguments passed to a Setup support library routine

[Setup]

One of the Setup information (.INF) files may be corrupted, or something is wrong with the distribution media.

Contact the supplier of the Windows NT distribution media and get another copy.

Bad arguments passed to a Setup support library routine

[Repair Disk]

One of the Setup information (.INF) files may be corrupted, or something is wrong with the distribution media.

Contact the supplier of the Windows NT distribution media and get another copy.

Bad block detected (unrecoverable read error).From device: *name*

[QIC117]

Data might have been lost, due to a bad block on the tape.

Reformat the tape or use a new tape.

Bad clusters in EA file header relocated.

[Chkdsk]

Bad clusters in the extended attribute file have been replaced with clusters taken from free space on the disk. The bad clusters have been marked in the file allocation table so that they will not be reused.

No action is needed.

Bad command line syntax

[File Compare]

The Comp command contained too many filename parameters, or your response to the Option prompt was not preceded by a slash (/) character or a minus (-) character.

To check the syntax for this command, type HELP at the command prompt followed by the command name (in this case, Comp).

Bad data

[Backup]

The media may not be recognized by the tape drive media in the drive may be corrupted.

Make sure compatible media is in the drive. If not, try user an older version of the tape.

Bad numeric argument : *number*

[File Compare]

You did not supply a valid number for the /n switch with the Comp command. The number field can only contain numbers between 0 and 9.

Bad or missing LAN Manager root directory.

[Network]

This message should occur only on a down-level computer. Any action to correct the problem should be performed on that computer.

Bad protocol option *text*

This option was mistyped or is not available for this command.

Make sure you have the correct syntax for the command. Then try again, making sure the command is typed correctly.

Bad prototype for routine.

[Help]

This error is from the Macro Language Editor for online help, and should not appear while using the Help file. Report this error to the provider of the Help file.

Bad routine name.

[Help]

This error is from the Macro Language Editor for online help, and should not appear while using the Help file. Report this error to the provider of the Help file.

Bad source disk specified on line *number* **in section** *number.*

[Setup]

Contact the supplier for another copy of the installation media.

Bad Window Class, ignored.

[Help]

This error is from the Macro Language Editor for online help, and should not appear while using the Help file. Report this error to the provider of the Help file.

Badly formed registry data on line *number* **in section** *number.*

[Setup]

Contact the supplier for another copy of the installation media.

Badly formed Setup UI Script Command.

[Setup]

When you select OK, Setup will automatically exit. First, retry the Setup operation from the beginning. If you get the same message and if you are running maintenance Setup, you can try replacing the .INF file with one from the distribution medium (you will have to decompress the file). Otherwise, contact your technical support group.

Badly formed Setup UI Script Command.

[Repair Disk]

When you select OK, Setup will automatically exit. First, retry the Setup operation from the beginning. If you get the same message and if you are running maintenance Setup, you can try replacing the .INF file with one from the distribution medium (you will have to decompress the file). Otherwise, contact your technical support group.

Beginning of tape or partition was encountered.

[Kernel32]

No user action is possible. If the application does not continue to run, contact the supplier of the application.

Binding algorithm failed

[Control Panel]

The Network option is currently unable to bind the components necessary for a usable network connection. A binding algorithm can fail because of an internal software error, or because the networking software produced inaccurate data.

Consult the event log in Event Viewer for details. Then contact your system administrator.

Binding algorithm query failed

[Control Panel]

The Network option in Control Panel is currently unable to bind the components necessary for a usable network connection. A binding algorithm query can fail because of an internal software error, or because the networking software produced inaccurate data.

Consult the event log in Event Viewer for details. Then contact your system administrator.

Binding preparation failed

[Control Panel]

The Networks option in Control Panel is currently unable to bind the components necessary for a usable network connection. A binding preparation can fail because of an internal software error, or because the networking software produced inaccurate data.

Consult the event log in Event Viewer for details. Then contact your system administrator.

Binding to SAP Socket failed. The Nw Sap Agent cannot continue.

[Netevent]

The application could not be started because a resource is in use by another application or otherwise unavailable. Often the problem is insufficient free memory.

Close one or more applications and try again.

Binding to wan socket failed. The Nw Sap Agent cannot continue.

[Netevent]

The application is unable to get status information about the Wide Area Network (WAN). Resources that are accessed via the SAP Agent and services that depend on the SAP Agent will not be available.

Call technical support. Report both this message and the message that accompanies it.

Binding too long.

[Help]

This error is from the Macro Language Editor for online help, and should not appear while using the Help file. Report this error to the provider of the Help file.

Bindings file specifies non-existent Registry key

[Control Panel]

The file that contains bindings information specifies a key in the Registry that does not exist.

Contact technical support.

Biplex port initializing. Wait a few seconds and redial.

[Remote Access Service]

This error can occur on a port configured for dialing out and receiving calls (biplex port). It happens when you dial out at the same time the server is initializing the port for receiving calls. Remote Access solves this problem for you by redialing in a few seconds.

Bookmark does not exist.

[Help]

The active application or the system has attempted to access a bookmark that does not exist.

In the Bookmark Define dialog box, select the name of an existing bookmark.

Bookmark with this name already exists.

[Help]

In the Bookmark Define dialog box, you attempted to assign to a bookmark the name of an already existing bookmark.

Assign the new bookmark a unique name.

Bookmarks are damaged; please exit WinHelp and delete WINHELP.BMK.

[Help]

The WINHELP.BMK file is located in your Windows NT SYSTEM32 directory.

Delete this file, then restart Help.

Boot-start or system-start driver (*name* **) must not depend on a service.**

[Netevent]

A boot-start or system-start driver is dependent on another driver or service to start. These drivers should depend only on a group.

Ask your system administrator to change the dependency to refer to a group rather than another driver.

Bus reset

[Backup]

If your tape drive uses the same controller as your SCSI device and the SCSI device times out, the controller driver resets the bus. This is fatal to tape drives.

Try putting your tape drive on a separate controller.

Caller's buffer is too small.

[Remote Access Service]

This error should not occur under normal circumstances.

Restart your computer to make sure that all recent configuration changes have taken effect. If the error persists, consult the Windows NT event log for detailed warnings or errors.

Can not install typeface due to copyright. Copyright holder: *name*

[Fonts (CP)]

The font cannot be installed because the system has not obtained the right to do so.

Contact the vendor of the font and report this message.

Can only search on text containing no more than 255 characters. Search for the first 255 characters entered?

[Write]

Choosing the Find option, you specified a search criteria longer than 255 characters. Write will only search on the basis of the first 255 characters specified.

To initiate the search on the basis of the first 255 characters that you have entered, choose Yes.

Can't access a needed shared library *name*

The operation cannot continue until the library file is accessed.

Make sure that the library file exists and that your process has permission to read the file and any directories that the file is in. Then try again.

Can't access user settings.

[Telnet]

The file in which your user settings were saved is probably missing or corrupt.

Use the Options menu to establish and save your settings.

Can't find file *filename*

[Print]

Make sure the file you specified in the Print command exists in the specified directory, and that you typed the filename and path correctly. If this message appears on the printer screen, the file has been removed, renamed, or deleted between the time it was queued for printing and the time it actually began printing.

can't find list of remote files, oops

[FTP Server]

The Ftp command was unable to retrieve the list of remote files to transfer.

Check the path and filename spelling used in the Ftp command against the actual name and location of the remote file list. If there is no problem there, contact your network administrator.

Can't find/open file: *filename*

[File Compare]

Make sure the filename is correct, and that it is not the name of a directory.

Can't nest calls to LoadModule.

[Kernel32]

Contact the supplier of the running application.

Can't open input file: ***filename*****.**

[Command Prompt]

The specified file cannot be opened. There may be too many files open already, the path may not be valid, and the destination filename may be the same as an existing directory name. Also, the file may be read-only, locked, or on a write-protected disk.

Make sure you have correctly specified the path and filenames, and that the filename is not the same as an existing directory name. Use the Attrib command to see if the file is read-only, and make sure the Share command has not locked the file. If the destination file is on a floppy disk, make sure the disk is not write-protected. If you have other files open, close some files so the new file can be opened.

Can't read file: *filename*

[File Compare]

The Comp command cannot read the specified file.

Make sure the file is not locked or in use by another program. The file might also be corrupted or located on a bad sector. If this is the case, use a backup copy of the file.

Can't read from input file: ***filename*****.**

[Command Prompt]

The input (source) file may be corrupted.

There is no remedy for this situation.

Can't send after socket shutdown *text*

No data can be sent because the socket has shut down.

Cannot access file *filename*

[More]

The More command cannot find the file you specified as an argument.

Check the spelling of the filename and the path of the file. Retry the More command with a corrected file specification.

Cannot access Registry key values.

[Remote Access Service]

The Remote Access Service failed to start because required Registry keys may be missing from the Registry.

Remove and then reinstall the Remote Access Service using the Network option in Control Panel. If after reinstalling the service you continue to see this message, contact technical support.

Cannot access service controller.

[Control Panel]

The service controller is a component that loads and unloads network drivers. Because the Network option cannot access the service controller, you cannot perform the current operation.

Contact technical support.

Cannot access TCPCFG library or it's entry points.

[Remote Access Service]

RAS could not find the TCPCFG.DLL file.

Use the Network option in Control Panel to remove and reinstall the TCP/IP protocol.

Cannot add ***name*** **to list**

[Remote Access Service]

This is an out of memory condition. RASADMIN is not able to add the specified item to a list of names (ports, users, or servers, etc.).

Try closing other applications to allow RASADMIN more memory.

Cannot add the remote computer group name ***name*** **on LANA** ***number*****. The error code is the data.**

[Remote Access Service]

A computer has the same name as the remote computer group name.

Remove the computer with the duplicate name from the network.

Cannot add the remote computer name ***computer name*** **on LANA** ***number*** **.The error code is the data.**

[Remote Access Service]

Another computer on the network has the same name as the remote computer.

Remove the other computer from the network or rename the remote computer.

Cannot adjust the logon rights and group membership of account ***account*****. The startup parameters for the** ***name*** **service may be in an inconsistent state. Error** ***number*** **occurred:** ***text***

[Server Manager]

An unexpected error occurred while the system was attempting to assign an account to the Replicator local group.

Consult the event log in Event Viewer for details on this error. Then, if necessary, contact your technical support group.

Cannot allocate memory in the admin support thread for the Remote Access Service.

[Remote Access Service]

A request from the Remote Access admin (RASADMIN.EXE) failed.

Restart your computer. If the problem persists, check your system's configuration, quotas, and resources. There may be problems with your system's memory. For further information, consult your Windows NT documentation.

Cannot allocate memory.

[Remote Access Service]

The system has run out of memory.

Close some applications, and redial.

Cannot allocate memory. Close some applications, and retry.

[Remote Access Service]

A system call to allocate memory failed.

Close some applications to reduce system memory usage and retry the operation that failed.

Cannot carry out the Word Wrap command because there is too much text in the file.

[Notepad]

Because your computer is low on memory, Notepad cannot wrap the text that you have typed.

To free memory, close one or more of the applications that you have running, then try again.

Cannot change Boot.ini file. Operating System and Timeout changes will not be saved.

[Program Manager]

Most likely, you do not have Write permission on the BOOT.INI file.

Change the permissions on this file so that you can write to the file, or ask the system administrator to do so for you. Then try again.

Cannot change Boot.ini file. Operating System and Timeout changes will not be saved.

[Program Manager]

Log on as an administrator and try again.

Cannot change Windows Default.

[Program Manager]

In the Color Schemes list, you attempted to remove the Windows default color scheme. Windows NT does not permit the removal of this scheme.

Choose OK.

Cannot change Windows Default.

[Program Manager]

In the Color Schemes list, you attempted to remove the Windows default color scheme. Windows NT does not permit the removal of this scheme.

Choose OK.

Cannot CHKDSK a network drive.

[Chkdsk]

You cannot use the Chkdsk command with a local drive letter that has been redirected over the network.

If you must run Chkdsk on the drive that is on the network, you will have to use the computer that is local to that drive.

Cannot CHKDSK a SUBSTed or ASSIGNed drive.

[Chkdsk]

A SUBSTed drive is a virtual drive hosted on another volume, and cannot be checked. The host volume must be checked instead. The Chkdsk command does not work on drives formed by the Subst or Assign commands.

Determine the host volume of the SUBSTed drive and run Chkdsk on that volume.

Cannot clear port statistics on server *computer name*

[Remote Access Service]

The server may be down or you may have too many applications running. A network or system error may have occurred.

At the command prompt, use the net view command to verify that you can see the server. If so, stop some applications running on the server. Also, check the Event Log in Event Viewer for information about related errors. Event Viewer is found in the Administrative Tools group.

Cannot clear port statistics.

[Remote Access Service]

The server may be down or you may have too many applications running. A network or system error may have occurred.

At the command prompt, use the net view command to verify that you can see the server. If so, stop some applications running on the server. Also, use the Event Log in Event Viewer to see information about related errors. Event Viewer is found in the Administrative Tools group.

Cannot close while DDE conversations are in progress. WM_CLOSE ignored.

[Dynamic Data Exchange]

You tried to close the Dynamic Data Exchange (DDE) while an application was using it. Do so would disrupt the application and could cause data corruption.

Try again later.

Cannot complete this function.

[Kernel32]

The function was called in an inappropriate context. For example, the GetSelection() API will return this message if it is called when there is no selection.

Contact the supplier of the running application.

Cannot connect network drive

[File Manager]

The computer sharing this drive might not be running on the network or might already have the maximum number of connections to it. Or, there may be a problem with the hardware or software that connects your computer to the network. Or, you might not be logged on to the network.

If you are able to connect to other network resources, check to make sure the remote computer is running and is able to accept connections. If you are not able to connect to any resources, and you are logged on, check the event log for errors involving network adapter cards and their drivers or protocols, and take the appropriate action on these errors. Then try again.

Cannot connect to OS2 SubSystem

[OS/2 Subsystem]

The Windows NT OS/2 subsystem cannot start up because the OS/2 subsystem client cannot connect to the OS/2 subsystem server. The server may be busy.

This may be a temporary condition. Wait, then retry running the OS/2 application. If you continue to get this message, contact your technical support staff.

Cannot construct accelerators.

[Remote Access Service]

An internal problem has occurred. RAS, Windows NT, or NETUI*.dll might need to be replaced.

Use the Network option in Control Panel to remove and reinstall RAS. If you continue to see this message, try replacing NETUI*.DLL from the distribution media. If you still receive this message, contact technical support.

Cannot construct application.

[Remote Access Service]

An internal problem has occurred. RAS, Windows NT, or NETUI*.dll might need to be replaced.

Use the Network option in Control Panel to remove and reinstall RAS. If you continue to see this message, try replacing NETUI*.DLL from the distribution media. If you still receive this message, contact technical support.

Cannot construct dialog

[Remote Access Service]

This indicates a low memory problem. Depending on which dialog failed to construct, you may not be able to perform the required operation. RAS, Windows NT, or NETUI*.DLL may need to be replaced.

Try closing other Windows applications, or try restarting the system.

Cannot convert *file system* **volumes to** *filename* **.**

[Convert]

The Convert utility cannot make the specified file system conversion. In this version of Windows NT, two conversions are possible: (1) FAT to NTFS, or (2) HPFS to NTFS.

Verify that the file system you are attempting to convert is either FAT or HPFS.

Cannot CONVERT a network drive.

[Convert]

You cannot use the Convert command on drives that have been redirected over the network.

Run the Convert utility on the computer that is local to the drive you want to convert.

Cannot convert an extended attribute

[Convert]

During a FAT to NTFS file system conversion, the Convert utility was unable to convert an extended attribute.

The FAT partition is still in its original (unconverted) state. Run the Chkdsk command with the /f option and try the conversion again.

Cannot copy file to itself

[Program Manager]

Try again, specifying a different filename to copy the file to.

Cannot copy to *filename* **from** *filename*

[Program Manager]

You attempted to copy a file to itself, and this action is not permitted.

No action is needed.

Cannot copy to *filename* from *filename*

[Program Manager]

You attempted to copy a file to itself, and this action is not permitted.

No action is needed.

Cannot copy to Clipboard; close one or more Windows applications and try again.

[Help]

The applications that you have running are making demands upon your system's memory that make it temporarily impossible for Windows NT to access the Clipboard.

Perform the action prescribed in the message.

Cannot create *filename* file.

[TCP/IP]

Try again, providing a different filename.

Cannot create *filename*

[Program Manager]

This message occurs when a file cannot be created for the copy operation. For example, you attempted to copy a font from one device to another, and the font file could not be created on the target device.

Choose OK.

Cannot create *filename*

[Program Manager]

This message occurs when a file cannot be created for the copy operation. For example, you attempted to copy a font from one device to another, and the font file could not be created on the target device.

Choose OK.

Cannot create a file when that file already exists.

[Kernel32]

If you can do it at the user interface, specify a different filename. Otherwise, contact the supplier of the running application.

Cannot create a named pipe instance in the admin support thread for the Remote Access Service.

[Remote Access Service]

Restart your computer. If the problem persists, check your system's configuration, quotas, and resources. There may be problems with your system's memory. For further information, consult your Windows NT documentation.

Cannot create a stable subkey under a volatile parent key.

[Kernel32]

In the Registry, if the parent key of a subtree is volatile then all descendants must be volatile too.

Contact the supplier of the running application.

Cannot create a top-level child window.

[Kernel32]

As part of its user interface, an application has tried to create a child window at an inappropriate level.

Contact the supplier of the running application.

Cannot create a value entry without a title. Please enter a title.

[Registry Editor]

You attempted to create a value entry in Registry Editor, but did not assign a title to it.

Assign the entry a title, then choose OK.

Cannot create an instance thread in the admin support thread for the Remote Access Service.

[Remote Access Service]

A request from the Remote Access admin (RASADMIN.EXE) failed.

Restart your computer. If the problem persists, check your system's configuration, quotas, and resources. There may be problems with your system's memory. For further information, consult your Windows NT documentation.

Cannot create another system semaphore.

[Kernel32]

All the system semaphore slots have been used. Another system semaphore cannot be created until one has been freed.

Try again later.

Cannot create another thread.

[Kernel32]

The thread table for the process is full; another thread cannot be added.

Remove some idle threads and try again, or use a different process.

Cannot create bookmark file.

[Help]

You have attempted to create a bookmark in a Help file to which you do not have write access.

Remove the read-only protection from the file, then try again.

Cannot create bookmark; remove the Read Only attribute for .BMK files.

[Help]

You attempted to create a bookmark when the .BMK file in your Windows NT directory is read-only protected.

In your Windows NT root directory in File Manager, use the Properties option to remove read-only protection, particularly from the WINHELP.BMK file.

Cannot Create CONOUT

[OS/2 Subsystem]

The Windows NT OS/2 subsystem cannot start up because standard output cannot be redirected to a file. The disk to which you are trying to redirect the output may be full, or you may not have write access to the disk.

Run the OS/2 application again, specifying a different destination for standard output. If you continue to get this message, contact your technical support staff.

Cannot create LMHOSTS file.

[Control Panel]

Your computer does not have sufficient disk space for the LMHOSTS file.

Verify that your computer has enough disk space. If so, contact your system administrator because there may be other problems with your system.

Cannot create new phone book.

[Remote Access Service]

CreateFile failed. The system may be running out of memory.

Check for an existing phone book file with protected attributes using the Properties from the File menu in File Manager. Check available disk space. Try closing other applications and services that are not in use. You might also want to remove any unneeded files and applications from your disk.

Cannot create or modify annotations; please exit WinHelp and remove the Read Only attribute for *filename* .

[Help]

Because the permissions on your annotation file do not allow it to be written to, no annotations can be added to the file.

Exit WinHelp and remove the Read Only attribute for the annotation file. Then try again.

Cannot create specified file. Make sure that: You have enough disk space. The file is not read-only. The filename is valid.

[Terminal]

Terminal is presently unable to create a temporary file that must be created for a file to be saved.

Follow the user action specified in the message.

Cannot create the *filename* file. Make sure that the path and filename are correct.

[Notepad]

In the Open dialog box, or from the command prompt, you specified the name of a file or a command path that does not exist.

In the Open dialog box, browse through the directories until you locate the file for which you are searching. Or, at the command prompt, specify a valid filename.

Cannot create the elementary file system structures.

[Convert]

During a FAT to NTFS file system conversion, the Convert utility could not create the elementary NTFS file system structures on the target volume.

Delete unnecessary files and retry the conversion. If this message reappears, the volume may not be suitable for conversion.

Cannot delete existing annotation.

[Help]

You attempted to delete an annotation when the .ANN file is either read-only or is saved to a network connection.

If you are sure you want to delete the annotation, copy the appropriate .ANN file to your hard disk, then delete it. Or, if the file is read-only, use the Properties option in File Manager to remove this protection, then delete the file.

Cannot delete system group

[User Manager]

When you install Windows NT, certain built-in user groups already appear in your User Manager window, and you cannot delete these groups.

Select OK.

Cannot delete the remote computer group name *name* from LANA *number* .The error code is the data.

[Remote Access Service]

An internal system error occurred.

Contact technical support.

Cannot delete the remote computer name *computer name* from LANA *number* .The error code is the data.

[Remote Access Service]

An internal system error occurred.

Contact technical support.

Cannot destroy object created by another thread.

[Kernel32]

One part of an application, as part of its user interface, has tried to delete a window owned by another part of the application.

Contact the supplier of the running application.

Cannot detect carrier.

[Remote Access Service]

A modem did not pick up the phone. Many modems return this error if the remote modem does not pick up the phone.

Please check the number and dial again. To automate redialing, set the Redial Settings option on the Phone Book's Options menu. For more information, see "Redialing" in the Remote Access Service online Help.

Cannot determine file system of drive *drive letter* **.**

[Utilities]

The utility cannot determine the file system (FAT, HPFS, or NTFS) for the volume, and cannot proceed.

Make sure you have administrative privilege, then try the operation again.

Cannot determine location of system directory.

[Convert]

The Convert utility needs to use files that it assumes are in the system directory, but it cannot find the system directory.

Make sure you have the privileges associated with the administrator group and that you have access to the system directory.

Cannot disconnect *user name* **from server** *computer name*

[Remote Access Service]

An error occurred while trying to disconnect the specified user from the Remote Access server.

Check the Event Log in Event Viewer in the Administrative Tools group for other errors related to this one.

Cannot disconnect phone book entry.

[Remote Access Service]

RasHangUp failed.

Try stopping and restarting RAS using the Services option in Control Panel. If this does not solve the problem, try restarting your computer. And finally, use the Network option in Control Panel to remove and reinstall RAS.

Cannot DISKCOPY to or from a network drive

[Disk Copy]

Diskcopy can be used only with local drives.

Verify that your are using the Diskcopy command on a local drive.

Cannot dismount the drive.

[Utilities]

No action is needed but you may have to restart the computer to access the drive.

Cannot display cursor blinking rate; to display rate, close one or more Windows applications and try again

[Program Manager]

There is not enough free memory to display the cursor blinking rate.

Cannot display cursor blinking rate; to display rate, close one or more Windows applications and try again

[Program Manager]

You are low on system memory.

Follow the action specified in the message.

Cannot display data.

[Remote Access Service]

Usually this message indicates a character set conversion problem. There is an internal problem with RAS.

Use the Network option in Control panel to remove and reinstall RAS.

Cannot divide by zero

[Calculator]

You have attempted to divide a number by zero.

Choose the C or CE button (or press ESC) to clear the calculation and start again. If you are using the recall memory as a divisor, verify that the value in memory is non-zero by pressing MR.

Cannot enumerate a non-container.

[Kernel32]

Windows NT organizes a network logically as a hierarchy. An application program can request a list of all resources below a specified network resource in the hierarchy, but in this case an application specified a network resource at the bottom of the hierarchy.

If you have a user interface, retry the request with a different network resource specified (for example, the resource at the root of the tree). Otherwise, contact the supplier of the running application.

Cannot enumerate Adapters in Registry

[Control Panel]

The Network option is having difficulty accessing the node in the Registry that contains information on adapters.

Contact technical support.

Cannot enumerate ports on server *computer name*

[Remote Access Service]

The server may be down or you may have too many applications running. A network or system error may have occurred.

At the command prompt, use the net view command to verify that you can see the server. If so, stop some applications running on the server. Also, use the Event Log in Event Viewer to see information about related errors. Event Viewer is found in the Administrative Tools group.

Cannot enumerate Products in Registry

[Control Panel]

The Network option is having difficulty accessing the node in the Registry that contains information on products.

Contact technical support.

Cannot enumerate Registry key values.

[Remote Access Service]

The Remote Access Service failed to start because required Registry keys may be missing from the Registry.

Use the Network option in Control Panel to remove and reinstall the Remote Access Service.

Cannot enumerate Remote Access ports.

[Remote Access Service]

The server may be down or you may have too many applications running. A network or system error may have occurred.

At the command prompt, use the net view command to verify that you can see the server. If so, stop some applications running on the server. Also, use the Event Log in Event Viewer to see information about related errors. Event Viewer is found in the Administrative Tools group.

Cannot enumerate servers on focus domain

[Remote Access Service]

The focus domain you specified either does not exist or no domain controllers exist in the domain.

Use the Remote Access Admin option in the Remote Access group to change the focus to a valid domain. From the Server menu, select Domain or Server. Then type the domain or server name in the Domain box.

Cannot enumerate Services in Registry

[Control Panel]

The Network option is having difficulty accessing the node in the Registry that contains information on services.

Contact technical support.

Cannot enumerate the Remote Access Connection Manager ports.

[Remote Access Service]

Your adapter card and its driver may be configured incorrectly.

Make sure the multiport adapter card and software have been correctly installed and configured. If so, remove and reinstall the Remote Access Service using the Network option in Control Panel.

Cannot enumerate users on focus domain - *name*

[Remote Access Service]

Verify that the Remote Access Server that contains user accounts is accessible.

Cannot enumerate users on focus domain or server

[Remote Access Service]

There is a problem with the server that contains user accounts. Until the problem is corrected, you will be unable to view the Remote Access permissions of user accounts or modify them.

Verify that the server with user accounts is working properly and is accessible.

Cannot enumerate users on focus server - *name*

[Remote Access Service]

.

Verify that the Remote Access Server that contains user accounts is accessible.

Cannot execute second macro while first is in process.

[Help]

This error is from the Macro Language Editor for online help, and should not appear while using the Help file. Report this error to the provider of the Help file.

Cannot find ***filename*****.**

[Cardfile]

In the Open File dialog box, you directed Cardfile to find a file that does not exist on the currently selected directory.

Make sure that both the path and filename are correct.

Cannot find a user or group account with name *name* on the indicated domain(s).

[Network]

Either the name was mistyped, or it has been removed from the domain(s), or it has not yet been added to the domain(s). In some cases the account has been added to the domain but has not yet been replicated to the Backup Domain Controller that this computer is getting information from.

Wait and try again, making sure the name is typed correctly. You might want to ask the network administrator to add the name.

Cannot find any icons in this file

[Program Manager]

In the Change Icon dialog box, you specified a file in which no icons exist.

Choose OK, then specify another file.

Cannot find file *filename* (or one of its components); check to ensure the path and filename are correct and that all required libraries are available.

[Program Manager]

In Program Manager, you selected an icon that is not attached to an executable program file. Or, using the Run option on the File menu, you specified the name of a file that does not designate an executable program.

Select the icon, and then choose the Properties option on the File menu. When the Program Item Properties dialog box appears, the name of the selected program's executable file appears in the Command Line option box. Ensure that the file listed here is the executable file for the selected program.

Cannot find file *filename* (or one of its components); check to ensure the path and filename are correct and that all required libraries are available.

[Task Manager]

The application cannot continue without information contained in the indicated file.

If the path and filename are correct, make sure that none of the executable (.EXE) or library (.DLL) files are missing or corrupt. You might need to restore files from a backup copy or reinstall the software.

Cannot find key.

[Remote Access Service]

One of the Remote Access configuration files probably contains invalid information.

The easiest way to resolve this problem is to reinstall Remote Access. If you are using a modem that is not supported by Remote Access, switch to a supported modem. For more information about modem script files, see "Modem Script File" in the Remote Access Service online Help. The Remote Access script files (PAD.INF, MODEM.INF, and SWITCH.INF) are in the \SYSTEM32\RAS subdirectory of your Windows NT directory.

Cannot find Primary for *computer name*. Continuing with the promotion may result in errors when *computer name*'s old Primary comes back on line. Do you want to continue with the promotion?

[Server Manager]

If you choose to promote a computer to domain controller, the system usually automatically demotes the previous domain controller to server status. The previous domain controller is currently not available. When it comes back online, it will not run the Netlogon service, and it will not participate in authentication of user logons.

Choose Yes. Then, when the previous domain controller comes back online, demote it manually.

Cannot find printer or printer driver.

[Help]

Either your computer is not connected physically to a printer, or the printer has not been properly configured on your system.

Check your physical connections. Or use Printers in Control Panel to configure your printer.

Cannot find the *filename* file. Do you want to create a new file?

[Notepad]

In Notepad, you attempted to open a file that does not exist in the location that you have specified in the Open dialog box.

If you want to create the file, select Yes. If not, select No. If you wish to return to the currently opened Notepad file, select Cancel.

Cannot find the Control Panel components (files with .CPL extension). Verify that they are installed in your Windows NT SYSTEM32 directory.

[Control Panel]

To run Control Panel, files with a .CPL extension must appear in your Windows NT SYSTEM32 directory.

Do a search in File Manager for .CPL files, then drag and drop these files into your Windows NT SYSTEM32 directory.

Cannot find the phone book entry.

[Remote Access Service]

Remote Access has located the Phone Book but cannot find the specified entry. This error should not occur unless you are writing to Remote Access APIs, and have specified an incorrect entry name. The Remote Access Service uses the file RASPHONE.PBK, located in the \SYSTEM32\RAS subdirectory of your Windows NT directory.

Cannot find the Primary DC for *name*. You may administer this domain, but certain domain-wide operations will be disabled.

[Server Manager]

The domain controller for the domain of focus cannot be found, possibly because the computer that serves as domain controller is not started.

If the administrative actions you want to perform must apply to all of the workstations in the selected domain, and the action is disabled, wait until the domain controller of the selected domain comes back online, then try again.

Cannot find the settings file *filename* .Insert the disk with the file in drive A.

[Terminal]

You attempted to call a file from the command line, the file could not be located.

Follow the user action specified in the message.

Cannot find the specified drive or directory. Make sure the path is correct.

[Terminal]

You have specified a directory that does not exist in the path that you have specified.

Specify the correct drive and directory, then try again.

Cannot find the specified file. Make sure the path and filename are correct.

[Terminal]

You attempted to open a file and have specified a path that does not lead to the file.

Make sure that the path and filename are correct. Or do a search for the file in File Manager.

Cannot find window class.

[Kernel32]

An application tried to use a window class that was not an application-specific class registered with the system or one of the predefined control classes (such as BUTTON, LISTBOX, SCROLLBAR, etc.).

Contact the supplier of the running application.

Cannot format a network drive.

[Format]

You specified a network drive in the Format command.

You cannot format drives that are redirected over the network.

Cannot format a RAM DISK drive.

[Format]

You specified a RAM disk in a Format command. You cannot format a RAM disk.

Cannot format an ASSIGNed or SUBSTed drive.

[Format]

ASSIGNed or SUBSTed drives aren't really disks, they're just part of other disks. Also, the Format command ignores drive reassignments.

No action is needed.

Cannot format. This media is write protected.

[Format]

You cannot format a write-protected disk.

Either remove the write-protection or use another disk.

Cannot get account information for user *user name*

[Remote Access Service]

Verify that the Remote Access Server that contains user accounts is accessible.

Cannot get information from server *computer name*

[Remote Access Service]

The server may be down or you may have too many applications running. A network or system error may have occurred.

At the command prompt, use the Net View command to verify that you can see the server. If so, stop some applications running on the server. Also, check the Event Log in Event Viewer for information about related errors. Event Viewer is found in the Administrative Tools group.

Cannot get list of Adapters

[Control Panel]

The Network option is having difficulty accessing the node in the Registry that contains the list of adapters. Therefore, you cannot complete the current operation.

Contact technical support.

Cannot get list of Products

[Control Panel]

The Network option is having difficulty accessing the node in the Registry that contains the list of products. Therefore, you cannot complete the current operation.

Contact technical support.

Cannot get port information from server *computer name*

[Remote Access Service]

The server may be down or you may have too many applications running. A network or system error may have occurred.

At the command prompt, use the net view command to verify that you can see the server. If so, stop some applications running on the server. Also, use the Event Log in Event Viewer to see information about related errors. Event Viewer is found in the Administrative Tools group.

Cannot get port information.

[Remote Access Service]

The server may be down or you may have too many applications running. A network or system error may have occurred.

At the command prompt, use the net view command to verify that you can see the server. If so, stop some applications running on the server. Also, use the Event Log in Event Viewer to see information about related errors. Event Viewer is found in the Administrative Tools group.

Cannot get port statistics.

[Remote Access Service]

RAS Manager call RasPortGetStatistics failed.

Try stopping and restarting RAS using the Services option in Control Panel. If this does not solve the problem, try restarting your computer. And finally, use the Network option in Control Panel to remove and reinstall RAS.

Cannot get port status. Reconfigure Remote Access for the correct port.

[Remote Access Service]

The specified port is not configured to use RAS. This situation might also occur if RAS values in the Registry have been changed to invalid values.

Use the Network option in Control Panel to reconfigure RAS. In the Installed Network Software box select Remote Access Service. Then choose Configure to configure a port for RAS to use. If the Registry has been corrupted, remove and reinstall RAS.

Cannot get send/receive buffer.

[Remote Access Service]

This message indicates an internal problem with RAS Phone or RAS Manager.

Try stopping and restarting RAS using the Services option in Control Panel. If this does not solve the problem, try restarting your computer. And finally, use the Network option in Control Panel to remove and reinstall RAS.

Cannot get status information for a connection.

[Remote Access Service]

RAS API call RasGetConnectStatus failed.

Try stopping and restarting RAS using the Services option in Control Panel. If this does not solve the problem, try restarting your computer. And finally, use the Network option in Control Panel to remove and reinstall RAS.

Cannot get status information for a port.

[Remote Access Service]

RAS Manager call RasGetInfo failed.

Try stopping and restarting RAS using the Services option in Control Panel. If this does not solve the problem, try restarting your computer. And finally, use the Network option in Control Panel to remove and reinstall RAS.

Cannot get timer. Close Mail and/or Fax (if they are running), and retry.

[Remote Access Service]

The SetTimer Win32 API failed. This indicates a timer, which is a finite system resource, was not available.

Close other running applications that might be using up timers.

Cannot hang up the Remote Access connection.

[Remote Access Service]

RAS API call RasHangUp failed.

Wait a few minutes and then try disconnect again. If waiting is unsuccessful, try stopping and restarting RAS using the Services option in Control Panel. If this does not solve the problem, try restarting your computer. And finally, use the Network option in Control Panel to remove and reinstall RAS.

Cannot initialize IP address control.

[Remote Access Service]

An internal problem has occurred. RAS, Windows NT, or NETUI*.dll might need to be replaced.

Use the Network option in Control Panel to remove and reinstall RAS. If you continue to see this message, try replacing NETUI*.DLL from the distribution media. If you still receive this message, contact technical support.

Cannot load a string.

[Remote Access Service]

This error should not occur under normal circumstances.

Restart your computer to make sure that all recent configuration changes have taken effect. If the error persists, consult the Windows NT event log for detailed warnings or errors.

Cannot load extension *name* **.Error** *number*

[Server Manager]

The functionality supplied by the specified extension will not be available.

Make sure the .DLL file for the extension is present. Restore it from a backup copy if necessary.

Cannot load extension *name* **.Error** *number* **:** *text*

[Server Manager]

The functionality supplied by the specified extension will not be available.

Make sure the .DLL file for the extension is present. Restore it from a backup copy if necessary.

Cannot load function address of "*name* " from "*filename* " DLL

[Dynamic Data Exchange]

The indicated function will not be available because the application will not be able to find the instructions to it. Commands using this function will not work.

Cannot load phone book or RAS Manager data.

[Remote Access Service]

RAS Manager or phone book file operation failed during initial data loading.

Try stopping and restarting RAS using the Services option in Control Panel. If this does not solve the problem, try restarting your computer. And finally, use the Network option in Control Panel to remove and reinstall RAS.

Cannot load RASMAN functions. Remove and reinstall Remote Access.

[Remote Access Service]

Use the Network option in Control Panel to remove and then reinstall RAS. In the Installed Network Software box select Remote Access Service and then choose Remove. Restart your computer. Select Network in Control Panel and choose Add Software to reinstall RAS.

Cannot load Shell32 library.

[Remote Access Service]

SHELL32.DLL file was not found.

No action is needed.

Cannot load the *filename* driver. The driver file may be missing. Try installing the driver again, or contact your system administrator.

[Drivers (CP)]

A device cannot function properly without a driver, and the specified driver file is missing. It should appear in your SYSTEM32 directory.

Locate the file in File Manager, then move it to your SYSTEM32 directory.

Cannot load the About Box.

[Remote Access Service]

The standard SHELL32.DLL ShellAbout call failed. The About box contains copy written information about the product and version numbers.

No action is needed.

Cannot load the NetBIOS gateway DLL component.

[Remote Access Service]

RASGTWY.DLL is missing or corrupted.

Either copy RASGTWY.DLL from your installation disks or reinstall the Remote Access Service. Use Network in Control Panel to remove and then reinstall the Remote Access Service.

Cannot load the phone book file.

[Remote Access Service]

The Remote Access Service uses the RASPHONE.PBK file in the \SYSTEM32\RAS subdirectory of your Windows NT directory.

Make sure the file is on this path, and restart Remote Access.

Cannot load Windows Help application.

[Backup]

Backup cannot display online Help. This problem can occur due to a lack of system resources or because the file containing Help for backup has been deleted from your drive.

To increase system resources, close one or more of the applications that you have running. To ensure that the file is on your disk, exit or minimize Backup, open File Manager, then do a search for BACKUP.HLP.

Cannot locate *name* **service for protocol** *name* **in the TCP/IP network services database. The service could not be started.**

[Netevent]

The services file is corrupted or does not exist.

Verify that the services file is present and in the proper location.

Cannot locate or create an NTFS index

[Convert]

During a FAT to NTFS file system conversion, the Convert utility was unable to create an NTFS root index.

The FAT partition is still in its original (unconverted) state. Delete some files from the partition and run the Chkdsk utility with the /r option. Then retry the conversion.

Cannot lock current drive.

[Utilities]

The utility cannot gain exclusive access to a volume that is the current drive for any process.

Check the current drive for all console windows and applications and try again.

Cannot lock the drive. The volume is still in use.

[Utilities]

The file system utility requires exclusive use of a volume (for example, to format it). However, the utility cannot lock the volume for your exclusive use right now. Somebody else may be using it.

Shut down other applications and console windows that are using the drive, and try again.

Cannot log on. User is currently logged on and argument TRYUSER is set to NO.

[Network]

This message should occur only on a down-level computer. Any action to correct the problem should be performed on that computer. The computer cannot update its copies of the replicated files while a user is logged on and the TRYUSER option is set to NO.

No action is needed. The computer will update the files when no user is logged on. To have the local computer update files while users are logged on, change the value of the TRYUSER entry in the [replicator] section of the configuration file to YES.

Cannot multiplex module *name*.The service could not be started.

[Netevent]

The specified module was installed incorrectly.

Remove the TCP/IP protocol and then reinstall it using the Network option in Control Panel.

Cannot open *filename* .

[Aclconv]

The Aclconv utility was unable to open the specified file. It may have been attempting to query an existing data file, set the file pointer to the top of an existing log file, or create a new log file.

Check to make sure that the file names are valid in the command line, and that the data file (if specified) and log file (if specified) exist and are accessible.

Cannot open an anonymous level security token.

[Kernel32]

An attempt was made to open a client's anonymous-level security token. A token must have an impersonation level of at least "Identification" to be opened.

Contact the supplier of the running application. A general workaround, if the application interface allows it, is to avoid trying to open the anonymous token, or to specify a higher level of impersonation for the client program.

Cannot open Clipboard.

[Calculator]

You tried to paste from the Clipboard, but another application has the Clipboard locked open. Most likely, this indicates a bug in the application that has the Clipboard locked open.

Choose OK, then try again later. Or attempt to close the application that is using the Clipboard.

Cannot open file. Start the application used to create this file, and open it from there.

[Program Manager]

A system error occurred while you were querying for a file association.

Perform the action specified in the message.

Cannot open Help file.

[Help]

Either the help file is corrupt, or there is not enough free memory to open the file, or you do not have sufficient permissions on either the file or a directory that it is in to read the file.

If this message was accompanied by a message citing insufficient memory, close some applications and try again. Otherwise, make sure you have Read permission on every directory leading to the .HLP file, and to the file itself, and try again. If you still get this message, restore the file from a backup copy and try again.

Cannot open program group *group*

[Program Manager]

You have attempted to delete from Program Manager a group that has been damaged or deleted from the Registry.

There is no user action for this situation.

Cannot open program group *group*. **Do you want the Program Manager to still try to load it in future ?**

[Program Manager]

One of the two following circumstances exist: (1) you lack the permission to access the REGEDT32 key that contains the user profile; or (2) the group was corrupted and cannot be read from the Registry.

If you want Program Manager to load the specified group in the future, choose Yes. If not, choose No.

Cannot open SYSTEM Environment section in Registry. Possible registry corruption.

[Program Manager]

Check the SYSTEM Environment section in the Registry for this computer. Also, make sure the security settings on this Registry key allow you to read it. If you still get this error, restart the computer, and press the spacebar immediately after selecting Windows NT at the Boot Loader prompt. Then choose Last Known Good.

Cannot open the *name* **file. Make sure a disk is in the drive you specified.**

[Notepad]

You designated an empty drive for the location of a file.

Either insert the disk that contains the file into the appropriate disk drive, or select a different disk drive.

Cannot open the *filename* **file. Please make sure that you specified the correct path for the LMHOSTS file.**

[TCP/IP]

The LMHOSTS file is a local text file that maps IP addresses to the NetBIOS names of computer outside of the local subnet. Without this file, you may be unable to communicate with these computers.

Make sure that you have specified the correct path and filename for this file.

Cannot open the LMHOSTS file. Please make sure that you specified the correct path for the LMHOSTS file.

[Control Panel]

The LMHOSTS file is a local text file that maps IP addresses to the NetBIOS names of computer outside of the local subnet. Without this file, you may be unable to communicate with these computers.

Make sure that you have specified the correct path to this file.

Cannot open the MIDIMAP.CFG file. Make sure the file is available.

[MIDI Mapper (Control Panel)]

The MIDIMAP.CFG file, which configures your MIDI Mapper options, must be in your Windows NT SYSTEM32 directory before Windows NT can initialize the MIDI Mapper dialog.

Exit or minimize Control Panel, and open File Manager. Search for the file, then move it into your SYSTEM32 directory.

Cannot open the phone book file.

[Remote Access Service]

The Remote Access Service uses the RASPHONE.PBK file in the \SYSTEM32\RAS subdirectory of your Windows NT directory.

Make sure the file is on this path, and restart Remote Access.

Cannot open the RasServer parameters Registry key.

[Remote Access Service]

The specified Registry key may be missing from the Registry.

Remove and then reinstall the Remote Access Service using the Network option in Control Panel. If after reinstalling the service you continue to see this message, contact technical support.

Cannot open the settings file because it is invalid. Specify the settings you want to use, and then save them to a new file.

[Terminal]

The settings file that you want to open is corrupted.

Follow the user action specified in the message.

Cannot open USER Environment section in Registry. Possible registry corruption.

[Program Manager]

The HKEY_CURRENT_USER\\Environment section of REGEDT32 may be corrupted.

See your system administrator. Or contact technical support, and report the content of this message.

Cannot open USER Environment section in Registry. Possible registry corruption.

[Program Manager]

The HKEY_CURRENT_USER\\Environment section of REGEDT32 may be corrupt.

Check the USER Environment section in the Registry for this computer. Also, make sure the security settings on this Registry key allow you to read it. If you still get this error, restart the computer, and press the spacebar immediately after selecting Windows NT at the Boot Loader prompt. Then choose Last Known Good.

Cannot open volume for direct access.

[Utilities]

Make sure the floppy disk is in the drive and the drive is ready.

Cannot operate on file. Make sure the file or disk is not damaged or write-protected.

[Write]

You have attempted an operation on a file that is damaged or that is write-protected. This message can also appear if you attempt to open or save changes to a file that is saved to a network server to which you are no longer connected.

Remove the write-protection. Or, if the file is saved to a network connection, reestablish the network connection, then try again to operate on the file.

Cannot paste from Clipboard. Please verify that the Clipboard contains text.

[Cardfile]

If you have made an error in copying a picture to the Clipboard, the Clipboard may not contain the picture that you are attempting to paste into a file.

Double-click the Clipbook Viewer icon. Select Clipboard in the Window menu, and the object appears in the Clipbook Viewer window. If the object does not appear, return to the source file, and copy the object again.

Cannot perform a cyclic copy

[Xcopy]

When using the Xcopy command, followed by the /s switch, you cannot copy to any subdirectories that are a subset of the directory you are copying from.

Specify a destination that is not a subdirectory of the source directory.

Cannot perform this operation on built-in accounts.

[Kernel32]

An operation has been attempted on a built-in account which is incompatible with the nature of built-in accounts. For example, built-in accounts cannot be renamed or deleted.

Contact the supplier of the running application.

Cannot perform this operation on this built-in special group.

[Kernel32]

Contact the supplier of the running application.

Cannot plumb unknown driver/module *name*.The service could not be started.

[Netevent]

The driver or module was installed incorrectly.

Remove the TCP/IP protocol and then reinstall it using the Network option in Control Panel.

Cannot print. Be sure that the printer is connected and set up properly.

[Cardfile]

Choose the Print Setup command from the File menu to verify that the default printer is active. Or choose Print Manager from the program group Main in Program Manager to verify current printer status.

Cannot print; run Control Panel to install and set up printers.

[Help]

Nothing can be printed because your system is not aware of any printers.

Choose Printers from the Control Panel to set up at least one printer. For more information choose Help in the Print Manager dialog box.

Cannot process a message from a window that is not a multiple document interface (MDI) window.

[Kernel32]

An application, as part of its user interface, has operated on a window that is part of an MDI window set as if it were an independent window.

Contact the supplier of the running application.

Cannot read boot sector.

[Utilities]

A critical sector near the beginning of the volume is unreadable. Back up files from the drive and replace the disk.

Cannot read file allocation table

[Recover-FAT/HPFS]

Use the Chkdsk command with the /f switch to correct the problem. If you still get this message, you may have to reformat the disk. After that, if you are using a hard disk and you still get this message, contact the hardware vendor.

Cannot read information from the registry.

[Remote Access Service]

Either the Registry is corrupted or another application is using the Registry.

Try closing other running applications.

Cannot read the device name from the media .INI file.

[Remote Access Service]

One of the Remote Access configuration files probably contains invalid information.

The easiest way to resolve this problem is to reinstall Remote Access. Use the Network option in Control Panel to remove and reinstall RAS. If you are using a modem that is not supported by Remote Access, switch to a supported modem, or see "Modem Script File" in the Remote Access Service online Help for information about modifying the modem script file for your modem. The Remote Access script files (PAD.INF, MODEM.INF, and SWITCH.INF) are in the \SYSTEM32\RAS subdirectory of your Windows NT directory.

Cannot read the device type from the media .INI file.

[Remote Access Service]

One of the Remote Access configuration files probably contains invalid information.

The easiest way to resolve this problem is to reinstall Remote Access. Use the Network option in Control Panel to remove and reinstall RAS. If you are using a modem that is not supported by Remote Access, switch to a supported modem, or see "Modem Script File" in the Remote Access Service online Help for information about modifying the modem script file for your modem. The Remote Access script files (PAD.INF, MODEM.INF, and SWITCH.INF) are in the \SYSTEM32\RAS subdirectory of your Windows NT directory.

Cannot read the maximum carrier BPS rate from the media .INI file.

[Remote Access Service]

One of the Remote Access configuration files probably contains invalid information.

The easiest way to resolve this problem is to reinstall Remote Access. Use the Network option in Control Panel to remove and reinstall RAS. If you are using a modem that is not supported by Remote Access, switch to a supported modem, or see "Modem Script File" in the Remote Access Service online Help for information about modifying the modem script file for your modem. The Remote Access script files (PAD.INF, MODEM.INF, and SWITCH.INF) are in the \SYSTEM32\RAS subdirectory of your Windows NT directory.

Cannot read the maximum connection BPS rate from the media .INI file.

[Remote Access Service]

One of the Remote Access configuration files probably contains invalid information.

The easiest way to resolve this problem is to reinstall Remote Access. Use the Network option in Control Panel to remove and reinstall RAS. If you are using a modem that is not supported by Remote Access, switch to a supported modem, or see "Modem Script File" in the Remote Access Service online Help for information about modifying the modem script file for your modem. The Remote Access script files (PAD.INF, MODEM.INF, and SWITCH.INF) are in the \SYSTEM32\RAS subdirectory of your Windows NT directory.

Cannot read the media .INI file.

[Remote Access Service]

One of the Remote Access configuration files probably contains invalid information.

The easiest way to resolve this problem is to reinstall Remote Access. Use the Network option in Control Panel to remove and reinstall RAS. If you are using a modem that is not supported by Remote Access, switch to a supported modem, or see "Modem Script File" in the Remote Access Service online Help for information about modifying the modem script file for your modem. The Remote Access script files (PAD.INF, MODEM.INF, and SWITCH.INF) are in the \SYSTEM32\RAS subdirectory of your Windows NT directory.

Cannot read the section name from the media .INI file.

[Remote Access Service]

One of the Remote Access configuration files probably contains invalid information.

The easiest way to resolve this problem is to reinstall Remote Access. Use the Network option in Control Panel to remove and reinstall RAS. If you are using a modem that is not supported by Remote Access, switch to a supported modem, or see "Modem Script File" in the Remote Access Service online Help for information about modifying the modem script file for your modem. The Remote Access script files (PAD.INF, MODEM.INF, and SWITCH.INF) are in the \SYSTEM32\RAS subdirectory of your Windows NT directory.

Cannot read the specified file. Make sure the path and filename are correct.

[Terminal]

You attempted to open a file that does not exist in the path that you have specified.

Click the OK button to return to the Open dialog box. Then, if necessary, type "*.TRM" in the File Name box, then open the individual directories in the Directories box until the Terminal file that you are looking for appears in the File Name box.

Cannot read the usage from the media .INI file.

[Remote Access Service]

One of the Remote Access configuration files probably contains invalid information.

The easiest way to resolve this problem is to reinstall Remote Access. Use the Network option in Control Panel to remove and reinstall RAS. If you are using a modem that is not supported by Remote Access, switch to a supported modem, or see "Modem Script File" in the Remote Access Service online Help for information about modifying the modem script file for your modem. The Remote Access script files (PAD.INF, MODEM.INF, and SWITCH.INF) are in the \SYSTEM32\RAS subdirectory of your Windows NT directory.

Cannot read/save UPS information in the registry.

[Control Panel]

UPS configuration information cannot be accessed or written to the Registry.

Make sure that you have access to the Registry key that contains UPS's configuration information.

Cannot receive buffer from device.

[Remote Access Service]

RAS Manager call RasPortReceive failed.

Try stopping and restarting RAS using the Services option in Control Panel. If this does not solve the problem, try restarting your computer. And finally, use the Network option in Control Panel to remove and reinstall RAS.

Cannot receive initial frame on port *address* .The user has been disconnected.

[Remote Access Service]

There could be a problem with the modem connection.

Make sure you're using a supported modem. If so, try using a lower baud rate. If you continue to see this message, contact technical support.

Cannot RECOVER a network drive

[Recover-FAT/HPFS]

You cannot recover files on drives that are redirected over a network, or files that are located on a network drive.

Cannot RECOVER an ASSIGNed or SUBSTed drive

[Utilities]

The Recover command does not work on a drive formed by the Assign, Join, or Subst command.

Cannot register help file.

[Remote Access Service]

An internal problem has occurred. RAS, Windows NT, or NETUI*.dll might need to be replaced.

Use the Network option in Control Panel to remove and reinstall RAS. If you continue to see this message, try replacing NETUI*.DLL from the distribution media. If you still receive this message, contact technical support.

Cannot register your computer on the remote network.

[Remote Access Service]

The Remote Access server was unable to register your computer's name on the network.

Contact your system administrator.

Cannot relocate existing file system structures

[Convert]

During a FAT to NTFS file system conversion, the Convert utility was unable to find contiguous space on the volume for the NTFS structures that have to be at a fixed location on the disk.

Delete unnecessary files and retry the conversion. If this message reappears, the volume may not be suitable for conversion.

Cannot remove *name*

[Program Manager]

In the Color Schemes scrolling list in the Control Panel's Color option box, you have attempted to remove the Windows default color scheme. Windows NT does not permit the removal of this option.

Choose OK.

Cannot remove *name*

[Program Manager]

You have attempted to remove the Windows default color scheme. Windows NT does not permit the removal of this option.

Choose OK.

Cannot remove phone book entry.

[Remote Access Service]

There may be a problem with the phone book file attributes or the file is locked.

If you can, determine why the file cannot be written to. Try closing other running applications.

Cannot rename to a different directory or disk. Use the File Move command instead.

[File Manager]

Using the Rename command on the File menu, you included the name of another drive in the new name that you want to assign to your directory or file.

To perform this operation, you must use the Move command.

Cannot request exclusive semaphores at interrupt time.

[Kernel32]

Exclusive system semaphores are owned by a task. The system checks to make sure that only the owner modifies the semaphore. It is impossible to determine the requester at interrupt time, so exclusive semaphores may not be modified then.

End your requested operation, wait awhile, and retry. If you still get this message, contact the supplier of the running application.

Cannot reroute printer output to serial device *name* **.**

[Mode]

You may not have sufficient privilege to make this change that you have requested with the Mode command.

Change your privilege level and retry the command. You may have to contact your system administrator in order to change your privilege level.

Cannot reset the network adapter for LANA *number*. The error code is the data.

[Remote Access Service]

The Remote Access Service or other network software is configured incorrectly.

Use the Network option in Control Panel to reconfigure the Remote Access Service by removing and then reinstalling it. If the problem persists, use Network to reconfigure other network software. Otherwise, contact technical support.

Cannot retrieve current system uppercase table. CHKDSK aborted.

[Chkdsk-NTFS]

The uppercase table is used for Unicode translation.

Contact the disk hardware vendor.

Cannot retrieve data from Windows.

[Remote Access Service]

There is an internal problem with RAS.

Try stopping and restarting RAS using the Services option in Control Panel. If this does not solve the problem, try restarting your computer. And finally, use the Network option in Control Panel to remove and reinstall RAS.

Cannot retrieve protocol information.

[Remote Access Service]

RAS Manager call RasGetProtocolInfo failed.

Try stopping and restarting RAS using the Services option in Control Panel. If this does not solve the problem, try restarting your computer. And finally, use the Network option in Control Panel to remove and reinstall RAS.

Cannot retrieve the security descriptor for this printer.

[Print Manager]

You cannot get security information from this printer because you do not have the necessary access privileges.

Ask the administrator to give you permission to connect to this printer. Or, if you are the administrator, take ownership of this printer.

Cannot run *application* in Windows NT mode.

[Kernel32]

The specified file or program is not compatible with Windows NT.

If the specified application is an MS-DOS program, switch to an MS-DOS session and retry the command. Otherwise, reinstall the application and retry the command. If you get this message again, contact the supplier of the application program.

Cannot save changes to phone book.

[Remote Access Service]

There may be a problem with the phone book file attributes or the file is locked. The server may be running out of disk space.

If you can, determine if the problem with the file is its attributes, or its use by another application or disk space. Try closing other running applications and services. Also use File Manager to check available disk space and file attributes.

Cannot save file on a different disk in the same drive. Insert the disk that originally contained the file into the drive or change drives, and then save the file.

[Cardfile]

After accessing a file from one floppy disk, you removed the disk, then attempted to save the original file on another floppy disk.

Follow the user action specified in the message.

Cannot save new Environment variables in Registry. Possible registry corruption.

[Program Manager]

The HKEY_CURRENT_USER\\ Environment section of REGEDT32 may be corrupted.

See your system administrator. Or contact technical support.

Cannot save new Environment variables in Registry. Possible registry corruption.

[Program Manager]

The HKEY_CURRENT_USER\\ Environment section of REGEDT32 may be corrupted.

Check the SYSTEM Environment and USER Environment sections in the Registry for this computer. Also, make sure the security settings on these Registry keys allow you to read them. If you still get this error, restart the computer, and press the spacebar immediately after selecting Windows NT at the Boot Loader prompt. Then choose Last Known Good.

Cannot save new settings

[Program Manager]

The system is unable to save the settings that you have made in the International dialog box.

Exit and restart the application, then try again.

Cannot save new settings

[Program Manager]

The color settings you selected could not be written to the WIN.INI file.

Make sure the permissions on the USER Environment keys allow you Write access and try again

Cannot save program group ' *group* **' because of insufficient memory.**

[Program Manager]

Close some applications and try again.

Cannot send buffer to device.

[Remote Access Service]

RAS Manager call RasPortSend failed.

Try stopping and restarting RAS using the Services option in Control Panel. If this does not solve the problem, try restarting your computer. And finally, use the Network option in Control Panel to remove and reinstall RAS.

Cannot send message to user *user name*, **who is connected to server** *name* **from computer** *computer name*

[Remote Access Service]

The messenger service may not be started on the client. Otherwise, a network or system error occurred.

Check the Event Log in Event Viewer for information about related errors. Event Viewer is found in the Administrative Tools group.

Cannot set account information for user *user name*

[Remote Access Service]

The specified user will be unable to use the Remote Access Service to connect to the network. Also, you cannot revoke the specified user's permissions.

Verify that the Remote Access Server that contains user accounts is accessible.

Cannot set non-local hook without a module handle.

[Kernel32]

An application, as part of its user interface, has tried to install a procedure to monitor system events throughout the application without supplying all the information about that procedure.

Contact the supplier of the running application.

Cannot set port information.

[Remote Access Service]

The Remote Access Phone Book file and the current Remote Access configuration are probably inconsistent.

If you have changed your communications equipment (such as your serial port or modem), be sure to reconfigure Remote Access. Use the Network option in Control Panel to reconfigure Remote Access. If the error persists, remove and recreate the affected Phone Book entry or, reinstall the Remote Access Service. The Remote Access Phone Book (RASPHONE.PBK) is in the SYSTEM32\RAS subdirectory of your Windows NT directory.

Cannot set stop time before start time.

[Performance Monitor]

In the Time dialog, you attempted to select a bookmark as a start time, but its time mark is later than the current stop time. Or you attempted to select a bookmark as a stop time, and the stop time is earlier than your current start time.

Ensure that your start time precedes your stop time.

Cannot set the startup parameters for the *name* service. Error *number* occurred: *text*

[Server Manager]

An unexpected error occurred when the system tried to configure the startup parameters for the specified service.

Consult the event log in Event Viewer for details on the error. Then, if necessary, contact your technical support group.

Cannot show or remove the window in the way specified.

[Kernel32]

An application, as part of its user interface, has tried to change the way a window is displayed. This was done in an inappropriate way, given the set of windows available to it. For example, the application may have tried to hide a window and activate another window, but there was no other window to activate.

Contact the supplier of the running application.

Cannot start a new logon session with an ID that is already in use.

[Kernel32]

Contact the supplier of the running application.

Cannot start disconnect monitor.

[Remote Access Service]

There is an internal problem with RAS.

Try stopping and restarting RAS using the Services option in Control Panel. If this does not solve the problem, try restarting your computer. And finally, use the Network option in Control Panel to remove and reinstall RAS.

Cannot start more than one copy of the specified program.

[Program Manager] [Task Manager]

You already have one copy of the specified program running, and you have attempted to open another.

Choose OK, then select the copy of this program that you already have running.

Cannot start RAS Manager.

[Remote Access Service]

RAS Manager call RasInitialize failed.

Try stopping and restarting RAS using the Services option in Control Panel. If this does not solve the problem, try restarting your computer. And finally, use the Network option in Control Panel to remove and reinstall RAS.

Cannot start ShellAbout dialog.

[Remote Access Service]

SHELL32.DLL standard About box call failed.

No action is needed.

Cannot stop printer rerouting at this time.

[Mode]

You cannot use the Mode command to end the rerouting the LPTn: device at this time. It may be busy.

Try the command again at a later time.

Cannot transfer multiple files. Wait until one file has been transferred before transferring another file

[Terminal]

You attempted to send a file while another file is in the process of being transferred. Terminal does not support this function.

Follow the user action specified in the message.

Cannot update the alert list on *computer name* **.**

[Server Manager]

You tried to update the Alerts list on a computer that does not support remote alert list updating. Alert lists on LAN Manager servers running versions of LAN Manager earlier than 2.1 cannot be updated remotely

Go to the computer for which you want to update the Alerts list and update it there. You might want to use Windows NT on that computer.

Cannot use 'all' as the device name with the specified command.

Try again, specifying a device by name.

Cannot verify the update setting for the linked object. Delete the card, and then create the link again.

[Cardfile]

When you link an object to a Cardfile file, you have the option to update the object either manually or automatically. Cardfile cannot determine which of these settings you have chosen.

To recreate the link, open the application in which the object was created, and copy the object, using the Copy option on the Edit menu. Then return to Cardfile, and in the Edit menu, select Paste Link.

Cannot write annotations; delete one or more files from the disk.

[Help]

You are low on disk space, and therefore cannot save annotations.

Perform the action prescribed in the message.

Cannot write boot sector.

[Utilities]

A critical sector near the beginning of the volume is unwriteable. Back up files from the drive and replace the disk.

Cannot write file allocation table

[Recover-FAT/HPFS]

Use the Chkdsk command with the /f switch to identify the problem. If you still get this message, you may have to reformat the disk. If you continue to get this message with a hard disk, contact the hardware vendor.

Cannot write information to the registry.

[Remote Access Service]

Either the Registry is corrupted or another application is using the Registry.

Try closing other running applications.

Cannot write the phone book file.

[Remote Access Service]

The Remote Access Service uses the RASPHONE.PBK file in the \SYSTEM32\RAS subdirectory of your Windows NT directory.

Make sure your disk is not full and that you have write access to this file.

Cannot write to the disk. There may be a problem with your disk or network connection. Check your disk or network connection, correct the problem, and then try again.

[MIDI Mapper (Control Panel)]

This message should appear only when you attempt to edit an object that has been saved to a network connection that is no longer available, or when the disk is write-protected.

Check your network connections. If the disk is write-protected, remove its write protection.

Cannot write to the file. Make sure the disk is not full or write-protected.

[Registry Editor]

The Registry Editor cannot write to the file.

Make sure that the disk is not write protected. Check to see that the amount of free space on the disk is equal to or greater than the size of the file. Then try again.

Cardfile cannot save *filename*.

[Cardfile]

When you make changes to a file, Cardfile locates these changes in a temporary file until you save these changes. Currently, the temporary file cannot be created.

Check to ensure that you are not low on disk space. Then, open your AUTOEXEC.BAT file and ensure that it contains both a TEMP and a TMP setting.

CD Player: Fatal Error

[CD Player]

An error was encountered by the CD Player program that will cause the program to stop.

Use Event Viewer to find out what errors preceded this one. Then look up those errors and take the appropriate action.

Challenge thread is shutting down due to some error condition.

[WINS Service]

Other activity on the computer has affected the activity of the specified thread.

Reboot the WINS server. If you still get this message, restore the WINS database from a backup copy.

Changes have been made to your disk configuration. Do you want to save the changes?

[Disk Administrator]

When you make changes in Disk Administrator, and then attempt to exit the application, you are presented with this standard confirmation message.

If you want to save the changes to your disk configuration, choose Yes. If not, choose No.

Changes have been made which require you to restart your computer. Click OK to initiate system shutdown.

[Disk Administrator]

Any time that you make changes to your disk configuration, you must restart your computer for these changes to take effect.

Choose the Shutdown option that is presented to you in Disk Administrator. If this attempt fails, shut down your system from Program Manager.

Changes will not be saved. Exit setup?

[Remote Access Service]

Cancel was chosen after some changes were made to the configuration of RAS.

Choose Yes to Exit Setup or choose No to continue configuring RAS.

Changing machine account password for account *name* failed with the following error: *text*

[Network] Net Message ID: 3224

This server found an error while changing the computer's password at the domain controller.

If you are using Windows NT, ask your network administrator to set your computer value back to the default value. Then, using the Services option in Control Panel, leave and rejoin the domain. If you are using Windows NT Advanced Server, use the Synchronize With Domain option in Server Manager to synchronize the servers.

Changing the computer name will not take effect until the system is restart. Do you wish to continue?

[Control Panel]

You chose to change the name of your computer, and this is a standard confirmation message.

If you choose to restart, the system will restart immediately.

Changing the computer name without the domain administrator first changing its name on the domain will result in domain

[Control Panel]

When a computer logs on to the domain, the computer name is compared to the list of computer names that the administrator has given to the domain. If the computer name of this computer does not match a name on this list, no one can log on from this computer, and no one can access this computer from elsewhere in the domain.

If you are sure you want to change the computer name (for example, if the administrator has already changed the name on the domain), choose Yes. Otherwise choose No.

Changing the domain name will require you to change the domain name on all Advanced Servers and Windows NT workstations in the domain. Also, any trust relationships with other domains will have to be reestablished using the User Manager for Domains. Are you sure you want to do this?

[Control Panel]

After you change the domain name, this domain will not be recognized by any Windows NT Servers, Window NT Workstations, or other domains until the name has been changed on those computers or domains.

Choose Yes to change the domain name, or No to cancel the change.

Changing the Startup Type for the *name* device may leave the system in an unusable state. Do you want to make the change?

[Server Manager]

The device might be needed to allow the system to start.

Check your documentation to make sure you want to change the startup type for this device.

Check printer on *name name*

[Network]

Something has stopped the indicated printer. It might be jammed, or out of paper or other supplies.

Check the printer.

Child windows cannot have menus.

[Kernel32]

An application, as part of its user interface, has tried to use a menu on a child window.

Contact the supplier of the running application.

CHKDSK cannot delete all corrupt directory entries.

[Chkdsk]

Due to resource constraints, Chkdsk could not remove all corrupt directory entries.

Run Chkdsk /f again.

CHKDSK could not create a directory to hold recovered files.

[Chkdsk-HPFS]

Delete any unneeded files and run the Chkdsk command with the /f switch again.

CHKDSK could not ensure the consistency of the recovered files.

[Chkdsk-HPFS]

Run the Chkdsk command with the /f switch again.

Chkdsk could not schedule this volume to be checked the next time the system boots.

[Chkdsk]

Chkdsk either couldn't mark the volume for checking using the file system FSCTL, or it couldn't insert the appropriate entries in the Registry.

Contact technical support.

CHKDSK detected an allocation error on the volume.

[Chkdsk-HPFS]

Use the Chkdsk command with the /f switch to correct the problem.

CHKDSK detected minor inconsistencies on the drive.

[Chkdsk]

CHKDSK found file system inconsistencies on the volume which do not affect file system usage.

No action is needed. The inconsistencies can be safely ignored.

CHKDSK discovered free space marked as allocated in the MFT Bitmap.

[Chkdsk-NTFS]

Chkdsk will mark the space as free so the file system can use it.

No action is needed.

CHKDSK discovered free space marked as allocated in the Volume Bitmap.

[Chkdsk-NTFS]

Chkdsk will mark the space as free so the file system can use it.

No action is needed.

CHKDSK does not run on CD-ROM drives.

[Chkdsk]

You cannot use Chkdsk on the specified drive, which is a read-only CD-ROM drive.

CHKDSK found lost data on the disk.

[Chkdsk]

CHKDSK has found data on the disk which it may be able to recover. If any files are recovered, they will appear in FOUND.xxx.

No action is needed.

CHKDSK was not able to delete all corrupted files.

[Chkdsk-HPFS]

Run the Chkdsk command with the /f switch again to delete the rest of the corrupted files.

CHKDSK was not able to resolve all hotfix references on the drive.

[Chkdsk-HPFS]

When the HPFS file system cannot write data to its proper place on the disk, it writes the data to a temporary replacement sector; these are called hot fixes. The Chkdsk utility is attempting to move the data it found in a temporary replacement sector to its correct location on the disk, but not enough disk space is available.

Delete any files you do not currently need from the disk, and then try the Chkdsk command again.

CHKDSK was not able to save all recovered data.

[Chkdsk-HPFS]

The Chkdsk utility found lost data on an HPFS volume, but was unable to recover the data by writing it to the disk in one or more files.

Delete any files you do not currently need from the disk, and then run the Chkdsk command again.

CHKDSK was not able to sort all badly-ordered directories.

[Chkdsk-HPFS]

Delete any unneeded files and run the Chkdsk command with the /f switch again.

CHKDSK was not able to write the bitmap.

[Chkdsk-HPFS]

Delete any unneeded files and run the Chkdsk command with the /f switch again.

CHKDSK was unable to adjust the size of the log file.

[Chkdsk]

There is not enough space to increase the size of the log file, or Chkdsk encountered file system corruption on a clean volume.

Delete some unneeded files and then run Chkdsk /f again.

Circular dependency: The *name* service depends on a group which starts later.

[Netevent]

The service specified depends on a group which is configured to start later than the specified service.

Ask your system administrator to either change the dependency or change the order of the GroupOrderList in the Registry.

Circular dependency: The *name* service depends on a service in a group which starts later.

[Netevent]

The service specified depends on another service that is in a group which is configured to start later than the specified service.

Ask your system administrator to either change the dependency or change the order of the GroupOrderList in the Registry.

Circular service dependency was specified.

[Kernel32]

An application tried to change the service dependency list for a service. A check of the other service dependency lists in the service database reveals at least one circular relationship between the proposed new list and existing lists. For instance, service A must start before service B in one list, but service B must start before service A in another list. Your computer has not been configured properly.

The system may not have been setup properly to run this application. Contact your system administrator.

Class already exists.

[Kernel32]

An application tried to register an application-specific window class with the system that had already been registered.

Contact the supplier of the running application.

Class does not exist.

[Kernel32]

An application tried to use an application-specific window class that had not been registered.

Contact the supplier of the running application.

Class still has open windows.

[Kernel32]

An application, as part of its user interface, has tried to unregister a class of windows, but there is at least one window of that class open in the user interface.

Contact the supplier of the running application.

Close an application and try again.

[Program Manager]

The applications that you have running are making demands on your computer's available memory that make it impossible for it to perform the requested operation.

Choose OK, close some of the applications that you have running, and then try again.

Code page operation not supported on this device

[Mode]

You have specified an invalid device and code page combination.

The Windows NT Mode command does not support changing code pages on an LPTn: device.

Command cannot be processed because the server application is busy. Wait until the server becomes available. Or try to determine which application is busy, switch to it, and then complete or cancel the action which is causing it to be busy.

[Cardfile]

A server application is the application providing the object that you want to link or embed into this Cardfile file.

Follow the user action specified in the message.

Command line too long.

[Virtual DOS Machine (VDM)]

NTVDM was unable to use the command line in the PIF file.

Use the PIF editor to change the command line in the PIF file.

Command missing from syntaxUsage : OS2 /C [*path*]command [*args*]

[OS/2 Subsystem]

The command has failed because incorrect parameters were used. The correct syntax is OS2 /P [<path>]command [<args>]

Try again, using the correct syntax for the command and the arguments.

Command read-after-write error. From device: *name*

[QIC117]

There is potentially a serious problem with the device.

Contact the hardware manufacturer or technical support.

Compare error on side *number*, **track** *number*

[Disk Compare]

The floppy disks are not identical. They differ on the specified side and track. The comparison of these two particular disks failed.

Component configuration file name missing in Registry

[Control Panel]

A file that is necessary to your configuration is missing from the Registry. Therefore, the current operation cannot be completed.

Contact technical support.

Component configuration option value missing in Registry

[Control Panel]

A value entry necessary to your configuration is missing in the Registry. Therefore, the current operation cannot be completed.

Contact technical support.

Component key missing from Configuration Registry

[Control Panel]

A component key necessary to your configuration is missing in the Registry. Therefore, the current operation cannot be completed. This message is most likely to appear after a new network component has been installed.

Reboot the computer and try again. If you still get this error remove the recently installed network component and reboot the computer, then reinstall it and reboot the computer again. If the problem continues, ask the administrator to edit the registry, removing the variable \Software\Microsoft\Ncpa\CurrentVersion\Bindfile; then choose Network from the Control Panel and choose Binding to redo the binding.

Computer name change cannot be changed at the same time as domain or workgroup information.

[Control Panel]

Finish changing the domain or workgroup information, then change the computer name.

Computer name not found

[Performance Monitor]

The computer you specified is not currently online, or the computer name was mistyped. Or, you do not have permission to access this computer, particularly if it is in a different domain.

Make sure the computer is running on the network and then try again, making sure that you have the correct computer name and that it is typed correctly. If you still get this message ask the network administrator to make sure you have permission to access that computer.

Computer not responding

[Performance Monitor]

The remote computer whose performance you are trying to monitor is not answering requests for data.

Make sure the computer is currently running on the network.

Computer name mask is not valid.

[WINS Service]

You specified an invalid computer name, or used wildcard characters incorrectly, in the Computer Name text box of the Filter.

Make sure that, except for wildcard characters, you have entered a valid computer name. The asterisk (*) wildcard can only be placed at the end of the computer name; the question mark (?) wildcard can appear anywhere.

Configuration operation attempt failed

[Control Panel]

When this message appears, you should have seen directly preceding it a message that more specifically addressing the problem.

If this message fails to help you, contact technical support.

Configuration operation was canceled by user

[Control Panel]

You canceled the setup of a software component or network adapter card. Any changes that were made will not take effect.

No action is needed.

Configuration Registry is currently locked by another process

[Control Panel]

Possibly, you attempted to activate another Setup application at the same time that you are using the Network option.

Wait until the other application that is using the process is complete, then try again.

Connect request failed

[TFTP]

The Tftp utility could not begin the file transfer process because it could not establish a network connection with the remote computer. The remote computer may be too busy at the moment, or out of resources.

Wait, then retry the Tftp command. If you still get this message, ask your network administrator to check what is happening at the remote computer.

Connection closed by remote host.

[FTP Server]

If you expected this message, no direct user action is necessary. If it is unexpected, ask your network administrator to check the condition of the remote computer.

Connection refused *text*

The attempt to connect was not successful.

Connection to device *name* **has been lost.**

[Backup]

There is no longer a connection to the named device. The physical connection (for example, the cable) may be loose, or the device may have been turned off, or in the case of a device connected to a remote computer, the remote computer may be turned off.

Make sure the physical connections are secure, that the device is turned on, and that any computer acting as a server for the device is turned on.

Connection was aborted by the remote client

[WINS Service]

Make sure that the remote WINS server and the router are both running. Then try again.

Consult your User's Guide and Reference before using the RECOVER command.

[Recover-FAT/HPFS]

Recover recovers readable data from a bad or defective disk. Data could be lost if you use the Recover command without knowing the restrictions of the command.

Continuing will cancel the connections.

[Network]

You had open connections on the network when you issued the net stop workstation command. If you have files open on any of the connections listed before this message appeared, and you continue to stop the workstation service, the files could be corrupted.

If you are sure you have no open files on any of your network connections, answer Yes to continue. Otherwise, answer No, close the open files, and try again.

Control ID not found.

[Kernel32]

An application, as part of its user interface, has requested an operation on a control (BUTTON, LISTBOX, SCROLLBAR, etc.) that does not exist in the user interface.

Contact the supplier of the running application.

Conversion ceased due to error.

[Aclconv]

The Aclconv utility was unable to convert an access control list.

Examine the log file you specified as a parameter in the Aclconv command. Resolve any problems that are listed there, then try the conversion again. Before you try again, free up as many Windows NT resources as you can. If this message persists, you will have to apply the file permissions manually, using File Manager.

Convert cannot gain exclusive access to the *drive letter* **drive, so it cannot convert it now. Would you like to schedule it to be converted the next time the system reboots (Y/N)?** *text*

[Convert]

A user or system process is using the specified drive. User processes are processes executed by running applications. System processes are processes from volumes with active paging files. An active paging file cannot be locked.

Stop other running applications and try the conversion again. Or, type Y and Convert will schedule the volume to be converted the next time the system restarts.

Convert cannot read the name translation table from *filename* **.**

[Convert]

Autoconv could not read the filename translation table created by Convert.

Run the Convert command again. Ensure that the file containing the filename translation table is not erased before the system is restarted.

Convert cannot write the name translation table to disk.

[Convert]

Either there is insufficient free space on the volume to write the name translation table, or the write failed which indicates that there are bad sectors on the volume.

Remove any unneeded files to free disk space. Also run Chkdsk /r to map bad sectors out of free space.

Convert directory to file (Y/N)? *text*

[Convert]

If a directory is too corrupt to repair, it can be converted into a file or released into free space.

Choose Yes to convert the directory into a file. Choose No to release the directory's clusters into free space.

Convert encountered a name in the root directory which could not be converted to Unicode.

[Convert]

Rerun Convert with the Nametable option, or delete files with extended characters in their names from the specified directory.

Convert encountered a name which could not be converted to Unicode in the directory *name* **.**

[Convert]

Rerun Convert with the Nametable option, or delete files with extended characters in their names from the specified directory.

Convert encountered duplicate names in the directory *name* **.**

[Convert]

Convert detected duplicate names in the specified directory. Convert failed because duplicate names are not allowed in the target file system.

Rename or delete files with duplicate names in the specified directory. Note that Convert recognizes as duplicates any names which differ only by case. For example, Convert would consider Differ.txt and differ.txt duplicate filenames.

Convert lost chains to files (Y/N)? *text*

[Chkdsk]

FAT Chkdsk has found chains of clusters that do not belong to any file. These chains can be converted to files in which case they will appear as FILExxxx.CHK in FOUND.xxx, or they can be released to free space.

Choose Y to recover the data as files. Choose N to release the data to free space.

Copy Disk Error

[File Manager]

The attempt to copy the disk failed.

Check the Event Log in Event Viewer for messages involving the disks you were copying to and from. Look up those messages, take appropriate action, and try again.

Copy process ended

[Disk Copy]

Diskcopy stopped because an error occurred. Another message about the error should follow this one.

No action is needed.

Correcting error in index *number* **for file** *filename* **.**

[Chkdsk]

Chkdsk found an error in the specified index and is correcting it.

No action is needed.

Correcting errors in the MFT mirror.

[Chkdsk-NTFS]

The backup copy of the beginning of the master file table was corrupt. Chkdsk is correcting this error.

No action is needed.

Corrupt Attribute Definition Table. CHKDSK is assuming the default.

[Chkdsk-NTFS]

The Attribute Definition Table on the NTFS volume is corrupt. NTFS will replace it with the default table.

No action is needed.

Corrupt master file table. CHKDSK aborted.

[Chkdsk-NTFS]

Chkdsk could not interpret the master file table or its mirror on the NTFS volume.

Reformat the NTFS volume. Then restore the data from a backup.

Corrupt Uppercase Table. Using current system Uppercase Table.

[Chkdsk-NTFS]

Chkdsk found that the table stored on volume to convert filenames to uppercase for collation was corrupt. Chkdsk has fixed this table.

No action is needed.

Could not accept on a socket

[WINS Service]

The computer was unable to accept a connection.

Reboot the computer.

Could not access *name* **:** *name*

[Print Manager]

An error occurred when you attempted to access a printer from Print Manager.

See the event log in Event Viewer for details on the error. Or contact your system administrator.

Could not add port: *name*

[Print Manager]

An error occurred when you attempted to add a port in Print Manager.

See the event log in Event Viewer for details on the error. Or contact your system administrator.

Could not add the form: *name*

[Print Manager]

The indicated system error prevented Print Manager from adding the form to the printer.

Look up the error message that is included at the end of this message, and take appropriate action. Then try again.

Could not allocate a responder association

[WINS Service]

WINS was unable to perform a preliminary task due to a shortage of some resource.

Check the amount of free disk space, and delete some files if necessary. Then reboot the computer.

Could not allocate a UDP Buffer

[WINS Service]

The WINS server is short of some resource, probably memory.

Close some applications and try again.

Could not allocate an explicit dialogue

[WINS Service]

The WINS server is short of some resource, probably memory.

Close some applications and try again.

Could not allocate an implicit dialogue

[WINS Service]

The WINS server is short of some resource, probably memory.

Close some applications and try again.

Could not allocate an initiator association

[WINS Service]

The WINS server is short of some resource, probably memory.

Close some applications and try again.

Could not bind an address to a socket

[WINS Service]

The WINS server is short of some resource, probably memory.

Reboot the computer.

Could not check volume *drive letter* **for errors. The conversion to** *file system* **did not take place.**

[Convert]

The Autoconv utility cannot run the Chkdsk utility on the target drive to fix any errors that may exist before the conversion is done. This may be because the drive could not be opened for the exclusive write access that Chkdsk needs.

Once your computer restart is complete, run the Convert utility from the command line.

Could not close a socket

[WINS Service]

There was a problem with the TCP/IP stack.

Reboot the computer.

Could not connect to the printer: *name*

[Print Manager]

The indicated system error prevented Print Manager from making the connection to the printer.

Look up the error message that is included at the end of this message, and take appropriate action. Then try again.

Could not continue the *name* **service on** *computer name* **.Error** *number* **:** *text*

[Server Manager]

You are temporarily unable to continue this service on the specified target server, possibly because the computer is temporarily malfunctioning.

See the event log in Event Viewer for details on this error. Then, if necessary, contact technical support.

Could not create a communication subsystem thread

[WINS Service]

The WINS server is short of some resource, probably memory.

Close some applications and try again.

Could not create printer: *name*

[Print Manager]

An error occurred when you attempted to create a printer in Print Manager.

See the event log in Event Viewer for details on the error. Or contact your system administrator.

Could not delete printer: *name*

[Print Manager]

The indicated system error prevented Print Manager from deleting the printer. It might be that you do not have permission to delete this printer. Or, the printer might be paused, with jobs waiting, in which case it cannot be deleted

Look up the error message that is included at the end of this message, and take appropriate action. If the printer is paused, resume printing. Also, make sure that you have permission to delete this printer. Then try again.

Could not delete the group ***group*****.**

[Program Manager]

The specified group has been damaged or deleted from the Registry, and as a result, Program Manager is unable to delete that group.

Attempt to recreate the group, then try again to delete it.

Could not delete the port: *text*

[Print Manager]

An error occurred when you attempted to delete a port in Print Manager.

See the event log in Event Viewer for details. Or contact your system administrator.

Could not determine the selected server. Try reselecting the server.

[Services for Macintosh (SFM)]

If reselecting the server does not work, try restarting the application. Also try restarting your system. Otherwise, contact technical support.

Could not determine the type of input.

[Network] Net Message ID: 2357

A software error occurred.

Contact technical support.

Could Not Find *filename*

[Command Prompt]

Command Prompt did not find the file or files that you specified.

Make sure you typed the filename and path correctly.

Could Not Find *filename*

[Command]

Command Prompt did not find the file or files that you specified.

Make sure you typed the filename and path correctly.

Could not find a domain controller for domain *name* **.**

[Network] Net Message ID: 3713

Either this domain does not have logon security and therefore does not have a domain controller, or its domain controller is currently unavailable.

If this domain does not have logon security, you cannot use this domain. Otherwise, retry the command. If the problem persists, ask your network administrator if the domain controller is running.

Could not find domain controller for this domain.

[Network] Net Message ID: 2453

Windows NT could not find the domain controller for this domain. This task cannot be completed unless the domain controller is running in this domain.

Start the Netlogon service on the domain controller.

Could not find file *filename* **Make sure that the required file exists and try again.**

[Convert]

The Convert utility could not find the programs that do automatic disk checking and file system conversion in the SYSTEM32 directory (in Version 1.0 of Windows NT, these two programs are named AUTOCHK.EXE and AUTOCONV.EXE). No conversion was done.

Restore those two program files from the Windows NT distribution medium to the Windows NT SYSTEM32 directory (you will have to decompress the files). Then retry the Convert command.

Could not find procedure *filename* **in** *name* **.DLL**

[Print Manager]

The specified .DLL file is corrupted, or has been overwritten by another file of the same name.

Recopy the specified .DLL from the installation disk(s).

Could not find setup file *filename*

[Print Manager]

Print Manager was unable to locate a necessary Setup file, most likely PRINTER.INF.

Ensure that this file is in your SYSTEM32 directory.

Could not find subprogram *name* **.**

[Network] Net Message ID: 3511

The specified program file could not be found.

Check that the program is in the same directory as NET.EXE, which is usually in your system directory.

Could not find the computer name *computer name* **.**

[Network]

The local computer name could not be found. This message rarely appears.

Contact technical support.

Could not find the domain controller for domain *name* **.**

[Network]

Either this domain does not have logon security and therefore does not have a domain controller, or its domain controller is unavailable.

If this domain does not have logon security, you cannot use this command. Otherwise, retry the command. If the problem persists, ask your network administrator if the domain controller is running.

Could not free a UDP Buffer

[WINS Service]

The WINS server is short of some resource, probably memory.

Check the memory resources on the computer. Stop and restart the WINS service, or reboot the computer.

Could not invoke help application.

[Disk Administrator]

Either you are low on memory, or the file containing Disk Administrator Help is not present in your Windows NT SYSTEM 32 directory.

If you have applications running, close one or more of them, then try again. If you have no other applications running, do a Search in File Manager for WINDISK.HLP and ensure that this file is in your SYSTEM32 directory.

Could not listen on the listening socket

[WINS Service]

A TCP/IP stack error has occurred. This is a serious and unlikely occurrence.

Call technical support.

Could not load *filename* **device driver.**

[Network]

Because this device driver could not be loaded, you will be unable to use the device. The problem could be due to either insufficient memory to load the device driver, or an absent or corrupt file. If this message occurs while starting the Workstation service, the service will not start.

Close some other applications and try again. If you still get this message, make sure the device driver software is on your path and is not corrupt. You might need to re-install the driver.

Could not load any transport.

[Network]

The workstation could not bind to any communications protocols.

Check the event log for other errors that occurred at the same time, and take the appropriate action. Also, choose Network in the Control Panel and make sure the configuration for the installed protocols is correct.

Could not load library *filename* .DLL

[Print Manager]

The specified .DLL file is corrupted, or has been overwritten by another file of the same name.

Recopy the specified .DLL from the installation disk(s).

Could not load library *filename* .DLL

[Print Manager]

Either the .DLL file referred to in the error message is corrupted or was overwritten by a file of the same name.

Recopy the file from the installation disks.

Could not locate a time-server.

[Network]

No computer is specified as a time-server in the configuration for the Server service.

This setting must be made in the Registry. Set the parameter in HKEY_LOCAL_MACHINE\System\CurrentControlSet\Services\LanmanServer\Para eters\TimeSource.

Could not lock the group '*name*'.

[User Profile Editor]

An attempt to lock a program group failed, most likely because User Profile Editor is unable to make necessary contact with the Registry key in which user profiles are located. This inability may be due to the permissions that have been set on the key.

In Registry Editor, make sure that the security on the key for the program group(s) that you are attempting to lock allow you Create Subkey, Delete, and Set Value permissions.

Could not look up the assoc block for an NBT association. Check if the message read is corrupted. WINS looks at bit 11-14 of the message to determine if the assoc. is from another WINS or from an NBT node. It is possible that the bits are corrupted or that there is a mismatch between what the two WINS servers expect to see in those bits (maybe you changed the value to be put in code and not increment the version number sent during assoc. setup.

[WINS Service]

Contact technical support.

Could not open *name* **:** *name*

[Print Manager]

An error occurred when you attempted to open a printer.

Consult this database for a detailed explanation of the second half of this message. Or see the event log in Event Viewer for details.

Could not open the file: *filename*

[Print Manager]

The system might be running low on disk space or access to the file might have been denied. Other problems might have occurred, but they should be specified in the message.

If you can, correct the problem specified in the message, otherwise, contact your system administrator.

Could not open the printer: *name*

[Print Manager]

An error occurred when you attempted to open a printer.

Consult this database for a detailed explanation of the second half of this message. Or see the event log in Event Viewer for details.

Could not pause document: *name*

[Print Manager]

The indicated system error prevented Print Manager from pausing the document.

Look up the error message that is included at the end of this message, and take appropriate action. Then try again.

Could not pause printer: *name*

[Print Manager]

The indicated system error prevented Print Manager from pausing the printer.

Look up the error message that is included at the end of this message, and take appropriate action. Then try again.

Could not pause the *name* **service on** *computer name* **.Error** *name* **:** *text*

[Server Manager]

You are temporarily unable to pause the specified service on the target server, possibly because the server is not started.

See the event log in Event Viewer for details on the error.

Could not purge printer: *name*

[Print Manager]

The indicated system error prevented Print Manager from purging all documents from this printer.

Look up the error message that is included at the end of this message, and take appropriate action. Also, make sure you have Full Control privileges on this printer. Then try again.

Could not read from NETBT

[WINS Service]

The WINS service will terminate due to this error.

Choose Network from the Control Panel and make sure the TCP/IP driver is installed and running. Then restart WINS.

Could not read from the UDP socket.

[WINS Service]

WINS was unable to receive a name packet.

Stop the WINS service. Then choose Network from the Control Panel and make sure the TCP/IP driver is installed and running. Finally, restart WINS.

Could not read the current virtual memory settings.

[Program Manager]

The System applet in the Control Panel cannot read Page File information from the Registry. The Registry is probably corrupt.

Contact technical support. The value of REG_MULTI_SZ in HKEY_LOCAL_MACHINE\SYSTEM\CurrentControlSet\Control\SessionManager|MemoryManagement|\PagingFiles needs to be checked by someone who is an expert user of Regedit32.

Could not register control handler with service controller *name* **.**

[Network] Net Message ID: 5724

The service controller did not start.

Check the event log with Event Viewer for more details about related errors.

Could not restart the document: *text*

[Print Manager]

The indicated system error prevented Print Manager from restarting the document.

Look up the error message that is included at the end of this message, and take appropriate action. Then try again.

Could not resume printing document: *filename*

[Print Manager]

Either the .DLL file referred to in the error message is corrupted or was overwritten by a file of the same name.

Recopy the file from the installation disks.

Could not resume printing document: *name*

[Print Manager]

The indicated system error prevented Print Manager from resuming printing of the document.

Look up the error message that is included at the end of this message, and take appropriate action. Then try again.

Could not resume printing: *text*

[Print Manager]

The indicated system error prevented Print Manager from resuming printing.

Look up the error message that is included at the end of this message, and take appropriate action. Then try again.

Could not run SETUP: *text*

[Print Manager]

The indicated system error prevented Print Manager from creating a process for Setup.

Look up the error message that is included at the end of this message, and take appropriate action. Then try again.

Could not save settings to Registry Serial Parameters area.

[Program Manager]

Either security settings prevent access to the required Registry keys, or the Registry is corrupt.

Contact technical support. The keys in Machine\System\CurrentControlSet\Services\Serial\Parameters need to be checked by someone who is an expert user of Regedit32.

Could not schedule an automatic conversion of the drive.

[Convert]

The Convert utility tried to schedule an automatic file system conversion of a drive because it could not be done now (because, for example, the drive could not be locked). The conversion could not be scheduled.

Make sure you have the privileges associated with the administrator group.

Could not set logon information for this user.

[Network] Net Message ID: 2454

This message should occur only on a down-level computer. Any action to correct the problem should be performed on that computer. The logon server could not update the logon or logoff information.

Stop and restart the Netlogon service at the server that returned this error.

Could not set printer: *name*

[Print Manager]

The indicated system error prevented Print Manager from changing one or more settings for this printer.

Look up the error message that is included at the end of this message, and take appropriate action. Then try again.

Could not set service status with service controller *name* **.**

[Network] Net Message ID: 5725

The service controller did not start.

Check the event log with the Event Viewer for more details about the service errors.

Could not set the device mode for this printer: *text*

[Print Manager]

The indicated system error prevented Print Manager from creating a new printer or changing job defaults.

Look up the error message that is included at the end of this message, and take appropriate action. Then try again.

Could not set the document details: *text*

[Print Manager]

The indicated system error prevented Print Manager from changing the details for a document.

Look up the error message that is included at the end of this message, and take appropriate action. Then try again.

Could not set the form: *name*

[Print Manager]

The indicated system error prevented Print Manager from setting the form.

Look up the error message that is included at the end of this message, and take appropriate action. Then try again.

Could not set the position of the document: *text*

[Print Manager]

The indicated system error prevented Print Manager from setting the position of the document.

Look up the error message that is included at the end of this message, and take appropriate action. Then try again.

Could not show help.

[Print Manager]

Help cannot be displayed for Print Manager. You may be low on system resources. Or PRINTMAN.HLP may be missing from your SYSTEM32 directory.

If you have a number of applications running, try closing some of them, then try again. Or place PRINTMAN.HLP in your SYSTEM32 directory.

Could not show help.

[Print Manager]

An error occurred when you attempted to open a printer.

Consult this database for a detailed explanation of the second half of this message. Or see the event log in Event Viewer for details.

Could not start one or more of the NetDDE related services. Consult your system administrator for help.

[Dynamic Data Exchange]

One or more of the following services cannot be started, possibly because it is disabled: ClipBook Server Network DDE Network DDE DSDM

Choose Services from the Control Panel and make sure these services are not disabled.

Could not start the *name* **device on** *computer name* **.Error** *number* **:** *text*

[Server Manager]

You are temporarily unable to start the specified device on the target server.

See the event log in Event Viewer for details on the error.

Could not start the *name* **service on** *computer name* **.Error** *number* **:** *text*

[Server Manager]

You are temporarily unable to start the specified service on the target server.

See the event log in Event Viewer for details on the error.

Could not stop the *name* **device on** *computer name* **.Error** *name* **:** *text*

[Server Manager]

You are temporarily unable to stop the specified device on the target server, possibly because the server is not started.

See the event log in Event Viewer for details on the error.

Could not stop the *name* **service on** *computer name* **.Error** *number* **:** *text*

[Server Manager]

You are temporarily unable to stop the specified service on the target server, possibly because the server is not started.

See the event log in Event Viewer for details on the error.

Could not transfer the file because of an invalid packet number. Try sending or receiving the file again.

[Terminal]

The term packet number designates the number of bits in a data packet. Most characters are transmitted in 7 or 8 data bits, though some computers require a setting of 5 or 6 data bits. You specified in the Communications dialog box a number of data bits Terminal cannot send.

Select the Communications option on the Settings menu, and select a different number of bits for your data packet.

Could not transfer the file because of too many tries to send or receive a data packet. Try sending or receiving the file again.

[Terminal]

When you use KERMIT protocol to send a packet, and there is a crash or malfunction on the system to which the packet is being sent, Terminal limits the times that you can try to send or receive a data packet.

When this occurs, you must begin again the entire process of sending or receiving a file.

Could not update the security descriptor for this printer: *text*

[Print Manager]

The indicated system error prevented Print Manager from updating the security descriptor for this printer.

Look up the error message that is included at the end of this message, and take appropriate action. Then try again.

Could not view the printer properties: *text*

[Print Manager]

The indicated system error prevented Print Manager from displaying the properties for this printer.

Look up the error message that is included at the end of this message, and take appropriate action. Then try again.

Couldn't determine user's logon name

[TCP/IP]

A TCP/IP utility that performs remote operations is trying to match a Windows NT user's unique security identifier (SID) with their user name and is unable to do so. This can happen, for instance, when a domain controller is not running and the utility is unable to make the match using the user names cached on your computer.

Log on to your computer with a user name that is sure to be recognized by the local computer without the use of a domain controller.

Critical resource missing from resource file

[Control Panel]

The binary file that enables the current process is corrupted. Or you are very low on memory.

If you have a number of applications running, close one or more of these, then try again. Or contact technical support.

Currency symbol cannot be empty or contain digits

[Program Manager]

The Symbol text box in the International - Currency Format dialog is blank or contains a number.

Enter one or more letters or symbols in this text box.

Current disk configuration information will be overwritten! Are you absolutely sure you want to continue?

[Disk Administrator]

If you continue, the current disk configuration information will be replaced with the specified configuration. It is advisable to have a backup copy of this information before continuing.

Current File: *filename* **Continue to finish writing this file to disk, or Abort the restore immediately without finishing the current file.**

[Backup]

A file is being written to the disk. You can either finish writing this file, or stop writing immediately.

Choose Continue to finish writing this file to disk, or choose Abort to stop the backup immediately.

Current File: *filename* **Continue to finish writing this file to tape, or Abort the backup immediately without finishing the current file.**

[Backup]

A file is being written to the tape. You can either finish writing this file, or stop writing immediately.

Choose Continue to finish writing this file to tape, or choose Abort to stop the backup immediately.

Current keyboard does not support this code page

[Mode]

Use the International option in Control Panel to select a valid code page.

Current tape is from a different tape family.

[Backup]

The tape that was just inserted is from another tape family. A tape family is a group of tapes in which backup data is continued from one tape to the next. A tape family can have one or more backup sets.

Remove the tape, and replace it with a tape from the family that you have been working with.

Current user trusted shares are inaccessible

[Dynamic Data Exchange]

You probably do not have permission to access the key HKEY_CURRENT_USER\Software\Microsoft\NetDDE in the Registry.

An experienced user of Regedit32 should check the permissions on these keys. Or, that person can delete the key and then run Setup to re-configure these keys.

Data error (cyclic redundancy check)

[Kernel32]

The operating system cannot read or write the data correctly.

If the error occurred on a hard disk, retry the command. If the error occurs again, the hard disk my have to be reformatted. If the error occurred on a floppy disk, insert a formatted floppy disk or the backup floppy disk, and retry the command.

Data of type MULTI_SZ cannot contain empty strings. Registry Editor will remove all empty strings found.

[Registry Editor]

Since the data type for this Registry entry is REG_MULTI_SZ, no empty strings are permitted. One NULL character acts as a separator; two NULL characters are interpreted as a separator followed by an empty string.

No action is needed. The empty string will be removed.

Data of type MULTI_SZ cannot contain empty strings. Registry Editor will remove the empty string found.

[Registry Editor]

Since the data type for this Registry entry is REG_MULTI_SZ, no empty strings are permitted. One NULL character acts as a separator; two NULL characters are interpreted as a separator followed by an empty string.

No action is needed. The empty string will be removed.

Data or no disc loaded

[CD Player]

You have attempted to play from an empty drive. Or you have attempted to play a disc that contains only data.

Insert an audio disc, then try again.

Date separator cannot be empty

[Program Manager]

The Separator text box in the International - Date Format dialog is blank.

Enter a separator, such as a slash, backslash, or comma, in this text box

DDE conversation is not valid.

A DDE (dynamic data exchange) is rendered invalid when the server application receives an unexpected command to paste an object.

Try the operation again. Or quit and restart.

Decimal separator cannot be empty or contain digits

[Program Manager]

The Decimal Separator text box in the International - Number Format dialog is blank or contains a number.

Enter a letter or symbol in this text box.

Default zone specified was invalid for adapter "*name* ".

[Services for Macintosh (SFM)]

The default zone name exceeded 32 characters. This will occur only if the zone name was changed by directly accessing the Registry instead of using the Network option in Control Panel.

Change the default zone name so that it is not more than 32 characters.

Delete group: *name*

[User Manager]

If you have selected the Confirmation option on the Options menu, User Manager prompts you for confirmation every time you choose to delete a user account or a user group.

If you are certain that you want to delete the selected user group, choose Yes. If not, select No to return to the User Manager menu.

Delete user: *username*

[User Manager]

If you set the Confirmation option in the Options menu, User Manager prompts you for confirmation every time you choose to delete a user account or user group.

If you are certain that you want to delete this user account or user group, select Yes. If not, choose No to return to the User Manager window.

Deleted data address mark found. From device: *name*

[QIC117]

An unexpected address mark was found on the tape.

Bulk-erase and reformat the tape, or replace it.

Deleting a user with a session is not allowed.

[Network] Net Message ID: 2231

This message should occur only on a down-level computer. Any action to correct the problem should be performed on that computer. The user currently has a session with the server.

The session must be ended before you can delete a user.

Demoting *computer name* **to Server may take a few minutes. Do you want to make the change?**

[Server Manager]

This message is intended to verify your decision to demote the specified server from the role of primary domain controller.

If you want to continue with the demotion, choose Yes. If not, choose No.

Desired zone invalid or not specified.

[Services for Macintosh (SFM)]

An incorrect value for the zone was specified directly in the Registry instead of with the Network option in Control Panel.

Use the Network option in Control Panel to set valid zones for all adapters. Then, restart the computer for the changes to take effect.

Desktop database for volume "*filename* **" could not be loaded. Starting with an empty database.**

[Services for Macintosh (SFM)]

The volume may be corrupted.

No action is needed.

Destination address required *text.*

You cannot send data without specifying a destination address.

Try again, but include a destination address.

Destination is not a directory: *text***.**

[Command Prompt]

The destination that you have specified for your expanded files is not a directory.

Specify a directory. If you are unsure of the correct syntax of the Expand command, type the command and /? at the command prompt.

Detected circular dependencies auto-starting services.

[Netevent]

An auto-start service is dependent on a chain of other services. One of the services in that chain is dependent on another service that appears earlier in the chain.

Ask your system administrator to check the configuration of your system to review the chain of dependencies. Your administrator should remove the dependency that loops back.

Detected circular dependencies demand starting *name*.

[Netevent]

The specified service is dependent on a chain of other services. One of the other services is dependent on another service that appears earlier in the chain.

Ask your system administrator to check the configuration of your system to review the chain of dependencies. Your administrator should remove the dependency that loops back.

Device *name* is not currently available.

[Utilities]

The device may be in use by another program, or it may not be online.

Make sure that the device is not in use by another program and that it is online. Then try the operation again.

Device block size differs from size with which tape was written

[Backup]

Use the device that was used to create the tape. Also, contact technical support. Be sure to record any messages and information you see for them.

Device driver *name* sent a bad BiosLinkage response.

[Network] Net Message ID: 3407

This message should occur only on a down-level computer. Any action to correct the problem should be performed on that computer. The device driver specified is incorrect. It may be incompatible with the network adapter card, or it may be out-of-date.

Use a different device driver.

Device response received when none expected.

[Remote Access Service]

One of the Remote Access configuration files probably contains invalid information.

The easiest way to resolve this problem is to reinstall Remote Access. Use the Network option in Control Panel to remove and reinstall RAS. If you are using a modem that is not supported by Remote Access, switch to a supported modem, or see "Modem Script File" in the Remote Access Service online Help for information about modifying the modem script file for your modem. The Remote Access script files (PAD.INF, MODEM.INF, and SWITCH.INF) are in the \SYSTEM32\RAS subdirectory of your Windows NT directory.

DHCP enables automatic configuration of TCP/IP parameters for your computer. Your internetwork must have a DHCP server if you want to take advantage of this feature.

[TCP/IP]

In addition to making it easier to configure your TCP/IP parameters, DHCP prevents problems that can arise when addresses are entered incorrectly, or when one address is entered on more than one computer, or when computers are moved from one area to another.

If you are not sure whether your internetwork has a DHCP server, ask your system administrator.

DHCP enables automatic configuration of TCP/IP parameters for your computer. Your internetwork must have a DHCP server running if you want to take advantage of this feature for easy configuration.

[TCP/IP]

In addition to making it easier to configure your TCP/IP parameters, DHCP prevents problems that can arise when addresses are entered incorrectly, or when one address is entered on more than one computer, or when computers are moved from one area to another.

If you are not sure whether your internetwork has a DHCP server, ask your system administrator.

DHCP failed to obtain a lease for the card with network address *address*.**On multi-homed machine all subsequent adapters will also fail to obtain lease. The following error occurred :** *text text*

[DHCP]

The network adapter card with this network address has not been leased a TCP/IP address by the DHCP server. Possibly the computer is not connected to the network or the card is not configured correctly. Or, there might be no DHCP server on this network.

Make sure the computer is physically connected to the network and the network card is correctly configured. Check with the network administrator to make sure that there is a DHCP server and that it is currently running the DHCP service.

DHCP failed to obtain a lease for the card with network address *address*. **The following error occurred :** *text*

The computer with this network address has not been leased a TCP/IP address by the DHCP server.

Ask your network administrator to look up the associated error and take the appropriate action.

DHCP failed to renew a lease for the card with network address *address*. **The following error occurred :** *text*

When the current lease for the computer with this network address expires, it will no longer have a TCP/IP address.

Ask your network administrator to look up the associated error and take the appropriate action.

DHCP failed to renew a lease for the card with network address *address*. The following error occurred : *text*

[DHCP]

When the current lease for the computer with this network address expires, it will no longer have a TCP/IP address.

Make sure the computer is physically connected to the network and the network card is correctly configured. Check with the network administrator to make sure that there is a DHCP server and that it is currently running the DHCP service.

DHCP IP address lease *name* for the card with network address *address* has been denied.

The computer using the network card with this address will not have an IP address.

Ask your network administrator to make sure that there are addresses in the free address pool of this scope. The administrator might need to add more addresses, stop excluding addresses that are no longer manually allocated.

DHCP IP address lease *name* for the card with network address *address* has been denied.

[DHCP]

The computer using the network card with this address will not have an IP address.

Ask your network administrator to make sure that there are addresses in the free address pool of this scope. The administrator might need to add more addresses, stop excluding addresses that are no longer manually allocated.

DHCP is unable to renew a lease for the card with network address *address*. The lease for IP address *address* has been terminated.

The computer using the network card with this address will not have an IP address.

DHCP is unable to renew a lease for the card with network address *address*. The lease for IP address *address* has been terminated.

[DHCP]

The computer using the network card with this address will not have an IP address.

Make sure the computer is physically connected to the network and the network card is correctly configured. Check with the network administrator to make sure that there is a DHCP server and that it is currently running the DHCP service.

DHCP received an unknown option *text* of length *number*. The raw option data is given below.

The option code was mistyped, or the option has not been defined.

Check the option code against the list of predefined options and against your custom parameters, if any. Then try again.

Dialog construction error ***text*****.**

[Remote Access Service]

The server may be running out of memory.

Try stopping other running applications and services. Also try removing and reinstalling RAS and restarting the server.

Difference encountered in alternate file data.

[Backup]

After a backup or restore operation, a difference was detected between the data in a file on the disk and the data in the same file on the tape. More information about the difference will follow in a subsequent message.

Difference encountered in Extended Attribute information.

[Backup]

A difference was detected between the permissions on a file on the disk and the permissions on the same file on the tape.

No action is needed. However, you might want to make sure the permissions are set correctly for this data.

Difference encountered in file data.

[Backup]

A difference was detected between the data in a file on the disk and the data in the same file on the tape.

No action is needed. However you might want to repeat the backup or restore operation for this file.

Difference encountered in security information.

[Backup]

A difference was detected between the permissions on a file on the disk and the permissions on the same file on the tape.

No action is needed. However, you might want to make sure the permissions are set correctly for this data.

DigiBoard adapter ***name*** **was unable to initialize properly.**

[Digi]

The specified adapter configuration could not be started.

directly access an incompatible diskette format

[Virtual DOS Machine (VDM)]

Insert a different floppy disk in the floppy disk drive and retry the operation.

Directory *name* does not exist. Do you want to create it?

[File Manager]

Using the Copy or Move command in the File menu, you specified in your destination file path the name of a directory that does not exist.

If you want to create the directory, choose Yes. If not, choose No.

Directory *directory* not found on the disk.

[Backup]

The named directory was not found on the target disk. If the directory by that name on the backup tape was restored, it did not overwrite an existing directory.

No action is needed.

Directory already exists.

[File Manager]

Using the Create Directory command on the File menu, you attempted to assign to a new directory a name assigned to a previously existing directory.

Use the Create Directory command again, and assign to the new directory a unique name.

Directory truncated.

[Chkdsk]

The directory was corrupted.

No action is needed.

Disable the write-protection on this disk or use another disk, and then try again.

[File Manager]

You attempted to write to a disk that is either write-protected or that is of the wrong density rating.

Remove the write-protection on the disk. If you still get this message, use a disk of a different density rating.

Disk *drive letter* : is write-protected. A file cannot be saved on a write-protected disk.

[Common Dialog]

Remove the disk and either replace it with a disk that is not write-protected, or remove the write protection on this disk and put it back in the drive. Then try again.

Disk Administrator can only create one partition on a removable disk.

[Disk Administrator]

If you create a partition that does not use the entire removable disk, you will not be able to use the remaining free space.

Do not partition this disk.

Disk Administrator cannot convert the active partition on disk 0 into a volume set.

[Disk Administrator]

X86 computers use the active partition on disk 0 to initiate starting the system. The system BIOS does not know how to support volume sets on this partition. Therefore, the partition cannot be part of a volume set.

Select a different partition for the volume set.

Disk Administrator cannot create extended partitions on removable media.

[Disk Administrator]

If you create a partition that does not use the entire disk, you will not be able to use the remaining free space.

Disk Administrator cannot delete the active partition on disk 0.

[Disk Administrator]

Replace the disk and put it in a disk 1 slot, then try to delete the partition. You might also try removing the active bit and then deleting the partition. This may require creating a new partition and making it active.

Disk Administrator cannot delete the partition containing Windows NT system files.

[Disk Administrator]

Windows NT is using the system files on the partition to run. In order to delete the partition where the system files are located, you would have to start another operating system and then delete the partition. If you delete the partition that contains Windows NT system files, Windows NT may not be able to start.

Disk Administrator cannot format a volume containing Windows NT system files.

[Disk Administrator]

Start a different installation of Windows NT.

Disk Administrator cannot format a volume that is not assigned a drive letter.

[Disk Administrator]

This is by design.

Assign a drive letter to this volume and try again.

Disk Administrator cannot locate fmifs.dll to perform this action.

[Disk Administrator]

Make sure the file is available. It should be the SYSTEM32 subdirectory of your Windows NT root directory. If necessary, restore the file from a backup copy.

Disk Administrator cannot mark the System Partition as non-secure.

[Disk Administrator]

You do not have the proper permission to mark the system partition as non-secure.

Disk Administrator cannot mark the System Partition secure.

[Disk Administrator]

You do not have the proper permission to mark the system partition secure.

Disk Administrator could not create a thread to perform this operation.

[Disk Administrator]

The operation could not be completed, probably due to a shortage of some resource such as memory.

Try again later. If you still get this message, close some applications and try again.

Disk Administrator has determined that one or more disks have been removed from your computer since Disk Administrator was last run, or that one or more disks are off-line. Configuration information about the missing disk(s) will be retained.

[Disk Administrator]

This is a status message, identifying the information that Disk Administrator has retained about your system configuration.

No action is needed.

Disk Administrator has determined that there are no fixed disks attached to the system, or all such disks are off-line. Click OK to exit.

[Disk Administrator]

Your system is low on memory.

Close one or more of the applications you have running, then try again to open Disk Administrator. Or use the System option in Control Panel to increase your Virtual Memory settings.

Disk Administrator has determined that this is the first time Disk Administrator has been run, or that one or more disks have been added to your computer since Disk Administrator was last run. System configuration will now be updated.

[Disk Administrator]

When you start Disk Administrator, it immediately checks your disk configuration and registers any changes that have been made to it. If disks have been removed or taken off-line, Disk Administrator retains the configuration information on these disks.

No action is needed.

Disk Administrator is already running.

[Disk Administrator]

You have attempted to activate Disk Administrator in Program Manager when a copy of Disk Administrator is already running.

Choose OK, then use the Disk Administrator that is already running.

Disk Administrator was unable to configure the Fault Tolerance Device. Mirrors and stripe sets with parity will not be initialized or regenerated.

[Disk Administrator]

The driver necessary for this operation is not present. Or, Disk Administrator was unable to access the Registry.

Attempt restarting your computer. If Disk Administrator is still unable to configure the Fault Tolerance Device, contact your technical support group.

Disk Administrator was unable to create its windows. Click OK to exit.

[Disk Administrator]

Try stopping other running applications and try the operation again.

Disk Administrator was unable to restart your computer. To ensure the integrity of your disks and data, you should initiate system shutdown from the Program Manager. Click OK to exit Disk Administrator.

[Disk Administrator]

You made changes to Disk Administrator and you were asked to restart your system from Disk Administrator for these changes to take effect. You attempted to do this, but Disk Administrator was unable to restart your computer.

Choose OK, then choose the Shutdown option from the File menu in Program Manager to initiate a system shutdown.

Disk error reading FAT *number*

[Chkdsk]

The Chkdsk command could not read one of the two file allocation tables on a FAT partition. The partition is still usable, because one of the file allocation tables can still be read. However, if the other file allocation table goes bad, the partition will be unusable.

Use the Chkdsk command with the /f option to correct the problem in the FAT partition. If you still get this message with a hard disk, back up any information you can and reformat the disk.

Disk error writing FAT

[Chkdsk]

The Chkdsk command could not write to the file allocation tables (FAT).

Use the Chkdsk command with the /f switch to correct the error. If you still get this message with a hard disk, back up any information you can and reformat the disk.

Disk Fault Tolerance Error *code*

[Network] Net Message ID: 3221

This message should occur only on a down-level computer. Any action to correct the problem should be performed on that computer. An error was recorded by the fault-tolerance system. The error is explained in the original error message.

Follow the action recommended in the original message.

Disk is full.

[Help]

You will need to free disk space to make any modifications to the currently active Help file.

Delete the unnecessary files from the disk.

Disk is not formatted.

[Utilities]

The volume has not been formatted.

Use the Format command, without the /q switch, to format the media.

Diskette has been removed or file damaged. Please verify that the diskette with the file is in the correct drive.

[Cardfile]

The file that you have attempted either to access, save, or print is saved to a floppy disk that you have removed from a disk drive.

Follow the user action specified in the message.

Do you want AUTOCHK to be run the next time that the machine reboots? [Y] [N]

[Chkdsk]

This message appears because you have attempted to run Chkdsk /f but the utility cannot lock the drive. Because Chkdsk /f cannot have exclusive access to the drive, you are asked if you want the utility to run the next time the computer is started.

Do you want to append data to this tape?

[Backup]

This is a confirmation message that appears after you have indicated that you do not want to overwrite existing data on a tape.

Choose Yes to append data or choose No to continue without appending data.

Do you want to capture this AppleTalk printing device?

[Services for Macintosh (SFM)]

Capturing a printing device means that you are configuring the device for your network. When the printing device (printer) was uncaptured, it could receive only one print job at a time. Once the device is captured, it will spool print jobs.

If you choose No, all users (including Apple® Macintosh users) will continue to be able to see the AppleTalk printing device on the network, but the device will not spool print jobs. If you select Yes, and decide to capture the printing device, Macintosh users will be able to see the printing device only under the new name given it when you selected Yes and configured the printer for the network.

Do you want to replace the data on this tape?

[Backup]

You chose to back up files onto a tape that already contains data. If you do this, the data that you back up will replace the tape's current contents.

If you want to continue with this operation, choose Yes.

Do you want to replace the security information on all existing subdirectories within *name* **?**

[Security]

You chose the "Replace Permissions on existing Subdirectories" option.

If you want the permissions that you are setting on the currently selected directory to override permissions set previously on files or subdirectories of that directory, choose Yes. If not, choose No.

Do you want to restore this file?

[Backup]

If there is a copy of the file in the target directory, you might not want to restore the file from this tape.

Choose Yes to overwrite the file on the target directory, or No to cancel the operation.

Do you want to start the Workstation service? *text* **:** *text*

[Network]

The Workstation service must be started in order to log on to the network or start other services.

Answer Yes to start the Workstation service, or answer No.

Do you want to use DHCP service to configure your IP Addresses?

[TCP/IP]

DHCP enables automatic configuration of TCP/IP parameters for your computer. It prevents problems that can arise when addresses are entered incorrectly, or when one address is entered on more than one computer, or when computers are moved from one area to another. Your internetwork must have a DHCP server if you want to take advantage of this feature.

Choose Yes to use the DHCP service, or choose No if your internetwork does not have a DHCP server.

Do you wish to delete all documents on *name* **?**

[Print Manager]

When you attempt to delete all documents (purge a printer), you are presented with this standard confirmation message.

If you want to delete all documents, choose Yes. If not, choose No.

Document item name is not valid.

[Paintbrush]

An error occurred while you were attempting to retrieve a linked object or part of an image.

Choose OK, then try again.

DosMuxSemWait did not execute; too many semaphores are already set.

[Kernel32]

All the system slots for semaphores have been taken in the function that waits for one of several semaphores to clear. This is a temporary condition; a slot will come free.

Try again later.

Drive *drive letter* **is already** *file system.*

[Convert]

The automatic file system conversion utility (Autoconv) had been scheduled to convert the file system on the specified drive the next time the computer was restarted. At restart time, Autoconv is running, but has found that the drive already has the target file system. No conversion is necessary, so no conversion will take place.

Drive *drive letter* **is nearly full.** *number* **bytes are available. Please warn users and delete unneeded files.**

[Network]

If the drive becomes too full, programs that need disk space for temporary files will fail.

Warn the users and either ask them to delete unneeded files or tell them that you will delete certain files and that they need to make copies of the files they want to keep.

Drive *drive letter* **: does not exist. Please verify that the correct drive is given.**

[Common Dialog]

Make sure you have a local or network drive assign to this drive letter. You might need to connect to a network drive using this drive letter, or you might need to connect a removable drive to your computer.

Drive *drive letter* **: does not have enough free space for the maximum paging file size specified. If you continue with this setting, the paging file will only grow to the size of the available free space.**

[Program Manager]

If all free space on the disk is taken up by the paging file, you might be unable to create new files or save your work on that disk.

Either delete some files on the drive, or reduce the maximum paging file size, or both. You can check the amount of space on the disk in File Manager.

Drive *drive letter* **: does not have enough free space for the maximum paging file size specified. If you continue with this setting, the paging file will only grow to the size of the available free space.**

[Program Manager]

While attempting to set the maximum size for a paging file, you chose a maximum size that is bigger than the current free space on that drive.

Either delete some files on the drive, or reduce the maximum paging file size, or both. You can check the amount of space on the disk in File Manager.

Drive *drive letter* **: is too small for the maximum paging file size specified. Please enter a smaller number.**

[Program Manager]

Enter a number that is smaller than the available space on the disk. You can check the amount of space on the disk in File Manager.

Drive *drive letter* **: is too small for the maximum paging file size specified. Please enter a smaller number.**

[Program Manager]

While setting the maximum size for a page file, you chose a value that is bigger than the partition containing the page file

Enter a number that is smaller than the total disk size, which you can view in File Manager. It should also be smaller than the current free space on the disk.

Drive *drive letter* **will not have the attribute bits reset during backup.**

[Backup]

The drive is read-only.

Drive *drive letter* **: does not exist. Please verify the appropriate drive was given.**

[Common Dialog]

Make sure you have a local or network drive assign to this drive letter. You might need to connect to a network drive using this drive letter, or you might need to connect a removable drive to your computer.

Drive *drive letter***: is busy and cannot be accessed. File Manager is formatting this disk.**

[File Manager]

You directed File Manager to format a disk, then attempted to access the drive on which the disk was being formatted before the formatting was completed.

Select the OK button on the Error Selecting Drive dialog box, wait until the disk is formatted, then try again.

Drive *drive letter***: is busy and cannot be accessed. File Manager is performing a disk copy.**

[File Manager]

You directed File Manager to copy a disk from one drive to another, then attempted to access one of the drives involved in this operation before the operation was complete.

Select OK, wait until the disk is copied, then try again.

Drive already SUBSTed

[Subst]

You tried to use the Subst command to assign a virtual drive to a virtual drive.

Use the Subst command to assign a physical drive to a virtual drive; that is the only way it can be used.

Drive door open

[Program Manager]

Nothing can be written to or read from the disk while the drive door is open.

Close the drive door. This might involve turning a lever or pushing the disk all the way in.

Drive not responding.

[Backup]

While enumerating the contents of the disk drive, Backup received a device error that the drive is no longer responding.

If the drive is a remote disk drive, check that the drive is available. Then try again. If the drive still does not respond, use the Hardware Setup option to test your hardware.

Drive types or diskette types not compatible

[Disk Compare]

The formats of the disks you want to copy with the Diskcopy command must be identical. This message is displayed only if the disks you have specified have different formats. For example, one floppy disk may be a 5.25-inch disk and the other may be a 3.5-inch disk.

Retry the Diskcopy command, using floppy disks with the same format.

Drive types or diskette types not compatible

[Disk Compare]

Diskcomp cannot compare unlike disks. For example, Diskcomp cannot compare a single-sided disk with a double-sided disk, nor a high-density disk with a double-density disk.

Make sure that the disks you are trying to compare are of the same type.

Drive types or diskette types not compatible

[Disk Copy]

The formats of the disks you want to copy with the Diskcopy command must be identical. This message is displayed only if the disks you have specified have different formats. For example, one floppy disk may be a 5.25-inch disk and the other may be a 3.5-inch disk.

Retry the Diskcopy command, using floppy disks with the same format.

Driver detect an internal error in its data structures for *name*.

Contact the supplier of the driver software for the named device. You might need to contact the supplier of the hardware in addition to, or instead of, the software supplier.

Driver does not support selected Baud Rate

[Virtual DOS Machine (VDM)]

Try the operation again, using a different baud rate.

Driver or device is incorrectly configured for *name*.

Contact your system administrator to reconfigure the driver or the named device.

Drives and Directories only allowed at the beginning of list

[Program Manager]

Re-write the list so that all the drives and directories are at the beginning of the list.

Due to an unexpected error the system cannot be restarted

[Drivers (CP)]

Drivers could not force the system to restart.

Shutdown the system from Program Manager, and then restart it.

During a logon attempt, the user's security context accumulated too many security IDs.

[Kernel32]

The user is a member of too many groups.

Remove the user from some groups or aliases to reduce the number of security IDs which have to be incorporated into the user's security context.

During the recovery process, the fault tolerance driver was not able to allocate needed memory.

[Disk Administrator]

Terminate some running applications and then retry the recovery process.

EA File contains no extended attributes. File deleted.

[Chkdsk]

The system file which contains extended attribute information for the FAT volume is empty, and therefore superfluous. It is removed to improve system performance.

No action is needed.

EA File has handle. Handle removed.

[Chkdsk]

The handle is an offset which contains the location of the extended attribute file. Since the extended attribute file is a system file, it cannot have extended attributes itself.

No action is needed.

EA log is unintelligible. Ignore log and Continue? (Y/N) *text*

[Chkdsk]

The extended attribute log on the FAT volume is corrupted. Continuing may cause some extended attribute information to be lost.

Each group is represented by a unique identifier which is independent of the group name. Once this group is deleted, *name* **even creating an identically named group in the future will not restore access to resources which currently name this group in the access control list.**

[User Manager]

When you choose to delete a user group in User Manager, you are presented with this standard warning.

If you still want to delete the selected user group, choose OK. If not, choose Cancel to return to the User Manager window.

Each user account is represented by a unique identifier which is independent of the username. Once this user account is deleted, *name* **even creating an identically named user account in the future will not restore access to resources which currently name this user account in the access control list.**

[User Manager]

When you choose to delete a user account in User Manager, you are presented with this warning.

If you still want to delete the selected user account, choose OK. If not, select Cancel to return to the User Manager window.

Either a required impersonation level was not provided, or the provided impersonation level is invalid.

[Kernel32]

A server has requested a security subsystem service by impersonating its client, but the client did not provide the necessary impersonation level.

Contact the supplier of the application that is running.

Either the default zone was null or the zone list was empty on a LocalTalkadapter "*name* ".

[Services for Macintosh (SFM)]

The default zone or zone list was deleted by directly accessing the Registry. The default zone could not have been made null, nor the zone list emptied if the Network option in Control Panel were used.

Use the Network option in Control Panel to specify a default zone for the LocalTalk adapter. Select Services for Macintosh and then choose Configure. Check the Enable Routing check box and then choose Advanced. Check the Seed this Network check box.

Either the specified user account is already a member of the specified group, or the specified group cannot be deleted because it contains a member.

[Kernel32]

An application has requested a change to the security accounts database that could not be carried out.

If the account is already a member of the group, there is no need to retry this. If the group cannot be deleted because it contains members, delete all members from the group and then retry.

Emulation selected is not available.

[Terminal]

Terminal is unable to emulate the type that you have designated.

Select another of the terminal emulation types listed in the Terminal Emulation dialog box. If you are unsure which terminal emulation type to use, select the DEC VT-100 (ANSI) option.

End of tape (end of tape when not expected). From device: *name*

[QIC117]

Use a different tape.

Error 87 occurred adding user ' *user name* **'. User information:**

[PORTUAS]

Error 87 indicates that PortUAS encountered an invalid parameter. The user accounts database may be corrupted.

Contact technical support.

Error 87 occurred changing user ' *user name* **'. User information:**

[PORTUAS]

Error 87 indicates that PortUAS encountered an invalid parameter. The user accounts database may be corrupted.

Contact technical support.

Error Adding Adapter Information To The Registry

[Digi]

Verify that you have the proper permissions to add the Registry key.

Error allocating buffer to hold LPC worker thread handles. The Nw Sap Agent cannot continue.

[Netevent]

There was not enough free memory for this application to run. Resources that are accessed via the SAP Agent and services that depend on the SAP Agent will not be available.

Close some applications and try again. If you get this message often you might want to install more memory.

Error allocating buffer to hold WAN notify thread handles. The Nw Sap Agent cannot continue.

[Netevent]

There was not enough free memory for this application to run. Resources that are accessed via the SAP Agent and services that depend on the SAP Agent will not be available.

Close some applications and try again. If you get this message often you might want to install more memory.

Error allocating database array. The Nw Sap Agent cannot continue.

[Netevent]

There was not enough free memory for this application to run. Resources that are accessed via the SAP Agent and services that depend on the SAP Agent will not be available.

Close some applications and try again. If you get this message often you might want to install more memory.

Error allocating hash table. The Nw Sap Agent cannot continue.

[Netevent]

There was not enough free memory for this application to run. Resources that are accessed via the SAP Agent and services that depend on the SAP Agent will not be available.

Close some applications and try again. If you get this message often you might want to install more memory.

Error allocating memory for an LPC Client structure. The Nw Sap Agent cannot continue.

[Netevent]

A client tried to communicate with this server, but the necessary memory could not be allocated on the server.

Close some applications and ask the client to try again. If you get this message often you might want to install more memory.

Error allocating memory has occurred

[Dynamic Data Exchange]

The application cannot start because there is not enough memory available.

Close some applications and try again.

Error allocating memory to hold a card structure. The Nw Sap Agent cannot continue.

[Netevent]

If this message appears during initialization, the SAP Agent cannot start and resources that are accessed via the SAP Agent and services that depend on the SAP Agent will not be available. If this message appears while the SAP Agent is running, the SAP Agent was unable to connect to a Wide Area Network (WAN) but will try again later.

If this message appears during initialization, close some applications and try again. If you get this message often you might want to install more memory. If this message appears while the SAP Agent is running, no action is needed.

Error changing *user name* **'s password. Error** *number* **occurred:** *text*

[Server Manager]

You are temporarily unable to set the password on the specified computer.

See the event log in Event Viewer for details on the error.

Error changing *computer name* **'s server role to** *name*. **Error** *name* **occurred:** *text*

[Server Manager]

You are temporarily unable to change the server role on the specified computer.

See the event log in Event Viewer for details on the error.

Error changing password on domain.

[Remote Access Service]

Try changing your password again. If you still get this message, contact your system administrator.

Error continuing Remote Access Server Service on *computer name*

[Remote Access Service]

New users cannot dial in to the Remote Access Server, but connected users can continue using the server.

Use the Event Log in Event Viewer for more information about related errors. Event Viewer is found in the Administrative Tools group. Also try stopping and restarting the Remote Access Service.

Error converting directory *name*

[Convert]

During a file system conversion from FAT to NTFS, the Convert utility was unable to convert the specified directory. Conversion was aborted at that point.

The FAT partition is still in its original (unconverted) state. Run the Chkdsk command with the /f option, then try the conversion again.

Error converting file *filename*

[Convert]

During a file system conversion from FAT to NTFS, the Convert utility was unable to convert the specified file. It will not be included in the NTFS volume file set.

The FAT partition is still in its original (unconverted) state. Run the Chkdsk command with the /f option, then try the conversion again.

Error converting file data

[Convert]

During a file system conversion from FAT to NTFS, the Convert utility was unable to move the data for a file into the NTFS file structure.

The FAT partition is still in its original (unconverted) state. Run the Chkdsk command with the /f option, then try the conversion again.

Error correction failed to correct data on tape. From device: *name*

[QIC117]

Data has been lost on the tape. The files are corrupt.

Bulk erase and reformat the tape, or replace it.

Error creating automatic statistics refresh thread.

[WINS Service]

The feature of the application that automatically refreshes statistics was unable to start, probably due to a shortage of some resource such as memory.

Close some applications and try again.

Error creating event for card list access synchronization. The Nw Sap Agent cannot continue.

[Netevent]

The application could not start because a needed resource could not be created. Resources that are accessed via the SAP Agent and services that depend on the SAP Agent will not be available.

Call technical support. Report both this message and the message that accompanies it.

Error creating event for database access synchronization. The Nw Sap Agent cannot continue.

[Netevent]

The application could not start because a needed resource could not be created. Resources that are accessed via the SAP Agent and services that depend on the SAP Agent will not be available.

Call technical support. Report both this message and the message that accompanies it.

Error creating file SERIAL.INI in the RAS directory.

[Remote Access Service]

A system error may have occurred. Serial port information is written to the SERIAL.INI file.

Verify that the SERIAL.INI file has not been deleted from the \<systemroot>\system32\ras directory.

Error Creating PCIMAC Registry Entry

[Digi]

An error occurred while writing to the Registry.

Verify that you have the proper permissions to update the Registry.

Error creating receive semaphore. The Nw Sap Agent cannot continue.

[Netevent]

The application could not start because a needed resource could not be created. Resources that are accessed via the SAP Agent and services that depend on the SAP Agent will not be available.

Call technical support. Report both this message and the message that accompanies it.

Error creating send event. The Nw Sap Agent cannot continue.

[Netevent]

The application could not start because a needed resource could not be created. Resources that are accessed via the SAP Agent and services that depend on the SAP Agent will not be available.

Call technical support. Report both this message and the message that accompanies it.

Error creating the LPC port. The Nw Sap Agent cannot continue.

[Netevent]

The application could not start because a needed resource could not be created. Resources that are accessed via the SAP Agent and services that depend on the SAP Agent will not be available.

Call technical support. Report both this message and the message that accompanies it.

Error creating the LPC thread event. The Nw Sap Agent cannot continue.

[Netevent]

The application could not start because a needed resource could not be created. Resources that are accessed via the SAP Agent and services that depend on the SAP Agent will not be available.

Call technical support. Report both this message and the message that accompanies it.

Error creating the modem detect strings.

[Remote Access Service]

Either the MODEM.INF file is corrupted or the server may be running out of memory.

Verify that the MODEM.INF file in your \<systemroot>\system32\ras directory is not corrupted. Compare the MODEM.INF file with the one on the distribution media. The structure of MODEM.INF is also covered in the Remote Access Service Administrator's Guide. Also check available disk space. Try closing other running applications and services.

Error creating thread counting event. The Nw Sap Agent cannot continue.

[Netevent]

The application could not start because a needed resource could not be created. Resources that are accessed via the SAP Agent and services that depend on the SAP Agent will not be available.

Call technical support. Report both this message and the message that accompanies it.

Error creating wan control semaphore. The Nw Sap Agent cannot continue.

[Netevent]

The application could not start because a needed resource could not be created. Resources that are accessed via the SAP Agent and services that depend on the SAP Agent will not be available.

Call technical support. Report both this message and the message that accompanies it.

Error determining role of ***computer name*****. Error** ***name*** **occurred:** ***text***

[Server Manager]

Server Manager is temporarily unable to determine the role that the specified server plays within the domain.

See the event log in Event Viewer for details on the error.

Error during disk read

[Convert]

During a file system conversion from FAT to NTFS, the Convert utility was unable to read a structure that is part of the FAT file system description.

The FAT partition is still in its original (unconverted) state. Run the Chkdsk command with the /r option on the FAT partition to map out bad (unreadable) sectors. Then try the conversion again.

Error during disk write

[Convert]

During a file system conversion from FAT to NTFS, the Convert utility was unable to write a structure that is part of the NTFS file system description.

The FAT partition is still in its original (unconverted) state. Run the Chkdsk command with the /r option on the FAT partition to map out bad (unwriteable) sectors. Then try the conversion again.

Error encountered during configuration/reconfiguration of WINS.

[WINS Service]

The computer might be running out of memory.

Close some applications and try setting your WINS configurations again. If you still get this message, reboot the computer and try again.

Error encountered reading data file.

[Aclconv]

The Aclconv utility was either unable to read the next access control list from the input data file, or was unable to write the converted access control list to the Windows NT resource.

The data file which is associated with this access control list, which had been imported into the NTFS file system earlier by the Convert utility, is still good. It is only the access control list that cannot be converted. Use Windows NT File Manager to locate any converted files that do not have access control lists associated with them, and add file security manually, using File Manager.

Error encountered reading log file.

[Aclconv]

The disk may have a bad sector. The Aclconv log file cannot be read. Results for this run of Aclconv cannot be displayed.

Error encountered while getting the selected server name.

[FTP Server]

Reboot the computer.

Error encountered writing log file.

[Aclconv]

The Aclconv utility was unable to write an entry to the log file.

Since the log file is suspect, you will have to use Windows NT File Manager to manually confirm that all the access control list (ACL) conversions you specified were completed.

Error getting ComputerName.

[Program Manager]

The System option box currently cannot display the name of the computer, possibly due to a network problem.

Choose OK and continue.

Error getting ComputerName.

[Program Manager]

The System option box currently cannot display the name of the computer, possibly due to a network problem.

Choose OK and continue.

error getting console input handle, code *code*

[FTP Server]

The FTP service could not complete a preliminary step toward asking for your password. The service has failed.

Restart your computer and try again. If you still get this message, call technical support, and report this message and the error code displayed at the end of the message.

error getting console mode, code *code*

[FTP Server]

The FTP service could not complete a preliminary step toward asking for your password. The service has failed.

Restart your computer and try again. If you still get this message, call technical support, and report this message and the error code displayed at the end of the message.

error getting console output handle, code *code*

[FTP Server]

The FTP service could not complete a preliminary step toward asking for your password. The service has failed.

Restart your computer and try again. If you still get this message, call technical support, and report this message and the error code displayed at the end of the message.

Error getting TCP/IP information from the registry.

[Remote Access Service]

The Registry is corrupted. The information is needed to be able to read messages that are sent using this protocol. Also, the server may be running out of memory.

Remove and reinstall RAS. Try closing other running application and services to free memory.

Error getting UserName.

[Program Manager]

The System option box currently cannot display the user name, possibly due to a network problem.

Choose OK and continue.

Error getting UserName.

[Program Manager]

The System option box currently cannot display the user name, possibly due to a network problem.

Choose OK and continue.

Error in compressed input file format: ***filename*****.**

[Command Prompt]

The compressed file contains an error.

Use the file from the MS-DOS installation disk to make another copy. If the error is on the installation disk, contact technical support for a new disk.

Error in extended attribute log.

[Chkdsk]

Chkdsk found that the extended attribute log was corrupt. If Chkdsk was invoked with the /f parameter, it will fix the corruption.

No action is needed.

Error in IOCTL call.

[Format]

Make sure the floppy disk is in the drive and that the drive is ready. After that, if this message reappears, there may be a hardware problem with the drive or controller. Run hardware diagnostics and/or contact the hardware supplier.

Error Init routine failed

[OS/2 Subsystem]

The Windows NT OS/2 subsystem cannot start up. A required dynamic-link library may be missing or corrupted.

Try running the OS/2 application again. If you still get this message, contact your system administrator. The Windows NT OS/2 subsystem may need to be reinstalled.

Error invalid segment number

[OS/2 Subsystem]

The OS/2 subsystem detected a segment number that was not correct in a .DLL or .EXE file, or the file is unusable.

Either restart the OS/2 subsystem or replace the .DLL or .EXE file. Then retry the application. If you still get this message, run these same application files under the OS/2 operating system, if you can. If you get a comparable message under OS/2, then contact the supplier of the application. If the application runs under OS/2, contact your technical support group about a problem with the Windows NT OS/2 subsystem.

Error loading "*filename* " DLL functions

[Dynamic Data Exchange]

Functions in the .DLL file will not be available because the instructions could not be loaded. Commands using these functions will not work.

Error loading "*filename* " DLL:*text.*

[Dynamic Data Exchange]

Functions in the .DLL file will not be available because the instructions could not be loaded. Commands using these functions will not work.

Error locating domain controller with user account information

[Remote Access Service]

Use the Event Log in Event Viewer to see information about related errors. Event Viewer is found in the Administrative Tools group.

Error module marked invalid

[OS/2 Subsystem]

The OS/2 subsystem task manager cannot run an application.

There were probably errors when the application was created. If you can, run these same application files under the OS/2 operating system. If you get a comparable message under OS/2, then contact the supplier of the application. If the application runs under OS/2, contact your technical support group about a problem with the Windows NT OS/2 subsystem.

Error occurred while processing: *text.*

[Command]

See the event log in Event Viewer for details on the error. Then contact your system administrator.

Error occurred while processing: *text.*

[Command Prompt]

See the event log in Event Viewer for details on the error. Then contact your system administrator.

Error on *drive letter*.

[Backup]

You have attempted to use a tape that Backup does not support.

Insert a different tape, then try again.

Error on getsockopt IPX_MAX_ADAPTER_NUM. Data is the error code. The Nw Sap Agent cannot continue.

[Netevent]

The application could not start because needed information could not be obtained. It might be that you do not have enough free memory. Resources that are accessed via the SAP Agent and services that depend on the SAP Agent will not be available.

Close some applications and try again. If you still get this message, call technical support and report both this message and the message that accompanies it.

Error on server : *text*

[TCP/IP]

Look up the indicated error and take appropriate action. Then try again.

Error on the tape in *drive letter*.

[Backup]

You have attempted to use a tape that Backup does not support.

Insert a tape with a different format into the drive.

Error opening a catalog file, check available disk space.

[Backup]

An error occurred while an internal catalog file was being opened.

Use File Manager to check the available disk space. Select the root directory and then read the disk space statistics from the status line at the bottom of the window. If necessary, delete some files to free disk space. Then return to the Backup window and retry the catalog operation.

Error opening file MODEM.INF in the RAS directory.

[Remote Access Service]

The server may be running out of memory or the MODEM.INF file has been deleted or is corrupted.

Try stopping other running applications and services. Also try removing and reinstalling RAS and restarting the server. Compare the MODEM.INF file in your \<systemroot>\system32\ras directory with the one from the distribution media.

Error opening file PAD.INF in the RAS directory.

[Remote Access Service]

The server may be running out of memory or the PAD.INF file may have been deleted or is corrupted.

Try stopping other running applications and services. Also try removing and reinstalling RAS and restarting the server. Compare the MODEM.INF file in your \<systemroot>\system32\ras directory with the one from the distribution media.

Error opening local file *filename*

[FTP Server]

During an Ftp file transfer, the Ftp utility was unable to open a file on your computer.

Make sure the file is not opened or locked by another user or application, and make sure that you have permissions to read this file and the directory it is in. Then try again.

error opening script file *filename*

[FTP Server]

You specified the -s switch with the TCP/IP Ftp command, along with the name of a text file that contains commands the Ftp utility will automatically run when it starts up (a script file). The Ftp utility was unable to open the script file.

Determine the correct path to the script file and retry the Ftp command, using that path with the -s switch.

Error opening the log file *filename***.**

[Backup]

The log file contains all the messages that were sent during a backup or restore. This file could not be opened, and therefore was not written to.

No action is needed.

Error ordinal not found *application.*

[OS/2 Subsystem]

The Windows NT OS/2 subsystem task manager cannot run this application. The application might not be supported by the Windows NT OS/2 subsystem, or it might not be correctly installed.

Reinstall the application and try to run it again. If you still get this message, contact your technical support group.

Error OS/2 error code *code.*

[OS/2 Subsystem]

The OS/2 subsystem task manager was unable to run an application because the relocation chain for the OS/2 application exceeded the segment limit.

Ask your system administrator or technical support staff to interpret the OS/2 error code that is displayed at the end of the message. Use OS/2 documentation to do that. Then take appropriate action.

Error pausing Remote Access Server Service on *computer name*

[Remote Access Service]

The server may be down or you may have too many applications running. A network or system error may have occurred.

Use the Event Log in Event Viewer to see information about related errors. Event Viewer is found in the Administrative Tools group.

Error performing inpage operation.

[Kernel32]

Retry the operation. If you still get this message, contact your system administrator. You may need to relocate your paging file.

Error positioning in a catalog file. The file may be corrupt.

[Backup]

An error occurred while finding the physical location of part of an internal catalog file. A corrupted catalog file renders Backup unable to position on a tape.

Exit the application (which will delete catalog files), then try again.

Error procedure not found *name*.

[OS/2 Subsystem]

The OS/2 subsystem cannot find the procedure named in the message in an application.

Reinstall the application and try to run it again. If you get this same message, contact your technical support staff.

Error reading a catalog file, the file may be corrupt.

[Backup]

An error occurred while a tape catalog file was being read. You may have a corrupted catalog file. It may not be possible to use the catalog to make selections.

Exit the application, which will delete disk catalog files, then recatalog the tape.

Error reading alternate file data.

[Backup]

Another process may be accessing the file in an exclusive mode.

Verify that another process is using the file. If not, then use the Chkdsk /f command to verify that the file is closed.

Error reading backup file.

[Repair Disk]

Restore could not read this backup file. The file is probably corrupt.

Try again, using a different backup file.

Error reading configured ISDN port information from the registry.

[Remote Access Service]

An inconsistency exists between what is configured on the computer and what is installed.

Delete the \\HKEY_LOCAL_MACHINE\SOFTWARE\Microsoft\Ras\TapiDevices key from the Registry and then reconfigure RAS.

Error reading directory *name*

[Convert]

The FAT or HPFS volume may be corrupted. Run the Chkdsk utility with the /f option and try the conversion again.

Error reading directory.

[Format]

There was an error reading a directory during a disk formatting operation.

If the error occurred on your hard disk, try to format it again. Then, if you still get this message, call your hardware supplier to determine the problem. If the error occurred on a floppy disk, discard the disk.

Error reading Extended Attribute information.

[Backup]

An error occurred while the application was reading security information for one or more files.

No action is needed. However, you might want to make sure the permissions are set correctly for this data.

Error reading file data.

[Backup]

An error occurred while the data in the file was being read.

Look up the accompanying error message for more details and suggested action.

Error reading file MODEM.INF in the RAS directory. Reading modem entry *text*

[Remote Access Service]

The server may be running out of memory.

Try stopping other running applications and services. Also try removing and reinstalling RAS and restarting the server.

Error reading file PAD.INF in the RAS directory.

[Remote Access Service]

The server may be running out of memory.

Try stopping other running applications and services. Also try restarting the server. If you continue to see this message, contact technical support.

Error reading file SERIAL.INI in the RAS directory.

[Remote Access Service]

Verify that the SERIAL.INI file is in your \<systemroot>\system32\ras directory. If so, then use the Network option in Control panel to reconfigure RAS.

Error reading help file.

[Help]

There may be an error in the DOSHELP.HLP file.

If you continue to see this message, create a new copy of the file from your Windows NT installation medium (you will have to decompress the file).

Error reading partition table.

[Format]

The Format command could not read the partition table.

Use Disk Administrator to repartition the hard disk, then try formatting it again. After that, if this message reappears, run hardware diagnostics on the drive and controller and/or contact the hardware supplier.

error reading password

[FTP Server]

The password in an Ftp utility script file is invalid.

Use the text editor of your choice to change the password in the script file so that the Ftp utility can carry out the rest of the script file commands. Then try again.

Error registering window class

[Volume Control]

You attempted to run Volume Control, and the application was unable to generate a window.

Contact your system administrator.

Error Removing Adapter Information From The Registry

[Digi]

An error occurred while deleting a Registry key.

Verify that you have the proper permissions to remove the Registry key.

Error requesting data from Device IO Control. Returning IO Status Block.

[Services for Macintosh (SFM)]

Performance Monitor is unable to query the AppleTalk protocol driver for performance data. Your system may be low on resources.

Check the Event Log in Event Viewer for related errors. Be sure to make a note of this information to relay it to technical support.

error restoring console mode, code *code*

[FTP Server]

The FTP service could not complete a preliminary step toward asking for your password. The service has failed.

Restart your computer and try again. If you still get this message, call technical support, and report this message and the error code displayed at the end of the message.

Error restoring the file ***filename*.**

[Backup]

The named file could not be restored. An accompanying message provides more information.

Examine the accompanying message for information about the specific errors.

Error sending an AT command to the modem. Make sure the modem is powered on and connected to the port.

[Remote Access Service]

The modem cannot be used to dial out or receive calls until the modem is properly connected to the port.

error setting console mode, code *code*

[FTP Server]

The FTP service could not complete a preliminary step toward asking for your password. The service has failed.

Reboot your computer and try again. If you still get this message, call technical support, and report this message and the error code displayed at the end of the message.

Error starting LPC worker thread. The Nw Sap Agent cannot continue.

[Netevent]

The application could not start because a needed resource could not be created. Resources that are accessed via the SAP Agent and services that depend on the SAP Agent will not be available.

Call technical support. Report both this message and the message that accompanies it.

Error starting receive thread. The Nw Sap Agent cannot continue.

[Netevent]

The application could not start because a needed resource could not be created. Resources that are accessed via the SAP Agent and services that depend on the SAP Agent will not be available.

Call technical support. Report both this message and the message that accompanies it.

Error starting the *name* **service on** *computer name*. **Error** *number* **occurred:** *text*

[Server Manager]

The specified service on the specified target server cannot be started.

See the event log in Event Viewer for details on the error. Then, if necessary, start the service on the local computer itself.

Error starting wan check thread. The Nw Sap Agent cannot continue.

[Netevent]

The application could not start because a needed resource could not be created. Resources that are accessed via the SAP Agent and services that depend on the SAP Agent will not be available.

Call technical support. Report both this message and the message that accompanies it.

Error starting wan worker thread. The Nw Sap Agent cannot continue.

[Netevent]

The application could not start because a needed resource could not be created. Resources that are accessed via the SAP Agent and services that depend on the SAP Agent will not be available.

Call technical support. Report both this message and the message that accompanies it.

Error starting worker thread. The Nw Sap Agent cannot continue.

[Netevent]

The application could not start because a needed resource could not be created. Resources that are accessed via the SAP Agent and services that depend on the SAP Agent will not be available.

Call technical support. Report both this message and the message that accompanies it.

Error stopping Remote Access Server Service on *computer name*

[Remote Access Service]

You will not be able to prevent users from dialing in using the Remote Access Service.

Restart the system.

Error stopping the *name* **service on** *computer name*. **Error** *number* **occurred:** *text*

[Server Manager]

The specified service on the specified target server cannot be stopped at this time.

See the event log in Event Viewer for details on the error. Then, if necessary, stop the service on the local computer itself.

Error synchronizing *computer name* **with its primary. Error** *name* **occurred:** *text*

[Server Manager]

Server Manager is temporarily unable to resync the specified target server with its domain controller.

See the event log in Event Viewer for details on the error. Then, if necessary, contact technical support.

Error while setting up environment for the application.

[Virtual DOS Machine (VDM)]

This occurs either because there is not enough disk space for the page file, or because of problems with entries in the Registry.

Delete some files to free disk space and try again. If you still get this message, reinstall Windows NT.

Error writing a catalog file, check available disk space.

[Backup]

An error occurred while an internal catalog file was being written to. A bad spot has been detected on your disk. Or there is not enough space on the target disk.

Use File Manager to check the available disk space. Select the root directory and then read the disk space statistics from the status line at the bottom of the window. If necessary, delete some files to free disk space. Then return to the Backup window and retry the catalog operation.

Error writing alternate file data.

[Backup]

Another process may be accessing the file in an exclusive mode.

Verify that another process is using the file. If not, then use the Chkdsk /f command to verify that the file is closed.

Error writing directory.

[Format]

There was an error writing to a directory.

If the error occurred on your hard disk, try to format it again. Then, if you still get this message, call your hardware vendor to determine the problem. If the error occurred on a floppy disk, discard the disk.

Error writing Extended Attribute information.

[Backup]

An error occurred while the application was writing security information for one or more files.

No action is needed. However, you might want to make sure the permissions are set correctly for this data.

Error writing FAT.

[Format]

There was an error while writing to your file allocation table (FAT).

If the error occurred on your hard disk, try to format it again. Then, if you still get this message, call your hardware vendor to determine the problem. If the error occurred on a floppy disk, discard the disk.

Error writing file data.

[Backup]

An error occurred while the data in the file was being written.

Look up the accompanying error message for more details and suggested action.

Error writing file SERIAL.INI in the RAS directory.

[Remote Access Service]

The server may be running out of memory.

Try stopping other running applications and services. Also try removing and reinstalling RAS and restarting the server. If you continue to see this message, contact technical support.

Error writing partition table.

[Format]

The Format command could not write the partition table.

Use Disk Administrator to repartition the hard disk and then try formatting it again. After that, if this message reappears, run hardware diagnostics on the drive and controller and/or contact the hardware vendor.

Error writing to *name* **for Document** *name* **:** *name* **Do you wish to retry or cancel the job?**

[Print Manager]

If you choose Retry and still get this message, check the device to make sure it is working properly. Also, check the event log for messages that appeared about the same time as this one involving this device or the connection to it. If you choose Cancel, the job will have to be resubmitted.

Error writing to *name* **:** *name* **Do you wish to retry or cancel the job?**

[Print Manager]

If you choose Retry and still get this message, check the device to make sure it is working properly. Also, check the event log for messages that appeared about the same time as this one involving this device or the connection to it. If you choose Cancel, the job will have to be resubmitted.

Error writing to disk for Document *name* **:** *name* **Do you wish to retry or cancel the job?**

[Print Manager]

Make sure that the disk has enough room for the document and that it is working properly. Then choose Retry. Also, check the event log for messages that appeared about the same time as this one involving this drive or the connection to it. If you choose Cancel, the job will have to be resubmitted. If you choose Cancel, the job will have to be resubmitted.

Error(s) were found during the operation.

[Backup]

One or more errors occurred during the most recent operation.

Examine the backup error log or the summary window for more information about the specific errors.

Error: *text* **: Adapter "***text* **" is not enabled for DHCP**

[IP]

You tried to perform a DHCP operation, but the adapter card does not support DHCP.

Error: *number*

[Minesweeper]

This is a general error message, designed to inform you of unusual conditions in the system.

See the Applications log in Event Viewer for details. Or exit and restart Minesweeper.

Error: Adapter "*name* **" is not bound to TCP/IP**

[IP]

You tried to perform an action that requires that the adapter be bound to TCP/IP.

Choose the Network option from Control Panel. Select TCP/IP Protocol from the Installed Network Software text box. Then choose Configure, and select the adapter specified in this message from the Adapter list box.

Error: Command line arguments conflict

[IP]

You tried to release and renew the same IP address.

Try again, making sure you do not specify the same address for the /release and /renew options.

Error: No adapters bound to TCP/IP

[IP]

Choose Network from the Control Panel. Select TCP/IP Protocol from the Installed Network Software text box. Then choose Configure, and choose an adapter from the Adapter drop-down list.

Error: No adapters bound to TCP/IP are enabled for DHCP

[IP]

You tried to perform a DHCP operation, but the adapter card does not support DHCP.

ERROR: Out Of Memory

[User Manager]

Close some applications and try again.

Error: Releasing adapter "*name* "

[IP]

An error occurred while attempting to release the DHCP lease on the adapter. It might be that the system is out of memory. This problem should be very rare.

Try again later. Or, reboot your computer and try again.

Error: Renewing adapter "*name* "

[IP]

An error occurred while attempting to renew the DHCP lease on the adapter. It might be that the system is out of memory. This problem should be very rare.

Try again later. Or, reboot your computer and try again.

Error: The adapter name "*name* " is invalid

[IP]

The adapter name you specified on the IPCONFIG command line is not valid.

For a list of available adapters, type IPCONFIG/ALL. Then enter the correct information for one of these adapters.

ERROR: Unable to create terminal thread

[TCP/IP]

The TCP/IP remote utility operation cannot be carried out now because a necessary system resource is not available.

This is probably a temporary condition. Wait a few seconds and retry the remote command. If you still get this message, contact your technical support group.

Error: Unrecognized command line argument "*text* "

[IP]

For a list of valid arguments, type IPCONFIG/? at the command prompt.

Errors found, F parameter not specified Corrections will not be written to disk.

[Chkdsk]

The Chkdsk command found errors on the disk, but Chkdsk will not correct them because you did not specify the /f switch.

To correct disk errors, use the Chkdsk command with the /f switch.

Errors found. CHKDSK cannot continue in read-only mode.

[Chkdsk-NTFS]

When Chkdsk runs on an NTFS volume, it uses several passes (unlike Chkdsk on a FAT volume, which uses one pass). Passes of NTFS Chkdsk depend on previous passes to write error information to disk, which cannot be done in read-only mode.

To fix the errors on the NTFS volume, rerun Chkdsk with the /f option.

Errors occurred while saving the profile file. The profile was partially saved.

[Network] Net Message ID: 2375

This message should occur only on a down-level computer. Any action to correct the problem should be performed on that computer. You are logged on with an account that does not have sufficient privilege to save the server's entire current configuration. Only part of the configuration was saved to the profile.

Log on with an account that has administrative privilege (or server operator privilege) before saving a server profile.

Exec format error *filename.*

The executable file cannot be used. It might be corrupt.

Restore the file from a backup copy and try again

EXPORT path *path* **cannot be found.**

[Network] Net Message ID: 3219

This message should occur only on a down-level computer. Any action to correct the problem should be performed on that computer. The specified export path does not exist.

Check the spelling of the EXPORTPATH entry in the configuration file. This entry must specify a directory that exists.

Extended Error *number*

[Mode]

A Windows NT system utility tried to access an error message stored in the system files, but a problem occurred.

Retry the operation. If you still get this message, contact your system administrator. You may have to reinstall one or more system files.

Extended Error *number*

[Replace]

A Windows NT system utility tried to access an error message stored in the system files, but a problem occurred.

Retry the operation. If you still get this message, contact your system administrator. You may have to reinstall one or more system files.

Extended Error *number*

[Xcopy]

A Windows NT system utility tried to access an error message stored in the system files, but a problem occurred.

Retry the operation. If you still get this message, contact your system administrator. You may have to reinstall one or more system files.

Extremely Low on Memory, unable to load group ***group*****.**

[Program Manager]

Choose System from Control Panel. Then choose Virtual Memory and increase the size of your paging file. Restart your computer. If you still get this message, contact technical support.

Facts dialog creation failure

[Control Panel]

An internal error occurred in the Network component of the Control Panel.

Reboot the computer, then choose Network from the Control Panel and choose Binding to redo the binding. If the problem continues, ask the administrator to do the following: Edit the registry, removing the variable \Software\Microsoft\Ncpa\CurrentVersion\Bindfile. Then choose Network from the Control Panel and choose Binding to redo the binding. If the problem still occurs, remove the recently installed network components, reboot the computer, and reinstall the network components.

Failed to access copyright data base.

[Fonts (CP)]

The Registry has not been set for typeface conversion, or it has become corrupt.

Re-install Windows NT.

Failed to access NBT driver *name*

[TCP/IP]

The TCP/IP NBTSTAT utility is unable to gather statistics about the TCP/IP connections using NetBIOS over TCP/IP (NBT).

Ask your system administrator to check the Windows NT Registry in your computer to make sure the driver named in the message is installed properly.

Failed to authenticate with *computer name***, a Windows NT domain controller for domain** *name***.**

[Network] Net Message ID: 3210

This server was denied access to the security database by the domain controller. Until this problem is corrected, the server cannot synchronize user account information with the domain controller.

Stop and restart the Netlogon service at this server.

Failed to carry out command.

Specify a valid command.

Failed to change link update options.

[Write]

You are probably low on memory.

Close one or more of the applications that you have running, then try again.

Failed to communicate with the source application.

[Write]

You attempted an OLE (object linking and embedding) operation on a Write document, but Write was unable to communicate with the application in which the object was created. You may be low on memory.

Close one or more of the applications that you have running, then try again.

Failed to convert input strings to unicode strings.

[AT-Network]

An application failed to convert input text to unicode text. Your system may be out of memory.

Contact your system administrator.

Failed to create child window.

Most likely, you are low on system resources, and as a result, Object Packager was unable to create a window.

Close one or more open applications or windows, then try the operation again.

Failed to create new object.

An internal software error has occurred. Or you are low on system resources.

Close one or more of the applications or windows that you have open. If the problem persists, shut down and restart Windows NT.

Failed to create object.

[Write]

You attempted unsuccessfully to embed an object into a Write document. You may be low in memory.

Close one or more of the applications that you have running, then try again.

Failed to delete object.

[Write]

You attempted unsuccessfully to delete an object from a Write document. You may be low on memory.

Close one or more of the applications that you have running, then try again.

Failed to edit/play object.

[Write]

You attempted unsuccessfully to edit an embedded or linked sound object in a Write document. You may be low on memory.

Close one or more of the applications that you have running, then try again.

Failed to freeze object.

The server application has malfunctioned. Or you have attempted to perform an operation on an object that no longer exists.

Try the operation again. Then contact your system administrator.

Failed to gather NBT status *code*

[TCP/IP]

The NBTSTAT utility was unable to complete the system call or a sockets library call named in the message.

Ask your network administrator to interpret the error code displayed at the end of this message, and take appropriate action.

Failed to gather NBT status *code*

[NBTSTAT-TCP/IP]

The NBTSTAT utility was unable to complete the system call or a sockets library call named in the message.

Ask your network administrator to interpret the error code displayed at the end of this message, and take appropriate action.

Failed to initialize device list. *text*

[Remote Access Service]

The device list could not be read because it is corrupted.

Use the Network option in Control Panel to remove and reinstall RAS from the installation disks. Also, compare the MODEM.INF and PAD.INF RAS information files with the distributed files. The files should be in your \<systemroot>\system32\ras directory.

Failed to initialize port list. *text*

[Remote Access Service]

The port list could not be read so available ports cannot be configured to use RAS.

Use the Network option in Control Panel to remove and reinstall RAS from the installation disks.

Failed to initialize the card with network address *address***.**

The computer using this network card will not be able to use the TCP/IP protocol because it could not receive TCP/IP configuration information from the DHCP server.

Failed to initialize *application*

[IP]

The application could not start. This is probably due to insufficient free memory. Or, an error might have been introduced while editing the Registry.

Correct any recent changes to the Registry and try again. If you still get this message, close some applications to free memory and try again.

Failed to launch help.

[WINS Service]

Either the help file could not be found, or there was not enough of some resource such as memory.

Make sure the .HLP file is present and is not corrupt. If necessary, restore the file from a backup copy. If the file is available, close some applications and try again.

Failed to load object. Close other applications to free memory, then reopen this document.

[Write]

Write was unable to load an object due to a lack of system resources.

Follow the user action specified in the message.

Failed to load the profile *text* for user *user name*.

[Workstation-Logon]

Because the specified profile could not be loaded, you will use the settings provided by the default profile during this session.

Ask the administrator to look up the accompanying error and take appropriate action. Then try logging in again.

Failed to load the profile *text* for user *user name*. See below for error code.

[Workstation-Logon]

Because the specified profile could not be loaded, you will use the settings provided by the default profile during this session.

Ask the administrator to look up the accompanying error and take appropriate action. Then try logging in again.

Failed to make unicode string out of *text*.

[AT-Network]

An application failed to convert input text to unicode text.

Contact your system administrator.

Failed to obtain Clipboard.

[Cardfile]

You attempted to paste text to the Clipboard, and it is either being used, or is locked open by another application.

If the Clipboard is locked open, close the application that has it locked open. Or wait for the application to finish using the Clipboard, then try again.

Failed to obtain necessary Local Security information.

[Control Panel]

The Network application was unable to determine the domain of which you are a member. You may be very low on memory.

Close some of the applications that you have running, then try again.

Failed to read file.

The server application has malfunctioned. Or you have attempted to perform an operation on an object that no longer exists.

Try the operation again. Then contact your system administrator.

Failed to read object.

The server application has malfunctioned. Or you have attempted to perform an operation on an object that no longer exists.

Try the operation again. Then contact your system administrator.

Failed to read object.

[Write]

Write cannot read the currently selected object, most likely because of a lack of system resources.

Close one or more of the applications that you have running, and then try again.

Failed to receive NEB message *code*

[TCP/IP]

The NBTSTAT utility was unable to complete the system call or a sockets library call named in the message.

Ask your network administrator to interpret the error code displayed at the end of this message, and take appropriate action.

Failed to receive NEB message *code*

[NBTSTAT-TCP/IP]

The NBTSTAT utility was unable to complete the system call or a sockets library call named in the message.

Ask your network administrator to interpret the error code displayed at the end of this message, and take appropriate action.

Failed to receive XEB message *code*

[TCP/IP]

The NBTSTAT utility was unable to complete the system call or a sockets library call named in the message.

Ask your network administrator to interpret the error code displayed at the end of this message, and take appropriate action.

Failed to receive XEB message *code*

[NBTSTAT-TCP/IP]

The NBTSTAT utility was unable to complete the system call or a sockets library call named in the message.

Ask your network administrator to interpret the error code displayed at the end of this message, and take appropriate action.

Failed to reconnect link to server.

You attempted to reconnect an object to its server application, and this attempt failed. The server application has malfunctioned, or you have attempted to perform an operation on an object that no longer exists.

Try the operation again. Then contact your system administrator.

Failed to register document.

The server application has malfunctioned. Or you have attempted to perform an operation on an object that no longer exists.

Try the operation again. Then contact your system administrator.

Failed to register document.

[Paintbrush]

The link between a Paintbrush file and a document has been broken.

Reestablish the broken link.

Failed to register icon "*name* " with the File Server for Macintosh service.

[Services for Macintosh (SFM)]

The server may be running out of memory or the Registry is corrupted.

First, try stopping other running applications and services. If you continue to see this message, use the Network option in Control Panel to remove and reinstall Services for Macintosh.

Failed to register server.

The server application has malfunctioned. Or you have attempted to perform an operation on an object that no longer exists.

Try the operation again. Then contact your system administrator.

Failed to register server.

[Paintbrush]

The link between Paintbrush and the application to which a bitmap is linked has been broken.

Reestablish the link.

Failed to save file.

Most likely, your disk is full. Or you attempted to save the file to a network share to which you are no longer connected.

If your disk is full, delete unnecessary files, then try again. If you have lost the connection, reestablish the connection, then try again to save the file.

Failed to save the system default profile to a local profile for user *user name*.

[Workstation-Logon]

Normally a user profile would be created for you, with the settings you used during this session. However, this could not be done. The next time you log on to this computer you will again have the default settings.

Failed to unlink workfile

[FTP Server]

The Ftp command was unable to close a temporary file it used to expand wildcard characters in a list of filenames.

No user action is necessary.

Failed to update link information.

[Write]

You attempted unsuccessfully to link an object to a Write document. You may be low on memory.

Close one or more of the applications that you have running, then try again.

Failed to update object.

The server application has malfunctioned. Or you have attempted to perform an operation on an object that no longer exists.

Try again. Then contact your system administrator.

Failed to update object.

[Write]

You attempted unsuccessfully to update an object in Write. You may be low on memory.

Close one or more of the applications that you have running, then try again.

Failure to access device: *name*

[Mode]

The Mode command was either trying to get the status of the COM port parameters (baud rate, parity, etc.), or was trying to set the COM port parameters. The Mode command was unable to open the specified COM port.

The device may be in use by another process. Either close down the other process or wait for it to finish, then retry the operation.

Failure to allocate the requested number of Expanded Memory pages.

[Virtual DOS Machine (VDM)]

The virtual DOS machine could not allocate the requested amount of memory for the specified EMS size.

Close down some running applications and then continue to retry the EMS allocation. To avoid this message in the future, change your expanded memory request in the PIF file for the application you are running.

Fatal error encountered.

[Utilities]

Retry the command. If you still get this message, contact technical support.

Fatal error: *text*

[IP]

The application could not continue, due to the indicated error.

Look up the indicated error and take appropriate action. Then try again.

Fatal: Cannot find dynamic link library "*filename* "

[IP]

The indicated file could not be found, and the application cannot continue without it.

Restore the file from a backup copy, or reinstall TCP/IP.

Fatal: Cannot find function "*name* " **in library** "*name* "

[IP]

The indicated file is probably corrupt.

Restore the file from a backup copy, or reinstall TCP/IP if you have no backup copy, and try again. If you still get this message, contact technical support.

FC: *filename* **longer than** *filename*

[File Compare]

The Fc (File Compare) command will only compare binary files that are the same length. Fc will compare the two files until it reaches the end of the shorter file.

FC: cannot open *filename* **- No such file or directory**

[File Compare]

The file cannot be opened.

Make sure the file exists in the specified directory, and that you typed the filename and path correctly.

FC: Incompatible Switches

[File Compare]

Two of the switches you specified cannot be used together. A switch is a parameter beginning with a slash, such as /s.

To check which switches can be used together in the same use of the command, type HELP at the command prompt followed by the command name (in this case, Fc).

FC: Insufficient number of file specifications

[File Compare]

The Fc (File Compare) command requires two file specifications.

To check the syntax of the command, type HELP at the command prompt followed by the command name (Fc, in this case).

FC: Unable to open *filename*. File unavailable for read access

[File Compare]

Fc could not read the file. It may be in use by another program, or the user may not have permission to access this file.

Make sure that the file exists, that it is not in use by another program, and that you have permissions to access it.

February only has 28 days in this year.

[Network]

Specify a number smaller than or equal to 28 for the date.

February only has 29 days in this year.

[Network]

Specify a number smaller than or equal to 29 for the date.

File "*filename*" in use - Backed up.

[Backup]

No action is needed. However, since the file was in use, another application might have been writing to it. This could mean that the file on tape reflects a version of the file that will not work with the creating application.

File *filename* not found

[Control Panel]

The specified file does not appear in your Windows NT SYSTEM32 directory.

Do a search for the file, then move it to your SYSTEM32 directory.

File *filename* access error: unable to export data.

[Performance Monitor]

You have attempted to export data to a full disk. Or you have attempted to export data to a server, and the server is not running.

If the disk if full, files must be deleted before you can export your data. If the server is not started, wait, then try again. You might need to ask your network administrator to start the server.

File *filename* access error: unable to write Log data.

[Performance Monitor]

You have attempted to write log data to a full disk or to a temporarily disabled server.

If the disk is full, some files must be deleted before you can complete this operation. If the server is down, wait and try again.

File *filename* access error: unable to write setting data.

[Performance Monitor]

You have attempted to write your Performance Monitor settings to a full disk or to a temporarily disabled server.

If the disk is full, unnecessary files must be deleted before you can complete this operation. If the server is down, wait and try again.

File *filename* was compressed with an algorithm unknown to Windows NT Setup. It cannot be decompressed.

[Setup]

Select Retry in the message box to retry the operation. If you get the same message, select Exit Setup and then retry the Setup operation from the beginning. If you still get this message, contact your technical support group.

File *filename* was compressed with an algorithm unknown to Windows NT Setup. It cannot be decompressed.

[Repair Disk]

Select Retry in the message box to retry the operation. If you get the same message, select Exit Setup and then retry the Setup operation from the beginning. If you still get this message, contact your technical support group.

File *filename* : cannot open this file.

[Performance Monitor]

You have attempted to open a file to which you do not have access or that is being used by another process.

If you lack the permission to open the file, log on under an account that has this permission, or contact your system administrator. If the file is in use by another process, close the application that is using the file, then try again to open it from Performance Monitor.

File *filename* : no Log data available. This may be a corrupt file.

[Performance Monitor]

The file named as a log file could not be read as such by Performance Monitor. The file might be corrupt, or might have been created by a different program.

Make sure you have supplied the correct name and path. You might need to restore this file from a backup copy.

File *filename* : this is an invalid Log file.

[Performance Monitor]

The log file could not be read by Performance Monitor. Either the file was created by a different application, or the file is corrupt.

Try again, making sure you have entered the name of the Performance Monitor log file. If you still get this message, restore the log file from a backup copy and try again.

File ***filename*** **: this is an invalid setting file.**

[Performance Monitor]

The log file could not be read by Performance Monitor. Either the file was created by a different application, or the file is corrupt.

Try again, making sure you have entered the name of the Performance Monitor log file. If you still get this message, restore the log file from a backup copy and try again.

File access error of a temporary file, during initialization.

[Virtual DOS Machine (VDM)]

You may be out of disk space, or the \TMP directory may not exist on your computer.

Either delete some unneeded files from your disk or create a \TMP directory that matches the path shown in your startup files. You can view that path by using the System icon in the Windows NT Control Panel. The path Windows NT expects to use for storing temporary files is displayed in the User Environment Variables box.

File allocation table bad, drive ***drive letter*****.**

[Chkdsk]

The utility could not write the file allocation table.

Back up all data on the specified drive and reformat the volume.

File cannot be copied onto itself

[Replace]

Specify a destination file that is different from the source file.

File cannot be copied onto itself

[Xcopy]

Specify a destination file that is different from the source file.

File creation error - ***code***

[Xcopy]

Make sure you typed valid path and filenames. If you specified a destination filename, use the Dir command with the /a switch to make sure you did not specify a read-only, hidden, or system file, or an existing subdirectory. Confirm that there is enough space for the file in the current directory and in your temporary directory, if appropriate. If the disk is write-protected, use another disk or remove the write-protection tab.

File in use by Windows.

[File Manager]

You cannot perform this action on this file while it is used by Windows.

Close the application that is using this file and try again. If the file is used by the Windows NT operating system, you cannot perform this operation on this file directly.

File Manager - Out of Memory

[File Manager]

Close some applications and try again.

File Manager cannot change attributes.

[File Manager]

You do not have the necessary permissions to change the attributes of this file.

Change the permissions on this file or directory to allow you to change these attributes, or ask the administrator to make those changes for you. Then try again.

File Manager cannot copy *filename* **:** *name*

[File Manager]

Take the appropriate action for the reason given for the failure. For example, if the destination disk is full, either delete some files or use a different disk; if you do not have write permission on the destination disk, change the permission or specify a different disk. Then try again.

File manager cannot copy multiple files or directories to the Clipboard. Select a single file, and then try again.

[File Manager]

In the Copy to Clipboard dialog box, you typed a filename. As a result, more than one filename now appears in the dialog box. File Manager does not permit this.

Follow the user action specified in the message.

File Manager cannot create directory *drive letter* **:** *name*

[File Manager]

Take the appropriate action for the reason given for the failure. For example, if you do not have write permission on the destination disk, change the permission or specify a different disk. Then try again.

File Manager cannot create or replace *filename* **:** *text*

[File Manager]

Take the appropriate action for the reason given for the failure. For example, if you do not have write permission on the destination disk, change the permission or specify a different disk. Then try again.

File Manager cannot delete *computer name* **:** *filename*

[File Manager]

Take the appropriate action for the reason given for the failure. For example, if you do not have write permission on the destination disk, change the permission or specify a different disk. Then try again.

File Manager cannot disconnect network drive. Files are open on this drive.

[File Manager]

Some of the files that you used while connected to a network drive are still open.

Choose OK, then close the open files and try again.

File Manager cannot find file (or one of its components).Make sure the path and filename are correct and that all required libraries are available.

[File Manager]

Applications in Windows NT require certain files to run. Using the Run command on the File menu, you specified a command path that does not contain all of the files necessary to run your application.

Follow the user action specified in the message.

File Manager cannot format disk. Make sure the disk is in the drive and not write-protected, damaged, or of wrong density rating.

[File Manager]

Make sure that the disk not write-protected, that it is all the way in the drive, and that the drive door, if any, is closed. If you still get this error, try using a different disk.

File Manager cannot lock volume.

[File Manager]

You attempted to Format or Copy a disk, and File Manager cannot gain exclusive access to the target disk. It is important that File Manager gain this access to ensure that no files are being accessed on the disk that is about to be formatted.

Make sure that no files are open on the target disk, then try again.

File Manager cannot move *filename* **:** *name*

[File Manager]

Take the appropriate action for the reason given for the failure. For example, if you do not have write permission on the destination disk, change the permission or specify a different disk. Then try again. a different disk. Then try again.

File manager cannot obtain disk information. Make sure the disk is in the drive.

[File Manager]

You selected the Format Disk option in the Disk menu, but have not placed a disk in the disk drive.

Follow the user action specified in the message.

File Manager cannot open or print file. Start the application used to create this file and open or print it from there.

[File Manager]

The file that you attempted to print is either not associated with an application, or is associated with an application that does not support printing from File Manager.

File Manager cannot perform a quick format. Continue with normal format?

[File Manager]

In the Format Disk dialog box, you specified the Quick Format option for a disk that has never been formatted. Or you attempted to quick format a disk that was previously formatted at a different density rating. You can only quick format a disk that has been previously formatted. In addition, you must quick format a disk to its present density.

If you want to continue with a normal format, choose Yes in the Format Disk Error dialog box. If not, choose No.

File Manager cannot print multiple files. Select only one file, and then try again.

[File Manager]

You selected multiple files from the right pane of the File Manager window, then have selected the Print command from the File menu. File Manager only supports the printing of one file at a time.

Follow the user action specified in the message.

File Manager cannot remove directory *drive letter* **:** *name*

[File Manager]

Take the appropriate action for the reason given for the failure. For example, if you do not have write permission on the destination disk, change the permission or specify a different disk. Then try again.

File Manager cannot rename *filename* **:** *name*

[File Manager]

Take the appropriate action for the reason given for the failure. For example, if you do not have write permission on the destination disk, change the permission or specify a different disk. Then try again.

File Manager is currently copying a disk. Exiting File Manager will abort this operation.

[File Manager]

Wait until File Manager is finished copying the disk and try again. Or, exit File Manager now and try copying the disk again at a later time.

File mark encountered

[Backup]

This message indicates a non-critical condition and should be followed with additional information, however it may indicate a problem with backup.

Contact technical support. Be sure to record any messages and information you see for technical support.

File name is invalid

[Dynamic Data Exchange]

The filename you typed does not fit the criteria for a valid filename. If you are using NTFS, the name can be up to 256 characters long, including extension. You can use any letters or numbers in the filename, plus any of the following characters:? \ * " < > | /If you are using the High Performance File System (HPFS) or file allocation tables (FAT), you must follow the filename convention for that system.

Try again, using a filename that is valid for the file system you are using. Note that File Manager will truncate long names to fit the FAT filename requirements so that computers using MS-DOS can see and use the file.

File Not Found

[Command]

Make sure the file exists in the specified directory, and that you typed the filename and path correctly.

File not found - *filename*

[Attrib]

Make sure the file exists in the specified directory, and that you typed the filename and path correctly.

File not found - *filename*

[Chkdsk]

Make sure the file exists in the specified directory, and that you typed the filename and path correctly.

File not found - *filename*

[File Compare]

Make sure the file exists in the specified directory, and that you typed the filename and path correctly.

File not found - *filename*

[Find]

Make sure the file exists in the specified directory, and that you typed the filename and path correctly.

File not found - *filename*

[Xcopy]

Make sure the file exists in the specified directory, and that you typed the filename and path correctly.

File not found *filename*

[FTP Server]

The global file list was expanded for use by the Ftp utility, but the expansion was invalid.

Ask your network administrator to interpret the error code displayed at the end of the message, and take appropriate action. You may have to edit the global file list.

File read/write failure; Assure correct disk is in the drive.

The application was unable to read from or write to the file.

Check the drive where the Help file is expected to be. The file is of type .HLP.

File record segment *number* **is unreadable.**

[Chkdsk-NTFS]

A file, part of a file, or a directory on an NTFS volume is unreadable.

There may be a loss of data. Look at subsequent Chkdsk messages for more information and decide if the missing data is important enough to be restored from backup.

File Server for Macintosh service has not been started. Would you like to start it?

[Services for Macintosh (SFM)]

Use the Services option in Control Panel to start the File Server for Macintosh.

File Server for Macintosh service only supports NTFS partitions. Please choose a directory on an NTFS partition.

[Services for Macintosh (SFM)]

File Manager shows which directories are FAT, HPFS, NTFS.

File verification failed.

[Xcopy]

Xcopy detected that the copied file does not have the same size as the original.

Run the Xcopy command again.

File1 Only Has *number* **Lines**

[File Compare]

You specified too many lines for the /n switch of the Comp command. You can only specify a number less than or equal to the number of lines in the specified file.

Try the Comp command again, using a smaller number in the /n switch.

File2 Only Has *number* **Lines**

[File Compare]

You specified too many lines for the /n switch of the Comp command. You can only specify a number less than or equal to the number of lines in the specified file.

Try the Comp command again, using a smaller number in the /n switch.

Filename not valid. Please verify that a valid filename is given.

[Cardfile]

You have attempted to access from File Manager a Cardfile file that was saved with an extension other than .CRD.

Select this file in File Manager, select the Rename option in the File menu, and assign a .CRD extension to the file.

Files are different sizes

[File Compare]

You used the Comp command to compare two files and the files are different sizes. No comparison was made.

You can compare the first 'n' bytes of the two files, even though they are of different sizes, by using the /n=number switch in the Comp command. If you specify a number larger than the number of lines in the smallest file, a warning message will appear and you can try again with a smaller number. To review the syntax of the Comp command, type HELP at the command prompt, followed by the command name (in this case, Comp).

Files on this volume cannot be recovered with this version of UNTFS.DLL.

[Recover-NTFS]

The file system version number on the NTFS volume indicates that it was created with a later release of Windows NT than this version of UNTFS.DLL.

Files with the extension *name* are programs and cannot be associated with another application.

[File Manager]

Most programs have either a .PIF, .COM, or .EXE extension, and you attempted to associate one of these executable program files with another program. Windows NT does not permit this operation.

Choose OK.

FIND: Parameter format not correct

[Find]

The parameters used with the Find command were not correct.

To see the valid syntax for the Find command, type HELP and the command name (in this case Find) at the command prompt.

finger: WSAStartup: *text*

[TCP/IP]

The TCP/IP utility named at the beginning of the message was unable to start up due to a socket error.

Wait, then retry the TCP/IP utility. If you still get this message, contact your network administrator to interpret the error code displayed at the end of the message. The appropriate action depends on the meaning of this code.

FIRST diskette bad or incompatible

[Disk Compare]

The Diskcomp command cannot recognize the format of the source floppy disk.

Make sure the floppy disk is in the drive and the drive door is closed. If it is, then try removing the disk and reinserting it. After that, if this message reappears, you will not be able to use this disk with the Diskcomp command.

Fixing critical MFT files with MFT mirror.

[Chkdsk-NTFS]

The beginning of the master file table (MFT) on this NTFS volume is corrupt, so CHKDSK is using the backup copy of the MFT instead.

No action is needed.

Floppy controller failed to respond or driver could not communicate with the floppy controller. Check that the IRQ is set correctly. From device: *name*

[QIC117]

Verify the configuration of the system. Make sure that this device is using the IRQ setting specified in the documentation for the device.

Floppy controller is in use by another device. From device: *name*

[QIC117]

Another application is using the floppy controller.

Close any applications that are accessing the floppy disk drives, and try again.

Force user logoff how long after time expires?: *text*

[Network]

After the end of the time period that the user is allowed on the network, how long to you want to let the user to continue to use resources in order to gracefully close files and applications?

Enter a time interval in minutes.

FORCEDOS: _default.pif corrupted

[ForceDOS]

Restore the DEFAULT.PIF file to your Windows NT directory from a backup copy.

FORCEDOS: _default.pif not found

[ForceDOS]

Restore the DEFAULT.PIF file to your Windows NT directory from a backup copy.

FORCEDOS: Bad directory name

[ForceDOS]

The directory you specified with the /d parameter is not a valid directory name.

Try again, making sure to specify an existing directory and making sure you type the name correctly.

FORCEDOS: Bad program path name

[ForceDOS]

The path name you entered did not meet the criteria for an MS-DOS path.

Check to make sure you have the correct path to the executable file, then try again. Make sure the directory names are separated with backslashes (\) and not forward slashes (/).

FORCEDOS: Cannot create temporary file

[ForceDOS]

Your program could not run because it could not create a required temporary file. There probably is not enough free space on the disk to create the file.

Check the available space on the disk. If necessary, delete some files to make room for the temporary file.

FORCEDOS: Command line too long

[ForceDOS]

The command line cannot be longer than 125 characters.

Try again, using abbreviations for parameters wherever possible. If the directory where the program resides is in the Windows NT path, you do not need to include the path when specifying the program filename.

FORCEDOS: Failed to create the process

[ForceDOS]

The command won't work. There is probably not enough free memory.

Close some applications and try again.

FORCEDOS: Not enough memory

[ForceDOS]

Close some applications and try again.

FORCEDOS: Program file not found

[ForceDOS]

Make sure you have typed the program name correctly. If the directory in which the program's executable file resides is not on the Windows NT path, you must specify the entire path to the program. Or, change to the directory where the program resides and try again.

Forcing ***user name*** **to close** ***filename*** **may result in loss of data. Do you want to continue?**

[Network]

The specified user is currently using the file you chose to close. The file should be closed from within the application the user used to open it if possible

If you want to continue, choose Yes. If not, choose No.

Forcing *computer name* to close *name* may result in loss of data. Do you want to continue?

[Server Manager]

When you choose to force a computer to close a shared directory, you risk causing the server to lose changes made to the shared directory.

If you still want to force the user to close the directory, choose Yes. If not, choose No.

Forcing *user name* to close *name* may result in loss of data. Do you want to continue?

[Services for Macintosh (SFM)]

Use Server Manager or File Manager to send a disconnect message to the specified user. In using either manager, select the MacFile menu. In Server Manager, select Send Message. In File Manager, select View/Modify Volumes and then select Send Message.

Forcing all file forks closed on *computer name* may result in loss of data. Do you want to continue?

[Services for Macintosh (SFM)]

Use Server Manager or File Manager to send a disconnect message to users. In using either manager, select the MacFile menu. In Server Manager, select Send Message. In File Manager, select View/Modify Volumes and then select Send Message.

Forcing all files on *computer name* to close may result in loss of data. Do you want to continue?

[Network] [Server Manager]

When you chose to close files remotely, you run the risk that users using those files may lose changes made to them. Consequently, Server Manager presents you with this confirmation message when you choose the Close All Resources button in the Open Resources dialog box.

If you still want to close all resources, choose the Yes option. If not, choose No.

Forcing all files on *computer name* to close may result in loss of data. Do you want to continue?

[Services for Macintosh (SFM)]

Use Server Manager or File Manager to send a disconnect message to the specified user. In using either manager, select the MacFile menu. In Server Manager, select Send Message. In File Manager, select View/Modify Volumes and then select Send Message.

Forcing the application to close may lose data. Do you wish to force the application to close?

[Program Manager] [Task Manager]

The safest way to close an application is to close files that the application has open from within the application window, and then close that window.

The best course is to choose No, and close the application from the application window. If this is not possible, choose Yes to force the application to close.

Foreign Tape

[Backup]

The data on the tape is not recognizable.

Use the application that was used to place the data on the tape to retrieve the data.

Format error in bindings storage file

[Control Panel]

The file in which variable names are paired with essential information does not have the expected file format. The file, which typically has a filetype of .INF, may be corrupt. This usually occurs after a new network component has been installed. In some cases the hardware or installation procedure provided with the component is at fault.

First, reboot the computer, then choose Network from the Control Panel and choose Binding to redo the binding. If the problem continues, remove any recently installed network component, reboot, reinstall the component, and reboot again. If you still get this error, ask the administrator to edit the registry, removing the variable \Software\Microsoft\Ncpa\CurrentVersion\Bindfile; then choose Network from the Control Panel and choose Binding to redo the binding. You may need to contact the vendor of the network component to resolve the problem.

Format failed.

[Format]

The formatting of an NTFS partition could not be completed, possibly because of unsuccessful write operations due to bad sectors on the disk.

Do not use the /q switch on the Format command. Reformat the disk without the /q switch, which will avoid writing to the bad sectors. If this message reappears, there is a hardware problem. Either run hardware diagnostics on the disk and its controller, or contact the supplier of the disk.

FORMAT is unable to enable the file system.

[Format]

There might be a problem with the system because the I/O subsystem should automatically recognize and enable file systems.

Contact technical support.

FormatMessage(*number* **) fails with winError =** *code*

[AT-Network]

The AT command did not load a message in the FormatMessage function.

Contact your system administrator.

Formatting will erase ALL data from your disk. Are you sure that you want to format the disk in drive *drive letter***?**

[File Manager]

You chose to format a floppy disk. Any time that you format a floppy disk in Windows NT, all data is removed from the disk.

If you do not wish to continue with this operation, select Yes. If not, select No to return to the Format disk dialog box, then choose Cancel.

FTP Server could not create a client worker thread for user at host *computer name*. The connection to this user is terminated. The data is the error.

[FTP Server]

Wait a few minutes and then try to reconnect the user.

FTP Server could not create the main connection thread. The data is the error.

[FTP Server]

When the main connection thread cannot be created, the FTP Service cannot start. Your system is out of virtual memory.

Increase the size of the paging file or stop some processes.

FTP Server could not initialize its security. The data is the error.

[FTP Server]

FTP Server cannot initialize unless it can register with the Windows NT security subsystem.

Contact technical support.

FTP Server could not initialize the socket library. The data is the error.

[FTP Server]

FTP Server could not connect to its protocol on the network.

Contact technical support.

FTP Server could not locate the FTP/TCP service. The data is the error.

[FTP Server]

The port number for the FTP/TCP service may have been deleted, renamed, or corrupted. The GetServByName call failed.

If the file has been deleted or corrupted, remove and then reinstall the TCP/IP protocol. Otherwise, change the name of the file back to Services.

FTP Server was unable to initialize due to a shortage of available memory. The data is the error.

[FTP Server]

The Ftp Server service is unable to run due to insufficient memory. Clients on this network will not be able to transfer files to & from other computers running FTP and TCP/IP unless another server on the LAN is running FTP Server.

Close some applications and try again. If you still get this error you might want to install more memory on the computer running FTP Server.

ftp: error allocating memory

[FTP Server]

There is insufficient memory for the data structures required by the Ftp utility to make the file transfer.

Wait a few seconds, then retry the Ftp operation. If you still get this message, quit some applications and then try again.

GATE Table alloc error *code*

[FTP Server] [TCP/IP]

There is not enough memory available to display the TCP/IP Gateway table.

Wait a few seconds and retry the operation. If you still get this message, quit some unneeded applications that are running, and then retry the operation.

GATE Table read error *code*

[FTP Server] [TCP/IP]

During a TCP/IP operation that uses a gateway, a problem occurred with the IP driver sometime between the request to read the routing table and actually reading it.

This is an extremely unusual event. Contact your network administrator to interpret the error code displayed at the end of the message, and then take appropriate action.

General Error has occurred Check if: Printer is out of paper; Printer is off line; Printer is being used by another process.

[Registry Editor]

An error occurred as you were attempting to print, and Registry Editor cannot determine the nature of this error.

Try again. If the problem recurs, make sure that your physical connections to the printer are secure, that the printer is properly configured, and that the printer is not out of paper or other supplies.

General error reported by device.

[Remote Access Service]

One of the Remote Access configuration files probably contains invalid information.

The easiest way to resolve this problem is to reinstall Remote Access. Use the Network option in Control Panel to remove and reinstall RAS. If you are using a modem that is not supported by Remote Access, switch to a supported modem, or see "Modem Script File" in the Remote Access Service online Help for information about modifying the modem script file for your modem. The Remote Access script files (PAD.INF, MODEM.INF, and SWITCH.INF) are in the \SYSTEM32\RAS subdirectory of your Windows NT directory.

General INF file error in file ***filename*****.**

[Setup]

Setup was in the process of loading and interpreting an .INF file.

Select Retry to retry the operation. If you get the same message, the .INF file is corrupted. Note the name of the .INF file that is displayed in the message box and then select the Exit Setup option. Then restore the named .INF file from the distribution medium (you will have to decompress the file). Retry the Setup operation. If you get this same message, contact your technical support group.

General INF file error in file *filename*.

[Repair Disk]

Setup was in the process of loading and interpreting an .INF file.

Select Retry to retry the operation. If you get the same message, the .INF file is corrupted. Note the name of the .INF file that is displayed in the message box and then select the Exit Setup option. Then restore the named .INF file from the distribution medium (you will have to decompress the file). Retry the Setup operation. If you get this same message, contact your technical support group.

General named pipe failure occurred in the admin support thread for the Remote Access Service.

[Remote Access Service]

Restart your computer. If the problem persists, check your system's configuration, quotas, and resources. For further information, consult your Windows NT documentation.

General named pipe failure occurred in the Point to Point Protocol engine.

[Remote Access Service]

Check the Event Log in Event Viewer for other errors related to system resources. Event Viewer is found in the Administrative Tools group. Also, restart the computer. If the problem persists, contact technical support.

Generic access types were contained in an access mask which should already be mapped to non-generic types.

[Kernel32]

Contact the supplier of the running application.

GetModuleFileName did not return a full path.

[Setup]

Select OK to exit Setup. Retry the Setup operation from the beginning. If you get this message again, contact your technical support group.

GetModuleFileName did not return a full path.

[Repair Disk]

Select OK to exit Setup. Retry the Setup operation from the beginning. If you get this message again, contact your technical support group.

GetSockName returned with an error. WINS created a socket and asked bind to bind a handle to it. On calling getsockname to determine the address bound, it got an error.

[WINS Service]

This is a severe error in the TCP/IP stack.

Contact technical support.

Getting bound address of socket failed. The Nw Sap Agent cannot continue.

[Netevent]

There was not enough memory to perform this operation. Resources that are accessed via the SAP Agent and services that depend on the SAP Agent will not be available.

Close some applications and try again. If you get this message often you might want to install more memory.

Grant Remote Access permissions to all *number* users?

[Remote Access Service]

When the system administrator grants RAS permissions to all users with accounts in the SAM on a server, it allows the users to remotely access the server. This is done usually when granting permissions to a block of users.

Choose Yes to grant access to all users in the local security database, or No to limit users access to the specified server.

group ' *group* ' already exists as a local group name in the Windows NT security database.

[PORTUAS]

No action is needed.

group ' *group* ' is already used as a user name in the Windows NT security database.

[PORTUAS]

PortUAS will ask you for another name for the group, unless the Force Ignore option has been implemented.

Hanging up a stuck session to *computer name*.

[Network] Net Message ID: 3194

This message should occur only on a down-level computer. Any action to correct the problem should be performed on that computer. The session with the specified server was ended because the server stopped responding.

Ask your network administrator if the server is running. If so, reconnect to the server. The amount of time a workstation waits for a server to respond to a request is determined by the SESSTIMEOUT entry in the workstation's configuration file. If your sessions with servers are frequently ended by this error, you may want to increase the value of SESSTIMEOUT. If you need assistance, contact your network administrator.

Hardware error on NetBIOS card.

[Dynamic Data Exchange]

The network adapter card used by NetBIOS has produced an error. The card may be defective or damaged, or it may be loose in its slot, or the connection to it may be loose.

Make sure that the network card is properly seated and that the cable connection is snug. If you still get this error, replace the card.

Hardware failure

[Backup]

Try cleaning the heads of the tape drive. If you continue to receive this message, contact the supplier of the tape drive. Be sure to record any messages and information you see for the supplier.

Hardware failure

[Remote Access Service]

This indicates a problem with the modem.

The modem should be reconfigured or replaced. Consult the documentation that accompanied your modem.

Hardware failure in port or attached device.

[Remote Access Service]

Your modem (or other connecting device) is not responding because the modem has been turned off, or the modem is not securely connected to your computer, or the serial cable does not have the correct specifications required by Remote Access, or the modem has experienced a hardware glitch.

Make sure your cable is securely fastened to both the modem and the computer. If so, verify that the serial cable has the correct specifications. For more information, see "Cabling Requirements" in the Remote Access Service online Help. If the modem has experienced a hardware glitch, turn off the modem, wait for 20 seconds, and then restart it.

Height must be less than 256.

[Kernel32]

As part of its user interface, an application has attempted an unsupported operation.

Contact the supplier of the running application.

Help application corrupt; reinstall WINHELP.EXE.

[Help]

Help cannot be started.

Copy WINHELP.EXE to your Windows NT SYSTEM32 directory.

Help file "*filename*" was not found.

[Backup]

The Help you requested cannot be loaded because the file is not available.

Use the application's Setup program to install Help.

Help file could not be found.

[Help]

Make sure the DOSHELP.HLP file exists and that the directory containing DOSHELP.HLP is in your search path. If you cannot find DOSHELP.HLP, you can copy it from your Windows NT installation medium (you will have to decompress the file).

Help file does not contain keywords.

[Help]

You have attempted to search for a word in a file that does not allow for a keyword search. Or, in an application that offers search capability, you have attempted to locate a word in a Help file that does not offer this capability.

No action is needed.

Help file has changed.

[Help]

Someone has deleted or changed the Help file you are viewing since you opened Help. For example, an updated copy of the file might have been installed.

Close and reopen Help.

Help is unavailable while printers are being set up from Windows Help.

[Help]

You cannot open a new Help window while you are using the Print Setup dialog in an existing Help window.

Finish setting up the printers and exit that dialog box.

Help is unavailable while printing from Windows Help.

[Help]

You cannot open a new Help window while you are printing from an existing Help window.

Finish printing in the existing help window and exit that dialog box.

Help On Help not available; rerun Setup.

[Help]

The file showing how to use Help was not loaded during installation, was loaded into the incorrect directory, or is damaged.

After rerunning Setup, ensure that the file is located in your Windows NT SYSTEM32 directory.

Help topic does not exist.

[Help]

In a search, you have found the name of a topic that does not exist. Or you have pressed a Help button for which there exists no corresponding Help file.

Consult your written documentation for help on the topic.

Help unavailable while printers are being set up from Windows Help.

[Help]

You have attempted to use Help while setting up a printer from Windows Help.

Wait until the printer is set up, then try again.

Help unavailable while printing from Windows Help.

[Help]

You have attempted to access a Help topic while printing a topic from Windows NT Help.

Wait until printing is completed, then try again.

Hot key is already registered.

[Kernel32]

Hot keys are keystroke combinations that have the highest priority in the user interface. An application tried to register a keystroke combination that had already been registered.

Contact the supplier of the running application.

Hot key is not registered.

[Kernel32]

Hot keys are keystroke combinations that have the highest priority in the user interface. An application tried to use a keystroke combination without first registering it with the system.

Contact the supplier of the running application.

HPFS partition has unreadable root.

[Utilities]

A critical sector near the beginning of the volume is unreadable. Back up files from the drive and replace the disk.

HPFS RECOVER does not support recovering directories.

[Recover-FAT/HPFS]

HPFS Recover can be used to recover file data only.

Retry the Recover command, specifying a filename (you can use wildcards in the file specification).

HPFS will only run on volumes with 512 bytes per sector.

[Format]

The sector size is determined by the disk drive manufacturer and you cannot change it.

Either do not use the HPFS file system on this drive or purchase a different drive. If you purchased this drive with the understanding that it had 512 bytes per sector, contact the hardware manufacturer.

IBM LAN support program internal error

[Dynamic Data Exchange]

NetBIOS has encountered an internal error in the IBM LAN Support program.

See the documentation for the IBM LAN Support program for the appropriate action.

ICMP network unreachable *text.*

The network running the Internet Control Message Protocol (ICMP) could not be reached.

Try again later.

Id index database for volume "*name* **" could not be loaded. Starting with an empty database.**

[Services for Macintosh (SFM)]

The volume information is corrupted.

The defaults were set so no action is needed.

If you enter multiple names, they must all be user accounts. You can only work with one global group or local group at a time.

[User Manager]

You are using the Low Speed Connection option, and you tried to perform some action from the User menu on several accounts. No group names can be included in this list of accounts.

Enter the name of a single user or group account, or enter several user names separated by semicolons (;).

If you have no other network components to install, click OK. Otherwise, use this dialog to add additional network adapters or software using 'Add Adapter' or 'Add Software'.

[Control Panel]

You can make further changes to your network settings, or choose OK to keep the changes you have made.

Choose a button to make further changes, or choose OK. For more information, choose Help.

If you save this document in the Write 3.0 format, the linked or embedded objects will be deleted from the saved file. Do you want to save this document in Write 3.0 format?

[Write]

When you save a document in a 3.0 Write (.WRI) format, linked or embedded pictures disappear though static pictures will remain.

If you want to save the document in a Write 3.0 format, choose Yes. If not, choose No. Choose Cancel to return to the document.

If you save this document in this format no pictures, including linked or embedded objects, will be saved. Do you want to save?

[Write]

Most likely, you attempted to save a Write document in a Word for MS-DOS format. This format deletes all pictures.

If you still want to save the document, choose Yes. If not, choose No. To return to the document, choose Cancel.

If you wish to create a new domain, indicate so. If the domain name is in error, you may correct it. your system is connected over a Wide-Area Network, or other special connection method, you may enter the domain controller name explicitly.

[Control Panel]

The domain name you entered does not currently exist on this network.

If you want to create a new domain with this domain name choose New. Otherwise, retype the domain name.

Ignoring redundant group ' *group* **'...**

[PORTUAS]

Groups with the same names are merged.

No action is needed.

Ignoring the communication operator flag for user *user name*...

[PORTUAS]

A resource on a LAN Manager server is flagged as having Communication Operators privilege. Since Windows NT has no corresponding group, this flag is being ignored.

No action is needed.

Illegal device name - *name*

[Mode]

Your computer does not recognize the device name. For example, you may have used the device name COM3: in a Mode command and your computer does not have a COM3: port installed.

Make sure you typed the device name correctly in the command. Also make sure that you've correctly set up and configured the device.

Illegal operation attempted on a Registry key which has been marked for deletion.

[Kernel32]

A Registry key can be marked for deletion and still have open handles.

Close out all uses of the key, or wait for them to be closed. Then retry the operation.

Illegal or missing file types specified in section *number*.

[Setup]

Contact the supplier for another copy of the installation media.

Illegal return type.

[Help]

This error is from the Macro Language Editor for online help, and should not appear while using the Help file. Report this error to the provider of the Help file.

Illegal to append data from an earlier log to data collected later.

[Performance Monitor]

You tried to place the data from one log file at the end of a file of data that was collected later. This would result in the data sample time being out of chronological order.

Relog the data to a new log file.

Image backups cannot be viewed or restored.

[Backup]

An image backup is essentially a snapshot of the backed up data. Inherently, such backups involve positioning problems, and Backup is unable to read the tape that you have used.

Use a different type of backup.

IMPORT path *path* cannot be found.

[Network] Net Message ID: 3218

The import path specified either from the command line or in the configuration file does not exist.

Check the spelling of the IMPORTPATH entry in the configuration file. This entry must specify a directory that exists.

Incompatible file system.

[File Manager]

You tried to copy data to or from a disk that was formatted for a different file system.

Use a different disk.

Incompatible files are installed in the LANMAN tree.

[Network]

This message should occur only on a down-level computer. Any action to correct the problem should be performed on that computer.

Incomplete directory tree displayed

[File Manager]

The directory tree is too long to be displayed in File Manager.

No action is needed.

Incorrect duplicate information in file *filename*.

[Chkdsk]

No action is needed. If the Chkdsk /f command was used, it will fix the incorrect duplicate information.

Incorrect modem response

[Remote Access Service]

When the Remote Access Service sends a string to the modem, it expects a certain response. If the response is different than expected, you see this message. The modem may not be functioning properly or the modem is incompatible with the Remote Access Service.

Reset the modem. If the problem persists, check the modem's configuration. Verify that the modem is compatible with the Remote Access Service.

Incorrect number of parameters - *text*

[Subst]

You typed the wrong number of parameters in a Subst command.

To find out the correct syntax for the Subst command, at the command prompt type Help, followed by the command name (in this case, Subst).

Incorrect Operating System version

[Utilities]

The utility does not match the version number of Windows NT.

Do not run this binary on this version of Windows NT. Run the binary that came with the version of Windows NT you are using.

Incorrect or missing signature in the Repair Information File.

[Setup]

The SETUP.LOG file on the Emergency Repair Disk might be corrupted or bad.

Make sure you have inserted the correct Emergency Repair Disk for your computer. If you don't have the correct disk, let Setup attempt to locate your Windows NT installation.

Incorrect value. Enter a maximum page file size that is greater than or equal to the initial page file size.

[Program Manager]

The Virtual Memory option in the System dialog allows you to set minimum and maximum paging file sizes. The Maximum Size setting must always be equal to larger than the Initial Size setting, and you have entered a Maximum Size setting that is smaller than the Initial Size setting.

Follow the action specified in the message.

Incorrect value. Enter a maximum page file size that is greater than or equal to the initial page file size.

[Program Manager]

The Virtual Memory option in the System dialog allows you to set minimum and maximum paging file sizes. The Maximum Size setting must always be equal to larger than the Initial Size setting, and you have entered a Maximum Size setting that is smaller than the Initial Size setting.

Follow the action specified in the message.

Incorrect value. Enter an initial page file size between 2 and the free space available on the drive.

[Program Manager]

In the Initial Size option in the Virtual Memory dialog box, you have designated less than 2 megabytes for your paging file. Windows NT requires that you enter at least 2 megabytes in this space, and that you enter a number no greater than the one that appears to the right of Space Available.

Follow the action specified in the message. Or leave the option blank if you do not want a page file on this volume.

Incorrect value. Enter an initial page file size between 2 and the free space available on the drive.

[Program Manager]

In the Initial Size option in the Virtual Memory dialog box, you have designated less than 2 megabytes for your paging file. Windows NT requires that you enter at least 2 megabytes in this space, and that you enter a number no greater than the one that appears to the right of Space Available.

Follow the action specified in the message. Or leave the option blank if you do not want a page file on this volume.

Incorrect Windows NT version

[File Compare]

Make sure the directory that contains the correct version of this utility appears in the path before any other directories containing a copy of this utility. Also, confirm that the current directory does not contain another copy of this file. If you cannot find the correct version of this utility, copy it from the Windows NT distribution medium (you will have to decompress the file).

Incorrect Windows NT version

[Find]

Make sure the directory that contains the correct version of this utility appears in the path before any other directories containing a copy of this utility. Also, confirm that the current directory does not contain another copy of this file. If you cannot find the correct version of this utility, copy it from the Windows NT distribution medium (you will have to decompress the file).

Incorrect Windows NT version

[Help]

Make sure the directory that contains the correct version of this utility appears in the path before any other directories containing a copy of this utility. Also, confirm that the current directory does not contain another copy of this file. If you cannot find the correct version of this utility, copy it from the Windows NT distribution medium (you will have to decompress the file).

Incorrect Windows NT version

[Replace]

Make sure the directory that contains the correct version of this utility appears in the path before any other directories containing a copy of this utility. Also, confirm that the current directory does not contain another copy of this file. If you cannot find the correct version of this utility, copy it from the Windows NT distribution medium (you will have to decompress the file).

Incorrect Windows NT version

[Utilities]

Make sure the directory that contains the correct version of this utility appears in the path before any other directories containing a copy of this utility. Also, confirm that the current directory does not contain another copy of this file. If you cannot find the correct version of this utility, copy it from the Windows NT distribution medium (you will have to decompress the file).

Index entries referencing file *filename* will not be validated because this file contains too many file names.

[Chkdsk]

Try breaking the specified file into two or more parts and run the Chkdsk command again.

Indicates a Windows NT Advanced Server could not be contacted or that objects within the domain are protected such that necessary information could not be retrieved.

[Kernel32]

Contact the supplier of the running application.

Indicates an ACL contains no inheritable components

[Kernel32]

Contact the supplier of the running application.

Indicates two revision levels are incompatible.

[Kernel32]

Contact the supplier of the running application.

Initialization failed because account file *filename* is either incorrect or not present.

[Network] Net Message ID: 3122

This message should occur only on a down-level computer. Any action to correct the problem should be performed on that computer. The user accounts database, NET.ACC, is missing, damaged, or in a format that is incompatible with this version of LAN Manager.

Copy the backup file, NETACC.BKP, to NET.ACC. If NETACC.BKP does not exist, copy NET.ACC or NETACC.BKP from a backup floppy or from the LAN Manager distribution disks. If you have upgraded your LAN Manager software, you may need to convert the user accounts database to a new format. See the instructions that came with your upgrade.

Initialization failed because network *name* was not started.

[Network] Net Message ID: 3123

This message should occur only on a down-level computer. Any action to correct the problem should be performed on that computer. All networks named in the SRVNETS entry of the server's configuration file must use the LAN Manager workstation software.

Be sure that all networks named in the SRVNETS entry of the server's configuration file are also named in the WRKNETS entry of that file.

Initialization failed because of a system execution failure on path *path*. The system error code is the data.

[Network] Net Message ID: 3105

This message should occur only on a down-level computer. Any action to correct the problem should be performed on that computer. A software error occurred.

Contact technical support.

Initialization failed because of a system execution failure on path *path*. There is not enough memory to start the process. The system error code is the data.

[Network] Net Message ID: 3131

This message should occur only on a down-level computer. Any action to correct the problem should be performed on that computer. There is not enough memory available to run the Server service.

Stop other applications and services (except the Workstation service) that are running on the computer and try again. If the problem continues, you will have to add more memory to the computer.

Initialization failed because of an error in the configuration file *filename*.

[Network]

This message should occur only on a down-level computer. Any action to correct the problem should be performed on that computer. The Remoteboot service failed to start because of an error in the listed configuration file.

Check the listed file.

Initialization failed because of an invalid line in the configuration file *filename*. The invalid line is the data.

[Network]

This message should occur only on a down-level computer. Any action to correct the problem should be performed on that computer. The Remoteboot service could not start because of an invalid line in the listed configuration file.

Check the listed line.

Initialization failed because of an invalid or missing parameter in the configuration file *filename*.

[Network]

This message should occur only on a down-level computer. Any action to correct the problem should be performed on that computer. The Remoteboot service could not start because the listed entry was missing from the configuration file.

Add the listed entry to the server's configuration file.

Initialization failed because of an open/create error on the file *filename*. The system error code is the data.

[Network] Net Message ID: 3110

This message should occur only on a down-level computer. Any action to correct the problem should be performed on that computer. A software error occurred.

Contact technical support.

Initialization failed because the dynamic-link library *name* returned an incorrect version number.

[Network]

This message should occur only on a down-level computer. Any action to correct the problem should be performed on that computer. The Remoteboot service could not start because the listed dynamic-link library returned the incorrect version number.

Be sure you are using the correct versions of the dynamic-link libraries.

Initialization failed because the requested service *name* could not be started.

[Network] Net Message ID: 3113

A software error occurred.

Contact technical support.

Initialization of "*filename* " DLL failed

[Dynamic Data Exchange]

Functions in the .DLL file will not be available because the instructions could not be loaded. Commands using these functions will not work.

Initialization of a mirror failed.

[Disk Administrator]

Because the mirror could not be initialized, the drive is not protected by Fault Tolerance.

Make sure the drives are on-line and are functioning properly. Check for Eventlog entries close to this one that indicate a hardware problem with one or both drives.

Initialization of a stripe with parity set failed.

[Disk Administrator]

Retry the initialization. If you get this same message, contact your system administrator.

Initialization parameters controlling resource usage other than net buffers are sized so that too much memory is needed.

[Network] Net Message ID: 3120

This message should occur only on a down-level computer. Any action to correct the problem should be performed on that computer. The server's main information segment is larger than the largest segment that can be allocated.

Decrease the values for one or more of the following entries in the server's configuration file: MAXCHDEVJOB, MAXCONNECTIONS, MAXOPENS, MAXCHDEVQ, MAXLOCKS, MAXSHARES, MAXCHDEVS. Then restart the Server service.

Insert a tape in *drive letter*.

[Backup]

The application is ready for a new tape.

Insert a blank tape, or one you are willing to erase, in the specified drive.

Insert tape #*number* in *drive letter*.

[Backup]

The application is ready for the next tape.

Insert the specified tape from the current tape family into the specified drive.

Insert the disk with the unlisted, updated, or vendor-provided driver in:

[Drivers (CP)]

You are attempting to install a device for which Windows NT does not provide a device driver. In this event, a driver should have been provided by your vendor with the device itself.

Insert the disk containing the device driver into the specified disk drive, and copy the driver file to your Windows NT SYSTEM32 directory.

Insert the following tape in *drive letter*:*name* Tape #*number*.

[Backup]

The application is ready for the specified tape.

Insufficient buffer size, unable to proceed.

[Graphics]

Either the display driver and the miniport expect the same structure to have different sizes or there is insufficient space_ina miniport structure to hold mode tables for all the graphics modes supported by a particular card. The former could occur if the software has been compiled with different versions of a header file. The latter could occur if support for more modes has been added or the structure has been shrunk.

Contact technical support.

Insufficient disk space

[Program Manager]

Delete some files and try again.

Insufficient disk space

[Program Manager]

Delete some files and try again.

Insufficient disk space

[Utilities]

The system is running out of disk space.

If you cannot increase your system's disk space, try removing any unneeded applications, programs, and files.

Insufficient disk space

[Repair Disk]

There is not enough disk space to restore the files you specified.

Delete some unneeded files, or specify fewer files to restore.

Insufficient disk space for CHKDSK to recover lost files.

[Chkdsk-NTFS]

Delete some unneeded files from the NTFS volume and then retry the Chkdsk command.

Insufficient disk space for conversion

[Convert]

In order to do the FAT to NTFS or HPFS to NTFS conversion, you will have to delete some unneeded files of the volume to be converted. Then retry the conversion.

Insufficient disk space for security descriptor for file ***filename*****.**

[Chkdsk-NTFS]

Delete some unneeded files from the NTFS volume and then retry the Chkdsk command.

Insufficient disk space to copy cross-linked portion. File being truncated.

[Chkdsk]

When FAT Chkdsk finds that two files claim the same disk sectors, it attempts to resolve this cross-link by copying the data in order to preserve both files. If there is not enough space to copy the cross-linked data, one of the files must be truncated to bring the disk into a consistent state.

No action is needed.

Insufficient disk space to correct disk error. Please free up some disk space and run CHKDSK again.

[Chkdsk]

Delete some unneeded files from the disk volume, then retry the Chkdsk utility.

Insufficient disk space to correct errors in index *number* **of file** *filename***.**

[Chkdsk]

Delete some unneeded files and run Chkdsk /f command again.

Insufficient disk space to create new root directory.

[Chkdsk]

Delete some unneeded files from the NTFS volume, if you can, and then retry the Chkdsk command. If you are unable to delete any files, reformat the volume and restore data from backup.

Insufficient disk space to fix master file table. CHKDSK aborted.

[Chkdsk-NTFS]

The master file table is still intact, so delete some unneeded files from the NTFS volume, then retry the Chkdsk command.

Insufficient disk space to fix the attribute definition table. CHKDSK aborted.

[Chkdsk-NTFS]

Delete some unneeded files from the NTFS volume and then retry the Chkdsk command.

Insufficient disk space to fix the bad clusters file. CHKDSK aborted.

[Chkdsk-NTFS]

Delete some unneeded files from the NTFS volume and then retry the Chkdsk command with the /r switch.

Insufficient disk space to fix the boot file. CHKDSK aborted.

[Chkdsk-NTFS]

Delete some unneeded files from the NTFS volume and then retry the Chkdsk command.

Insufficient disk space to fix the log file. CHKDSK aborted.

[Chkdsk-NTFS]

Delete some unneeded files from the NTFS volume, if you can, and then retry the Chkdsk command. If you cannot delete any files, reformat the NTFS volume and restore files from backup.

Insufficient disk space to fix the uppercase file. CHKDSK aborted.

[Chkdsk-NTFS]

Delete some unneeded files from the NTFS volume and then retry the Chkdsk command.

Insufficient disk space to fix volume bitmap. CHKDSK aborted.

[Chkdsk-NTFS]

Delete some unneeded files from the NTFS volume, if you can, and then retry the Chkdsk command. If you cannot delete any files, you will have to reformat the NTFS volume and restore data from backup.

Insufficient disk space to hotfix unreadable system file ***filename*** **.CHKDSK Aborted.**

[Chkdsk-NTFS]

There is not enough free disk space to replace the damaged file record. This file record is crucial to the proper functioning of the file system.

Delete some unneeded files from the NTFS volume, if you can, and then retry the Chkdsk command. If you cannot delete any files, you will have to reformat the NTFS volume and restore data from backup.

Insufficient disk space to hotfix unreadable user file ***filename*****.**

[Chkdsk-NTFS]

Delete some unneeded files from the NTFS volume and then retry the Chkdsk command.

Insufficient disk space to insert missing data attribute.

[Chkdsk-NTFS]

Chkdsk inserts a marker in NTFS files that are empty (have no data attribute). There was no free disk space to write such a marker.

Delete some unneeded files from the NTFS volume and then retry the Chkdsk command.

Insufficient disk space to print.

[Help]

You lack the disk space to print the selected topic.

Delete unnecessary files from your hard disk, then try again.

Insufficient disk space to record bad clusters.

[Chkdsk-NTFS]

Delete some unneeded files from the NTFS volume and then retry the Chkdsk command with the /r switch.

Insufficient disk space to recover lost data.

[Chkdsk-NTFS]

Move or delete some files to free disk space, then retry the Chkdsk utility.

Insufficient disk space to repair master file table mirror. CHKDSK aborted.

[Chkdsk-NTFS]

The master file table mirror must not be damaged for the file system to function properly.

Delete some unneeded files from the NTFS volume, if you can, and then retry the Chkdsk command. If you cannot delete any files, you will have to reformat the NTFS volume and restore data from backup.

Insufficient disk space to replace bad clusters detected in file *filename*.

[Chkdsk]

There is not enough free space on the disk to allocate new clusters to replace bad clusters found in the specified file.

Delete unneeded files and run Chkdsk /r again.

Insufficient disk space.

[Backup] [Replace] [Xcopy]

The disk is full and the process cannot be completed.

Move or delete some files to free disk space, or use another disk. Then retry the operation.

Insufficient Memory

[OS/2 Subsystem]

There is not enough memory right now for the Windows NT OS/2 subsystem to run this application.

Wait, then restart the application. If you get this message again, quit some running applications and then restart the application. If you still get this message, contact your system administrator. You may need more memory installed in your computer.

Insufficient memory available.

[Backup] [Network] [Performance Monitor] [Program Manager] [Repair Disk]

You do not have sufficient memory to perform the specified operation.

Close one or more of the Windows NT applications that you have running, then try again.

Insufficient memory for buffers.

[Command Prompt]

There was not enough memory for the internal buffers of the Expand command.

Free memory by closing files and programs you no longer use. If you still get this message, remove memory-resident (TSR) programs or unnecessary device drivers from your CONFIG.SYS file, then restart your computer.

Insufficient memory for dialog box.

[Help]

The system is low on memory. Therefore, Help cannot display a dialog box.

Close one or more of the applications that you have running to free system memory.

Insufficient memory resources.

[Virtual DOS Machine (VDM)]

Terminate the application, and quit any unneeded applications that are running. Then restart your application.

Insufficient memory to complete this operation.

[Remote Access Service]

Close other Windows applications.

Insufficient memory to continue operation. From device: *name*

[QIC117]

Close some applications and try again.

Insufficient memory to display all fonts

[Program Manager]

Close some applications and try again.

Insufficient memory to grow DOSKEY list.

[Doskey]

Delete any unneeded commands in the command history list and try the operation again. For example, you can clear all the buffered commands by pressing Alt+F7. If this message occurs often, use the /listsize switch on the Doskey command to increase the number of commands that can be remembered.

Insufficient memory to load installable Virtual Device Drivers.

[Virtual DOS Machine (VDM)]

Quit some unneeded application programs, then restart your virtual DOS machine. If you still get this message, ask your system administrator to check the Virtual Device Drivers key in the Registry of your computer.

Insufficient memory to print.

[Help]

The applications that are already running are making demands upon system memory. Consequently, you cannot print the currently selected topic.

Close one or more of the applications that you have running, then try again.

Insufficient memory.

[Format]

There was not enough memory to carry out this command.

Free memory by closing files and programs you no longer use.

Insufficient privilege for the file *filename* **- skipped.**

[Backup]

You do not have the necessary privileges to restore the named file. Therefore, this file was not restored.

Either ask that permission be given to you to write to the named file (and to access and write in the directory it is in), or log in with a username that has this permission. Then repeat the restore operation, specify this file.

Insufficient privilege to load the key.

[Registry Editor]

To load a hive, you must have Restore privilege on the Registry.

Ask your network administration to give you the permissions to restore the hive. Then try again.

Insufficient privilege to perform requested operation.

[Registry Editor]

You attempted to perform in Registry Editor an operation that you do not have adequate permission.

See your system administrator. If you are the administrator, log on under your administrative account, and then try again to perform the operation.

Insufficient privilege to save the key.

[Registry Editor]

To use the Save Key command, you need Backup privileges.

Log on as a different user, for example as an Administrator, and try again.

Insufficient privilege to unload the key.

[Registry Editor]

To unload a hive, you must have Backup privilege on the Registry.

Ask your network administrator to give you the necessary permissions, then try again.

Insufficient room in root directory   Move files from root directory and repeat CHKDSK

[Chkdsk]

When the Chkdsk command converts lost chains into files, it creates a directory for the found files in the root directory. There was not room in the root for this new directory.

Copy one or more files from the root directory into a subdirectory and use the Chkdsk command with the /f switch again.

Interface failure occurred

[Dynamic Data Exchange]

NetBIOS failed.

Use Event Viewer to find out what errors may have cause NetBIOS to fail. Then look up those errors and take the appropriate action.

Internal authentication error.

[Remote Access Service]

This error should not occur under normal circumstances.

Restart your computer to make sure that all recent configuration changes have taken effect. If the error persists, consult the Windows NT event log for detailed warnings or errors. Please record the Fail Code (a NetBIOS error code), and make it available to your technical support staff if you call for help.

Internal consistency error.

[Recover-FAT/HPFS]

The recover process did not complete because of the internal error that was encountered.

Retry the Recover command. You might want to investigate your system's file allocation table (FAT) and the high-performance (HPFS) file systems. They are probably corrupted.

Internal error in NCPA.CPL: LMUICMN DLL Initialization failed

[Control Panel]

One of the information sources required for this operation could not be made available.

Try again later. If you still get this message, see the event log in Event Viewer for details. Then contact your network administrator.

Internal error in NCPA.CPL: LMUICMN DLL Initialization failed

[TCP/IP]

Close and re-open the Control Panel, and try again.

Internal error in NTVDM procedure.

[Virtual DOS Machine (VDM)]

Terminate the application, then restart it. If you still get this message, contact technical support.

Internal Error in Query: *text*

[Control Panel]

The specified error occurred, probably during the binding operation.

Reboot the computer, then choose Network from the Control Panel and choose Binding to redo the binding. If the problem continues, ask the administrator to do the following: Edit the registry, removing the variable \Software\Microsoft\Ncpa\CurrentVersion\Bindfile. Then choose Network from Control Panel and choose Binding to redo the binding. If the problem still occurs, remove the recently installed network components, reboot the computer, and reinstall the network components.

Internal error on NetBIOS card

[Dynamic Data Exchange]

The network adapter card used by the NetBIOS interface had an internal error.

Make sure that the card is properly seated and that the cable plug is snug. It might be necessary to replace the card.

Internal Error.

[More]

This message indicates a severe system error occurred while running the More command.

Contact technical support to help you identify the problem.

Internal OS/2 Subsystem Error - application terminated

[OS/2 Subsystem]

An error has occurred in the Windows NT OS/2 subsystem. The application you were running in this subsystem has consequently stopped.

Contact technical support, and report what application was being run and what activities had taken place in that application immediately before this message appeared.

Invalid accelerator table handle.

[Kernel32]

As part of its user interface, an application has tried to operate on a keyboard accelerator table without specifying which one.

Contact the supplier of the running application.

Invalid access to memory location.

[Kernel32]

Contact the supplier of the running application.

Invalid Base I/O Port Address.

[Program Manager]

In the Base I/O Port Address list in the Advanced Settings dialog box, you entered a port address in a format other than hexadecimal.

Enter the address in hexadecimal format, without the 0x prefix.

Invalid Base I/O Port Address.

[Program Manager]

In the Base I/O Port Address list in the Advanced Settings dialog box, you entered a port address other than one of the addresses listed. The list contains all of the options that you can select.

Select one of these options, then choose OK.

Invalid baud rate specified

[Utilities]

The baud rate specified was invalid.

Use the Ports option in Control Panel to select a valid baud rate.

Invalid baud rate; the baud rate must be a positive value.

[Program Manager]

In the Baud Rate option of the Settings dialog box, you specified a negative integer as a baud rate for the selected serial port. You must specify a positive number for this option.

From the Baud Rate list, select one of the listed baud bates, then choose OK.

Invalid baud rate; the baud rate must be a positive value.

[Program Manager]

In the Baud Rate option of the Settings dialog box, you specified a negative integer as a baud rate for the selected serial port. You must specify a positive number for this option.

From the Baud Rate list, select one of the listed baud bates, then choose OK.

Invalid Border Width entry. Specify a number between 1 and 50.

[Program Manager]

In the Desktop option's Border Width box, you entered a zero, a negative number, or a number larger than fifty. This Desktop setting must contain a number between 1 and 50.

Specify a number between 1 and 50.

Invalid Border Width entry. Specify a number between 1 and 50.

[Program Manager]

In the Desktop option's Border Width box, you entered a zero, a negative number, or a number larger than fifty. This Desktop setting must contain a number between 1 and 50.

Specify a number between 1 and 50.

Invalid characters in volume label

[Utilities]

Verify that the characters in the volume label are compatible with the file system.

Invalid code page

[Chcp]

The code page number you used as a parameter in the Chcp command is invalid. Chcp cannot set the active code page number to that value.

Try the Chcp command again, with a valid parameter value, or use the International icon in Control Panel.

Invalid code page specified

[Chcp]

Use the International option in Control Panel to select a valid code page.

Invalid code page specified

[Utilities]

Use the International option in Control Panel to select a valid code page.

Invalid command

[Backup]

The tape drive and backup may be incompatible.

Check the Hardware Compatibility List for the compatible version of the tape drive. You might also want to contact the supplier of the drive. Be sure to record any messages and information you see for them.

Invalid command.

[AT-Network]

You used invalid switches in the command.

Type AT /? to see the correct syntax for the command.

Invalid compression specified.

[Remote Access Service]

This error should not occur under normal circumstances.

Restart your computer to make sure that all recent configuration changes have taken effect. If the error persists, consult the Windows NT event log for detailed warnings or errors.

Invalid cursor handle.

[Kernel32]

As part of its user interface, an application has tried to operate on a mouse cursor without specifying which one.

Contact the supplier of the running application.

Invalid date

[Repair Disk]

You specified a date that does not exist or used a format that Restore does not recognize.

Try again, using a format recognized by Restore. To see the recognized formats, type restore /?

Invalid decimal digit entry

[Program Manager]

In the Decimal Digits option box of the International-Number Format dialog box, you entered nothing, or you deleted the 2 that appears in this box by default. A number must appear in this box.

Enter a single digit number from 0 to 9.

Invalid decimal digit entry

[Program Manager]

In the Decimal Digits option box of the International-Number Format dialog box, you entered nothing, or you deleted the 2 that appears in this box by default. A number must appear in this box.

Enter a single digit number from 0 to 9.

Invalid decimal entry

[Program Manager]

In the Decimal Digits option box of the International-Currency Format dialog box, you entered nothing, or you deleted the 2 that appears in this box by default. A number must appear in this box.

Enter a single digit number from 0 to 9.

Invalid default gateway address *address* **was specified for adapter** *name***. Some remote networks may not be reachable as a result.**

[Netevent]

Get the correct gateway address from your network administrator. Then use the Network applet in the Control Panel to specify this address in the TCP/IP configuration. Then try again.

Invalid device context (DC) handle.

[Kernel32]

An application, as part of its user interface, has tried to release a system resource but did not specify which one.

Contact the supplier of the running application.

Invalid device name or path specified.

[Setup]

Retry initial installation from the start. If you get the same message, contact your technical support group.

Invalid device name or path specified.

[Repair Disk]

Retry initial installation from the start. If you get the same message, contact your technical support group.

Invalid Domain or Server name.

[Event Viewer]

The domain name or server name that you specified does not conform to the rules for naming domains and servers.

Make sure you have the correct domain name or server name. Then try again, making sure the name is typed correctly. Remember that server names must be preceded with a double backslash (\\).

Invalid Domain or Server name.

[Server Manager]

There is no domain or server with the name you entered.

Make sure you have the correct name. Then try again, making sure the name is typed correctly.

Invalid drive - *drive letter*

[Convert]

When you specified the drive for the Convert utility to convert to the NTFS file system, either you specified a drive that does not exist or you specified a redirected drive.

Convert cannot be run on a remote drive. If you simply mistyped the drive letter in the Convert command line, retry the command with the correct drive letter.

Invalid drive or file name

[Recover-FAT/HPFS]

Make sure the drive exists and that the filename is valid and exists on the path specified.

Invalid drive or file name

[Edlin]

Make sure the drive exists and that the filename is valid and exists on the path specified.

Invalid drive specification

[Xcopy]

The drive specified either for the source or destination of the Xcopy command does not exist.

Check that you entered the correct source and target paths.

Invalid drive specification

[Repair Disk]

The drive specification must be in the form of the drive letter followed by a colon (:). For example, B: and D: are valid drive specifications.

Try again, using a valid drive specification.

Invalid drive specification Specified drive does not exist or is non-removable

[Disk Compare]

The Diskcopy and Diskcomp commands work only on local, removable drives. You may have specified a non-existent drive letter, a hard disk, or a drive letter that was assigned or substituted.

Specify the name of a valid floppy disk drive.

Invalid drive specification Specified drive does not exist or is non-removable

[Disk Copy]

The Diskcopy and Diskcomp commands work only on local, removable drives. You may have specified a non-existent drive letter, a hard disk, or a drive letter that was assigned or substituted.

Specify the name of a valid floppy disk drive.

Invalid drive specification Specified drive does not exist or is non-removable

[Tree]

The Diskcopy and Diskcomp commands work only on local, removable drives. You may have specified a non-existent drive letter, a hard disk, or a drive letter that was assigned or substituted.

Specify the name of a valid floppy disk drive.

Invalid drive specification Specified drive does not exist or is non-removable

[Xcopy]

The Diskcopy and Diskcomp commands work only on local, removable drives. You may have specified a non-existent drive letter, a hard disk, or a drive letter that was assigned or substituted.

Specify the name of a valid floppy disk drive.

Invalid drive.

[Help]

You have attempted to select a drive that does not exist on your system.

Select a drive that exists.

Invalid existing format. This disk cannot be QuickFormatted. Proceed with Unconditional Format (Y/N)? *text*

[Format]

The format of the disk is not supported by Windows NT. The disk cannot be QuickFormatted because QuickFormat preserves the existing format.

Either proceed with unconditional format, which will create a valid disk format, or supply a validly formatted disk.

Invalid filename: *filename.*

[Backup]

Backup uses only log files, and you have attempted to use a file of a different type.

Select a log file, then try again.

Invalid flags.

[Kernel32]

Contact the supplier of the running application.

Invalid Grid Granularity entry. Specify a number between 0 and 49.

[Program Manager]

The Grid Granularity setting in the Desktop option determines both the position and the size of the windows you manipulate. If you set this option at zero, the windows appear where you place them. If you set the option at larger than zero, all items on your desktop align in an orderly fashion. This number must be set between zero and 49, and you have selected a number either less than zero or greater than 49.

Select a number between 0 and 49, then select OK.

Invalid Grid Granularity entry. Specify a number between 0 and 49.

[Program Manager]

The Grid Granularity setting in the Desktop option determines both the position and the size of the windows you manipulate. If you set this option at zero, the windows appear where you place them. If you set the option at larger than zero, all items on your desktop align in an orderly fashion. This number must be set between zero and 49, and you have selected a number either less than zero or greater than 49.

Select a number between 0 and 49, then select OK.

Invalid GW_* command.

[Kernel32]

As part of its user interface, an application used an invalid operation.

Contact the supplier of the running application.

Invalid handle to a multiple-window position structure.

[Kernel32]

As part of its user interface, an application has tried to operate on a multiple-window structure without specifying which one.

Contact the supplier of the running application.

Invalid hook handle.

[Kernel32]

As part of its user interface, an application has tried to operate on a procedure that monitors the system for certain events, without specifying which one.

Contact the supplier of the running application.

Invalid hook procedure type.

[Kernel32]

As part of its user interface, an application has tried to install a procedure to monitor the system for certain events, but the type of procedure was not recognized by Windows NT.

Contact the supplier of the running application.

Invalid hook procedure.

[Kernel32]

As part of its user interface, an application has tried to install a procedure to monitor the system for certain events, but the procedure format is invalid.

Contact the supplier of the running application.

Invalid host name.

[Control Panel]

The host name was specified in an incorrect format.

Correct the host name of your computer by reconfiguring the TCP/IP protocol. Use the Network option in Control Panel to configure the TCP/IP protocol. Select Connectivity and then change the host name.

Invalid host name.

[TCP/IP]

The host name was specified in an incorrect format.

Correct the host name of your computer by reconfiguring the TCP/IP protocol. Use the Network option in Control Panel to configure the TCP/IP protocol. Select Connectivity and then change the host name.

Invalid icon handle.

[Kernel32]

As part of its user interface, an application has tried to operate on an icon without specifying which one.

Contact the supplier of the running application.

Invalid Icon Spacing entry

[Program Manager]

The Icon Spacing setting in the Desktop option allows you to arrange your icons in relation to one another. You can space your icons from 32 to 512 pixels apart. Any other setting is invalid.

In the Spacing option, specify a number between 32 and 512. When you exit the Desktop option, select the Arrange Icons option in the Program Manager Window menu, and your Icon Spacing entry takes effect.

Invalid Icon Spacing entry

[Program Manager]

The Icon Spacing setting in the Desktop option allows you to arrange your icons in relation to one another. You can space your icons from 32 to 512 pixels apart. Any other setting is invalid.

In the Spacing option, specify a number between 32 and 512. When you exit the Desktop option, select the Arrange Icons option in the Program Manager Window menu, and your Icon Spacing entry takes effect.

Invalid index.

[Kernel32]

Contact the supplier of the running application.

Invalid information found in the phone book file.

[Remote Access Service]

The Remote Access Service uses the file RASPHONE.PBK, located in the SYSTEM32\RAS subdirectory of your Windows NT directory.

Delete this file, and restart Remote Access.

Invalid input for function

[Calculator]

The number that you have entered is not appropriate to the function that you are attempting to perform. For example, you cannot request the factorial for a negative number.

Enter a number that corresponds to the function that you are attempting to perform.

Invalid instance number *number* specified for module *name*. The service could not be started.

[Netevent]

The specified module was installed incorrectly.

Remove the TCP/IP protocol and then reinstall it using the Network option in Control Panel.

Invalid IP Address entered.

[WINS Service]

The value you entered is not in the valid format for an IP address. IP addresses must be of the form w.x.y.z, where w, x, y, and z are decimal numbers between 0 and 255 representing the four bytes of the IP address.

Enter a different IP address.

Invalid IP address.

[Control Panel]

You specified the IP address of the protocol in an incorrect format.

Use Network in Control Panel to configure the TCP/IP protocol and correct the IP address.

Invalid IP or Subnet Mask address.

[TCP/IP]

While using the TCP/IP Configuration dialog, you specified the IP address or the subnet mask in an incorrect format.

Ask your system administrator for the correct IP address and subnet mask. Then use the Network option in the Control panel to configure the TCP/IP protocol and correct the IP address or subnet mask.

Invalid Item List

[Dynamic Data Exchange]

Report this error message to the vendor of the application you were using when the message appeared.

Invalid keyboard code specified

[Keyb]

Make sure the keyboard code value you specified in the Keyb command is correct, and then try again.

Invalid keyboard delay

[Mode]

You specified an invalid value for the Typematic delay for the console keyboard, using the Mode command.

Retry the command, using a valid Delay= parameter value.

Invalid keyboard ID specified

[Keyb]

Use the International option in Control Panel to select a valid keyboard ID.

Invalid keyboard rate

[Mode]

You specified an invalid value for the Typematic rate for the console keyboard, using the Mode command.

Retry the command, using a valid Rate= parameter value.

Invalid keyword.

[Help]

The currently active application attempted to search the Help file on the basis of a keyword that does not exist in the Help file.

Specify a keyword that appears in the keyword list, then try again.

Invalid level in call

[Dynamic Data Exchange]

Report this error message to the vendor of the application you were using when the message appeared.

Invalid library handle: *name*.

[Setup]

This is a warning message. SETUP.EXE was trying to unload a dynamic-link library (DLL), but the handle to the library was invalid.

Retry Setup. If you get the same message, contact your technical support group.

Invalid library handle: *name*.

[Repair Disk]

This is a warning message. SETUP.EXE was trying to unload a dynamic-link library (DLL), but the handle to the library was invalid.

Retry Setup. If you get the same message, contact your technical support group.

Invalid library procedure: *name*.

[Setup]

Setup opened a dynamic-link library (DLL) on the path specified in the SETUP.INF file, but could not find a required procedure within that DLL.

Exit Setup, then retry the Setup operation from the beginning. If you get the message again, contact your technical support group.

Invalid library procedure: *name*.

[Repair Disk]

Setup opened a dynamic-link library (DLL) on the path specified in the SETUP.INF file, but could not find a required procedure within that DLL.

Exit Setup, then retry the Setup operation from the beginning. If you get the message again, contact your technical support group.

Invalid log file format.

[Aclconv]

The log file specified is not a valid Aclconv log file. The Aclconv /list command can only display log files created by Aclconv.

Invalid logical sector specification in read/write. From device: *name*

[QIC117]

The application using the QIC117 device has made an illegal request.

Contact technical support.

Invalid macro definition.

[Doskey]

Windows NT cannot interpret a new Doskey macro definition. You may have used a metacharacter that the Doskey command does not recognize in the macro, or tried to nest one macro inside another.

Edit the macro and retry it.

Invalid media or Track 0 bad - disk unusable.

[Format]

The disk may be unusable, or you may be trying to format the disk to an incorrect format.

Make sure you are formatting the correct density. For example, you cannot format a double-density disk as a high-density disk. If you continue to get this message, the disk may have bad sectors near the beginning of the disk. The Format command can accommodate defective sectors on the disk, except those near the beginning. If the disk is a floppy disk, use another disk. If the disk is a hard disk, contact your hardware vendor.

Invalid menu handle.

[Kernel32]

As part of its user interface, an application has tried to operate on a menu without specifying which one.

Contact the supplier of the running application.

Invalid message box style.

[Kernel32]

An application, as part of its user interface, has specified a style for a message box that cannot be interpreted or acted upon by Windows NT.

Contact the supplier of the running application.

Invalid message for a combo box because it does not have an edit control.

[Kernel32]

An application, as part of its user interface, has tried to get input typed by the user from a control that does not have that capability.

Contact the supplier of the running application.

Invalid message for single-selection list box.

[Kernel32]

An application, as part of its user interface, tried to operate on a list box in an inappropriate way, given its contents.

Contact the supplier of the running application.

Invalid muxid specified for upper driver *name*. The service could not be started.

[Netevent]

The driver was installed incorrectly.

Remove the TCP/IP protocol and then reinstall it using the Network option in Control Panel.

invalid name syntax ' *name* '

[PORTUAS]

Make sure you have the correct the username or group name. Then try again, making sure to type the name correctly.

Invalid network range specified for adapter "*name* ".

[Services for Macintosh (SFM)]

For a LocalTalk adapter, the low end of the network range must be equal to the high end of the network range. For example, a LocalTalk adapter range would be 1 to 1 or 3 to 3. For adapters that are not LocalTalk, the low end of the range must be less than the high end. For example, an invalid range for a non-LocalTalk adapter would be 4 to 1. A valid range would be 1 to 4.

Use the Network option in Control Panel to change the ranges. In the Installed Network Software box, choose Services for Macintosh and then choose Configure. In the Advanced Configuration dialog box, change the ranges for the network adapters to satisfy the criteria mentioned.

Invalid number of parameters

[Xcopy]

You specified too many or too few parameters for this command.

To find out the syntax of this command, type HELP at the command prompt followed by the command name.

Invalid number of parameters

[Restore]

You specified too many or too few parameters for this command.

To find out the syntax of this command, type HELP at the command prompt followed by the command name.

Invalid number of parameters

[Repair Disk]

For a list of valid parameters, use the command restore /?Then try again, using only the valid parameters.

Invalid option: *text*

[TCP/IP]

You specified an invalid switch in the NBTSTAT command. Valid switches are: -A, to display server connections; -R, to reread the LMHOSTS file; -N to list local NetBIOS names, -C to list the NetBIOS name cache, and -C to list the NetBIOS name cache using IP addresses.

Retry the NBTSTAT command using one or more of the valid options.

Invalid option: *text*

[NBTSTAT-TCP/IP]

You specified an invalid switch in the NBTSTAT command. Valid switches are: -A, to display server connections; -R, to reread the LMHOSTS file; -N to list local NetBIOS names, -C to list the NetBIOS name cache, and -C to list the NetBIOS name cache using IP addresses.

Retry the NBTSTAT command using one or more of the valid options.

Invalid options in a file description line in a .INF file.

[Setup]

While generating the file copy list from an .INF file, Setup encountered a File Description line with invalid options.

Select Retry to retry the operation. If you still get this message, select Exit Setup. Restore all the .INF files from the distribution medium (you will have to decompress the files). Then rerun the Setup operation from the beginning. If you get this message again, contact your technical support group.

Invalid options in a file description line in a .INF file.

[Repair Disk]

While generating the file copy list from an .INF file, Setup encountered a File Description line with invalid options.

Select Retry to retry the operation. If you still get this message, select Exit Setup. Restore all the .INF files from the distribution medium (you will have to decompress the files). Then rerun the Setup operation from the beginning. If you get this message again, contact your technical support group.

Invalid parameter - *parameter*

[Convert]

You specified a parameter that is not valid for this command.

To find out which parameters are valid for a command, type HELP at the command prompt followed by the command name.

Invalid parameter - *parameter*

[Mode]

You specified a parameter that is not valid for this command.

To find out which parameters are valid for a command, type HELP at the command prompt followed by the command name.

Invalid parameter - *parameter*

[Xcopy]

You specified a parameter that is not valid for this command.

To find out which parameters are valid for a command, type HELP at the command prompt followed by the command name.

Invalid parameter - *parameter*

[Subst]

You specified a parameter that is not valid for this command.

To find out which parameters are valid for a command, type HELP at the command prompt followed by the command name.

Invalid parameter - *parameter*

[Utilities]

You specified a parameter that is not valid for this command.

To find out which parameters are valid for a command, type HELP at the command prompt followed by the command name.

Invalid parameter combination

[Utilities]

Type HELP followed by the command name at the command prompt to find out which parameters can be combined.

Invalid path

[Utilities]

Either the source or destination supplied with the Xcopy command is invalid.

Make sure that the specified source path is valid and exists, and that the specified destination is valid.

Invalid path

[Repair Disk]

Either the source or destination supplied with the Restore command is invalid.

Make sure that the specified source path is valid and exists, and that the specified destination is valid. Remember to separate directory names with a backslash (\) and not a forward slash (/).

Invalid path created by combining *text* and *text*.

[Setup]

Setup created a path by combining partial path specifications in an .INF file, and the created path was invalid.

Select the Exit Setup option. Then retry the Setup operation from the beginning. If you still get this message, contact your technical support group.

Invalid path created by combining *text* and *text*.

[Repair Disk]

Setup created a path by combining partial path specifications in an .INF file, and the created path was invalid.

Select the Exit Setup option. Then retry the Setup operation from the beginning. If you still get this message, contact your technical support group.

Invalid path specification.

[Help]

The application that you are using has attempted to access a Help file that does not exist in the expected location.

Make sure that the Help file exists either in the same directory in which the application's executable file exists, or that the Help file is located in the Windows NT SYSTEM32 directory.

Invalid program file name, please check your pif file.

[Virtual DOS Machine (VDM)]

The program filename in the PIF file is invalid. For example, it may not have a .COM or .EXE extension.

Use the PIF editor to change the executable filename in the PIF file.

Invalid Screen Saver Delay entry

[Program Manager]

When you select a Screen Saver in the Desktop option in Control Panel, you must indicate the time that must pass before the screen saver appears on the screen. This entry must be between 1 and 99 minutes, and you entered a number that does not fall in this range.

Enter a number between 1 and 99, then choose OK.

Invalid Screen Saver Delay entry

[Program Manager]

When you select a Screen Saver in the Desktop option in Control Panel, you must indicate the time that must pass before the screen saver appears on the screen. This entry must be between 1 and 99 minutes, and you entered a number that does not fall in this range.

Enter a number between 1 and 99, then choose OK.

Invalid section name in .INF file ***filename*****.**

[Setup]

For example, Setup expects section names in an .INF file to be enclosed in square brackets. The .INF file may be corrupted.

Select Retry to retry the operation. If you get the same message, select Exit Setup. Restore the .INF file from the distribution medium (you will have to decompress it). Then rerun the Setup operation from the beginning. If you get this message again, contact your technical support group.

Invalid section name in .INF file ***filename*****.**

[Repair Disk]

For example, Setup expects section names in an .INF file to be enclosed in square brackets. The .INF file may be corrupted.

Select Retry to retry the operation. If you get the same message, select Exit Setup. Restore the .INF file from the distribution medium (you will have to decompress it). Then rerun the Setup operation from the beginning. If you get this message again, contact your technical support group.

Invalid size.

[Disk Administrator]

When you create a partition, volume set, or stripe set, you are presented with a message telling you the minimum and maximum sizes that the partition, volume set, or stripe set can be. You have attempted to create one of these entities and have not observed the specified maximum or minimum size.

Double-check to ensure that your partition, volume set, or stripe set fulfills the size specifications of the message that appeared when you created them.

Invalid startup directory, please check your pif file.

[Virtual DOS Machine (VDM)]

NTVDM was unable to find the application in the startup directory specified by the PIF file.

NTVDM was unable to find the application in the startup directory specified by the PIF file.

Invalid subnet mask *number* **was specified for address** *address* **on adapter** *number*. **This interface cannot be initialized.**

[Netevent]

Get the correct subnet mask address from your network administrator. Then use the Network applet in the Control Panel to specify this address in the TCP/IP configuration. Then try again.

Invalid switch - "*text* **".**

[Command]

You have entered with a command a switch that does not correspond to that command.

To determine which switches are available for the command you want to use, type the command at the command prompt, then type /?. Command prompt now displays and defines the valid switches.

Invalid switch - *parameter*

[Attrib] [File Compare] [Find] [Print] [Replace] [Sort] [Tree] [Xcopy]

You typed a switch that is not valid for this command. In general, a switch is a parameter beginning with a slash, such as /s. (Some switches may start with a - or +).

To check which switches are valid for this command, type HELP at the command prompt followed by the command name.

Invalid Switch - *name*

[Repair Disk]

You included a switch that is not used with the Restore command.

For a list of accepted switches, type restore /?

Invalid system-wide (SPI_*) parameter.

[Kernel32]

An application, as part of its user interface, has used a system-wide parameter not recognized by Windows NT.

Contact the supplier of the running application.

Invalid TCP Domain Name.

[TCP/IP]

You specified the domain name in an incorrect format.

Use the Network option in Control Panel to change the TCP domain name of the TCP/IP protocol.

Invalid thread identifier.

[Kernel32]

An application, as part of its user interface, has tried to use a particular set of running code, but did not identify which one.

Contact the supplier of the running application.

Invalid time

[Repair Disk]

You specified a time that does not exist, for example 25:00:00, or you specified the time in an invalid format, or a character was included in your time specification that is not used in time formats.

Try again. Be sure to use a format recognized by Restore. To see the recognized formats, type restore /?

Invalid time separator entry

[Program Manager]

In the Separator option box in the International-Time Format dialog box, you entered a time separator option that the Control Panel does not accept, or you deleted the (:) that appears in the option box by default.

Enter the separator that you want to appear with times on your system.

Invalid timeout entry

[Program Manager]

If you are running a dual boot system, you can indicate how many seconds pass before the default operating system automatically starts. This entry appears in the Show list for option, and you must enter in this option a number between 0 and 999. You have entered a negative number in this option.

Enter a number between 0 and 999 and try again.

Invalid timeout entry

[Program Manager]

If you are running a dual boot system, you can indicate how many seconds pass before the default operating system automatically starts. This entry appears in the Show list for option, and you must enter in this option a number between 0 and 999. You have entered a negative number in this option.

Enter a number between 0 and 999 and try again.

Invalid Update Frequency. Minimum value is 100 ms.

[Remote Access Service]

You attempted to enter an update frequency of less than 100ms. Such values are disallowed since they don't result in faster updates, but do result in unnecessary loads on the system.

Specify a number greater than 99.

Invalid value for the Time Interval. It should be between 0 and 2000000

[Performance Monitor]

This number represents the number of seconds between updates.

Enter a number in this range.

Invalid value for the Vertical Maximum. It should be between 1 and 2000000000.

[Performance Monitor]

This number represents the maximum value used for the vertical axis in the chart view.

Enter a number in this range. It should be slightly larger than the maximum value you expect to log.

Invalid volume label

[Utilities]

Verify that the volume label is supported by the file system being used.

Invalid window handle.

[Kernel32]

As part of its user interface, an application has tried to operate on a window without specifying which one.

Contact the supplier of the running application.

Invalid window, belongs to other thread.

[Kernel32]

As part of its user interface, an application has tried to operate on the wrong window.

Contact the supplier of the running application.

IO error on both the source and destination disks.

[File Manager]

An I/O error occurred on both the source and destination disks while you were attempting to perform a disk copy.

Make sure that the disks are not damaged, then try again.

IO error on the destination disk.

[File Manager]

An I/O error occurred when trying to write to the target disk during a disk copy.

Make sure that the disk is not damaged, then try again.

IO error on the source disk.

[File Manager]

An I/O error occurred when you were trying to read from the target disk during a disk copy.

Make sure that the disk is not damaged, then try again.

IoCreateDevice failed on port *address*.

[Digi]

The Windows NT name space device could not be created.

Contact Digi technical support. The support number should be given in the configuration help dialogs.

IP address *address* is not valid. No link to this network was established.

[Netevent]

The IP address specified during Setup is invalid.

Use Network in Control Panel to reconfigure the TCP/IP and to correct the IP address.

IP address must be unique for each network card.

[TCP/IP]

If you have more than one network card in your computer, you must specify different IP addresses for each card.

Specify a unique IP address for each network card by selecting TCP/IP protocol in Network in Control Panel.

IP broadcast attempted to invalid address *address*.

[Netevent]

The interface specified by the IP address is not configured to accept subnet broadcasts.

No action is needed.

IP cannot source-route a broadcast packet. Source *address*, Destination *address*.

[Netevent]

Broadcast packets cannot be source-routed using IP. Since these packets are sent to everyone, do not specify the path the packets are to use to reach their destinations.

Ask your system administrator to correct the packets generated by the computer at the specified source IP address.

IP could not transmit a packet of size *number* marked Don't Fragment. Source *address*, Destination *address*.

[Netevent]

The packet is too large to send without fragmenting it.

Ask your system administrator to correct the packet sizes generated by the computer at the specified source IP address or to increase your network's maximum transmission unit.

IP has received *number* packets with invalid header checksums.

[Netevent]

IP received packets with bad checksums.

Ask your system administrator to correct the packets generated by the computer at the specified source IP address.

IP has received *number* packets with invalid lengths.

[Netevent]

IP received several invalid packets.

Ask your system administrator to correct the packets generated by the computer at the specified source IP address.

IP received a packet with incompatible header version *number*.

[Netevent]

Packets received by the IP should be version 4.

Ask your system administrator to correct the packets generated by the computer at the specified source IP address.

IP received a packet with option *name* of invalid length *number*. Source *address*, Destination *address*.

[Netevent]

Ask your system administrator to correct the packets generated by the computer at the specified source IP address.

IP received an ICMP packet with a bad checksum. Source *address*, Destination *address*.

[Netevent]

IP received an ICMP packet with an invalid checksum.

Ask your system administrator to correct the packets generated by the computer at the specified source IP address.

IP received an ICMP packet with invalid destination protocol *name*, muxid *name*. Type *name*, Code *code*, Source *address*, Destination *address*.

[Netevent]

IP received an invalid protocol identification with the ICMP packet.

Ask your system administrator to correct the packets generated by the computer at the specified source IP address.

IP received an ICMP packet with invalid destination protocol *name*. Type *name*, Code *code*, Source *address*, Destination *address*.

[Netevent]

IP received the specified invalid protocol identification.

Ask your system administrator to correct the packets generated by the computer at the specified source IP address.

IP received an ICMP packet with invalid type *name*. Source *address*, Destination *address*.

[Netevent]

IP received an invalid ICMP packet.

Ask your system administrator to correct the packets generated by the computer at the specified source IP address.

IP received an ICMP packet with option *name* of invalid length *number*. Type *name*, Code *code*, Source *address*, Destination *address*.

[Netevent]

Ask your system administrator to correct the packets generated by the computer at the specified source IP address.

IP received error *code* on network *name*. Marking network as down.

[Netevent]

A lower layer of the protocol sent an M_ERROR message to the IP which will register the network as being down.

Ask your network administrator to check the network interface card.

Is it OK to continue disconnecting and force them closed? *text* : *text*

[Network]

You have tried to break the connection to a resource on which you have open files.

Answer No, close the files from within the application that opened them, and try again. If you cannot close the files from within the application, answer Yes at this prompt.

Job canceled from Print Manager

[Registry Editor]

You have attempted to print Registry data, then canceled the job from Print Manager.

No action is needed.

Key name *name* not found in Configuration Registry

[Control Panel]

The current operation could not be completed because an essential entry in the Registry could not be found.

Restart the computer, then choose the Network option from Control Panel and choose Binding to redo the binding. If the problem continues, ask the administrator to do the following: Edit the registry, removing the variable \Software\Microsoft\Ncpa\CurrentVersion\Bindfile. Then choose Network from Control Panel and choose Binding to redo the binding. If the problem still occurs, remove the recently installed network components, reboot the computer, and reinstall the network components.

Key not found in Configuration Registry

[Control Panel]

The current operation could not be completed because an essential entry in the Registry could not be found.

Reboot the computer, then choose Network from the Control Panel and choose Binding to redo the binding. If the problem continues, ask the administrator to do the following: Edit the registry, removing the variable \Software\Microsoft\Ncpa\CurrentVersion\Bindfile. Then choose Network from the Control Panel and choose Binding to redo the binding. If the problem still occurs, remove the recently installed network components, reboot the computer, and reinstall the network components.

Lan Adapter number information mismatch in Configuration Registry

[Control Panel]

In the Registry, each Local Area Network Adapter (LANA) is mapped to a number. A problem has been detected in this mapping

Ask your network administrator to examine the registry values in \system\CurrentControlSet\Services\NetBIOSInformation\Parameters and resolve the mismatch.

LAN Manager does not recognize "*name* " as a valid option.

[Network] Net Message ID: 3053

This message should occur only on a down-level computer. Any action to correct the problem should be performed on that computer. This option is not valid for this service.

Check the spelling of this option. If you did not type it from the command line, check the configuration file.

LAN Manager error *number* occurred.

[Network]

A LAN Manager error has occurred, and the system was unable to determine the specific nature of the problem.

Look up the LAN Manager message by typing NET HELPMSG <code> at the command prompt and follow the action recommended in the message.

LAN Manager error *code* occurred.

[Services for Macintosh (SFM)]

Contact technical support.

LANA numbers must be less than 256 for each protocol.

[Control Panel]

Configure the NetBIOS interface to change the LANA number of the protocol to 128 or less.

LB_SETCOUNT sent to non-lazy listbox.

[Kernel32]

An application, as part of its user interface, has attempted an invalid operation.

Contact the supplier of the running application.

Length mismatch in received IP packet header. Specified length *number*, **actual** *number*. **Source** *address*, **Destination** *address*.

[Netevent]

IP received an invalid packet.

Ask your system administrator to correct the packets generated by the computer at the specified source IP address.

Lesson not supported by this version of Help.

[Help]

A CBT (computer-based tutorial) is attempting to interface with a version of Help that does not support it.

Close Help, then start the tutorial again.

LFB Aperture conflict, disabling aperture.

[Graphics]

This warning message appears if the linear frame buffer (LFB) conflicts with system memory, or if two drivers clam the same address range in system memory. In either case, it is a hardware conflict. When the aperture is disabled the VGA aperture is used, if it's available, or draw using the engine. Performance is lower than if the LFB were available.

No action is needed.

Line *number* **contains a syntax error.**

[Setup]

Contact the supplier for another copy of the installation media.

Line *path* **!u! contains a syntax error.**

[Setup]

The SETUP.LOG file on the Emergency Repair Disk might be corrupted or bad.

Make sure you have inserted the correct Emergency Repair Disk for your computer. If you don't have the correct disk, let Setup attempt to locate your Windows NT installation.

Line non-operational

[Remote Access Service]

This usually indicates a hardware problem. The modem can be in a weird state.

The user can power cycle the modem.

Listen failed: *text*

[Dynamic Data Exchange]

The computer was expecting data from another computer but has not received it. Either the other computer is not sending, or the thread on this computer that listens for data has encountered an error.

LoadLibrary() fails with winError = *code*

[AT-Network]

Files that are required to run the AT command did not load.

Verify that your system directory contains all files required to run the AT command.

Local security could not be started because an error occurred during initialization. The error code returned is *code*. **THE SYSTEM IS NOT SECURE.**

[Network] Net Message ID: 3186

This message should occur only on a down-level computer. Any action to correct the problem should be performed on that computer. Local security could not start because of the listed error.

Find and correct the cause of the listed error, and then restart the computer.

Local security could not be started because the user accounts database(NET.ACC) was missing or corrupted, and no usable backup database was present. THE SYSTEM IS NOT SECURE.

[Network] Net Message ID: 3185

This message should occur only on a down-level computer. Any action to correct the problem should be performed on that computer. Local security could not start because the user accounts database file, NET.ACC, is missing or damaged and no backup file exists on the hard disk.

Restore NET.ACC from a backup. The backup file will be named either NET.ACC or NETACC.BKP. Then restart the computer. If there is no backup, reinstall LAN Manager using the Setup program.

Lock violation

[Xcopy]

A file that Xcopy was trying to access is locked by another program.

Log file *filename* **is corrupt.**

[Network]

The indicated log file could not be read because it is corrupt or not in the expected format.

Restore the file from a backup copy and try again.

Log file *name* is full.

[Network] Net Message ID: 2377

This message should occur only on a down-level computer. Any action to correct the problem should be performed on that computer. The log file is too large.

Clear the log file or increase the MAXERRORLOG entry in the computer's configuration file. If you need assistance, contact your network administrator.

Logging error

[Backup]

Most likely, your hard disk is full.

Delete unnecessary files from your hard disk, then try again.

Login failed.

[FTP Server]

The name and/or password information entered for the account on the remote procedure is invalid.

Retry the login with a different name and/or password information. If you still get this message, contact the administrator of the remote machine to get a valid name and/or password.

Logon attempt with current password failed with the following error: *text*

[Netevent]

An attempt to log on to a service account failed.

Ask your system administrator to verify the current configured account information for the service. Use Event Viewer to examine the event log and identify the service.

Logon failure: account currently disabled.

[Kernel32]

An administrator has disabled your account to prevent you from logging on.

Ask your administrator to enable your account.

Logon failure: account logon time restriction violation.

[Kernel32]

The user name, domain, and password were accepted, but it is the wrong time-of-day to log on. For example, the request came at midnight and the account is restricted to log ons between 9 a.m. and 5 p.m.

Ask your administrator what restrictions have been applied to your account. Or, if you can, try to log on to a different account which may have no logon restrictions.

Logon failure: the specified account password has expired.

[Kernel32]

Your password has expired and must be changed before you can log on.

Change your password or get an administrator to assign you a new password before you attempt to log on again.

Logon failure: the user has not been granted the requested logon type at this computer.

[Kernel32]

You may be trying to log on interactively to a computer you can only access over a network, or vice versa.

Change your logon location. Try to log on either locally (interactively) or remotely (over the network), as appropriate. You may want to ask the person who administers computer security to change the security database so you can log on either locally or remotely.

Logon failure: unknown user name or bad password.

[Kernel32]

You mistyped either your user name or password, or have selected the wrong domain.

Check your user name and password entries and, if necessary, find out what domain you should be using. Then try to log on again.

Logon failure: user account restriction.

[Kernel32]

The user name, domain, and password were accepted, but then an administrative restriction was encountered, such as the hours you may log on.

Ask an administrator to find out what restrictions have been applied to your account. If you need to get some work done right away, log on at a different computer (if you can).

Logon failure: user not allowed to log on to this computer.

[Kernel32]

The user name, domain, and password were accepted, but the logon request was made from a computer that is not in the account's list of logon computers.

Ask an administrator to find out what restrictions have been applied to your account. If you need to get work done right away, log on at another computer (if you can).

Longterm lock of the server buffers failed. Check swap disk's free space and restart the system to start the server.

[Network] Net Message ID: 3132

This message should occur only on a down-level computer. Any action to correct the problem should be performed on that computer. The server was unable to access required memory.

Be sure there is a least one megabyte of free space on the swap disk. The swap disk is specified by the SWAPPATH entry in the CONFIG.SYS file. Then restart the computer and try to start the Server service again.

Margin values are not within expected ranges. Please verify that margin values are valid positive numbers.

[Cardfile]

You have specified a negative number as a margin, or have specified margins that exceed the height or width of the Cardfile.

Return to the Page Setup dialog box, and specify valid margins.

Master *computer name* **did not send an update notice for directory** *name* **at the expected time.**

[Network]

This alert is raised by the Replicator service if it cannot connect to the master replicator.

Be sure the Server and Replicator services are running on the export server.

Master *computer name* **did not send an update notice for directory** *name* **at the expected time.**

[Network] Net Message ID: 3209

This server's Replicator service lost contact with the export server for the listed directory.

Be sure the Server and Replicator services are running on the export server.

Measurement not in expected range. Please enter a valid positive number.

[Write]

You entered a negative margin or a zero in one of the measurement options in the Page Layout dialog box. Or you entered a number that is too large to fit the page.

Follow the user action specified in the message.

Media in drive may have changed.

[Kernel32]

This is an informational message. The I/O operation was halted because the media in the drive changed unexpectedly.

Retry the operation. Do not change the media unless prompted to do so.

Memory allocation failure.

[Remote Access Service]

Either the server does not have enough virtual memory, or the system quota settings are too low, or the server does not have enough physical memory.

Free memory on the server by optimizing memory allocations to different resources, or by stopping some nonessential services, or by installing more memory on the server.

Memory error during initialization.

[Virtual DOS Machine (VDM)]

Terminate the application, and quit any unneeded applications that are running. Then restart your application.

Message has been sent, but not all recipients have received it.

[Server Manager]

This status message arises because of two possible circumstances. One or more of the workstations to which you sent the message is not running. Or the messenger service on one or more of the workstations in the selected domain is not started.

Wait and try again. Or use the Services option to select the computer and to start its Messenger service remotely.

Message returned in transaction has incorrect size.

[Netevent]

The service controller cannot communicate with the service due to a problem with the system.

Contact technical support.

Messages cannot be forwarded back to the same workstation.

[Network] Net Message ID: 2279

This message should occur only on a down-level computer. Any action to correct the problem should be performed on that computer. You cannot forward a message to yourself at your own workstation.

No action is needed.

Messages for this alias are not currently being forwarded.

[Network] Net Message ID: 2288

This message should occur only on a down-level computer. Any action to correct the problem should be performed on that computer. Messages for this alias are not being forwarded.

No action is needed.

MIDI Mapper could not find a valid MIDIMAP.CFG file in your Windows SYSTEM directory. It cannot run without this file. Do you want to create and initialize a new MIDIMAP.CFG file?

[MIDI Mapper (Control Panel)]

The MIDIMAP.CFG file configures the MIDI Mapper options and contains a record of the sound maps that are already saved to your system. MIDI Mapper cannot run without this file.

Before you select the Yes option, it is advisable to do a search in File Manager for the MIDIMAP.CFG file. If this search fails to produce the file, create and initialize a new MIDIMAP.CFG file by selecting the Yes option, and by filling in the options in the new MIDIMAP.CFG.

Mirror pairs cannot include partitions on removable media.

[Disk Administrator]

Because it is impossible to maintain a mirror if one of the drives is removed, Disk Administrator does not allow removable media to be mirrored or to serve as a mirror.

Mismatch between the floppy disk sector ID field and the floppy disk controller track address.

[Kernel32]

Retry the operation, using a different floppy disk or a floppy disk with a different density. If this message reappears, contact the hardware supplier or the floppy disk driver software supplier.

Mismatch return type.

[Help]

This error is from the Macro Language Editor for online help, and should not appear while using the Help file. Report this error to the provider of the Help file.

Missing ')'

[Help]

This error is from the Macro Language Editor for online help, and should not appear while using the Help file. Report this error to the provider of the Help file.

Missing *configname* **(field 3) on line** *number* **!u! in section** *number***.**

[Setup]

Contact the supplier for another copy of the installation media.

Missing colon or semicolon.

[Help]

This error is from the Macro Language Editor for online help, and should not appear while using the Help file. Report this error to the provider of the Help file.

Missing end quote.

[Help]

This error is from the Macro Language Editor for online help, and should not appear while using the Help file. Report this error to the provider of the Help file.

Modem not responding

[Remote Access Service]

The Remote Access Service did not receive a response from the modem. Remote users will be unable to connect to the server.

The modem should be reconfigured or replaced. Verify that the modem is compatible with the Remote Access Service.

Monitoring Alert on Computer *name* **-** *path* **HP PaintJet XL**

[Performance Monitor]

The indicated computer was disconnected while Performance Monitor was monitoring it.

No action is needed. You will get another message when the remote computer is connected again.

More data is available than can be returned by Windows NT.

[Network] Net Message ID: 3513

Windows NT could not display all available data.

The action required depends on the command that returned the error. Contact your network administrator.

More data is available.

[Kernel32]

A read operation on a pipe has read the requested amount, but the pipe contains more data to read.

Contact the supplier of the running application.

More help is available by typing NET HELPMSG ***number*****.**

[Network]

For more information, at the command prompt type net helpmsg <message number>

More memory needed to complete Setup. Try shutting down some other active programs.

[Setup]

This can be a critical or non-critical error within Setup.

If this is a non-critical error, Setup will present an Ignore option which you should select, and Setup may be able to continue. Otherwise, select Exit Setup and restart the Setup operation. If you get the same message, contact your technical support group.

More memory needed to complete Setup. Try shutting down some other active programs.

[Repair Disk]

This can be a critical or non-critical error within Setup.

If this is a non-critical error, Setup will present an Ignore option which you should select, and Setup may be able to continue. Otherwise, select Exit Setup and restart the Setup operation. If you get the same message, contact your technical support group.

More than the maximum number of default gateways were specified for adapter ***name*****. Some remote networks may not be reachable as a result.**

[Netevent]

Use the Network option in Control Panel to remove some default gateways from the configuration for this adapter. Then try again.

Moving this computer out of the ***name*** **domain may result in loss of access by some domain user accounts. Are you sure you want to move this computer out of the** ***name*** **domain?**

[Control Panel]

Choose Yes if you are sure you want to move this computer out of the domain. Otherwise choose No.

Multiple requests were made for the same session

[Dynamic Data Exchange]

Only one request for the session can be successful.

No action is needed.

Must enter both /t and /n parameters.

[Format]

Type both switches with this command.

Must specify a file system

[Convert]

The Convert command takes two parameters: the volume to be converted and the target file system. You did not supply the second parameter.

To check which parameters are valid for this command, type HELP at the command prompt followed by the command name (in this case, Convert).

name ' *name* **' conflicts with a domain name** *name*

[PORTUAS]

A user or global group name from the down-level database that is being upgraded is a duplicate of the domain name.

PortUAS will ask you for another name for the user or global group, unless the Force Ignore option has been implemented.

Name not found

[Dynamic Data Exchange]

NetBIOS tried to send a message to a computer whose NetBIOS name could not be found. The computer is probably not active on the network at this time.

No action is needed. You might want to make sure the computer is running and on the network, and try again.

Name table translation is not available for conversion to *file system***.**

[Convert]

Name table translation is required only when converting from HPFS to NTFS.

Omit the /Nametable parameter when converting from FAT to NTFS.

Name too long in key *name* **: Name =** *text***. The Nw Sap Agent cannot continue.**

[Netevent]

The specified name in the specified key of the Registry is not a valid name because it is too long. The application will work as usual except that this server name will be ignored during this session.

The server name should be changed in the Registry by someone experienced with Regedit32.

Name was not found or no valid name exists

[Dynamic Data Exchange]

The NetBIOS name of this computer could not be found when an application tried to start. The application cannot be started without knowing the NetBIOS name of the computer it is running on.

NEC chip out of spec. From device: *name*

[QIC117]

The floppy tape device cannot be used on this controller.

Contact the vendor.

Need count entry for EA set at cluster *name* **corrected.**

[Chkdsk]

This field is redundant, and can be reconstructed from other information on the volume.

No action is needed.

Neither the Owner nor the Primary Group account names are valid. Please specify valid account names for the Owner and Primary Group of this directory.

[Services for Macintosh (SFM)]

The account names specified do not exist. The account names were typed incorrectly.

NetBIOS Adapter Status Query on Lana number *number* **failed:** *text*

[Dynamic Data Exchange]

The NetBIOS protocol is unable to communicate through the network adapter card with the indicated LANA number.

Make sure that the card is properly seated and is functioning correctly.

NetBIOS program not loaded in PC

[Dynamic Data Exchange]

The NetBIOS software has not been loaded.

Use the Network option in Control Panel to make sure the NetBIOS interface is properly configured and has the necessary bindings.

NetBIOS Reset Adapter Command on Lana number *number* **failed:** *text*

[Dynamic Data Exchange]

The NetBIOS protocol needs to send a command to the indicated Local Area Network Adapter (LANA) number, but was unable to do so. It is therefore unable to use the card assigned to that LANA number.

Netcard detection service failed to start

[Control Panel]

Normally, the network adapter card is detected automatically, but because the Netcard Detection service did not start you will need to supply this information in the dialog box that follows this one.

Choose Continue. In the dialog box that follows, manually add the netcard.

Netcard detection service is not installed

[Control Panel]

Normally, the network adapter card is detected automatically, but because the Netcard Detection service is not installed you will need to supply this information in the dialog box that follows this one.

Choose Continue. In the dialog box that follows, manually add the netcard.

Netcard DMA Channel setting is currently in use by another device.

[Control Panel]

The DMA channel setting assigned to the network adapter card is already assigned to some other device.

Choose a different DMA setting for the network adapter card you just installed. Begin by choosing Network from the Control Panel.

Netcard I/O Port Address setting is currently in use by another device.

[Control Panel]

The address assigned to the I/O port used by the network adapter card is already assigned to some other I/O port.

Choose a different I/O base address for the network adapter card you just installed. Begin by choosing Network from the Control Panel.

Netcard Memory Buffer Address setting is currently in use by another device.

[Control Panel]

The Memory Buffer address assigned to the network adapter card is already assigned to some other device.

Choose a different Memory Buffer address for the network adapter card you just installed. Begin by choosing Network from the Control Panel.

NetDDE Agent Already running

[Dynamic Data Exchange]

You tried to start NetDDE Agent, but it is already running.

No action is needed.

NetDDE Agent unable to initialize

[Dynamic Data Exchange]

Either there is too little free memory, or some of the system files are not available.

Close some applications and try again. If this message still appears, some of the system files might be corrupt or missing, and should be restored from a backup copy.

NetDDE Service on node "*name* " has been stopped.

[Dynamic Data Exchange]

You will be unable to use Dynamic Data Exchange to communicate with the specified computer until the NetDDE service is started again.

Start the NetDDE service on that computer.

Netlogon has detected two machine accounts for server "*name* ". The server can be either an NTAS server that is a member of the domain or the server can be a LanMan server with an account in the SERVERS global group. It cannot be both.

[Network]

Either remove the indicated server from the SERVERS global group or use Server Manager to remove the computer from the domain.

Network access is denied.

[Kernel32]

You attempted to access a resource that is not available to you. It is possible that: (1) you do not have a valid account on the server sharing the resource; or (2) your account on this server has not been granted the permissions necessary to access the resource.

Make sure you specify the correct name of the resource that you want to use, then retry the command. If you are still denied access, contact your network administrator.

Network adapter malfunctioned

[Dynamic Data Exchange]

The network adapter card has malfunctioned.

Replace the network adapter card.

Network drive is not available.

[File Manager]

You attempted to connect to a network server that is either not functioning properly or is not turned on.

If you have physical access to the server, you can start it or reactivate the connection. Otherwise, wait until the server is started, then try again.

Network error *number* occurred.

[Network]

An unexpected network error has occurred.

Contact your technical support group.

Network error *code* occurred.

[Network] Net Message ID: 3212

The Replicator service stopped because the listed Windows NT error occurred.

To see more information about the error, type NET HELPMSG <message>#, where <message># is the error number.

Network error *code* occurred.

[Services for Macintosh (SFM)]

Contact technical support.

Network identifications must be unique. Please check your subnet mask.

[Control Panel]

Your adapter cards have identical subnet masks and IP addresses. Each card must have a unique subnet mask and IP address.

Make sure the subnet mask and IP address of each adapter card is different.

Network identifications must be unique. Please check your subnet mask.

[TCP/IP]

Your adapter cards have identical subnet masks and IP addresses. Each card must have a unique subnet mask and IP address.

Make sure the subnet mask and IP address of each adapter card is different.

Network is down

Try again later.

Network logons are paused.

[Network] Net Message ID: 2209

This message should occur only on a down-level computer. Any action to correct the problem should be performed on that computer. An administrator has paused the Netlogon service. No one can log on until the Netlogon service is continued.

The administrator must continue the Netlogon service by typing NET CONTINUE NETLOGON.

Network Number conflicts with an existing router.

[Services for Macintosh (SFM)]

The network is already being seeded by another router with a different network number.

Use the Network option in Control Panel to either disable seeding on the LocalTalk adapter or change the network range to reflect the network number being seeded on the network.

Network service not responding.

[Common Dialog]

The network driver did not respond to a request to display its dialog box.

Try again. If you still get this message, reboot your computer and try again. If you get this message after rebooting, contact your network administrator.

New connections will be remembered.

[Network]

The connections that you have at the end of this session will be remembered and, if possible, restored the next time you log on.

No action is needed.

New connections will not be remembered.

[Network]

Any changes that you make to your network connections during this session will not be remembered when you log off. The next time you log on you will have the connections you had when you logged on this time.

No action is needed.

No access permissions are explicitly assigned to *filename*, and so it inherits permissions from *path*. Do you want to assign permissions to *filename* explicitly?

[Security]

You selected a LAN Manager 2.x directory/file that does not have an explicit ACL (access control list) but which does inherit permissions from the specified resource path.

If you want to assign explicit permissions on the file, choose Yes in the dialog box. Then use the Permissions option in the Security menu to assign permissions on the files in the selected directory.

No active ISDN lines are available.

[Remote Access Service]

Make sure that your ISDN line is plugged in correctly, make sure that the terminating resistors are installed correctly (see the documentation for your ISDN card), and then redial. If you still get this error, contact DigiBoard Customer Service or your ISDN telephone company.

No adapter is configured to be the default adapter.

[Services for Macintosh (SFM)]

The default adapter setting was deleted by directly accessing the Registry instead of using the Network option in Control Panel.

Use NCPA to set a default adapter in the Services for Macintosh configuration section by choosing an adapter to be the Default Network.

No AppleTalk printing devices were found in this zone.

[Services for Macintosh (SFM)]

Ask your system administrator if printing devices were configured for the zone you specified. Otherwise, try using another zone.

No application is associated with this file.

You attempted to open a file in Object Packager that lacks an association.

Choose an associated file. Or open File Manager and create an association for the file.

No application is associated with this file. Choose Associate from the File menu to create an association.

[File Manager]

Before you can access a file from File Manager, the file must be associated with one of the applications installed on your workstation.

Select the Associate option in the File menu. When the Associate dialog box appears, select one of the options in the Associate With File Type box, then choose OK.

No association exists for the specified file.

[Program Manager]

Using the Run command in the File menu, you have attempted to run a file that lacks an extension.

Locate the file in File Manager, associate the file with an application, and then try again to run the file.

No association exists for the specified file.

[Task Manager]

The system does not know what application to use to open files with this file extension.

Assign an application to files with this extension (begin by choosing Associate from the File menu of File Manager). Or, choose Run from the File menu of File Manager to specify both the application and the file in a command line.

No asynchronous net available.

[Remote Access Service]

Most likely, your network configuration is wrong.

Restart your computer to make sure that all recent configuration changes have taken effect. If error persists, consult the Windows NT event log for detailed warnings or errors. Please record the Fail Code (a NetBIOS error code), and make it available to your technical support staff if you call for help.

No backslash is in the account name.

[Netevent]

The account name for the account in which the service is to run must contain a backslash. Unless the service is to run as a local system account, account names should contain a backslash, as in <domain name>\\<user name>.

If this error occurs when setting up or configuring the system, create the account again using a backslash to separate the domain name from the unique portion of the account name. Otherwise, contact the vendor of the service for which the account is being created.

No buffer space is available.

The operation could not be carried out due to the lack of buffer space.

No CDROM devices were found. App will exit.

[CD Player]

You attempted to activate CD Player, and there is no CD-ROM attached to your computer.

Attach a CD-ROM, make sure the attachments are secure, then try again.

No connection to *computer name*

[Chat]

Chat was terminated on the remote computer before the conversation could be established (for example, the other user might have closed Chat before responding to your call). Or, the connection to that computer was disrupted by a network failure or because the remote computer was turned off.

No control connection for command *command*

[FTP Server]

There is no control connection to pass the command to the remote host.

Ask your network administrator to interpret the error code displayed at the end of the message, and take appropriate action.

No data

[Backup]

Backup has encountered space on the tape where no data exists. The tape may be incomplete because a power outage occurred.

Use another backup of the tape if you have it. If you contact technical support, be sure to record any messages and information you see for them.

No data detected on this medium.

[File Manager]

Make sure the correct disk or tape is loaded.

No default zone was specified for adapter "*name* ".

[Services for Macintosh (SFM)]

The adapter's default zone was deleted from the Registry by directly by directly accessing it instead of using the Network option in Control Panel. Network would not allow a default zone to be deleted.

Set a default zone for the adapter using the Network option in Control Panel. Then, restart your computer for the changes to take effect.

No destination specified for: ***filename*.**

[Command Prompt]

You attempted an expand operation, but did not specify a destination for the expanded files.

For the correct format of the Expand command, type the name of the command, then /?, at the command prompt.

No driver was specified under module *name*. **The service could not be started.**

[Netevent]

Remove the TCP/IP protocol and then reinstall it using the Network option in Control Panel.

No encryption key is available. A well-known encryption key was returned.

[Kernel32]

Contact the supplier of the running application.

No endpoint was found.

[Kernel32]

An endpoint identifies a particular server instance (or address space) on a host computer in a distributed computing environment. The client part of a distributed (RPC) application is seeking an endpoint that cannot be found.

Contact the supplier of the running distributed application.

No file to print

[Print]

You must specify at least one file to print when you use the Print command (there must be one filename parameter).

Retry the Print command, specifying a file to print.

No files found - *path*

[Replace]

The Replace command could not find the files specified in the source path.

Retype the command with the correct source path for the files.

No files found.

[File Manager]

You inserted a blank formatted floppy disk, then selected the root directory in the Tree view of File Manager. This message appears in the file pane of the File Manager window.

No action is needed.

No files specified.

[Command Prompt]

You typed Expand at the command prompt, but did not specify which file you wanted to expand.

Type a filename after the Expand command, then try again.

No files were selected for Backup.

[Backup]

You selected the Backup option on the Operations menu, but have not selected the files that you want to back up.

Select the files that you want to back up, then try again.

No files were selected for Restore.

[Backup]

You selected the Restore option in the Operations menu before selecting the files that you want to restore.

Choose the files or directories that you want to restore, then try again.

No fonts found.

[Program Manager]

No font files were found in the selected directory.

In the Directories box, choose a different directory. For example, the System subdirectory in the WINNT directory might have the font files. If you aren't sure where the files might be, use File Manager to search for files of type .FON. Then select that directory in the Add Fonts dialog box.

No fonts found.

[Program Manager]

No font files were found in the selected directory.

In the Directories box, choose a different directory. For example, the System subdirectory in the WINNT directory might have the font files. If you aren't sure where the files might be, use File Manager to search for files of type .FON. Then select that directory in the Add Fonts dialog box.

No fonts installed

[Program Manager]

Although font files might be available on this computer, none of the fonts have been loaded in memory.

Choose Add to install fonts.

No fonts installed

[Program Manager]

No installed fonts of any kind were found. This includes TrueType fonts, bitmaps, etc.

Choose Add to install fonts.

No fonts selected.

[Program Manager]

To see a sample of a font, select one font in the Installed Fonts box.

No ID address mark was found on the floppy disk.

[Kernel32]

Retry the operation using a different floppy disk or a floppy disk with a different density. If this message reappears, contact the hardware supplier or the floppy disk driver software supplier.

No interfaces have been exported.

[Kernel32]

In a distributed (RPC) application, a request was made for a list of RPC interfaces that a server has assigned (exported) to a name-service database entry. This message indicates that no interfaces were exported.

Contact the supplier of the running distributed application.

No ISDN channels are available to make the call.

[Remote Access Service]

All of the available ISDN channels are busy.

Hang up one call and redial.

No longer attempting to connect

[Chat]

You hung up while Chat was attempting to connect to another computer.

This message requires no user action.

No mapping between account names and security IDs was done.

[Kernel32]

A request for mapping between the Unicode form of domain, user, group, or alias names and their security ID form could not be carried out. No mapping was done.

Contact the supplier of the running application.

No matching files were found.

[File Manager]

Using the Search option on the File menu, you specified as a search criterion the name of a file that does not appear in the path that you have specified.

Open the root directory, then do another search. If the search still fails to produce the desired file, the file does not exist on the currently active drive.

No matching mappings found.

[WINS Service]

The database has no entries that match the criteria you specified.

No action is needed.

No matching static mappings found.

[WINS Service]

The database has no entries that match the criteria you specified.

No action is needed.

No media in drive.

[Kernel32]

Insert the media in the drive and retry the operation. If you still get this message, contact the supplier of the running application.

No memory available

[File Compare]

There is not enough free memory available to use the Comp command.

Free memory by closing files and programs you no longer use, then retry the operation.

No message text was found for this error code (The data is the error code).

[Services for Macintosh (SFM)]

Contact technical support.

No more data is available.

[Kernel32]

A read operation on a pipe has not read the requested amount, but the pipe is out of data.

Contact the supplier of the running application.

No more data is on the tape.

[Kernel32]

No user action is possible. If the application does not continue to run, contact the supplier of the application.

No more IP addresses can be added.

[WINS Service]

You cannot add more static addresses because you have reached the maximum number of IP addresses (25) for this Internet Group or Multihomed address.

If you want, you can remove unused static addresses.

No more local user identifiers (LUIDs) are available.

[Kernel32]

The Windows NT security subsystem creates unique identifiers on each computer to identify objects a user creates during a user session. The limit for this session has been reached.

Contact the supplier of the running application. A general workaround you may want to try is to restart the local system.

No more memory is available for security information updates.

[Kernel32]

Delete any unnecessary changes from the request, or recreate the object using all the dynamic security information that exists now, plus the changes. You may have to contact the supplier of the running application to do this.

No more ports are available for this printer.

[Program Manager]

Free a port by disconnecting a printer or other device from one of the ports. Then try again.

No more primary partitions can be created on the disk. A disk cannot hold more than four partitions (including the extended partition but not including logical drives).

[Disk Administrator]

You have attempted to create a primary partition when there are already four on your disk.

Create volume or stripe sets from the partitions that you have already created.

No more print jobs can be added.

[Network] Net Message ID: 2156

This message should occur only on a down-level computer. Any action to correct the problem should be performed on that computer. The server does not have enough memory available to add another print job.

Wait a while, then send the print job again. If the problem persists, you may want to contact your network administrator about changing the MAXJOBS entry in the server's configuration file. This entry defines the maximum number of print jobs allowed on the server at one time. If the configuration file is changed, you must stop and restart the server's spooler for the changes to take effect.

No more printer destinations can be added.

[Network] Net Message ID: 2157

This message should occur only on a down-level computer. Any action to correct the problem should be performed on that computer. The server does not have enough memory available to add another printer.

Change the MAXPRINTERS entry in the server's configuration file. This entry defines the maximum number of printers the server can share. Then stop and restart the spooler for the changes to take effect.

No more printers can be added.

[Network] Net Message ID: 2155

This message should occur only on a down-level computer. Any action to correct the problem should be performed on that computer. The server does not have enough memory available to add another printer queue.

To free memory, delete an existing printer queue. Then create and share the new queue. You can also reconfigure the server to allow more printer queues by increasing the value of the MAXQUEUES entry in the server's configuration file. This entry defines the maximum number of queues the server can share. After you edit the configuration file, stop and start the server's spooler for the changes to take effect.

No more threads can be created in the system.

[Kernel32]

All system slots for threads have been used; no more threads can be created until some threads have been released.

Free some threads or processes, and try again. You may be able to do this by waiting, then retrying the operation. If you continue to get this message, contact the supplier of the running application.

No names in cache

[TCP/IP]

This is an informational message. The NBTSTAT utility cannot display NetBIOS connection information because there are no entries in the current NetBIOS cache.

No direct user action is necessary.

No netcard detection DLLs were found

[Control Panel]

The application could not detect the network adapter card because the required .DLL files were missing.

Reinstall the new network component. If the problem continues, contact the vendor for a new .DLL file.

No network adapters found

[Control Panel]

You have attempted to enable networking when there are no network adapters attached to your system.

Install a network adapter, then try again.

No network address is available to use to construct a universal unique identifier (UUID).

[Kernel32]

In a distributed (RPC) application, an attempt was made to create a unique object identifier. The address of the network adapter for the computer that will contain the object is used as the basis for the generated object identifier. But no such address was available, so the unique object identifier could not be created.

Make sure you are running the application on a computer with a network card. If you are, and this message is displayed, contact the supplier of the running application.

No network provider accepted the given network path.

[Kernel32]

An application was unable to connect a local device to a network resource. Either the network resource is not started, or the name of the network resource in the connection request was not recognized by any network providers.

Make sure all expected network resources are started. Or, if you have a user interface, enumerate the names of all the network resources your computer knows about. Then, either change the name in the request, or add it to the list of resources your computer knows about.

No network services are started.

[Network]

You cannot use the network because no network services have been started.

Start the Workstation service, and any other services that you want to use such as the Messenger service.

No Parameters subkey was found for user defined data. This is odd, and it also means no user configuration can be found.

A required key was deleted from the Registry by an application or by someone using Regedit.

In the Registry, add a parameters key below the Serial node.

No permissions are explicitly assigned to *filename* and it does not inherit permissions. Only administrators can access *filename*. Do you want to assign access permissions to *filename* to allow other users to access it?

[Security]

You have selected a LAN Manager 2.x directory/file that does not have an explicit ACL (access control list) and that does not inherit permissions.

If you want to set explicit permissions on the specified resource, choose Yes, then use the Permissions option in File Manager to set permissions.

No PPP control protocols configured.

[Remote Access Service]

The PPP connection was established without any Network Control Protocols configured. This error should not occur under normal circumstances.

No printer selected. Use Print Setup.

[Help]

You have selected the Print command before selecting and configuring a printer.

You should first run the Print Setup command, and select the appropriate options in the Print Setup dialog box.

No printers installed

[Program Manager]

To install a printer, choose Create Printer from the Print menu in the Print Manager dialog box.

No printers installed; use Control Panel to install printers.

[Help]

You cannot use Print Setup until a printer has been installed.

Choose Printers from the Control Panel to set up at least one printer. For more information choose Help in the Print Manager dialog box.

No process is on the other end of the pipe.

[Kernel32]

The specified pipe was disconnected at its other end.

Try the program again later. If you continue to get this message, contact the supplier of the running application.

No protocol sequences have been registered.

[Kernel32]

A protocol sequence identifies the network protocols used to establish a connection between the client and server parts of a distributed (RPC) application. A server in a distributed application tried to put itself in a state of listening for calls from clients without specifying a protocol sequence for receiving those calls.

Contact the supplier of the running distributed application.

No security context is available to allow impersonation.

[Kernel32]

The client must specify the security information which allows the server to impersonate the client.

Contact the supplier of the running application.

No serial device was successfully initialized. The serial driver will unload.

[Kernel32]

Contact your system administrator and look at the event log together. There will be several messages in the log that contain the keywords "serial I/O" and which give details about this event. The system administrator may have to reconfigure your computer.

No serial port setting changed.

This message should have been preceded with another one that explained why the port settings have not changed.

No source drive specified

[Repair Disk]

You must specify the drive on which the backup files are stored.

Try again, specifying both the source and destination drives. For a description of the command syntax, type restore /?

No such page.

[Write]

Using the Go To option, you specified a page that does not exist in the currently active document.

Specify a valid page number.

No system quota limits are specifically set for this account.

[Kernel32]

Contact the supplier of the running application.

No tape device detected. If you have a tape device attached, make sure that the appropriate tape driver has been installed using the Add/Remove Tape Devices option in the Options menu of Windows NT Setup. Also check that tape device power is on, and cables are properly connected.

[Backup]

Backup is unable to detect a tape device.

Follow the action specified in the message.

No target drive specified

[Repair Disk]

You must specify the drive to which you want the backup files restored.

Try again, specifying both the source and destination drives. For a description of the command syntax, type restore /?

No uncataloged sets were found on the tape.

[Backup]

The catalog operation determined that there was no additional information to catalog. All sets on the tape were accounted for in the catalog before the operation was started.

No action is needed.

No updates are necessary to this replicant network/local security database.

[Network] Net Message ID: 2248

This message should occur only on a down-level computer. Any action to correct the problem should be performed on that computer. A server requested an update of the user accounts database, even though no update was required.

No action is needed.

No users have sessions with this server.

[Network]

No users are currently connected any shares on this server.

No action is needed.

No valid response was provided.

[Network] Net Message ID: 3757

You did not provide a valid response to a Windows NT prompt.

Type a valid response.

No wildcards were found.

[Kernel32]

Contact the supplier of the running application.

No Windows NT Domain Controller is available for domain ***name*** **for the following reason:** ***text***

[Network] Net Message ID: 5719

Both the domain controller and the backup domain controllers are down.

Wait a few minutes and then retry your command or action. If the problem persists, contact your network administrator.

No zones were detected on the network. An internal error occurred.

[Services for Macintosh (SFM)]

A call to the protocol stack failed.

Try stopping and restarting the AppleTalk protocol stack using the Devices option in Control Panel. If you continue to receive this error message, try restarting your system. If this does not correct the problem, contact technical support.

No zones were detected on the network. Searching for AppleTalk printing devices in the default zone.

[Services for Macintosh (SFM)]

If your network is supposed to have zones, the network may not be available or there are problems with the router.

Contact technical support.

Non-clone open of *application* attempted.

[Netevent]

Windows NT supports only clone opens by streams modules.

Contact the vendor of the application.

Not a valid file name.

[Notepad]

If saving a Notepad file to a FAT volume, you can assign a filename of up to eight characters with a three character extension. The filename that you have assigned violates one of these specifications or contains illegal characters.

Type a valid name, then try again.

Not able to paste as a bitmap. Use the Clipboard Viewer to make sure the Clipboard contains a bitmap.

[Paintbrush]

You tried to paste something other than a bitmap where Paintbrush expected a bitmap. The Clipboard might contain text or some other kind of graphic instead of a bitmap.

Make sure the Clipboard contains a bitmap and try again. You might want to copy the bitmap again. Or, use the Paste from command in the Edit menu to select a file to paste from.

Not all privileges referenced are assigned to the caller.

[Kernel32]

The service was asked to make a set of changes to the privileges in a user account. The requested changes were made for all privileges assigned to the account. One or more of the change requests were for unassigned privileges, so they were not made.

This is probably not a problem. Try your privileged operation and see if it fails. If it does, see your administrator for help in obtaining the needed privilege.

Not enough disk space save card. Delete one or more files from the directory to which you are saving this card to increase the available disk space and then try again.

[Cardfile]

Your disk may be full. Or the setting of the temp path in your AUTOEXEC.BAT file may be incorrect.

Go to the command prompt, and type the Dir command to determine how much disk space you have available. If you have plenty of disk space, you probably need to check the temp setting in your AUTOEXEC.BAT file and to ensure that the file contains both a TEMP and TMP setting.

Not enough memory

[More]

Not enough memory was available to complete the process.

Free memory by closing files and programs you no longer use, then retry the operation.

Not enough memory available for this task. Quit one or more applications to increase available memory, and then try again.

[Control Panel]

The applications that you already have running are making demands upon your computer's memory so that Control Panel cannot perform the desired function.

Close the applications that you do not need, then try again.

Not enough memory available to complete this operation. Quit one or more applications to increase available memory, and then try again.

[Notepad]

Your system is low on memory, probably because you have too many applications currently running.

Close one or more of the applications that you have running, and then try again.

Not enough memory for this operation.

[Paintbrush]

Close some applications and try again.

Not enough memory or unable to load resource.

[Network]

A required resource could not be loaded into memory. This error is usually caused by a missing or corrupt file, but it could also be due to insufficient memory.

Close some applications and try again. If you still get this message, check the event log to find out what file could not be opened. Restore that file from a backup copy or reinstall from the setup disk for the application, and try again.

Not enough memory or unable to load resource.

[Services for Macintosh (SFM)]

Try closing other running applications and services. Also use the Network option in Control Panel to remove and reinstall Services for Macintosh. If you continue to see this message, contact technical support.

Not enough memory to cancel the link. Quit one or more applications to increase available memory, and then try again.

[Cardfile]

You have applications running that make it impossible for Windows NT to cancel the link between the server application (the application in which the object was created) and the currently active Cardfile file.

Exit or minimize Cardfile, and close some of the applications that you are running. Then, returning to Cardfile, repeat the canceling operation; select the linked object and choose the Link option in the Edit menu. When the Link dialog box appears, select the Cancel option.

Not enough memory to copy the object. Quit one or more applications to increase available memory, and then try again.

[Cardfile]

You have a number of Windows NT applications running which make it impossible for you to copy a the object to the Clipboard.

Quit one or more of the applications that you have running, then try again.

Not enough memory to determine the link update setting. Quit one or more applications to increase available memory, and then try again.

[Cardfile]

When you choose the Links option from the Edit menu in Cardfile, the Links dialog box appears and indicates whether your links are updated manually or automatically. If you have too many applications running in Windows NT, your computer cannot make this determination.

Close some of the Windows NT applications that you have running, and attempt again to access the Links dialog box by using the Links option in the Cardfile Edit menu.

Not enough memory to print. Quit one or more applications, and then try again.

[File Manager]

The applications that you have running or minimized are making demands upon your workstation's available memory, making it impossible for you to print.

Follow the user action specified in the message.

Not enough memory to start the specified application. Quit one or more applications, and then try again.

[File Manager]

The applications that you have running or minimized are making demands upon your workstation's available memory, making it impossible for you to start a new application.

Follow the user action specified in the message.

Not enough memory was available to allocate internal storage needed for *name*.

Close some applications and try again. If you get this message often, you might want to install more memory, or start the driver earlier during startup.

Not enough memory was available to allocate internal storage needed for the device *name*.

[Digi]

Try stopping other running applications. Also try removing unneeded files from your disk. If you can, add more memory.*

Not enough quota is available to process this command.

[Program Manager]

Close some applications and try again. If you still get this message, choose System from Control Panel, then choose Virtual Memory and increase the size of your paging file.

Not enough resources are available to complete this operation.

[Kernel32]

In a distributed (RPC) application, either a client or a server has run out of a resource (such as memory) while carrying out an operation.

Increase the amount of memory available to the client or server, or both, and retry the operation.

Not enough resources are available to process this command.

[Kernel32]

All available storage is in use.

Retry the operation later.

Not enough storage is available to complete this operation.

[Kernel32]

Do one of the following, then retry the operation: (1) reduce the number of running programs; (2) remove unwanted files from the disk the paging file is on and restart the system; (3) check the paging file disk for an I/O error; or (4) install additional memory in your system.

Not enough storage is available to process this command.

[Kernel32]

Do one of the following, then retry the command: (1) reduce the number of running programs; (2) remove unwanted files from the disk the paging file is on and restart the system; (3) check the paging file disk for an I/O error; or (4) install additional memory in your system.

Not resetting hidden file - *filename*

[Attrib]

The specified files already had hidden attributes, so none of their attributes may be reset with the Attrib command unless you specify a +h or -h switch in the list of file attributes to change.

Retry the command, adding the +h or -h switch to the list of attribute switches.

Not resetting system file - *filename*

[Attrib]

The specified files already had system attributes, so none of their attributes may be reset with the Attrib command unless you specify a +s or -s switch in the list of file attributes to change.

Retry the command, adding the +s or -s switch to the list of attribute switches.

Not super user

[FTP Server] [TCP/IP]

You do not have the privilege to do this operation with TCP/IP gateways.

Log on as a member of the Administrator group and retry the operation.

NT LanMan error *number*

[Network]

Look up the LAN Manager message by typing NET HELPMSG <code> at the command prompt and follow the action recommended in the message.

NTFS RECOVER cannot be used to recover system files; use CHKDSK instead.

[Recover-NTFS]

System files cannot be accessed directly by users.

Run Chkdsk /f to correct file system errors.

NTFS RECOVER failed.

[Recover-NTFS]

NTFS Recover encountered file system errors on the volume or the system might be running out of memory.

Try stopping other running applications in order to free more memory. Also run Chkdsk /f to correct file system errors and try the operation again.

NTVDM does not support a ROM BASIC.

[Virtual DOS Machine (VDM)]

This is an informational message. Try running the application with Microsoft QBASIC, which is shipped with Windows NT as the replacement for ROM BASIC.

NTVDM has encountered a System Error

[Virtual DOS Machine (VDM)]

The Windows NT operating system function that failed will be displayed with the message. Write it down. Then terminate the application and restart it. If you still get this message, contact your technical support group.

Number is invalid.

[WINS Service]

The number you entered includes non-numeric characters, or is outside the allowed range.

Enter a different number.

Once the server is stopped, it cannot be restarted remotely. Are you sure you wish to stop *computer name*

[Server Manager]

When you use the Services option to stop a Server, Server Manager presents you with this confirmation message, indicating that once you stop the Server service remotely, it can only be restarted locally.

If you are sure that you want to stop the selected computer, choose Yes. If not, choose No.

One file was not found.

[Backup]

One file was not found on the target disk.

Try using an older version of the tape that was backed up.

One of the library files needed to run this application is damaged. Please reinstall this application.

Contact your system administrator to reinstall the application.

One of your NetBIOS names is already registered on the remote network.

[Remote Access Service]

Networking architecture requires each computer on the network to be registered with a unique name. This rule applies to both the LAN and remote workstations. Because unique names are required, you cannot have both a Remote Access and a direct connection (such as Ethernet connector) to the same network. If you are evaluating Remote Access in such a situation, you need to unplug the network connector before attempting to connect through Remote Access.

Make sure your computer name is different from all other computer names on the network. To change your computer name, use the Network option in Control Panel. If the name is not your computer name, another computer may have registered a computer name matching your domain name, or you are running a NetBIOS application that has added a conflicting name. If the problem persists after changing the name, contact your system administrator.

One or more of the items selected is a directory. Do you want to take ownership of all the files and subdirectories contained in the selected directories?

[Security]

When you opt to take ownership of a directory, you are given the option of taking ownership of all of the files in the directory.

If you want to do this, choose Yes. If not, choose No.

One or more of the specified properties cannot currently be set.

[Print Manager]

You tried change to direct printing while jobs are in the queue for this printer.

Wait until the queue is empty, then change to direct printing.

One or more parameters are invalid

[Dynamic Data Exchange]

Report this error message to the vendor of the application you were using when the message appeared.

One or more selected users have Logon Hours settings which are not specified in days-per-week or hours-per-week. You may edit these settings, but they will be initially reset. Do you wish to reset and edit these Logon Hours settings?

[User Manager]

You have edited the Logon Hours for a group of users directly through the API. If you choose to reset these Logon Hours now, all of the selected users will be allowed access to the server at all times.

If you wish to reset the Logon Hours for the specified users, choose OK.

One or more selected users have Logon Hours settings which are specified as days-per-week. Is it OK to convert these settings to hours-per-week?

[User Manager]

You have edited the Logon Hours setting for a group of users directly through the API. If you choose to reset these Logon Hours now, all of the selected users will be allowed access to the server at all times.

If you want to convert these settings, choose Yes.

Open of *name* attempted prior to initialization.

[Netevent]

Drivers must be initialized before they can be opened by TCP/IP.

Start the driver by selecting the Services option in Control Panel. Then choose TCP/IP protocol and then select Start.

Operation not fully completed

[File Manager]

You ignored a message informing you that you lacked adequate permission to perform an operation. Windows NT cannot complete this operation.

No action is needed.

Option *name* is ambiguous.

[Network] Net Message ID: 3507

The specified option can be confused with other options.

Type enough letters of the option so that it is unambiguous. If the command has two options that both begin with /OPT, such as /OPT and /OPTION, you must type at least four letters to designate the second option. To see a list of options for this command, type NET HELP <command>.

Out of buffers.

[Remote Access Service]

This error should not occur under normal circumstances.

Restart your computer to make sure that all recent configuration changes have taken effect. If the error persists, consult the Windows NT event log for detailed warnings or errors.

Out of Disk Space

[Disk Administrator]

There is not enough space on the hard disk for the current operation.

Delete some files that you don't need, or that you have backed up and are not currently using, and try again.

Out of disk space

[Registry Editor]

You cannot print because you are out of disk space.

In File Manager, delete unnecessary files, then try again.

Out of disk space writing output file: ***filename*****.**

[Command Prompt]

Your destination disk is full, so the rest of the file will not fit on the disk.

Delete some files to make room or use another disk.

Out of Memory

[Minesweeper]

Minesweeper is currently out of memory.

Close one or more of the applications that you have running, then try again.

Out of memory

[FTP Server]

There was insufficient memory for the data structures the Ftp utility needs to complete a file transfer.

Try again in a few seconds. If you still get this message, quit some applications and retry the file transfer.

Out of memory (IP ADDR)

[IP]

Close some applications and try again. Or, close and restart the current application.

Out of memory *code*

[FTP Server]

The Ftp utility was unable to get enough memory to hold the global file list.

Wait a few seconds, then try again. If you still get this message, quit some running applications and try again. If you still get this message, ask your network administrator to interpret the error code displayed at the end of the message, and take appropriate action.

Out of memory.

[Control Panel]

Try closing one or more applications, then try again.

Out of memory.

[Command] [File Compare] [Fonts (CP)] [Mode] [Replace] [Utilities]

The utility ran out of memory before it could finish.

You can free memory by closing files and programs you are no longer using. If you still get this message, remove memory-resident programs (TSRs) or unnecessary device drivers from your CONFIG.NT file, and restart your computer.

Out of memory.

[Help]

Close some applications and try again. Also, you can increase the size of the page file used by virtual memory by choosing System from the Control Panel and then choosing Virtual Memory.

Out of memory.

[TCP/IP]

Try again in a few seconds. If you still get this message, quit some unneeded applications that are running, and retry the file transfer.

Overlapped I/O event is not in a signaled state.

[Kernel32]

Contact the supplier of the running application.

Overlapped I/O operation is in progress.

[Kernel32]

Contact the supplier of the running application.

Ownership was not successfully taken on all of the files/directories. Error *code* **occurred:** *text*

[Security]

You have attempted to take ownership of files/directories, and you are not an administrator. Unless you are given full control of files/directories by their owner, or are assigned by an administrator the right to take ownership, you cannot do so.

Contact the owner of the files/directories, or contact your system administrator. If you are the system administrator, log on under your administrator account, and take ownership of the files/directories.

Package not installed *name*

Install the package, then try again.

Packet received on adapter "*name* **" contained errors and is not being accepted.**

[Services for Macintosh (SFM)]

This message is for your information only.

No action is needed.

Parameter *parameter* **has an invalid type.**

[Remote Access Service]

The Remote Access Service is configured incorrectly because the type of the specified parameter was changed. When the Remote Access Service is installed, it supplies the correct types for Registry parameters.

Reconfigure the Remote Access Service by removing and then reinstalling it. Use the Network option in Control Panel to remove and reinstall the service.

Parameter format not correct -

[Attrib] [Chcp] [Find] [Tree]

You typed one or more parameters that do not have a valid format for this command. For instance, you may have added a numerical value for a switch that will not allow a value to be specified. Or you may have used an incompatible combination of parameters.

To find out which parameters are valid for this command, type HELP at the command prompt followed by the command name.

Parameter format not correct - "*text* ".

[Command] [Command Prompt] [Utilities]

You typed a parameter that is not correct for the format of this command. For instance, you may have added a numerical value for a switch that will not allow a numerical value to be specified.

To find out which parameters are valid for this command, type the Help command at the command prompt, then type /?.

Parameter type wrong.

[Help]

This error is from the Macro Language Editor for online help, and should not appear while using the Help file. Report this error to the provider of the Help file.

Parameter value not in allowed range

[Sort]

You typed a numeric parameter value that is not in the range of values allowed by this command. For example, in the Sort command, you may have specified a column number that is too large for the input you are sorting.

Retype the command, using a different numeric parameter value.

Parameters not compatible.

[Format]

You specified switches that cannot be used together.

To find out which switches are valid for this command, type HELP at the command prompt followed by the command name (in this case, Format).

Parameters not compatible with fixed disk.

[Format]

You used a parameter that is not compatible with the specified drive.

To find out which Format command parameters can be used with a fixed disk, type HELP at the command prompt followed by the command name, Format.

Parameters not supported by drive.

[Format]

Type the Format command again and specify the correct format with the /f switch. To see all the /f switch options, type HELP at the command prompt followed by the command name (in this case, Format).

Parameters not supported.

[Format]

You have specified parameters that the Format utility does not support for the type of drive you are working on.

To check which parameters are valid, type HELP at the command prompt followed by the command name (in this case, Format).

Parameters passed from SETUP were invalid

[Control Panel]

The network information that was provided during Setup is incorrect.

Reinstall Windows NT and provide the correct Setup information.

Parse Error *text*

[Mode]

An error occurred on the command line.

Check the syntax for the command by typing HELP at the command prompt, followed by the command name. Then retry the command using the correct syntax.

Parse Error *text*

[Replace]

An error occurred on the command line.

Check the syntax for the command by typing HELP at the command prompt, followed by the command name. Then retry the command using the correct syntax.

Parse Error *text*

[Xcopy]

An error occurred on the command line.

Check the syntax for the command by typing HELP at the command prompt, followed by the command name. Then retry the command using the correct syntax.

Pasted text too long; excess has been cut from annotation.

[Help]

You can only paste 32 kilobytes of text from a file into the Annotate dialog box, and you have exceeded this limit.

No action is needed.

Pasting from MSP files is not supported. Open the MSP file, use the Save As command to save it as a bitmap file, and then paste it into your image.

[Paintbrush]

Windows 3.1 and Windows NT do not support some of the functions and applications from earlier versions of Windows. MSP (Microsoft Paint) is one such application.

Follow the user action specified in the message.

Path not found - ***path***

[Utilities]

The path might have been typed incorrectly. Also, verify that your network connections still exist.

Physical end of tape encountered.

[Kernel32]

No user action is possible. If the application does not continue to run, contact the supplier of the application.

PIF file not found or bad file format.

[Virtual DOS Machine (VDM)]

NTVDM cannot find the PIF file specified in the command line, or the file was found but it does not have a PIF format (for instance, it may be an MS-DOS batch file instead of a PIF file).

Retry the running application, specifying a different path to the PIF file.

Please be sure to confirm the computer password exactly

[Control Panel]

The password must be typed in exactly the same way (including capitalization) both times.

Retype the password.

Please enter a threshold value in the Alert if option box.

[Performance Monitor]

In the Add to Alert dialog box, you did not make an entry in the Alert If option box.

In the Alert If option box, enter a value appropriate to the counter.

Please enter the path for your LMHOSTS file first.

[TCP/IP]

You selected Import without specifying the path of the LMHOSTS file.

Specify a path for the file or select Cancel to dismiss the dialog box.

Please select a valid modem to view or change settings.

[Remote Access Service]

You tried to change or view the settings of an invalid modem.

Select a valid modem.

Please select an excluded range from the list before attempting to delete it.

[Remote Access Service]

Exclude ranges cannot be specified before the start and end IP addresses are entered. If you select an included range, any addresses in that range will be disconnected and data may be lost.

Type the start and end IP addresses in the appropriate places in the dialog box. Be sure the end address is greater than the start address.

Please specify a start and end exclude address before attempting to add the exclude range.

[Remote Access Service]

Exclude ranges cannot be specified before the start and end IP addresses are entered.

Type the start and end IP addresses in the appropriate places in the dialog box. Be sure the end address is greater than the start address.

Please specify a start and end IP address before attempting to add the exclude range.

[Remote Access Service]

Exclude ranges cannot be specified before the start and end IP addresses are entered.

Type the start and end IP addresses in the appropriate places in the dialog box. Be sure the end address is greater than the start address.

Poll drive is disabled.

[Backup]

Because of an unexpected error, the application will no longer poll the tape drive looking for events such as “new tape,” “no tape,” or “busy.”

Exit the application and restart. If the message reappears try a fresh tape in the drive. If it still happens then make sure your tape drive has the correct version of ROM chip installed.

poll failed *code*

[FTP Server] [TCP/IP]

The data connection in use by a TCP/IP utility was not properly closed down due to failure in a poll system call.

Retry the TCP/IP utility operation. If you still get this message, contact your network administrator to interpret the error code displayed at the end of the message and take appropriate action.

Popup menu already active.

[Kernel32]

An application, as part of its user interface, tried to pass control to a popup menu that already had control.

Contact the supplier of the running application.

Port *address* **(** *code* **) was unable to initialize properly.**

[Digi]

The specified port will not be accessible.

Contact Digi technical support.

Port *name* **already exists.**

[Print Manager]

You have attempted to assign to a port a name that already designates another port.

Select another name, then choose OK.

PortUAS must be run on a Windows/NT Advanced Server domain controller or Windows/NT system, not a server.

[PORTUAS]

Run PortUAS on the Primary Domain Controller (PDC), not the Backup Domain Controller (BDC). The servers in the domain that are running Windows NT Advanced Server will automatically be updated.

PortUAS returned - *code***. More information about this and other error codes greater than 2100 may be available by typing NET HELPMSG** *number* **at the command prompt. A zero indicates that no errors were detected when the database was converted.**

[PORTUAS]

The name of the database is invalid or does not exist.

Contact technical support if help is not available for the error code that appears in this message.

PPP terminated by remote machine.

[Remote Access Service]

A PPP conversation was started, but was terminated at the request of the remote computer. Most likely an error occurred on the server.

PPP timeout.

[Remote Access Service]

A PPP conversation was started, but was terminated because the remote computer did not respond within an appropriate time. This can be caused by poor line quality or by a problem at the server.

Press OK to cancel modem detection and select a modem from the device list.

[Remote Access Service]

Setup could not detect a modem.

Primary rule base consultation error

[Control Panel]

A internal software error has occurred.

Consult the error log in Event Viewer to determine more specifically the nature of the problem. Or contact technical support.

Print job *name* has been canceled while printing on *name*.

[Network]

Either the user or an administer canceled the print job before it finished.

No action is needed. You can resubmit the print job if you want, but you should find out why the job was canceled first. There may have been a problem with the output format.

Print job *name* has been deleted and will not print.

[Network]

Either the user or an administer canceled the print job before it started.

No action is needed. You can resubmit the print job if you want.

Print job *name* has not completed printing on *name*.

[Network]

The print job has started but has not finished.

Use Print Manager to find out whether the job has started and whether there is a problem with the printer. There may be several jobs ahead of this one.

Print job *name* has paused printing on *name*.

[Network]

The job has been temporarily suspended and can be continued rather than resubmitted

Use Print Manager to continue the job.

Print job *name* is being held from printing.

[Network]

The print job has been set to print during a specified time period.

No action is needed. However, the owner of the document or the administrator can change the printing hours for the document using Print Manager.

Print job *name* is being spooled.

[Network]

The print job is being copied to the printer server's memory. When that is done you will be able to continue using your computer without waiting for the job to print.

No action is needed.

Print job *name* is queued for printing.

[Network]

The print job has been copied to the printer server's memory. It will be printed when the printer becomes available.

No action is needed,

Print Manager was unable to retrieve printer information. This may be because the spooler is not running. Print Manager cannot continue.

[Print Manager]

Start the Spooler service from the Services applet in the Control Panel.

Print Manager was unable to retrieve printer information. This may be because the spooler is not running. Print Manager cannot continue.

[Print Manager]

Ask your system administrator to verify that the Spooler service is running on the server. Use the Services option in Control Panel to start the Spooler service.

Printer creation cannot continue: *text*

[Print Manager]

The indicated system error prevented Print Manager from creating this printer.

Look up the error message that is included at the end of this message, and take appropriate action. Then try again.

Probable non-Windows NT disk Continue (Y/N)? *text*

[Utilities]

The elementary structures on the disk are not consistent with the FAT file system definition. The disk may be a corrupted FAT volume, or it may have been formatted for another operating system.

If you are certain that this is a FAT volume, choose Yes; otherwise, choose No.

Problem drawing or printing object.

[Write]

Most likely, you are low on memory.

Close one or more applications, and then try again.

Problem executing macro.

[Help]

This error is from the Macro Language Editor for online help, and should not appear while using the Help file. Report this error to the provider of the Help file.

Problem with object/link.

[Write]

There is a problem between your Write document and a linked or embedded object.

Reestablish the link between Write and the object.

Processed or skipped *number* users out of *number* total users.

[PORTUAS]

The two numbers should be the same unless you used the -u option. If the numbers do not match, your down-level user accounts database may be corrupted.

Contact technical support.

Profile files cannot exceed 64K.

[Network] Net Message ID: 2370

This message should occur only on a down-level computer. Any action to correct the problem should be performed on that computer. The profile is too large. Profile files can be no larger than 64 kilobytes.

Remove unnecessary commands from the profile and try loading it again.

Program filenames must end with .EXE.

[Network] Net Message ID: 3718

This message should occur only on a down-level computer. Any action to correct the problem should be performed on that computer. The Netrun service runs only programs with the filename extension .EXE.

To use a program with a .COM extension, an administrator must rename it to an .EXE file.

Program group ' *group* ' is write-protected. Its icons cannot be updated for the new display device.

[Program Manager]

You have attempted to modify a program group that has been specified as read-only in the Registry.

In REGEDT32, locate this program group, then remove its read-only protection.

Program group *group* is invalid or damaged; recreate the group.

[Program Manager]

The specified group must be recreated.

To recreate the group, choose the New option on the File Menu in Program Manager.

Program group *group* is write-protected. Its contents will not be updated.

[Program Manager]

You have attempted to modify a program group that has been specified as read-only in the Registry.

In REGEDT32, locate this program group, then remove its read-only protection.

Program group *group* is write-protected. The program group cannot be modified.

[Program Manager]

You have attempted to write to or delete a group that has been locked in the User Profile Editor.

Log on under a user account that has permission to unlock the group in the User Profile Editor.

Promoting *computer name* to Primary may take a few minutes. Do you want to make the change?

[Server Manager]

This message is intended to verify your decision to promote the specified server to the role of domain controller.

If you want to continue with the promotion, choose Yes. If not, choose No.

Protocol driver not attached *text*

The required protocol cannot be used until the driver is attached.

Protocol family not supported.

Use a protocol from a different protocol family.

Protocol not supported *name*

Use a different protocol.

Query result parsing failure

[Control Panel]

The network bindings could not be interpreted. This usually occurs after a new network component has been installed. In some cases the hardware or installation procedure provided with the component is at fault.

First, reboot the computer, then choose Network from the Control Panel and choose Binding to redo the binding. If the problem continues, remove any recently installed network component, reboot, reinstall the component, and reboot again. If you still get this error, ask the administrator to edit the registry, removing the variable \Software\Microsoft\Ncpa\CurrentVersion\Bindfile; then choose Network from the Control Panel and choose Binding to redo the binding. You may need to contact the vendor of the network component to resolve the problem.

Quick format is not allowed on this volume.

[Disk Administrator]

Quick Format is not available for formatting mirror sets or stripe sets with parity. This allows the format process to perform a surface scan and locate any bad sectors on the volume.

Continue without choosing Quick Format.

RasMan initialization failure. Check the event log.

[Remote Access Service]

This error should not occur under normal circumstances.

Restart your computer to make sure that all recent configuration changes have taken effect. If the error persists, consult the Windows NT event log for detailed warnings or errors.

RASMXS.DLL cannot load RASSER.DLL.

[Remote Access Service]

Remove and reinstall the Remote Access Service.

RasPortEnum failed.

[Remote Access Service]

Possibly, RAS cannot be started because the ports could not be opened. There was a problem with the Performance Monitor call to RAS.

Use the Network option in Control Panel to reconfigure RAS. Select RAS from the list of installed software and then choose Configure.

RASSER.DLL cannot open the SERIAL.INI file.

[Remote Access Service]

Check the configuration of the Remote Access Service with the Network option in Control Panel.

name **p:** *name code*: **name too long**

[TCP/IP]

This is an internal error in the TCP/IP utility, Rcp.

Retry the operation. If you still get this message, contact your technical support group.

rcp: *filename* **: file changed size**

[TCP/IP]

The file unexpectedly changed size during the remote copy operation.

Retry the remote file copy operation. If you continue to get this message, contact your network administrator.

rcp: *filename* **: file not found**

[TCP/IP]

The file named in the message cannot be accessed, because it cannot be found.

Check the spelling of the file specification in the Rcp command. If it is correct, you may need to use File Manager to search for the file. In either case, retry the Rcp command, using a correct file specification.

rcp: *name* **: name too long.**

[TCP/IP]

This is an internal error in the TCP/IP utility, Rcp.

Retry the operation. If you still get this message, contact your technical support group.

rcp: *filename* **: not a plain file**

[TCP/IP]

You specified a directory as a source for a remote copy, without using the -r option.

Retry the Rcp command, using the -r option. Then the Rcp utility will copy all the files in the directory.

rcp: *name* **: not a regular file or directory**

[TCP/IP]

The Rcp utility will not do a remote copy of the file that is named in the message because it is not a regular file. For example, a file with the system attribute is not a regular file.

If you can change the file or directory attributes so it can be copied by the Rcp command, do so. Otherwise, find a different way to do the remote copy.

rcp: *path* **: path too long**

[TCP/IP]

This is an internal error in the TCP/IP utility, Rcp.

Retry the operation. If you still get this message, contact your technical support group.

rcp: *text* **: permission denied**

[TCP/IP]

The remote file copy operation failed because file permissions on the local or remote host did not permit it. For example, you may have tried to copy a file onto the local host when that filename already exists on the local host with read-only permission.

You may have to ask your system administrator for different permissions before you can use the Rcp command in this way.

rcp: ambiguous target

[TCP/IP]

You specified several files or directories on the Rcp command line for the destination of the remote copy operation.

Retype the Rcp command, specifying an unambiguous destination for the remote file copy operation.

rcp: Cannot specify both ascii and binary modes

[TCP/IP]

You cannot use both the -a and -b switches in an Rcp command. In other words, a file transfer cannot be done in both ASCII and binary modes at the same time.

Review the usage information about the Rcp command displayed after this message. Then retry the Rcp command, using that information.

rcp: invalid user name *name*

[TCP/IP]

The user name displayed in the message is invalid. The only valid characters in the Rcp command user parameter are letters, numbers, underscore (_), and dash(-).

Retry the Rcp command, using a valid user name.

rcp: lost connection

[TCP/IP]

The connection to the remote host closed before the remote copy (Rcp) operation was complete. The problem could be at the remote host or at one of the computers on your current route to the remote host.

Retry the Rcp command. If you cannot reestablish the remote connection or you get this same message, contact your network administrator to check the condition of the remote computer.

rcp: protocol error: bad mode

[TCP/IP]

An error in the Rpc protocol occurred between the local and remote hosts. For instance, there may be a mismatch between the implementations of the TCP/IP protocol on the two computers.

Retry the Rcp command. If you continue to get this message, contact your network administrator

rcp: protocol error: expected control record

[TCP/IP]

An error in the Rpc protocol occurred between the local and remote hosts. For instance, there may be a mismatch between the implementations of the TCP/IP protocol on the two computers.

Retry the Rcp command. If you continue to get this message, contact your network administrator

rcp: protocol error: lost connection

[TCP/IP]

An error in the Rpc protocol occurred between the local and remote hosts. For instance, there may be a mismatch between the implementations of the TCP/IP protocol on the two computers.

Retry the Rcp command. If you continue to get this message, contact your network administrator

rcp: protocol error: mode not delimited

[TCP/IP]

An error in the Rpc protocol occurred between the local and remote hosts. For instance, there may be a mismatch between the implementations of the TCP/IP protocol on the two computers.

Retry the Rcp command. If you continue to get this message, contact your network administrator

rcp: protocol error: size not delimited

[TCP/IP]

An error in the Rpc protocol occurred between the local and remote hosts. For instance, there may be a mismatch between the implementations of the TCP/IP protocol on the two computers.

Retry the Rcp command. If you continue to get this message, contact your network administrator

rcp: protocol error: unexpected '\\'

[TCP/IP]

An error in the Rpc protocol occurred between the local and remote hosts. For instance, there may be a mismatch between the implementations of the TCP/IP protocol on the two computers.

Retry the Rcp command. If you continue to get this message, contact your network administrator.

rcp: setsockopt (SO_KEEPALIVE) *name*

[TCP/IP]

While sending a command to the remote host, the Rcp utility detected a failed Sockets library call. This may be because the remote host will not accept the command at all, in which case the Rcp utility quits execution. Or, it may be that the remote host has begun to accept the command, and the Sockets library call failed. In that case, the Rcp utility will display this message and continue trying to send the command.

If the Rcp utility quit, the remote host may be unavailable. For example, it may be shut down. Ask your network administrator to check the condition of the remote computer. If the Rcp utility continued executing, no direct user action is required.

rcp: WSAStartup: *code*

[TCP/IP]

The TCP/IP utility named at the beginning of the message was unable to start up due to a socket error.

Wait, then retry the TCP/IP utility. If you still get this message, contact your network administrator to interpret the error code displayed at the end of the message. The appropriate action depends on the meaning of this code.

Read error on local file *filename* **disk read error occurred** *text.*

[TFTP]

The TCP/IP utility was transferring a file from your computer to a remote computer, but was unable to read part of the file on your computer in order to transfer it.

Try the file transfer again. If you still get this message, restore a backup copy of the file you want to transfer. Then retry the file transfer.

Read error.

[Recover-FAT/HPFS]

HFPS Recover could not read file system structures.

Run Chkdsk /f to correct file system errors.

Read from ConsoleIn error == *code*

[FTP Server]

An error occurred while the FTP service was trying to read your password. The service cannot continue.

Ask your network administrator to interpret the error code displayed at the end of the message, and take appropriate action.

Read Only Drive Encountered!

[Backup]

The media in the drive cannot be written to, or is write-protected. Therefore no files can be copied to this drive. If you are backing up from this drive and have specified a Normal backup a Copy backup will be performed instead. Or, if you have specified an Incremental backup from this drive, a Differential backup will be performed instead.

No action is needed. However, you can specify a different target drive if you want to.

Receive error. Session to *name* **closed abnormally:** *text*

[Dynamic Data Exchange]

Your connection to the indicated resource was lost due to the indicated error. Any files that you had open on the resource might have been corrupted.

Re-establish the connection. Check any files that were open for corruption, and restore them from a backup if necessary.

Received unknown request *text* from NBT.

[Netevent]

Use the Network option in Control Panel to remove and then reinstall the driver. Select RFC NetBIOS, choose Remove, and then choose Add.

Recent bindings review changes will be lost during this process; reapply them after operation completes.

[Control Panel]

After this process is finished, choose Network from the Control Panel and then choose Bindings to reconfigure the binding information.

Record with name (*name* **) could not replace another record in the db. The Version number of the record is (** *number* **). The version number of record in db is (** *number* **)**

[WINS Service]

If this message appears often, call technical support. Otherwise, ignore this message.

Record with name (*name* **) has bad address. It has not been put in the WINS database.**

[WINS Service]

This message can appear when WINS is being initialized with static records from a static initialization file.

In the initialization file, correct the address assigned to the indicated name.

Recover mode not supported by HPFS CHKDSK.

[Chkdsk-HPFS]

The recover mode is supported by NTFS and FAT Chkdsk.

If you really want to try to use the recover mode on the volume, you might try converting the volume to NTFS or FAT and then use recover.

RECOVER on an entire volume is no longer supported. To get equivalent functionality use CHKDSK.

[Recover-FAT/HPFS]

For more information about the Chkdsk command, type Chkdsk /? at the command prompt.

Recursion too deep, stack overflowed.

[Kernel32]

Contact the supplier of the running application.

Recv failed *code*

[TCP/IP]

Input was received from the remote host, but it was invalid. For example, the input may have had no content.

Retry the remote command. If you get this same message, ask your network administrator to interpret the error code displayed at the end of the message, and take appropriate action.

Regeneration of a stripe with parity or mirror set failed.

[Disk Administrator]

Fault tolerance was unable to recover from a previous failure. The stripe is not currently protected by Fault Tolerance.

Make sure the drives are on-line and are functioning properly. Check for Eventlog entries close to this one that indicate a hardware problem with one or both drives.

Registry access error: unable to read or create software product information

[Control Panel]

The Network option is unable to access a node in the Registry that contains vital information.

Contact technical support.

Registry component improperly installed

[Control Panel]

A component in the Registry necessary to the completion of this operation has not been installed correctly.

Consult the event log in Event Viewer for details, then contact your system administrator.

Registry component section mismatch

[Control Panel]

Two places in the Registry contain vital information that does not agree.

Consult the event log in Event Viewer for details, then contact your system administrator.

Registry Editor cannot access registry

[Registry Editor]

The Registry might be corrupt.

Restart the computer, and press the spacebar immediately after selecting Windows NT at the Boot Loader prompt. Then choose Last Known Good.

Registry Editor cannot connect to the remote machine

[Registry Editor]

The computer you are trying to connect to cannot be accessed. The computer might be down, or there might be a problem with the network.

Make sure the remote computer is running. Also make sure that other computers can access the target computer, and that this computer can make other network connections.

Registry Editor cannot create a key without a name. Please enter a key name.

[Registry Editor]

Each key in the Registry must have a name, a data type, and a value or values.

Enter a name for the key.

Registry Editor cannot create a value entry without a name. Please enter a value name.

[Registry Editor]

You attempted to create a value entry in Registry Editor, but did not assign it a name.

Assign a name to the value entry, then choose OK.

Registry Editor cannot find the desired key

[Registry Editor]

The key that you are trying to find does not exist. The key name might have been mistyped.

If you are sure there is a key by this name, try again, making sure to type the key name correctly.

Registry Editor cannot read the predefined key HKEY_CLASSES_ROOT

[Registry Editor]

The Registry might be corrupt.

Restart the computer, and press the spacebar immediately after selecting Windows NT at the Boot Loader prompt. Then choose Last Known Good.

Registry Editor cannot read the predefined key HKEY_CURRENT_USER

[Registry Editor]

The Registry might be corrupt.

Restart the computer, and press the spacebar immediately after selecting Windows NT at the Boot Loader prompt. Then choose Last Known Good.

Registry Editor cannot read the predefined key HKEY_LOCAL_MACHINE

[Registry Editor]

The Registry might be corrupt.

Restart the computer, and press the spacebar immediately after selecting Windows NT at the Boot Loader prompt. Then choose Last Known Good.

Registry Editor cannot read the predefined key HKEY_USERS

[Registry Editor]

The Registry might be corrupt.

Restart the computer, and press the spacebar immediately after selecting Windows NT at the Boot Loader prompt. Then choose Last Known Good.

Registry Editor cannot restore a non-volatile key on top of a volatile key.

[Registry Editor]

Volatile keys are created each time the system is started, and deleted when you turn the system off. Non-volatile keys are kept in a file between startups. You have tried to restore a non-volatile key that would overwrite a volatile key.

No action is needed. You might want to try again, specifying a different target.

Registry Editor could not accomplish the requested operation.

[Registry Editor]

This is a general message, and appears when Registry Editor cannot perform an operation, but cannot determine specifically the nature of the problem. For example, you attempted to access a remote computer, the network was down, and Registry Editor could not determine the specific nature of the network problem.

Try again to perform the operation. If this message reappears, try restarting Windows NT.

Registry Editor could not add the value entry. The key currently does not give you access to create a value entry.

[Registry Editor]

The access permissions on this key do not allow you to create new value entries.

Change permissions on this key so that you can create a value entry, and try again.

Registry Editor could not add the value entry. The key currently selected is marked for deletion.

[Registry Editor]

A process has marked this key in the Registry for deletion, but it has not yet been deleted because other processes are using it. It will be deleted when it is no longer in use, along with any subkeys. Therefore you cannot take any action on this key or any of its subkeys at this time.

No action is needed.

Registry Editor could not add the value entry. The key currently selected is not accessible.

[Registry Editor]

This key cannot be accessed. It has probably been deleted by another process since the Registry Editor window was last updated.

Choose Refresh All or Refresh Active from the View menu to refresh the screen. Or enable Auto Refresh (in the Options menu).If the problem persists, the registry might be corrupt.

Registry Editor could not create the key. The key already exists.

[Registry Editor]

A key by this name already exists on this node.

Create a new key with a different name.

Registry Editor could not create the subkey. The key currently selected does not give you access to create a subkey.

[Registry Editor]

The permissions on this key do not allow you to add a subkey.

Change permissions on this key so that you can create a subkey, and try again.

Registry Editor could not create the subkey. The key currently selected is marked for deletion.

[Registry Editor]

A process has marked this key in the Registry for deletion, but it has not yet been deleted because other processes are using it. It will be deleted when it is no longer in use, along with any subkeys. Therefore you cannot create a subkey to this key at this time.

No action is needed.

Registry Editor could not create the subkey. The key currently selected is not accessible.

[Registry Editor]

This key cannot be accessed. It has probably been deleted by another process since the Registry Editor window was last updated.

Choose Refresh All or Refresh Active from the View menu to refresh the screen. Or enable Auto Refresh (in the Options menu).If the problem persists, the registry might be corrupt.

Registry Editor could not create the value entry. The value entry already exists. Please enter a new name.

[Registry Editor]

A value entry by this name already exists in this key.

You can change the value of the existing entry, or create a new entry with a different name.

Registry Editor could not delete the key currently selected. The key, or one of its subkeys does not give you DELETE access.

[Registry Editor]

When a key is deleted, all of its subkeys are also deleted. Therefore you must have DELETE access on the key and on all of its subkeys in order to delete the key.

Change permissions on this key so that you can delete a subkey, and try again.

Registry Editor could not delete the key currently selected. The key, or one of its subkeys is not accessible.

[Registry Editor]

This key cannot be accessed. It has probably been deleted by another process since the Registry Editor window was last updated.

Choose Refresh All or Refresh Active from the View menu to refresh the screen. Or enable Auto Refresh (in the Options menu).If the problem persists, the registry might be corrupt.

Registry Editor could not delete the value entry. The key currently selected is marked for deletion.

[Registry Editor]

A process has marked this key in the Registry for deletion, but it has not yet been deleted because other processes are using it. It will be deleted when it is no longer in use, along with any subkeys. Therefore you cannot take any action, including deletions, on this key or any of its subkeys at this time.

No action is needed.

Registry Editor could not delete the value entry. The key currently selected is not accessible.

[Registry Editor]

This key cannot be accessed. It has probably been deleted by another process since the Registry Editor window was last updated.

Choose Refresh All or Refresh Active from the View menu to refresh the screen. Or enable Auto Refresh (in the Options menu).If the problem persists, the registry might be corrupt.

Registry Editor could not delete the value entry. The Key currently selected does not give you access to delete a value entry.

[Registry Editor]

The access permissions on this key do not allow you to delete value entries.

Change permissions on this key so that you can delete a value entry, and try again.

Registry Editor could not load the key. The file is not a valid registry file.

[Registry Editor]

You tried to load a file that does not contain a hive. You might have mistyped the filename, or this file might be corrupt.

Try again, making sure that you type the filename correctly. If the file appears to be corrupt, specify a different file.

Registry Editor could not load the key. The key already exists.

[Registry Editor]

There is already a key by this name in the Registry. You cannot load to an existing key.

Enter a key name that is not already used.

Registry Editor could not restore the key. The key currently selected is not accessible.

[Registry Editor]

This key cannot be accessed. It has probably been deleted by another process since the Registry Editor window was last updated.

Choose Refresh All or Refresh Active from the View menu to refresh the screen. Or enable Auto Refresh (in the Options menu).If the problem persists, the registry might be corrupt.

Registry Editor could not retrieve the security information. The key currently selected does not give you access to retrieve such information.

[Registry Editor]

The security settings on this key do not allow you to obtain security information about the key.

Ask your network administrator to give you the appropriate permissions and try again. Or, log on as a different user, for example as an Administrator, and try again.

Registry Editor could not retrieve the security information. The key currently selected is marked for deletion.

[Registry Editor]

A process has marked this key in the Registry for deletion, but it has not yet been deleted because other processes are using it. It will be deleted when it is no longer in use, along with any subkeys. Therefore Registry Editor cannot retrieve information about the key..

No action is needed.

Registry Editor could not retrieve the security information. The key currently selected is not accessible.

[Registry Editor]

This key cannot be accessed. It has probably been deleted by another process since the Registry Editor window was last updated.

Choose Refresh All or Refresh Active from the View menu to refresh the screen. Or enable Auto Refresh (in the Options menu).If the problem persists, the registry might be corrupt.

Registry Editor could not save the key. The key currently selected is not accessible.

[Registry Editor]

This key cannot be accessed. It has probably been deleted by another process since the Registry Editor window was last updated.

Choose Refresh All or Refresh Active from the View menu to refresh the screen. Or enable Auto Refresh (in the Options menu).If the problem persists, the registry might be corrupt.

Registry Editor could not save the security information. The key currently selected does not give you access to save such information.

[Registry Editor]

The security settings on this key do not allow you to change security information.

Ask your network administrator to give you the appropriate permissions and try again. Or, log on as a different user, for example as an Administrator, and try again.

Registry Editor could not save the security information. The key currently selected is marked for deletion.

[Registry Editor]

A process has marked this key in the Registry for deletion, but it has not yet been deleted because other processes are using it. It will be deleted when it is no longer in use, along with any subkeys. No changes can be made to this key or any of its subkeys.

No action is needed.

Registry Editor could not save the value entry. The key currently selected does not give you access to set a value entry.

[Registry Editor]

The security settings on this key do not allow you to change value entries.

Change permissions on this key so that you can delete a subkey, and try again.

Registry Editor could not save the value entry. The key currently selected is marked for deletion.

[Registry Editor]

A process has marked this key in the Registry for deletion, but it has not yet been deleted because other processes are using it. It will be deleted when it is no longer in use, along with any subkeys. Therefore you cannot take any action, including deletions, on this key or any of its subkeys at this time.

No action is needed.

Registry Editor could not save the value entry. The key currently selected is not accessible.

[Registry Editor]

This key cannot be accessed. It has probably been deleted by another process since the Registry Editor window was last updated.

Choose Refresh All or Refresh Active from the View menu to refresh the screen. Or enable Auto Refresh (in the Options menu).If the problem persists, the registry might be corrupt.

Registry Editor could not set security in all subkeys. The key currently selected contains one or more inaccessible subkeys.

[Registry Editor]

This key cannot be accessed. It has probably been deleted by another process since the Registry Editor window was last updated.

Choose Refresh All or Refresh Active from the View menu to refresh the screen. Or enable Auto Refresh (in the Options menu).If the problem persists, the registry might be corrupt.

Registry Editor could not set security in all subkeys. The key currently selected contains one or more subkeys marked for deletion.

[Registry Editor]

Registry Editor could to set security in all subkeys because some of them are marked for deletion.

No action is needed.

Registry Editor could not set security in the key currently selected, or some of its subkeys. These keys do not give you access to change security information.

[Registry Editor]

Since security settings for a key affect its subkeys as well, you must have permission to change security information for the key and all its subkeys in order to change security information for the key.

Ask your network administrator to give you the appropriate permissions and try again. Or, log on as a different user, for example as an Administrator, and try again.

Registry Editor is operating in the Read Only Mode. Changes made to this key will not be saved in the registry.

[Registry Editor]

Generally, changes to values in the Registry should be made using the graphical tools in Windows NT. By using the Registry Editor in Read Only mode, you are protected from making accidental changes that could impair or disable Windows NT.

If you are sure you want to make changes to this key, and cannot make the changes using any of the graphical tools in Windows NT, clear Read Only in the Options menu and try again.

Registry Editor is operating in the Read Only Mode. Changes made to this value entry will not be saved in the registry.

[Registry Editor]

Generally, changes to values in the Registry should be made using the graphical tools in Windows NT. By using the Registry Editor in Read Only mode, you are protected from making accidental changes that could impair or disable Windows NT.

If you are sure you want to change this value entry, and cannot change it using any of the graphical tools in Windows NT, clear Read Only in the Options menu and try changing the value again.

Registry Editor will delete the currently selected key and all its subkeys. Do you want to continue the operation?

[Registry Editor]

If you continue the operation, all the information in this key and all its subkeys will be lost. There is no Undo command for deletions.

Make sure you have selected an entry you want to delete before continuing.

Registry Editor will delete the currently selected value entry. Do you want to continue the operation?

[Registry Editor]

There is no Undo command for deletions. If you delete this value entry and it has a predefined default value, the default will be used.

Make sure you have selected an entry you want to delete before continuing.

Registry Editor will restore a key on top of the currently selected key. All value entries and subkeys of this key will be deleted. Do you want to continue the operation?

[Registry Editor]

When a key is restored, the values that were saved to the hive file overwrite the current values for that key in the Registry.

Choose Yes to restore the key and its subkeys, or choose Cancel to cancel the operation.

Registry Editor will unload the currently selected key and all its subkeys. Do you want to continue the operation?

[Registry Editor]

The key will be removed from the Registry.

Choose Yes to unload the key and its subkeys, or choose Cancel to cancel the operation.

Registry Enumeration Failed

[Control Panel]

The Registry is currently unable to perform a vital function.

Consult the event log in Event Viewer for details, then contact your system administrator.

Registry error: bad database

[Control Panel]

The Registry, which is a database, is corrupted.

Reinstall Windows NT.

Registry error: cannot access key

[Control Panel]

Either an internal software error has occurred, or permissions have been set upon a necessary Registry key which forbid you from accessing it.

See the event log in Event Viewer for details. Then contact your system administrator.

Registry error: cannot modify key

[Control Panel]

The Network option needs to alter information in the Registry and cannot alter the appropriate Registry key. Consequently, the current configuration operation cannot be completed.

Consult the event log in Event Viewer for details, then contact your system administrator.

Registry error: cannot open key

[Control Panel]

The Network option cannot open a Registry key that contains information necessary to the current operation. Possibly, permissions have been set upon this key that make render it impossible for you to access it.

Consult the event log in Event Viewer for details, then contact your system administrator.

Registry error: no such key

[Control Panel]

The registry tried to use a key that does not exist.

Reboot the computer, then choose Network from the Control Panel and choose Binding to redo the binding. If the problem continues, ask the administrator to do the following: Edit the registry, removing the variable \Software\Microsoft\Ncpa\CurrentVersion\Bindfile. Then choose Network from the Control Panel and choose Binding to redo the binding. If the problem still occurs, remove the recently installed network components, reboot the computer, and reinstall the network components.

Registry error: out of memory

[Control Panel]

Close one or more of the applications that you have running to increase available memory.

Registry Fact Consultation Failed

[Control Panel]

An error occurred, probably during the binding operation.

Reboot the computer, then choose Network from the Control Panel and choose Binding to redo the binding. If the problem continues, ask the administrator to do the following: Edit the registry, removing the variable \Software\Microsoft\Ncpa\CurrentVersion\Bindfile. Then choose Network from the Control Panel and choose Binding to redo the binding. If the problem still occurs, remove the recently installed network components, reboot the computer, and reinstall the network components.

Registry format error: no bindfile location

[Control Panel]

The registry has no record of the location of the file in which network binding information is stored.

Ask your network administrator to remove the registry value \Software\Microsoft\Ncpa\Bindfile. Then reboot the computer, choose Network from the Control Panel, and choose Binding. If the problem still occurs, remove any recently installed network components, reboot the computer, and reinstall the network components.

Registry key *name* could not be opened. Check current configuration.

[Digi]

The specified key could not be opened because it either doesn't exist or because you do not have the proper privilege to access it.

Use the Registry Editor to verify that the key exists. If not, reinstall the Digi driver. If the key exists, contact your system administrator to change your access to the key.

Registry rule base consultation error

[Control Panel]

An internal error occurred, probably in connection with a new network component.

If you just installed a new network component, remove it and reboot the computer, then reinstall it and reboot the computer again. If the problem continues, ask the administrator to edit the registry, removing the variable \Software\Microsoft\Ncpa\CurrentVersion\Bindfile; then choose Network from the Control Panel and choose Binding to redo the binding.

Releasing a node acquired on the adapter "*name* " because the connected network is not seeded by any router on the net

[Services for Macintosh (SFM)]

No router on the LocalTalk network which is connected to a LocalTalk adapter is seeding the network. A LocalTalk network must be seeded by at least one router.

Check if the seed router is down. If necessary, seed the LocalTalk adapter. Select Services for Macintosh and then choose Configure. Check the Enable Routing check box and then choose Advanced. Check the Seed this Network check box.

Releasing a node acquired on the adapter "*name* " because the node was obtained in the initial range. A node is now being acquired in the seeded range.

[Services for Macintosh (SFM)]

This message is for your information only. The AppleTalk protocol has determined that the network has a seeded range, and it is now starting in that range.

No action is needed.

Relocation Chain Exceeds Limit

[OS/2 Subsystem]

The OS/2 subsystem task manager was unable to run an application because the relocation chain for an OS/2 application segment exceeded the segment limit.

There were probably errors when the application was created. If you can, run these same application files under the OS/2 operating system. If you get a comparable message under OS/2, then contact the supplier of the application. If the application runs under OS/2, contact your technical support group about a problem with the Windows NT OS/2 subsystem.

Remote Access Connection Manager failed to start because the Point to Point Protocol failed to initialize.

[Remote Access Service]

A system error has occurred.

Check the Event Log in Event Viewer for other errors related to system resources. Event Viewer is found in the Administrative Tools group. Also, restart the computer. If the problem persists, contact technical support.

Remote Access error *text* **-**

[Remote Access Service]

This message is followed by other information which should give more information about the nature of the error.

Contact technical support.

Remote Access Server Configuration Failure. Cannot find the LANA numbers for the network adapters.

[Remote Access Service]

The Remote Access Service is configured incorrectly. Or the configuration of the Remote Access Service conflicts with other network software.

Use the Network option in Control Panel to remove and reinstall the Remote Access Service. If you continue to see this message, remove and reinstall all network software. If the problem continues to persist, contact technical support.

Remote Access Service failed to start because the Remote Access Connection Manager failed to initialize.

[Remote Access Service]

The Remote Access Connection Manager is configured incorrectly.

Use the Network option in Control Panel to remove and reinstall the Remote Access Service. Check the event log with Event Viewer in the Administrative Tools group for related errors to determine the configuration problem.

Remote PPP peer is not responding.

[Remote Access Service]

PPP was attempted but the remote computers did not respond. This error occurs because the server does not support PPP, such as a down-level Remote Access server.

Removing invalid long directory entry from *text*

[Chkdsk]

The directory entry is invalid.

No action is needed.

Removing orphan long directory entry: *name*

[Chkdsk]

FAT supports long filenames by using long directory entries. Every long directory entry must have an associated short entry. A long entry without a corresponding short entry is superfluous and will be removed by Chkdsk. Such orphaned entries can be created by running an operating system which does not recognize FAT long filenames.

No action is needed.

Removing the server *computer name* from the domain will render it incapable of sharing resources or authenticating domain logons until it is added to another domain. Are you sure you want to remove the server *name* from the *name* domain?

[Server Manager]

When you choose the Remove From Domain option in the Computer menu, this confirmation message appears.

If you still want to remove the server from the domain, choose Yes. If not, choose No.

Removing the workstation *computer name* from the domain will render it incapable of authenticating domain logons until it is added to another domain. Are you sure you want to remove the workstation *computer name* from the *name* domain?

[Server Manager]

When you choose the Remove From Domain option in the Computer menu, this confirmation message appears. If you remove the specified computer from the domain, you will render it incapable of accepting connections from other members of the domain from which you have removed it.

If you still want to remove the computer from the domain, choose Yes. If not, choose No.

Removing trailing directory entries from *name*.

[Chkdsk]

Chkdsk cleans up unused directory entries after the end of the directory is reached. This action does not affect user data.

No action is needed.

Reopen of same *name* stream attempted.

[Netevent]

A component's stream has been opened for the second time.

No action is needed.

Replicated data has changed in directory *name*.

[Network]

Data in the indicated replicated directory on an import computer has changed independent of changes in the master directory. This message is sent by the Replicator service.

Replication of the *text* Account Object "*name* " from primary domain controller *name* failed with the following error: *text*

[Network]

This event is logged by the Netlogon service.

Look up the indicated error and take appropriate action.

Replication of the *name* **Domain Object "***name* **" from primary domain controller** *name* **failed with the following error:** *text*

[Network]

Look up the indicated error and take appropriate action.

Replication of the *text* **Global Group "***name* **" from primary domain controller** *name* **failed with the following error:** *code*

[Network]

Look up the indicated error and take appropriate action.

Replication of the *text* **Local Group "***name* **" from primary domain controller** *name* **failed with the following error:** *text*

[Network]

Look up the indicated error and take appropriate action.

Replication of the *text* **Policy Object "***name* **" from primary domain controller** *name* **failed with the following error:** *text*

[Network]

Look up the indicated error and take appropriate action.

Replication of the *text* **Secret "***name* **" from primary domain controller** *name* **failed with the following error:** *text*

[Network]

Look up the indicated error and take appropriate action.

Replication of the *text* **Trusted Domain Object "***name* **" from primary domain controller** *name* **failed with the following error:** *name*

[Network]

Look up the indicated error and take appropriate action.

Replication of the *text* **User "***user name* **" from primary domain controller** *name* **failed with the following error:** *text*

[Network]

Look up the indicated error and take appropriate action.

Replicator could not access *name* **on** *name* **due to system error** *code***.**

[Network]

Look up the indicated error and take appropriate action. Also, check that the account under which the replicator is running has access to the specified file or directory.

Replicator could not access *name* on *computer name* due to system error *code*.

[Network]

Because of the listed system error, the Replicator service could not access a file on the listed export server.

Be sure the Replicator service's account on the export server has permission to read the directories that are being replicated. The name of this account can be displayed and changed using the Services option in Control Panel.

Replicator failed to update signal file in directory *name* due to *code* system error.

[Network] Net Message ID: 3220

This message should occur only on a down-level computer. Any action to correct the problem should be performed on that computer. The listed system error caused the Replicator service to fail to update its status.

Check the cause of the system error.

Replicator limit for files in a directory has been exceeded.

[Network]

The actual limit depends on the length of the file and directory names, and on the depth of the directory tree.

Delete some files or directories.

Replicator limit for tree depth has been exceeded.

[Network] Net Message ID: 3214

This message should occur only on a down-level computer. Any action to correct the problem should be performed on that computer. The replication tree can be no more than 32 levels deep.

Reorganize the replicated directories so that no path is more than 32 levels deep.

Requested addition of items exceeds the maximum allowed.

[Network] Net Message ID: 2121

The list of items in the command is too long.

If your command included a list of items, split the list into two smaller lists. Type the command with the first list, and then again with the second list.

Required Registry key *name* is missing. The service could not be started.

[Netevent]

Either the Registry is corrupted or the specified key was removed from the Registry.

Reinstall the specified Registry key using the Network option in Control Panel.

Required Registry value *name* is missing. The service could not be started.

[Netevent]

Either the Registry is corrupted or the specified value was removed from the Registry.

Reinstall the specified Registry value using the Network option in Control Panel.

Reserved name specified for Add Group Name

[Dynamic Data Exchange]

The name

Resetting image attributes will clear the current image and start a new editing session. Do you want to start a new session with the new image attributes?

[Paintbrush]

Using the Image Attributes option in the Options menu, you have attempted to reset the Image Attributes on a Paintbrush image in progress. Paintbrush does not support this option. Therefore, if you want to reset the image attributes, you must restart your Paintbrush image.

If you wish to start over, select the Yes option, and Paintbrush will give you an opportunity to save the currently opened Paintbrush image. If you do not wish to begin creating the image again, select the No option, and Paintbrush will return you to the currently opened Paintbrush image.

Resolver linkage problem.

[Network] Net Message ID: 3412

This message should occur only on a down-level computer. Any action to correct the problem should be performed on that computer. An internal error occurred.

Contact technical support.

Restore failed.

[WINS Service]

The WINS database could not be restored. This may be because of insufficient space on the target disk, or insufficient permissions to write to the target directory.

Make sure that the account from which you started the restore has write privilege on the target directory, and that the target has enough free space for the data. If another message accompanied this one, check it for additional suggestions.

Result is too large

[Calculator]

You have entered a number which is larger than 1.e+308, or have attempted to perform a function that results in a number larger than 1.e+308.

Choose the C or the CE button, then perform a function that results in a number less than 1.e+308.

Result of function is undefined

[Calculator]

You have entered the tangent of a very large number or the log of a negative number.

Choose the C or the CE button, then enter another number.

Resync Failed. Files are too different

[File Compare]

The Fc (File Compare) command could not find enough similarities to continue comparing the files.

You can only use the Fc command to compare these two files in binary mode.

Resyncing *computer name* with its Primary may take a few minutes. Do you want to make the change?

[Server Manager]

This message appears when you choose to resynchronize a computer with the domain controller. You should be aware that choosing the Yes option initiates the replication of the current SAM database from the domain controller to Backup.

If you still want to resynchronize the computer with its domain controller, choose Yes.

Resyncing the *name* domain may take a few minutes. Do you want to make the change?

[Server Manager]

When you choose the Synchronize Entire Domain option in the Computer menu, you are presented with this confirmation message.

If you want to synchronize the entire domain despite the time demands, choose Yes. If not, choose No.

Routine not found.

[Help]

When a Help file references FTUI32.DLL or FTENG32.DLL, and these files are not found, this message appears.

Make sure that these files are located in your Windows NT SYSTEM32 directory.

Rpl Pull thread is shutting down due to some error condition.

[WINS Service]

Other activity on the computer has affected the activity of the specified thread.

Stop and restart the WINS service.

Rpl Push thread is shutting down due to some error condition.

[WINS Service]

Other activity on the computer has affected the activity of the specified thread.

Stop and restart the WINS service.

Saving file in Cardfile 3.0 format.

[Cardfile]

Cardfile was unable to load the Object Linking and Embedding libraries, so it cannot support the Cardfile 3.1 format. If Cardfile saves your file in a Cardfile 3.0 format, be aware that any embedded object becomes a static object, which means that you cannot edit it from within Cardfile. Also, if the object is in color, saving it in Cardfile 3.0 converts the object to black-and-white.

Choose OK.

Scheme name cannot be blank.

[Program Manager]

In the Color option in Control Panel, you created a custom color, then attempted in the Save Scheme dialog box to save the scheme with no name. Windows NT does not support this naming selection.

Assign a name to your color scheme.

Scheme name cannot be blank.

[Program Manager]

In the Color option in Control Panel, you created a custom color, then attempted in the Save Scheme dialog box to save the scheme with no name. Windows NT does not support this naming selection.

Assign a name to your color scheme.

Scheme name cannot contain equals sign.

[Program Manager]

In the Color option in Control Panel, you created a custom color, then have assigned to it (in the Save Scheme dialog box) a name that contains an equals sign. Windows NT does not permit this naming selection.

Enter a different scheme name without an equals sign (=).

Scheme name cannot contain equals sign.

[Program Manager]

In the Color option in Control Panel, you created a custom color, then have assigned to it (in the Save Scheme dialog box) a name that contains an equals sign. Windows NT does not permit this naming selection.

Enter a different scheme name without an equals sign (=).

Scheme name cannot contain left or right brace.

[Program Manager]

In the Color option in the Control Panel, you have attempted to save a Custom Color Scheme that you have created, and in the Save Scheme dialog box, you have entered a name that contains a brace ([ ]). While you can include brackets (\(\)) in the names of Color Schemes, you cannot include braces.

Remove the brace(s) from the name of your color scheme, then select OK.

Scheme name cannot contain left or right brace.

[Program Manager]

In the Color option in the Control Panel, you have attempted to save a Custom Color Scheme that you have created, and in the Save Scheme dialog box, you have entered a name that contains a brace ([ ]). While you can include brackets (\(\)) in the names of Color Schemes, you cannot include braces.

Remove the brace(s) from the name of your color scheme, then select OK.

Screen already locked.

[Kernel32]

Contact the supplier of the running application.

Scroll bar range cannot be greater than 0x7FFF.

[Kernel32]

As part of its user interface, an application specified an invalid value.

Contact the supplier of the running application.

Search failed, end of log reached.

[Event Viewer]

You searched the event log, and the search produced no results.

Try again, specifying a different search criterion. Or search a different log.

SECOND diskette bad or incompatible

[Disk Compare]

The second floppy disk used in a Diskcomp command does not have the same format as the first floppy disk, is unformatted, or has an unrecognizable format.

Make sure the floppy disk is in the drive and the drive door is closed. If it is, then try removing the disk and reinserting it. After that, if this message reappears, you will not be able to use this disk with the Diskcomp command.

Second logon attempt with old password also failed with the following error: *text*

[Netevent]

The service controller made a second attempt to log on to a service using an old password.

Ask your system administrator to verify the current configured account information for the service. Use Event Viewer to examine the event log and identify the service.

Section *number* **missing or empty.**

[Setup]

Contact the supplier for another copy of the installation media.

Security information for the *name* directory is different.

[Backup]

The security information may be different because the backup may have been made while the directory was in use. Or a problem may have occurred during the backup or restore operation.

Use the Security menu in File Manager to view the security information on both versions of the directory. If the information is not different, try backing up or restoring the directory again.

Security information for the file *filename* is different.

[Backup]

The security information may be different because the backup may have been made while the file was in use. Or a problem may have occurred during the backup or restore operations.

Use the Security menu in File Manager to view the security information on both versions of the file. If the information is not different, try backing up or restoring the file again.

Security logging has been disabled. Use the Event Viewer to reduce the retention period and then enable security logging.

[Workstation-Logon]

Because the audit log is full, security logging has been disabled.

Use the Log Settings option in Event Viewer to determine how long audited events will be saved and how much space will be allotted to log size.

Select an AppleTalk printing device or choose Cancel.

[Services for Macintosh (SFM)]

Double-click a zone to select a printing device. If you choose Cancel, you will not configure a printer.

Select only one file to rename, or use wildcards (for example, *.TXT) to rename a group of files with similar names.

[File Manager]

You attempted to rename a number of files at once. File Manager does not allow this operation, unless you are simply changing a number of files to the same extension.

In the Error Renaming File dialog box, choose OK, then rename your files one at a time.

Select returned with an error

[WINS Service]

The WINS service shut down abruptly or is encountering problems with a resource on the computer or with the stack.

Restart the WINS service.

Send error. Session to *name* closed abnormally: *text*

[Dynamic Data Exchange]

Your connection to the indicated resource was lost due to the indicated error. Any files that you had open on the resource might have been corrupted.

Re-establish the connection. Check any files that were open for corruption, and restore them from a backup if necessary.

Sending files is no longer supported.

[Network] Net Message ID: 3777

The Net Send command no longer sends files.

Type the message you wish to send on the same line as Net Send.

Send to could not send all the bytes

[WINS Service]

Call technical support.

Send to could not send UDP message.

[WINS Service]

The computer might be running short of some resource.

Reboot the computer. If you see this message often, call technical support.

Send to returned with an error

[WINS Service]

Reboot the computer. If you see this message often, call technical support.

Serial overrun errors were detected while communicating with your modem.

[Remote Access Service]

Lower the modem's initial speed (bits per second), and redial. For instructions about lowering the initial speed, see "Setting Modem Features" in Remote Access online Help.

Serial port not initialized; please check your communication settings and try again.

[Terminal]

Before exchanging information with a remote computer, certain communications settings (baud rate, data bits, parity, flow control) must be set.

To determine your communications settings, select the Communications option from the Settings menu. For information about the correct options to select in this dialog box, see your modem documentation and the remote service package, or call the remote system's information number and request the settings.

Server port *number* in use!

[TCP/IP]

The Tftp server cannot start up because the port specified for it to use for a connection is already in use.

Wait, then retry the operation. If you still get this message, contact your system administrator.

Server port *number* in use!

[FTP Server]

The Tftp server cannot start up because the port specified for it to use for a connection is already in use.

Wait, then retry the operation. If you still get this message, contact your system administrator.

Server Unavailable

[Registry Editor]

The server might not be running, or the connections to it might be down.

Make sure the server is running, and that both it and this computer are connected to the network.

Service binding reconfiguration failed.

[Control Panel]

The application attempted to change the values associated with a service, but failed.

Reboot the computer, then choose Network from the Control Panel and choose Binding to redo the binding. If the problem continues, ask the administrator to do the following: Edit the Registry, removing the variable \Software\Microsoft\Ncpa\CurrentVersion\Bindfile. Then choose Network from the Control Panel and choose Binding to redo the binding. If the problem still occurs, remove the recently installed network components, reboot the machine, and reinstall the network components.

Service dependency update failed.

[Control Panel]

The application attempted to change the dependencies associated with a service, but failed.

Try again later. If you still get this message, contact your network administrator.

Setting broadcast option on socket failed. The Nw Sap Agent cannot continue.

[Netevent]

The SAP Agent encountered an error while setting a broadcast option on a socket.

Reboot your computer and try again. If you still get this message, call technical support.

Setting option EXTENDED_ADDRESS failed. The Nw Sap Agent cannot continue.

[Netevent]

The application could not start because a needed option could not be set. Resources that are accessed via the SAP Agent and services that depend on the SAP Agent will not be available.

Call technical support. Report both this message and the message that accompanies it.

Setup cannot bind the AppleTalk socket to the AppleTalk Protocol.

[Services for Macintosh (SFM)]

The AppleTalk protocol may not have been started.

To start the AppleTalk protocol, select the Devices option in Control Panel. Select AppleTalk Protocol and then choose Start.

Setup cannot find any AppleTalk routers on the network. Check your AppleTalk network configuration.

[Services for Macintosh (SFM)]

The zone list is empty. This may be due to an invalid configuration or a network error that prevents Setup from getting the AppleTalk information from the network.

Verify that a valid list of zones is in the zone list. Use the Network option in Control Panel to check the configuration of AppleTalk. Select Services for Macintosh and choose the Configure button.

Setup cannot initialize the Windows socket protocol. The Windows socket protocol may not be ready at this time or you could have an out of date Windows socket version.

[Services for Macintosh (SFM)]

The AppleTalk protocol or the AFD service may not be started or an internal error may have occurred.

Use the Network option in Control Panel to verify that Services for Macintosh have been configured. If so, try restarting your system because it may be having other problems. Then, contact technical support.

Setup cannot save AppleTalk Protocol information to the registry. The changes you have made will not take effect.

[Services for Macintosh (SFM)]

The Registry handle may be locked by someone else or an internal error has occurred.

Verify that the Registry has not been corrupted. Then restart your system and try the operation again. Otherwise, contact technical support.

Setup could not get the zone list from the AppleTalk network. The AppleTalk protocol or the AFD network service may not be started. Do you want to continue configuration?

[Services for Macintosh (SFM)]

If you select Yes, Setup will be unable to verify that you have specified the correct configuration information for the network.

Select Services for Macintosh in the Network option in Control Panel to verify that the AppleTalk Protocol and AFD service have been started. If so, contact your network administrator because there is a problem with the network.

Setup does not have the privilege to perform this operation.

[Setup]

This message is most likely to occur in maintenance Setup, rather than in the use of Setup for initial installation of Windows NT.

Select Retry in the message box to retry the operation. If you get the message again, select the Exit Setup button. If you were doing maintenance Setup, retry the Setup operation. If you were doing an initial installation, start it again from the beginning. If the message still occurs, contact your technical support group.

Setup does not have the privilege to perform this operation.

[Repair Disk]

This message is most likely to occur in maintenance Setup, rather than in the use of Setup for initial installation of Windows NT.

Select Retry in the message box to retry the operation. If you get the message again, select the Exit Setup button. If you were doing maintenance Setup, retry the Setup operation. If you were doing an initial installation, start it again from the beginning. If the message still occurs, contact your technical support group.

Setup encountered an error while updating partition information on *name*. This error prevents Setup from continuing. Press F3 to exit Setup.

[Setup]

There might be a problem with your hard disk or other hardware.

Consult the documentation that accompanied your disk or other hardware.

Setup expanded the full path of a symbolic link and it overflowed the specified buffer.

[Setup]

Select Retry in the message box to retry the operation. If you get the message again, select the Exit Setup button and begin the initial installation again. If the message still occurs, contact your technical support group.

Setup expanded the full path of a symbolic link and it overflowed the specified buffer.

[Repair Disk]

Select Retry in the message box to retry the operation. If you get the message again, select the Exit Setup button and begin the initial installation again. If the message still occurs, contact your technical support group.

Setup is out of memory and cannot continue. Press F3 to exit Setup.

[Setup]

The computer is running out of memory.

Remove any unneeded files and applications from your disk. If possible, increase disk space.

Setup is out of memory, cannot continue.

[Setup]

This can happen during initial installation of Windows NT, or during maintenance Setup.

Select Retry in the message box to retry the operation. If you get the message again, select the Exit Setup button and begin the initial installation again. If the message still occurs, contact your technical support group.

Setup is out of memory, cannot continue.

[Repair Disk]

This can happen during initial installation of Windows NT, or during maintenance Setup.

Select Retry in the message box to retry the operation. If you get the message again, select the Exit Setup button and begin the initial installation again. If the message still occurs, contact your technical support group.

Setup Script must end with an EXIT command

[Setup]

Setup is unable to finish interpreting a Setup script in an .INF file because it is not certain the script is complete.

Select OK to exit Setup. Restore all the .INF files from the distribution medium (you will have to decompress the files). Then rerun Setup. If you get this message again, contact your technical support group.

Setup Script must end with an EXIT command

[Repair Disk]

Setup is unable to finish interpreting a Setup script in an .INF file because it is not certain the script is complete.

Select OK to exit Setup. Restore all the .INF files from the distribution medium (you will have to decompress the files). Then rerun Setup. If you get this message again, contact your technical support group.

Setup was denied access to a remote resource on the network.

[Setup]

Setup attempted to redirect (connect) a local device to a remote resource on the network, but access to the remote resource was denied. This is most likely to happen during maintenance Setup, rather than at initial installation.

Select the Retry button in the message box to retry the operation. If you get the same message, contact your network administrator to find out the state of the remote resource and how you can access it. After you resolve that, retry the operation.

Setup was denied access to a remote resource on the network.

[Repair Disk]

Setup attempted to redirect (connect) a local device to a remote resource on the network, but access to the remote resource was denied. This is most likely to happen during maintenance Setup, rather than at initial installation.

Select the Retry button in the message box to retry the operation. If you get the same message, contact your network administrator to find out the state of the remote resource and how you can access it. After you resolve that, retry the operation.

Setup was unable to copy the file *filename*. \a To retry the copy, press ENTER. Make sure the proper Windows NT floppy disk or CD-ROM is in the drive. \a To skip this file, press ESC. WARNING: this option is intended for advanced users who understand the ramifications of the absence of the various Windows NT files. If you choose to skip this file, Setup cannot guarantee successful installation of Windows NT. To exit Setup, press F3.

[Setup]

If the file won't copy after repeating pressing ENTER, you might have corrupted media or there might be a problem with your hardware.

Contact the supplier of the installation media,

Setup was unable to copy the key *number* from the existing configuration data file *name* to your existing configuration. NOTE: Setup may not be able to upgrade your system properly. Retry this operation and if it continues to fail press F3to exit Setup. To retry copying the key, press ENTER. To skip this operation, press ESC. To exit Setup, press F3.

[Setup]

Contact technical support and report the Registry key that couldn't be copied.

Setup was unable to create an AppleTalk socket. Windows socket support for the AppleTalk Protocol may not be installed.

[Services for Macintosh (SFM)]

Check the Registry entry for Winsock to verify that the AppleTalk protocol is in the transport list.

Setup was unable to create the directory *name*. Setup cannot continue until the directory has been successfully created. \a To retry the operation, press ENTER. \a To exit Setup, press F3.

[Setup]

A file might exist with the name of the directory Setup attempted to create.

Exit Setup. Then determine if a file exists on the disk with a duplicate name. Delete the file from the disk. Otherwise, contact the supplier for replacement installation media.

Setup was unable to find or load the file.

[Setup]

The SETUP.LOG file on the Emergency Repair Disk might be corrupted or bad.

Make sure you have inserted the correct Emergency Repair Disk for your computer. If you don't have the correct disk, let Setup attempt to locate your Windows NT installation.

Setup was unable to initialize an internal database used to formulate device names. This indicates an internal Setup error or a serious system problem. Setup cannot continue. Press F3 to exit.

[Setup]

Contact technical support,

Setup was unable to load the file.

[Setup]

The file is corrupted or is missing.

Contact the supplier for another copy of the installation media.

Share data has been corrupted

[Dynamic Data Exchange]

The NetDDE DSDM database has been corrupted. Either it was administered incorrectly, or the Registry is corrupt.

Use DDEShare to delete all DDE shares, and then re-enter the shares. If you are unable to correct the problem that way, use Regedit32 to delete the DSDM information. Then use DDEShare to re-enter the shares.

Share name already exists

[Dynamic Data Exchange]

You attempted to add a share that already exists.

Specify a different name for this share, or delete the old share and create the new one.

Share name does not exist

[Dynamic Data Exchange]

There is no share by this name.

Check to make sure you have the correct name for the share. Then try again, making sure to type the name correctly.

Share name is invalid

[Dynamic Data Exchange]

The word you typed does not meet the requirements for a share name. Share names can have up to 256 characters. The equals sign (=) and backslash(\) cannot be used in the share name.

Enter a different share name.

Sharing violation

[Xcopy]

Xcopy failed because a file it is trying to copy, or a file to which it is trying to copy, is in use by another program.

Short Date Separator cannot be empty

[Program Manager]

In the International-Date Format dialog box in Control Panel, you left empty the Separator option in the Short Date Format box. Control Panel does not permit this action.

Make an entry in the Separator box, then select OK.

Short Date Separator cannot be empty

[Program Manager]

In the International-Date Format dialog box in Control Panel, you left empty the Separator option in the Short Date Format box. Control Panel does not permit this action.

Make an entry in the Separator box, then select OK.

Skip this file?

[Backup]

You attempted to back up a file that is in use.

If you want to skip this file, choose Yes. Then back up this file at a later time.

Skipping user *user name*...

[PORTUAS]

The username you specified with the /u or -u on the command line will just be ported.

No action is needed.

SNMP service encountered a fatal error.

[TCP/IP]

The SNMP component was not installed correctly.

Remove the SNMP service and then reinstall it.

Socket create call failed for main socket. The NwSapAgent cannot continue.

[Netevent]

The application could not start because a needed resource could not be obtained. The most likely reasons are that the Internetwork Packet Exchange (IPX) protocol could not be found or that the IPX WinSock information in the Registry is missing or in error.

Use the Network applet in the Control Panel to make sure the NWLink IPX/SPX Compatible Transport Driver is installed. If you still get this message, remove and re-install the NWLink IPX/SPX Compatible Transport Driver or have someone who is proficient in the user of Regedit32 edit the Registry to correct the entries affecting IPX WinSock information.

Socket create call failed for wan socket. The Nw Sap Agent cannot continue.

[Netevent]

The application could not start because a needed resource could not be obtained. The most likely reasons are that the Internetwork Packet Exchange (IPX) protocol could not be found or that the IPX WinSock information in the Registry is missing or in error.

Use the Network applet in the Control Panel to make sure the NWLink IPX/SPX Compatible Transport Driver is installed. If you still get this message, remove and re-install the NWLink IPX/SPX Compatible Transport Driver or have someone who is proficient in the user of Regedit32 edit the Registry to correct the entries affecting IPX WinSock information.

Socket operation on non-socket *name*

This operation cannot be performed on this connection.

Some entries in the error log were lost because of a buffer overflow.

[Network] Net Message ID: 3114

This message should occur only on a down-level computer. Any action to correct the problem should be performed on that computer. The error log is full, and one or more error log entries have been lost.

If you want to save the current error log file, copy it to another filename. Then clear the error log. You may do this remotely with Event Viewer.

Some firmware configuration information was incomplete.

Contact Microsoft Product Support.

Some mapping between account names and security IDs was not done.

[Kernel32]

During the mapping of Unicode strings to Security IDs (or vice versa), some names could not be mapped. This is an informational message and typically means that either an account has been deleted or a domain controller could not be located to map some of the names.

Either ignore the message, or wait and retry when the domain controller will be available.

Some of the users have open files. Disconnecting these users may cause loss of their data. Are you sure you want to disconnect all users from the Macintosh-Accessible volume *name* ?

[Services for Macintosh (SFM)]

Use Server Manager or File Manager to send a disconnect message to users. In using either manager, select the MacFile menu. In Server Manager, select Send Message. In File Manager, select View/Modify Volumes and then select Send Message.

Some of the users have open resources, disconnecting these users may cause loss of data. Are you sure you want to disconnect all users connected to the *computer name* share from all connected resources?

[Server Manager]

When you choose to disconnect all users from all resources, you run a risk that these users will lose changes that they have made to shared files. Consequently, Server Manager presents you with this confirmation message.

If you are sure you want to disconnect all users from all shares, choose Yes. If not, choose No. Then, before selecting this option again, alert all users that they are about to be disconnected.

Some of the users have open resources, disconnecting these users may cause loss of data. Are you sure you want to disconnect all users from all connected resources?

[Server Manager]

When you choose to disconnect all users from all resources, you run a risk that these users will lose changes that they have made to shared files. Consequently, Server Manager presents you with this confirmation message.

If you are sure you want to disconnect all users from all shares, choose Yes. If not, choose No. Then, before selecting this option again, alert all users that they are about to be disconnected.

Some of the users have resources open for *name*, closing these open resources may result in loss of data. Are you sure you want to close all open resources?

[Network]

To avoid data loss, resources should be closed from within the appropriate program.

Warn users that these resources need to be closed, and give them time to close the resources gracefully. Then try again.

Some of the users have resources open for *name*, closing these open resources may result in loss of data. Are you sure you want to close all open resources?

[Server Manager]

When you choose to disconnect a user from a shared resource, you risk causing the user to lose unsaved data. Consequently, any time that you choose to remotely disconnect a user, Server Manager presents you with a confirmation message.

If you are sure that you want to disconnect the user, choose Yes. If not, choose No, and before selecting this option again, alert the user of the imminent disconnect.

Some of the users have resources open for *name*, closing these open resources may result in loss of data. Are you sure you want to close all open resources?

[Security]

Because of the potential for data loss, you might try waiting a while before closing the open resources.

Some of the users have resources open for *text*, closing these open resources may result in loss of data. Are you sure you want to close all open resources?

[Services for Macintosh (SFM)]

Use Server Manager or File Manager to send a disconnect message to the users. In using either manager, select the MacFile menu. In Server Manager, select Send Message. In File Manager, select View/Modify Volumes and then select Send Message.

Some users have open files. Disconnecting these users may result in loss of their data. Are you sure you want to disconnect all users from all connected volumes?

[Services for Macintosh (SFM)]

Use Server Manager or File Manager to send a disconnect message to users. In using either manager, select the MacFile menu. In Server Manager, select Send Message. In File Manager, select View/Modify Volumes and then select Send Message.

SORT: Parameter value not in allowed range

[Sort]

You typed a numeric parameter value that is not in the range of values allowed by this command. For example, in the Sort command, you may have specified a column number that is too large for the input you are sorting.

Retype the command, using a different numeric parameter value.

Source and destination are the same.

[File Manager]

You directed File Manager to copy a file to the directory in which the file is already located.

In the Error Copying File dialog box, choose the OK button. Then in the Copy dialog box, specify a different directory as the destination directory.

Source and destination disks are incompatible.

[File Manager]

You attempted to perform a disk copy between disks that are incompatible, either because they are formatted to different capacities, or because the destination disk does not support formatting to the same capacity as the source disk. Or you attempted to perform a disk copy between disks of different sizes.

Make sure that both disks are the same size and formatted to the same capacities, then try again.

Source and target drives are the same

[Repair Disk]

The source and target directories must be on different drives.

Try again, specifying both the source and destination drives. For a description of the command syntax, type restore /?

SOURCE diskette bad or incompatible.

[Disk Copy]

Your disk has an unrecognizable format.

Make sure the floppy disk is in the drive and the drive door is closed. If it is, then try removing the disk and reinserting it. After that, if this message reappears, use a different disk.

Source does not contain backup files

[Repair Disk]

This disk does not contain backup files, so none can be restored.

Insert a disk containing backup files.

Source path required

[Replace]

You must specify a path to one or more source files as the first parameter in the Replace command.

To check the syntax of this command, type HELP at the command prompt followed by the command name (in this case, Replace).

Space to store the file waiting to be printed is not available on the server.

[Kernel32]

The server that is sharing the printer does not have space available to store the file waiting to be printed.

Retry the command at a later time.

Specified drive does not exist.

[Utilities]

Either the specified drive is not in use or the drive has been typed incorrectly.

Use File Manager or the Net Use command to verify your network connections.

Specify a value of 30 or greater for the Timeout If Not Connected In option.

[Terminal]

The minimum amount of time that Terminal waits for a signal from the remote computer is 30 seconds, and you specified a smaller number.

Follow the action specified in the message.

Specify only one file or directory in the To box. Or, if you want to specify a group of files, use wildcards (for example, *.TXT).

[File Manager]

In the To option of the Copy dialog box, you specified more than one file.

Specify only one drive and directory name, then try again.

speed sense failed (unsupported transfer rate).From device: *name*

[QIC117]

The tape device cannot be used.

Report this message to the hardware vendor and technical support.

Started with no bindings. The protocol must be bound to at least one adapter.

[Services for Macintosh (SFM)]

Try removing and reinstalling Services for Macintosh.

Startup failed to create critical resource: *name***.**

[Netevent]

Stop other services from running and retry the operation in few minutes. If the problem persists, your system administrator may need to add more memory to your system.

STOP: 0x00000001 (*parameter*, *parameter*, *parameter*, *parameter*)
APC_INDEX_MISMATCH

[Executive STOP]

This is a Windows NT Executive character-mode STOP message. It indicates a mismatch of thread and APC indexes. The most common reason to see this message is if a file system has a mismatched number of KeEnterCriticalRegion compared to KeLeaveCriticalRegion.

Restart and set the Recovery options in the System Control Panel or the /CRASHDEBUG system start option. If this message reappears, contact your system administrator or technical support group.

STOP: 0x00000002 (*parameter*, *parameter*, *parameter*, *parameter*)
DEVICE_QUEUE_NOT_BUSY

This is a Windows NT Executive character-mode STOP message. It indicates that a device queue was expected to be busy, but was not.

Restart and set the Recovery options in the System Control Panel or the /CRASHDEBUG system start option. If this message reappears, contact your system administrator or technical support group.

STOP: 0x00000003 (*parameter*, *parameter*, *parameter*, *parameter*)
INVALID_AFFINITY_SET

This is a Windows NT Executive character-mode STOP message. It indicates a null of nonproper subset affinity.

Restart and set the Recovery options in the System Control Panel or the /CRASHDEBUG system start option. If this message reappears, contact your system administrator or technical support group.

STOP: 0x00000004 (*parameter*, *parameter*, *parameter*, *parameter*)
INVALID_DATA_ACCESS_TRAP

This is a Windows NT Executive character-mode STOP message. It indicates an invalid data access trap.

Restart and set the Recovery options in the System Control Panel or the /CRASHDEBUG system start option. If this message reappears, contact your system administrator or technical support group.

STOP: 0x00000005 (*parameter*, *parameter*, *parameter*, *parameter*)
INVALID_PROCESS_ATTACH_ATTEMPT

This is a Windows NT Executive character-mode STOP message. It indicates a problem with an owned mutex or a mutex with a process already attached.

Restart and set the Recovery options in the System Control Panel or the /CRASHDEBUG system start option. If this message reappears, contact your system administrator or technical support group.

STOP: 0x00000006 (*parameter*, *parameter*, *parameter*, *parameter*)
INVALID_PROCESS_DETACH_ATTEMPT

This is a Windows NT Executive character-mode STOP message. It indicates a problem with an owned mutex or an unclean APC state.

Restart and set the Recovery options in the System Control Panel or the /CRASHDEBUG system start option. If this message reappears, contact your system administrator or technical support group.

STOP: 0x00000007 (*parameter*, *parameter*, *parameter*, *parameter*)
INVALID_SOFTWARE_INTERRUPT

This is a Windows NT Executive character-mode STOP message. It indicates a level not within the software range.

Restart and set the Recovery options in the System Control Panel or the /CRASHDEBUG system start option. If this message reappears, contact your system administrator or technical support group.

STOP: 0x00000008 (*parameter*, *parameter*, *parameter*, *parameter*)
IRQL_NOT_DISPATCH_LEVEL

This is a Windows NT Executive character-mode STOP message. It indicates an attempt to remove a device not at the dispatch level.

Restart and set the Recovery options in the System Control Panel or the /CRASHDEBUG system start option. If this message reappears, contact your system administrator or technical support group.

STOP: 0x00000009 (*parameter, parameter, parameter, parameter*)
IRQL_NOT_GREATER_OR_EQUAL

This is a Windows NT Executive character-mode STOP message. It indicates an IRQL that was expected to be greater or equal, but was not.

Restart and set the Recovery options in the System Control Panel or the /CRASHDEBUG system start option. If this message reappears, contact your system administrator or technical support group.

STOP: 0x0000000A (*parameter, parameter, parameter, parameter*)
IRQL_NOT_LESS_OR_EQUAL

This is a Windows NT Executive character-mode STOP message. It indicates an attempt was made to touch pagable memory at a process internal request level (IRQL) that is too high. This is usually caused by drivers using improper addresses. The fourth parameter in the message parameter list is the memory address at which the fault happened. The second parameter shows the IRQL. If the IRQL was not equal to 2, then the interrupt most likely came from a driver. Compare the memory address in the fourth parameter with the base addresses of the drivers in the driver table on the STOP screen to find the driver that is the problem. Note that the third parameter encodes read/write access (0 = read, 1= write).

Restart and set the Recovery options in the System Control Panel or the /CRASHDEBUG system start option. If this message reappears, contact your system administrator or technical support group. If a kernel debugger is available, try to get a stack backtrace.

STOP: 0x0000000B (*parameter, parameter, parameter, parameter*)
NO_EXCEPTION_HANDLING_SUPPORT

This is a Windows NT Executive character-mode STOP message. It indicates that exception handling was not supported.

Restart and set the Recovery options in the System Control Panel or the /CRASHDEBUG system start option. If this message reappears, contact your system administrator or technical support group.

STOP: 0x0000000C (*parameter, parameter, parameter, parameter*)
MAXIMUM_WAIT_OBJECTS_EXCEEDED

This is a Windows NT Executive character-mode STOP message. It indicates too many wait objects in a wait multiple structure.

Restart and set the Recovery options in the System Control Panel or the /CRASHDEBUG system start option. If this message reappears, contact your system administrator or technical support group.

STOP: 0x0000000D (*parameter, parameter, parameter, parameter*)
MUTEX_LEVEL_NUMBER_VIOLATION

This is a Windows NT Executive character-mode STOP message. It indicates an attempt to acquire a lower level mutex.

Restart and set the Recovery options in the System Control Panel or the /CRASHDEBUG system start option. If this message reappears, contact your system administrator or technical support group.

STOP: 0x0000000E (*parameter*, *parameter*, *parameter*, *parameter*)
NO_USER_MODE_CONTEXT

This is a Windows NT Executive character-mode STOP message. It indicates an attempt to enter user mode with no context.

Restart and set the Recovery options in the System Control Panel or the /CRASHDEBUG system start option. If this message reappears, contact your system administrator or technical support group.

STOP: 0x0000000F (*parameter*, *parameter*, *parameter*, *parameter*)
SPIN_LOCK_ALREADY_OWNED

This is a Windows NT Executive character-mode STOP message. It indicates an attempt to acquire an owned spin lock.

Restart and set the Recovery options in the System Control Panel or the /CRASHDEBUG system start option. If this message reappears, contact your system administrator or technical support group.

STOP: 0x00000010 (*parameter*, *parameter*, *parameter*, *parameter*)
SPIN_LOCK_NOT_OWNED

This is a Windows NT Executive character-mode STOP message. It indicates an attempt to release an unowned spin lock.

Restart and set the Recovery options in the System Control Panel or the /CRASHDEBUG system start option. If this message reappears, contact your system administrator or technical support group.

STOP: 0x00000011 (*parameter*, *parameter*, *parameter*, *parameter*)
THREAD_NOT_MUTEX_OWNER

This is a Windows NT Executive character-mode STOP message. It indicates an attempt to release a thread by a mutex non-owner.

Restart and set the Recovery options in the System Control Panel or the /CRASHDEBUG system start option. If this message reappears, contact your system administrator or technical support group.

STOP: 0x00000012 (*parameter*, *parameter*, *parameter*, *parameter*)
TRAP_CAUSE_UNKNOWN

This is a Windows NT Executive character-mode STOP message. It indicates a trap from an unknown cause.

Restart and set the Recovery options in the System Control Panel or the /CRASHDEBUG system start option. If this message reappears, contact your system administrator or technical support group.

STOP: 0x00000013 (*parameter, parameter, parameter, parameter*)
EMPTY_THREAD_REAPER_LIST

This is a Windows NT Executive character-mode STOP message. It indicates the thread reaper list is corrupted (the reaper list became signaled, but no threads were present on the list).

Restart and set the Recovery options in the System Control Panel or the /CRASHDEBUG system start option. If this message reappears, contact your system administrator or technical support group.

STOP: 0x00000014 (*parameter, parameter, parameter, parameter*)
CREATE_DELETE_LOCK_NOT_LOCKED

This is a Windows NT Executive character-mode STOP message. It indicates that the thread reaper was handed a thread to reap, but the CreateDeleteLock for the process was not locked.

Restart and set the Recovery options in the System Control Panel or the /CRASHDEBUG system start option. If this message reappears, contact your system administrator or technical support group.

STOP: 0x00000015 (*parameter, parameter, parameter, parameter*)
LAST_CHANCE_CALLED_FROM_KMODE

This is a Windows NT Executive character-mode STOP message. This indicates that the last chance exception service was called from kernel mode.

Restart and set the Recovery options in the System Control Panel or the /CRASHDEBUG system start option. If this message reappears, contact your system administrator or technical support group.

STOP: 0x00000016 (*parameter, parameter, parameter, parameter*)
CID_HANDLE_CREATION

This is a Windows NT Executive character-mode STOP message. This indicates a failure occurred creating a handle to represent a client ID.

Restart and set the Recovery options in the System Control Panel or the /CRASHDEBUG system start option. If this message reappears, contact your system administrator or technical support group.

STOP: 0x00000017 (*parameter, parameter, parameter, parameter*)
CID_HANDLE_DELETION

This is a Windows NT Executive character-mode STOP message. This indicates that a failure occurred deleting a handle to represent a client ID.

Restart and set the Recovery options in the System Control Panel or the /CRASHDEBUG system start option. If this message reappears, contact your system administrator or technical support group.

STOP: 0x00000018 (*parameter, parameter, parameter, parameter*)
REFERENCE_BY_POINTER

This is a Windows NT Executive character-mode STOP message. This indicates a failure occurred referencing an object by what should be a referenced pointer.

Restart and set the Recovery options in the System Control Panel or the /CRASHDEBUG system start option. If this message reappears, contact your system administrator or technical support group.

STOP: 0x00000019 (*parameter, parameter, parameter, parameter*)
BAD_POOL_HEADER

This is a Windows NT Executive character-mode STOP message. This indicates a block of pool with a bad header was returned to the pool.

Restart and set the Recovery options in the System Control Panel or the /CRASHDEBUG system start option. If this message reappears, contact your system administrator or technical support group.

STOP: 0x0000001A (*parameter, parameter, parameter, parameter*)
MEMORY_MANAGEMENT

This is a Windows NT Executive character-mode STOP message. It indicates a general memory management problem.

Restart and set the Recovery options in the System Control Panel or the /CRASHDEBUG system start option. If this message reappears, contact your system administrator or technical support group.

STOP: 0x0000001B (*parameter, parameter, parameter, parameter*)
PFN_SHARE_COUNT

This is a Windows NT Executive character-mode STOP message. It indicates a memory management page frame number (PFN) database element has a corrupt share count.

Restart and set the Recovery options in the System Control Panel or the /CRASHDEBUG system start option. If this message reappears, contact your system administrator or technical support group.

STOP: 0x0000001C (*parameter, parameter, parameter, parameter*)
PFN_REFERENCE_COUNT

This is a Windows NT Executive character-mode STOP message. It indicates a memory management page frame number (PFN) database element has a corrupt reference count.

Restart and set the Recovery options in the System Control Panel or the /CRASHDEBUG system start option. If this message reappears, contact your system administrator or technical support group.

STOP: 0x0000001D (*parameter, parameter, parameter, parameter*)
NO_SPIN_LOCK_AVAILABLE

This is a Windows NT Executive character-mode STOP message. It indicates no spin locks are available to allocate.

Restart and set the Recovery options in the System Control Panel or the /CRASHDEBUG system start option. If this message reappears, contact your system administrator or technical support group.

STOP: 0x0000001E (*parameter, parameter, parameter, parameter*)
KMODE_EXCEPTION_NOT_HANDLED

This is a Windows NT Executive character-mode STOP message. It indicates a kernel mode exception was not handled. The second parameter in the parameter list is the memory address at which the unhandled exception occurred. Usually, the exception address pinpoints the driver/function that caused the problem. A common problem is 0x80000003 which means a hard coded breakpoint or assertion was hit but the system started \NODEBUG

Restart and set the Recovery options in the System Control Panel or the /CRASHDEBUG system start option. If this message reappears, contact your system administrator or technical support group. Make sure that a debugger is attached to the computer and that the system is started /DEBUG. Always note the address where the exception occurred as well as the link date of the driver/image that contains the address.

STOP: 0x0000001F (*parameter, parameter, parameter, parameter*)
SHARED_RESOURCE_CONV_ERROR

This is a Windows NT Executive character-mode STOP message. It indicates a shared resource conversion problem.

Restart and set the Recovery options in the System Control Panel or the /CRASHDEBUG system start option. If this message reappears, contact your system administrator or technical support group.

STOP: 0x00000020 (*parameter, parameter, parameter, parameter*)
KERNEL_APC_PENDING_DURING_EXIT

This is a Windows NT Executive character-mode STOP message. It indicates a kernel mode asynchronous procedure call (APC) found pending during thread termination. The first parameter is the address of the APC found pending during exit. The second parameter is the thread's APC disable count. And the third parameter is the current IRQL (internal request level). If the thread's disable count is non-zero, it is the source of the problem. The current IRQL should be 0. If not, a driver's cancellation routine returned at an elevated IRQL.

Restart and set the Recovery options in the System Control Panel or the /CRASHDEBUG system start option. If this message reappears, contact your system administrator or technical support group. Check the file systems and drivers installed on your computer.

STOP: 0x00000021 (*parameter*, *parameter*, *parameter*, *parameter*)
QUOTA_UNDERFLOW

This is a Windows NT Executive character-mode STOP message. It indicates that quota was returned to a process, but that process was not using the amount of quota being returned.

Restart and set the Recovery options in the System Control Panel or the /CRASHDEBUG system start option. If this message reappears, contact your system administrator or technical support group.

STOP: 0x00000022 (*parameter*, *parameter*, *parameter*, *parameter*) **FILE_SYSTEM**

This is a Windows NT Executive character-mode STOP message. This indicates a generic file system problem.

Restart and set the Recovery options in the System Control Panel or the /CRASHDEBUG system start option. If this message reappears, contact your system administrator or technical support group.

STOP: 0x00000023 (*parameter*, *parameter*, *parameter*, *parameter*)
FAT_FILE_SYSTEM

This is a Windows NT Executive character-mode STOP message. It indicates a FAT file system problem.

Restart and set the Recovery options in the System Control Panel or the /CRASHDEBUG system start option. If this message reappears, contact your system administrator or technical support group. Be sure to note any messages you see to pass on to your technical support group.

STOP: 0x00000024 (*parameter*, *parameter*, *parameter*, *parameter*)
NTFS_FILE_SYSTEM

This is a Windows NT Executive character-mode STOP message. It indicates an NTFS file system problem.

Restart and set the Recovery options in the System Control Panel or the /CRASHDEBUG system start option. If this message reappears, contact your system administrator or technical support group. Be sure to note any messages you see to pass on to your technical support group.

STOP: 0x00000025 (*parameter*, *parameter*, *parameter*, *parameter*)
NPFS_FILE_SYSTEM

This is a Windows NT Executive character-mode STOP message. It indicates a named pipe file system problem.

Restart and set the Recovery options in the System Control Panel or the /CRASHDEBUG system start option. If this message reappears, contact your system administrator or technical support group. Be sure to note any messages you see to pass on to your technical support group.

STOP: 0x00000026 (*parameter, parameter, parameter, parameter*)
CDFS_FILE_SYSTEM

This is a Windows NT Executive character-mode STOP message. This indicates a CD-ROM file system problem.

Restart and set the Recovery options in the System Control Panel or the /CRASHDEBUG system start option. If this message reappears, contact your system administrator or technical support group. Be sure to note any messages you see to pass on to your technical support group.

STOP: 0x00000027 (*parameter, parameter, parameter, parameter*)
RDR_FILE_SYSTEM

This is a Windows NT Executive character-mode STOP message. It indicates a redirector file system problem.

Restart and set the Recovery options in the System Control Panel or the /CRASHDEBUG system start option. If this message reappears, contact your system administrator or technical support group.

STOP: 0x00000028 (*parameter, parameter, parameter, parameter*)
CORRUPT_ACCESS_TOKEN

This is a Windows NT Executive character-mode STOP message. It indicates the security system encountered an invalid access token.

Restart and set the Recovery options in the System Control Panel or the /CRASHDEBUG system start option. If this message reappears, contact your system administrator or technical support group.

STOP: 0x00000029 (*parameter, parameter, parameter, parameter*)
SECURITY_SYSTEM

This is a Windows NT Executive character-mode STOP message. It indicates a problem internal to the security system.

Restart and set the Recovery options in the System Control Panel or the /CRASHDEBUG system start option. If this message reappears, contact your system administrator or technical support group.

STOP: 0x0000002A (*parameter, parameter, parameter, parameter*)
INCONSISTENT_IRP

This is a Windows NT Executive character-mode STOP message. It indicates that an IRP (I/O request packet) was encountered in an inconsistent state. For example, some field or fields of the IRP were inconsistent with the remaining state of the IRP.

Restart and set the Recovery options in the System Control Panel or the /CRASHDEBUG system start option. If this message reappears, contact your system administrator or technical support group.

STOP: 0x0000002B (*parameter, parameter, parameter, parameter*)
PANIC_STACK_SWITCH

This is a Windows NT Executive character-mode STOP message. It indicates a panic switch to the kernel stack because of stack overflow. This error may be caused by the kernel-mode driver using too much stack space. Or a data corruption has occurred in the kernel.

Restart and set the Recovery options in the System Control Panel or the /CRASHDEBUG system start option. If this message reappears, contact your system administrator or technical support group.

STOP: 0x0000002C (*parameter, parameter, parameter, parameter*)
PORT_DRIVER_INTERNAL

This is a Windows NT Executive character-mode STOP message. It indicates an internal error in a port driver.

Restart and set the Recovery options in the System Control Panel or the /CRASHDEBUG system start option. If this message reappears, contact your system administrator or technical support group.

STOP: 0x0000002D (*parameter, parameter, parameter, parameter*)
SCSI_DISK_DRIVER_INTERNAL

This is a Windows NT Executive character-mode STOP message. It indicates an internal error in a SCSI hard disk driver.

Restart and set the Recovery options in the System Control Panel or the /CRASHDEBUG system start option. If this message reappears, contact your system administrator or technical support group.

STOP: 0x0000002E (*parameter, parameter, parameter, parameter*)
DATA_BUS_ERROR

This is a Windows NT Executive character-mode STOP message. It indicates a data bus error which can be caused by a parity error in the system memory. This error could also be caused by a driver accessing an address that does not exist.

Restart and set the Recovery options in the System Control Panel or the /CRASHDEBUG system start option. If this message reappears, contact your system administrator or technical support group.

STOP: 0x0000002F (*parameter, parameter, parameter, parameter*)
INSTRUCTION_BUS_ERROR

This is a Windows NT Executive character-mode STOP message. It indicates an instruction bus error.

Restart and set the Recovery options in the System Control Panel or the /CRASHDEBUG system start option. If this message reappears, contact your system administrator or technical support group.

STOP: 0x00000030 (*parameter, parameter, parameter, parameter*)
SET_OF_INVALID_CONTEXT

This is a Windows NT Executive character-mode STOP message. It indicates an attempt to edit values of SS or ESP when returning to kernel mode code.

Restart and set the Recovery options in the System Control Panel or the /CRASHDEBUG system start option. If this message reappears, contact your system administrator or technical support group.

STOP: 0x00000031 (*parameter, parameter, parameter, parameter*)
PHASE0_INITIALIZATION_FAILED

This is a Windows NT Executive character-mode STOP message. Initialization of the Windows NT executive failed during phase 0 (this is during phase 4 of system startup). This can only happen during the relatively short period of time that the Windows NT executive is being initialized. There may be a hardware problem.

Restart and set the Recovery options in the System Control Panel or the /CRASHDEBUG system start option. If this message reappears, contact your system administrator or technical support group.

STOP: 0x00000032 (*parameter, parameter, parameter, parameter*)
PHASE1_INITIALIZATION_FAILED

This is a Windows NT Executive character-mode STOP message. Initialization of the Windows NT executive failed during phase 1 (this is during phase 4 of system startup). This can only happen during the relatively short period of time the Windows NT executive is being initialized. There may be a problem with a device driver.

Restart and set the Recovery options in the System Control Panel or the /CRASHDEBUG system start option. If this message reappears, contact your system administrator or technical support group.

STOP: 0x00000033 (*parameter, parameter, parameter, parameter*)
UNEXPECTED_INITIALIZATION_CALL

This is a Windows NT Executive character-mode STOP message. Initialization of the Windows NT executive failed during phase 1 (this is during phase 4 of system startup). This can only happen during the relatively short period of time the Windows NT executive is being initialized. There may be a problem with a device driver.

Restart and set the Recovery options in the System Control Panel or the /CRASHDEBUG system start option. If this message reappears, contact your system administrator or technical support group.

STOP: 0x00000034 (*parameter, parameter, parameter, parameter*)
CACHE_MANAGER

This is a Windows NT Executive character-mode STOP message. Initialization of the Windows NT executive failed during phase 1 (this is during phase 4 of system startup). This can only happen during the relatively short period of time the Windows NT executive is being initialized. There may be a problem with a device driver.

Restart and set the Recovery options in the System Control Panel or the /CRASHDEBUG system start option. If this message reappears, contact your system administrator or technical support group. Be sure to note any messages you see to pass on to your technical support group.

STOP: 0x00000035 (*parameter, parameter, parameter, parameter*)
NO_MORE_IRP_STACK_LOCATIONS

This is a Windows NT Executive character-mode STOP message. It indicates that the I/O system detected a call from one driver to another with no available IRP (I/O request packet) stack locations remaining in the packet for the invoked driver to use. Other memory problems may accompany this error.

Restart and set the Recovery options in the System Control Panel or the /CRASHDEBUG system start option. If this message reappears, contact your system administrator or technical support group.

STOP: 0x00000036 (*parameter, parameter, parameter, parameter*)
DEVICE_REFERENCE_COUNT_NOT_ZERO

This is a Windows NT Executive character-mode STOP message. It indicates an attempt was made to delete a device object whose reference count was non-zero. A non-zero reference count means that there are still outstanding references to the device. There may be a problem in calling the device driver.

Restart and set the Recovery options in the System Control Panel or the /CRASHDEBUG system start option. If this message reappears, contact your system administrator or technical support group.

STOP: 0x00000037 (*parameter, parameter, parameter, parameter*)
FLOPPY_INTERNAL_ERROR

This is a Windows NT Executive character-mode STOP message. It indicates a floppy disk driver internal error.

Restart and set the Recovery options in the System Control Panel or the /CRASHDEBUG system start option. If this message reappears, contact your system administrator or technical support group.

STOP: 0x00000038 (*parameter, parameter, parameter, parameter*)
SERIAL_DRIVER_INTERNAL

This is a Windows NT Executive character-mode STOP message. It indicates a serial device driver internal error.

Restart and set the Recovery options in the System Control Panel or the /CRASHDEBUG system start option. If this message reappears, contact your system administrator or technical support group.

STOP: 0x00000039 (*parameter, parameter, parameter, parameter*)
SYSTEM_EXIT_OWNED_MUTEX

This is a Windows NT Executive character-mode STOP message. It indicates an attempt was made to exit a system service while owning one or more mutexes.

Restart and set the Recovery options in the System Control Panel or the /CRASHDEBUG system start option. If this message reappears, contact your system administrator or technical support group.

STOP: 0x0000003A (*parameter, parameter, parameter, parameter*)
SYSTEM_UNWIND_PREVIOUS_USER

This is a Windows NT Executive character-mode STOP message. It indicates an attempt was made to unwind through the system service dispatcher into user mode.

Restart and set the Recovery options in the System Control Panel or the /CRASHDEBUG system start option. If this message reappears, contact your system administrator or technical support group.

STOP: 0x0000003B (*parameter, parameter, parameter, parameter*)
SYSTEM_SERVICE_EXCEPTION

This is a Windows NT Executive character-mode STOP message. It indicates an exception was raised in a system service which was not handled by the system service.

Restart and set the Recovery options in the System Control Panel or the /CRASHDEBUG system start option. If this message reappears, contact your system administrator or technical support group.

STOP: 0x0000003C (*parameter, parameter, parameter, parameter*)
INTERRUPT_UNWIND_ATTEMPTED

This is a Windows NT Executive character-mode STOP message. It indicates an unwind operation was initiated in an interrupt service routine that attempted to unwind through the interrupt dispatcher.

Restart and set the Recovery options in the System Control Panel or the /CRASHDEBUG system start option. If this message reappears, contact your system administrator or technical support group.

STOP: 0x0000003D (*parameter, parameter, parameter, parameter*)
INTERRUPT_EXCEPTION_NOT_HANDLED

This is a Windows NT Executive character-mode STOP message. It indicates an exception was raised in an interrupt service routine which was not handled by the interrupt service routine.

Restart and set the Recovery options in the System Control Panel or the /CRASHDEBUG system start option. If this message reappears, contact your system administrator or technical support group.

STOP: 0x0000003E (*parameter, parameter, parameter, parameter*)
MULTIPROCESSOR_CONFIGURATION_NOT_SUPPORTED

This is a Windows NT Executive character-mode STOP message. It indicates the multiprocessor configuration is not supported. For example, not all processors are at the same level or of the same type. There might also be mismatched coprocessor support.

Restart and set the Recovery options in the System Control Panel or the /CRASHDEBUG system start option. If this message reappears, contact your system administrator or technical support group.

STOP: 0x0000003F (*parameter*, *parameter*, *parameter*, *parameter*)
NO_MORE_SYSTEM_PTES

This is a Windows NT Executive character-mode STOP message. It indicates no more system page table entries (PTEs) exist for mapping non-paged entities.

Restart and set the Recovery options in the System Control Panel or the /CRASHDEBUG system start option. If this message reappears, contact your system administrator or technical support group.

STOP: 0x00000040 (*parameter*, *parameter*, *parameter*, *parameter*)
TARGET_MDL_TOO_SMALL

This is a Windows NT Executive character-mode STOP message. It indicates an MDL that was allocated to map a buffer is not large enough to contain the page frame numbers (PFNs) required to map the desired buffer. There might be a problem with the driver.

Restart and set the Recovery options in the System Control Panel or the /CRASHDEBUG system start option. If this message reappears, contact your system administrator or technical support group.

STOP: 0x00000041 (*parameter*, *parameter*, *parameter*, *parameter*)
MUST_SUCCEED_POOL_EMPTY

This is a Windows NT Executive character-mode STOP message. It indicates there is no more must-succeed pool.

Restart and set the Recovery options in the System Control Panel or the /CRASHDEBUG system start option. If this message reappears, contact your system administrator or technical support group.

STOP: 0x00000042 (*parameter*, *parameter*, *parameter*, *parameter*)
ATDISK_DRIVER_INTERNAL

This is a Windows NT Executive character-mode STOP message. It indicates a hard disk device driver internal error.

Restart and set the Recovery options in the System Control Panel or the /CRASHDEBUG system start option. If this message reappears, contact your system administrator or technical support group.

STOP: 0x00000043 (*parameter*, *parameter*, *parameter*, *parameter*)
NO_SUCH_PARTITION

This is a Windows NT Executive character-mode STOP message. It indicates a disk device driver called the I/O system to change a partition type on a specified partition, but the partition does not exist.

Restart and set the Recovery options in the System Control Panel or the /CRASHDEBUG system start option. If this message reappears, contact your system administrator or technical support group.

STOP: 0x00000044 (*parameter, parameter, parameter, parameter*)
MULTIPLE_IRP_COMPLETE_REQUESTS

This is a Windows NT Executive character-mode STOP message. It indicates an attempt was made to complete an IRP (I/O request packet) more than once, possibly by more than one driver.

Restart and set the Recovery options in the System Control Panel or the /CRASHDEBUG system start option. If this message reappears, contact your system administrator or technical support group.

STOP: 0x00000045 (*parameter, parameter, parameter, parameter*)
INSUFFICIENT_SYSTEM_MAP_REGS

This is a Windows NT Executive character-mode STOP message. It indicates an attempt was made to allocate more map registers than are allocated to an adapter.

Restart and set the Recovery options in the System Control Panel or the /CRASHDEBUG system start option. If this message reappears, contact your system administrator or technical support group.

STOP: 0x00000046 (*parameter, parameter, parameter, parameter*)
DEREF_UNKNOWN_LOGON_SESSION

This is a Windows NT Executive character-mode STOP message. It indicates a token was deleted that was not part of any known logon session.

Restart and set the Recovery options in the System Control Panel or the /CRASHDEBUG system start option. If this message reappears, contact your system administrator or technical support group.

STOP: 0x00000047 (*parameter, parameter, parameter, parameter*)
REF_UNKNOWN_LOGON_SESSION

This is a Windows NT Executive character-mode STOP message. It indicates a token was created that was not part of any known logon session.

Restart and set the Recovery options in the System Control Panel or the /CRASHDEBUG system start option. If this message reappears, contact your system administrator or technical support group.

STOP: 0x00000048 (*parameter, parameter, parameter, parameter*)
CANCEL_STATE_IN_COMPLETED_IRP

This is a Windows NT Executive character-mode STOP message. Indicates that an attempt was made to cancel an IRP (I/O request packet), but the packet had already been completed so it was not in a cancelable state. There may be a problem with the driver. Or, although unlikely, more than one driver may be accessing the same packet.

Restart and set the Recovery options in the System Control Panel or the /CRASHDEBUG system start option. If this message reappears, contact your system administrator or technical support group.

STOP: 0x00000049 (*parameter*, *parameter*, *parameter*, *parameter*)
PAGE_FAULT_WITH_INTERRUPTS_OFF

This is a Windows NT Executive character-mode STOP message. It indicates a page fault occurred when interrupts were disabled.

Restart and set the Recovery options in the System Control Panel or the /CRASHDEBUG system start option. If this message reappears, contact your system administrator or technical support group.

STOP: 0x0000004A (*parameter*, *parameter*, *parameter*, *parameter*)
IRQL_GT_ZERO_AT_SYSTEM_SERVICE

This is a Windows NT Executive character-mode STOP message. It indicates an attempt to exit from a system service with an IRQL greater than 0.

Restart and set the Recovery options in the System Control Panel or the /CRASHDEBUG system start option. If this message reappears, contact your system administrator or technical support group.

STOP: 0x0000004B (*parameter*, *parameter*, *parameter*, *parameter*)
STREAMS_INTERNAL_ERROR

This is a Windows NT Executive character-mode STOP message. This indicates an internal error in the Streams environment or in a Streams driver.

Restart and set the Recovery options in the System Control Panel or the /CRASHDEBUG system start option. If this message reappears, contact your system administrator or technical support group.

STOP: 0x0000004C (*parameter*, *parameter*, *parameter*, *parameter*)
FATAL_UNHANDLED_HARD_ERROR

This is a Windows NT Executive character-mode STOP message. This indicates a fatal hard error (STATUS error) occurred before the hard error handler was available. There are several reasons why this error might occur: a Registry hive file could not be loaded because it is either corrupt or missing; Winlogon or Windows unexpectedly did not start; or a driver or system dynamic link library is corrupt.

Restart and set the Recovery options in the System Control Panel or the /CRASHDEBUG system start option. If this message reappears, contact your system administrator or technical support group. If you can, start an alternate operating system. If none is available, try reinstalling Windows NT after replacing the specified file with a new file.

STOP: 0x0000004D (*parameter*, *parameter*, *parameter*, *parameter*)
NO_PAGES_AVAILABLE

This is a Windows NT Executive character-mode STOP message. It indicates there are no physical pages available.

Restart and set the Recovery options in the System Control Panel or the /CRASHDEBUG system start option. If this message reappears, contact your system administrator or technical support group.

STOP: 0x0000004E (*parameter, parameter, parameter, parameter*)
PFN_LIST_CORRUPT

This is a Windows NT Executive character-mode STOP message. It indicates the memory management page file number (PFN) list is corrupt.

Restart and set the Recovery options in the System Control Panel or the /CRASHDEBUG system start option. If this message reappears, contact your system administrator or technical support group.

STOP: 0x0000004F (*parameter, parameter, parameter, parameter*)
NDIS_INTERNAL_ERROR

This is a Windows NT Executive character-mode STOP message. It indicates an internal error in the NDIS wrapper or an NDIS driver.

Restart and set the Recovery options in the System Control Panel or the /CRASHDEBUG system start option. If this message reappears, contact your system administrator or technical support group.

STOP: 0x00000050 (*parameter, parameter, parameter, parameter*)
PAGE_FAULT_IN_NONPAGED_AREA

This is a Windows NT Executive character-mode STOP message. It indicates a page fault in the address space reserved for non paged data.

Restart and set the Recovery options in the System Control Panel or the /CRASHDEBUG system start option. If this message reappears, contact your system administrator or technical support group.

STOP: 0x00000051 (*parameter, parameter, parameter, parameter*)
REGISTRY_ERROR

This is a Windows NT Executive character-mode STOP message. It indicates a Registry or configuration manager problem. An I/O error may have occurred while the Registry was trying to read one of its files. This could be caused by hardware or file system problems. Another reason this message may appear is because of a failure in a refresh operation which occurs when resource limits are encountered.

Restart and set the Recovery options in the System Control Panel or the /CRASHDEBUG system start option. If this message reappears, contact your system administrator or technical support group.

STOP: 0x00000052 (*parameter, parameter, parameter, parameter*)
MAILSLOT_FILE_SYSTEM

This is a Windows NT Executive character-mode STOP message. It indicates a mailslot file system problem.

Restart and set the Recovery options in the System Control Panel or the /CRASHDEBUG system start option. If this message reappears, contact your system administrator or technical support group.

STOP: 0x00000053 (*parameter*, *parameter*, *parameter*, *parameter*)
NO_BOOT_DEVICE

This is a Windows NT Executive character-mode STOP message. It indicates no boot device driver was successfully initialized.

Restart and set the Recovery options in the System Control Panel or the /CRASHDEBUG system start option. If this message reappears, contact your system administrator or technical support group.

STOP: 0x00000054 (*parameter*, *parameter*, *parameter*, *parameter*)
LM_SERVER_INTERNAL_ERROR

This is a Windows NT Executive character-mode STOP message. It indicates an internal error in the Windows NT Server.

Restart and set the Recovery options in the System Control Panel or the /CRASHDEBUG system start option. If this message reappears, contact your system administrator or technical support group.

STOP: 0x00000055 (*parameter*, *parameter*, *parameter*, *parameter*)
DATA_COHERENCY_EXCEPTION

This is a Windows NT Executive character-mode STOP message. It indicates an inconsistency between pages in the primary and secondary data caches.

Restart and set the Recovery options in the System Control Panel or the /CRASHDEBUG system start option. If this message reappears, contact your system administrator or technical support group.

STOP: 0x00000056 (*parameter*, *parameter*, *parameter*, *parameter*)
INSTRUCTION_COHERENCY_EXCEPTION

This is a Windows NT Executive character-mode STOP message. It indicates an inconsistency between pages in the primary and secondary instruction caches.

Restart and set the Recovery options in the System Control Panel or the /CRASHDEBUG system start option. If this message reappears, contact your system administrator or technical support group.

STOP: 0x00000057 (*parameter*, *parameter*, *parameter*, *parameter*)
XNS_INTERNAL_ERROR

This is a Windows NT Executive character-mode STOP message. It indicates an XNS internal error. You may need to replace your network card.

Restart and set the Recovery options in the System Control Panel or the /CRASHDEBUG system start option. If this message reappears, contact your system administrator or technical support group.

STOP: 0x00000058 (*parameter*, *parameter*, *parameter*, *parameter*)
FTDISK_INTERNAL_ERROR

This is a Windows NT Executive character-mode STOP message. It indicates an inconsistency between pages in the primary and secondary data caches. It indicates a fault-tolerant disk driver internal error.

Restart and set the Recovery options in the System Control Panel or the /CRASHDEBUG system start option. If this message reappears, contact your system administrator or technical support group.

STOP: 0x00000059 (*parameter*, *parameter*, *parameter*, *parameter*)
PINBALL_FILE_SYSTEM

This is a Windows NT Executive character-mode STOP message. It indicates an inconsistency between pages in the primary and secondary data caches. It indicates an HPFS problem.

Restart and set the Recovery options in the System Control Panel or the /CRASHDEBUG system start option. If this message reappears, contact your system administrator or technical support group.

STOP: 0x0000005A (*parameter*, *parameter*, *parameter*, *parameter*)
CRITICAL_SERVICE_FAILED

This is a Windows NT Executive character-mode STOP message. It indicates that a critical service failed to initialize while booting the LastKnownGood control set.

Restart and set the Recovery options in the System Control Panel or the /CRASHDEBUG system start option. If this message reappears, contact your system administrator or technical support group.

STOP: 0x0000005B (*parameter*, *parameter*, *parameter*, *parameter*)
SET_ENV_VAR_FAILED

This is a Windows NT Executive character-mode STOP message. It indicates a critical service failed to initialize, but the LastKnownGood environment variable could not be set.

Restart and set the Recovery options in the System Control Panel or the /CRASHDEBUG system start option. If this message reappears, contact your system administrator or technical support group.

STOP: 0x0000005C (*parameter*, *parameter*, *parameter*, *parameter*)
HAL_INITIALIZATION_FAILED

This is a Windows NT Executive character-mode STOP message. Phase 0 initialization of the Hardware Abstraction Layer (HAL) failed. This can only happen during the relatively short period of time that the Windows NT executive is being initialized, during phase 4 of Windows NT startup. This may be a hardware problem.

Restart and set the Recovery options in the System Control Panel or the /CRASHDEBUG system start option. If this message reappears, contact your system administrator or technical support group.

STOP: 0x0000005D (*parameter*, *parameter*, *parameter*, *parameter*)
HEAP_INITIALIZATION_FAILED

This is a Windows NT Executive character-mode STOP message. Phase 0 initialization of the heap failed. This can only happen during the relatively short period of time that the Windows NT executive is being initialized, during phase 4 of Windows NT startup. This may be a hardware problem.

Restart and set the Recovery options in the System Control Panel or the /CRASHDEBUG system start option. If this message reappears, contact your system administrator or technical support group.

STOP: 0x0000005E (*parameter*, *parameter*, *parameter*, *parameter*)
OBJECT_INITIALIZATION_FAILED

This is a Windows NT Executive character-mode STOP message. Phase 0 initialization of the object manager failed. This can only happen during the relatively short period of time that the Windows NT executive is being initialized, during phase 4 of Windows NT startup. This may be a hardware problem.

Restart and set the Recovery options in the System Control Panel or the /CRASHDEBUG system start option. If this message reappears, contact your system administrator or technical support group.

STOP: 0x0000005F (*parameter*, *parameter*, *parameter*, *parameter*)
SECURITY_INITIALIZATION_FAILED

This is a Windows NT Executive character-mode STOP message. Phase 0 security initialization failed. This can only happen during the relatively short period of time that the Windows NT executive is being initialized, during phase 4 of Windows NT startup. This may be a hardware problem.

Restart and set the Recovery options in the System Control Panel or the /CRASHDEBUG system start option. If this message reappears, contact your system administrator or technical support group.

STOP: 0x00000060 (*parameter*, *parameter*, *parameter*, *parameter*)
PROCESS_INITIALIZATION_FAILED

This is a Windows NT Executive character-mode STOP message. Phase 0 process initialization failed. This can only happen during the relatively short period of time that the Windows NT executive is being initialized, during phase 4 of Windows NT startup. This may be a hardware problem.

Restart and set the Recovery options in the System Control Panel or the /CRASHDEBUG system start option. If this message reappears, contact your system administrator or technical support group.

STOP: 0x00000061 (*parameter*, *parameter*, *parameter*, *parameter*)
HAL1_INITIALIZATION_FAILED

This is a Windows NT Executive character-mode STOP message. Phase 1 initialization of the Hardware Abstraction Layer (HAL) failed. This can only happen during the relatively short period of time that the Windows NT executive is being initialized, during phase 4 of Windows NT startup. There may be a problem with a device driver.

Restart and set the Recovery options in the System Control Panel or the /CRASHDEBUG system start option. If this message reappears, contact your system administrator or technical support group.

STOP: 0x00000062 (*parameter*, *parameter*, *parameter*, *parameter*)
OBJECT1_INITIALIZATION_FAILED

This is a Windows NT Executive character-mode STOP message. Phase 1 initialization of the object manager failed. This can only happen during the relatively short period of time that the Windows NT executive is being initialized, during phase 4 of Windows NT startup. There may be a problem with a device driver.

Restart and set the Recovery options in the System Control Panel or the /CRASHDEBUG system start option. If this message reappears, contact your system administrator or technical support group.

STOP: 0x00000063 (*parameter*, *parameter*, *parameter*, *parameter*)
SECURITY1_INITIALIZATION_FAILED

This is a Windows NT Executive character-mode STOP message. Phase 1 security initialization failed. This can only happen during the relatively short period of time that the Windows NT executive is being initialized, during phase 4 of Windows NT startup. There may be a problem with a device driver.

Restart and set the Recovery options in the System Control Panel or the /CRASHDEBUG system start option. If this message reappears, contact your system administrator or technical support group.

STOP: 0x00000064 (*parameter*, *parameter*, *parameter*, *parameter*)
SYMBOLIC_INITIALIZATION_FAILED

This is a Windows NT Executive character-mode STOP message. Symbolic link initialization failed. This can only happen during the relatively short period of time that the Windows NT executive is being initialized, during phase 4 of Windows NT startup. There may be a problem with a device driver.

Restart and set the Recovery options in the System Control Panel or the /CRASHDEBUG system start option. If this message reappears, contact your system administrator or technical support group.

STOP: 0x00000065 (*parameter*, *parameter*, *parameter*, *parameter*)
MEMORY1_INITIALIZATION_FAILED

This is a Windows NT Executive character-mode STOP message. Phase 1 memory initialization failed. This can only happen during the relatively short period of time that the Windows NT executive is being initialized, during phase 4 of Windows NT startup. There may be a problem with a device driver.

Restart and set the Recovery options in the System Control Panel or the /CRASHDEBUG system start option. If this message reappears, contact your system administrator or technical support group.

STOP: 0x00000066 (*parameter, parameter, parameter, parameter*)
CACHE_INITIALIZATION_FAILED

This is a Windows NT Executive character-mode STOP message. Cache initialization failed. This can only happen during the relatively short period of time that the Windows NT executive is being initialized, during phase 4 of Windows NT startup. There may be a problem with a device driver.

Restart and set the Recovery options in the System Control Panel or the /CRASHDEBUG system start option. If this message reappears, contact your system administrator or technical support group.

STOP: 0x00000067 (*parameter, parameter, parameter, parameter*)
CONFIG_INITIALIZATION_FAILED

This is a Windows NT Executive character-mode STOP message. Configuration initialization failed because the Registry couldn't allocate the pool needed to contain the Registry files. This can only happen during the relatively short period of time that the Windows NT executive is being initialized, during phase 4 of Windows NT startup. There may be a problem with a device driver.

Restart and set the Recovery options in the System Control Panel or the /CRASHDEBUG system start option. If this message reappears, contact your system administrator or technical support group.

STOP: 0x00000068 (*parameter, parameter, parameter, parameter*)
FILE_INITIALIZATION_FAILED

This is a Windows NT Executive character-mode STOP message. File system initialization failed. This can only happen during the relatively short period of time that the Windows NT executive is being initialized, during phase 4 of Windows NT startup. There may be a problem with a device driver.

Restart and set the Recovery options in the System Control Panel or the /CRASHDEBUG system start option. If this message reappears, contact your system administrator or technical support group.

STOP: 0x00000069 (*parameter, parameter, parameter, parameter*)
IO1_INITIALIZATION_FAILED

This is a Windows NT Executive character-mode STOP message. Phase 1 I/O initialization failed. This can only happen during the relatively short period of time that the Windows NT executive is being initialized, during phase 4 of Windows NT startup. There may be a problem with a device driver.

Restart and set the Recovery options in the System Control Panel or the /CRASHDEBUG system start option. If this message reappears, contact your system administrator or technical support group.

STOP: 0x0000006A (*parameter, parameter, parameter, parameter*)
LPC_INITIALIZATION_FAILED

This is a Windows NT Executive character-mode STOP message. Local procedure call (LPC) initialization failed. This can only happen during the relatively short period of time that the Windows NT executive is being initialized, during phase 4 of Windows NT startup. There may be a problem with a device driver.

Restart and set the Recovery options in the System Control Panel or the /CRASHDEBUG system start option. If this message reappears, contact your system administrator or technical support group.

STOP: 0x0000006B (*parameter, parameter, parameter, parameter*)
PROCESS1_INITIALIZATION_FAILED

This is a Windows NT Executive character-mode STOP message. Phase 1 process initialization failed. This can only happen during the relatively short period of time that the Windows NT executive is being initialized, during phase 4 of Windows NT startup. There may be a problem with a device driver.

Restart and set the Recovery options in the System Control Panel or the /CRASHDEBUG system start option. If this message reappears, contact your system administrator or technical support group.

STOP: 0x0000006C (*parameter, parameter, parameter, parameter*)
REFMON_INITIALIZATION_FAILED

This is a Windows NT Executive character-mode STOP message. Reference monitor initialization failed. This can only happen during the relatively short period of time that Windows NT executive is being initialized. There may be a problem with a device driver.

Restart and set the Recovery options in the System Control Panel or the /CRASHDEBUG system start option. If this message reappears, contact your system administrator or technical support group.

STOP: 0x0000006D (*parameter, parameter, parameter, parameter*)
SESSION1_INITIALIZATION_FAILED

This is a Windows NT Executive character-mode STOP message. Session manager virtual memory allocation parameters failed during session manager initialization. This can only happen during the relatively short period of time that the Windows NT executive is being initialized, during phase 4 of Windows NT startup. There may be a problem with a device driver.

Restart and set the Recovery options in the System Control Panel or the /CRASHDEBUG system start option. If this message reappears, contact your system administrator or technical support group.

STOP: 0x0000006E (*parameter*, *parameter*, *parameter*, *parameter*)
SESSION2_INITIALIZATION_FAILED

This is a Windows NT Executive character-mode STOP message. Session manager virtual memory environment failed to initialize. This can only happen during the relatively short period of time that the Windows NT executive is being initialized, during phase 4 of Windows NT startup. There may be a problem with a device driver.

Restart and set the Recovery options in the System Control Panel or the /CRASHDEBUG system start option. If this message reappears, contact your system administrator or technical support group.

STOP: 0x0000006F (*parameter*, *parameter*, *parameter*, *parameter*)
SESSION3_INITIALIZATION_FAILED

This is a Windows NT Executive character-mode STOP message. Session manager process creation failed. This can only happen during the relatively short period of time that the Windows NT executive is being initialized, during phase 4 of Windows NT startup. There may be a problem with a device driver.

Restart and set the Recovery options in the System Control Panel or the /CRASHDEBUG system start option. If this message reappears, contact your system administrator or technical support group.

STOP: 0x00000070 (*parameter*, *parameter*, *parameter*, *parameter*)
SESSION4_INITIALIZATION_FAILED

This is a Windows NT Executive character-mode STOP message. During session manager initialization, a resume thread operation failed. This can only happen during the relatively short period of time that the Windows NT executive is being initialized, during phase 4 of Windows NT startup. There may be a problem with a device driver.

Restart and set the Recovery options in the System Control Panel or the /CRASHDEBUG system start option. If this message reappears, contact your system administrator or technical support group.

STOP: 0x00000071 (*parameter*, *parameter*, *parameter*, *parameter*)
SESSION5_INITIALIZATION_FAILED

This is a Windows NT Executive character-mode STOP message. During Phase 1 initialization of the Windows NT executive, the session manager terminated. This can only happen during the relatively short period of time that the Windows NT executive is being initialized, during phase 4 of Windows NT startup. There may be a problem with a device driver.

Restart and set the Recovery options in the System Control Panel or the /CRASHDEBUG system start option. If this message reappears, contact your system administrator or technical support group.

STOP: 0x00000072 (*parameter*, *parameter*, *parameter*, *parameter*)
ASSIGN_DRIVE_LETTERS_FAILED

This is a Windows NT Executive character-mode STOP message. It indicates a drive letter assignment failed.

Restart and set the Recovery options in the System Control Panel or the /CRASHDEBUG system start option. If this message reappears, contact your system administrator or technical support group.

STOP: 0x00000073 (*parameter*, *parameter*, *parameter*, *parameter*)
CONFIG_LIST_FAILED

This is a Windows NT Executive character-mode STOP message. It indicates the system configuration link list failed. One of the core system hives is corrupt or unreadable. Or, some critical Registry keys and values are not present.

Restart and set the Recovery options in the System Control Panel or the /CRASHDEBUG system start option. If this message reappears, contact your system administrator or technical support group. Try starting the Last Known Good Configuration.

STOP: 0x00000074 (*parameter*, *parameter*, *parameter*, *parameter*)
BAD_SYSTEM_CONFIG_INFO

This is a Windows NT Executive character-mode STOP message. It indicates the system configuration information is corrupted.

Restart and set the Recovery options in the System Control Panel or the /CRASHDEBUG system start option. If this message reappears, contact your system administrator or technical support group.

STOP: 0x00000075 (*parameter*, *parameter*, *parameter*, *parameter*)
CANNOT_WRITE_CONFIGURATION

This is a Windows NT Executive character-mode STOP message. It indicates the system configuration information cannot be written. The system hive files cannot be expanded to accommodate additional data written to it between Registry initialization and phase 1 initialization. There may be no free space on the drive.

Restart and set the Recovery options in the System Control Panel or the /CRASHDEBUG system start option. If this message reappears, contact your system administrator or technical support group.

STOP: 0x00000076 (*parameter*, *parameter*, *parameter*, *parameter*)
PROCESS_HAS_LOCKED_PAGES

This is a Windows NT Executive character-mode STOP message. It indicates that a process terminated with pages locked for I/O.

Restart and set the Recovery options in the System Control Panel or the /CRASHDEBUG system start option. If this message reappears, contact your system administrator or technical support group.

STOP: 0x00000077 (*parameter*, *parameter*, *parameter*, *parameter*)
KERNEL_STACK_INPAGE_ERROR

This is a Windows NT Executive character-mode STOP message. It indicates an I/O error during a kernel stack paging operation. The requested page of kernel data could not be read in. This is caused by a bad block in the paging file or a disk controller error. If the error was caused by a bad block, when your system is restarted, Autocheck will run and attempt to find the bad sector.

Restart and set the Recovery options in the System Control Panel or the /CRASHDEBUG system start option. If this message reappears, contact your system administrator or technical support group.

STOP: 0x00000078 (*parameter*, *parameter*, *parameter*, *parameter*)
PHASE0_EXCEPTION

This is a Windows NT Executive character-mode STOP message. It indicates an exception during phase 0 of the Windows NT executive.

Restart and set the Recovery options in the System Control Panel or the /CRASHDEBUG system start option. If this message reappears, contact your system administrator or technical support group.

STOP: 0x00000079 (*parameter*, *parameter*, *parameter*, *parameter*)
MISMATCHED_HAL

This is a Windows NT Executive character-mode STOP message. It indicates a mismatched kernel and Hardware Abstraction Layer (HAL) image.

Restart and set the Recovery options in the System Control Panel or the /CRASHDEBUG system start option. If this message reappears, contact your system administrator or technical support group.

STOP: 0x00000079 (*parameter*, *parameter*, *parameter*, *parameter*)
MISMATCHED_HAL

This is a Windows NT Executive character-mode STOP message. It indicates a mismatched kernel and Hardware Abstraction Layer (HAL) image.

Restart and set the Recovery options in the System Control Panel or the /CRASHDEBUG system start option. If this message reappears, contact your system administrator or technical support group.

STOP: 0x0000007A (*parameter*, *parameter*, *parameter*, *parameter*)
KERNEL_DATA_INPAGE_ERROR

This is a Windows NT Executive character-mode STOP message.

Restart and set the Recovery options in the System Control Panel or the /CRASHDEBUG system start option. If this message reappears, contact your system administrator or technical support group.

STOP: 0x0000007B (*parameter*, *parameter*, *parameter*, *parameter*)
INACCESSIBLE_BOOT_DEVICE

This is a Windows NT Executive character-mode STOP message. During I/O system initialization, the driver for the boot device may have failed to initialize the device the system is attempting to boot from. It is also possible that the file system failed to initialize because it did not recognize the data on the boot device. If this error occurs during initial system setup, the system may have been installed on an unsupported disk or SCSI controller. Also, this error may occur because of the installation of a new SCSI adapter or disk controller or if the disk was repartitioned with the system partition.

Restart and set the Recovery options in the System Control Panel or the /CRASHDEBUG system start option. If this message reappears, contact your system administrator or technical support group.

STOP: 0x0000007D (*parameter, parameter, parameter, parameter*)
INSTALL_MORE_MEMORY

This is a Windows NT Executive character-mode STOP message. Windows NT requires at least 5 MB of memory to start.

Restart your computer. If this message reappears, do not restart. Contact your system administrator or someone capable of checking out the physical memory that is currently installed in your computer.

STOP: 0x0000007F (*parameter, parameter, parameter, parameter*)
UNEXPECTED_KERNEL_MODE_TRAP

This is a Windows NT Executive character-mode STOP message. It indicates that a trap occurred in kernel mode.

Restart and set the Recovery options in the System Control Panel or the /CRASHDEBUG system start option. If this message reappears, contact your system administrator or technical support group.

STOP: 0x00000080 (*parameter, parameter, parameter, parameter*)
NMI_HARDWARE_FAILURE

This is a Windows NT Executive character-mode STOP message.

Restart and set the Recovery options in the System Control Panel or the /CRASHDEBUG system start option. If this message reappears, contact your system administrator or technical support group.

STOP: 0x00000080 (*parameter, parameter, parameter, parameter*)
NMI_HARDWARE_FAILURE

This is a Windows NT Executive character-mode STOP message.

Restart and set the Recovery options in the System Control Panel or the /CRASHDEBUG system start option. If this message reappears, contact your system administrator or technical support group. You might also want to contact the supplier of your hardware.

STOP: 0x00000081 (*parameter, parameter, parameter, parameter*)
SPIN_LOCK_INIT_FAILURE

This is a Windows NT Executive character-mode STOP message.

Restart and set the Recovery options in the System Control Panel or the /CRASHDEBUG system start option. If this message reappears, contact your system administrator or technical support group.

Storage to process this request is not available.

[Kernel32]

The system has more requests to process than it can currently handle.

Try the request again later.

Stripe sets cannot include partitions on removable media.

[Disk Administrator]

Because it is impossible to maintain a stripe if one of the drives is removed, Disk Administrator does not allow removable media to be part of a stripe set.

Subnet mask *name* for IP address *address* is not valid. No link to this network was established.

[Netevent]

The subnet mask specified during Setup is invalid.

Use the Network option in Control Panel to reconfigure the subnet mask.

Supplied buffer is too small

[Dynamic Data Exchange]

You have reached the limits of the buffer size specified by the application.

If possible, shorten any names used for shares, topics, or application names. If you still get this message, report it to the vendor of your application.

Switch *parameter* is not implemented

[Print]

A switch is a parameter that begins with a slash, such as /s. The /b, /u, /m, /s, /q, /t, /c, and /p switches are not implemented for the Print command.

To check which switches are implemented for the Print command, type HELP at the command line followed by Print.

Synchronization of a stripe with parity set failed.

[Disk Administrator]

Retry the initialization. If you get this same message, contact your system administrator.

Syntax error on line *number* in section *number*

[Setup]

Contact the supplier for another copy of the installation media.

Syntax error.

[Help]

This error is from the Macro Language Editor for online help, and should not appear while using the Help file. Report this error to the provider of the Help file.

System could not allocate the required space in a Registry log.

[Kernel32]

There is not enough room on the disk, in the system partition, for the Registry log.

Delete unneeded files from the system partition and then retry the operation.

System error *number*

[Network]

An unexpected software error occurred.

Contact your technical support group. Tell the support person what error number appeared and the circumstances that caused the error to appear.

System error *code*

[Services for Macintosh (SFM)]

Contact technical support.

System error *code* occurred.

[Network] Net Message ID: 3216

The Replicator service stopped because the listed system error occurred.

Check the cause of the system error.

System error *code* occurred.

[Services for Macintosh (SFM)]

Contact technical support.

System memory heap allocation error.

[Setup]

This can occur during the initial installation of Windows NT.

Select Retry in the message box to retry the operation. If you get the same message, select Exit Setup and begin the initial installation again. If the message still occurs, contact your technical support group.

System memory heap allocation error.

[Repair Disk]

This can occur during the initial installation of Windows NT.

Select Retry in the message box to retry the operation. If you get the same message, select Exit Setup and begin the initial installation again. If the message still occurs, contact your technical support group.

System not ready.

Try again later.

Sytos ECC translation error. Please check the manual for possible solutions.

[Backup]

An error occurred while reading a Sytos plus tape. The ECC data written to the tape was not in the expected location.

Check the Sytos manual for possible solutions. If you use REGEDIT32 to modify the Registry, the change should be made to the Sytos Plus ECC flag under \Software\Microsoft\ntbackup\Translators in the HKEY_CURRENT_USER pane, as specified in the Sytos Plus manual.

t_look returned *code* **or** *number*

[FTP Server] [TCP/IP]

The data connection in use by a TCP/IP utility, was not properly closed down due to an unexpected event.

Retry the TCP/IP utility operation. If you still get this message, contact your network administrator to interpret the meaning of the code displayed at the end of the message, and take appropriate action.

Tape could not be partitioned.

[Kernel32]

The application is attempting to partition a tape on a drive that does not support this.

Either use different functionality in the application, use a different application, or use a different tape drive.

Tape Eject Failed. Not possible to eject tape now.

[Backup]

Contact the supplier of the tape drive.

Tape is not formatted

[Backup]

The tape may not have been completely formatted when backup was started.

Use backup to reformat the tape. Then retry the backup operation. If you receive this error during a restore operation, use an older backup of the tape.

Tape partition information could not be found when loading a tape.

[Kernel32]

The application requires partition information to be on the tape. Either the tape that is in the drive has not been prepared, or the partition information on the tape is not recognized by the application.

Either prepare the tape, use a different tape, or contact the supplier of the application.

Tape positioning error on ***drive letter*****.**

[Backup]

Backup is experiencing difficulty positioning correctly in the current tape.

If doing a restore operation, attempting to restore an entire set may remedy this situation. If this does not solve the problem, as a last resort, modify the Registry so that backup will not do positioning. Use REGEDT32 to change the \USR\SOFTWARE\MICROSOFT\NTBACKUP\BACKUP ENGINE\USE FAST FILE RESTORE key to 0.

Tape unusable (too many bad sectors).From device: *name*

[QIC117]

Discard this tape and use a different one.

TARGET diskette bad or incompatible.

[Disk Copy]

The formats of the disks you want to copy must be identical. This message is displayed only if the disks you have specified have different formats.

Make sure the floppy disk is in the drive and the drive door is closed. If it is, then try removing the disk and reinserting it. After that, if this message reappears, use a different disk.

Target diskette may be unusable

[Disk Copy]

Try using another floppy disk.

Target diskette unusable

[Disk Copy]

Diskcopy cannot write to the supplied target disk.

Discard the unusable floppy disk and try another.

TCP received a SYN packet with no options. Source *address*, **Destination** *address*.

[Netevent]

The MSS_LENGTH option must be specified in SYN packets sent to the TCP.

Ask your system administrator to correct the packets generated by the computer at the specified source IP address.

TCP received a TLI write message of unknown type *name*.

[Netevent]

Ask your system administrator to correct the packets generated by the computer.

tcp/finger: unknown service

[TCP/IP]

You cannot use the TCP/IP Finger command to get information about a user on a remote server right now because the TCP/IP Finger service is not running on that server.

Contact your network administrator or someone at the remote server to find out why the Finger service is not running.

TCP/IP is not completely configured. If you cancel now, TCP/IP will be disabled. Do you want to cancel TCP/IP configuration?

[TCP/IP]

Select No to correct the TCP/IP configuration or Yes to restart your computer with the incorrect protocol configuration.

TCP/IP is not running on this system

[IP]

TCP/IP must be installed and running in order to use IPCONFIG.

Install TCP/IP and try again. If TCP/IP is already installed, enable the binding and try again. To enable the binding, choose Network from the Control Panel, choose Bindings, select TCP/IP, and choose Enable.

TCP/IP not bound to any adapters

[IP]

Choose the Network option from Control Panel. Select TCP/IP Protocol from the Installed Network Software text box. Then choose Configure, and select the adapter TCP/IP is to use from the Adapter list box.

Terminal could not receive the binary file *filename*.Verify that you are using the correct protocol and try again.

[Terminal]

Terminal recognizes two protocols: KERMIT and XOFF. Possibly, you have attempted to use one protocol to receive a packet that was sent in the other.

Contact the person sending the packet and verify that the sending and receiving protocols are the same.

Terminal could not send the binary file *filename*.Verify that you are using the correct protocol and try again.

[Terminal]

Terminal cannot send your binary file, possibly because you have not chosen the correct protocol.

From the Settings menu, choose the Binary Transfers option. In the Binary Transfers dialog box, select either the XModem/CRC or the Kermit option.

Terminal failed to set the new communication settings. Verify that the hardware supports these settings.

[Terminal]

Check the documentation that came with your hardware to find out what settings are supported. Then try again, specifying only supported settings.

Text not found.

[Write]

You searched for a string of text in a Write document and the search produced no matches.

No action is needed.

The *filename* file already exists. Do you want to overwrite it?

[Notepad]

You attempted to save a Notepad file under the name of a Notepad file that already exists.

If you want the currently open Notepad file to replace the older file of the same name, select Yes. If not, select No option, then assign the current file a different name. If you want to return to the currently active file, select Cancel.

The *filename* file is empty and will be deleted. This file cannot be saved because it is empty.

[Notepad]

You deleted the contents of a Notepad file, then attempted to save it as an empty file. Notepad will not save an empty file.

If you do not want to keep the file, select OK. If you want to return to the Notepad file, select Cancel. Then, attempt to exit Notepad. When a dialog box appears asking you if you want to save the changes that you have made, select the No option, and the text that you deleted will appear in the Notepad file the next time you open it.

The *filename* file is too large for Notepad. Use another editor to edit the file.

[Notepad]

You attempted to open in Notepad a file that is larger than one megabyte.

To open this file, you will need to use a text editor that is capable of displaying a file of this size.

The *name* call failed for *name* with the following error: *text*

[Netevent]

The service controller could not set a Registry value for a function that it requires for operation.

Contact technical support.

The *name* call failed with the following error: *text*

[Netevent]

In order for the service controller to operate properly, the specified function call must be completed.

Contact technical support.

The *filename* log file cannot be opened.

[Network]

Either the indicated log file is locked by another process, or you do not have permission to open this file.

Make sure you have the necessary permissions on this file and on the path to the file and try again.

The *filename* log file cannot be opened.

[Netevent]

The log file may be read-only.

Ask your system administrator to examine the log files to determine why the specified file will not open. Events will be logged in the default log file.

The *filename* log file is corrupted and will be cleared.

[Network]

The contents of the corrupt file will be deleted so that new data can be written to and read from the file.

No action is needed.

The *name* log file is full.

[Netevent]

The specified log file contains the maximum configured number of events.

Clear the log using Event Viewer from the Administrative Tools group. Open Event Viewer, select Log, and then select Clear All Events.

The *name* log has been reduced in size. The new setting will not take effect until you clear the log.

[Event Viewer]

In the Event Log Settings dialog box, you set the Maximum Log Size at less than the current Maximum Log Size, and the current log size may already be larger than the maximum size that you specified. Consequently, the new Maximum Log Size will not take effect until you clear the log(s).

No action is needed.

The *name* log is corrupt. Do you want to clear it now?

[Event Viewer]

For an unknown reason, the log is corrupted.

Clear the specified log.

The *name* logs have been reduced in size. The new settings will not take effect until you clear the logs.

[Event Viewer]

In the Event Log Settings dialog box, you set the Maximum Log Size at less than the current Maximum Log Size, and the current size of one or more of your logs may already be larger than the maximum size that you specified. Consequently, the new Maximum Log Size will not take effect until you clear the logs.

No action is needed.

The *text* NETWORKS entry in the LANMAN.INI file has a syntax error and will be ignored.

[Network] Net Message ID: 3403

This message should occur only on a down-level computer. Any action to correct the problem should be performed on that computer. The listed entry in the [networks] section of the LANMAN.INI file has a syntax error.

Check the format of the listed entry.

The *name* Registry key denied access to SYSTEM account programs so the Service Control Manager took ownership of the Registry key.

[Netevent]

The current permissions on the specified key in the control set do not allow full access to programs running in the Local System account (such as the Service Control Manager).

Use the Registry editor to find the key in the current control set and make sure the Local System account is given full access.

The *name* service continue is pending

[Network]

No action is needed.

The *name* service could not be started.

[Network]

See the accompanying error for more details.

The *name* service could not be stopped.

[Network]

This service is currently performing a task, and cannot be stopped at this time.

Try again later. If you still cannot stop the service, you might need to reboot the computer.

The *name* service depends on the *name* group and no member of this group started.

[Netevent]

None of the services in the specified group started. Because the service is dependent on other members of the group, the service did not start.

Ask your system administrator to check the event log with Event Viewer to locate any service related errors that may have caused this error. Your system administrator should also check your computer's configuration.

The *name* service depends on the *name* service which failed to start because of the following error: *text*

[Netevent]

The specified service failed to start.

Contact your system administrator.

The *name* **service depends on the following nonexistent service:** *name*

[Netevent]

The specified service could not be started because it is configured to depend on another service that does not exist.

Ask your system administrator to check your computer's configuration.

The *name* **service failed to pause.**

[Network]

This service is currently performing a task, and cannot be paused at this time.

Try again later. If you still cannot stop the service, you might need to reboot the computer.

The *name* **service failed to resume.**

[Network]

This service is currently performing a task, and cannot be paused at this time.

Try again later. If you still cannot stop the service, you might need to reboot the computer.

The *name* **service failed to start due to the following error:** *text*

[Netevent]

The service could not be started.

Contact your system administrator.

The *name* **service has been started by another process and is pending.**

[Network]

No action is needed.

The *name* **service has reported an invalid current state** *code***.**

[Netevent]

The service controller cannot recognize the state code reported by the service specified.

Report the code number to the service vendor's technical support group.

The *name* **service hung on starting.**

[Netevent]

The service specified is stuck in the start pending state. The service failed to indicate that it is making progress within the time period specified in its last status message.

Wait a few minutes to see if the service starts eventually. If the service does not start, use the Services option in Control Panel to start the service manually. If the problem persists, contact the service vendor.

The *name* **service is not started. Is it OK to start it?** *text*: *text*

[Network]

You tried to perform a task that requires the indicated service. The task cannot be performed until the service is started. Or, you tried to stop a service that is not started.

If you need to use a command that requires this service, start the service or ask your network administrator to do so.

The *name* **service pause is pending**

[Network]

This service is in the process of being paused.

No action is needed.

The *name* **service returned service specific error** *number*.

[Server Manager]

The indicated error was encountered by the specified service.

Look up the indicated error and take the appropriate action.

The *name* **service terminated with service-specific error** *code*.

[Netevent]

The service stopped due to an error.

Contact your system administrator.

The *name* **service terminated with the following error:** *text*

[Netevent]

The service stopped due to an error.

Depending on the error, you should either restart the service using the Services option in Control Panel, contact your system administrator, or contact the service vendor.

The *name* **Registry parameter** *name* **was set to invalid value** *name*. **Setting to the default value of** *number*.

[Netevent]

The device used the default value for the parameter because the value specified in the Registry is illegal.

Ask your system administrator to correct the parameter's value in the Registry.

The *filename* **driver has been added. For the new driver to take effect, you must quit and restart Windows NT.**

[Drivers (CP)]

Any time that you add or remove a driver, you must restart Windows NT before the driver takes effect.

Shut down and restart your computer.

The *filename* driver has been removed. To remove the driver from your system, you must quit and restart Windows NT.

[Drivers (CP)]

Any time that you add or remove a device driver, you must restart Windows NT before the new device driver actually goes into effect.

Exit and restart Windows NT.

The 'Copies' number is not in the expected range. Make sure that the entry is a positive number.

[Paintbrush]

Using the Print option in the File menu, you have invoked the Print dialog box, then have specified a negative number in the Number of Copies option. Also note that Paintbrush will not permit you to make more than 999 copies of an image.

Change the number in the Number of Copies option to a positive number, then select OK.

The 'Margin' settings leave no room for the image. Please adjust the margins to increase available space.

[Paintbrush]

Change the settings so that the margins are smaller and the space within the margins is larger. If necessary, print to a larger page size.

The *defaultoff* macro in the device.INF file section contains an undefined macro.

[Remote Access Service]

One of the Remote Access configuration files probably contains invalid information.

The easiest way to resolve this problem is to reinstall Remote Access. Use the Network option in Control Panel to remove and reinstall RAS. If you are using a modem that is not supported by Remote Access, switch to a supported modem, or see "Modem Script File" in the Remote Access Service online Help for information about modifying the modem script file for your modem. The Remote Access script files (PAD.INF, MODEM.INF, and SWITCH.INF) are in the \SYSTEM32\RAS subdirectory of your Windows NT directory.

The *message* macro was not found in the device .INF file section.

[Remote Access Service]

One of the Remote Access configuration files probably contains invalid information.

The easiest way to resolve this problem is to reinstall Remote Access. Use the Network option in Control Panel to remove and then reinstall RAS. If you are using a modem that is not supported by Remote Access, switch to a supported modem, or see "Modem Script File" in the Remote Access Service online Help for information about modifying the modem script file for your modem. The Remote Access script files (PAD.INF, MODEM.INF, and SWITCH.INF) are in the \SYSTEM32\RAS subdirectory of your Windows NT directory.

The access control list (ACL) structure is invalid.

[Kernel32]

For example, the length of the access control list (ACL) may be shorter than the sum of the lengths of the access control entries (ACEs) in the ACL.

Use the access control list editor to fix up the structure of the ACL.

The account *account* could not be found.

[Network]

There is no user account by that name in this group.

Make sure you have the correct account name and try again, making sure you type the name correctly. You might need to add the user account, or ask the domain administrator to add it.

The account *name* could not be found.

[Security]

You have attempted to search for an account, and have specified an account that cannot be found.

Select another account or another domain.

The account *account* is a global group account. The application will not accept global group accounts.

[Network]

You supplied a global group account name, and this application accepts only local groups or user accounts.

Type the name of a user account or local group.

The account *name* is a global group account. The application will not accept global group accounts.

[Security]

You supplied a global group account name, and this application accepts only local groups or user accounts.

Type the name of a user account or local group.

The account *account* is a local group account. The application will not accept local group accounts.

[Network]

You attempted to add a local group account to an application that does not accept them. This message occurs, for example, if you attempt to add a local group to User Profile Editor.

Add an account of a type that the application can accept.

The account *account* is a user account. The application will not accept user accounts.

[Network]

Check the documentation supplied with the application, or contact the application vendor, to find out what the application will accept. Then try again.

The account *name* is a user account. The application will not accept user accounts.

[Security]

You have typed a name in the Add Names dialog box that the client did not request.

Type the name of a user group.

The account *account* is a well known group account. The application will not accept well known group accounts.

[Network] [Security]

You attempted to add a well-known group account (for example, System or Everyone) to an application that does not accept them.

Specify a different group name, then try again.

The account *name* is a local group account. The application will not accept local group accounts.

[Security]

You attempted to add a local group account to an application that does not accept them. This message occurs, for example, if you attempt to add a local group to User Profile Editor.

Add an account of a type that the application can accept.

The account could not be found.

[Security]

The account specified as the owner of a resource has been deleted.

Select a new owner for the resource.

The account does not have Remote Access permission.

[Remote Access Service]

You have a valid account on the domain you selected, but your account does not have permission to access the network remotely.

Ask your system administrator to give you dial-in permission. If you have an account with dial-in permission on another domain, do the following to use your account on that domain:1) Edit the Phone Book entry and clear the Authenticate using current user name and password check box; 2) dial; 3) specify the appropriate user name, password, and domain.

The account has expired.

[Remote Access Service]

Ask your system administrator to reactivate your account.

The account is disabled.

[Remote Access Service]

Ask your system administrator to enable your account.

The account is not permitted to logon at this time of day.

[Remote Access Service]

Your account has been configured for limited access to the network.

If you need to access the network at a different time of day than what's presently configured, ask your system administrator to change the configuration.

The account name is invalid or does not exist.

[Kernel32]

An application attempted to create a service or change the configuration of a service in the service database. However, it used the wrong account name or a badly formatted account name.

Use User Manager to verify that a service account exists for this service, and that the password has not expired. Then try the request again.

The account used is a Computer Account. Use your global user account or local user account to access this server.

[Kernel32]

You used the wrong account to logon to the server.

Try again, but this time use your normal user account or your remote user account.

The account used is an interdomain trust account. Use your global user account or local user account to access this server.

[Kernel32]

You used the wrong account to logon to the server.

Try again, but this time use your normal user account or your remote user account.

The account used is an server trust account. Use your global user account or local user account to access this server.

[Kernel32]

You used the wrong account to logon to the server.

Try again, but this time use your normal user account or your remote user account.

The account you typed is invalid.

[Server Manager]

In the Service Config dialog box, you have entered an account name that contains invalid characters.

Type the name of a valid account.

The action cannot be completed because the application needed by the object is busy. Switch to the unavailable application and complete or cancel the action that is causing it to be unavailable.

[Write]

You attempted an OLE (object linking and embedding) operation, and the server application (Paintbrush or Sound Recorder, for example) is busy.

Close the server application, and then try again.

The active files restored will not become usable until the computer is restarted.

[Backup]

Some of the files that were just restored either contain configuration information, or they were in use or otherwise not openable when they were restored.

Restart the computer for the changes to take effect.

The address database already has 25 ACTIVE address owners which is the maximum. This error was noticed while attempting to add the address given below.

[WINS Service]

A maximum of 25 WINS servers can have addresses in the database. During replication, a 26th WINS servers address was seen.

It is possible that one or more WINS servers that have records in the database are no longer active. Ask the network administrator to delete obsolete WINS servers from the database.

The address for the thread ID is not correct.

[Kernel32]

The thread ID address passed to the DosCreateThread function was not correct.

Correct the thread ID address. You may have to contact the supplier of the running application.

The Address Mapping Table for adapter "*name* " was not updated because the incoming packet contained an invalid source address

[Services for Macintosh (SFM)]

This message is for your information only. It notifies the network administrator that bad packets are on the network.

No action is needed. However, if you see this message frequently, contact your network administrator.

The alert recipient is invalid.

[Network] Net Message ID: 2433

This message should occur only on a down-level computer. Any action to correct the problem should be performed on that computer. A software error occurred.

Contact technical support.

The alert table is full.

[Network] Net Message ID: 2431

This message should occur only on a down-level computer. Any action to correct the problem should be performed on that computer. The number of alert notifications requested exceeded the number specified by the NUMALERTS entry in your configuration file.

Increase the value of the NUMALERTS entry. Then stop and restart the Workstation service.

The Alerter service had a problem creating the list of alert recipients. The error code is *code*.

[Network] Net Message ID: 3170

A software error occurred.

Contact technical support.

The amount of resource *name* requested was more than the maximum. The maximum amount was allocated.

[Network] Net Message ID: 3198

This message should occur only on a down-level computer. Any action to correct the problem should be performed on that computer. The amount of the listed resource requested was more than the maximum allocated amount.

Ask your network administrator to check the workstation's configuration.

The announcement of the server name failed.

[Network]

This message should occur only on a down-level computer. Any action to correct the problem should be performed on that computer.

The API return buffer is too small.

[Network] Net Message ID: 2123

The program you are running created a buffer that is too small for the data being used.

The program should correct this problem. If it does not, see your network administrator or the vendor who supplied the program. Tell your network administrator that the API return buffer is too small.

The AppleTalk Protocol Registry parameters cannot be read. One or more parameters might be missing or contain invalid values.

[Services for Macintosh (SFM)]

The Setup program may have failed to store default adapter values in the Registry.

Check the appendix of the Services for Macintosh book to determine the Registry parameters for the AppleTalk key values and their ranges. You may need to remove and reinstall Services for Macintosh.

The AppleTalk Protocol was configured successfully. Changes will take effect when you restart AppleTalk.

[Services for Macintosh (SFM)]

Use the Devices option in Control Panel to stop the AppleTalk protocol. Select AppleTalk Protocol and then choose Stop. Other services related to the AppleTalk protocol may also be stopped. With AppleTalk Protocol selected, choose Start. You might want to use the Services option to restart services that were stopped when the protocol was stopped.

The AppleTalk zone list could not be obtained from the network.

[Services for Macintosh (SFM)]

The AppleTalk network is not available.

Ask your network administrator to verify that all AppleTalk routers are working properly.

The application cannot start.

[Chat]

A system error has prevented Chat from starting.

Try to start the application again. If this message reappears, restart Windows NT.

The application has chosen not to close. It may be completing a lengthy task.

[Program Manager]

Try again later.

The application has chosen not to close. It may be completing a lengthy task.

[Task Manager]

Try again later.

The Application log file could not be opened. *filename* **will be used as the default log file.**

[Netevent]

The Application log file is corrupted. The default log file will continue to be used as the log file until the Application log file is repaired and the system is restarted.

Ask your system administrator to determine the cause of the corruption.

No action is needed.

The application program is not compatible with the version of the operating system being used.

[Command Prompt]

You have attempted to run in Windows NT an executable file that is corrupted or that Windows NT does not support.

No user action can remedy this situation.

The argument string passed to DosExecPgm is not correct.

[Kernel32]

The argument (command parameters) string passed to DosExecPgm was not in the proper format.

Correct the argument string. You may have to contact the supplier of the running application.

The array bounds are invalid.

[Kernel32]

There is a problem with a remote procedure call (RPC) in a distributed application.

Contact the supplier of the running distributed application.

The AT command has timed-out. Please try again later.

[Network] Net Message ID: 3815

The command could not be completed because another scheduled command is currently running.

Try the command later.

The AT command processor could not run *application*.

[Network] Net Message ID: 3178

This message should occur only on a down-level computer. Any action to correct the problem should be performed on that computer. You used the AT utility to specify a program that could not run.

Check the filename of the program you tried to schedule. If it is in a directory that is not on the computer's search path, be sure to specify its full path. Be sure that all programs you schedule are executable.

The AT job ID does not exist.

[Network] Net Message ID: 3806

You specified a job identification number that does not exist.

To see the list of jobs and identification numbers in the schedule file, type AT.

The AT schedule file could not be updated because the disk is full.

[Network] Net Message ID: 3810

This message should occur only on a down-level computer. Any action to correct the problem should be performed on that computer. You cannot update the schedule file because the disk is full.

Make room on the disk by deleting unnecessary files.

The AT schedule file is corrupted.

[Network] Net Message ID: 3807

This message should occur only on a down-level computer. Any action to correct the problem should be performed on that computer. The schedule file is damaged.

Restore the schedule file, SCHED.LOG, from a backup copy, or delete the file and create a new one with the AT utility. SCHED.LOG is in the LANMAN\\ LOGS directory.

The AT schedule file is invalid. Please delete the file and create a new one.

[Network] Net Message ID: 3812

This message should occur only on a down-level computer. Any action to correct the problem should be performed on that computer. The schedule file has been damaged, possibly by system errors.

Restore the schedule file, SCHED.LOG, from a backup copy, or delete the file and create a new one with the AT utility. SCHED.LOG is in the LANMAN\\LOGS directory.

The AT schedule file was deleted.

[Network]

The schedule file was cleared.

No action is needed.

The attempt to restart the system failed. You should restart the system manually.

[Control Panel]

The system failed to restart itself when you selected the specified button.

To restart the system, choose the Shutdown option on the File menu in Program Manager.

The Auditing Dialog failed: *text*

[Print Manager]

The indicated system error prevented Print Manager from opening the Auditing dialog.

Look up the error message that is included at the end of this message, and take appropriate action. Then try again.

The authentication level is unknown.

[Kernel32]

Contact the supplier of the running application.

The authentication service is unknown.

[Kernel32]

In a distributed (RPC) application, either the client or server attempted to set authentication and authorization information for the binding between the client and server. However, the authentication service named by the application client or server is unknown to Windows NT.

Contact the supplier of the running distributed application.

The authentication type is unknown.

[Kernel32]

Contact the supplier of the running application.

The authorization service is unknown.

[Kernel32]

Contact the supplier of the running application.

The batch file cannot be found.

[Command Prompt]

Make sure the batch program exists and that you've typed the name correctly. Also confirm that it is in the search path or in the current directory. If this message occurs while running the batch program, there may be a command in the batch program that deletes or renames the batch program, or makes it inaccessible. Check the syntax of the command to determine the cause.

The batch file cannot be found.

[Command]

Make sure the batch program exists and that you've typed the name correctly. Also confirm that it is in the search path or in the current directory. If this message occurs while running the batch program, there may be a command in the batch program that deletes or renames the batch program, or makes it inaccessible. Check the syntax of the command to determine the cause.

The baud clock rate configuration is not supported on device *name*.

Contact the vendor of the device and report this message.

The binary data entered does not represent a whole number of bytes. Registry Editor will pad the binary data with 0s.

[Registry Editor]

No action is needed.

The binding does not contain an entry name.

[Kernel32]

In a distributed (RPC) application, a client attempted to reference information in an entry in the name-service database, but the information referenced was from a different source. Only binding handles obtained from a name-service database can have their entry name referenced.

Contact the supplier of the running distributed application.

The binding does not contain any authentication information.

[Kernel32]

While a distributed (RPC) application was running, either the client or server inquired about the security information associated with the relationship (binding) between the client and server. There was none.

Contact the supplier of the running distributed application.

The binding handle is invalid.

[Kernel32]

Windows NT is unable to use the information supplied by a distributed (RPC) application to establish a client-server relationship which will enable a remote procedure call.

Contact the supplier of the running distributed application.

The binding handle is not the correct type.

[Kernel32]

During an operation on the information that binds a client and server during a remote procedure call, the wrong type of binding was specified. There are two types of bindings: client and server.

Contact the supplier of the running distributed application.

The binding handles passed to a remote procedure call do not match.

[Kernel32]

Contact the supplier of the running distributed application.

The broadcast message was truncated.

[Network] Net Message ID: 2289

The broadcast message was too long. Only the first 128 characters of the message were sent.

Keep broadcast messages to 128 characters or less.

The browser driver has forced an election on network *number* because it was unable to find a master browser for that network.

[Netevent]

No action is needed.

The browser driver has forced an election on network *number* because it was unable to find a master browser to retrieve a backup list on that network.

[Netevent]

No action is needed.

The browser driver has received an election packet from computer *computer name* on network *name*. The data is the packet received.

[Netevent]

If the user or system administrator sets log election in the computer's configuration information, each time an election occurs, the computer will register this information.

No action is needed.

The browser driver has received too many illegal datagrams from the remote computer *computer name* to name *computer name* on transport *name*. The data is the datagram. No more events will be generated until the reset frequency has expired.

[Netevent]

The limit for the number of illegal datagrams that can be logged per minute has been exceeded.

No action is needed.

The browser driver was unable to convert a character string to a unicode string.

[Netevent]

The conversion of a name failed.

No action is needed.

The browser driver was unable to initialize variables from the Registry.

[Netevent]

The Registry contains invalid parameters.

Check the configuration parameters in the Registry. See the operating system documentation for information about valid configuration parameters.

The browser has failed to start because the dependent service *name* had invalid service status *code*.

[Netevent]

You may have attempted to start the browser while the Server or Workstation services were paused. Start or continue the Server or Workstation services.

The browser has forced an election on network *number* because a master browser was stopped.

[Netevent]

The network must have a master browser.

No action is needed.

The browser has forced an election on network *number* because a Windows NT Advanced Server (or domain master) browser is started.

[Netevent]

No action is needed.

The browser has forced an election on network *number* because the Domain Controller (or Server) has changed its role

[Netevent]

A network administrator promoted or demoted a domain controller, so another master browser must be elected in order to keep the network functioning.

No action is needed.

The browser has received a server announcement indicating that the computer *computer name* is a master browser, but this computer is not a master browser.

[Netevent]

An inconsistency exists between the Browser service and the Server service.

Contact your network administrator if this message is in the event log in Event Viewer more than 6 times. Otherwise, stopping and restarting the server will eliminate the error.

The browser has received an illegal datagram from the remote computer *computer name* to name *computer name* on transport *name*. The data is the datagram.

[Netevent]

Another computer sent a packet that could not be recognized by your local computer.

No action is needed.

The browser service has failed to retrieve the backup list too many times on transport *name*.The backup browser is stopping.

[Netevent]

The backup browser will stop being a backup when it tries and fails to retrieve the list more than 5 times. It will start again after one hour.

No action is needed unless you see this message on several different computers. Then, there may be problems with the master browser.

The browser service was configured with MaintainServerList=No.

[Network]

This computer is not a browse server. It does not maintain a current browse list, nor does it contact the Master Browse server for a browse list.

Set MaintainServerList=Yes or = Auto in the Registry. If you do not want to run the browser, disable it in Services in the Control Panel.

The browser was unable to add the configuration parameter *text*.

[Netevent]

Contact your network administrator.

The browser was unable to promote itself to master browser. The browser will continue to attempt to promote itself to the master browser, but will no longer log any events in the event log in Event Viewer.

[Netevent]

The browser has attempted to promote itself to the master browser more than 25 times.

Contact your network administrator.

The browser was unable to promote itself to master browser. The computer that currently believes it is the master browser is ***computer name*****.**

[Netevent]

In any workgroup or domain, only one computer is allowed to be the master browser. Another computer in the workgroup or domain is functioning incorrectly as the master browser.

Contact your network administrator to stop the specified computer by exiting Windows.

The browser was unable to promote itself to master browser. The computer that currently believes it is the master browser is unknown.

[Netevent]

In any workgroup or domain, only one computer is allowed to be the master browser. Another computer in the workgroup or domain is functioning incorrectly as the master browser, but the computer is not recognized.

Contact your network administrator to find the other computer.

The browser was unable to retrieve a list of domains from the browser master ***computer name*** **on the network** ***name*****.The data is the error code.**

[Netevent]

The browser requested a list of domains from the master browser but did not receive the list.

Contact your network administrator.

The browser was unable to retrieve a list of servers from the browser master ***computer name*** **on the network** ***name*****.The data is the error code.**

[Netevent]

The browser requested a list of servers from the master browser but did not receive the list.

Contact your network administrator.

The browser was unable to update its role. The data is the error.

[Netevent]

Usually the browser cannot update its role if another computer in the domain has the same computer name.

No action is needed.

The browser was unable to update the service status bits. The data is the error.

[Netevent]

An error occurred in the Server service.

Check the event log with Event Viewer for more details about the error.

The buffer for types is not big enough.

[Network] Net Message ID: 2362

A software error occurred.

Contact technical support.

The buffer is invalid.

[Remote Access Service]

This error should not occur under normal circumstances.

Restart your computer to make sure that all recent configuration changes have taken effect. If the error persists, consult the Windows NT event log for detailed warnings or errors.

The byte count is too small.

[Kernel32]

Contact the supplier of the running distributed application.

The change log cache maintained by the Netlogon service for database changes is corrupted. The Netlogon service is resetting the change log.

[Network] Net Message ID: 5705

The NETLOGON.CHG file is corrupted or your computer does not have enough disk space.

Ask your system administrator to check the amount of disk space on your computer. If you have sufficient space, your administrator should delete the NETLOGON.CHG file from your system directory and then restart the service.

The client does not have the permissions required to execute the function.

[WINS Service]

You need Administrator, Account Operator, or System Operator privileges to execute this function.

Ask the administrator to assign the necessary permissions to you. Then try again. Or, ask someone with the necessary privileges to execute the function for you.

The client name is invalid.

[DHCP]

Make sure you have the correct computer name for the client computer, and that you have typed the name in correctly.

The Clipboard line is too long to paste. Copy and paste smaller portions of the line.

[Notepad]

Because your computer is low on memory, Notepad cannot paste the line that you have copied to the Clipboard.

Close one or more of the applications that you have running, then try again.

The ClipBook Viewer cannot display the information you have copied. To view the information, try pasting it into a document.

[Clipboard]

ClipBook Viewer is either low on memory, or the information that you have copied is in a format that ClipBook Viewer does not support (a binary format, for example).

Follow the user action specified in the message.

The CMOS file cmos.ram could not be created.

[Virtual DOS Machine (VDM)]

The file that holds the internal CMOS state could not be created.

Check that you have permission to create the CMOS.RAM file, which is in the SYSTEM32 subdirectory. You may need to ask your system administrator to give you permission to do so. Then restart the virtual DOS machine.

The CMOS file cmos.ram could not be updated.

[Virtual DOS Machine (VDM)]

The file that holds the internal CMOS state could not be updated.

Check that you have permission to update the CMOS.RAM file, which is in the SYSTEM32 subdirectory. You may need to ask your system administrator to give you write permission on this file. Then restart the virtual DOS machine.

The code page specified is not valid.

[Mode]

Find out the code page values supported by your keyboard and then retry the Mode command, using a valid code page value in the Select= parameter. Or you may want to use the International icon in Control Panel to examine and modify the code page.

The command completed with one or more errors.

[Network] Net Message ID: 3504

The command tried to perform multiple tasks and some of them could not be completed.

No action is needed.

The command contains an invalid number of arguments.

[Network] Net Message ID: 3503

The command has an invalid number of options or variables.

To see the syntax of this command, type NET HELP <command>.

The command finished; the name has active sessions and is no longer registered.

[Dynamic Data Exchange]

The application tried to delete a NetBIOS name, but the computer using that name is using connections to remote resources at this time. When it has finished using those resources it will be disconnected from them, and the NetBIOS name will then be deleted from the list of active NetBIOS names on this network.

No action is needed.

The command line cannot exceed 259 characters.

[Network] Net Message ID: 3809

Commands used with the AT utility cannot exceed 259 characters.

Type a command with 259 or fewer characters.

The Common Program Groups cannot be accessed. Do you want to create a Personal Program Group?

[Program Manager]

Only users with Admin privileges can create or change common groups. However, you can create a personal group.

Choose Yes to create a personal group at this time, or choose No.

The communication device attached to port *address* is not functioning.

[Remote Access Service]

Verify that the modem is properly connected and is on. Check the cabling. Do not use one of the 9-25 pin converters that come with most mouse hardware because some of these converters do not carry modem signals. To be safe, use a converter made especially for this purpose. Also try turning the modem off and then back on.

The component cannot be run in Windows NT mode.

[File Manager]

You have attempted to run an executable file that has a bad format. Or you have attempted to load a .DLL file that lacks an ordinal.

The computer *computer name* already exists.

[Network] Net Message ID: 3782

The computer account specified already exists.

Choose a different computer name.

The computer *computer name* is not configured for remote administration.

[Server Manager]

You have attempted to remotely administer a computer that does not support remote administration (such as a Windows for Workgroups workstation).

No action is needed.

The computer *computer name* tried to connect to the server *computer name* using the trust relationship established by the *name* domain. However, the computer lost the correct security identifier (SID)when the domain was reconfigured. Reestablish the trust relationship.

[Network]

When a Windows NT computer joins a domain, it obtains the domain SID from the domain controller. The computer retains the SID in its local security database.

Remove and then add the computer to the domain again.

The computer has rebooted from a bug check. The bug check was: *text* . *text* A dump was saved in: *filename*.

[Network]

Contact technical support.

The computer has rebooted from a bug check. The bug check was: *text***.** *text* **A full dump was not saved.**

[Network]

Contact technical support.

The computer is not active in this domain.

[Network] Net Message ID: 2320

This message should occur only on a down-level computer. Any action to correct the problem should be performed on that computer. Your computer is not active in the domain you specified.

To perform tasks in the specified domain, you must add the domain to the list of domains in which the workstation is a member.

The computer name already exists on the network. Change it and restart the computer.

[Network] Net Message ID: 2144

The computer name already exists on the network. Each workstation must have a unique computer name.

Change the computer name and restart the computer before restarting the Workstation service.

The computer name could not be added as a message alias. The name may already exist on the network.

[Network] Net Message ID: 2270

A software error occurred.

Contact technical support.

The computer name could not be deleted.

[Network] Net Message ID: 2278

You cannot delete a message alias that is also a computer name.

No action is needed.

The computer name entered is already in use by another computer. Are you sure you want to change your computer name to this name?

[Control Panel]

Each computer name on the network should be unique. Some services cannot start if another computer with the same name is on the network.

If you are sure you want to give this computer this computer name (for example if it is to replace the computer with this computer name), choose Yes. Usually, you should choose No and then specify a different computer name.

The computer name entered is not properly formatted.

[Control Panel]

The computer name option in the Network dialog box can consist of no more than 15 characters, and cannot contain any of the following characters: ; : " < > * + = \\ | ? ,. The computer name that you have specified contains one of these characters.

Remove the character that you have entered, then try again.

The Computer Name has been successfully changed to ***computer name*****. This change will not take effect until the computer is restarted.**

[Control Panel]

No action is needed. You can continue to use the computer under the old computer name until you restart your computer. To use the new computer name, press Ctrl + Alt + Delete, and log in.

The computer name is being used as a message alias on another computer.

[Network]

This message should occur only on a down-level computer. Any action to correct the problem should be performed on that computer.

The computer name you typed is invalid.

[Server Manager]

In the Add Computer dialog box, you entered a computer name that contains invalid characters.

Enter a valid computer name, then try again.

The computer or username you typed is invalid.

[Server Manager]

Make sure you have the correct computer name or username. Then try again, making sure to type the name correctly.

The configuration file contains an invalid service program name.

[Network]

This message should occur only on a down-level computer. Any action to correct the problem should be performed on that computer. Your configuration file has associated a service with a nonexistent program file.

Be sure that each entry shown in the [services] section of your configuration file lists a valid pathname for the service's executable file. If you need assistance, contact your network administrator.

The configuration file or the command line has a duplicate parameter.

[Network]

This message should occur only on a down-level computer. Any action to correct the problem should be performed on that computer. An option was used more than once in your command or in the configuration file. An option can be used only once in a command and once in the configuration file. If an option is typed from the command line, it overrides the value in the configuration file.

Do not type the same option twice in a command. Be sure not to use different abbreviations that can specify the same option, such as wrkserv and wrkservices. If the error was not caused by a command, check the configuration file for duplicate options.

The configuration file or the command line has an ambiguous option.

[Network] Net Message ID: 3058

This message should occur only on a down-level computer. Any action to correct the problem should be performed on that computer. Some options can be confused with other options that start with the same letter.

Spell out enough of the option so that it cannot be confused with other command options.

The configuration registry database is corrupt.

[Kernel32]

The structure of one of the files that contains Registry data is corrupted, or the image of the file in memory is corrupted, or the file could not be recovered because an alternate copy or log was absent or corrupted.

Use the Emergency Repair Disk to restore the configuration information.

The configuration registry key is invalid.

[Kernel32]

The system is unable to open or create a Registry key that does not have a name.

Provide a key name.

The connection dropped.

[Remote Access Service]

Redial the entry. If you continue to get this message, reduce the modem's initial speed, and turn off the advanced modem features. For more information, see "Setting Modem Features" in the Remote Access Service online Help. If the problem persists, contact your system administrator. If you're dialing manually, make sure you're connected before you click Done.

The connection identification does not specify a valid connection.

[Network] Net Message ID: 2462

This message should occur only on a down-level computer. Any action to correct the problem should be performed on that computer. A software error occurred.

If this error persists or causes other errors, contact technical support.

The contents of Clipboard cannot be deleted.

[Clipboard]

Currently, a malfunctioning application is holding the Clipboard open.

Exit or minimize Clipboard, close the other application, then try again.

The contents of the *name* is not valid. You must type a value between *number* and *number*.

[Network]

In the specified text box, enter a value in the specified range.

The contents of the *name* is not valid. You must type a value between *number* and *number*.

[Services for Macintosh (SFM)]

Contact technical support.

The contents of the target file were lost.

[Command Prompt]

You tried to combine several sources into one file. The destination file was also one of the source files. Therefore, instead of adding the other source files to the destination files, the destination file was overwritten before it could be copied. The original content of this file is lost.

If you want to combine files with the destination file, list the destination file as the first source file.

The contents of the target file were lost.

[Command]

You tried to combine several sources into one file. The destination file was also one of the source files. Therefore, instead of adding the other source files to the destination files, the destination file was overwritten before it could be copied. The original content of this file is lost.

If you want to combine files with the destination file, list the destination file as the first source file.

The contents of this drive have changed. Do you want to update the Search Results window?

[File Manager]

You searched for a file, then having found the file, you renamed it or copied it to a different directory. When you do this, File Manager presents you with this message.

If you want to update the Search Results window, select Yes. If not, choose No.

The context handle changed during a remote procedure call.

[Kernel32]

Contact the supplier of the running distributed application.

The control registers for *name* overlaps the *name* status register.

The multiport card is incorrectly configured.

If the configuration was done by a setup program, contact the vendor of the device that included the setup program. If the configuration was performed using Regedit, delete that configuration information from the Registry and try again.

The control registers for *name* overlaps with the *name* control registers.

You used Ports in the Control Panel to add a port, but the address you specified overlaps an existing address.

The conversion failed. ***file system*** **was not converted to** ***file system***

[Convert]

The file conversion from a FAT partition or HPFS volume to an NTFS volume is not complete.

The FAT partition or HPFS volume is still in its original (unconverted state). Free up some system resources and try the conversion again.

The Copy API cannot be used.

[Kernel32]

Contact the supplier of the running application.

The Creator/Type item is invalid.

[Services for Macintosh (SFM)]

The Creator/Type item must contain between 1 to 4 characters.

The credentials supplied conflict with an existing set of credentials.

[Kernel32]

Credentials are a username/password combination. In this case, you already have a logon session started with a set of credentials and have tried to start another session between the same computers, using the same set of credentials.

Either end the existing session, or log on with a different set of credentials. Note that this message may not be caused by anything you did at the user interface, but can be caused by a running application (applications can log on as users). In that case, contact the supplier of the running application.

The current image will be replaced by the contents of the Clipboard. Do you want to continue?

[Paintbrush]

If you want to continue, select Yes. If not, select No. If unsure, select No, open the Clipboard to see the contents of the clipboard, then return to Paintbrush.

The current local clock is ***time*** **Do you want to set the local computer's time to match the time at** ***computer name*** **?** ***time*** **:** ***text***

[Network]

Choose Yes to synchronize your computer with the indicated server, or choose No to leave your clock at the current setting.

The current MIDI setup references a MIDI device which is not installed on your system. Do you want to continue?

[MIDI Mapper (Control Panel)]

In the MIDI Mapper dialog box, you attempted to edit a Setup that is not installed on your system.

In the Name list in the MIDI Mapper dialog box, select the name of a Setup that is installed on your system. Or select one of the other two options in the Show box. Or select the Close button on the MIDI Mapper dialog box.

The data returned from a remote administration command has been truncated to 64K.

[Network]

When remotely administering a LAN Manager 2.x server, only the first 64K of the information can be received successfully.

No action is needed.

The data type is not supported by the print processor.

[Network] Net Message ID: 2167

This message should occur only on a down-level computer. Any action to correct the problem should be performed on that computer. The data type of the print job is not supported by the queue's print processor.

Use a different print processor for jobs that have this data type, or rewrite the application so that it uses a data type the print processor can recognize.

The Database has been found to be inconsistent. More specifically, the number of owners found in the Name Address Mapping table are different from the number found in the Owner Address Mapping table

[WINS Service]

The database is corrupt.

Restore the database from a backup copy.

The Database of Name to Address Mappings is empty. It could mean that a previous invocation of WINS created the database and then went down before any registration could be done.

[WINS Service]

No action is needed. WINS will recover automatically.

The database specified does not exist.

[Kernel32]

Verify that the database specified is the Services Active database. You may have to contact the supplier of the running application.

The datafiles key could not be opened

[WINS Service]

A key in the Registry (under WINS\Parameters) that is created when WINS is installed has been deleted.

No action is needed. If you want, you can replace the keys using Regedit or by reinstalling WINS.

The day field is too big.

[Network]

The value in the day field must be no larger than the number of days in a month.

Try again, using a smaller value.

The day field is too big.

[Services for Macintosh (SFM)]

Contact technical support.

The decimal value entered is greater than the maximum value of a DWORD. Registry Editor will truncate the value entered.

[Registry Editor]

The maximum decimal value of a DWORD is 2 to the 32nd power minus 1. You have entered for a DWORD value entry a decimal number that exceeds this.

Enter a decimal value entry less than this number, then choose OK.

The default/desired zone name specified is not in the zone list for adapter "*name* ".

[Services for Macintosh (SFM)]

The value for the default/desired zone name were incorrectly modified by directly accessing the Registry instead of using the Network option in Control Panel.

Use the Network option in Control Panel to reset the default/desired zones from the zone list. Then, restart the computer for the changes to take effect.

The delete failed due to a problem with the AT schedule file.

[Network] Net Message ID: 3808

This message should occur only on a down-level computer. Any action to correct the problem should be performed on that computer. LAN Manager cannot find the job you are trying to delete.

Check the job identification number by typing AT. Try again to delete the job, using the correct job identification number. If the error persists, the schedule file, SCHED.LOG, may be damaged. Restore SCHED.LOG from a backup copy, or delete it and create a new one with the AT utility. SCHED.LOG is in the LANMAN\\LOGS directory.

The dependency service does not exist or has been marked for deletion.

[Kernel32]

An application has attempted to start a service. However, a service that this service depends on is not installed or is in the process of being deleted.

Either remove the dependency between the services or install the service upon which the other service depends.

The dependency service or group failed to start.

[Kernel32]

An application has attempted to start a service. However, the service did not start because one or more services that it depends on failed to start.

Use Event Viewer to look in the event log for details about the dependent service or group that failed to start.

The description for Event ID (*number* **) in Source (** *number* **) could not be found. It contains the following insertion string(s):**

[Network] [Security]

No description can be found for the event ID. Very likely, the Registry is not configured properly, or a necessary .DLL file is missing.

Contact technical support and report the content of the message, as well as of the insertion strings that follow the colon.

The description for Event ID (*number* **) in Source (** *number* **) could not be found. It contains the following insertion string(s):**

[Services for Macintosh (SFM)]

Contact technical support.

The destination directory is a subdirectory of the source.

[File Manager]

Using either the Move or the Copy command, you did not designate a drive name in the To section of the dialog box.

Return to the dialog box, and then specify a drive name.

The destination disk is full.

[Setup]

Select the Exit Setup option. Then, either install Windows NT on another drive, or delete some unneeded files from this destination disk and rerun the Setup installation process from the beginning.

The destination disk is full.

[Repair Disk]

Select the Exit Setup option. Then, either install Windows NT on another drive, or delete some unneeded files from this destination disk and rerun the Setup installation process from the beginning.

The destination disk is full. Please insert another disk to continue.

[File Manager]

You copied the contents of one drive to a disk, and the disk in your disk drive cannot contain any more information.

Insert a new disk, and choose the OK button on the dialog. Or insert a new disk and press the ENTER key.

The destination list provided does not match the destination list of the printer queue.

[Network] Net Message ID: 3758

This message should occur only on a down-level computer. Any action to correct the problem should be performed on that computer. When you share an existing printer queue, you cannot specify a list of printers different from those already assigned for the queue.

To share the printer queue, type NET SHARE <queue name> /PRINT. Then, to change the list of printers the queue uses, type NET PRINT <share name> /ROUTE:<device names>.

The destination path is illegal.

[Network] Net Message ID: 2382

This message should occur only on a down-level computer. Any action to correct the problem should be performed on that computer. The destination path does not exist.

Check the spelling of the destination path. If you need more information, see your network administrator.

The destination path specified in the Setup command is invalid. Check the /d switch.

[Setup]

Correct the path specified in the /d switch of the Setup command and retry the command.

The destination path specified in the Setup command is invalid. Check the /d switch.

[Repair Disk]

Correct the path specified in the /d switch of the Setup command and retry the command.

The device *name* that is part of a fault tolerance set has failed and will no longer be used.

[Disk Administrator]

The drive that contains the fault tolerance member named in the message has failed. A copy of the data contained on the drive still exists.

Contact your system administrator to replace the failed drive and to reestablish your fault tolerance set.

The device .INF file contains no responses for the command.

[Remote Access Service]

One of the Remote Access configuration files probably contains invalid information.

The easiest way to resolve this problem is to reinstall Remote Access. Use the Network option in Control Panel to remove and reinstall RAS. If you are using a modem that is not supported by Remote Access, switch to a supported modem, or see "Modem Script File" in the Remote Access Service online Help for information about modifying the modem script file for your modem. The Remote Access script files (PAD.INF, MODEM.INF, and SWITCH.INF) are in the \SYSTEM32\RAS subdirectory of your Windows NT directory.

The device .INF file could not be opened.

[Remote Access Service]

One of the Remote Access configuration files probably contains invalid information.

The easiest way to resolve this problem is to reinstall Remote Access. Use the Network option in Control Panel to remove and reinstall RAS. If you are using a modem that is not supported by Remote Access, switch to a supported modem, or see "Modem Script File" in the Remote Access Service online Help for information about modifying the modem script file for your modem. The Remote Access script files (PAD.INF, MODEM.INF, and SWITCH.INF) are in the \SYSTEM32\RAS subdirectory of your Windows NT directory.

The device .INF file is missing a command.

[Remote Access Service]

One of the Remote Access configuration files probably contains invalid information.

The easiest way to resolve this problem is to reinstall Remote Access. Use the Network option in Control Panel to remove and reinstall RAS. If you are using a modem that is not supported by Remote Access, switch to a supported modem, or see "Modem Script File" in the Remote Access Service online Help for information about modifying the modem script file for your modem. The Remote Access script files (PAD.INF, MODEM.INF, and SWITCH.INF) are in the \SYSTEM32\RAS subdirectory of your Windows NT directory.

The device cannot be set to the specified number of lines and/or columns.

[Mode]

You specified invalid values for the rows and columns parameters while using the Mode command to change the LPTn: (printer) device resolution.

Retry the command, using valid values.

The device could not allocate one or more required resources due to conflicts with other devices. The device interrupt setting of ' *number* **' could not be satisfied due to a conflict with Driver '** *name* **'.**

Two drivers are requesting exclusive use of the same interrupt setting (IRQ). The second driver cannot be loaded, and functionality dependent on this driver will not be available.

Change the IRQ setting for the driver that was being loaded when the message appeared, or for the driver specified in this message. Then try again.

The device could not allocate one or more required resources due to conflicts with other devices. The device port setting of '*name*' could not be satisfied due to a conflict with Driver '*name*'.

Two drivers are requesting exclusive use of the same port. The second driver cannot be loaded, and functionality dependent on this driver will not be available.

Change the port for the driver that was being loaded when the message appeared, or for the driver specified in this message. Then try again.

The device does not exist.

[Remote Access Service]

The Remote Access Phone Book file and the current Remote Access configuration are probably inconsistent.

If you have changed your communications equipment (such as your serial port or modem), be sure to reconfigure Remote Access. Use the Network option in Control Panel to reconfigure Remote Access. If the error persists, remove and recreate the affected Phone Book entry or, reinstall the Remote Access Service. The Remote Access Phone Book (RASPHONE.PBK) is in the SYSTEM32\RAS subdirectory of your Windows NT directory.

The device driver does not exist.

[Network] Net Message ID: 2166

This message should occur only on a down-level computer. Any action to correct the problem should be performed on that computer. The device driver you specified has not been installed for the printer queue.

Check the spelling of the name of the device driver. To use a new device driver with this printer queue, you must first use Control Panel to install the device driver. For more information about Control Panel, see your operating system manual(s).

The device is being accessed by an active process.

[Network] Net Message ID: 2404

The drive letter you specified is the current drive of a session. You tried to delete a drive redirection (x:) while it is in use, possibly as your current drive.

Be sure the drive you are trying to delete is not the current drive in any of your sessions.

The device is busy.

[Utilities]

The device is initializing or regenerating a fault-tolerance construct (mirror or stripe with parity).

Wait until the device is not busy and try again.

The device is in use by an active process and cannot be disconnected.

[Kernel32]

An application tried to cancel a network connection that was in use by one or more active processes.

Either wait for the process to quit using the connection and retry your operation or, if the user interface enables you to, force the disconnection and retry.

The device is not connected.

[Network] Net Message ID: 2107

This message should occur only on a down-level computer. Any action to correct the problem should be performed on that computer. This device name is not assigned to a shared resource.

Check the spelling of the device name first. To see which local device names are assigned to shared resources, type NET USE.

The device is not currently connected but it is a remembered connection.

[Kernel32]

An application requested the name of the network resource associated with a particular local device. That device is not currently connected, but it is a remembered connection.

This message is for your information; direct user action is not necessary.

The device is not ready.

[Kernel32]

One of the following errors occurred: (1) the drive is empty; (2) the drive door is open; or (3) the drive is in use.

Do one of the following: (1) insert a floppy disk in the drive and retry the command; (2) close the drive door and retry the command; or (3) wait until the device is available and retry the command.

The device moved to a BPS rate not supported by the COM driver.

[Remote Access Service]

Your modem tried to connect at a speed that the serial port cannot interpret.

Reset your initial speed to the next lowest standard bps rate: 38400, 19200, 9600, 2400.

The device name in the device .INF or media .INI file is too long.

[Remote Access Service]

One of the Remote Access configuration files probably contains invalid information.

The easiest way to resolve this problem is to reinstall Remote Access. Use the Network option in Control Panel to remove and reinstall RAS. If you are using a modem that is not supported by Remote Access, switch to a supported modem, or see "Modem Script File" in the Remote Access Service online Help for information about modifying the modem script file for your modem. The Remote Access script files (PAD.INF, MODEM.INF, and SWITCH.INF) are in the \SYSTEM32\RAS subdirectory of your Windows NT directory.

The device or directory does not exist.

[Network] Net Message ID: 2116

You specified an unknown device or directory.

Check the spelling of the device or directory name.

The device response caused buffer overflow.

[Remote Access Service]

This error should not occur under normal circumstances.

Restart your computer to make sure that all recent configuration changes have taken effect. If the error persists, consult the Windows NT event log for detailed warnings or errors.

The device type does not exist.

[Remote Access Service]

The Remote Access Phone Book file and the current Remote Access configuration are probably inconsistent.

If you have changed your communications equipment (such as your serial port or modem), be sure to reconfigure Remote Access. Use the Network option in Control Panel to reconfigure Remote Access. If the error persists, remove and recreate the affected Phone Book entry or, reinstall the Remote Access Service. The Remote Access Phone Book (RASPHONE.PBK) is in the SYSTEM32\RAS subdirectory of your Windows NT directory.

The device type is unknown.

[Network] Net Message ID: 3716

You typed an invalid device name.

Check the spelling of the device name. Valid device names are LPT1: to LPT9: and COM1: to COM9: for printers and communication devices, and A: to Z: for disk devices.

The device, *name* **, did not respond within the timeout period.**

Check the cabling on the device named in the message. After that, if you still get this message, run hardware diagnostics on the disk drive named in the message, and on its controller. You may have to contact the vendor of the device.

The device, *name* **, had a seek error.**

Retry the operation. If you still get this message, run hardware diagnostics on the disk drive named in the message, and on its controller. You may have to contact the vendor of the device, and you may have to replace the controller, the disk drive, or both.

The device, *name* **, has a bad block.**

Run the Chkdsk utility, with the /r option, on the named partition. After that, if you still get this message, run hardware diagnostics on the disk drive named in the message, and on its controller. You may have to contact the vendor of the device, and you may have to replace the controller, the disk drive, or both.

The device, *name* **, has been reset.**

You can ignore this message. It is for informational purposes only.

The device, *name* **, is not ready for access yet.**

Retry the operation. If you still get this message, run hardware diagnostics on the disk drive named in the message, and on its controller. You may have to contact the vendor of the device, and you may have to replace the controller, the disk drive, or both.

The DHCP client could not obtain an IP address. If you want to see DHCP messages in the future, choose YES. If you do not want to see DHCP messages choose NO.

[DHCP]

Make sure the computer is physically connected to the network and the network card is correctly configured. Check with the network administrator to make sure that there is a DHCP server and that it is currently running the DHCP service.

The DHCP client could not renew the IP address lease. If you want to see DHCP messages in the future, choose YES. If you do not want to see DHCP messages choose NO.

[DHCP]

Make sure the computer is physically connected to the network and the network card is correctly configured. Check with the network administrator to make sure that there is a DHCP server and that it is currently running the DHCP service.

The DHCP client couldn't obtain an IP address.

Ask your network administrator to make sure that there are addresses in the free address pool of this scope. The administrator might need to add more addresses, stop excluding addresses that are no longer manually allocated.

The DHCP client lost the lease. The network is brought down. If you want to see DHCP messages in the future, choose YES. If you do not want to see DHCP messages choose NO.

[DHCP]

Make sure the computer is physically connected to the network and the network card is correctly configured. Check with the network administrator to make sure that there is a DHCP server and that it is currently running the DHCP service.

The DHCP protocol will attempt to automatically configure your workstation during system initialization. Any parameters specified in these configuration dialogs will override any values obtained by DHCP. Do you want to enable DHCP?

[TCP/IP]

If you enable DHCP, the IP Address and Subnet Mask will assume the values assigned by the DHCP server, regardless of whether you have specified values for them. Any other parameters that are specified manually will override the values supplied by the DHCP server.

Choose Yes if you want to let DHCP assign your IP Address and Subnet Mask. In this case you might also want to delete any values you have entered for the other parameters, and let DHCP assign them too. Choose No if you to not want to use DHCP to assign values for you.

The DHCP server encountered the following error when cleaning up the pending user records: *text text*

[DHCP]

An internal error occurred in the DHCP server.

Look up the indicated error and take appropriate action. If this message appears often, you might want to restore an earlier version of your DHCP database.

The DHCP server encountered the following error when backing up the registry configuration: *text text*

[DHCP]

An internal error occurred in the DHCP server.

Look up the indicated error and take appropriate action. If this message appears often, you might want to restore an earlier version of your DHCP database.

The DHCP server encountered the following error when backing up the user database: *text text*

[DHCP]

An internal error occurred in the DHCP server.

Look up the indicated error and take appropriate action. If this message appears often, you might want to restore an earlier version of your DHCP database.

The DHCP server encountered the following error when cleaning up the user database: *text text*

[DHCP]

An internal error occurred in the DHCP server.

Look up the indicated error and take appropriate action. If this message appears often, you might want to restore an earlier version of your DHCP database.

The DHCP server failed to initialize its global data. The following error occurred: *text text*

[DHCP]

The DHCP Server service could not start. The system is probably out of memory.

Reboot the system and try again.

The DHCP server failed to initialize its registry data. The following error occurred: *text text*

[DHCP]

The DHCP Server service could not start. The system is probably out of memory, or the Registry might be corrupt.

Reboot the system and try again.

The DHCP server failed to initialize the database. The following error occurred: *text text*

[DHCP]

The DHCP Server service could not start. The system is probably out of memory, or the Registry might be corrupt.

Reboot the system and try again.

The DHCP server failed to initialize winsock data. The following error occurred: *text text*

[DHCP]

The DHCP Server service could not start. The system is probably out of memory, or the Registry might be corrupt.

Reboot the system and try again.

The DHCP server failed to initialize Winsock startup. The following error occurred: *text text*

[DHCP]

The DHCP Server service could not start. The system is probably out of memory, or the Registry might be corrupt.

Reboot the system and try again.

The DHCP Server failed to register with Service Controller. The following error occurred: *text text***.**

[DHCP]

The DHCP Server service could not start. The system is probably out of memory, or the Registry might be corrupt.

Reboot the system and try again.

The DHCP server failed to restore the database. The following error occurred: *text text*

[DHCP]

The DHCP Server service could not start.

Look up the indicated error and take appropriate action. Then try again. You might need to revert to a backup copy of the DHCP database.

The DHCP server failed to restore the dhcp registry configuration. The following error occurred: *text text*

[DHCP]

The DHCP Server service could not start.

Reboot and try again.

The DHCP Server Failed to start the RPC server. The following error occurred : *text text*

[DHCP]

The DHCP Server service could not start.

Reboot and try again.

The DHCP server initialization parameters are invalid.

[DHCP]

The DHCP Server service could not start.

Use Regedit to correct the parameter values.

The DHCP server is shutting down due to the following error: *text text*

[DHCP]

Look up the indicated error and take appropriate action. Then try again.

The DHCP server received a message from an invalid client.

[DHCP]

Make sure you are using the current version of this application.

The DHCP server received an invalid message.

[DHCP]

Make sure you are using the current version of this application.

The DHCP Server received an unknown option *name* **of length** *number*. **The raw option data is given below.**

[DHCP]

The option has not been defined.

No action is needed. All other options have been configured.

The DHCP server was unable establish a sockets connection.

[DHCP]

Your computer is probably out of memory.

Reboot your computer and try again.

The DHCP server was unable to start as an RPC server.

[DHCP]

The DHCP Server service could not start.

Reboot the computer and try again.

The directory cannot be removed.

[Kernel32]

The directory cannot be removed for one of the following reasons: (1) it does not exist, or the directory name is misspelled; (2) it contains files or other subdirectories; (3) it is the current directory in this session or another session that is in process, or is a directory on a drive that is not current in any session; or (4) it has the same name as a reserved device name.

Do one of the following, then retry the command: (1) correct the directory name; (2) remove all files and subdirectories from the directory; (3) use the Chdir command to change the current directory in all sessions that might be using it; or (4) if the directory name is the same as an installed device, remove the device.

The directory is not a subdirectory of the root directory.

[Kernel32]

The directory specified in the Join command must be a subdirectory of the root directory.

Retry the command, specifying a different directory.

The directory is not empty.

[Kernel32]

The Join command requires that the directory be empty.

Retry the command, specifying an empty directory.

The directory name is invalid.

[Kernel32]

If you can do it through a user interface, correct the directory name. Otherwise, contact the supplier of the running application.

The directory or file cannot be created.

[Kernel32]

One of the following errors occurred: (1) the file or directory name already exists; (2) the directory path cannot be found; (3) the root directory is full or there is not enough space on the disk for the new file or directory; (4) the directory name contains unacceptable characters or is a reserved file name; or (5) the disk is not properly formatted.

Correct the problem, then retry the command.

The disk containing one of the free spaces you have chosen is not able to accept any more partitions.

[Disk Administrator]

You can only create four primary partitions on a hard disk, and the disk containing free space already contains four partitions.

Choose another disk. Or create a volume set within the free space on the currently selected disk.

The disk contains no support files for the component you are attempting to change.

[Setup]

Contact the supplier for another copy of the installation media.

The disk file was not found or was inaccessible.

[Backup]

The copy of the file that should be on the disk could not be found.

Make sure you specified the file name correctly. Also, make sure the file has not been locked by another application.

The disk in drive *drive letter* is not formatted. Do you want to format it now?

[File Manager]

Before you can write to the disk, you must format it.

To format the disk, choose Yes.

The disk is full.

[Kernel32]

Delete some unneeded files from the disk, then try again.

The disk is in use or locked by another process.

[Kernel32]

A process has exclusive use of this disk, prohibiting another process from accessing it at this time.

Retry the operation later, or try it on another disk.

The disk is too large to format for the specified file system.

[Utilities]

Use another file system, or repartition the disk with Disk Administrator.

The disk is write-protected.

[File Manager]

You have attempted an operation on a disk that is write-protected.

Remove the disk, remove the write protection (by flipping a tab on the disk), then try again.

The disk media is not recognized. It may not be formatted.

[Kernel32]

Reformat the media, or use a different media, and then retry the operation.

The display driver on this computer cannot display this information in bitmap format.

[Clipboard]

The display driver on a computer determines whether you can view the contents from another computer's ClipBook in bitmap format. You have attempted to view ClipBook information in a bitmap format, but do not have the necessary driver.

Install the necessary video driver.

The domain controller for this domain cannot be located.

[Control Panel]

You must specify a domain name other than the computer name.

Enter a different name.

The domain entered is already permitted to trust this domain.

[User Manager]

If you are not able to grant permissions on resources in the domain whose name you entered to users in this domain, make sure that this domain trusts the domain whose name you entered and that the trust passwords match.

The domain entered is already trusted.

[User Manager]

If you are not able to grant permissions on resources in the domain whose name you entered to users in this domain, make sure that this domain trusts the domain whose name you entered and that the trust passwords match.

The domain entered is not a Windows NT domain.

[Control Panel]

The domain name you entered is not the name of any Windows NT domain on this network. You can only join Windows NT domains from a Windows NT computer, although you may be able to access information on computers in other domains.

Enter the name of a Windows NT domain.

The domain name entered does not exist or is not properly formatted.

[Control Panel]

The domain name option in the Network dialog box can consist of no more than 15 characters, and cannot contain any of the following characters: ; : " < > * + = \\ | ? ,. The domain name that you have selected contains one of these characters.

Remove the character, then try again.

The domain name entered is already in use by other computers.

[Control Panel]

You tried to create a domain with a domain name that is already in use.

Specify a different domain name, or use the domain that already exists.

The domain name entered is the same as this domain name.

[User Manager]

You can only establish trust relationships with another domain.

No action is needed.

The domain name you entered cannot be accepted for this server. If this domain has been renamed at the domain controller,

[Control Panel]

Because servers are also backup domain controllers, they cannot change domains after initial setup. However, if the domain has been renamed at the controller, you need to enter the new domain name.

If the domain has not been renamed, choose Cancel. If the domain has been renamed, enter the new name. If you want to remove this server from this domain and add it to another domain, you must reinstall Windows NT on the computer, and use Server Manager on the old domain to remove this Backup Domain Controller.

The domain name you typed is invalid.

[User Manager]

The name you typed does not meet the naming requirements for domains. Domain names cannot contain spaces (blank characters).

Try again, specifying a valid domain name.

The domain specified could not be used.

[Network]

This message should occur only on a down-level computer. Any action to correct the problem should be performed on that computer.

The domain was in the wrong state to perform the security operation.

[Kernel32]

For instance, the password associated with a user cannot be changed by the Windows NT security subsystem if the security database is stored on a domain server that is in a disabled state.

Contact the supplier of the running application.

The DosMuxSemWait list is not correct.

[Kernel32]

The list passed to the function that waits for one of several semaphores to clear is not in the proper format.

Correct the format of the semaphore wait list. You may have to contact the supplier of the running application.

The down-level logoff request for the user *user name* from *name* failed.

[Network] Net Message ID: 5708

You may have specified an invalid user name.

Ask your system administrator to verify that the security database includes the user's name.

The down-level logon request for the user *user name* from *computer name* failed.

[Network] Net Message ID: 5707

You have specified an invalid user name.

Ask your system administrator to verify that the security database includes the user name. Then make sure that the user's password matches the password for the user in the database.

The drive cannot find the sector requested.

[Kernel32]

The disk or floppy disk may be damaged, unformatted, or not compatible with the operating system.

Retry the command after you do one of the following: (1) make sure the disk is properly inserted; (2) use the Chkdsk utility to check that the disk is not damaged; (3) format the disk or floppy disk for the appropriate file system (realize that when you format a disk, any information that was previously on the disk will be erased); or (4) check to make sure you do not have a high density floppy disk in a low density floppy drive.

The drive cannot locate a specific area or track on the disk.

[Kernel32]

The disk may be damaged, unformatted, or not compatible with the operating system.

Do one of the following: (1) make sure the floppy disk is properly inserted; (2) check that the disk is not damaged; or format the disk for the appropriate file system.

The drive letter is in use locally.

[Network] Net Message ID: 2405

This message should occur only on a down-level computer. Any action to correct the problem should be performed on that computer. You tried to assign a local drive letter to a shared resource.

Use a drive letter that does not correspond to a local drive.

The driver beneath this one has failed in some way for *text*.

Contact your system administrator to check the configuration of the driver software on your computer, especially the drivers for the device named in the message. You may have to contact the driver suppliers.

The driver could not allocate something necessary for the request for *name*.

The request for the named device could not be carried out because there were not enough resources, typically memory.

Increase the paging file size. If you still get this message, add more physical memory to your computer.

The driver detected a controller error on *name*.

Check the cabling on the device named in the message. After that, if you still get this message, run hardware diagnostics. You may have to contact the vendor of the device or you may have to replace the controller.

The driver detected an internal driver error on *name*.

Contact the supplier of the driver for the device named in the message.

The driver detected an unexpected sequence by the device, *name*.

Check the cabling on the device named in the message. After that, if you still get this message, run hardware diagnostics. You may have to contact the vendor of the device.

The driver has detected a device with old or out-of-date firmware. The device will not be used.

Contact the hardware manufacturer for an upgrade the firmware for this device.

The driver has detected that device *name* has old or out-of-date firmware. Reduced performance may result.

The device and driver could be running at a faster rate.

No action is needed. However, you might want to contact the hardware manufacturer for an upgrade to the firmware for this device.

The driver was configured with an incorrect interrupt for *name*.

Contact your system administrator to reconfigure the device named in the message.

The driver was configured with an invalid I/O base address for *name*.

Contact your system administrator to reconfigure the device named in the message.

The dynamic-link library *name* could not be loaded, or an error occurred while trying to use it.

[Network] Net Message ID: 3776

A system dynamic-link library could not be loaded.

Make sure the file specified is in your system directory. If it is not, contact your network administrator.

The elementary file-system structures are corrupt. CHKDSK cannot check this drive.

[Chkdsk-HPFS]

This volume is unrecoverably corrupted. Reformat it and restore backed up data.

The Emergency Repair Disk is not startable. Repairing a damaged Windows NT installation is an option available at the beginning of Windows NT Setup. To start Setup, insert the Windows NT Setup Disk into drive A:. Press control+alt+delete to restart your computer.

[Repair Disk]

In order to use the Emergency Repair Disk, you must start your computer from the Windows NT Setup disk as directed in the message.

The endpoint cannot be created.

[Kernel32]

In a distributed (RPC) application, a server was unable to create a specific destination in one of the interfaces it offers to clients.

Contact the supplier of the running application.

The endpoint format is invalid.

[Kernel32]

An endpoint identifies a particular server instance (or address space) on a host computer in a distributed computing environment. A distributed (RPC) application has generated badly-formatted endpoint identification information.

Contact the supplier of the running application.

The endpoint is a duplicate.

[Kernel32]

An application tried to use the same endpoint.

Contact the supplier of the running application.

The endpoint mapper database could not be created.

[Kernel32]

Contact the supplier of the running distributed application.

The entry already exists.

[Kernel32]

In a distributed (RPC) application, an attempt was made to create an entry in the name-service database with an entry name that already exists in the database.

Contact the supplier of the running distributed application.

The entry is not found.

[Kernel32]

In a distributed (RPC) application, an attempt was made to operate on a named entry in the name-service database. An entry with that name could not be found.

Contact the supplier of the running distributed application.

The entry name is incomplete.

[Kernel32]

In a distributed (RPC) application, the name of a name-service database entry is incompletely specified, compared to its assigned format.

Contact the supplier of the running distributed application.

The entry selected is not an AppleTalk printing device. Are you sure you want to despool to an AppleTalk spooler?

[Services for Macintosh (SFM)]

Despooling to an AppleTalk spooler is a very indirect way to print.

If you want to despool directly to a printer, try another device in the list.

The enumeration value is out of range.

[Kernel32]

Contact the supplier of the running distributed application.

The error code is *code*.There was an error retrieving the message. Make sure the fileNET.MSG is available.

[Network]

This alert appears if the error message text could not be retrieved from NETMSG.DLL.

Make sure the file NETMSG.DLL is available and can be written to and read from.

The error log is full. No errors will be logged until the file is cleared or the limit is raised.

[Network]

This message should occur only on a down-level computer. Any action to correct the problem should be performed on that computer.

The event is invalid.

[Remote Access Service]

This error should not occur under normal circumstances.

Restart your computer to make sure that all recent configuration changes have taken effect. If the error persists, consult the Windows NT event log for detailed warnings or errors.

The event log file is corrupt.

[Kernel32]

Run Chkdsk with the /f option on the disk that contains the event log file.

The event log record is misformed.

[Network] [Security]

The log file is probably corrupt.

Reboot your computer and try again. If you still get this message, run chkdsk to see if the log files are corrupted on the disk, and restore the files from backup copies if they are. If the error continues, clear the log file so new entries are not corrupted.

The event name is invalid.

[Network] Net Message ID: 2143

This message should occur only on a down-level computer. Any action to correct the problem should be performed on that computer. A software error occurred.

Contact technical support.

The Eventlog service is not started.

[Event Viewer]

You have attempted to access information in Event Viewer, and the service is not started.

Use the Services option in Control Panel to start the event log service.

The Eventlog service is paused.

[Event Viewer]

You attempted to access information in the Event Viewer when the Eventlog service has been paused.

Use the Services option in Control Panel to continue this service.

The Eventlog service on the local machine is not started.

[Event Viewer]

You have attempted to access the Eventlog service, and the service is not started.

Wait until the service has been started on the remote computer, then try again. Or, if you are administering a Windows NT Advanced Server, and the computer is not a LAN Manager 2.x computer, use Server Manager to start the service remotely.

The Eventlog service on the local machine is paused.

[Event Viewer]

You have attempted to access information on a remote computer when the Eventlog service on that computer is paused.

Wait until the service is continued, then try again. Or, if you are administering a Windows NT Advanced Server, and the computer is not a LAN Manager 2.x computer, use Server Manager to continue the service remotely.

The exception 0x*code* occurred in the application *application* at location 0x*code*.

[Network]

Restart the computer that issued the alert message.

The exception was encountered during the processing of a grp member.

[WINS Service]

WINS will try to recover automatically. If this message appears often, restore the WINS database from a backup copy.

The exclusive semaphore is owned by another process.

[Kernel32]

This is an exclusive system semaphore, and only the owner can modify it.

End your requested operation. You may have to contact the supplier of the running application.

The expanded command in the device .INF file is too long.

[Remote Access Service]

The limit for commands in the script file is 256 characters.

Break the command into multiple commands. For more information, see "Commands" in the Remote Access Service online Help.

The export path you typed is invalid.

[Server Manager]

The path you typed is not a valid pathname. It may have been mistyped.

Retype the path name. The pathname must use the following format, with no spaces:\\computername\sharename\subdirectory. You can specify many subdirectories or none, but each subdirectory name must be preceded with a backslash.

The extended attribute file on the mounted file system is corrupt.

[Kernel32]

The extended attributes for the specified disk are not usable.

Run the Chkdsk utility with the /f switch on the disk.

The extended attribute table file is full.

[Kernel32]

The number of files containing extended attributes has reached the system limit.

Delete any files containing attributes that you no longer need.

The extended attributes are inconsistent.

[Kernel32]

Contact the supplier of the running application.

The extended attributes did not fit in the buffer.

[Kernel32]

Contact the supplier of the running application.

The extension ' *application* **' is currently associated with '** *name*.**' Continue and overwrite this association?**

[File Manager]

If you want to change the association for files with this extension, choose Yes. Otherwise choose No.

The external process was canceled by a Ctrl+Break or another process.

[Command]

You attempted to establish a network connection at the command prompt, then pressed CTRL+BREAK to cancel the process.

No action is needed.

The external process was canceled by a Ctrl+Break or another process.

[Command Prompt]

You attempted to establish a network connection at the command prompt, then pressed CTRL+BREAK to cancel the process.

No action is needed.

The fault tolerance driver configuration information is corrupt.

[Disk Administrator]

Ask your system administrator to check the disk configuration information on your computer. The disk configuration information may have to be restored from a backup, using Windows NT Disk Administrator.

The fault tolerance driver was able to map a faulty sector from use by the system on *name*.

[Disk Administrator]

This is not a fatal error. However, a bad spot has developed on the disk. The information that was on this block has been mapped to one of the disk's spare blocks, using the redundant data.

This disk is beginning to fail. At the next scheduled maintenance, low-level format the drive. If the problem persists, replace the drive.

The fault tolerance driver was able to recover data from the duplicate copy for an I/O failure on *name*.

[Disk Administrator]

The failure on the specified disk would have resulted in loss of data if the fault tolerance system had not recovered the data.

This disk is beginning to fail. At the next scheduled maintenance, low-level format the drive. If the problem persists, replace the drive.

The fault tolerance driver was unable to map a faulty sector from use by the system on *name*.

[Disk Administrator]

The specified name is a fault tolerance set member name; it refers to a fault tolerance partition. There is a bad sector on one of the disks on one side of the mirror set. Your data security is at some risk. There is still a good sector on the other side of the mirror set, and the probability that the same sector number will go bad on both sides of the mirror is quite low.

To regain complete data security, do the following: (1) examine the event logs to identify which drive has the bad sector; (2) back up all data on that drive; (3) reformat the drive, using the verify switch to map out the bad sector; and (4) restore the backed up data.

The fault tolerance member *name* data was recovered from redundant copy.

[Disk Administrator]

Data was lost from the specified member due to some problem such as failure of a sector, but the data has been copied from the mirror copy.

No action is needed. However you might want to be sure that the faulty sector is mapped from use by the system.

The fault tolerance set containing device *name* has been disabled.

[Disk Administrator]

Either a single device has failed in a stripe or volume set, or two devices have failed in a stripe set with parity or in a mirror set.

Contact your system administrator to repair or replace the drive and restore data from backup.

The fault tolerant driver detected the system was shutdown dirty.

[Disk Administrator]

The system was shut down or crashed before newly written data could be written to the redundant copy. The data will be resynchronized automatically.

No action is needed.

The fault-tolerance error log file, LANROOT\\LOGS\\FT.LOG,is more than 64K.

[Network] Net Message ID: 3258

This message should occur only on a down-level computer. Any action to correct the problem should be performed on that computer. The fault-tolerance system error log is larger than 64K.

Run FTADMIN to fix any existing errors and clear them from the error log.

The fault-tolerance error-log file, LANROOT\\LOGS\\FT.LOG, had the update in progress bit set upon opening, which means that the system crashed while working on the error log.

[Network] Net Message ID: 3259

This message should occur only on a down-level computer. Any action to correct the problem should be performed on that computer. The server crashed while accessing the fault-tolerance error log, possibly damaging that log. The damaged fault-tolerance error log was cleared after its contents were backed up to LANMAN\\LOGS\\FT.ERR.

No action is needed.

The file *filename* has been changed after initialization. The boot-block loading was temporarily terminated.

[Network]

This message should occur only on a down-level computer. Any action to correct the problem should be performed on that computer. The listed file was changed after the Remoteboot service was started. Loading the boot-block stopped temporarily.

Stop and restart the Remoteboot service.

The file *filename* has a bad executable format

[OS/2 Subsystem]

The OS/2 subsystem task manager attempted to load a program that has an incorrect format.

No direct user action is necessary. If you continue to get this message, contact your technical support group.

The file *filename* has a bad format

[OS/2 Subsystem]

The Windows NT OS/2 subsystem is unable to run the program file named in the message. The specified file or program is either an MS-DOS application program or not compatible with OS/2.

If the specified application is an MS-DOS program, switch to an MS-DOS session and retry the command. Otherwise, reinstall the application and retry the command. If the error occurs again, contact the supplier of the application.

The file *filename* has an invalid stack address

[OS/2 Subsystem]

The OS/2 subsystem cannot run the file that is named in the message. It does not contain a correct stack segment.

There were probably errors when the application was created. If you can, run these same application files under the OS/2 operating system. If you get a comparable message under OS/2, then contact the supplier of the application. If the application runs under OS/2, contact your technical support group about a problem with the Windows NT OS/2 subsystem.

The file *filename* has an invalid starting address

[OS/2 Subsystem]

The Windows NT OS/2 subsystem task manager cannot run this application.

There were probably errors when the application was created. If you can, run these same application files under the OS/2 operating system. If you get a comparable message under OS/2, then contact the supplier of the application. If the application runs under OS/2, contact your technical support group about a problem with the Windows NT OS/2 subsystem.

The file *filename* in use - skipped.

[Backup]

The named file was in use on the disk, and therefore was not backed up.

No action is needed. When the file is no longer in use, you can repeat the operation, specifying only the named file.

The file *filename* is different.

[Backup]

The named file was different in the target directory than on the backup tape.

No action is needed.

The file *filename* is in use - waiting.

[Backup]

This is a status message, and it appears when you attempt to back up a file that is in use.

If you want to discontinue waiting, you can choose the Skip option.

The file *filename* was not found on disk.

[Backup]

The named file was not found on the target disk. If the file by that name on the backup tape was restored, it did not overwrite an existing file.

No action is needed.

The file cannot be copied onto itself.

[Command]

You have used the Copy command at the command prompt to copy a file onto itself, and this action is not permitted.

At the command prompt, specify a different source and destination directory.

The file cannot be copied onto itself.

[Command Prompt]

You have used the Copy command at the command prompt to copy a file onto itself, and this action is not permitted.

At the command prompt, specify a different source and destination directory.

The file extension is invalid.

[Services for Macintosh (SFM)]

The file extension contains more than 3 characters.

The file is read-only. Use a different filename.

[Write]

You have attempted to save changes made to a file that is read-only protected.

Follow the user action specified in the message.

The file name is too long.

[Kernel32]

Rename the file using a shorter filename.

The file pointer cannot be set on the specified device or file.

[Kernel32]

Contact the supplier of the running application.

The File Server for Macintosh service failed to start because it was unable to load the AppleTalk Filing Protocol file system driver.

[Services for Macintosh (SFM)]

Contact technical support.

The File Server for Macintosh service failed to start because a fatal error occurred while trying to initialize Macintosh-Accessible volumes.

[Services for Macintosh (SFM)]

Contact technical support.

The File Server for Macintosh service failed to start because a fatal error occurred while trying to initialize the AppleTalk Filing Protocol driver(SfmSrv.sys) with the extension/type/creator associations.

[Services for Macintosh (SFM)]

Use the Registry Editor to try to remove all Type/Creator pairs from the Registry. Remove the pair using the \\HKEY_LOCAL_MACHINE\System\CurrentControlSet\Services\MacFile\Parameters\Type_Creators Registry key.

The File Server for Macintosh service failed to start because a fatal error occurred while trying to initialize the AppleTalk Filing Protocol driver(SfmSrv.sys) with the server icons.

[Services for Macintosh (SFM)]

The server may be running out of memory or the Registry is corrupted.

First, try stopping other running applications and services. If you continue to see this message, use the Network option in Control Panel to remove and reinstall Services for Macintosh.

The File Server for Macintosh service failed to start because it was unable to open the AppleTalk Filing Protocol file system driver (SfmSrv.sys).

[Services for Macintosh (SFM)]

The file may be missing from the <systemroot>\system32 directory.

Use File Manager to verify the existence and location of the file. If the file is missing, remove and reinstall Services for Macintosh.

The File Server for Macintosh service failed to start. Security access checking of administrators could not be setup correctly.

[Services for Macintosh (SFM)]

Contact technical support.

The File Server for Macintosh service failed to start. The registry configuration database could not be opened.

[Services for Macintosh (SFM)]

Sometimes using the Network option in Control Panel locks the Registry.

Close the Network option. If the File Server for Macintosh still fails to start, contact technical support.

The File Server for Macintosh service failed to start. Unable to setup the server to accept Remote Procedure Calls.

[Services for Macintosh (SFM)]

Contact technical support.

The File Server for Macintosh service is not installed on the server *computer name*.

[Services for Macintosh (SFM)]

Use the Network option in Control Panel to install the service. Choose Add Software and then select Services for Macintosh.

The File Server for Macintosh service was unable to load a resource string(s).

[Services for Macintosh (SFM)]

Services for Macintosh will not start.

Contact technical support.

The file system does not support atomic changes to the lock type.

[Kernel32]

Contact the supplier of the running application.

The file system structures on the specified volume are corrupt; the volume cannot be converted. Run CHKDSK /f to correct this problem.

[Chkdsk-HPFS]

Run the Chkdsk command with the /f switch on the HPFS volume to correct the problem. Then retry the HPFS to NTFS conversion.

The file transfer failed because the transmission was stopped by the receiver.

[Terminal]

In the course of a file transfer, either the sender or the receiver has the option to stop the transfer of the file, and the person to whom you were sending a file has elected to do this. In Terminal, if you are the receiver, you may do this by selecting the Stop option on the Transfers menu.

Contact the receiver.

The file transfer failed because the transmission was stopped by the sender.

[Terminal]

In the course of a file transfer, either the sender or the receiver has the option to stop the transfer of the file, and the person who was sending you a file has elected to do this. In Terminal, if you are the sender, you may do this by selecting the Stop option on the Transfers menu.

Contact the sender.

The File Transfer Protocol relies on the ability to pass user passwords over the network without data encryption. A user with physical access to the network may be able to examine users' passwords during FTP validation.

[Control Panel]

Choose Yes to continue installing the FTP Server service, or No to cancel installation.

The File Transfer Protocol relies on the ability to pass user passwords over the network without data encryption. A user with physical access to the network may be able to examine users' passwords during FTP validation. Are you sure you want to continue?

[TCP/IP]

Choose Yes to continue installing the FTP Server service, or No to cancel installation.

The File Type description cannot be empty. Please type in a new File Type.

[File Manager]

You tried to create a new file type without entering anything in the File Type box at the top of the dialog.

Type a descriptive name in the File Type box. This name will appear in the Associate With box of the Associate dialog box.

The File Type must have a command for at least one of its Actions. Please type in an application in the command field.

[File Manager]

You tried to create a new file type without specify the command to be run when files assigned to this file type are opened.

Type in a command, or an executable file including the relative path, or choose Browse to view and select from the available executables.

The filename is invalid. Make sure the filename is not longer than 8 characters, followed by a period and an extension.

The filename can include any combination of letters and numbers, and any of the following characters:. " / \ [ ] ; : | = , ? * + < >

Try again, specifying a valid filename.

The filename or extension is too long.

[Kernel32]

The length of the filename or the extension is greater than the maximum length allowed.

Correct the filename or extension and then retry the command.

The filename, directory name, or volume label syntax is incorrect.

[Kernel32]

The system does not accept the keyboard combination Alt+0 through Alt+32 or the following characters: \\ \\ / [ ] : | < > + ; = . ? "

Correct the file name or volume label and try the command again.

The files do not fit to the boot-block configuration file *filename*. Change the BASE and ORG definitions or the order of the files.

[Network] Net Message ID: 3254

This message should occur only on a down-level computer. Any action to correct the problem should be performed on that computer. The files in the listed boot-block definition file do not fit in the boot block.

Change the order of the files or the value of BASE or ORG.

The first NTFS boot sector is unwriteable.

[NTFS]

Backup all files and reformat or replace the volume.

The flag passed is not correct.

[Kernel32]

The flag passed to the JOIN command or to the DosFlagProcess function is not correct.

Correct the flags. You may have to contact the supplier of the running application.

The floppy cannot be written to because it is write-protected.

[Repair Disk]

Take the disk out of the drive, remove the write-protection from the disk, replace the disk, and try again.

The floppy disk controller reported an error that is not recognized by the floppy disk driver.

[Kernel32]

Retry the operation, using a different floppy disk or a floppy disk with a different density. If this message reappears, contact the hardware supplier or the floppy disk driver software supplier.

The floppy disk controller returned inconsistent results in its registers.

[Kernel32]

This is either a hardware problem or a device driver problem. Check the hardware first. If you still get this message, contact the supplier of the floppy disk driver software and report your computer configuration.

The following boot-start or system-start driver(s) failed to load: *name*

[Netevent]

The drivers in the list failed to start.

Ask your system administrator to verify that the drivers in the list are not critical to your system's operation.

The following error occurred when trying to delete group *group***:***text.*

[User Manager]

You have attempted to delete one of User Manager's built-in groups. This action is not permitted.

The following error occurred when trying to delete user *user name***:***text.*

[User Manager]

You have attempted to delete one of User Manager's built-in user accounts. This action is not permitted.

The following error occurred when trying to delete user *user name* **:** *text* **Do you wish to continue with the next user?**

[User Manager]

The indicated error prevented User Manager from deleting this account.

Choose Yes to continue deleting user accounts or No to stop deleting them. Look up the indicated error message to find out what you need to do before trying to delete this account again.

The following error occurred accessing the properties of the group *group***:***text.* **The group properties cannot be edited or viewed at this time.**

[User Manager]

You are logged on to an account that does not have permission to view the properties of the selected group, and you have attempted to view these properties.

Contact your system administrator. If you are the system administrator, log off of the workstation, then log on again under your administrative account.

The following error occurred accessing the properties of the local group *group*:*text*. **The local group properties cannot be edited or viewed at this time.**

[User Manager]

You are logged on to an account that does not have permission to view the properties of the selected group, and you have attempted to view these properties.

Contact your system administrator. If you are the system administrator, log off of the workstation, then log on again under your administrative account.

The following error occurred accessing the properties of the user *user name*:*text*. **The user properties cannot be edited or viewed at this time.**

[User Manager]

You are logged on to an account that does not have permission to view the properties of the selected user account, and you have attempted to view these properties.

Contact your system administrator. If you are the system administrator, log off of the workstation, log on again under your administrative account, then try again.

The following error occurred adding the user *user name* **to the requested local groups:** *text*

[User Manager]

This user account has not been added to the local groups.

Look up the indicated error message to find out what you need to do before trying to add this account to the local groups again.

The following error occurred applying security information to *name* **:** *text* **Do you wish to continue?**

[Security]

The security information was not set on the specified file or directory.

An error message should have been displayed which gives more information about the error. You might also check the Event Log in Event Viewer for related information.

The following error occurred attempting to read the Directory *name* **:** *text* **Do you wish to continue?**

[Security]

An error occurred while writing security information to files and/or subdirectories. You may not have permission to read the named directory or there might be a problem on the disk.

If the error indicated you cannot read the directory, grant yourself read permission and retry the operation. To ignore the error and continue without applying the security information to some of the directories, press 'Yes'.

The following error occurred changing the properties of the group *group* **:** *text*

[User Manager]

The properties have not been changed.

Look up the indicated error message to find out what you need to do before trying to change the properties of this global group again

The following error occurred changing the properties of the local group *group* **:** *text*

[User Manager]

The properties have not been changed.

Look up the indicated error message to find out what you need to do before trying to delete this local group again,

The following error occurred changing the properties of the user *user name* **:** *text*

[User Manager]

The properties have not been changed.

Look up the indicated error message to find out what you need to do before trying to change the properties for this user again.

The following error occurred changing the properties of the user *user name* **:** *text* **Do you wish to continue with the next user?**

[User Manager]

The properties have not been changed.

Choose Yes to continue or No to stop changing properties for these user accounts. Look up the indicated error message to find out what you need to do before trying to change the properties of this user account again.

The following error occurred creating the group *name* **:** *text*

[User Manager]

The global group has not been created.

Look up the indicated error message to find out what you need to do before trying to create this global group again.

The following error occurred creating the local group *group* **:** *text*

[User Manager]

The local group has not been created, or some users were not added to the group.

Look up the indicated error message to find out what you need to do before trying to perform this operation again.

The following error occurred creating the user *user name* **:** *text*

[User Manager]

The user account has not been created.

Look up the indicated error message to find out what you need to do before trying to create this account again.

The following error occurred while preparing to create a new group: *text*

[User Manager]

The group has not been created.

Look up the indicated error message to find out what you need to do before trying to create this group again.

The following error occurred while preparing to create a new local group: *text*

[User Manager]

The local group has not been created.

Look up the indicated error message to find out what you need to do before trying to create this local group again.

The following error occurred while preparing to create a new user: *text*

[User Manager]

The user account has not been created.

Look up the indicated error message to find out what you need to do before trying to create this user account again.

The following error was returned by the Windows NT System: *code***.**

[Services for Macintosh (SFM)]

Contact technical support.

The following value in the Setup Information File is corrupt or missing: Value *number* **!u! on line** *name* **!u! in section [** *name* **]Setup cannot continue. Press F3 to exit.**

[Setup]

Contact the supplier for another copy of the installation media.

The following value in the Setup Information File is corrupt or missing: Value *number* **on the line in section [** *name* **]with key "***name***."Setup cannot continue. Press F3 to exit.**

[Setup]

Contact the supplier for another copy of the installation media.

The format of the specified computer name is invalid.

[Kernel32]

An application requested a network operation, but the format of the computer name included in the request was unrecognizable to Windows NT.

If you have a user interface in the application, reenter the computer name. A computer name can have up to 15 characters and must not include any spaces. Precede computer names with two backslashes, as in \\\\<computer name>.

The format of the specified domain name is invalid.

[Kernel32]

An application requested a network operation, but the format of the domain name included in the request was unrecognizable to Windows NT.

If you have a user interface in the application, reenter the domain name. A domain name can have up to 15 characters and cannot include spaces.

The format of the specified event name is invalid.

[Kernel32]

Check the format of the event name.

The format of the specified group name is invalid.

[Kernel32]

An application requested a network operation, but the format of the group name included in the request was unrecognizable to Windows NT.

Check the syntax of the group name. If you have a user interface in the application, reenter the group name. A group name can have up to 20 characters. You may also use the Windows NT User Manager application to edit group names.

The format of the specified message destination is invalid.

[Kernel32]

Find out the valid format of the destination name and retry.

The format of the specified message name is invalid.

[Kernel32]

Check the format of the message name.

The format of the specified network name is invalid.

[Kernel32]

An application requested a network operation, but the format of the network name included in the request was unrecognizable to Windows NT.

If you have a user interface in the application, reenter the network name. A network name can have up to 15 characters and cannot include spaces.

The format of the specified password is invalid.

[Kernel32]

An application attempted to connect a local device to a network resource, but the format of the password included in the request was unrecognizable to Windows NT.

If you have a user interface, retry the request with a different password. Otherwise, contact the supplier of the running application.

The format of the specified service name is invalid.

[Kernel32]

Check the format of the service name.

The format of the specified share name is invalid.

[Kernel32]

Check the format of the share name.

The format of this file is not supported.

[Paintbrush]

In some instances, Windows 3.1 or Windows NT does not support applications developed for earlier versions of Windows. For example, Windows NT does not support the .CPL format. When earlier applications are supported, text or format conversion is sometimes necessary.

If a format is unsupported, there is no user action.

The format of time should be hh:mm:ss. Check value of "SpTime" in the registry.

[WINS Service]

You entered the time in a format the application does not recognize.

Re-enter the time setting, and check carefully for a mistyped value. The administrator might want to check the registry to make sure the value of SpTime specifies this format. However, it is unlikely that this value has changed.

The forwarded message alias could not be found on the network.

[Network] Net Message ID: 2286

This message should occur only on a down-level computer. Any action to correct the problem should be performed on that computer. This alias no longer exists on the workstation that was receiving the alias's forwarded messages. The alias may have been deleted at that workstation, or the workstation may have been restarted.

Restart the workstation or add the alias to the workstation again.

The free space you have chosen is not large enough to contain a mirror of the partition you have chosen.

[Disk Administrator]

When you choose the mirroring option, the free space that you choose to mirror a partition must be equal to or larger than the partition that it is mirroring. You have chosen a free space that is smaller than the partition that it is intended to mirror.

Choose OK, then choose a free space that is equal to or larger than the partition that you want it to mirror, then try again.

The free space you have chosen is not large enough to contain an element in the stripe set you have chosen for regeneration.

[Disk Administrator]

When you choose to regenerate a stripe set, you must have enough free space available to contain all of the elements of the stripe set.

Choose a section of free space large enough to contain the elements in the stripe set.

The FT set containing *name* cannot be used.

[Disk Administrator]

One or more disks in this set have been lost.

Make sure the drives are on-line and are functioning properly. Check for Eventlog entries close to this one that indicate a hardware problem with one or both drives.

The FTP Server service has not been started. Would you like to start the FTP Server service?

[FTP Server]

You cannot administer the FTP Server service unless the service is started.

Choose Yes to start the service. Or choose No.

The FTP service is unavailable on *computer name*.

[FTP Server]

The indicated computer is not running the FTP Server service, or the FTP Server service is not installed..

Try again later. If you still get this message, ask the network administrator to make sure the FTP Server service is running on that computer.

The FTP service is unavailable.

[FTP Server]

The local computer is not running the FTP Server service, or the service is not responding. It might be stopped or paused. In rare instances it might be in a confused state.

Try again later. If you still get this message, ask the network administrator to make sure the FTP Server service is running.

The full domain list can not be generated at this time. Some domains may be missing from the list.

[Workstation-Logon]

Currently, you can only see the list of domains that trusts your own.

Choose OK to view the available list. Or wait and try again.

The full synchronization replication of the *name* database from the primary domain controller *computer name* failed with the following error: *text*

[Network] Net Message ID: 5718

The specified server is down or was restarted.

Ask your network administrator to check the specified server.

The full synchronization request from the server *computer name* failed with the following error: *text*

[Network] Net Message ID: 5714

The specified server is down or was restarted.

Verify that the specified server is running.

The given IP address already exists in the list box.

[WINS Service]

The IP address you entered as a new address already exists, and is listed in the list box.

No action is needed. If you want, specify a different address as the new address.

The given IP address is invalid

[DHCP]

The IP address must be in dotted decimal notation, such as 102.54.94.97 or 104.55.32.12.

Try again, using a valid IP address.

The global filename characters, * or ?, are entered incorrectly or too many global filename characters are specified.

[Kernel32]

If you can do it at the user interface, reenter the global filename characters. Otherwise, contact the supplier of the running application.

The group already exists.

[Network] Net Message ID: 2223

You tried to create a group with a group name that already exists.

Use a different group name for the new group. To display a list of group names established on the server, type NET GROUP if you are running the Windows NT Advanced Server. If you are running Windows NT, type NET GROUP /domain. Your Windows NT workstation must be a member of a domain that is running Windows NT Advanced Server. Otherwise, you will see a message that tells you that NET GROUP is a Windows NT Advanced Server command only.

The group may not be disabled.

[Kernel32]

Built-in system groups cannot be deleted. The group you have selected to be deleted is a system group.

The group name could not be found.

[Network] Net Message ID: 2220

You specified an unknown group name.

Check the spelling of the group name. To display a list of the groups in the security database, type NET GROUP if you are running the Windows NT Advanced Server. If you are running Windows NT, type NET GROUP /domain. Your Windows NT workstation must be a member of a domain that is running Windows NT Advanced Server. Otherwise, you will see a message that tells you that NET GROUP is a Windows NT Advanced Server command only.

The group SERVERS is not present in the local security database.

[Network]

This message should occur only on a down-level computer. Any action to correct the problem should be performed on that computer.

The hardware resources for *name* are already in use by another device.

An interrupt or port address that the indicated hardware needs to use is already in use by another device (probably by the network).

Use Port from the Control Panel to assign a different interrupt or port address to this device. Use Event Viewer to look for other messages that might provide more information about the problem.

The Help file is corrupted.

[Network] Net Message ID: 3712

Help file, NET.HLP, is damaged. The file is usually in your system directory.

Contact your network administrator. Your administrator should copy the Help file from the Windows NT distribution disks to your computer. If the problem persists, contact technical support.

The Help file is empty.

[Network] Net Message ID: 3711

Help file, NET.HLP, is damaged. The file is usually in your system directory.

Contact your network administrator. Your administrator should copy the Help file from the Windows NT distribution disks to your computer. If the problem persists, contact technical support.

The helper thread was unable to obtain a list of trusted domains.

[Services for Macintosh (SFM)]

This message should be followed by another message that indicates that Services for Macintosh could not be started.

Check the Event Log in Event Viewer for errors related to the File Server for Macintosh not starting. Be sure to make a note of this information to relay it to technical support.

The helper thread was unable to open Local Security Authority.

[Services for Macintosh (SFM)]

Check the Event Log in Event Viewer for related errors Be sure to make a note of this information to relay it to technical support.

The helper thread was unable to open the AppleTalk Filing Protocol file system driver.

[Services for Macintosh (SFM)]

Use File Manager to verify that the Srvsys.drv file is located in the <systemroot>\system32 directory. If the file is not there, remove and reinstall Services for Macintosh. Otherwise, contact technical support.

The helper thread was unable to send the list of trusted domains to the AppleTalk Filing Protocol file system driver.

[Services for Macintosh (SFM)]

Contact technical support.

The Home Directory specified is invalid.

[Control Panel]

The Home Directory must exist on this computer.

Make sure you have typed the directory path correctly, and that the directory exists.

The Home Directory specified is invalid.

[TCP/IP]

The Home Directory must exist on this computer.

Make sure you have typed the directory path correctly, and that the directory exists.

The Home Directory, *name* **, for** *user name* **could not be created. The User Account has been updated. You must create the Home Directory manually.**

[User Manager]

You have designated in the User Environment Profile option a Home Directory that exists on a remote computer which is either not running or to which you don't have access.

If you are sure that you have access to the computer, wait and try again. If you do not have access to this computer, log on under a user account that has access to the remote computer. Or consult your system administrator.

The hook procedure is not installed.

[Kernel32]

An application, as part of its user interface, tried to use a procedure to monitor system events which it had not installed.

Contact the supplier of the running application.

The HPFS file system does not support removable media.

[Format]

You specified the HPFS for a floppy disk. You cannot format a floppy disk as an HPFS disk.

The I/O bus was reset.

[Kernel32]

Check the cabling to your peripheral devices and retry the operation. If this message reappears, run hardware diagnostics. If the diagnostics do not detect a problem, contact the supplier of the running application.

The I/O operation has been aborted because of either a thread exit or an application request.

[Kernel32]

Contact the supplier of the running application.

The I/O ports for adapter *name* could not be translated to something the memory management system could understand.

[Digi]

The ports could not be mapped to the input/output registers.

Check the configuration of the adapter. You might want to consult the documentation that accompanied the adapter. If the problem persists, contact Digi technical support.

The identifier *name* already exists. Type a unique name in the Identifier box.

[Registry Editor]

You can have only one instance of each device type in the Registry.

Enter a name for a device type that is not already in use on this computer.

The import path you typed is invalid.

[Server Manager]

The path you typed is not a valid pathname. It may have been mistyped.

Retype the path name. The pathname must use the following format, with no spaces:\\computername\sharename\subdirectory. You can specify many subdirectories or none, but each subdirectory name must be preceded with a backslash.

The INF *filename* has a invalid file description line in section [*name*].

[Setup]

While interpreting a .INF file, Setup encountered a file description line it could not interpret.

Select Retry to retry the operation. If you still get this message, select Exit Setup. Restore all the .INF files from the distribution medium (you will have to decompress the files). Then rerun the Setup operation from the beginning. If you get this message again, contact your technical support group.

The INF *filename* has a invalid file description line in section [*name*].

[Repair Disk]

While interpreting a .INF file, Setup encountered a file description line it could not interpret.

Select Retry to retry the operation. If you still get this message, select Exit Setup. Restore all the .INF files from the distribution medium (you will have to decompress the files). Then rerun the Setup operation from the beginning. If you get this message again, contact your technical support group.

The INF *filename* is missing a referenced file description line in section [*name*].Check for missing lines.

[Repair Disk]

While interpreting a .INF file, Setup could not find a file that is referred to earlier in the .INF file.

Select Retry to retry the operation. If you still get this message, select Exit Setup. Restore all the .INF files from the distribution medium (you will have to decompress the files). Then rerun the Setup operation from the beginning. If you get this message again, contact your technical support group.

The INF *filename* is missing the referenced file description section [*name*].Check for missing lines.

[Setup]

Select the Retry button. If you get the same message, you will have to exit Setup. Try to replace the .INF file with the .INF file from the distribution medium (you will have to decompress the file). Then retry the Setup operation from the beginning. If you still get this message, contact your technical support group.

The INF *filename* is missing the referenced file description section [*name*].Check for missing lines.

[Repair Disk]

Select the Retry button. If you get the same message, you will have to exit Setup. Try to replace the .INF file with the .INF file from the distribution medium (you will have to decompress the file). Then retry the Setup operation from the beginning. If you still get this message, contact your technical support group.

The INF file contains an invalid read-syms script command.

[Setup]

Setup was unable to interpret a line in the .INF file.

Select Retry to retry the operation. If you still get this message, select Exit Setup. Restore all the .INF files from the distribution medium (you will have to decompress the files). Then rerun the Setup operation from the beginning. If you get this message again, contact your technical support group.

The INF file contains an invalid read-syms script command.

[Repair Disk]

Setup was unable to interpret a line in the .INF file.

Select Retry to retry the operation. If you still get this message, select Exit Setup. Restore all the .INF files from the distribution medium (you will have to decompress the files). Then rerun the Setup operation from the beginning. If you get this message again, contact your technical support group.

The information in the list of servers may be incorrect.

[Network] Net Message ID: 2319

This message should occur only on a down-level computer. Any action to correct the problem should be performed on that computer. A software error occurred.

Contact technical support.

The inherited access control list (ACL) or access control entry (ACE)could not be built.

[Kernel32]

The inheritance information on a directory is invalid.

You, or an administrator, should replace the directory protection with new permissions and then try to create the file again.

The Initial Password and Confirm Password fields do not match

[Control Panel]

When you select a password, you must always type the password twice to confirm it. You did this, and the two passwords you typed to not match.

Type both passwords again.

The interface is unknown.

[Kernel32]

In a distributed (RPC) application, servers present objects known as interfaces to clients. These interfaces have unique identifiers. The distributed application tried to use an interface that does not exist.

Contact the supplier of the running distributed application.

The interface was not found.

[Kernel32]

In a distributed (RPC) application, an attempt was made to remove an RPC interface from an entry in the name-service database, but the specified interface did not meet the conditions for removal.

Contact the supplier of the running distributed application.

The IPX protocol cannot be used for dial-out on more than one port at a time.

[Remote Access Service]

Only one port can be used to dial out using the IPX protocol.

The IPX protocol cannot dial-in on the port because the IPX router is not installed.

[Remote Access Service]

This indicates an inconsistency in the Remote Access IPX configuration.

Restart your computer to ensure all configuration changes have taken effect.

The IPX protocol cannot dial-out on the port because the machine is an IPX router.

[Remote Access Service]

This is a beta limitation that will be removed for final release.

The JET Database call returned the following Error : ***text*.**

[DHCP]

The cause of the problem is indicated by the error at the end of the message. The DHCP database might be corrupt.

Look up the indicated error and take appropriate action. If the database is corrupt, restore a previous version of the DHCP database, as described in your Windows NT Server documentation.

The JET Database call returned the following Warning : ***text*.**

[DHCP]

This message is informational only.

If you encounter other problems, look up the indicated error and take appropriate action.

The journal hook procedure is already installed.

[Kernel32]

An application, as part of its user interface, has tried to install a procedure to record and play back system events, but it had already installed that type of procedure.

Contact the supplier of the running application.

The key cannot be restored; either you have insufficient privilege, or the key or one of its subkeys is in use by another process.

[Registry Editor]

Ask your network administrator to give you the appropriate permissions and try again.

The key currently selected cannot be accessed.

[Registry Editor]

This key cannot be accessed. It has probably been deleted by another process since the Registry Editor window was last updated.

Choose Refresh All or Refresh Active from the View menu to refresh the screen. Or enable Auto Refresh (in the Options menu).If the problem persists, the registry might be corrupt.

The key currently selected is volatile. Registry Editor cannot create a non-volatile subkey on a volatile key.

[Registry Editor]

This key is created during system startup, and is deleted when the computer is turned off. (Other, non-volatile, keys are kept in a file between startups). Since this entire key is volatile, it cannot keep non-volatile information.

You might want to add the subkey to a non-volatile key.

The key name specified is not valid. A key name cannot contain \\.

[Registry Editor]

A key name cannot contain any backslashes.

Enter a key name that does not have the backslash character (\).

The label given is inappropriate for this volume.

[Disk Administrator]

FAT limits the length of the label and the characters used in the label.

Verify that the volume label you specified is compatible with FAT volumes.

The LAN adapter number is invalid.

[Network] Net Message ID: 2400

This message should occur only on a down-level computer. Any action to correct the problem should be performed on that computer. The LAN adapter number in the configuration file is incorrect.

A NET<n> entry in the [networks] section of the computer's configuration file needs to be corrected. See your network administrator if you need assistance.

The LANA number of each protocol must be unique.

[Control Panel]

Select NetBIOS interface in the Network option of Control Panel to specify unique LANA numbers for each protocol.

The LANMAN root directory is unavailable.

[Network] Net Message ID: 3803

This message should occur only on a down-level computer. Any action to correct the problem should be performed on that computer. The root directory for LAN Manager is unavailable.

Be sure the workstation is running and the directory containing the LAN Manager software is accessible.

The last file was not restored

[Repair Disk]

There was not enough room on the destination disk for the file, or the file was corrupted.

Use the Restore command to restore the file separately on another disk.

The last remaining administration account cannot be disabled or deleted.

[Kernel32]

You cannot delete or disable this account because it is the last locally-defined account that has administrative capabilities.

The length of a secret exceeds the maximum length allowed.

[Kernel32]

A secret is an encrypted piece of information, such as a password or user name.

Contact the supplier of the running application.

The limit of 64 entries per resource was exceeded.

[Network] Net Message ID: 2230

This message should occur only on a down-level computer. Any action to correct the problem should be performed on that computer. Each resource can have no more than 64 access records defined.

Put the users into groups and specify permissions for the groups rather than for each user.

The line is busy.

[Remote Access Service]

Redial the number. To automate redialing, set the Redial Settings feature on the Phone Book's Options menu. For more information, see "Redialing" in the Remote Access Service online Help.

The linked information cannot be updated. Either delete the link and recreate it or use the Change Link button in the Link dialog box to redefine the source document for the link.

[Cardfile]

The link between the object and the source file is broken, possibly because the name of the source document has been changed. Consequently, the link cannot be updated. You need either to delete then recreate the link or to redefine the source document for the link.

(1) If you have changed the name of the source document that contains the linked objects, you must go to the destination document, then change the name of the document that the object is linked to so that the link will work properly again. (2) If you need to delete the link (in order to recreate it), select the Picture option from the Edit menu, then select the object. From the Edit menu choose Cut. Now return to the actual linked object (the Paintbrush file, for example) and create the links again.

The list of RPC servers available for the binding of auto handle has been exhausted.

[Kernel32]

Contact the supplier of the running distributed application.

The list box identifier was not found.

[Kernel32]

An application, as part of its user interface, has requested an operation on a list box control that does not exist in the user interface.

Contact the supplier of the running application.

The LM386 server cannot be started because CACHE.EXE is not running.

[Network] Net Message ID: 3091

This message should occur only on a down-level computer. Any action to correct the problem should be performed on that computer. The CACHE.EXE program must be running before the LAN Manager 386 server can be started.

Run CACHE.EXE by typing CACHE. You can also add a RUN line to the configuration file to have CACHE.EXE start automatically whenever the computer starts.

The local device name is already in use.

[Kernel32]

You specified a resource with a local device name that is already being used.

Try the request again, using a different device name. Your choices are A: through Z: for directory device names, LPT1: through LPT9: for printer device names, and COM1: through COM9: for communications device names.

The local policy of this system does not permit you to logon interactively.

[Workstation-Logon]

You do not have the right to log on to this system locally, but you may have remote logon rights.

Try to log on to this system from a remote computer.

The local security authority database contains an internal inconsistency.

[Kernel32]

An error occurred from an operation on the local security policy database.

Restart the system. If that does not correct the problem, restore your last backup of the local security policy database.

The local WINS server received a request from a remote WINS server that is not of the same version. Because the WINS servers are not compatible, the connection was terminated. The version number of the remote WINS server is given below.

[WINS Service]

WINS servers share address database information. However, the servers sharing information must run the same version of WINS (the number to the left of the decimal must be the same, but the number to the right can vary). A server running a different version of WINS tried to communicate with the local WINS server.

Make sure that all of the servers that will be sharing address database information are using the same

The log file does not contain the requested record number.

[Network] Net Message ID: 2440

This message should occur only on a down-level computer. Any action to correct the problem should be performed on that computer. A software error occurred.

Contact technical support.

The log file has been corrupted.

[Network] Net Message ID: 3717

This message should occur only on a down-level computer. Any action to correct the problem should be performed on that computer. The log file you are using is damaged.

If you will need to refer to this log file in the future, copy it to another filename, and then clear it so that you can start another one.

The log size specified for the *name* log(s) is not a 64K increment. The size of the log(s) will be rounded upward to the next 64K increment.

[Event Viewer]

In the Event Log Settings dialog box, you manually changed the Maximum Log Size to a number that is not a 64K increment. Event Viewer rounds such numbers up to the nearest 64K increment.

Choose OK.

The logical drive created will not be accessible from other operating systems such as MS-DOS because the extended partition start or end cylinder value is too large. Do you want to create the logical drive anyway?

[Disk Administrator]

Some MS-DOS versions do not support disk drives with more than 1023 cylinders.

The logon processor did not add the message alias.

[Network] Net Message ID: 2204

This message should occur only on a down-level computer. Any action to correct the problem should be performed on that computer. Your user name was not added as a new message alias for one of the following reasons: the Messenger service is not started on your workstation; your user name and your workstation's computer name are the same, and your workstation's computer name is already a message alias; or your user name is in use as a message alias on another computer on the network. In this case, you cannot receive messages at the local workstation using this name.

Start the Messenger service on your workstation if it is not already started. Then use the Net Name command to add your user name as a message alias. If your user name is being used as a message alias on another computer, delete the alias on that computer. Then use the Net Name command to add your user name as a message alias on this computer.

The logon script path you typed is invalid.

[Server Manager]

The path you typed is not a valid pathname. It may have been mistyped.

Retype the path name. The pathname must use the following format, with no spaces:\\computername\sharename\subdirectory. You can specify many subdirectories or none, but each subdirectory name must be preceded with a backslash.

The logon server could not be found.

[Network] Net Message ID: 2215

This message should occur only on a down-level computer. Any action to correct the problem should be performed on that computer. No domain controller is responding to your command.

See your network administrator.

The logon server could not validate the logon.

[Network] Net Message ID: 2217

This message should occur only on a down-level computer. Any action to correct the problem should be performed on that computer. Your logon server is running an earlier version of LAN Manager.

No action is needed.

The logon server was not specified. Your computer will be logged on as STANDALONE.

[Network] Net Message ID: 2214

This message should occur only on a down-level computer. Any action to correct the problem should be performed on that computer. The logon was not validated by a logon server.

No action is needed.

The logon session ID is already in use.

[Kernel32]

Contact the supplier of the running application.

The logon session is not in a state that is consistent with the requested operation.

[Kernel32]

Contact the supplier of the running application.

The machine account for this computer either does not exist or is inaccessible.

[Control Panel]

There is no account for your computer on this domain, or the account information is not available.

Ask your network administrator to create an account for you.

The machine configuration has changed and should be restarted before this operation is attempted. Continue anyway?

[Control Panel]

Changes have been made to the configuration of this computer, but the changes will not take effect until the computer is restarted. This could cause problems with the operation you are trying to perform, because of differences between the configuration settings and the actual current configuration.

The safest course is to choose No, close open files and running applications, restart the computer, and then try the operation again. However, you can choose yes and continue the current operation if you want to.

The Macintosh-Accessible volume was created successfully, but an account name of an Owner or Group (or both) is invalid.

[Services for Macintosh (SFM)]

The owner or group name you specified may have been deleted.

Select Permissions from the MacFile menu in File Manager to change the owner or group of the Macintosh-accessible volume.

The MacPrint Service was unable to access its registry key. (The data is the Win32 error code.)

[Services for Macintosh (SFM)]

The Registry key might have been deleted or access to it has been limited.

Verify that the key is in the Registry. The path is \\HKEY_LOCAL_MACHINE\System\CurrentControlSet\Services\MacPrint. Also, contact your system administrator.

The manager type is unknown.

[Kernel32]

In a distributed (RPC) application, a manager type can be associated with a server interface. This message can occur when the server tries to delete or query an interface and specifies the wrong manager type.

Contact the supplier of the running application.

The Margin values are not correct. Either they are not numeric characters or they don't fit the dimensions of the page. Try either entering a number or decreasing the margins.

[Notepad]

Using the Page Setup option in the File menu, you designated a margin range that exceeds the height or width of the page, that is not a positive number, or that is not a numeric character.

Specify valid margins.

The master browser has received a server announcement from the computer *computer name* **that believes that it is the master browser for the domain on transport** *name*.**The master browser is stopping or an election is being forced.**

[Netevent]

Only one computer in a domain can be running as the master browser.

Contact your network administrator.

The maximum directory IDs have been reached on volume "*name* **"./n Copy contents to a newly created Macintosh-Accessible volume.**

[Services for Macintosh (SFM)]

Copy the contents to a newly created Macintosh-accessible volume.

The maximum number of added message aliases has been exceeded.

[Network] Net Message ID: 2277

The maximum number of message aliases on each computer is limited by the system hardware. You have reached this limit. This limit also affects the number of other domains you can specify with the Othdomains option of the Net Config Workstation command.

To find the limit for your system, see your hardware documentation or ask your administrator. To display a list of current message aliases, type NET NAME. To delete a message alias to make room for a new message alias or another domain specified by the Othdomains option, type NET NAME <alias>/DELETE.

The maximum number of calls is too small.

[Kernel32]

In a distributed (RPC) application, a server specified the maximum number of concurrent calls from clients that it will listen for, and that number is too small. For example, the server might have specified the number 0.

Contact the supplier of the running distributed application.

The maximum number of connections is invalid

[Control Panel]

Maximum Connections can be set to any value up to 50.

Specify a valid number of connections.

The maximum number of connections is invalid

[TCP/IP]

Maximum Connections can be set to any value up to 50.

Specify a valid number of connections.

The maximum number of secrets that may be stored in a single system has been exceeded.

[Kernel32]

A secret is an encrypted piece of information, such as a password or user name.

Contact the supplier of the running application.

The maximum timeout setting is invalid

[Control Panel]

Idle Timeout can be set to any value up to 60. If you set the Idle Timeout to 0 (zero), users are never automatically disconnected.

Specify a number from 0 to 60.

The maximum timeout setting is invalid

[TCP/IP]

Idle Timeout can be set to any value up to 60. If you set the Idle Timeout to 0 (zero), users are never automatically disconnected.

Specify a number from 0 to 60.

The media .INI file refers to an unknown device name.

[Remote Access Service]

One of the Remote Access configuration files probably contains invalid information.

The easiest way to resolve this problem is to reinstall Remote Access. Use the Network option in Control Panel to remove and reinstall RAS. If you are using a modem that is not supported by Remote Access, switch to a supported modem, or see "Modem Script File" in the Remote Access Service online Help for information about modifying the modem script file for your modem. The Remote Access script files (PAD.INF, MODEM.INF, and SWITCH.INF) are in the \SYSTEM32\RAS subdirectory of your Windows NT directory.

The media .INI file refers to an unknown device type.

[Remote Access Service]

One of the Remote Access configuration files probably contains invalid information.

The easiest way to resolve this problem is to reinstall Remote Access. Use the Network option in Control Panel to remove and reinstall RAS. If you are using a modem that is not supported by Remote Access, switch to a supported modem, or see "Modem Script File" in the Remote Access Service online Help for information about modifying the modem script file for your modem. The Remote Access script files (PAD.INF, MODEM.INF, and SWITCH.INF) are in the \SYSTEM32\RAS subdirectory of your Windows NT directory.

The media is write protected.

[Kernel32]

No information can be changed or added to a write-protected drive.

If this is a removable media drive, make sure that the proper disk is being used, or remove the write-protection. Then retry the command.

The media selected cannot support the file system selected.

[Disk Administrator]

HPFS does not support removable drives.

Choose a different file system for this media.

The memory range for adapter *name* could not be translated to something the memory management system could understand.

[Digi]

The adapter's memory range could not be mapped.

Verify that the specified memory address range is correct. If the problem persists, contact Digi technical support.

The memory resources needed by NTVDM could not be allocated.

[Virtual DOS Machine (VDM)]

The virtual DOS machine could not allocate the required amount of memory.

Close down some running applications and then continue.

The message alias could not be found on the network.

[Network]

The message could not be delivered because the addressee is not logged on, or is not using the name you sent the message to as a computer name or message alias.

No action is needed.

The message alias is currently in use. Try again later.

[Network]

The computer to which you tried to send a message was receiving another message. A computer can receive only one message at a time.

Send the message again later.

The message alias table on the remote station is full.

[Network] Net Message ID: 2287

This message should occur only on a down-level computer. Any action to correct the problem should be performed on that computer. The workstation to which you are trying to forward the message alias has no room for new aliases.

Ask the user on that workstation if an existing alias can be deleted so yours can be added, or forward your alias to a different workstation.

The message alias was not successfully deleted from all networks.

[Network] Net Message ID: 2299

The message alias could not be deleted from all networks of which this computer is a member. This should cause no problems.

If this error occurs frequently, contact technical support.

The message contains too many characters. Please type a shorter message.

[Services for Macintosh (SFM)]

Messages are limited to 199 characters.

The message has been sent, but the connected workstation has not received it. The workstation is running an unsupported version of System software.

[Services for Macintosh (SFM)]

In order for Services for Macintosh to be able to communicate with the System software, the software needs to be upgraded.

The Message server has stopped due to a lock on the Message server shared data segment.

[Network] Net Message ID: 3141

This message should occur only on a down-level computer. Any action to correct the problem should be performed on that computer. A software error occurred.

Contact technical support.

The message text is empty. Send anyway?

[Remote Access Service]

You pressed send before actually entering any text.

Enter text before pressing Enter or choose Cancel to exit the dialog.

The message was sent but not received.

[Network] Net Message ID: 2282

The remote workstation was unable to receive your message. The Workstation or Messenger service may not be running on that workstation, it may have been receiving another message as yours arrived, or its message buffer may be too small.

Send your message again later. If the error persists, see your network administrator.

The message was sent, but the recipient has paused the Messenger service.

[Network] Net Message ID: 2281

The person receiving your message has paused the Messenger service, so your message could not be received.

Send your message again later. If the error persists, see your network administrator.

The Messenger service failed to start.

[Network] Net Message ID: 2272

This message should occur only on a down-level computer. Any action to correct the problem should be performed on that computer. The initialization sequence of the Messenger service failed, so the service could not start.

Check the error log for error messages related to the Messenger service failing to start. This problem may be caused by the way your workstation or server is configured, or by hardware or software errors.

The Messenger service has not been started.

[Network] Net Message ID: 2284

This message should occur only on a down-level computer. Any action to correct the problem should be performed on that computer. The Messenger service must be running for you to use this command.

To start the Messenger service, type NET START MESSENGER.

The Messenger service is already started.

[Network]

This message should occur only on a down-level computer. Any action to correct the problem should be performed on that computer. You tried to start the Messenger service, but it is already running.

No action is needed. If this error occurs often, contact technical support.

The Method has been changed to COPY.

[Backup]

This is an informational message which appears if a read-only (CD-ROM) drive is being backed up. Backup usually resets the read-only attribute. However, because the attribute cannot be reset, the method has been changed to copy.

The minimum password age for user accounts cannot be greater than the maximum password age.

[Network]

The minimum password age specified must not be greater than the maximum.

Specify a minimum password age that is less than the maximum password age.

The minimum password age must be less than the maximum password age.

[User Manager]

Change the number in the Expires In box, or the number in the Allow Changes In box, or both, so that the number in the first box is larger than the number in the second.

The modem on *number* moved to an unsupported BPS rate.

[Remote Access Service]

The communications port does not support the speed that the modem tried to use.

Put in a different communications port or choose a lower initial baud rate by selecting initial speed Modem Settings. If this does not work, you might need to change your modem.

The module *name* has an invalid module type

[OS/2 Subsystem]

The Windows NT OS/2 subsystem cannot run the application that contains the module named in the message. A dynamic link library file cannot be used as an executable module of an application. And an executable file cannot be used as a dynamic link library.

Reinstall the application and try running it again in the Windows NT environment. If you get this same message, there were probably errors when the application was created. If you can, run these same application files under the OS/2 operating system. If you get a comparable message under OS/2, then contact the supplier of the application. If the application runs under OS/2, contact your technical support group about a problem with the Windows NT OS/2 subsystem.

The mounted file system does not support extended attributes.

[Kernel32]

An attempt was made to save extended attributes using a file system that does not have the ability to save extended attributes.

Save the file or directory using a file system that can save extended attributes.

The Name Challenge Request thread could not be created

[WINS Service]

There is a shortage of some resource, such as memory, on the computer.

Reboot the computer.

The name entered is not properly formatted.

[Control Panel]

The name option in the Network dialog box can consist of no more than 15 characters, and cannot contain any of the following characters: ; : " < > * + = \\ | ? ,. The name that you have selected contains one of these characters.

Remove the character, then try again.

The name has already been shared.

[Network]

The share name is already in use on this server.

Choose a share name that is not currently used on this server. To see a list of resources currently shared on this server, type NET SHARE. Any name that is not on this list can be used as a share name.

The name is already being used. Use another name.

[Clipboard]

You have attempted to assign to a page a name that you have already assigned to another page.

Follow the action specified in the message.

The name is not on the local computer.

[Network] Net Message ID: 2285

You tried to delete a message alias that is not on your computer.

To display a list of aliases on your computer and to check the spelling of the aliases, type NET NAME.

The name limit for the local computer network adapter card was exceeded.

[Kernel32]

The number of names allowed on the network adapter card for the local computer was exceeded.

Perform one of the following actions, then retry the operation: (1) disconnect from any resources that you are not currently using; or (2) reconfigure the network adapter card. If neither of these actions correct the problem, contact your network administrator.

The name of the file after expansion is bigger than WINS can handle. The unexpanded string is *text*.

[WINS Service]

The file was specified with an expansion string. When the expansion string was translated to the value set for it in this computer's environment, the resulting filename was too large for WINS to use.

Move the file to a different directory, such that the full path name is less than 255 characters. Change the name specification to match the new location, and try again.

The name or security ID (SID) of the domain specified is inconsistent with the trust information for that domain.

[Kernel32]

Contact your system administrator or domain administrator to resolve the inconsistency.

The name provided is not a properly formed account name.

[Kernel32]

A client has used a badly formatted account name as part of a security service request. An account name cannot be NULL, and can have no more than 512 characters.

Change the account name, then retry the operation.

The name registration packet that was just received has too many addresses. The maximum number of addresses for a multi-homed client is 25. The number of addresses found in the packet is given below.

[WINS Service]

A client has sent a name registration packet for a multi-homed client. A multi-homed client is one with more than address to register. Each network adapter card can register up to five addresses. After you have set the addresses in the computer's configuration, the request packets are sent automatically. This packet had more addresses than are allowed, and has been discarded. Depending on the software on the client computer, the first 25 addresses may or may not be registered for the client computer.

Check the Event log to find out which client sent the name registration packet. Then reconfigure that client so that it has 25 or fewer addresses.

The name service is unavailable.

[Kernel32]

In a distributed (RPC) application, an operation on the name-service database was attempted, but the database was unavailable.

Contact the supplier of the running distributed application.

The name specified for the user's home directory (*path* **) is not a universal naming convention (UNC) name.**

[Network] Net Message ID: 3917

Your home directory is not a network path that can be connected to. The directory must specify a full path, including the server and share names.

Ask your network administrator to verify that the home directory path specified in the user account is correct.

The name specified is not recognized as an internal or external command, operable program or batch file.

[Command Prompt]

At the command prompt, you have entered characters that do not correspond with any command that Command Prompt recognizes. For example, this message would appear if you misspelled a legitimate Command Prompt command.

Ensure that the command that you have typed is spelled correctly and corresponds to a recognized Command Prompt command.

The name specified is not recognized as an internal or external command, operable program or batch file.

[Command]

At the command prompt, you have entered characters that do not correspond with any command that Command Prompt recognizes. For example, this message would appear if you misspelled a legitimate Command Prompt command.

Ensure that the command that you have typed is spelled correctly and corresponds to a recognized Command Prompt command.

The name syntax is invalid.

[Kernel32]

In a distributed (RPC) application, a client may have specified a name-service database entry name that did not conform to the syntax of such a name.

Contact the supplier of the running distributed application.

The name syntax is not supported.

[Kernel32]

In a distributed (RPC) application, a client may have specified a syntax for a name-service database entry name that is not supported by Windows NT.

Contact the supplier of the running distributed application.

The NBT LMHOSTS file could not be loaded.

[Netevent]

The NBT LMHOSTS file could not be opened.

Ask your system administrator to make sure the LMHOSTS file is present in the Database Path Registry parameter.

The NCBCANCEL command was not valid; the command was not canceled.

[Dynamic Data Exchange]

Contact your application vendor.

The NEAR value must be an integer between 1 and 50,000

[Disk Administrator]

Enter a number between 1 and 50,000.

The NetBIOS name is invalid. It may be too long, or contain one or more invalid characters.

[WINS Service]

The name you specified when adding a WINS server is not a valid NetBIOS computer name.

Make sure that you have the correct computer name. Then try again, making sure to type the name correctly.

The NETBT key could not be opened

[WINS Service]

The NETBT configuration is stored in the Registry, under Current Control Set\Services\NETBT key. The LINKAGE key could not be opened. WINS uses NETBT to send and receive client responses and request.

Ask the administrator to check the Registry and reinstall TCP/IP.

The NETBT key could not be queried

[WINS Service]

This could indicate a problem with the general health of the system.

Do a general checkup of this computer. Call technical support.

The netcard detection DLL is incomplete (export missing)

[Control Panel]

The application could not detect the network adapter card because a portion of the required .DLL file was missing.

Reinstall the new network component. If the problem continues, contact the vendor for a new .DLL file.

The Netlogon service could not add the RPC interface. The service was terminated. The following error occurred: *text*

[Network] Net Message ID: 5702

Other network services that are required to run the RPC interface have failed.

Check the event log with Event Viewer for more details about other service errors.

The Netlogon service could not create server share *name*. **The following error occurred:** *text*

[Network] Net Message ID: 5706

The Server service did not start.

Check the event log with Event Viewer for more details about related errors.

The Netlogon service could not initialize the replication data structures successfully. The service was terminated. The following error occurred: *text*

[Network] Net Message ID: 5700

Your system does not have enough disk space to start the service.

Ask your system administrator to check the amount of disk space on your computer.

The Netlogon service could not read a mailslot message from *name* **due to the following error:** *text*

[Network] Net Message ID: 5703

The Mailslot service did not start because the driver is missing.

Ask your system administrator to verify that the Windows NT installation completed successfully.

The Netlogon service failed to register the service with the service controller. The service was terminated. The following error occurred: *text*

[Network] Net Message ID: 5704

The service controller is not running.

Check the event log with Event Viewer for more details about related errors.

The Netlogon service failed to update the domain trust list. The following error occurred: *text*

[Network] Net Message ID: 5701

Your computer does not have sufficient disk space or the local security database is corrupted.

Contact your system administrator.

The Netlogon service has not been started.

[Network] Net Message ID: 2455

This message should occur only on a down-level computer. Any action to correct the problem should be performed on that computer. The Netlogon service is not running.

Start the Netlogon service at the server, and then type the command again.

The network *name* **ran out of network control blocks (NCBs). You may need to increase NCBs for this network. The following information includes the number of NCBs submitted by the server when this error occurred:**

[Network] Net Message ID: 3126

This message should occur only on a down-level computer. Any action to correct the problem should be performed on that computer. The server found a resource shortage in a network driver when it tried to issue an NCB.

Be sure that the NET<n> entries in the configuration file specify valid NetBIOS device drivers and that these device drivers are in the LANMAN\\DRIVERS directory. Also be sure that the CONFIG.SYS file contains a DEVICE line specifying the absolute paths of the device drivers. You may be able to increase the NCBs for the listed network by changing an option in the network's NET<n> entry in the configuration file. See the installation guide that came with your network adapter for information about those options. If you need assistance, contact your network administrator.

The network address is invalid.

[Kernel32]

The network address contained in a remote procedure call (RPC) is invalid.

Contact the supplier of the running distributed application.

The network BIOS command limit has been reached.

[Kernel32]

The network currently has too many NetBIOS requests waiting to be processed.

Retry the command at a later time. If you continue to have problems, contact your network administrator.

The network BIOS session limit was exceeded.

[Kernel32]

Your computer network adapter card has too many NetBIOS sessions currently active.

Disconnect from any resources that you are not currently using and then retry the command. Contact your network administrator if you continue to have problems.

The network connection could not be found.

[Network]

This network connection does not exist.

To display a list of shared resources to which your computer is connected, type NET USE.

The network disk drive has stopped responding. Backup set aborted.

[Backup]

Use File Manager to verify your network connection.

The network end number for this network is invalid.

[Services for Macintosh (SFM)]

The network end number is outside the range of 1 to 65,279.

Specify a number between 1 and 65,279.

The network is busy.

[Kernel32]

The network is currently busy processing other requests, or is out of resources.

Retry the command at a later time or verify your network configuration to be sure enough network resources are specified.

The network is down

[FTP Server] [TCP/IP]

The TCP/IP utility cannot run because the networking software is not running on the local computer.

Ask your network administrator to get the network software running on your computer.

The network is not installed or enabled. You will not be able to make a remote connection. Do you wish to continue dialing?

[Chat]

You attempted to dial another computer from Chat, and network software is not properly installed on your computer.

Use the Network option in Control Panel to install network software, and then try again.

The network is not present or not started.

[Kernel32]

An application has initiated a network operation, such as redirecting a local device to a network resource or listing all current redirections, but there is no network.

Make sure the network adapter card is in the computer, that the cable connection into the network card is not loose, that the network software is properly installed, and that the network resource is started. You may need to contact your network administrator or technical support group to check these things.

The network is not started.

[Network] Net Message ID: 3107

This message should occur only on a down-level computer. Any action to correct the problem should be performed on that computer. A program or command could not run because LAN Manager is not started or installed.

Check that LAN Manager is installed and that the Workstation service is started. Then type the command again.

The network logon failed.

[Kernel32]

This may be due to a validation authority that cannot be reached.

Contact your system administrator or domain administrator to check why the trust relationship between the two computers has failed.

The network name cannot be found.

[File Manager]

You specified a network drive that does not exist as the source or destination. If the connection has been broken, or could not be made at startup, the icon for that drive is dimmed.

Connect or reconnect to the drive and try again.

The network name cannot be found.

[Kernel32]

The specified network name is not correct. You attempted to access a resource that is not shared by the server you specified.

Make sure the network name you specified is correct, then retry the command. If you continue to have problems, contact your network administrator.

The network options are invalid.

[Kernel32]

A distributed (RPC) application has tried to use the network, but cannot because the options included in its request are invalid.

Contact the supplier of the distributed application. The network options in the string binding may not have been programmed correctly.

The network path was not found.

[Kernel32]

The server that you specified does not exist or has not been started.

Do one of the following: (1) verify that you specified the path name correctly, then retry the command; (2) verify that the server specified is started, then retry the command; or (3) contact your network administrator if you continue to have problems.

The network range specified is in conflict with the network range of another network adapter. You must specify a network range that does not overlap other networks. The following ranges are being used by other adapters in the system. *number*

[Services for Macintosh (SFM)]

To determine which ranges overlap, you might want to make a note of each of the ranges. Select the Network option in Control Panel. Select Services for Macintosh in the Installed Network Software box. Then choose Configure. In the AppleTalk Protocol Configuration dialog box, choose the Advanced button. Specify a range not used by other adapters.

The network ranges specified for one or more adapters overlap with those of the adapter "*name* **".**

[Services for Macintosh (SFM)]

Use the Network option in Control Panel to determine which ranges overlap among the installed adapters. Select Service for Macintosh from the Installed Network Software box and then choose Configure. In the Advanced Configuration dialog box, specify different network adapter ranges to remove the overlap.

The network request is not supported.

[Kernel32]

You attempted an operation that cannot be performed from your computer or that is not supported on the specified remote server.

Verify that you are using the correct server for the command or task that you want to perform, then retry the command. If you continue to have problems, contact your network administrator to ensure that the correct software is installed on your system.

The network request was not accepted.

[Kernel32]

One of the following occurred: (1) the specified server cannot support the network request; (2) the maximum number of users for the alias may have been reached; or (3) the server might have run out of network resources, such as memory, network buffers, or NetBIOS commands necessary to process your request.

Retry the command at a later time. If the same error occurs, contact your network administrator. Network administrators should consult documentation for the server.

The network resource type is not correct.

[Kernel32]

The network directory or device name that you specified is not correct.

Retry the command using the correct network directory or device name. For example, valid directory device names are A: through Z:, valid printer names are LPT1: through LPT9:, and valid communications device names are COM1: through COM9:.

The network software is not installed.

[Network] Net Message ID: 3076

This message should occur only on a down-level computer. Any action to correct the problem should be performed on that computer. An operation was attempted that requires LAN Manager. The workstation will not start because either LAN Manager is not installed, or the MINSES.EXE file required for LAN Manager is not loaded.

Install LAN Manager. If LAN Manager is installed and you are using LAN Manager Enhanced, verify that the following entries are in the configuration file: [network] - netservices=minses; [services] - minses=\\NETPROG\\MINSES.EXE. If LAN Manager is installed and you are using LAN Manager Basic, verify that MINSES.EXE is listed in the [start workstation] section of the configuration file.

The network start number for this network is invalid.

[Services for Macintosh (SFM)]

The network start number is outside the range of 1 to 65,279.

Specify a number between 1 and 65,279.

The new password was not correctly confirmed. Be sure that the confirmation password exactly matches the new password.

[User Manager]

In the User Properties dialog box, you have assigned a password to a user account, but have not confirmed that password.

Select the OK button, return to the User Properties dialog box, and make sure that you have entries in both the Password and Confirm Password options.

The new password was not correctly confirmed. Be sure that the confirmation password matches exactly the new password.

[Server Manager]

In the Service Config dialog box, your new password and your confirmation passwords do not match.

Type the same password in both the New Password and the Confirm Password option boxes.

The NT password is too complex to be converted to a LAN Manager password. The LAN Manager password returned is a NULL string.

[Kernel32]

Contact the supplier of the running application. A general workaround is to change your password or run with no security between applications.

The NTFS file system does not function on floppies.

[NTFS]

Format floppy disks with the FAT file system only. When you are using the Format command to format a floppy disk, do not use the /fs: switch.

The NTVDM CPU has encountered an illegal instruction.

[Virtual DOS Machine (VDM)]

Retry the operation. If you still get this message, try to continue. If you are able to continue, you might want to check the results of the running application. Otherwise, terminate the application, then restart it. If you still get this message, contact your technical support group or the supplier of the running application.

The number of lines and columns cannot be changed in a full screen.

[Mode]

Retry the Mode command with a valid parameter.

The number of specified semaphore events for DosMuxSemWait is not correct.

[Kernel32]

Either no event or too many events were specified in a call to the function that waits for one of several semaphores to clear.

Correct the event count. You may have to contact the supplier of the running application.

The NWSap Registry Key *name* was not present. The NwSapAgent could not start.

[Netevent]

The application could not start because a key is missing from the Registry or is incorrect.

Use the Network applet from the Control Panel to remove and re-install the SAP Agent.

The object can not be deleted because the application needed by the object is busy. You may switch to the object's application and try to correct the problem.

Attempt to free the busy application, then try again to delete the object.

The object could not be deleted because the server application is busy. Wait until the server becomes available. Or try to determine which application is busy, switch to it, and then complete or cancel the action which is causing it to be busy.

[Cardfile]

The server application refers to the application (such as Paintbrush or Sound Recorder) in which the object was created.

Follow the user action specified in the message.

The object universal unique identifier (UUID) has already been registered.

[Kernel32]

A distributed (RPC) application tried to create a unique object identifier, but that identifier already exists.

Contact the supplier of the running distributed application.

The object universal unique identifier (UUID) was not found.

[Kernel32]

In a distributed (RPC) application, a unique object identifier was used that cannot be matched with an existing object. The object has not been registered with the Windows NT RPC run-time.

Contact the supplier of the running distributed application.

The old driver is still being used by Windows NT. You must quit and restart Windows NT before you can add the updated driver.

[Drivers (CP)]

Any time that you add or remove a device driver, you must restart Windows NT before the new device driver actually begins to function.

Exit and restart Windows NT.

The operating system cannot run ***application.***

[Kernel32]

The application program cannot run on this version of the operating system.

Reinstall the application program, then retry the command. If the message occurs again, contact the supplier of the application.

The operating system cannot run this component.

[File Manager]

You attempted to run an executable file that has a bad format. Or you have attempted to load a .DLL file that lacks an ordinal.

No action is needed.

The operating system cannot run this application program.

[Kernel32]

Contact the supplier of the application.

The operating system is not presently configured to run this application.

[Kernel32]

Contact your system administrator to check the configuration of Windows NT on your computer.

The operation failed because a network software error occurred.

[Network]

A software error occurred.

Contact technical support.

The operation is invalid for this device.

[Network] Net Message ID: 2331

This message should occur only on a down-level computer. Any action to correct the problem should be performed on that computer. The command cannot be used on a communication-device queue.

If you need further help, contact your network administrator.

The operation is invalid on a redirected resource.

[Network] Net Message ID: 2117

This message should occur only on a down-level computer. Any action to correct the problem should be performed on that computer. The device name you specified is assigned to a shared resource.

To perform this operation on this device name, you first must end its connection to the shared resource.

The operation is invalid on a redirected resource.

[Services for Macintosh (SFM)]

Creating a volume on a redirected resource is not currently supported.

In order to tell which drives on your computer are redirected, type Net Use at the command prompt. Any drives that are listed after you type the command are redirected drives.

The option *name* is unknown.

[Network] Net Message ID: 3506

The specified option is invalid.

Check the spelling of the option you typed. To see a list of options for this command, type NET HELP <command>.

The options of this command are:

[Network]

When using this command, include only those options listed here.

The other computer did not respond

[Chat]

You dialed a computer in Chat, and the computer did not respond. Most likely, the name that you specified designates a computer name that does not exist on the network or that is not started.

Wait, and then try again. Or specify a valid computer name.

The output file already exists. Click OK to overwrite.

[Print Manager]

You have attempted to print to a file and the filename already exists.

Before overwriting the existing output file, you might want to check the contents of the file.

The parent directory could not be located.

[Network] Net Message ID: 2232

This message should occur only on a down-level computer. Any action to correct the problem should be performed on that computer. No permissions have been assigned for the parent directory.

Your network administrator must assign permissions for this resource.

The partial synchronization replication of the *name* **database from the primary domain controller** *computer name* **failed with the following error:** *text*

[Network] Net Message ID: 5716

The specified server is down or was restarted.

Verify that the specified server is running.

The partial synchronization request from the server *computer name* **failed with the following error:** *text*

[Network] Net Message ID: 5712

The specified server is down or was restarted.

Verify that the specified server is running.

The partition number of the partition which contains your Windows NT system files has changed. The old partition number was *number* ; the new partition number is *number*. Edit BOOT.INI to reflect this change before shutting the system down.

[Disk Administrator]

Usually this message occurs only if you have repartitioned the boot partition on an x86 computer. In this case, you must manually edit your BOOT.INI, or you may be unable to start your system after Disk Administrator shuts it down.

At the command prompt, type EDIT BOOT.INI. When the file appears, find the word "partition" followed by parentheses and a number. Changed this number to the new partition number specified in the message.

The password entered is not properly formatted.

[Control Panel]

A password in the Network dialog box can consist of no more than 15 characters, and cannot contain any of the following characters: ; : " < > * + = \\ | ? ,. The password that you have entered contains one of these characters.

Remove the character, then try again.

The password for this computer is not found in the local security database.

[Network] Net Message ID: 5601

Either Windows NT did not install properly or the local security database is corrupted on your computer.

If you receive this message after your initial installation of the operating system, reinstall Windows NT. Otherwise, contact your system administrator.

The password has expired.

[Remote Access Service]

If you are connecting through the Remote Access Phone Book, you will automatically be prompted to change your password. If you are connecting through the RASDIAL command, you can change your password by 1) Pressing CTRL+ALT+DEL and 2) Selecting Change Password, and following the instructions on the screen.

The password is incorrect.

[User Manager]

Make sure you have the correct password and try again, taking care to type the password correctly including capitalization. Make sure the Caps Lock has not been accidentally turned on.

The password is invalid for *name*.

[Network]

You used an incorrect password.

Check that you have the correct password, and then retype it. If you cannot remember your password, see your network administrator to have your password changed.

The password is invalid.

[Network]

You typed an invalid password.

Retype the command, using a valid password.

The password is shorter than required.

[Network]

The password you specified is not long enough.

Use a longer password. See your network administrator to find the required length for passwords on your system.

The password of this user cannot change.

[Network] Net Message ID: 2243

This message should occur only on a down-level computer. Any action to correct the problem should be performed on that computer. You cannot change your password.

See your network administrator if you want your password changed.

The password of this user has expired.

[Network] Net Message ID: 2242

Your password has expired. You will not be able to perform any network tasks until you change your password.

To change your password, press Ctrl+Alt+Del and then select Change Password.

The password of this user is too recent to change.

[Network]

You cannot change your password again for a certain length of time.

No action is needed. See your network administrator to find the length of time that you must use your current password.

The password or user name is invalid for *name*.

[Network]

Either your password or your user name is incorrect.

Retry the operation with the correct password or user name. If you cannot remember your password, see your network administrator to have your password changed.

The password parameter is invalid.

[Network]

You specified an invalid password.

Use a valid password.

The password you typed is invalid.

[Server Manager]

The new password that you have typed in the Service Config dialog either (1) was typed incorrectly; or (2) violates the minimum and maximum password length defined in the system Account Policy.

Make sure that you have typed the correct password. Or see your system administrator to determine the password parameters defined in the system Account Policy.

The password you typed is invalid.

[User Manager]

In the Password option, you can specify a password of up to 14 characters. You have specified a password that is longer than 14 characters, or that is shorter than the minimum password length defined in your workstation's account policy.

Specify a password of no more than 14 characters and no less than the minimum length defined in your account policy, confirm the password, then choose OK.

The passwords do not match.

[Network]

The two passwords you typed did not match.

Be sure to type identical passwords.

The passwords you typed do not match. Type the new password in both text boxes.

[Workstation-Logon]

When you change your password, you must type it twice. You have typed two passwords that differ. The mismatch might be due to a mistyped word, or due to a difference in capitalization.

Type the new password in both text boxes again, making sure that they are exactly the same.

The path *path* is invalid.

Make sure the path and file you specified are valid and retry the operation.

The path *path* is invalid.

[Program Manager]

Attempting to create a new program item, you have specified an invalid path in the Command Line option.

Choose OK, then type in this option box a path that points to the program item's executable file.

The path is invalid.

[Task Manager]

The path you entered does not follow the rules for a valid path.

Make sure you have the correct path, and then try again, making sure to type the path correctly. Remember to use backslashes (\) rather than forward slashes (/) between directory names.

The path specified cannot be used at this time.

[Kernel32]

The path specified is being used by the current process or another process.

Try again later.

The path specified is being used in a substitute.

[Kernel32]

An attempt was made to join to a path which is being used in a substitute.

Retry the command, specifying another path.

The path you specified is not valid. Specify a path that is local to the selected server on which you want to create the Macintosh-Accessible volume.

[Services for Macintosh (SFM)]

You may have included a drive letter when you specified the path. Or, you tried to create a volume on a server that is not running Services for Macintosh.

The Peer service supports only two simultaneous users.

[Network] Net Message ID: 2122

This message should occur only on a down-level computer. Any action to correct the problem should be performed on that computer. On a workstation running the Peer service, only you and one other user can have connections to a shared resource at the same time.

Retype the command, specifying two as the maximum number of users for the resource.

The Permissions Editor failed: *text*

[Print Manager]

The indicated system error prevented Print Manager from opening the Printer Permissions dialog.

Look up the error message that is included at the end of this message, and take appropriate action. Then try again.

The permissions for the selected group or user cannot be displayed because they do not correspond to standard NTFS permissions. You can remove the permissions or replace them with standard NTFS permissions.

[Security]

The permissions editor cannot display all possible permission combinations on NTFS. The non-standard permissions may have been applied to the selected user or group through an application.

If you can, determine how the file was given the non-standard permissions.

The phone book file you specified does not exist.

[Remote Access Service]

Verify that you typed the name correctly. Also verify the path to the phone book file.

The phone number including prefix and suffix is too long.

[Remote Access Service]

The maximum length of the phone number, including prefix and suffix, is 128 characters.

The physical end of the tape has been reached.

[Kernel32]

For instance, some tapes have an end-of-tape mark (a hole for sensor light to shine through) when there is no more room to write data on the tape.

Insert another tape or rewind this one.

The pipe has been ended.

[Kernel32]

The using process has closed the pipe or, if you are trying to write to the pipe, there are no available readers.

End your requested operation. If this occurs often while running an application, contact the supplier of that application.

The pipe is being closed.

[Kernel32]

An attempt was made to read from a pipe, but no data was available.

Contact the supplier of the running application.

The pipe state is invalid.

[Kernel32]

A pipe operation cannot be performed on a file that does not refer to a pipe.

Contact the supplier of the running application.

The pixel format is invalid.

[Kernel32]

A valid pixel format identifies a pixel configuration supported on a drawing surface. DescribePixelFormat describes all the pixel formats supported on a given drawing surface. SetPixelFormat changes the pixel format of a window or drawing surface. The pixel format of a window or drawing surface can be modified only once. Once it is set, it cannot be changed to a different pixel format.

If you can, verify that the pixel format is supported by the drawing surface. If the pixel format was changed on another occasion, it cannot be changed again. Contact the supplier of the running distributed application.

The port handle is invalid.

[Remote Access Service]

This error should not occur under normal circumstances.

Restart your computer to make sure that all recent configuration changes have taken effect. If the error persists, consult the Windows NT event log for detailed warnings or errors.

The port is already in use or is not configured for Remote Access dial out.

[Remote Access Service]

If the port is already in use by another connection, hang up the connection on this port, or edit the entry to use another communication port. If the port is not already in use, reconfigure your Remote Access port for dial out. Use the Network option in Control Panel to reconfigure RAS. For more information see "Reconfiguring Remote Access" in the Remote Access Service online Help.

The port is already open.

[Remote Access Service]

Another application is using the port.

Close the application and redial.

The port is disconnected.

[Remote Access Service]

This error should not occur under normal circumstances.

Restart your computer to make sure that all recent configuration changes have taken effect. If the error persists, consult the Windows NT event log for detailed warnings or errors.

The port is not configured for Remote Access.

[Remote Access Service]

If the port is already being used for another connection, hang up that connection, or edit this entry to use another communications port. If the port is not already in use, reconfigure your Remote Access port for dialing out. Use the Network option in Control Panel to reconfigure RAS. For instructions, see "Reconfiguring Remote Access" in the Remote Access Service online Help.

The port is not connected.

[Remote Access Service]

This error should not occur under normal circumstances.

Restart your computer to make sure that all recent configuration changes have taken effect. If the error persists, consult the Windows NT event log for detailed warnings or errors.

The port is not open.

[Remote Access Service]

This error should not occur under normal circumstances.

Restart your computer to make sure that all recent configuration changes have taken effect. If the error persists, consult the Windows NT event log for detailed warnings or errors.

The port is probably being used for dialing out or is not a Remote Access port.

[Remote Access Service]

One of the ports you are trying to enumerate is being used to dial out using the Remote Access Service.

Either ignore this message, wait until the port is not being used, or stop attempting to use the port for dialing out.

The port or device is already disconnecting.

[Remote Access Service]

Wait for Remote Access to finish disconnecting the entry or close the Remote Access Service.

The port was disconnected by the remote machine.

[Remote Access Service]

The link has been disconnected for one of the following reasons: an unrecoverable phone line error; a noisy line; or disconnection by the system administrator.

To re-establish the link, redial. If you have enabled the Redial on link failure option, the entry is redialed automatically. You can enable automatic redialing through Redial Settings on the Options menu. For more information see "Setting Options" in the Remote Access Service online Help. If this error persists, lower the modem's initial speed (bps) setting, and dial again. Also see "Setting Modem Features" in the Remote Access Service online Help.

The port was disconnected by the user.

[Remote Access Service]

You have disconnected the line through an action on your computer.

Redial.

The port was disconnected due to hardware failure.

[Remote Access Service]

The link has been disconnected for one of the following reasons: an unrecoverable error occurred in your modem (or other communication device); an unrecoverable error occurred on your communications port; or your modem cable has come unplugged.

To diagnose and correct the problem make sure your modem is on and your cable is securely attached or make sure your modem is functioning properly. For instructions on testing your modem through Windows NT Terminal, see "Testing Your Modem" in the Remote Access Service online Help.

The port was disconnected.

[Remote Access Service]

Redial the entry. If you continue to get this message, reduce the modem's initial speed, and turn off the advanced modem features. For more information see "Setting Modem Features" in the Remote Access Service online Help. If the problem persists, contact your system administrator.

The port was not found.

[Remote Access Service]

The Remote Access Phone Book file and the current Remote Access configuration are probably inconsistent.

If you have changed your communications equipment (such as your serial port or modem), be sure to reconfigure Remote Access. Use the Network option in Control Panel to reconfigure RAS. For more information see "Reconfiguring Remote Access" in the Remote Access Service online Help. If the error persists, remove and recreate the affected Phone Book entry or, reinstall the Remote Access Service. The Remote Access Phone Book (RASPHONE.PBK) is in the SYSTEM32\RAS subdirectory of your Windows NT directory.

The primary domain controller for domain *name* failed.

[Network] Net Message ID: 3034

The domain controller for this domain has stopped.

Wait a few minutes, and then restart the domain controller. If this is not possible, you have the option of promoting another server with user-level security to be the domain controller.

The primary domain controller for domain *name* has apparently failed.

[Network] Net Message ID: 3223

The domain controller for this domain has stopped.

Wait a few minutes, and then restart the domain controller. If this is not possible, you have the option of promoting another server to be the domain controller.

The Primary Group account name is invalid. Please specify a valid account name for the Primary Group of this directory.

[Services for Macintosh (SFM)]

The account name does not exist in the security database.

Use User Manager to view existing groups in the security database.

The print job does not exist.

[Network] Net Message ID: 2151

There is no print job matching the print job identification number you typed.

Be sure you typed the correct print job identification number. To see a list of current print jobs, type NET PRINT \\\\<computer name>\\<share name>.

The print processor is not installed.

[Network] Net Message ID: 2168

This message should occur only on a down-level computer. Any action to correct the problem should be performed on that computer. The print processor you specified has not been installed on the server.

Use Control Panel to install a print processor. For more information about the Control Panel, see your operating system manual(s).

The print processor is not responding.

[Network] Net Message ID: 2160

This message should occur only on a down-level computer. Any action to correct the problem should be performed on that computer. The spooler is failing to communicate with the print processor.

See your network administrator. There may be software problems with the print processor or hardware problems with the associated printer.

The print processor is unknown.

[Kernel32]

The print processor is a dynamic-link library (DLL) which calls the printer driver. An application has tried to use a print processor which has not been installed on your computer.

Contact your system administrator to check the software that has been installed on your computer. If the required DLL cannot be installed on your system, you may have to contact the supplier of the running application.

The printer already exists.

[Kernel32]

You cannot create a printer with a name that already exists.

Try a different name.

The printer command is invalid.

[Kernel32]

An application has tried to use an invalid printer command. Examples of generic printer commands are things like: Initialize Printer, Pause Printer, or Purge Printer.

Contact the supplier of the running application.

The printer destination already exists.

[Network]

This message should occur only on a down-level computer. Any action to correct the problem should be performed on that computer. This printer has already been installed.

Be sure you typed the correct device name.

The printer destination cannot be found.

[Network] Net Message ID: 2152

This message should occur only on a down-level computer. Any action to correct the problem should be performed on that computer. This printer is not used by a printer queue.

Check the spelling of the printer name and then retype the command.

The printer does not exist.

[Network] Net Message ID: 2150

The printer you have specified is invalid.

Check the spelling of the printer name. To see the list of printers shared on this server, type NET PRINT \\\\<computer name>\\<share name>.

The printer driver is unknown.

[Kernel32]

An application has tried to use a printer driver which has not been installed.

Contact your system administrator to find out which printer drivers are installed on your system. You may have to contact the supplier of the running application.

The printer is offline.

[Network]

The physical printer is not connected to the network or is turned off or has gone offline.

Go to the printer and make sure that it is running and that all cables are secure. There might be a button to push to bring the printer online.

The printer is out of paper.

[Kernel32] [Network]

One of the following has occurred: (1) there is no paper in the printer; or (2) there is not enough disk space to create a spool file.

Do one of the following: (1) make sure the paper is loaded properly with paper; (2) make sure the printer is switched on; (3) make sure the printer is installed and connected; or (4) delete any unnecessary files from the disk that contains the spool directory. Then retry the command.

The printer name is invalid.

[Kernel32]

Either you specified no printer name where one is required, or you included a comma in the printer name.

Specify a valid printer name. Do not use any commas in the name.

The printer queue already exists.

[Network] Net Message ID: 2154

This message should occur only on a down-level computer. Any action to correct the problem should be performed on that computer. You tried to create a printer queue with a name that is already in use on this server.

Give the new queue a different name. To see a list of printer queues already existing on the server, type NET PRINT.

The printer that was selected for printing in Paintbrush has been changed or deleted. The current default printer will be selected.

[Paintbrush]

If you want, you can use Print Manager to set up this printer, if it is still available.

The procedure number is out of range.

[Kernel32]

Contact the supplier of the running distributed application. There is a version control problem in the application that can only be fixed by the application supplier (procedures were added to an .IDL file without changing the version number).

The process cannot access the file because another process has locked a portion of the file.

[Kernel32]

One process has locked a portion of a file, and a second process has attempted to use the same portion of the file.

Retry the operation later.

The process cannot access the file because it is being used by another process.

[Kernel32]

The file is already being used by another process.

Retry the operation later.

The process terminated unexpectedly.

[Kernel32]

The process in which the service runs terminated unexpectedly.

Start the service again. If the problem persists, contact your technical support group.

The profile for user *user name* is already loaded due to a previous unload failure. The profile will appear in the state in was during the last logon session.

[Workstation-Logon]

No action is needed.

The program cannot be used with this operating system.

[Network] Net Message ID: 3408

Your computer has an incorrect version of the operating system.

Upgrade your computer to the latest version of Windows NT.

The program group has been modified by another program or user and will be reloaded; try the operation again.

[Program Manager]

The program group will be reloaded automatically; however, you need to try the operation again.

The queue is empty.

[Network] Net Message ID: 2115

If you do not see your document listed, it has either completed printing, or the printer did not receive your document.

No action is needed.

The queue priority is invalid.

[Network] Net Message ID: 2335

This message should occur only on a down-level computer. Any action to correct the problem should be performed on that computer. A software error occurred.

Contact technical support.

The queue you specified does not exist.

[Network] Net Message ID: 2338

This message should occur only on a down-level computer. Any action to correct the problem should be performed on that computer. The queue name you typed does not exist.

Check the spelling of the queue name.

The recipient process has refused the signal.

[Kernel32]

Make sure the recipient process can handle the signal sent, or try a different signal. You may have to contact the supplier of the running application.

The redirector accessed a share-level server that indicates it encrypts passwords. This combination is not supported.

[Netevent]

The redirector does not support the security imposed by the server. The redirector will contact the server, but the connection will not be secure.

Contact your network administrator.

The redirector could not create a system thread.

[Netevent]

Your computer may not have enough memory. Some operations might not work.

If you see this message often, contact technical support.

The redirector could not create its device. The redirector could not be started.

[Netevent]

Another device may exist with the device name you are trying to create.

Contact technical support to locate the other device on your computer.

The redirector could not set the priority for a system thread.

[Netevent]

When the redirector creates system threads, the redirector sets the priority of these threads. The redirector was unable to set the priorities.

Contact technical support.

The redirector dereferenced a connection through zero.

[Netevent]

Contact technical support.

The redirector dereferenced the allocated SMB count through zero.

[Netevent]

Contact technical support.

The redirector failed to allocate a buffer for an oplock break.

[Netevent]

Your computer is running very low on memory. Other users may not be able to access any files that are shared.

Contact technical support.

The redirector failed to allocate a multiplex table entry. This indicates that the MAXCMDS parameter to the redirector is insufficient for the users needs.

[Netevent]

The MAXCMDS parameter of the redirector is insufficient for the users needs.

Ask your network administrator to change the MAXCMDS entry in the [LANMANWORKSTATION] section of the Registry.

The redirector failed to determine the connection type.

[Netevent]

The workstation passed an invalid connection type to the redirector.

Contact technical support.

The redirector failed to map the requested file disposition (for NtCreateFile).

[Netevent]

The kernel on your computer does not match the version of your redirector.

Ask your network administrator to check your computer's configuration.

The redirector failed to unlock part of a file on server *name*.

[Netevent]

Either the network went down or an application failure occurred. Data may have been lost.

Retry the command.

The redirector failed to write data to server *name* after the file was closed.

[Netevent]

Another error on the network may have caused this error. Data has been lost.

Retry the command. Check the event log with Event Viewer for information about other network errors that are related to this error.

The redirector has failed to connect to the server *computer name* on the primary transport. The data contains the error.

[Netevent]

Your workstation could not be connected to this server.

Look up the error that caused this operation to fail, and take appropriate action. Then try again.

The redirector has timed out a request to *name*.

[Netevent]

The server did not respond to a request from the redirector within the time specified by the SESSTIMEOUT entry in the configuration information. The default value for this entry is 45 seconds.

Retry the command. If this error occurs frequently, ask your network administrator to increase the value.

The redirector is allocating additional resources for input/output request packet contexts. This is probably caused by a resource leak in the redirector.

[Netevent]

A resource leak in the redirector may cause this error.

No action is needed.

The redirector is already installed.

[Network]

This message should occur only on a down-level computer. Any action to correct the problem should be performed on that computer.

No action is needed.

The redirector is in use and cannot be unloaded.

[Kernel32]

You have tried to stop the Workstation service, but it is being used by another application.

End the other application, or wait for it to end. Then retry the operation.

The redirector is out of a resource: ***name*****.**

[Network] Net Message ID: 3191

This message should occur only on a down-level computer. Any action to correct the problem should be performed on that computer. The workstation is out of the specified resource.

Adjust the workstation's configuration file to increase the amount of this resource. If you need assistance, contact your network administrator.

The redirector received an incorrect response from ***name*** **to a lock request.**

[Netevent]

The specified server did not respond correctly.

Contact your network administrator.

The redirector received an incorrectly formatted response from ***name*****.**

[Netevent]

The redirector received a bad packet from a server.

Your command could not be processed. Wait a few minutes, then retry the command. If you receive this message after retrying the command, contact your network administrator.

The redirector received an invalid oplock level from ***computer name*****.**

[Netevent]

No action is needed.

The redirector received an SMB that was too short.

[Netevent]

The redirector received a bad packet from a server.

Retry the command.

The redirector was unable to allocate memory.

[Netevent]

Ask your system administrator to add more memory to your computer and then retry the command.

The redirector was unable to create a worker thread because it has already created the maximum number of configured work threads.

[Netevent]

An operation required more threads than the MAXTHREADS entry in your configuration information allows.

Increase the number of MAXTHREADS in your configuration information.

The redirector was unable to delete the file specified on server *computer name* when it was closed by the application. The data contains the name of the file.

[Netevent]

Use File Manager to delete this file.

The redirector was unable to initialize variables from the Registry.

[Netevent]

At Startup, the redirector could not get the information it needed from the Registry because it is corrupted.

Contact your network administrator.

The registry contains an invalid value for the logon message parameter. The logon message parameter is located in the SYSTEM\\CurrentControlSet\\Service\\MacFile\\Parameters registry key.

[Services for Macintosh (SFM)]

The logon message parameter should have from 1 to 19 characters.

Use the Registry Editor to change the value of this parameter in the Registry.

The registry contains an invalid value for the maximum non-paged memoryparameter. The maximum non-paged memory parameter is located in the SYSTEM\\CurrentControlSet\\Service\\MacFile\\Parameters registry key.

[Services for Macintosh (SFM)]

The maximum non-paged memory parameter should not be more than 16,000. Non-paged memory should not be less than 256. If the invalid value is left in place, the default value will be used.

The registry contains an invalid value for the maximum paged memory The maximum paged memory is located in the SYSTEM\\CurrentControlSet\\Service\\MacFile\\Parameters registry key.parameter.

[Services for Macintosh (SFM)]

The maximum paged memory parameter should not be more than 256,000. Paged memory should not be less than 1000. If the invalid value is left in place, the default value will be used.

The registry contains an invalid value for the maximum sessions parameter. The maximum sessions parameter is located in the SYSTEM\\CurrentControlSet\\Service\\MacFile\\Parameters registry key.

[Services for Macintosh (SFM)]

The value in the Registry may have been changed to limit the number of sessions. Generally the number of maximum sessions is as much as a DWORD value can be.

The registry contains an invalid value for the path to the Macintosh code-page file.

[Services for Macintosh (SFM)]

Use the Registry Editor to change the invalid value for the path. The invalid path is located in the \\HKEY_LOCAL_MACHINE\System\CurrentControlSet\Control\Nls\CodePage\MACCP Registry key. The path is listed next to the value specified in this key.

The registry contains an invalid value for the server name parameter. The server name is located in the SYSTEM\\CurrentControlSet\\Service\\MacFile\\Parameters registry key.

[Services for Macintosh (SFM)]

The server name parameter should have from one to three characters.

Use Registry Editor to change the invalid value for the server name parameter in the Registry.

The registry contains an invalid value for the server options parameter. The server options is located in the SYSTEM\\CurrentControlSet\\Service\\MacFile\\Parameters registry key.

[Services for Macintosh (SFM)]

The range for the server options parameter is from 0 to 7.

Use Registry Editor to change the value of the parameter in the Registry.

The registry contains invalid information for the volume "*name* ". The value was ignored and processing was continued.

[Services for Macintosh (SFM)]

Use Server Manager or File Manager to view volumes and then delete the invalid volume.

The Registry event variable could not be created

[WINS Service]

Check the general health of the system. Reboot if necessary.

The Registry is corrupt. The structure of one of the files that contains Registry data is corrupt, or the system's image of the file in memory is corrupt, or the file could not be recovered because the alternate copy or log was absent or corrupt.

[Kernel32]

The structure of one of the files that contains Registry data is corrupted, or the image of the file in memory is corrupted, or the file could not be recovered because an alternate copy or log was absent or corrupted.

Use the Emergency Repair Disk to restore the configuration information.

The Registry Notify Function returned an error

[WINS Service]

Check the general health of the system. Reboot if necessary.

The Registry or the information you just typed includes an illegal value for "*text* ".

[Network] Net Message ID: 3051

You specified invalid values for one or more of the service's options.

Retype the command with correct values, or change the values for the listed options in the configuration file.

The registry structure is not set properly.

[Event Viewer]

Data related to Event Viewer is not configured correctly in the Registry.

Set the structure. Or contact technical support.

The Remote Access server cannot allocate a route for the user connected on port *number*. The user has been disconnected. Check the configuration of your Remote Access Service.

[Remote Access Service]

Use the Network option in Control Panel to remove and reinstall the Remote Access Service. If the problem persists, contact technical support.

The Remote Access Server encountered an internal error.

[Remote Access Service]

The Remote Access Server cannot recover from the internal error.

Restart the system.

The Remote Access server is not responding.

[Remote Access Service]

One of the following may have caused this error: the Remote Access server is not running; the line may be too noisy; or your modem may have failed to negotiate correctly with the Remote Access server's modem at the selected speed.

Contact your system administrator to make sure the server is running. Lower the modem's initial speed (bps), and dial again. For more information see "Setting Modem Features" in the Remote Access Service online Help. If the problem persists, lower the modem's initial speed (bps), and dial again.

The Remote Access Service is not configured to receive calls.

[Remote Access Service]

The Remote Access server is configured for dialing out only or some other program is using the port. The Remote Access Service will not start unless this error is corrected.

Use the Network option in Control Panel to reconfigure the Remote Access Service. Choose Configure Port and then select Dial out and Receive calls.

The remote adapter is not compatible.

[Kernel32]

Your computer cannot communicate with the specified remote computer because the two hardware network adapters are not compatible.

Retry the command, communicating with a different computer. If you continue to have problems, contact your network administrator.

The remote computer canceled the file transfer with this message: *text*

[Terminal]

The user action depends upon the message you receive.

Most likely, however, you will need to contact the sender to determine the problem.

The remote computer is not available.

[Kernel32]

You might have specified the wrong computer name, or the remote computer might be busy or turned off.

Perform one of the following actions, and then retry the operation: (1) specify the correct remote computer name; or (2) ensure that the specified remote computer is available. If neither of these actions corrects the problem, contact your network administrator.

The remote procedure call failed and did not execute.

[Kernel32]

A server connection was lost while the server was attempting to perform a remote procedure call. The remote procedure call did not execute. The connection may have broken because of a problem with the network hardware or because a process terminated.

Either restart the server or try to connect to another server. Also, ask your network administrator to check the integrity of the network. If the problem persists, contact the supplier of the running application.

The remote procedure call failed.

[Kernel32]

A server connection was lost while the server was attempting to perform a remote procedure call. It is unknown whether the remote procedure call executed, or how much of it executed. The connection may have broken because of a problem with the network hardware or because a process terminated.

Wait a few minutes and then try the operation again. If this message reappears, check the server or try to connect to another server. You may also have to check the integrity of the network. If the problem persists, contact the supplier of the running application.

The remote server has been paused or is in the process of being started.

[Kernel32]

The server you attempted to access is either in the paused state or is still being started.

Retry the command at a later time. If the same error occurs, contact your network administrator.

The replication server could not update directory *name* **from the source on** *computer name* **due to error** *code***.**

[Network] Net Message ID: 3208

An error prevented this server from updating the listed directory from the export server. The directory cannot be updated until the problem is corrected.

Copy the files manually, if necessary, and investigate the cause of the listed error.

The replicator attempted to log on at *computer name* **as** *name* **and failed.**

[Network]

Check that the user account under which the replicator is running is valid on the specified server or domain.

The replicator attempted to log on at *computer name* as *user name* and failed.

[Network] Net Message ID: 3211

This message should occur only on a down-level computer. Any action to correct the problem should be performed on that computer. The Replicator service was denied access to the listed export server. Until this problem is corrected, the replicator cannot update the local copies of files exported by that server.

Be sure that the local computer has an account on the export server. The user name and password for this account are specified by the LOGON and PASSWORD entries in the local computer's configuration file. If there is no LOGON entry, the local computer name is the user name and no password is necessary.

The replicator cannot update directory *name*. It has tree integrity and is the current directory for some process.

[Network] Net Message ID: 3206

A directory cannot be replicated when it is the current directory of a process and its value for INTEGRITY is TREE.

For the directory to be replicated, be sure it is not the current directory of any process.

The request could not be performed because of an I/O device error.

[Kernel32]

Check the cabling to your peripheral devices and retry the operation. If you still get this message, run hardware diagnostics. If the diagnostics do not detect a problem, contact the supplier of the running application.

The request for data from the ATK Device IO Control failed. Returning the IO Status Block.

[Services for Macintosh (SFM)]

The buffer might not be large enough. This is not something you can change.

Contact technical support.

The request has timed out.

[Remote Access Service]

This error should not occur under normal circumstances.

Restart your computer to make sure that all recent configuration changes have taken effect. If the error persists, consult the Windows NT event log for detailed warnings or errors.

The request is incorrectly formatted for *text*.

Contact the supplier of the driver for the device named in the message.

The requested action is restricted for use by logon processes only. The calling process has not registered as a logon process.

[Kernel32]

Contact the supplier of the running application.

The requested API is not supported on the remote server.

[Network] Net Message ID: 2142

The server does not support the request that was sent to it. This can happen if two or more versions of networking software are on the network. However, no program included with Windows NT should cause this error.

Contact the vendor of the program that was running when the error occurred. Tell the vendor that the program requested an API that is not supported on the remote server.

The requested control is not valid for this service

[Kernel32]

The control request was ignored. Stop, pause, continue, and interrogate are examples of standard control requests. There are also user-defined controls. This message could be returned, for instance, if an application sends a pause request to a service that does not support pause.

Contact the supplier of the running application.

The requested device is invalid.

[Network] Net Message ID: 2341

This message should occur only on a down-level computer. Any action to correct the problem should be performed on that computer. The device name is invalid because it does not represent a physical device or because the device hardware is faulty.

Check the spelling of the device name, and then retype the command. If the problem persists, contact your network administrator. Your administrator should use diagnostics to check that the device hardware is properly installed and working. For more assistance, contact your hardware dealer.

The requested information is not available.

[Network] Net Message ID: 2139

This message should occur only on a down-level computer. Any action to correct the problem should be performed on that computer. Your command could not be completed because the MAILSLOTS entry of your workstation's configuration file is incorrect.

Change the MAILSLOTS entry of the configuration file to YES. Then stop and restart the Workstation service.

The requested operation cannot be performed in full-screen mode.

[Kernel32]

Contact the supplier of the running application.

The requested operation is not supported.

[Kernel32]

This version of Windows NT does not support this remote procedure call (RPC) operation.

Contact the supplier of the running distributed application.

The requested pause or stop is not valid for this service.

[Network] Net Message ID: 2191

This command is invalid for this service, or the service cannot accept the command right now because it is still in the process of starting.

If the service normally accepts this command, try typing it again later. To display a list of valid commands, type NET HELP.

The requested service has already been started.

[Network] Net Message ID: 2182

You tried to start a service that is already running.

To display a list of active services, type NET START.

The required *filename* driver is already on the system. Do you want to use the current driver or install a new driver?

[Drivers (CP)]

You have attempted to install a driver that already exists in your Windows NT SYSTEM32\\Drivers directory.

If you want to use the Current driver, choose the Current option. If not, choose the New driver option.

The required parameter was not provided on the command line or in the configuration file.

[Network] Net Message ID: 3052

This message should occur only on a down-level computer. Any action to correct the problem should be performed on that computer. You must specify a value for the listed option.

Define a value for the option, either from the command line or in the configuration file.

The resource name could not be found.

[Network] Net Message ID: 2222

You tried to access the permissions for a resource that has no permissions assigned to it.

Check the spelling of the resource's name. Before you can assign user permissions for a particular resource, you must create a record of that resource in the database of resource permissions.

The resource named cannot be shared.

[Network]

You cannot share this resource.

No action is needed.

The resource permission list already exists.

[Network] Net Message ID: 2225

This message should occur only on a down-level computer. Any action to correct the problem should be performed on that computer. You tried to create an access record for a resource that already has one.

To view or change permissions for this resource, use the Permissions editor from File Manager.

The revision level is unknown.

[Kernel32]

The service has encountered a revision level in a security object that it does not recognize. For instance, this may be a more recent revision than the service knows about.

Rebuild the security object in the current Windows NT environment. Then the service will recognize its revision level.

The route is not allocated.

[Remote Access Service]

Most likely, your network configuration is wrong.

Restart your computer to make sure that all recent configuration changes have taken effect. If error persists, consult the Windows NT event log for detailed warnings or errors.

The route is not available.

[Remote Access Service]

Most likely, your network configuration is wrong.

Restart your computer to make sure that all recent configuration changes have taken effect. If error persists, consult the Windows NT event log for detailed warnings or errors.

The RPC protocol sequence is invalid.

[Kernel32]

A protocol sequence identifies the network protocols used to establish a connection between the client and server parts of a distributed (RPC) application. Windows NT recognizes this protocol sequence, but cannot interpret it.

Contact the supplier of the running application, or contact your technical support group to try to change the syntax of the protocol sequence. Servers can call the Windows NT API function RpcNetworkInqProtseqs( ) to obtain a list of the supported protocol sequences and their proper syntax.

The RPC protocol sequence is not supported.

[Kernel32]

A protocol sequence identifies the network protocols used to establish a connection between the client and server parts of a distributed (RPC) application. Windows NT does not support a protocol sequence used in this application.

Contact the supplier of the running application, or contact your technical support group to try to change the protocol sequence. Servers can call the Windows NT API function RpcNetworkInqProtseqs( ) to obtain a list of the supported protocol sequences.

The RPC protocol sequence was not found.

[Kernel32]

Contact the supplier of the running distributed application.

The RPC server attempted an integer division by zero.

[Kernel32]

In a distributed (RPC) application, the server attempted an integer divide by zero.

Contact the supplier of the running distributed application.

The RPC server is already listening.

[Kernel32]

In a distributed (RPC) application, a server can call Windows NT when it is ready to accept remote procedure calls from clients. In this case, Windows NT received such a call from a server that was already ready to receive remote procedure calls.

Contact the supplier of the running distributed application.

The RPC server is not listening.

[Kernel32]

In a distributed (RPC) application, a server is not listening for remote procedure calls, or could not be reached.

Contact the supplier of the running distributed application.

The RPC server is too busy to complete this operation.

[Kernel32]

A distributed (RPC) application has tried to reach a server that is temporarily too busy. The server may need more resources.

Wait a few minutes, then retry the operation. If this message keeps reappearing, you may want to ask your system administrator to give the server more base resources. You may also want to contact the supplier of the running application if this message appears often when a particular distributed application is running.

The RPC server is unavailable.

[Kernel32]

A distributed (RPC) application has tried to reach a server that is not available. For instance, the server may be shut down, there may be a network hardware problem, there may be no common transports, or the server may not exist.

Explore each of the possible problems and make the necessary changes. Then retry the operation.

The Run server you requested is paused.

[Network] Net Message ID: 2385

This message should occur only on a down-level computer. Any action to correct the problem should be performed on that computer. You tried to run a program or command on a server that is paused.

See your network administrator. Your administrator must continue the server for your command to run.

The SAM database on the Windows NT Advanced Server does not have a computer account for this workstation trust relationship.

[Kernel32]

Contact your system administrator to establish the computer account on the remote computer which is necessary for this trust relationship.

The Scale can only be a number between *number* and *number* percent.

[Paintbrush]

You can direct your printer to print a Paintbrush image on a 10% to 400% scale. The percentage that you have designated does not fall between these two numbers.

In the File menu, choose Print Setup. In the Print Setup dialog box, select the Options option. In the Scaling option in the Options dialog box, designate a scaling percentage between 10% and 400%.

The Scavenger thread encountered an exception while cleaning up the owner-add table. It will try again after the Verify Interval has elapsed.

[WINS Service]

The owner-add table lists the WINS servers that own records (addresses) in the database. Servers are deleted from this table if they no longer own any records in the database. The Verify Interval specifies how often this cleanup is done. Something interrupted the scavenger thread while it was performing this cleanup.

No action is needed. The cleanup will be tried again automatically when the number of seconds specified in the Verify Interval setting have passed. You can also initiate a cleanup directly, if you want.

The Scavenger thread was unable to change its priority level.

[WINS Service]

Call technical support.

The SCHED.LOG file could not be opened.

[Network] Net Message ID: 3804

This message should occur only on a down-level computer. Any action to correct the problem should be performed on that computer. Either the SCHED.LOG file has been opened by another process or the disk is full.

Be sure the disk is not full. If another process has opened the file, you will have to wait for it to close the file before you can open it.

The screen cannot be set to the number of lines and columns specified.

[Mode]

You specified invalid values for the rows and columns parameters while using the Mode command to change the console display size.

Retry the command, using valid values.

The second NTFS boot sector is unwriteable.

[NTFS]

The backup copy of the NTFS boot sector which was saved in the middle of the volume, cannot be written.

Back up all files and reformat the volume. If possible, repartition or replace the disk.

The security account database contains an internal inconsistency.

[Kernel32]

First, restart the system. If this message reappears, restore the most recent backup of the system.

The security account manager (SAM) or local security authority (LSA) server was in the wrong state to perform the security operation.

[Kernel32]

Contact the supplier of the running application.

The security context is invalid.

[Kernel32]

Contact the supplier of the running application.

The security database could not be found.

[Network] Net Message ID: 2219

Windows NT could not find the security database file.

Copy the backup version of the file.

The security database full synchronization has been initiated by the server *computer name*.

[Network]

This is an informational Alert. The system will operate as usual.

No action is needed.

The security database has not been started.

[Network] Net Message ID: 2227

The security database is not active. This database must be active for the command to run.

The security database should have started when the Workstation service started. Check the error log with Event Viewer to determine why the database did not start.

The security database is corrupted.

[Network]

The security database is damaged.

Restore the security database from a backup.

The security descriptor stored in the Registry for the share *name* was invalid. The share was not automatically recreated.

[Netevent]

The Registry is corrupted.

Contact your system administrator.

The security descriptor structure is invalid.

[Kernel32]

Contact the supplier of the running application. As a workaround, your system administrator or technical support group may know how to edit the structure of the security descriptor.

The security ID structure is invalid.

[Kernel32]

Contact the supplier of the running application. As a workaround, your system administrator or technical support group may know how to edit the security ID (SID) structure or values.

The security information cannot be displayed because it is different between *name* and *name*. Do you wish to reset the security information on all the selected items?

[Security]

You are trying to display the security information on multiple files and directories.

If you choose OK, both of the specified files or directories will be set to the permissions you have indicated.

The security information for *name* are not standard and cannot be displayed. Do you want to overwrite the current security information?

[Security]

You may overwrite this information.

To overwrite the current security information on the selected resource, choose Yes.

The security information for *name* are not standard and cannot be displayed. You do not have permission to change the security information for this resource.

[Security]

You have attempted to access the security information of a resource which cannot be displayed.

Contact your system administrator. The administrator will probably not be able to view the information but will be able to overwrite the security information.

The security log file is full, logging must be disabled to continue using the system. However, a problem prevented the disabling of logging.

[Workstation-Logon]

The Security log file is full.

In Event Viewer, clear the log. Or use Event Viewer to increase the size of space allotted to the event log.

The selected COM port is either not supported or is being used by another device. Select another port.

[Terminal]

Using the Communications option on the Settings menu, you have selected a COM (also called a Serial I/O) port that is being used by another device (a mouse, for example), or that Windows NT does not support.

Select another of the Ports listed in the Connector option on the Communications dialog box. Or select None, and Terminal will file through the list of ports until it finds an available one. NOTE: You cannot use the Ports option in Control Panel to set Terminal settings.

The selected Creator/Type item already exists.

[Services for Macintosh (SFM)]

Duplicate creator/type items are not allowed.

Verify that the information you have typed is not already in the list.

The selected directory does not belong to a Macintosh-Accessible volume. The Macintosh view of directory permissions is only available for directories that are part of a Macintosh-Accessible volume.

[Services for Macintosh (SFM)]

If you'd like to make the directory part of a Macintosh-accessible volume, select Create Volume from the MacFile menu in File Manager. In order to tell which volumes are Macintosh-accessible, use the MacFile menu in either Server Manager or File Manager. From the MacFile menu in Server Manager, select Volumes. From the MacFile menu in File Manager, select View/Modify Volumes.

The selected file fork has already been closed. It may have been forced to close by another administrator or a Macintosh user.

[Services for Macintosh (SFM)]

The lists of open files may not have been refreshed.

No action is needed. After this message appears, the screen refreshes automatically.

The selected file is not in the correct format for use with Cardfile. Create a new file or open a file with the .CRD extension.

[Cardfile]

You have saved a Cardfile file with an extension other than .CRD. Therefore, you cannot access the Cardfile file either using the Browse function in Cardfile or from File Manager.

Close or minimize Cardfile, go to the file in File Manager, and using the Rename option on the File menu, select the Cardfile file, and assign a .CRD extension to it.

The selected floppy drive is unable to support the required media type.

[Repair Disk]

In order to create an Emergency Repair Disk, the Rdisk utility requires that your a: drive support high capacity media. The Emergency Repair Disk cannot be created. However, all the repair information will be saved on your hard disk.

No action is needed.

The selected Macintosh user is no longer connected. The user may have logged off or been forced off by another administrator.

[Services for Macintosh (SFM)]

The window probably hasn't been refreshed recently.

Press F5 to refresh the window.

The selected Macintosh-Accessible volume is currently in use by Macintoshes. The selected volume may be removed only when no Macintosh workstations are connected to it.

[Services for Macintosh (SFM)]

Use Server Manager or File Manager to disconnect all connected users and then you can delete the volume. You might also want to use Server Manager or File Manager to send a disconnect message to the users to prevent data loss. In using either manager, select the MacFile menu. In Server Manager, select Send Message. In File Manager, select View/Modify Volumes and then select Send Message.

The selected user has open files. Disconnecting this user may result in the loss of data. Are you sure you want to disconnect *user name* from all connected volumes?

[Services for Macintosh (SFM)]

Use Server Manager or File Manager to send a disconnect message to the specified user. In using either manager, select the MacFile menu. In Server Manager, select Send Message. In File Manager, select View/Modify Volumes and then select Send Message.

The selected user has open resources. Disconnecting this user may cause loss of data. Are you sure you want to disconnect *user name* from all connected resources?

[Server Manager]

When you choose to disconnect a user from a shared resource, you risk causing the user to lose unsaved data. Consequently, any time that you choose to remotely disconnect a user, Server Manager presents you with a confirmation message.

If you are sure that you want to disconnect the user, choose Yes. If not, choose No, and before selecting this option again, alert the user of the imminent disconnect.

The selected users have different Logon Hours settings. You may edit these settings, but they will be initially reset. Do you wish to reset and edit the Logon Hours settings for these users?

[User Manager]

You have selected multiple users who don't have identical logon hours. Before these hours can be edited properly, they must be reset to the same initial state. If you do not want these hours reset, you must edit the logon hours of each user individually.

The semaphore cannot be set again.

[Kernel32]

Semaphores can be set and released in a nested fashion only a limited number of times. That limit has been reached.

Check semaphore request nesting and make sure that the semaphore is released before requesting it again. You may have to contact the supplier of the running application.

The semaphore is set and cannot be closed.

[Kernel32]

A semaphore cannot be closed while it is set.

Release the semaphore, or wait for it to be released. Then close it. You may have to contact the supplier of the running application.

The serial driver could not allocate adequate I/O queues. This may result in an unreliable connection.

[Remote Access Service]

If you are using a multiport adapter card, it may be configured to use too many ports. Otherwise your computer or the Remote Access server may be out of memory.

Reduce the number of ports being used on your multiport adapter card. Or check the memory on your computer and the Remote Access server. If neither is low on memory, contact technical support.

The server *name* and *name* both claim to be the primary domain controller for the *name* domain. One of the servers should be demoted or removed from the domain.

[Network]

Each domain should have only one primary domain controller (PDC). Two PDCs exist in the domain because one of the PDCs stopped working for an extended period. A backup domain controller (BDC) was then promoted to PDC. Now the original PDC is working again.

Demote one of the PDCs.

The server *computer name* cannot be located. You cannot administer the server at this time.

[Server Manager]

The server that you have selected is either down for repair or is not started.

Wait until the server is started, then try again.

The server cannot access the user accounts database (NET.ACC).

[Network]

This message should occur only on a down-level computer. Any action to correct the problem should be performed on that computer.

The server cannot allocate NetBIOS resources needed to support the client.

[Remote Access Service]

All of the NetBIOS names requested by Windows NT could not be added by a RAS server.

Ask your system administrator to increase the resource capacity of the Remote Access server, or through Services in Control Panel, stop nonessential services on your computer, such as Messenger, Alerter, Browser, and Network DDE. You may also have to disable Server.

The server cannot create the *name* mailslot needed to send the ReleaseMemory alert message. The error received is:

[Network] Net Message ID: 3127

This message should occur only on a down-level computer. Any action to correct the problem should be performed on that computer. The server cannot respond to a ReleaseMemory alert. Otherwise, the server is functioning normally.

No action is needed.

The server cannot export directory *name* to client *name*. It is exported from another server.

[Network] Net Message ID: 3207

This server found that another server is exporting the listed directory to the listed import server.

Be sure that only one computer is configured as the export server of this directory for the listed import computer. Check the EXPORTLIST and EXPORTPATH entries in the configuration files of the export server and the IMPORTLIST and IMPORTPATH entries in the configuration file of the import server.

The server cannot increase the size of a memory segment.

[Network] Net Message ID: 3121

This message should occur only on a down-level computer. Any action to correct the problem should be performed on that computer. The server cannot increase the size of a memory segment.

Be sure that the MEMMAN entry in the server's CONFIG.SYS file allows swapping and that there is at least 1 megabyte of free space on the swap disk. The swap disk is specified by the SWAPPATH entry in the CONFIG.SYS file. You could also decrease the value of the NUMBIGBUF entry in the server's configuration file.

The server cannot open more files because it has reached its maximum number.

[Network] Net Message ID: 2466

This message should occur only on a down-level computer. Any action to correct the problem should be performed on that computer. No more files on the server can be opened.

To open another file, you will first have to close a file or stop a network application that has open files. Also, see your network administrator. Your administrator may want to increase the value of the MAXOPENS entry in the server's configuration file.

The server cannot update the AT schedule file. The file is corrupted.

[Network] Net Message ID: 3129

This message should occur only on a down-level computer. Any action to correct the problem should be performed on that computer. The schedule file, SCHED.LOG, in the LANMAN\\LOGS directory, is damaged.

Restore the schedule file from a backup copy, or delete the file and create a new one using the AT utility.

The server could not access the *name* network with NetBiosOpen.

[Network] Net Message ID: 3177

This message should occur only on a down-level computer. Any action to correct the problem should be performed on that computer. The server could not start one of its networks.

Be sure that each network listed in the SRVNETS entry in the server's configuration file has a corresponding entry in the [networks] section of the configuration file.

The server could not be located.

[Network] Net Message ID: 2103

This message should occur only on a down-level computer. Any action to correct the problem should be performed on that computer. The server you specified does not exist.

You may have misspelled the server's computer name. To see a list of servers in your domain, type NET VIEW. Remember to precede computer names with two backslashes, as in \\\\<computer name>.

The server could not bind to the transport *name* because another computer on the network has the same name. The server could not start.

[Netevent]

Ask your network administrator to change the server's name or to change the name of the other network computer.

The server could not bind to the transport *name*.

[Netevent]

There may be a problem with the underlying transport because it did not load.

Check the event log with Event Viewer for information about related errors. Contact your network administrator.

The server could not close *filename*.The file is probably corrupted.

[Network] Net Message ID: 3205

This message should occur only on a down-level computer. Any action to correct the problem should be performed on that computer. The server found an error while closing the listed file.

The file may be damaged. If it is, restore it from a backup copy.

The server could not create a process. The server could not be started.

[Netevent]

The server was started on a computer that does not have any memory free.

Contact technical support.

The server could not create a startup thread. The server could not be started.

[Netevent]

The server was started on a computer that does not have any memory free.

Contact technical support.

The server could not create a thread. The THREADS parameter in the CONFIG.SYS file should be increased.

[Network] Net Message ID: 3204

This message should occur only on a down-level computer. Any action to correct the problem should be performed on that computer. The server was unable to create a thread.

Increase the value of the THREADS entry in the server's CONFIG.SYS file. The range for this value is 64 to 512.

The server could not create its device. The server could not be started.

[Netevent]

The server was started on a computer that does not have any memory free.

Contact technical support.

The server could not expand a table because the table reached the maximum size.

[Netevent]

A client opened too many files or had too many active directory searches on the server.

The client should either close some files or limit the number of simultaneous directory searches on the server.

The server could not find an AT schedule file so it created one.

[Network] Net Message ID: 3176

This message should occur only on a down-level computer. Any action to correct the problem should be performed on that computer. The server created a schedule file.

No action is needed.

The server could not open the named pipe file system. Remote named pipes are disabled.

[Netevent]

The server was started on a computer that does not have any memory free.

Contact technical support.

The server could not read the AT schedule file.

[Network] Net Message ID: 3174

This message should occur only on a down-level computer. Any action to correct the problem should be performed on that computer. LAN Manager cannot read the schedule file because the file is damaged.

Restore the schedule file from a backup copy, if you have one. If not, delete the file and create a new one with the AT utility.

The server could not start the scavenger thread. The server could not be started.

[Netevent]

The server was started on a computer that does not have any memory free.

Contact technical support.

The server did not bind to any transports. The server could not start.

[Netevent]

There may be a problem with the underlying transport(s) because it (they) did not load. If the server could bind to at least one transport, it would have started.

Check the event log with Event Viewer for information about related errors. Contact your network administrator.

The server encountered an error when callingNetIMakeLMFileName. The error code is the data.

[Network] Net Message ID: 3130

This message should occur only on a down-level computer. Any action to correct the problem should be performed on that computer. The server could not find the NET.MSG file.

The NET.MSG file should be in the LANMAN\\ NETPROG directory. If it is not there, copy it from the LAN Manager distribution disks.

The server endpoint cannot perform the operation.

[Kernel32]

In a distributed (RPC) application, the client failed to reach the server endpoint. The endpoint mapper may not be started or network communications may have failed.

Verify that the endpoint mapper can start and verify network communications. You may have to contact the supplier of the running distributed application.

The server failed to register for the ReleaseMemory alert, with recipient *computer name*. The error code fromNetAlertStart is the data.

[Network] Net Message ID: 3128

This message should occur only on a down-level computer. Any action to correct the problem should be performed on that computer. The server cannot respond to a ReleaseMemory alert. Otherwise, the server is functioning normally.

No action is needed.

The server failed to start. Either all three chdevparameters must be zero or all three must be non zero.

[Network] Net Message ID: 3124

This message should occur only on a down-level computer. Any action to correct the problem should be performed on that computer. The configuration file entries CHARWAIT, CHARTIME, and CHARCOUNT must all be zero or must all have non-zero values.

Correct the entries and then restart the Server service.

The server found an invalid AT schedule record.

[Network] Net Message ID: 3175

This message should occur only on a down-level computer. Any action to correct the problem should be performed on that computer. The schedule file contains a record with an invalid format.

Restore the schedule file from a backup copy. If you do not have one, delete the AT schedule file and create a new one with the AT utility.

The server has encountered a network error.

[Netevent]

If you see many errors of this type in the event log in Event Viewer, they indicate a network hardware or software problem.

Contact your network administrator.

The server has reached the maximum number of connections it supports.

[Network] Net Message ID: 2465

This message should occur only on a down-level computer. Any action to correct the problem should be performed on that computer. The server is supporting the maximum number of connections.

To make another connection to the server, first end a current connection. If you have no connections that you can end, try your command again later. You will be able to make your connection once another user's connection is ended. Also, see your network administrator. Your administrator may want to increase the value of the MAXCONNECTIONS entry of the server's configuration file.

The server has reached the maximum number of sessions it supports.

[Network] Net Message ID: 2464

This message should occur only on a down-level computer. Any action to correct the problem should be performed on that computer. The server is supporting the maximum number of sessions.

Try the command later. You will not be able to start a session with this server until another user's session has ended. Also, see your network administrator. Your administrator may want to purchase an Additional User Pak for the server or increase the value of the MAXUSERS entry of the server's configuration file.

The server identification does not specify a valid server.

[Network] Net Message ID: 2460

This message should occur only on a down-level computer. Any action to correct the problem should be performed on that computer. A software error occurred.

If this error persists or causes other errors, contact technical support.

The server is configured without a valid user path.

[Network] Net Message ID: 2211

The USERPATH entry in the server's configuration file does not list a valid directory.

Add a user path by creating the directory (if it does not already exist). Stop the Server service and type the path of the directory as the value for USERPATH in the server's configuration file. Then start the Server and Netlogon services.

The server is currently out of the requested resource.

[Network] Net Message ID: 2119

The server could not access enough of a resource, such as memory, to complete this task. Some resources are limited.

Try again later. If you continue to receive this message, stop some nonessential processes or applications and try to complete the task again. If you still have problems, your network administrator may need to reconfigure your system.

The server is in use and cannot be unloaded.

[Kernel32]

You tried to stop the Server service, but it is being used by another application.

End the other application or wait for it to finish. Then retry the operation.

The server is not configured for remote administration.

[Network] Net Message ID: 3743

The server is not set up to be administered remotely.

For the server to be administered remotely, you must share the server's ADMIN$ and IPC$ resources.

The server is not configured for transactions.

[Network] Net Message ID: 2141

The specified server is not configured to accept the command you typed.

Ask your network administrator if the server is configured properly. The administrator may choose to share the server's IPC$ resource to correct this problem.

The server is not running with user-level security.

[Network]

This message should occur only on a down-level computer. Any action to correct the problem should be performed on that computer.

The server name you typed is invalid.

[Network]

The server name you typed does not meet the criteria for server names, or was preceded with a double backslash (\\), which is redundant in this text box.

Make sure you have the correct name, and try again. Be careful not to mistype the server name.

The server received an incorrectly formatted request from *computer name*.

[Netevent]

The specified computer sent an invalid SMB which indicates a problem with the computer's redirector.

Contact the vendor of the redirector.

The server received an unexpected disconnection from a client.

[Netevent]

There is a problem with the underlying transport.

Contact the vendor of the transport.

The server service has not been started. Would you like to start the server service?

[Server Manager]

The Server service on the local computer is not running.

If you want to start this service, choose Yes.

The server service was unable to load the server driver.

[Netevent]

Either the SRV.SYS file is missing from your computer's driver directory or it is corrupted. The system refused to load the driver.

Contact your system administrator.

The server service was unable to map error code *code*.

[Netevent]

The server was unable to map a WIN32 error code to a LAN Manager error code.

Report this message to the vendor of application.

The server service was unable to recreate the share *name* because the directory *name* no longer exists.

[Netevent]

The directory that was previously shared has been deleted.

If you want to recreate the share, create the directory first.

The server service was unable to unload the server driver.

[Netevent]

Restart the server or, if the problem persists, contact your system administrator.

The server was unable to allocate from the system nonpaged pool because the pool was empty.

[Netevent]

The system ran out of its nonpaged pool.

Ask your system administrator to increase the system's memory.

The server was unable to allocate from the system nonpaged pool because the server reached the configured limit for nonpaged pool allocations.

[Netevent]

This is a non-critical message that appears if the server is configured to use limited resources. If the server is configured to use an unlimited number of connections, some hidden parameters may need to be changed.

No action is needed unless the server has reached the maximum configured Optimization setting. Then contact technical support. If the server is not configured to use the maximum number of connections, select Network in Control Panel. When the Installed Network Software box appears, select Server and then Configure. Select Maximize Connections in the Optimization box to increase the number of available resources.

The server was unable to allocate from the system paged pool because the pool was empty.

[Netevent]

The system ran out of its paged pool.

Ask your system administrator to increase the system's memory.

The server was unable to allocate from the system paged pool because the server reached the configured limit for paged pool allocations.

[Netevent]

This is a non-critical message that appears if the server is configured to use limited resources. If the server is configured to use an unlimited number of connections, some hidden parameters may need to be changed.

No action is needed unless the server has reached the maximum configured Optimization setting. Then contact technical support. If the server is not configured to use the maximum number of connections, select Network in Control Panel. When the Installed Network Software box appears, select Server and then Configure. Select Maximize Connections in the Optimization box to increase the number of available resources.

The server was unable to allocate virtual memory.

[Netevent]

The system's paging file is full.

Ask your system administrator to increase the paging file's size or to increase the server's memory.

The server was unable to perform an operation due to a shortage of available resources.

[Netevent]

This is a non-critical message that appears if the server is configured to use limited resources. If the server is configured to use an unlimited number of connections, some hidden parameters may need to be changed.

No action is needed unless the server has reached the maximum configured Optimization setting. Then contact technical support. If the server is not configured to use the maximum number of connections, select Network in Control Panel. When the Installed Network Software box appears, select Server and then Configure. Select Maximize Connections in the Optimization box to increase the number of available resources.

The server's call to a system service failed unexpectedly.

[Netevent]

Contact technical support.

The server's configuration parameter "irpstacksize" is too small for the server to use a local device. Please increase the value of this parameter.

[Netevent]

The server preallocates I/O request packets to be the size specified by the IRPSTACKSIZE parameter in the configuration information. The value of this parameter must be as large as the size required by any transport or file system in the network.

Ask your system administrator to change the parameter in the server's configuration information.

The server's Registry key *name* was not present and could not be created. The server could not start.

[Netevent]

The Registry is corrupted.

Ask your system administrator to reinstall the Registry from the Emergency Repair Disk that was made when Windows NT was installed.

The server's Registry key *name* was not present. The server could not start.

[Netevent]

The Registry is corrupted.

Ask your system administrator to reinstall the Registry from the Emergency Repair Disk that was made when Windows NT was installed.

name **e servers** ***computer name*** **and** ***name*** **both claim to be an NT Domain Controller for the** ***computer name*** **domain. One of the servers should be removed from the domain because the servers have different security identifiers(SID).**

[Network]

This can happen if identically named domains on different networks are placed on the same network.

Remove one of the servers from the domain.

The service cannot accept control messages at this time.

[Kernel32]

There is a temporary mismatch between the requested control and the state of the service to be controlled. The service may be in a state of start-pending, stop-pending, or stopped.

Wait a few minutes, then retry your operation.

The service control dispatcher could not find the service name in the dispatch table.

[Network]

This message should occur only on a down-level computer. Any action to correct the problem should be performed on that computer.

The service control is busy.

[Network] Net Message ID: 2187

The service is not responding to requests now. Another program may be controlling the service or there may be a software problem.

Try to stop the service by typing NET STOP <service>. If this fails, stop all programs running on the computer and try typing the Net Stop command again. If the problem persists, contact technical support. Be prepared to give the name of the service and other information about the system, such as the services and applications that were running on the computer, and the amount and type of network activity when the problem occurred.

The service could not be controlled in its present state.

[Network] Net Message ID: 2189

The service is not currently accepting requests. If the service is starting, it cannot process requests until it is fully started.

Try the operation again in a minute or two. If this problem persists, the service may be stuck in a partially running state. Contact technical support. Be prepared to give the name of the service and other information about the system, such as the services and applications that were running, and the type and amount of network activity on the computer at the time of the problem.

The service database is locked.

[Kernel32]

An application may have tried to lock a service database that was already locked. Or an application may have tried to start a service when the service database was locked.

Wait a few minutes, then try the operation again.

The service database is locked.

[Network] Net Message ID: 2180

A software error occurred.

Contact technical support.

The service did not report an error.

[Network] Net Message ID: 3534

Try the task later. If the problem persists, contact your network administrator.

The service did not respond to control and was stopped with the DosKillProc function.

[Network] Net Message ID: 3060

The service did not respond to a control signal. The service may not be running correctly or a fatal error might have occurred. Windows NT stopped the service.

Contact technical support.

The service did not respond to the start or control request in a timely fashion.

[Kernel32]

An application tried to start a service, or control a running service, and requested this be done within a certain time frame. It was not done within that time frame.

Wait a few minutes and then retry your request. If you receive this message again, contact your technical support group.

The service did not start due to a logon failure.

[Kernel32]

An application tried to start up a service, but the service could not log on.

Use the Event Viewer to look in the event log for details about the logon failure. If the service account is not a local account, verify that the domain controller is functioning.

The service does not respond to control actions.

[Network] Net Message ID: 2183

This message should occur only on a down-level computer. Any action to correct the problem should be performed on that computer. A software error occurred.

Contact technical support.

The service ended abnormally.

[Network] Net Message ID: 2190

This message should occur only on a down-level computer. Any action to correct the problem should be performed on that computer. The service was not running properly and would not respond to a command. The service was terminated.

Stop the service by typing NET STOP <service>. Then restart the service by typing NET START <service>. If the problem occurs frequently, contact technical support.

The service failed to authenticate with the primary domain controller.

[Network]

This message should occur only on a down-level computer. Any action to correct the problem should be performed on that computer.

The service failed to obtain a long-term lock on the segment for network control blocks (NCBs). The error code is the data.

[Network] Net Message ID: 3102

This message should occur only on a down-level computer. Any action to correct the problem should be performed on that computer. A software error occurred.

Contact technical support.

The service failed to release the long-term lock on the segment for network control blocks (NCBs). The error code is the data.

[Network] Net Message ID: 3103

This message should occur only on a down-level computer. Any action to correct the problem should be performed on that computer. A software error occurred.

Contact technical support.

The service has not been started.

[Kernel32] [Network] Net Message ID: 2184

You tried to use a service that is not running.

To display a list of active services, type NET START. To start a service, type NET START <service>.

The service has returned a service-specific error code.

[Kernel32]

You will have to check the documentation for the service to get an explanation of the service-specific error code.

The service has stopped due to repeated consecutive occurrences of a network control block (NCB) error. The last bad NCB follows in raw data.

[Network] Net Message ID: 3140

A software error occurred.

Contact technical support.

The service is in an unexpected state.

[Server Manager]

One of the Windows NT services is in an unexpected state.

Contact technical support.

The service is not responding to the control function.

[Network] Net Message ID: 2186

The service cannot run your command at this time.

Try the command again later. If the problem persists, stop and restart the service. However, if the problem continues after you have restarted the service, report the problem. Be sure to include the name of the service and the command that was refused, to technical support.

The service is not responding.

[Server Manager]

You have attempted to start a service that is not responding. The possible reasons for this depend on the specific service.

Try again later.

The service name is invalid.

[Network] Net Message ID: 2185

You tried to start a service that is not configured on this system.

Check the spelling of the service name or check the configuration information for the service using the Services option from Server Manager.

The service process could not connect to the service controller.

[Kernel32]

Contact the supplier of the running application.

The service table is full.

[Network] Net Message ID: 2181

This message should occur only on a down-level computer. Any action to correct the problem should be performed on that computer. You cannot start another service because you have reached the maximum number of services specified in your configuration file.

You can start another service if you first stop a nonessential one. To display the list of services that are running, type NET START. You could also change the maximum number of services allowed to run simultaneously on the computer by changing the value of the NUMSERVICES entry in the computer's configuration file. If you need assistance, contact your network administrator.

The session from *computer name* has open files.

[Network]

This message should occur only on a down-level computer. Any action to correct the problem should be performed on that computer.

The session identification does not specify a valid session.

[Network] Net Message ID: 2461

This message should occur only on a down-level computer. Any action to correct the problem should be performed on that computer. A software error occurred.

If this error persists or causes other errors, contact technical support.

The session setup from the computer *computer name* failed because there is no trust account in the security database for this computer. The name of the account referenced in the security database is *user name*.

[Network] Net Message ID: 5723

The account may not exist in the security database.

Verify that the account exists. If the account exists, contact your network administrator to check the cause of the problem.

The session setup from the computer *computer name* failed to authenticate. The name of the account referenced in the security database is *name*. The following error occurred: *text*

[Network] Net Message ID: 5722

The computer account may not exist.

Verify that the computer account exists. If the account exists, contact your network administrator to check the cause of the problem.

The session setup to the Windows NT Domain Controller *name* for the domain *name* failed because the computer *computer name* does not have a local security database account.

[Network] Net Message ID: 5720

The local security database is corrupted.

Contact your network administrator.

The session setup to the Windows NT Domain Controller *name* for the domain *name* failed because the Windows NT Domain Controller does not have an account for the computer *computer name*.

[Network] Net Message ID: 5721

The specified server's security database is corrupted.

Contact your network administrator.

The session was canceled.

[Kernel32]

Transmission errors caused the connection to the remote computer to be disconnected.

Run the application again to reestablish the connection.

The settings could not be saved.

[User Profile Editor]

User Profile Editor was unable to write to the Registry. Or the hard disk is full.

Make sure that permissions on the appropriate Registry key (HKEY_USERS\\ <user name>) are not configured to keep you from writing to this key. If your hard disk is full, delete unnecessary files, and then try again.

The setup .INF file ***filename*** **has a missing or invalid [Source Media Descriptions] section.**

[Setup]

Most of the .INF files used by Setup have a [Source Media Descriptions] section which identifies the media the source installation files, such as video adapter drivers, are on. If this section of the .INF file is missing or has a bad format, then Setup will not be able to find some files needed for installation.

Retry the Setup operation. If you get the same message, and you are running maintenance Setup, try replacing the file named in the message with the .INF file from the distribution medium (you will have to decompress the file). Otherwise, contact your technical support group.

The setup .INF file ***filename*** **has a missing or invalid [Source Media Descriptions] section.**

[Repair Disk]

Most of the .INF files used by Setup have a [Source Media Descriptions] section which identifies the media the source installation files, such as video adapter drivers, are on. If this section of the .INF file is missing or has a bad format, then Setup will not be able to find some files needed for installation.

Retry the Setup operation. If you get the same message, and you are running maintenance Setup, try replacing the file named in the message with the .INF file from the distribution medium (you will have to decompress the file). Otherwise, contact your technical support group.

The share could not be created. The gateway account could not access to the resource.

Verify that the gateway account has access to the share and that you supplied the correct credentials.

The share name entered may not be accessible from some MS-DOS workstations. Are you sure you want to use this share name? *name* **:** *text*

[Network]

MS-DOS workstations can only recognize share names that fit the file naming requirements in MS-DOS. If you assign this name to the share, MS-DOS workstations will not be able to access it.

If you are sure this share will not need to be accessed from MS-DOS workstations choose Yes. Otherwise choose No.

The share name which you have specified is not a valid 8.3 file name and may not be visible from non-NT machines, e.g. DOS machines.

[Print Manager]

If you want users at computers that are not running Windows NT to be able to see this shared printer, specify a name that follows the MS-DOS naming conventions, as follows: The name can contain up to eight characters, optionally followed by a period and an extension of up to three characters. It must start with either a letter or a number, and can contain any uppercase or lowercase characters except the following:. " \ / [ ] : ; | = , ? * + < >

The shared queue cannot be deleted while a print job is being spooled to the queue.

[Network]

This message should occur only on a down-level computer. Any action to correct the problem should be performed on that computer. You attempted to delete an active printer.

After the current print job has finished spooling, either print or delete the job. Then delete the printer.

The shared resource you are connected to could not be found.

[Network] Net Message ID: 2392

This message should occur only on a down-level computer. Any action to correct the problem should be performed on that computer. LAN Manager found a problem while trying to complete the task.

Type the command again in a few minutes. If you continue to receive this message, see your network administrator.

The signal handler cannot be set.

[Kernel32]

Signal handlers cannot be set when a process is ending.

Allow the process to end without setting a handler. You may have to contact the supplier of the running application.

The Simple TCP/IP Services could not find the TCP Chargen port. The TCP Chargen service was not started.

[Repair Disk]

This computer will be unable to respond to Chargen requests from other systems that use the Chargen protocol.

Make sure that the entry for this port is in the SERVICES file in the WINNT35\SYSTEM32\DRIVERS\ETC directory.

The Simple TCP/IP Services could not find the TCP Daytime port. The TCP Daytime service was not started.

[Repair Disk]

This computer will be unable to respond to Daytime requests from other systems that use the Daytime protocol.

Make sure that the entry for this port is in the SERVICES file in the WINNT35\SYSTEM32\DRIVERS\ETC directory.

The Simple TCP/IP Services could not find the TCP Discard port. The TCP Discard service was not started.

[Repair Disk]

This computer will be unable to respond to Discard requests from other systems that use the Discard protocol.

Make sure that the entry for this port is in the SERVICES file in the WINNT35\SYSTEM32\DRIVERS\ETC directory.

The Simple TCP/IP Services could not find the TCP Echo port. The TCP Echo service was not started.

[Repair Disk]

This computer will be unable to respond to Echo requests from other systems that use the Echo protocol.

Make sure that the entry for this port is in the SERVICES file in the WINNT35\SYSTEM32\DRIVERS\ETC directory.

The Simple TCP/IP Services could not find the TCP QOTD port. The TCP QOTD service was not started.

[Repair Disk]

This computer will be unable to respond to Quote of the Day requests from other systems that use the Quote of the Day protocol.

Make sure that the entry for this port is in the SERVICES file in the WINNT35\SYSTEM32\DRIVERS\ETC directory.

The Simple TCP/IP Services could not find the UDP Chargen port. The UDP Chargen service was not started.

[Repair Disk]

This computer will be unable to respond to Character Generator requests from other systems that use the Character Generator protocol.

Make sure that the entry for this port is in the SERVICES file in the WINNT35\SYSTEM32\DRIVERS\ETC directory.

The Simple TCP/IP Services could not find the UDP Daytime port. The UDP Daytime service was not started.

[Repair Disk]

This computer will be unable to respond to UDP Daytime requests from other systems that use the UDP Daytime protocol.

Make sure that the entry for this port is in the SERVICES file in the WINNT35\SYSTEM32\DRIVERS\ETC directory.

The Simple TCP/IP Services could not find the UDP Discard port. The UDP Discard service was not started.

[Repair Disk]

This computer will be unable to respond to UDP Discard requests from other systems that use the Discard protocol.

Make sure that the entry for this port is in the SERVICES file in the WINNT35\SYSTEM32\DRIVERS\ETC directory.

The Simple TCP/IP Services could not find the UDP Echo port. The UDP Echo service was not started.

[Repair Disk]

This computer will be unable to respond to UDP Echo requests from other systems that use the UDP Echo protocol.

Make sure that the entry for this port is in the SERVICES file in the WINNT35\SYSTEM32\DRIVERS\ETC directory.

The Simple TCP/IP Services could not find the UDP QOTD port. The UDP QOTD service was not started.

[Repair Disk]

This computer will be unable to respond to UDP Quote of the Day requests from other systems that use the UDP Quote of the Day protocol.

Make sure that the entry for this port is in the SERVICES file in the WINNT35\SYSTEM32\DRIVERS\ETC directory.

The Simple TCP/IP Services could not open the Quotes file. The UDP and TCP QOTD services were not started.

[Repair Disk]

This computer might be unable to respond to some requests from other systems that use the Quote of the Day protocol.

Make sure that the file is present and that you have the necessary permissions to open it. If the file is missing or corrupt, you might need to restore it from a backup copy, or re-install it.

The Simple TCP/IP Services could not open the TCP Chargen port. The TCP Chargen service was not started.

[Repair Disk]

This computer might be unable to respond to some requests from other systems that use the Quote of the Day protocol. There may not be enough free memory, or the port is open by another application.

Close some applications to free memory, and try again. To find out whether another application has the port open, use the netstat command.

The Simple TCP/IP Services could not open the TCP Daytime port. The TCP Daytime service was not started.

[Repair Disk]

This computer might be unable to respond to some requests from other systems that use the Quote of the Day protocol. There may not be enough free memory, or the port is open by another application.

Close some applications to free memory, and try again. To find out whether another application has the port open, use the netstat command.

The Simple TCP/IP Services could not open the TCP Discard port. The TCP Discard service was not started.

[Repair Disk]

This computer might be unable to respond to some requests from other systems that use the Discard protocol. There may not be enough free memory, or the port is open by another application.

Close some applications to free memory, and try again. To find out whether another application has the port open, use the netstat command.

The Simple TCP/IP Services could not open the TCP Echo port. The TCP Echo service was not started.

[Repair Disk]

This computer might be unable to respond to some requests from other systems that use the Echo protocol. There may not be enough free memory, or the port is open by another application.

Close some applications to free memory, and try again. To find out whether another application has the port open, use the netstat command.

The Simple TCP/IP Services could not open the TCP QOTD port. The TCP QOTD service was not started.

[Repair Disk]

This computer might be unable to respond to some requests from other systems that use the Quote of the Day protocol.

The Simple TCP/IP Services could not open the UDP Chargen port. The UDP Chargen service was not started.

[Repair Disk]

This computer might be unable to respond to some requests from other systems that use the Character Generator protocol. There may not be enough free memory, or the port is open by another application.

Close some applications to free memory, and try again. To find out whether another application has the port open, use the netstat command.

The Simple TCP/IP Services could not open the UDP Daytime port. The UDP Daytime service was not started.

[Repair Disk]

This computer might be unable to respond to some requests from other systems that use the Daytime protocol. There may not be enough free memory, or the port is open by another application.

Close some applications to free memory, and try again. To find out whether another application has the port open, use the netstat command.

The Simple TCP/IP Services could not open the UDP Discard port. The UDP Discard service was not started.

[Repair Disk]

This computer might be unable to respond to some requests from other systems that use the Discard protocol. There may not be enough free memory, or the port is open by another application.

Close some applications to free memory, and try again. To find out whether another application has the port open, use the netstat command.

The Simple TCP/IP Services could not open the UDP Echo port. The UDP Echo service was not started.

[Repair Disk]

This computer might be unable to respond to some requests from other systems that use the Echo protocol. There may not be enough free memory, or the port is open by another application.

Close some applications to free memory, and try again. To find out whether another application has the port open, use the netstat command.

The Simple TCP/IP Services could not open the UDP QOTD port. The UDP QOTD service was not started.

[Repair Disk]

This computer might be unable to respond to some requests from other systems that use the Quote of the Day protocol. There may not be enough free memory, or the port is open by another application.

Close some applications to free memory, and try again. To find out whether another application has the port open, use the netstat command.

The software requires a newer version of the operating system.

[Network] Net Message ID: 3512

This message should occur only on a down-level computer. Any action to correct the problem should be performed on that computer. The software you are attempting to run requires a more recent version of the operating system.

Run the software using a more recent version of the operating system.

The source and destination paths are on different servers.

[Network] Net Message ID: 2383

This message should occur only on a down-level computer. Any action to correct the problem should be performed on that computer. A software error occurred.

Contact technical support.

The source document cannot be found. Make sure that the object still exists in the source document, the link has not been corrupted or the source document has not been deleted, moved, or renamed.

[Write]

A document containing linked information cannot be found. Possibly, the document is saved to a network share to which you are not currently connected.

Follow the user action specified in the message.

The source path cannot be a directory.

[Network] Net Message ID: 2380

This message should occur only on a down-level computer. Any action to correct the problem should be performed on that computer. The source path you typed is a directory name, which is not allowed.

You must include a filename or wildcard in the path. To copy all files in a directory, type COPY [<source>]*.* <destination>.

The source path is illegal.

[Network] Net Message ID: 2381

This message should occur only on a down-level computer. Any action to correct the problem should be performed on that computer. You referred to a nonexistent drive, directory, or filename, or you typed the command incorrectly.

Check the spelling of the source or pathname you have typed. Remember to precede computer names with two backslashes, as in \\\\<computer name>.

The source path specified in the Setup command is invalid. Check the /s switch.

[Setup]

Select OK to exit Setup. Correct the source path specification on the Setup command line, especially if you are running Setup to a share point, and then retry the Setup command. If you still get this message, contact your technical support group.

The source path specified in the Setup command is invalid. Check the /s switch.

[Repair Disk]

Select OK to exit Setup. Correct the source path specification on the Setup command line, especially if you are running Setup to a share point, and then retry the Setup command. If you still get this message, contact your technical support group.

The specified .INF file could not be found.

[Display]

The application could not find the file you specified.

Make sure the file is in the directory you specified. Then try again, making sure you type the path correctly.

The specified account name is already a member of the local group.

[Kernel32]

Contact the supplier of the running application.

The specified account name is not a member of the local group.

[Kernel32]

For instance, the Windows NT security subsystem cannot delete an account from an alias when that account is not in the alias in the security database.

Contact the supplier of the running application.

The specified address is not available.

[DHCP]

The address that you tried to assign to a client is either not in the IP address range for this scope, or is already in use.

Try again, specifying a different address.

The specified application is not a Windows or DOS program.

[Program Manager]

The application was written for an operating system other than one of the Microsoft Windows operating systems or MS-DOS. It cannot be run on this computer.

Get a version of the application that was written for use with Microsoft Windows or MS-DOS.

The specified application is not a Windows or DOS program.

[Task Manager]

The application you specified was written for another operating system. It cannot be run from Windows NT.

Use a Windows or MS-DOS version of the application. Or, run the application on a computer that is using the operating system that the application was written for.

The specified attributes are invalid, or incompatible with the attributes for the group as a whole.

[Kernel32]

The Windows NT subsystem maintains a set of attributes for a group of accounts as a whole, such as whether the group can own objects. An application ownership change request on behalf of a user may conflict with these.

Contact the supplier of the running application.

The specified Client already exists in the database.

[DHCP]

An address has already been assigned to this client.

No action is needed.

The specified client is a reserved client.

[DHCP]

You cannot delete a reserved client.

If you want to remove this client, use the Reservations dialog.

The specified client is already registered for the specified event.

[Network] Net Message ID: 2430

This message should occur only on a down-level computer. Any action to correct the problem should be performed on that computer. A program requested the alerter to notify it of an event for which it is already receiving notifications.

Contact technical support.

The specified client is not a reserved client.

[DHCP]

You cannot change basic information for this client because this is not one of the clients that were explicitly assigned a reserved IP address.

No action is needed.

The specified codepage is invalid.

[PORTUAS]

The code page that you specified with the /c or -c option on the command line is not valid.

Check the code page and try again, making sure to type the code page correctly.

The specified code page is not valid.

[Aclconv]

The code page supplied in the /code page switch to the Aclconv command is invalid.

Use the International option in Control Panel to determine what code pages are valid. Or omit the /code page switch and use the system code page.

The specified component could not be found in the configuration information.

[Network] Net Message ID: 2146

Windows NT could not find the required information in your configuration.

Ask your network administrator to check your configuration. The administrator should make sure your system configuration contains all information required to run Windows NT and any associated applications.

The specified datatype is invalid.

[Kernel32]

Contact the supplier of the running application.

The specified device name is invalid.

[Kernel32]

An application program requested a connection between a local device and a network resource, but the local device name in the request was invalid.

If you have a user interface, try a different device name. For example, A: through Z: usually will work. Otherwise, contact the supplier of the application.

The specified DHCP element cannot be removed because it has been used.

[DHCP]

No action is needed.

The specified disk or diskette cannot be accessed.

[Kernel32]

The hard disk or floppy disk is not properly formatted for the appropriate file system.

Format the hard disk or floppy disk for the file system you are using.

The specified document times conflict with the printer's times.

[Print Manager]

You have specified that a document be printed at a time when the printer is scheduled to be turned off or unavailable.

Specify a different time for printing your document.

The specified domain already exists.

[Kernel32]

Contact the supplier of the running application.

The specified domain did not exist.

[Kernel32]

For example, an application requested the security ID of a domain served by a server, but the name of the domain supplied with the request did not exist on the server.

Find out what domain names can be used, check your spelling, and try again. You may have to contact the supplier of the running application.

The specified drive is the System Partition on an ARC-compliant system; its file system cannot be converted

[Convert]

The system partition on an ARC-compliant system must always be FAT. If the system partition is converted to another file system, the system will not be able to restart.

No action is needed.

The specified driver is invalid.

[Kernel32]

The driver might have been specified incorrectly in the Registry or the driver version may be incompatible with this version of Windows NT.

Verify that the driver is installed properly. You might want to try using the Drivers option in Control Panel to remove and reinstall the driver. If you continue to see this message, contact the supplier of the driver.

The specified extended attribute handle is invalid.

[Kernel32]

A file contains a reference to an extended attribute that does not exist. Either the disk partition is damaged or the extended attribute system file has been improperly modified.

Run the Chkdsk utility with the /f switch on the disk.

The specified extended attribute name was invalid.

[Kernel32]

The extended attribute name contains a character that is not correct.

Correct the extended attribute name and try the operation again.

The specified file cannot be played on the specified MCI device. The file may be corrupt, not in the correct format, or no file handler available for this format.

Try using either a different file with this device or a different device with this file. Or, restore this file from a backup copy and try again.

The specified group already exists.

[Kernel32]

A client requested the creation of new account (user, group, or alias), but the requested account name is already a group account name.

Use a different name, or delete the existing group account and retry with the same name.

The specified group does not exist.

[Kernel32]

A client requested a service for a group account, such as changing group security information, but the service could not find the account in this domain.

Use the correct group name. Check your spelling, then try again.

The specified IpRange already exists.

[DHCP]

You specified a range that has already been assigned to another scope.

View the existing scopes to find out what ranges are already in use. Then try again, specifying a range that is not already in use.

The specified local group already exists.

[Kernel32]

A request for a new alias specified an alias name that already exists in the security database.

Contact the supplier of the running application.

The specified local group does not exist.

[Kernel32]

Contact the supplier of the running application.

The specified module could not be found.

[Kernel32]

The requested module is not loaded.

Check which module is being requested, and make sure it has been loaded. You may have to contact the supplier of the running application.

The specified network name is no longer available.

[Kernel32]

The network resource that you specified was either temporarily taken offline or is no longer available. It is possible that: (1) the share at the server might have been temporarily deleted; (2) the server that shared the resource might have been turned off; or (3) the permissions might have been changed.

Retry the operation. If you continue to have difficulty accessing the resource: (1) contact the person who administers the server to find out why it is no longer available; or (2) contact the network administrator.

The specified network password is not correct.

[Kernel32]

The password that you specified is not correct for the account or resource you attempted to access.

Specify the correct password. Contact your network administrator if you continue to have problems.

The specified network provider name is invalid.

[Kernel32]

An application was browsing the resources on a network and specified a provider name that was unrecognizable by Windows NT.

Make sure you did not type the provider name incorrectly (if the running application has given you the ability to do that). If you cannot correct this condition through the application user interface, contact the supplier of the running application.

The specified network resource or device is no longer available.

[Kernel32]

The specified resource is not available. The computer that shared the resource might have been turned off, or the permissions might have changed.

Do one of the following: (1) check to see that the computer that is sharing resources is turned on, then retry the command; or (2) contact your network administrator to find out how you can use the resource.

The specified option already exists.

[DHCP]

This option is already defined.

No action is needed.

The specified option does not exist.

[DHCP]

You tried to use an option that has not been defined.

Define the option and try again.

The specified options are not supported by this serial device

[Mode]

While using the Mode command to change one or more options for a COMn: device, you specified at least one unsupported option. None of the option changes you specified were made.

To find out which serial port options can be changed with the Mode command, type HELP at the command prompt, followed by the command name (in this case, Mode).

The specified parameter could not be found in the configuration information.

[Network] Net Message ID: 2147

Windows NT could not find a particular entry in your configuration.

Ask your network administrator to check your configuration. The administrator should make sure your system configuration contains all information required to run Windows NT and any associated applications.

The specified path is invalid.

[File Manager] [Kernel32]

Check the path to the file and try again, making sure to type the pathname correctly. Start with the drive letter, followed by a colon (:) and a backslash (\), and be sure to separate directories from subdirectories with a backslash. In some cases you can use the Browse feature to specify a path.

The specified path is not valid.

[Backup]

The may be misspelled or a drive letter was specified where it shouldn't have been.

Check the spelling in the path or verify that the path should not be preceded with a drive letter.

The specified path points to a file that may not be available during later Windows sessions. Do you want to continue?

[Program Manager]

You have attempted to load into a Control Panel option a file (most likely, a font) from a network share or removable media. When you do this, Windows NT presents this message.

To ensure that the file will be available during later Windows NT sessions, copy the file to your Windows NT SYSTEM32 directory.

The specified path points to a file that may not be available during later Windows sessions. Do you want to continue?

[Program Manager]

You have attempted to load into a Control Panel option a file (most likely, a font) from a network share. When you do this, Windows NT presents this message.

To ensure that the file will be available during later Windows NT sessions, copy the file to your Windows NT SYSTEM32 directory.

The specified port is unknown.

[Kernel32]

The printer port name you specified does not currently exist on your computer.

Use Print Manager to look at the current list of ports you can print to and use one of those.

The specified printer driver is already installed.

[Kernel32]

This is an informational message. You cannot install a printer driver with the same name as a printer driver which is already installed.

No action is needed. The printer driver is already installed.

The specified printer or disk device has been paused.

[Kernel32]

The network printer or disk device that you specified has been paused.

Use the Net Continue command to reactivate the device, then retry the command.

The specified priority is invalid.

[Kernel32]

An application tried to use a document or printer priority outside the range of 1 to 99.

Unless you can specify a valid priority through the user interface of the application, you will have to contact the supplier of the running application.

The specified procedure could not be found.

[Kernel32]

The specified procedure is not in the module being searched.

Check which procedure is being requested and make sure that it is in the module. You may have to contact the supplier of the running application.

The specified range either overlaps with an range or is invalid.

[DHCP]

Make sure the End Address for the range is greater than the Start Address for the range. If you still get this message, look at the other scopes to see what ranges are already defined. Then try again, specifying a range that is not yet assigned.

The specified Range is full.

[DHCP]

All addresses in this range have been assigned.

If possible, extend the range.

The specified Reserved Ip already exists.

[DHCP]

You tried to assign an IP address that is already assigned or leased to another client.

Specify a different address.

The specified separator file is invalid.

[Kernel32]

A separator file is a file printed between print jobs to mark where the output from one job finishes and the output from the next job begins.

Use Print Manager to look at the printer details information, which lists all the separator files known to your computer. Either use one of those or install a new one.

The specified server cannot perform the requested operation.

[Kernel32]

You requested an operation that cannot be performed by the specified server.

Make sure you have specified the correct computer name and command, then retry the command. If you continue to have problems, contact your network administrator.

The specified service already exists.

[Kernel32]

An application tried to create a service that already exists on this computer.

Don't try the operation again without deleting the existing service.

The specified service database lock is invalid.

[Kernel32]

An application tried to unlock a service database without providing a previously acquired lock.

Contact the supplier of the running application. The database lock must be one obtained from the LockServiceDatabase API function call.

The specified service does not exist as an installed service.

[Kernel32]

Check the spelling of the service name and then retype it. If you still get this message, contact your system administrator.

The specified service has been marked for deletion.

[Kernel32]

For instance, an application may have tried to delete a service already marked for deletion, attempted to change the configuration or security for a service marked for deletion, or tried to start a service marked for deletion.

This message is for your information, no action is needed.

The specified service is disabled and cannot be started.

[Kernel32]

A service management user interface application has tried to start a service that is marked as disabled in the computer's service database.

If it was intended for this service to be enabled, then the Windows NT Setup program should have enabled it at system installation time, or the system administrator should have done so later. Contact your network administrator to see if the specified service was ever enabled. If it was, you may have to contact the supplier of the running application.

The specified Subnet already exists.

[DHCP]

You tried to create a scope for a subnet that already has a scope.

No action is needed.

The specified Subnet does not exist.

[DHCP]

You tried to delete a scope that does not exist.

No action is needed.

The specified system semaphore name was not found.

[Kernel32]

Make sure the semaphore name is correct and try again. You may have to contact the supplier of the running application.

The specified user account is not a member of the specified group account.

[Kernel32]

For instance, a client may have requested that a service delete a user account from a group and the user is not a member of the group.

You may want to add the user account to the group account before retrying, or you may have used the wrong group name in your request.

The specified user already exists.

[Kernel32]

A service request to create a new user, group, or alias account has been denied because the requested account name already exists.

Use a different name, or delete the existing account and retry with the same name.

The specified user does not exist.

[Kernel32]

A client requested an operation on a user account, such as changing the password, but the user account could not be found.

Check that you spelled the account name correctly, then retry.

The specified username is invalid.

[Kernel32]

An application has specified a user name as part of a network service request and the format of the user name is invalid.

Check the syntax of the user name.

The specified volume has hotfixes; it cannot be converted. Run CHKDSK /f to resolve these references.

[Convert-HPFS]

On the HPFS volume you specified as the source for a file system conversion from HPFS to NTFS, not all temporary areas (which were created to correct disk write errors) have been written to permanent areas on the volume.

Run the Chkdsk command with the /f switch on the HPFS volume. Then retry the conversion.

The specified volume is dirty; it cannot be converted. Run CHKDSK /f to correct this problem.

[Convert-HPFS]

On the HPFS volume you specified as the source for a file system conversion from HPFS to NTFS, not all file changes have been written to permanent areas on the volume.

Run the Chkdsk command with the /f switch on the HPFS volume. Then retry the conversion.

The spooler is not running.

[Network] Net Message ID: 2161

This message should occur only on a down-level computer. Any action to correct the problem should be performed on that computer. The spooler has not been started.

Use Print Manager to start the spooler.

The start offset is out of range.

[Network] Net Message ID: 2371

This message should occur only on a down-level computer. Any action to correct the problem should be performed on that computer. A software error occurred.

Contact technical support.

The start type for the Netlogon service could not be changed. Use the Services applet to correct the problem.

[Control Panel]

In order to change the domain, the application must change the start type for the Net Logon service. It was unable to do so.

Choose the Services icon from the Control Panel. Select the Net Logon service, and choose the Startup button. You can then specify how the service should be started.

The static data file that is used to initialize WINS database is too big.

[WINS Service]

The static initialization file you tried to use is too large. If the initialization was done automatically, the registry can provide the name of the file.

Split the file into two or more files, and try again

The status port for *name* overlaps the control registers for the device.

Either a newly installed device driver configured the port incorrectly, or an error was made while editing the Registry directly.

Contact the vendor of the driver and report this message. Or, if the error was introduced while editing the Registry, delete the nodes that were added and try again.

The status register for *name* overlaps the *name* control registers.

The multiport card is incorrectly configured.

Delete the configuration information from the Registry and try again.

The status register for *name* overlaps with the *name* status register.

The multiport card is incorrectly configured.

Delete the configuration information from the Registry and try again.

The string and prefix specified are too long.

[Network] Net Message ID: 2354

This message should occur only on a down-level computer. Any action to correct the problem should be performed on that computer. A software error occurred.

Contact technical support.

The string binding is invalid.

[Kernel32]

A string binding contains only some of the information necessary to make a remote procedure call. An application needs to map string bindings to bindings before attempting the call. In this case, the string binding submitted to the mapping procedure was invalid. For example, a string binding cannot contain white space.

Contact the supplier of the running distributed application.

The string could not be converted.

[Remote Access Service]

This error should not occur under normal circumstances.

Restart your computer to make sure that all recent configuration changes have taken effect. If the error persists, consult the Windows NT event log for detailed warnings or errors.

The string universal unique identifier (UUID) is invalid.

[Kernel32]

The unique object identifier part of a string binding in a distributed (RPC) application is incorrect.

Contact the supplier of the running distributed application.

The structure size is incorrect.

[Remote Access Service]

This error should not occur under normal circumstances.

Restart your computer to make sure that all recent configuration changes have taken effect. If the error persists, consult the Windows NT event log for detailed warnings or errors.

The stub is unable to get the remote procedure call handle.

[Kernel32]

Contact the supplier of the running distributed application.

The stub received bad data.

[Kernel32]

Contact the supplier of the running distributed application.

The sub-service failed to start.

[Network] Net Message ID: 3062

The specified service could not be started automatically when another service was started.

Start the service individually.

The subdirectory *name* is already in the list.

[Server Manager]

The subdirectory you specified cannot be added to this list because it is already there.

No action is needed.

The supplied user buffer is not valid for the requested operation.

[Kernel32]

Contact the supplier of the running application.

The syntax is incorrect.

[Network] Net Message ID: 3953

You did not use the correct syntax of this command.

To see the syntax of this command, type NET HELP <command>.

The syntax of the command is incorrect.

[Command]

Make sure you typed the command correctly and that the parameters are correct. To get help on this command, type the command, then /?. Or type HELP, followed by the command name.

The syntax of the command is incorrect.

[Command Prompt]

Make sure you typed the command correctly and that the parameters are correct. To get help on this command, type the command, then /?. Or type HELP, followed by the command name.

The system cannot accept the date entered.

[Command]

You have entered a date that does not correspond to the correct format for the Country that you have specified in the Country dialog in Control Panel. Or you have specified a date that does not follow the mm-dd-yyyy format. Or you have indicated that the year is before 1980 or after 2099.

Open the International option in Control Panel to determine the country that you have specified, then enter at the command prompt a date that corresponds to the specified country's format. Or specify a date that corresponds to the mm-dd-yyyy format. Or enter a year between 1980 and 2099.

The system cannot accept the date entered.

[Command Prompt]

You have entered a date that does not correspond to the correct format for the Country that you have specified in the Country dialog in Control Panel. Or you have specified a date that does not follow the mm-dd-yyyy format. Or you have indicated that the year is before 1980 or after 2099.

Open the International option in Control Panel to determine the country that you have specified, then enter at the command prompt a date that corresponds to the specified country's format. Or specify a date that corresponds to the mm-dd-yyyy format. Or enter a year between 1980 and 2099.

The system cannot accept the START command parameter *parameter*.

[Command Prompt]

You typed a parameter for the Start command that is invalid for that command.

To determine what parameters are valid for Start, type HELP START at the command prompt.

The system cannot accept the START command parameter *parameter*.

[Command]

You typed a parameter for the Start command that is invalid for that command.

To determine what parameters are valid for Start, type HELP START at the command prompt.

The system cannot accept the time entered.

[Command]

At the command prompt, you have invoked the Time command, and you have entered the time in an invalid format. The correct format for setting time is hours:minutes:seconds.hundredths:a|p. The a|p specifies a.m. or p.m., and if you do not include this setting, Command Prompt automatically uses a.m.

At the command prompt, enter a correctly formatted setting.

The system cannot accept the time entered.

[Command Prompt]

At the command prompt, you have invoked the Time command, and you have entered the time in an invalid format. The correct format for setting time is hours:minutes:seconds.hundredths:a|p. The a|p specifies a.m. or p.m., and if you do not include this setting, Command Prompt automatically uses a.m.

At the command prompt, enter a correctly formatted setting.

The system cannot change your password now because the domain *name* is not available.

[Workstation-Logon]

The domain on which you have an account is temporarily unavailable. The domain controller may not be started, or a trust relationship may have been broken.

Try again later. Or contact your domain administrator.

The system cannot complete the process.

[Command Prompt]

You may be low on memory.

Close one or more of the applications or windows that you have running, and then try again.

The system cannot complete the process.

[Command]

You may be low on memory.

Close one or more of the applications or windows that you have running, and then try again.

The system cannot delete current connections to network resources.

[Network] Net Message ID: 2372

This message should occur only on a down-level computer. Any action to correct the problem should be performed on that computer. Loading the profile failed because one or more connections between your computer and other network computers are active. LAN Manager could not delete the active connections.

If you were trying to load the profile onto a workstation, be sure the workstation is not actively using any shared resources. Be sure the current directory in each session is not a shared directory. If you were trying to load the profile onto a server, you must wait until none of the server's shared resources are being actively used. To see which users are actively using the server's resources, type NET FILE.

The system cannot execute the specified program.

[Command Prompt]

You directed the system to start an executable program file that may be corrupted or that is not compatible with Windows NT.

Run a valid program file.

The system cannot execute the specified program.

[Command]

You directed the system to start an executable program file that may be corrupted or that is not compatible with Windows NT.

Run a valid program file.

The system cannot find message for message number 0x*code* in message file for *filename*.

[Kernel32]

The message is not in the message file.

Enter the correct message number or reinstall the message file, and retry the command.

The system cannot find the batch label specified.

[Command]

Use the CD command to reach the directory that contains the batch file, then type the filename.

The system cannot find the batch label specified.

[Command Prompt]

Use the CD command to reach the directory that contains the batch file, then type the filename.

The system cannot find the device specified.

[Kernel32]

An unknown device was specified.

Retry the command, using a correct device name.

The system cannot find the drive specified.

[Kernel32]

One of the following has occurred: (1) the specified drive does not exist; (2) the drive letter is incorrect; (3) you are trying to restore to a redirected drive; or (4) you are trying to restore to a read-only drive.

For situations (1) and (2) above, retry the command using the correct drive letter. For situation (3), you cannot use the Restore command on a redirected drive.

The system cannot find the file *filename*.

[OS/2 Subsystem]

The OS/2 subsystem task manager cannot find the file that is named in the message. For example, the file does not exist in the current directory or on the specified search paths.

Retry the command specifying the correct filename.

The system cannot find the file specified.

[Kernel32]

The file named in the command does not exist in the current directory or search path specified. Or the filename was entered incorrectly.

Retry the command using the correct filename.

The system cannot find the path specified.

[Kernel32]

The path named in the command does not exist for the drive specified, or the path was entered incorrectly.

Retry the command using the correct path.

The system cannot find the command processor in the path specified.

[Command]

Type a valid path to the command processor.

The system cannot log you on to this domain because the system's computer account in its primary domain is missing or the password on that account is incorrect.

[Workstation-Logon]

You have typed the wrong password. Or the trust relationship between your domain and the domain onto which you are attempting a log on has been broken.

Retype the password. If this fails, contact your domain administrator. If you are the domain administrator, contact the administrator of the domain with which trust has been broken. Then use Server Manager to reestablish the relationship.

The system cannot log you on to this domain because the system's primary domain password is missing.

[Workstation-Logon]

The trust relationship between your domain and the domain that you are attempting to log on to may be broken.

Contact your system administrator. If you are the system administrator, contact the domain administrator. The domain administrator should use Server Manager to attempt to reestablish the broken trust relationship.

The system cannot log you on to this domain because the trust relationship between the primary domain and the trusted domain failed.

[Workstation-Logon]

The trust relationship between your domain and the domain that you are attempting to log on to has probably been broken.

Contact the system administrator. If you are the system administrator, contact the administrator of the domain that you attempted to log on to. The domain administrator should use Server Manager to reestablish the trust relationship.

The system cannot move the file to a different disk drive.

[Kernel32]

The file cannot be moved to a different disk drive at the same time you rename it using the Rename command.

Retry the command specifying the same drive for both the original and changed file names, or copy the file to the different drive and rename it by using different source and destination filenames.

The system cannot open *name* port requested by the application.

[Virtual DOS Machine (VDM)]

An application has attempted to use a communications (COM) port that NTVDM was unable to locate or open. The port that cannot be opened is named in the message.

Retry the operation using a different communications port (for instance, COM2 instead of COM1). If you still get this message, contact your system administrator to check the status of the communications ports on your computer.

The system cannot open the file.

[Kernel32]

The maximum number of open files has been reached.

Wait until another application has ended. Then retry the operation.

The system cannot open the device or file specified.

[Kernel32]

Contact the supplier of the running application.

The system cannot perform a JOIN or SUBST at this time.

[Kernel32]

The drive specified is being used by another process.

Retry the command later.

The system cannot read from the specified device.

[Kernel32]

The operating system detected an error while reading from this device.

Make sure the device is: (1) installed and connected; (2) switched on; (3) not being used by another process; (4) in the proper send mode; or (5) formatted, if the device is a disk. Then retry the command.

The system cannot start another process tattoos time.

[Kernel32]

The maximum number of running processes has been reached.

End a process or retry the command after the current process has completed.

The system cannot support a COM port number greater than 256.

[Program Manager]

Windows NT supports up to 256 COM ports.

Specify a COM port with a smaller number.

The system cannot support a COM port number greater than 256.

[Program Manager]

Specify a COM port with a smaller number.

The system cannot write to the specified device.

[Kernel32]

The operating system detected an error while writing to this device.

Make sure the device is: (1) installed and connected; (2) switched on; (3) not being used by another process; (4) in the proper receive mode; or (5) formatted, if the device is a disk. Then retry the command.

The system could not find message: ***text*****.**

[Network]

The system could not find the message.

Contact your system administrator.

The system detected a divide by zero error.

[Command Prompt]

The program attempted to divide by zero. There may be a problem in the program.

Contact technical support.

The system detected a divide by zero error.

[Command]

The program attempted to divide by zero. There may be a problem in the program.

Contact technical support.

The system detected a segment number that was not correct.

[Kernel32]

The .DLL or .EXE file contains a segment number that is not correct, or the file is unusable.

Do one of the following and then retry the command: (1) restart the system; or (2) replace the .DLL or .EXE file.

The system file is not suitable for running DOS and WINDOWS applications.

[Virtual DOS Machine (VDM)]

There is a problem with either CONFIG.NT or AUTOEXEC.NT. When NTVDM starts up, it edits these files to meet the requirements of MS-DOS and 16-bit Windows. If you get this message, NTVDM was not able to make all the edits necessary to meet all of those requirements.

Contact your system administrator.

The system has attempted to load or restore a file into the Registry, but the specified file is not in a Registry file format.

[Kernel32]

Specify the correct path to a file that has a Registry file format and retry the operation.

The system is not fully installed. Please run setup again.

[Workstation-Logon]

You chose to abort Setup.

If you want to install Windows NT on this workstation, you must run Setup again.

The system is out of environment space.

[Command]

The environment space cannot be expanded any further, so the specified environment variable cannot be added or redefined.

You can increase the size of the existing environment by using the Set command to delete some of the existing environment variables before redefining or adding new environment variables. If you are using the Set command within a batch file and get this message, try typing the Set command again at the command prompt. If you still get this message, specify a larger environment using the /e switch with the Shell command in your CONFIG.SYS or CONFIG.NT file, then restart your computer.

The system is out of environment space.

[Command Prompt]

The environment space cannot be expanded any further, so the specified environment variable cannot be added or redefined.

You can increase the size of the existing environment by using the Set command to delete some of the existing environment variables before redefining or adding new environment variables. If you are using the Set command within a batch file and get this message, try typing the Set command again at the command prompt. If you still get this message, specify a larger environment using the /e switch with the Shell command in your CONFIG.SYS or CONFIG.NT file, then restart your computer.

The system ran out of a resource controlled by the *name* option.

[Network] Net Message ID: 3101

This message should occur only on a down-level computer. Any action to correct the problem should be performed on that computer. The system required more of a resource than was available.

Change the value of the listed option in the configuration file to allow the system to access more of the resource.

The system returned an unexpected error code. The error code is the data.

[Network]

The system returned an unexpected error code. The error code is in the data.

Check the cause of the error.

The system returned the following unexpected error code: *code*

[Network]

This message is logged in the event log by the Netlogon service.

Look up the indicated error and take appropriate action

The system reverted to its last known good configuration. The system is restarting....

[Netevent]

The current system configuration was unacceptable so the system restarted with the last saved configuration that worked. A service may have had an error that caused it to fail to start.

Ask your system administrator to check the event log with Event Viewer to identify the configuration problems. The log has information about errors that preceded this one. Your system administrator may need to contact the vendor of the component that failed.

The system was unable to parse the command line in this file.

[Network] Net Message ID: 2373

This message should occur only on a down-level computer. Any action to correct the problem should be performed on that computer. The profile contains an invalid command.

Check the profile. See your network administrator if you need assistance.

The tag is invalid.

[Kernel32]

A remote procedure call (RPC) cannot be carried out in a distributed application.

Contact the supplier of the running distributed application.

The Take Ownership Dialog failed: *text*

[Print Manager]

The indicated system error prevented Print Manager from opening the Take Ownership dialog.

Look up the error message that is included at the end of this message, and take appropriate action. Then try again.

The tape device driver failed on a request to *drive letter***.**

[Backup]

Contact technical support. Be sure to record any messages and information you see for technical support.

The tape device failed on a request to *drive letter***.**

[Backup]

Contact technical support. Be sure to record any messages and information you see for technical support.

The tape device reported an error on a request to *drive letter***. Error reported:***code***.**

[Backup]

Contact technical support. Be sure to record any messages and information you see for technical support.

The tape has been rewound, insert tape #*number* **in** *drive letter***.**

[Backup]

The tape that is now in the specified drive has been rewound, and the application is ready for the specified tape to be inserted in its place

Remove the tape that is now in the specified drive, and replace it with the specified tape from the current tape family.

The tape in *drive letter* **cannot be read.**

[Backup]

You attempted to use a tape with a format that Backup does not support.

Insert a tape that is supported

The tape in *drive letter* **is not blank. It was created by another application.**

[Backup]

Backup requires that blank tapes or tapes formatted for backup be used.

Choose Yes to overwrite the contents of the tape or choose No. If you choose No, you will be prompted about aborting the backup operation.

The tape in *drive letter* is not blank. It was created by another application. Do you wish to continue?

[Backup]

You chose to erase a tape that contains data that Backup cannot read, but may contain valid data.

Before choosing Yes, you should probably determine the contents of the tape.

The tape in *drive letter* is not properly inserted.

[Backup]

The tape in the specified drive cannot be read until it is properly inserted.

Remove and re-insert the tape. Make sure that it is positioned correctly, and that the door to the tape drive is closed.

The tape in *drive letter* is unrecognizable and cannot be read.

[Backup]

Either the tape is bad, or is in a format that Backup does not support.

Insert another tape. Or if you can determine which application was used to create the tape, use the application to access the data.

The tape in *drive letter* is write-protected.

[Backup]

Remove the tape, and flip the tab that write-protects it.

The tape in the drive has an unrecognizable format or is not formatted.

[Backup]

This tape was created by another application. The current application cannot read the information on it.

If you are sure you want to overwrite the tape, use the Erase command. To read the tape, access it from within the application that created it.

The tape in the drive is "*name*" and was created by *name* on *date* at *time*.

[Backup]

If this is a tape you do not want to erase, cancel the operation. Otherwise, continue.

The tape in the drive is blank.

[Backup]

You do not need to erase the tape in the drive because it is already blank.

No action is needed.

The tape in the drive is unrecognizable.

[Backup]

The data on the tape was not created using the backup application.

Insert another tape. Or, use the application that was used to create the tape to access the data on the tape.

The tape in the drive is unrecognizable. Use another tape.

[Backup]

The tape in the drive cannot be erased because it is not recognizable. This could be caused by a damaged tape.

Use a different tape.

The tape in the drive must be erased before it can be used.

[Backup]

Backups can only be made on blank tapes. If old data were left on the tape and overwritten, there is a chance it could be extracted later, which would pose a security risk.

Erase the data on this tape, or use a blank tape.

The tape is out of sequence. Insert the first tape in this tape family.

[Backup]

The application is trying to catalog the contents of the tape or set. You must start with the first tape in the tape family for this operation to be successful.

Insert the first tape into the drive.

The tape operation was terminated by the user.

[Backup]

You canceled an operation on the tape that was in progress.

No action is needed.

The target drive is not formatted for NTFS; ACLCONV can only restore security information to NTFS volumes.

[Aclconv]

Convert the volume to NTFS before restoring permissions.

The target server is not setup to accept Remote Procedure Calls.

[Services for Macintosh (SFM)]

The target server has not been started.

Type NET START <MacFile> at the target server to enable it to accept remote procedure calls (RPCs).

The text in the *filename* file has changed. Do you want to save the changes?

[Notepad]

You tried to exit a Notepad file to which you have made changes, but you have not yet saved the changes to the document.

If you want to save the changes that you have made to your Notepad file, select Yes. If not, select No. If you want to return to the file, select Cancel.

The time range specified ends before it starts.

[Network] Net Message ID: 3761

You specified a time range that starts later than it ends. Time ranges must start and end on the same day.

Retype the command with a valid time range. You can use either the 12-hour or the 24-hour time format. When you use the 12-hour format, you must specify either AM or PM for each time. When you use the 24-hour format, do not specify AM or PM.

The time zone bias calculated between *computer name* **and the current workstation is too large. The data specifies the number of 100ns units between the workstation and server. Make sure that the time of day on the workstation and server are correct.**

[Netevent]

The time difference between the workstation and the server is larger than 24 hours which indicates a configuration failure in one of the computers.

Type TIME or DATE at the command prompt to determine whether the server or workstation has the incorrect time and then correct the time on that computer.

The Time Zone information cannot be found in the registry.

[Program Manager]

Either the location of time zone information specified in the Registry is incorrect, or the Registry is corrupt.

Contact technical support. The value of REG_MULTI_SZ in Machine\Software\Microsoft\WindowsNT\CurrentVersion\TimeZones needs to be checked by someone who is an expert user of Regedit32. If you still get this message, restart the computer, and press the spacebar immediately after selecting Windows NT at the Boot Loader prompt. Then choose Last Known Good.

The time/date in the View From box has to be less than the time/date you selected in the View Through box.

[Event Viewer]

The date that you have specified in the View Through box precedes that which you have specified in the View From box.

Make sure that the View From date precedes the View Through option.

The timeout period has expired on a call to another WINS server. Assuming that the network and routers are working properly, either the remote WINS server is overloaded, or its TCP listener thread has terminated.

[WINS Service]

This server tried to communicate with another WINS server, but got no response within the time-out period. The problem is with either the network or the other server. Either one may be slow (probably due to a temporary overload). Or WINS on the other server may have encountered an error that left it unable to respond.

Check the Event log to find out what push or pull partner WINS was trying to communicate with. Then check that server's Even log to find out what the problem is, and take appropriate action. If there appears to be no problem on the remote server, check the network and routers that connect the servers.

The timeout value is invalid.

[Kernel32]

In a distributed (RPC) application, the client can specify the relative amount of time that should be spent to establish a relationship to the server before giving up. There is a small set of numbers that can be specified to represent the relative time (it is not measured in seconds), and apparently an invalid number has been used.

Contact the supplier of the running distributed application.

The Tmm Thread could not be signaled. This indicates that this computer is extremely overloaded or that the WINS application has failed.

[WINS Service]

A component of WINS that keeps track of timeout periods could not be contacted.

Stop and restart WINS. Make sure that the computer is not overloaded (close some applications if necessary).

The token is already in use as a primary token.

[Kernel32]

Contact the supplier of the running application.

The TrueImage Interpreter experienced an access violation during job processing.(Document Name: *name*)

[Services for Macintosh (SFM)]

Contact technical support.

The TrueImage Interpreter experienced an access violation during initialization.(Document Name: *name*)

[Services for Macintosh (SFM)]

The document did not print.

Contact technical support.

The TrueImage Interpreter failed to allocate memory required to process a job.

[Services for Macintosh (SFM)]

The server may be running out of memory.

Try stopping other running applications. You might also need to remove unused files and applications from the server's disk.

The TrueImage Interpreter had an error string occur out of sequence.(Document Name: *name* **)**

[Services for Macintosh (SFM)]

Contact technical support.

The TrueImage Interpreter has reached its limit for internal fonts. No more fonts could be defined.

[Services for Macintosh (SFM)]

The system is out of resources.

Try stopping other running applications. You might also need to remove unused files and applications from your disk.

The TrueImage Interpreter process was unable to start succesfully. The error code returned from the system was *code*.

[Services for Macintosh (SFM)]

Contact technical support.

The TrueImage Interpreter was unable to allocate required memory.

[Services for Macintosh (SFM)]

Try stopping other running applications. You might also need to remove unused files and applications from your disk. Also try increasing the page file size. Otherwise, contact technical support.

The TrueImage Interpreter was unable to create a required Device Context. The error code returned from the system was *code*.

[Services for Macintosh (SFM)]

The system is out of resources.

Try stopping other running applications. You might also need to remove unused files and applications from your disk. Contact technical support.

The TrueImage Interpreter was unable to generate the Error Page. The error code returned from the system was *code*.

[Services for Macintosh (SFM)]

Contact technical support.

The TrueImage Interpreter was unable to image to the target printer. The error code returned from the system was *code*.

[Services for Macintosh (SFM)]

Contact technical support.

The TrueImage Interpreter was unable to initialize the required information to begin processing the job. The error code returned from the system was *code*.

[Services for Macintosh (SFM)]

Contact technical support.

The TrueImage Interpreter was unable to Initiate the Start of Document. The error code returned from the system was *code*.

[Services for Macintosh (SFM)]

Contact technical support.

The TrueImage Interpreter was unable to query the font list correctly to begin processing the job.

[Services for Macintosh (SFM)]

Contact technical support.

The TrueImage Interpreter was unable to reset page-level information, such as paper size or number of copies. The job printing may not be correct. The error code returned from the system was *code*.

[Services for Macintosh (SFM)]

Contact technical support.

The TrueImage Interpreter was unable to retrieve data from the printspooler. The error code returned from the system was *code*.

[Services for Macintosh (SFM)]

Contact technical support.

The TrueImage Interpreter was unable to retrieve the default printercharacteristics. The error code returned from the system was *code*.

[Services for Macintosh (SFM)]

There is a problem with the printer configuration.

Use Print Manager to recreate the printers.

The TrueImage Interpreter was unable to set its priority correctly. The error code returned from the system was *code*.

[Services for Macintosh (SFM)]

Contact technical support.

The TrueImage Interpreter was unable to set the correct security privilege and cannot print the Job. The error code returned from the system was *code*.

[Services for Macintosh (SFM)]

Contact technical support.

The trust relationship between the primary domain and the trusted domain failed.

[Kernel32]

Contact your system administrator to reestablish the trust relationship using Windows NT Server Manager.

The trust relationship between this workstation and the primary domain failed.

[Kernel32]

Contact your system administrator to reestablish the trust relationship, using Windows NT Server Manager.

The type of the token is inappropriate for its attempted use.

[Kernel32]

A security token was misapplied.

Contact the supplier of the running application.

The type universal unique identifier (UUID) has already been registered.

[Kernel32]

In a distributed (RPC) application, a server can specify the type of each object it offers to clients. In this case, that object type already existed when the server tried to establish an object type.

Contact the supplier of the running distributed application.

The universal unique identifier (UUID) type is not supported.

[Kernel32]

The client in a remote procedure call supplied an object universally unique identifier (UUID) of a type not supported by the server.

Contact the supplier of the running distributed application.

The UPS driver could not be opened. The error code is the data.

[Network]

The UPS service could not be started because the driver that accompanies your UPS hardware could not be opened. Either you do not have permission to open the file, or the file is corrupt.

Make sure you have the necessary permissions on the driver file and on all directories in the path to that file. If you still get this error you might need to reinstall the driver.

The UPS indicated a line fail or low battery situation. Service not started.

[Network] Net Message ID: 2483

The UPS service was not configured correctly when it was installed.

Contact your network administrator or consult the UPS battery documentation for the correct configuration information. Change the configuration of the service using Control Panel. Then restart the service.

The UPS must support signal on either low battery or power failure.

[Control Panel]

In the UPS Configuration box in the UPS window, you are provided with three options, including Power failure signal option and the Low battery signal at least 2 minutes before shutdown. You have indicated that your UPS is installed on a serial communications port, and have selected the OK button, but have not selected either of the first two options in the UPS Configuration box. The first of these options (Power signal failure) will alert you only if the main power supply on your computer fails. The second option will alert you when the battery on your UPS device is low two minutes before UPS automatically shuts down your computer.

Select the Power failure signal option if you wish to be alerted by your UPS only in the event of a power failure. Or select the Low battery signal at least 2 minutes before shutdown if you want to be notified before UPS shuts down your computer.

The UPS service could not access the specified Comm Port.

[Network] Net Message ID: 2482

Either the specified communications port does not exist, is in use by another application, or is malfunctioning.

Verify that the communications port exists and then verify that it is not being used by another application. If the port is being used, either close the other application or wait until the application has closed. If the communications port is malfunctioning, see if it will work with another application. If so, try to connect the UPS service again. If the service still cannot access the specified communications port, contact technical support.

The UPS service did not complete execution of the user specified shut down command file.

[Network] Net Message ID: 3232

The UPS service could not finish running the specified command file in less than 30 seconds.

Modify the contents of the command file so that it can be completed in 30 seconds or less.

The UPS service failed to execute a user specified shutdowncommand file *filename*. The error code is the data.

[Network]

Use Event Viewer to find the error code. Then look up the error and take appropriate action.

The UPS service failed to perform a system shut down.

[Network] Net Message ID: 2484

The UPS service attempted to perform a system shutdown because the UPS battery is low. The system was not shut down.

Contact technical support.

The UPS service is about to perform final shut down.

[Network]

Close any open files on this computer and disconnect from it.

The UPS service is not configured correctly.

[Network] Net Message ID: 2481

A configuration error occurred in the UPS service.

Check the UPS battery's documentation for the correct configuration information and reconfigure the UPS service.

The UPS service is starting shut down at *computer name* **due to low battery.**

[Network]

Close any open files on this computer and disconnect from it.

The UPS service is starting shut down at *computer name***.**

[Network]

Close any open files on this computer and disconnect from it.

The UPS service performed server shut down.

[Network] Net Message ID: 3231

The UPS battery is low, probably because of an extended power outage.

No action is needed. The system will start automatically when the power is restored.

The usage of this font on screen will require a translation from the Adobe Type 1 font format to Windows native format, TrueType. Before converting the font, please obtain the distributor's authorization.

[Fonts (CP)]

Contact the vendor of the font and request the necessary permission. Once you have permission, you can continue past this message.

The usage parameter in the media .INI file is invalid.

[Remote Access Service]

One of the Remote Access configuration files probably contains invalid information.

The easiest way to resolve this problem is to reinstall Remote Access. Use the Network option in Control Panel to remove and reinstall RAS. If you are using a modem that is not supported by Remote Access, switch to a supported modem, or see "Modem Script File" in the Remote Access Service on-line Help for information about modifying the modem script file for your modem. The Remote Access script files (PAD.INF, MODEM.INF, and SWITCH.INF) are in the \SYSTEM32\RAS subdirectory of your Windows NT directory.

The user *user name* has connected and failed to authenticate on port *address*. The line has been disconnected.

[Remote Access Service]

Check the user's permissions in the Administrator's utility. Make sure the user is typing the correct user name and password. Try again to connect.

The user *user name* has opened this resource for *text*. Are you sure you want to close *text*?

[Network] [Server Manager] [Services for Macintosh (SFM)]

To avoid data corruption, the resource should be closed by the process that opened it.

Ask the user to close this resource. If you must force the resource to close, check for data corruption afterward.

The user *name* \\ *user name* connected to port *address* has been disconnected because the computer could not be projected onto the network.

[Remote Access Service]

The Remote Access Service server is configured incorrectly if many users receive this message. If only one user receives this message, the user's remote computer may be configured incorrectly.

The user should disconnect and then reconnect to the network. Users' remote computers should have unique computer names. Remote users might also want to stop some services that are running on their computers. If the problem persists with several users, reconfigure the server.

The user account already exists.

[Network] Net Message ID: 2224

You tried to create a user account with a user name that already exists.

Use a different user name for the new user account. To display a list of existing user names, type NET USER.

The user accounts database (NET.ACC) is missing. The local security system is restoring the backup database made at *date*.Any updates made to the database made after this time are lost.

[Network] Net Message ID: 3184

This message should occur only on a down-level computer. Any action to correct the problem should be performed on that computer. The user accounts database file is missing, so the backup file made at the listed date is now being used. Changes made to the user accounts database since this time were lost. Local security is still in effect.

To update the user accounts database, retype changes made to it since the listed date.

The user accounts database is not configured correctly.

[Network] Net Message ID: 2450

This message should occur only on a down-level computer. Any action to correct the problem should be performed on that computer. The user accounts database is not configured properly. There may be a conflict between the computer's role, which defines how this server participates in logon security, and the server's record of the name of the primary domain controller. For example, the role of this computer may be set to PRIMARY while the primary domain controller entry names a different server.

Contact your network administrator.

The user already belongs to this group.

[Network]

The user you are trying to add to this group is already a member.

No action is needed.

The user cannot be removed from a group because the group is currently the user's primary group.

[Kernel32]

Contact the supplier of the running application.

The user connected to port *address* has been disconnected because an internal authentication error occurred.

[Remote Access Service]

The user should try to connect to the port again. If the problem persists, contact technical support.

The user connected to port *address* has been disconnected because of a failure to lock user memory.

[Remote Access Service]

If this message appears frequently, free memory on the server by optimizing memory allocations to different resources, or by stopping some nonessential services, or by installing more memory on the server.

The user connected to port *address* has been disconnected because there is not enough memory available in the system.

[Remote Access Service]

Either the server does not have enough virtual memory, or the system quota settings are too low, or the server does not have enough physical memory.

Free memory on the server by optimizing memory allocations to different resources, or by stopping some nonessential services, or by installing more memory on the server.

The user connected to port *address* has been disconnected because there was a transport-level error during the authentication conversation.

[Remote Access Service]

The modem being used may not be supported or users' modem baud rates may be too high.

If you see this message frequently, verify that the supported modems are being used. Also, advise users to try using lower baud rates. Redial and try to connect again.

The user connected to port *address* has been disconnected due to a critical network error on the async network.

[Remote Access Service]

Check the serial port connections. If the problem persists, contact technical support.

The user connected to port *address* has been disconnected due to a critical network error on the local network.

[Remote Access Service]

Verify that the network adapter card is connected and working properly. If so, and if the problem persists, contact technical support.

The user connected to port *address* has been disconnected due to an authentication timeout.

[Remote Access Service]

The user has taken too long to authenticate.

The user should try to connect to the port again. If the problem persists with this user and several others, considering increasing the authentication time.

The user connected to port *address* has been disconnected due to inactivity.

[Remote Access Service]

The Remote Access Service by default disconnects users after 20 minutes of inactivity. The amount of time to disconnect is configurable through the Autodisconnect parameter in the Remote Access parameters section of the Registry.

Redial and then reconnect to the port.

The user context supplied is invalid.

[Network] Net Message ID: 3775

The user context you supplied with /USER is invalid.

Retype the command with a valid user context which may be a simple user name or a qualified user name (in the form DOMAIN\\USER NAME).

The user does not belong to this group.

[Network] Net Message ID: 2237

This user is not a member of this group.

To see a list of users in this group, type NET GROUP <group name> if you are running the Windows NT Advanced Server. If you are using Windows NT, type NET GROUP <group name> /domain. The Windows NT workstation must be a member of a domain that is running Windows NT Advanced Server. Otherwise, you will see a message that tells you that NET GROUP is a Windows NT Advanced Server command only.

The user is not allowed to log on at this time.

[Network]

You are not allowed to log on at this time of day.

If you need to log on, have your network administrator change the logon hours listed in your account.

The user is not allowed to log on from this workstation.

[Network]

You are not allowed to log on from this workstation.

If you need to log on from this workstation, have your network administrator change the logon workstation(s) listed in your account.

The User Manager cannot administer Domain Controllers. Use the User Manager for Domains instead.

[User Manager]

If your system is a domain controller, you cannot administer the workstation using User Manager.

Select the User Manager for Domains icon.

The user must be a member of the primary group.

[User Manager]

You tried to remove one or more users from a group that is the primary group for the user or users.

To set a primary group for a set of users, choose Help and follow the procedure under Managing Group Accounts for Multiple User Accounts.

The user name could not be found.

[Network]

You specified an unknown user name.

Check the spelling of the user name. To display a list of the users in the security database, type NET USER.

The user name entered is not properly formatted.

[Control Panel]

A username in the Network dialog consists of no more than 15 characters, and cannot contain the following characters: : ; " <>*+= \\ | , ?. You have included one of these characters in your user name.

Remove the character from your user name, then try again.

The user name is invalid.

[Network]

You typed an invalid user name.

Retype the command with a valid user name.

The user name or group name parameter is invalid.

[Network]

You specified an invalid user name or group name.

Use a different user name or group name.

The user specified port for *name* is way too high in physical memory.

The port address that you specified is within 7 bytes of the last byte of virtual memory.

Change the address to one that is further from the end of virtual memory.

The user was successfully created but could not be added to the USERS local group.

[Network] Net Message ID: 3774

The user name was not added to the local group.

Try deleting the user. Then add the user to the local group again. If the problem persists, contact technical support.

The user's account has expired.

[Kernel32]

Contact your system administrator to reinstate your account.

The user's home directory could not be determined.

[Network]

The system could not determine your home directory.

Ask your network administrator to add a home directory for you.

The user's home directory has not been specified.

[Network]

The system could not determine your home directory.

Ask your network administrator to add a home directory for you.

The User/Group *name* no longer exists on this server. Do you want to continue writing the permissions on this resource without *name*?

[Security]

A user or group was deleted from the UAS of the server while an ACL (access control list) that contains that User/Group was being edited. You cannot write the resource to the server because the User/Group no longer exists on the server.

If you want to continue writing these permissions, choose Yes. If not, choose No.

The validation information class requested was invalid.

[Kernel32]

An authentication package could not interpret the specified information.

Contact the supplier of the running application.

The value for ENABLESCRIPT must be YES.

[Network] Net Message ID: 3771

The /ENABLESCRIPT option of the Net User command accepts only YES as a value.

Retype the command, either specifying /ENABLESCRIPT:YES, or not specifying /ENABLESCRIPT.

The value for the parameter *parameter* to the browser service was illegal.

[Netevent]

Ask your network administrator to correct the parameter in your configuration information.

The value for WANFilter in the registry must be 0-2. The Nw Sap Agent cannot continue.

[Netevent]

The application could not start because a key is missing from the Registry or is incorrect.

This key in the Registry should be changed to a value between 0 and 2, inclusive, by someone experienced with Regedit32.

The value named *name* in the server's Registry key *name* was invalid. The value was ignored, and processing continued.

[Netevent]

Ask your network administrator to remove the value from the Registry or to use the default for the Registry key.

The version of the file is not Windows NT 3.5.

[Setup]

The SETUP.LOG file on the Emergency Repair Disk might be corrupted or bad.

Make sure you have inserted the correct Emergency Repair Disk for your computer. If you don't have the correct disk, let Setup attempt to locate your Windows NT installation.

The version option is invalid.

[Kernel32]

In a distributed (RPC) application, an operation such as deleting entries was to be performed on the name-service database. Part of the request for such an operation specifies how to treat database entry version numbers. The operation was not performed.

Contact the supplier of the running distributed application.

The video device failed to initialize for full screen mode.

[Virtual DOS Machine (VDM)]

Some system resource could not be allocated because it is in use by another application.

Close any applications that might be competing for resources, and try again.

The volume does not contain a recognized file system. Please make sure that all required file system drivers are loaded and that the volume is not corrupt.

[Kernel32]

Run the Chkdsk utility to check for a corrupted volume. Contact your system administrator to make sure all required file system drivers are loaded.

The volume for a file has been externally altered such that the opened file is no longer valid.

[Kernel32]

Contact your system administrator.

The volume is too fragmented to be converted to NTFS.

[Convert]

Delete some unneeded files and retry the conversion. If this fails, back up all files, format the volume to NTFS, and then restore files.

The volume is too small for the specified file system.

Each file system requires a certain amount of space for its internal structures. The NTFS file system requires volumes to use the most space of the three file systems and FAT requires the least. NTFS typically requires at least 4 MB. Usually, any volume smaller than 10 MB should be formatted to FAT.

Format the volume to FAT instead of NTFS, or repartition the media to make the volume larger.

The volume set is not formatted to NTFS; only NTFS volume sets can be extended.

[Disk Administrator]

In order to extend this set, you must reformat the volume as NTFS. Since reformatting overwrites all data on the volume, be sure to back up the files on the volume first.

The Win 16 Subsystem was unable to end the selected task. The Subsystem will terminate.

The application will close. Any files were open by this application might be corrupted.

When you reopen the application, check the files that were open for corruption. If the files are corrupt you might need to restore them from backup copies.

The window cannot act on the sent message.

[Kernel32]

Contact the supplier of the running application.

The window does not have a system menu.

[Kernel32]

An application, as part of its user interface, has attempted an unsupported operation on a window.

Contact the supplier of the running application.

The window does not have scroll bars.

[Kernel32]

An application, as part of its user interface, tried to do an operation on a window that can only be done on a window that has scroll bars.

Contact the supplier of the running application.

The window is not a child window.

[Kernel32]

An application, as part of its user interface, tried to operate on a window as if it were part of a multiple-document interface set of windows, but it was not.

Contact the supplier of the running application.

The window is not a combo box.

[Kernel32]

An application, as part of its user interface, has tried to perform an operation on a window that can only be done on a combo box, and the specified window is not a combo box.

Contact the supplier of the running application.

The window is not a valid dialog window.

[Kernel32]

An application, as part of its user interface, has tried to get user input from a window that does not have that capability.

Contact the supplier of the running application.

The window style or class attribute is invalid for this operation.

[Kernel32]

SetPixelFormat requires that a window whose pixel format is to change has a compatible window style or class attribute.

Contact the supplier of the running distributed application.

The Windows Internet Naming Service is not running on the target machine.

[WINS Service]

Either start WINS on the target computer, or specify a different computer.

user name **Windows NT** *name* **logon request for the user** *computer name\\user name* **from** *computer name* **(via** *computer name***) failed.**

[Network] Net Message ID: 5709

The user or domain name may be invalid.

Ask your system administrator to verify that the domain and user name exist and that the password is valid.

The Windows NT domain controller for this domain could not be located.

[Network]

Try again later. If you still get this message, contact your system administrator.

The Windows NT Print System is not responding. (The data is the Win32 error code.)

[Services for Macintosh (SFM)]

Use the Services option in Control Panel to verify that the Spooler service is running. If so, stop and restart the service.

The Windows NT Service Controller reported an error. (The data is the Win32 error code.)

[Services for Macintosh (SFM)]

The system may be out of resources.

Verify the key values in the Registry. Otherwise, contact technical support.

The WINS configuration key could not be created/opened.

[WINS Service]

The WINS configuration is stored in the Registry, under Current Control Set\Software\WINS key. This key could not be created (or opened).

Ask the administrator to check that the entry is correct, or reinstall WINS.

The WINS PARAMETERS key could not be created/opened

[WINS Service]

The WINS configuration is stored in the Registry, under Current Control Set\Software\WINS key. The Parameters in this section could not be created (or opened).

Ask the administrator to check that the entry is correct, or reinstall WINS.

The WINS PULL configuration key could not be created/opened

[WINS Service]

The WINS configuration is stored in the Registry, under Current Control Set\Software\WINS key. The Pull key under WINS\Partners could not be created (or opened).

Ask the administrator to check that the entry is correct, or reinstall WINS.

The WINS PUSH configuration key could not be created/opened

[WINS Service]

The WINS configuration is stored in the Registry, under Current Control Set\Software\WINS key. The Push key under WINS\Partners could not be created (or opened).

Ask the administrator to check that the entry is correct, or reinstall WINS.

The workgroup name entered is not properly formatted.

[Control Panel]

This is not a valid workgroup name.

Type in a new workgroup name. A workgroup name can contain up to 15 characters, including letters, numbers, and the following characters: !@#$%^&()_-;:'",.It cannot contain any spaces, and must begin with a letter or number.

The working directory is invalid.

[Program Manager]

The directory specified in the Working Directory option or in the Command Path option does not exist.

Select OK, then specify the name of a directory that contains the program file and all of the required libraries.

The workstation could not initialize the Async NetBIOS Thread. The error code is the data.

[Network] Net Message ID: 3162

This message should occur only on a down-level computer. Any action to correct the problem should be performed on that computer. A software error occurred.

Contact technical support.

The workstation could not open the initial shared segment. The error code is the data.

[Network] Net Message ID: 3163

This message should occur only on a down-level computer. Any action to correct the problem should be performed on that computer. The Workstation service may have been started improperly. Always use the Net Start command to start the workstation; do not run WKSTA.EXE directly.

To start the Workstation service, type NET START WORKSTATION. If more problems occur, contact technical support.

The workstation does not have a trust secret.

[Kernel32]

Contact your system administrator to reestablish the trust secret on the your computer. This is a necessary part of any trust relationships between domains. If this trust relationship once functioned, the administrator may have to delete the relationship and reestablish it.

The workstation driver is not installed.

[Network] Net Message ID: 2102

Windows NT is not installed, or your configuration file is incorrect.

Install Windows NT, or see your network administrator about possible problems with your configuration file.

The workstation encountered an error while responding to an SSI revalidation request. The function code and the error codes are the data.

[Network] Net Message ID: 3167

This message should occur only on a down-level computer. Any action to correct the problem should be performed on that computer. A software error occurred.

Contact technical support.

The workstation encountered an error while trying to start the user accounts database. The error code is the data.

[Network] Net Message ID: 3166

This message should occur only on a down-level computer. Any action to correct the problem should be performed on that computer. The Workstation service failed to start the user accounts database.

Contact technical support.

The workstation has open files.

[Network]

This message should occur only on a down-level computer. Any action to correct the problem should be performed on that computer.

The workstation host table is full.

[Network] Net Message ID: 3164

This message should occur only on a down-level computer. Any action to correct the problem should be performed on that computer. The internal table that maintains information about network servers is full. You can access all network servers normally, but you may not be able to see all servers when you type the Net View command. This happens only on very large networks.

Contact your network administrator. Your administrator may want to divide the network into domains, using the DOMAIN entry in each computer's configuration file.

The workstation information segment is bigger than 64K. The size follows, in DWORD format:

[Network] Net Message ID: 3160

This message should occur only on a down-level computer. Any action to correct the problem should be performed on that computer. The workstation's main information segment is larger than the largest segment that can be allocated.

Decrease the values for one or more of the following entries in the [workstation] section of the configuration file. If you need assistance, contact your network administrator. MAXCMDS, NUMCHARBUF, NUMWORKBUF, MAXTHREADS, NUMDGRAMBUF, SIZCHARBUF, NUMALERTS, NUMSERVICES, SIZERROR. After you change the configuration file, restart the Workstation service. If you change the MAXCMDS or MAXTHREADS entry, you will have to restart the computer.

The workstation is not configured properly.

[Network]

This message should occur only on a down-level computer. Any action to correct the problem should be performed on that computer.

The workstation is not logged on to the local-area network.

[Network] Net Message ID: 2201

This message should occur only on a down-level computer. Any action to correct the problem should be performed on that computer. You must log on to the network before performing this operation.

To log on, type NET LOGON <user name>[<password>].

The Workstation must be started with the NET START command.

[Network]

This message should occur only on a down-level computer. Any action to correct the problem should be performed on that computer.

Type NET START at the MS-DOS prompt.

The Workstation service has not been started.

[Network] Net Message ID: 2138

You have tried to use the network before starting the Workstation service.

Start the Workstation service by typing NET START WORKSTATION.

The Workstation service is already running. Windows NT will ignore command options for the workstation.

[Network]

No action is needed.

The Workstation service is in an inconsistent state. Restart the computer before restarting the Workstation service.

[Network]

The workstation is in an inconsistent state.

Restart the computer.

The Workstation service or the Browser service has not been started.

[Network]

You cannot use the network until the Workstation service has been started. You cannot browse network resources until the Browser service has been started.

Start the Workstation and/or Browser services. The command is net start <service>

The Workstation service or the Browser service has not been started.

[Security]

Check the Event Log in Event Viewer for messages related to the services not starting.

The workstation was unable to get the name-number of the computer.

[Network] Net Message ID: 3161

This message should occur only on a down-level computer. Any action to correct the problem should be performed on that computer. A software error occurred.

Contact technical support.

The wrong device is attached to the port.

[Remote Access Service]

Your hardware configuration and the Remote Access setup are probably inconsistent with each other.

If you have changed your communications equipment (such as serial port or modem), be sure to reconfigure Remote Access accordingly. Use the Network option in Control Panel to reconfigure RAS. For more information see "Reconfiguring Remote Access" in the Remote Access Service online Help. This error also occurs when the section header in the MODEM.INF file is longer than 32 characters. Ensure that the section header in MODEM.INI for this device is less than 31 characters before attempting any other corrective action.

The wrong disk is in the drive.

[File Manager]

You have inserted into a drive a disk that is in the incorrect format, the wrong size, or that has an unacceptable density rating.

Try another disk.

The wrong version of the driver has been loaded.

Contact your system administrator to check the driver version installed on your computer. You may have to contact the driver suppliers.

The Zone Information Socket could not be opened on a new node being acquired, and the acquired node is being released on adapter "*number* ".

[Services for Macintosh (SFM)]

A Zone Information Protocol socket could not be opened by the protocol internally. This might mean the protocol is functioning improperly.

Use the Devices option in Control Panel to try stopping and restarting the AppleTalk protocol.

There already exists a WINS server entry with that address.

[WINS Service]

No action is needed; however, you can specify a different address for this entry if you want.

There are currently no logon servers available to service the logon request.

[Kernel32]

This may be due to a network failure, or because the computer is physically removed from the network (such as with laptop computers).

If you are using a network, make sure the domain controller you are trying to log on to is accessible. If necessary, obtain administrative assistance to do this. As an alternative, and in the case of laptops, log on to the machine locally as the primary user of the system.

There are no adapters configured for this protocol stack.

This protocol cannot be used to communicate over the network because none of the network adapter cards in this computer are currently configured to communicate using the protocol.

Use Network from the Control Panel to configure a network adapter card to use this protocol.

There are no alternate servers registered on this server.

[Network] Net Message ID: 2467

This message should occur only on a down-level computer. Any action to correct the problem should be performed on that computer. This server has no alternate servers registered.

Contact your network administrator.

There are no available drive letters left.

[Network]

You cannot connect to any more remote drives until you disconnect from one or more drives.

If you need to make a new connection, disconnect from at least one drive and try again.

There are no bindings.

[Kernel32]

In a distributed (RPC) application, there are currently no bindings over which a server can receive a remote procedure call.

Contact the supplier of the running distributed application.

There are no child processes to wait for.

[Kernel32]

Try the operation again (you may have to restart the application). If this message reappears, contact the supplier of the running application.

There are no drivers installed, and Print Manager cannot locate the file *filename*. No printers can be created.

[Print Manager]

The installation of the print drivers was not completed, either due to some error or because the user interrupted the process. There are no installed drivers on this computer at this time.

Install one or more printer drivers. If you continue to get this message, check the event log for errors that occurred at the same time as this one. Take appropriate action on those errors, and try again.

There are no endpoints.

[Remote Access Service]

Most likely, your network configuration is wrong.

Restart your computer to make sure that all recent configuration changes have taken effect. If error persists, consult the Windows NT event log for detailed warnings or errors.

There are no entries in the log to filter on.

[Event Viewer]

You chose the Filter option on a log that is empty.

If you want to filter another log, switch to a log that contains entries, then try again.

There are no entries in the log to filter on. The contents in the event viewer main window will be refreshed.

[Event Viewer]

You chose the Filter option while focused on a log that appears to contain log information. Event Viewer has determined that no log information exists, however, and will now update the Event Viewer window.

No action is needed.

There are no icons available for the file specified. You can choose an icon from those available for Program Manager.

[Program Manager]

The file that you have specified does not contain any icons.

To use the icons available in Program Manager, execute the following procedures: Choose the icon in Program Manager, and select the Properties option in the File menu. In the Program Item Properties dialog box, choose the Change Icon button, then type PROGMAN.EXE or MORICONS.DLL in the File Name option of the Change Icon dialog box. Then, select an icon and choose OK.

There are no more bindings.

[Kernel32]

A distributed application was unable to carry out a remote procedure call (RPC).

Contact the supplier of the running distributed application.

There are no more endpoints available from the endpoint mapper.

[Kernel32]

In a distributed (RPC) application, the client called a server endpoint but no server had registered that endpoint.

Make sure the server is started.

There are no more members.

[Kernel32]

In a distributed (RPC) application, an inquiry has been made repeatedly of one of the lists in the name-service database, and there are no more members in the list.

Contact the supplier of the running distributed application.

There are no more ports of the specified type to clone.

[Remote Access Service]

The local computer does not have any more ports to clone.

Add more ports to the computer before attempting to clone.

There are no protocol sequences.

[Kernel32]

In a distributed (RPC) application, a server can specify the protocol sequences it will use to receive calls. In this case, a server did not specify a protocol sequence that is supported by Windows NT.

Contact the supplier of the running distributed application.

There are no readable FATs.

[Utilities]

A critical sector near the beginning of the volume is unreadable. Back up files from the drive and replace the disk.

There are no selected servers.

[FTP Server]

Select a server from the main window of Server Manager.

There are no Serial Ports which can be setup on this system.

[Program Manager]

This message occurs when the Control Panel cannot access the key \\HARDWARE\\DeviceMap\\SerialComm.

Contact technical support.

There are no Serial Ports which can be setup on this system.

[Program Manager]

This message occurs when the Control Panel cannot access the key \\HARDWARE\\DeviceMap\\SerialComm.

Contact technical support.

There are no shared communication devices.

[Network] Net Message ID: 2337

This message should occur only on a down-level computer. Any action to correct the problem should be performed on that computer. The server is not sharing any communication-device queues, so the command you typed is invalid.

No action is needed.

There are no user configurable Advanced I/O parameters for this COM port.

[Program Manager]

Advanced I/O settings include such things as a base port address and an interrupt request (IRQ) line that Windows NT uses to send information to a serial port. For the device that you have attached to the selected port, no such advanced settings are necessary.

Select the OK button to return to the Settings for dialog box.

There are no user configurable Advanced I/O parameters for this COM port.

[Program Manager]

Advanced I/O settings include such things as a base port address and an interrupt request (IRQ) line that Windows NT uses to send information to a serial port. For the device that you have attached to the selected port, no such advanced settings are necessary.

Select the OK button to return to the Settings for dialog box.

There are open files and/or incomplete directory searches pending on the connection to *computer name*.

[Network]

Disconnecting from this resource at this time could result in locked files and/or data corruption. This message is followed by the message, "Do you want to continue?"

The best course is to answer No and try again later. If you must disconnect immediately, check the files that were open for possible corruption as soon as possible.

There are open files on the connection.

[Network] Net Message ID: 2401

You tried to delete an active connection. There are open files or requests pending on this connection.

Close all files and end all programs related to the connection before you try to delete it.

There are some unreadable FATs.

[Utilities]

A critical sector near the beginning of the volume is unreadable. Back up files from the drive and replace the disk.

There are some unwriteable FATs.

[Utilities]

A critical sector near the beginning of the volume is unwriteable. Back up files from the drive and replace the disk.

There are too many names in the user accounts database.

[Network] Net Message ID: 2228

This message should occur only on a down-level computer. Any action to correct the problem should be performed on that computer. The user accounts database is full.

Make space in the database by deleting users, groups, and resource permissions.

There are too many NETWORKS entries in the LANMAN.INI file.

[Network] Net Message ID: 3404

This message should occur only on a down-level computer. Any action to correct the problem should be performed on that computer. The LANMAN.INI file cannot have more than 12 entries in the [networks] section.

Remove entries from the [networks] section until 12 or fewer remain.

There is a conflict in the value or use of these options: ***text*****.**

[Network] Net Message ID: 3063

This message should occur only on a down-level computer. Any action to correct the problem should be performed on that computer. Two command-line options or configuration file entries have conflicting values.

Check the command you typed or the configuration file for conflicting options.

There is a problem with a configuration of user specified shut down command file.

[Network]

Examine your command file to make sure there are no special characters. Be sure to save it as an ASCII text file.

There is a problem with a configuration of user specified shut down command file. The UPS service started anyway.

[Network]

Examine your command file to make sure there are no special characters. Be sure to save it as an ASCII text file.

There is a problem with the file.

[Network] Net Message ID: 3064

A problem with the listed configuration file prevented the service from starting.

Check the listed file.

There is a problem with the font file. Cannot display font sample.

[Program Manager]

The font file might be corrupt.

Remove the font and replace the font file from a backup or from the installation disk.

There is a problem with the font file. Cannot display font sample.

[Program Manager]

The font file might be corrupt.

Remove the font and replace the font file from a backup or from the installation disk.

There is a problem with the printer; please check it.

[Network]

The printer might be jammed, out of paper or other supplies, or it might need to be reset, among other possibilities.

Go to the printer to check for and correct any problems.

There is a problem with the security database creation date or serial number.

[Network]

This message should occur only on a down-level computer. Any action to correct the problem should be performed on that computer.

There is a process on other end of the pipe.

[Kernel32]

This is an informational message. No action is needed.

There is a syntax error in the Setup information file at line ***number*** **!u!. This indicates an internal Setup error. Setup cannot continue. Press F3 to exit.**

[Setup]

Contact the supplier of the installation media.

There is already a logon domain for this computer.

[Network] Net Message ID: 2216

This message should occur only on a down-level computer. Any action to correct the problem should be performed on that computer. This workstation already has a logon domain established.

To log on in a different domain, you must first log off from the current domain and then log on again to a different domain.

There is no account for this computer in the security database.

[Network]

This message should occur only on a down-level computer. Any action to correct the problem should be performed on that computer.

There is no answer.

[Remote Access Service]

A modem did not pick up the phone.

Please check the number and dial again.

There is no association for ***filename*****.**

[Program Manager]

Using the Run command, you specified a file that is not executable or that is not associated with a Windows NT application.

In File Manager, associate the file that you are trying to run with an application, then try again to run it.

There is no current MIDI port.

None of your ports have been assigned to a MIDI device.

There is no dial tone.

[Remote Access Service]

Make sure the phone line is plugged into the correct socket in the modem. Also, make sure you've added any special access numbers, such as the prefix 9 followed by a comma, to connect to an outside line. For example: 9,555-8181

There is no mouse installed. Use Windows NT Setup to install a mouse.

[Program Manager]

You have attempted to set Mouse options in the Control Panel prior to installing a Mouse.

Install a mouse, then try again.

There is no mouse installed. Use Windows NT Setup to install a mouse.

[Program Manager]

You have attempted to set Mouse options in the Control Panel prior to installing a Mouse.

Install a mouse, then try again.

There is no space for another entry in the table of available servers.

[Network] Net Message ID: 2463

This message should occur only on a down-level computer. Any action to correct the problem should be performed on that computer. The table of available servers is full. You will not be able to see a complete list of network servers when you type the Net View command or use the LAN Manager Screen.

Stopping other processes or services on the workstation may free enough memory to correct this problem. MS-DOS workstations have a NUMSERVERS entry in the configuration file, which specifies the number of servers that the workstation can list with Net View. Increasing this value can solve this problem, but will also use more memory.

There is no such computer: ***computer name*.**

[Network]

The computer account specified does not exist.

Retype the command with a correct computer name.

There is no such global user or group: ***name*.**

[Network]

The name you specified is not used on this domain.

Check to make sure you have the correct name. Then try again, being careful to type the name correctly.

There is no such user or group: ***name*.**

[Network]

The user or group specified does not exist.

Retype the command with a correct user name or group name.

There is no such user: ***user name*.**

[Network]

You typed an unknown user name.

Check the spelling of the user name and then retype the command.

There is no tape in the drive.

[Backup]

You directed Backup to perform an erase or eject operation on a drive that contains no tape.

Insert a tape into the specified drive, then try again.

There is not a remote procedure call active in this thread.

[Kernel32]

In a distributed (RPC) application, a server can impersonate an active client (a client that is being served by this server thread). In this case, a server tried to impersonate a client but there was no active client to impersonate.

Contact the supplier of the running distributed application.

There is not an open file with that identification number.

[Network] Net Message ID: 2314

This message should occur only on a down-level computer. Any action to correct the problem should be performed on that computer. There is no open file on the server corresponding to the number you specified.

Check the identification number of the open file. To display a list of open files and their identification numbers, type NET FILE.

There is not enough free space on disk to save lost data.

[Chkdsk-HPFS]

The Chkdsk utility found some lost data on an HPFS volume, but there is not enough room on the disk to recover it.

Delete unneeded files from the volume, then try the Chkdsk command again.

There is not enough memory available for CHKDSK to fix the drive.

[Chkdsk-HPFS]

The Chkdsk utility is attempting to fix an HPFS volume, but not enough memory is available.

End one or more programs that are running in other processes, then run the Chkdsk utility again.

There is not enough memory available to CHKDSK to save lost data.

[Chkdsk-HPFS]

The Chkdsk utility has found lost data on an HPFS volume, but not enough memory is available to recover all the data.

End one or more programs that are running in other processes, then run the Chkdsk utility again.

There is not enough memory available to run CHKDSK.

[Chkdsk-HPFS]

The Chkdsk utility requires more memory than your system currently has available in order to check the HPFS volume.

End any programs that you no longer need that are running in other processes, then try the Chkdsk command again.

There is not enough memory to attempt to recover lost data.

[Chkdsk-HPFS]

The Chkdsk utility has found lost data on an HPFS volume, but not enough memory is available to recover all the data.

End one or more programs that are running in other processes, then run the Chkdsk utility again.

There is not enough memory to start the Workstation service.

[Network] Net Message ID: 3400

This message should occur only on a down-level computer. Any action to correct the problem should be performed on that computer. The computer does not have enough memory available to start the Workstation service.

Stop other applications that are running on the computer, and then start the Workstation service again.

There is not enough space on the disk.

[Kernel32]

The disk being written to has no more room.

Delete some unwanted files from the disk and retry the command.

There is not enough space on this drive for the paging file size specified. Please enter a smaller number or free some disk space.

[Program Manager]

In the Virtual Memory dialog in the Control Panel's System option, you have specified a Paging File Size that exceeds the amount of space on the drive that you are using.

Double-check the numbers that you have entered in the Initial Size and Maximum Size options in the Virtual Memory dialog. The Initial and Maximum Size options must be less than the Space Available. In addition, the number in the Maximum Size option must be equal to or larger than the number that appears in the Initial Size option. Change the numbers according to the criteria, or open File Manager and delete unnecessary files to free disk space.

There is nothing to configure for this port.

[Print Manager]

You have attempted to configure the file port, such as c:\file.txt. Ports such as this are files that are printed to instead of ports. This is why there is nothing to configure.

No action is needed.

There is nothing to unexport.

[Kernel32]

In a distributed (RPC) application, an attempt was made to remove objects from an entry in the name-service database, but there were no objects of the specified type to remove.

Contact the supplier of the running application.

There was an error expanding *name* as a group name. Try splitting the group into two or more smaller groups.

[Network] Net Message ID: 3171

This message should occur only on a down-level computer. Any action to correct the problem should be performed on that computer. An error occurred when LAN Manager tried to identify the members of the specified group. The group is probably too large.

Split the group into two or more smaller groups.

There was an error in creating or reading the alerter mailslot. The error code is *code*.

[Network] Net Message ID: 3173

A software error occurred.

Verify that the Alerter service has been started. If the service has already been started, contact technical support.

There was an error initializing the International dialog; ensure that you have valid language.inf and layout.inf files in your Windows NT system directory.

[Program Manager]

The International dialog in Control Panel requires the LANGUAGE.INF, LAYOUT.INF and the CONTROL.INI files to function. These files should appear in the Windows NT SYSTEM32 directory.

Exit or minimize Control Panel, open File Manager, and check for the presence of these files. If they are not present, copy them to your SYSTEM32 directory.

There was an error initializing the International dialog; ensure that you have valid language.inf and layout.inf files in your Windows NT system directory.

[Program Manager]

If necessary, restore these files from a backup copy.

There was an error installing NETWKSTA.SYS. Press ENTER to continue.

[Network]

This message should occur only on a down-level computer. Any action to correct the problem should be performed on that computer. The LAN Manager device driver NETWKSTA.SYS could not be installed.

Another error message that contains a more detailed explanation of the error should have been displayed prior to this message. See that message for the cause of the problem.

There was an error sending *user name* **the alert message -(** *text* **)The error code is** *code***.**

[Network] Net Message ID: 3172

An error occurred when an alert message was sent. The user name designated to receive the alert may no longer exist.

Use Server Manager to repair the error.

There was an error stopping service *name***.The error code from NetServiceControl is the data.**

[Network] Net Message ID: 3104

This message should occur only on a down-level computer. Any action to correct the problem should be performed on that computer. A software error occurred.

Contact technical support.

There was an unrecoverable error in the dynamic-link library of the service.

[Network] Net Message ID: 3256

This message should occur only on a down-level computer. Any action to correct the problem should be performed on that computer. An unrecoverable error occurred because of a problem with the dynamic-link library of the Remoteboot service.

Be sure you are using the correct versions of the dynamic-link libraries.

There was more than one zone specified in the zone list for a LocalTalk adapter "*name* **".**

[Services for Macintosh (SFM)]

More than one zone was specified in the zone list for a LocalTalk adapter by directly accessing the Registry instead of using the Network option in Control Panel.

Use the Network option in Control Panel to specify one zone in the zone list for the LocalTalk adapter. Select Services for Macintosh and then choose Configure. Check the Enable Routing check box and then choose Advanced. Check the Seed this Network check box.

There were *number* **access-denied errors in the last** *number* **minutes.**

[Network]

This message should occur only on a down-level computer. Any action to correct the problem should be performed on that computer.

There were *number* **access-denied errors in the last** *number* **minutes. Please review the server's audit trail.**

[Network]

This message should occur only on a down-level computer. Any action to correct the problem should be performed on that computer.

There were *number* bad password attempts in the last *number* minutes. Please review the server's audit trail.

[Network]

This message should occur only on a down-level computer. Any action to correct the problem should be performed on that computer.

This *filename* driver is required by the system. If you remove it, your system may not work properly. Are you sure you want to remove it?

[Drivers (CP)]

You have attempted to remove a device driver, and have not removed the device that requires the driver. Any device that you attach to your machine requires a driver file, and should you opt to remove the currently selected driver, the device to which it is linked will not function in Windows NT.

If you want to remove the driver, select Yes. If not select No.

This action will permanently remove the component from the system. If you wish to reinstall it, you will have to restart the system before doing so. Do you still wish to continue?

[Control Panel]

In the Network dialog box, you chose to remove either a piece of installed network software or an adapter card. This is a standard confirmation message.

If you are sure you want to remove the selected component, choose Yes.

This application requires a newer version of Microsoft Windows.

[Program Manager] [Task Manager]

You are trying to use an application that uses features of Microsoft Windows that were not available on the version of Windows you are using. You cannot use this application with the version of Windows you are using.

Upgrade to the current version of Microsoft Windows or Windows NT.

This application requires Standard or Enhanced Mode Windows.

[Program Manager]

The application you tried to run is an older version that uses Real Mode. It is not compatible with this operating system.

Upgrade the application to one that uses Standard or Enhanced Mode. Or, use a computer that is running Microsoft Windows version 3.0 to open this application.

This asg_type is invalid.

[Network] Net Message ID: 2251

A software error occurred.

Contact technical support.

This card cannot be viewed. Delete the card.

[Cardfile]

The selected card could not be read either from an original or a temporary file. Consequently, this card is not valid or viewable.

Choose OK, then delete the card.

This card contains an open embedded object. Before you can delete the object, you must close it by closing the server application.

[Cardfile]

The server application is the application through which the embedded object was created. You attempted to delete an embedded object, but the application through which the embedded object was created is still running.

Double-click on the embedded object. The application in which the object was created appears. Selecting the Exit option in the File menu, exit the application, then attempt again to delete the object from the destination file.

This change will take effect when File Server for Macintosh service is restarted.

[Services for Macintosh (SFM)]

Use the Services option in Control Panel to stop and then restart the service.

This computer is no longer a member of any domain.

[Control Panel]

Your computer is currently a stand-alone workstation and will be unable to access domain resources.

If you want to use domain resources, join a domain.

This computer name is already configured as a server on the domain. Please contact your domain administrator.

[Control Panel]

This name cannot be used as a computer name because it is already being used as a domain name.

Specify a different name.

This computer name is already configured as a workstation on the domain. Please contact your domain administrator.

[Control Panel]

This name cannot be used as a computer name because it is already being used as a workstation name on the current domain.

Specify a different name.

This computer name is invalid.

[Network]

The specified computer name is invalid.

Contact technical support.

This Counter Style Not Available For Display

[Performance Monitor]

This message appears when you choose a counter style that is presented by a vendor's application but is not supported in this release of Performance Monitor.

Contact the vendor.

This device cannot be shared as both a spooled and a non-spooled resource.

[Network] Net Message ID: 2318

This message should occur only on a down-level computer. Any action to correct the problem should be performed on that computer. You cannot route requests from both a printer queue and a communication-device queue to the same device.

To assign the device to a printer queue, you must first remove it from all communication-device queues. To assign the device to a communication-device queue, you must remove it from all printer queues.

This device cannot be shared.

[Network] Net Message ID: 2332

This message should occur only on a down-level computer. Any action to correct the problem should be performed on that computer. The device name you typed does not represent a valid local device that can be shared.

Select a valid device name.

This device is already in use as a communication device.

[Network] Net Message ID: 2343

This message should occur only on a down-level computer. Any action to correct the problem should be performed on that computer. This device is used with a communication-device queue. You cannot use a device with both communication-device queues and printer queues.

To use this device with a printer queue, you must disconnect all communication-device queues from it.

This device is already in use by the spooler.

[Network] Net Message ID: 2342

This message should occur only on a down-level computer. Any action to correct the problem should be performed on that computer. This device is used with a printer queue. You cannot use a device with both printer queues and communication-device queues.

To use this device with a communication-device queue, you must first disconnect all printer queues from it.

This device is currently being shared.

[Network] Net Message ID: 2252

This message should occur only on a down-level computer. Any action to correct the problem should be performed on that computer. The device name you have tried to assign to a shared resource represents a local device that is already being shared.

Select another device name or stop sharing the device you specified.

This device is not shared.

[Network] Net Message ID: 2311

The device you specified is not shared.

Check the spelling of the device name. To share the device, type NET SHARE <share name>=<device name>.

This device name list is invalid.

[Network] Net Message ID: 2334

This message should occur only on a down-level computer. Any action to correct the problem should be performed on that computer. A software error occurred.

Contact technical support.

This device was not open.

[Network] Net Message ID: 2333

This message should occur only on a down-level computer. Any action to correct the problem should be performed on that computer. You tried to purge an empty communication-device queue.

No action is needed.

This document is corrupt and cannot be accessed.

[Write]

You have attempted to open a corrupted document in Write.

No action is needed.

This domain has more global groups than can be replicated to a LanManBDC. Either delete some of your global groups or remove the LanManBDCs from the domain.

[Network]

Either delete some of your global groups or remove the LAN Manager\r\nBDCs from the domain.

This drive contains the Windows system files and cannot be disconnected.

[File Manager]

The drive from which you are attempting to disconnect contains the file that are required to run Windows NT.

Choose OK.

This file extension is already associated with a Creator/Type item.

[Services for Macintosh (SFM)]

File extensions can be associated with only one Creator/Type item.

Select another Creator/Type item to associate with the file extension.

This file is in use by some other application.

[File Manager] [Program Manager] [Task Manager]

You attempted to open a file that is in use by another application. This is a sharing violation.

If you know which application is using the file, close the application, then try again.

This file is not a Windows Help file.

[Help]

You have attempted to run in Windows NT a help file that Windows NT does not support.

Consult the written documentation that accompanied the application for help on the topic, or contact technical support.

This global group is in a domain which is not in the list of trusted domains. Have more trusted domains been added while new users were being selected?

[Network]

The specified global group was not in the list of trusted domains that appeared in the User Browser dialog, but does appear in the Local Group Membership dialog. Most likely, a trusted domain was added while new users were being selected.

Choose OK. Then close and reopen User Browser.

This global group is in a domain which is not in the list of trusted domains. Have more trusted domains been added while new users were being selected?

[Security]

The specified global group was not in the list of trusted domains that appeared in the User Browser dialog, but does appear in the Local Group Membership dialog. Most likely, a trusted domain was added while new users were being selected.

Close and then reopen the User Browser. Try the operation again.

This hook procedure can only be set globally.

[Kernel32]

An application, as part of its user interface, has tried to install the wrong type of procedure to monitor system events.

Contact the supplier of the running application.

This image was saved in an old format. Do you want to convert it into the standard bitmap format?

[Paintbrush]

Very often, Windows 3.1 or Windows NT does not support applications developed for earlier versions of Windows. When earlier applications are supported, text or format conversion is sometimes necessary.

If you want to convert to the standard bitmap format, select the Yes option. If not, select the No option.

This is a share-level server. You can only set permissions and auditing information on Windows NT File System (NTFS) volumes and LAN Manager 2.x user-level servers.

[Security]

From a Windows NT computer, you attempted to set permissions on a share-level resource. This action is not permitted.

No action is needed.

This is a system, hidden, or read-only file.

[File Manager]

When you attempt to delete a system, hidden, or read-only file, File Manager presents you with this message.

If you still want to delete the file, choose Yes. If not, choose No.

This is an invalid argument: *text*.

[Network] Net Message ID: 3402

This message should occur only on a down-level computer. Any action to correct the problem should be performed on that computer. The listed variable or option (from an entry in the [networks] section of the LANMAN.INI file) is invalid.

Check the format of the entries in the [networks] section of the LANMAN.INI file.

This is an invalid device name.

[Network] Net Message ID: 2294

You typed a command or ran a program that specified an invalid device name.

If you specified the device name, be sure that it is valid and that you have typed it correctly. If a program specified the device name, consult the program's documentation.

This is an invalid response.

[Network]

The only valid responses to the prompt are Yes and No.

Answer Yes or No at the prompt.

This is not a valid computer name or domain name.

[Network] Net Message ID: 3730

You typed an invalid computer name or domain.

Retype the command with a valid computer name or domain. If you need further assistance, contact your network administrator.

This is not an embedded or linked object. You cannot activate it.

[Cardfile]

The object that you have attempted to activate is a static object. This means that it cannot be edited in the document in which it is embedded.

Return to the actual Paintbrush file in which the object was originally created, and activate it from that file.

This is not an embedded or linked object. You cannot activate it.

[Write]

You have attempted to activate an object that is not linked to a server application.

No action is needed.

This is not an NTFS volume.

[Chkdsk-NTFS]

The NTFS volume is unrecoverably corrupted.

Reformat the NTFS volume. Then restore the data from a backup.

This keyboard cannot change its speed.

[Program Manager]

No action is needed.

This list box does not support tab stops.

[Kernel32]

An application, as part of its user interface, has tried to operate on a list box in a way that list box does not support.

Contact the supplier of the running application.

This list of devices is invalid.

[Network] Net Message ID: 2340

This message should occur only on a down-level computer. Any action to correct the problem should be performed on that computer. A software error occurred.

Contact technical support.

This message alias already exists locally.

[Network]

You tried to add a message alias that already exists on this computer.

Use a different name if you want to add a new message alias. To display the list of aliases on this computer, type NET NAME.

This message alias has been added but is still forwarded.

[Network]

This message should occur only on a down-level computer. Any action to correct the problem should be performed on that computer. Messages for this alias are being forwarded to another computer.

Stop forwarding messages and allow messages to be received by the local computer again.

This message alias will be deleted later.

[Network]

Some hardware configurations have a delay between the typing of a command and the deletion of an alias.

No action is needed. The deletion will occur soon.

This network connection does not exist.

[Kernel32]

An application tried to delete or retrieve information about an established network connection (such as the user name used to establish the connection), but the network connection does not exist.

Check the spelling of the connection name, and also make sure it is one that is currently connected.

This network connection has files open or requests pending.

[Kernel32]

An application tried to cancel a network connection that had one or more files open.

Either close the files or wait until the files are closed, then try to cancel the connection.

This new drive letter assignment will happen immediately. Do you wish to continue?

[Disk Administrator]

If there are no applications with open files or unsaved data on this computer, choose Yes. Otherwise, wait until you are ready for a graceful shutdown and restart.

This object has been changed. Update document before proceeding?

You attempted to exit Object Packager before saving the changes you made to an object, and this is a standard confirmation message.

If you want to save the changes you have made, choose Yes.

This operation cannot be performed on the print destination in its current state.

[Network] Net Message ID: 2162

This message should occur only on a down-level computer. Any action to correct the problem should be performed on that computer. The requested change cannot be made because a software error occurred.

Contact technical support.

This operation cannot be performed on the print job in its current state.

[Network] Net Message ID: 2164

This message should occur only on a down-level computer. Any action to correct the problem should be performed on that computer. The requested change cannot be made because a software error occurred.

Contact technical support.

This operation cannot be performed on the printer queue in its current state.

[Network] Net Message ID: 2163

This message should occur only on a down-level computer. Any action to correct the problem should be performed on that computer. The requested change cannot be made because a software error occurred.

Contact technical support.

This operation is not allowed on the last administrative account.

[Network] Net Message ID: 2452

This message should occur only on a down-level computer. Any action to correct the problem should be performed on that computer. This is the only account with administrative privilege. You cannot delete it.

You must add another account with administrative privilege before deleting this one.

This operation is not allowed on this special group.

[Network] Net Message ID: 2234

You cannot perform this task on special groups such as Users, Administrators and Guests.

No action is needed.

This operation is not permitted when the Netlogon service is running.

[Network] Net Message ID: 2451

This message should occur only on a down-level computer. Any action to correct the problem should be performed on that computer. You cannot perform this task while the Netlogon service is running.

To perform this task, stop the Netlogon service on the server. Retype the command, and then restart the Netlogon service.

This operation is not supported on computers with multiple networks.

[Network] Net Message ID: 2300

This message should occur only on a down-level computer. Any action to correct the problem should be performed on that computer. You cannot run this command on a computer that is on multiple networks.

No action is needed.

This operation is not supported on workstations.

[Network] Net Message ID: 2106

This operation can be performed only on a server.

See your network administrator if you need more information.

This operation is only allowed for the Primary Domain Controller of the domain.

[Kernel32]

For instance, the password associated with a user cannot be changed at a domain server that is in a backup, rather than primary, role.

Change the domain server role, or change domain servers, and retry the operation.

This operation is only allowed on the primary domain controller of the domain.

[Network] Net Message ID: 2226

The specified server is not the domain controller, so you cannot update its security database.

Run the command on the domain controller. If you are using User Manager, set the focus on the domain controller, and then retry the command.

This operation is privileged on systems with earlier versions of the software.

[Network] Net Message ID: 3714

This message should occur only on a down-level computer. Any action to correct the problem should be performed on that computer. You must have administrative privilege on the remote computer to perform this task because that computer is running a previous version of LAN Manager.

To complete this task, ask your administrator to give you administrative privilege on the remote computer, or have that computer upgraded to Windows NT.

This operation will delete all scheduled jobs.

[AT-Network]

You used the command AT /D and are being warned that all of your scheduled jobs are about to be deleted.

Type Y if you want to delete all scheduled jobs, or N if not.

This operation will erase ALL data from the destination disk. Are you sure you want to continue?

[File Manager]

When you use the Copy Disk option in the Edit menu to copy the contents of one floppy disk to another, File Manager presents you with this message.

If you want to continue, choose Yes. If not, choose No to return to the Copy Disk dialog box.

This operation will result in a disk whose partition scheme may not be compatible with MS-DOS. Some partitions may not be accessible if the disk is used with MS-DOS in the future. Do you want to continue and create the partition anyway?

[Disk Administrator]

MS-DOS is capable of seeing only one primary partition. If you add more than one (you can create up to four), MS-DOS is unable to see them, and you are unable to access those partitions from MS-DOS.

If you are sure that you want to create the partition, select Yes. If not, choose No to return to the Disk Administrator window.

This page could not be shared.

[Clipboard]

A networking error has prevented you from sharing a ClipBook page.

Wait, and try again later. Or save the page as a text file and locate it in a shared directory.

This password cannot be used now.

[Network] Net Message ID: 2244

This message should occur only on a down-level computer. Any action to correct the problem should be performed on that computer. You cannot use a password that has just expired. Your network administrator may also have configured your account so that you cannot use any of your previous passwords.

Change your password to one that you have not used before.

This path component is invalid.

[Network] Net Message ID: 2356

This message should occur only on a down-level computer. Any action to correct the problem should be performed on that computer. A software error occurred.

Contact technical support.

This printer destination is idle and cannot accept control operations.

[Network] Net Message ID: 2158

This message should occur only on a down-level computer. Any action to correct the problem should be performed on that computer. The specified printer is not in use.

Be sure you are referring to the correct printer.

This printer destination request contains an invalid control function.

[Network] Net Message ID: 2159

This message should occur only on a down-level computer. Any action to correct the problem should be performed on that computer. An internal control function is invalid.

Contact technical support.

This program can only be used by Administrators.

[User Profile Editor]

You do not possess the level of permission required to use User Profile Editor.

Contact your system administrator. If you are the administrator of this system, log off, then log on again under your administrative account.

This program group already contains the maximum number of items.

[Program Manager]

The maximum number of program items that a program group can contain is 50. The currently selected program group already contains that number.

Delete one of these items to create room for the new one.

This program is not a valid Windows NT application.

[File Manager]

The application cannot be started from within Windows NT. It may have been created for use with MS-DOS or some other operating system.

If the application was written for MS-DOS, open an MS-DOS command prompt window and run the application from there.

This program or one of its components is compressed. Please uncompress it and try again.

[Program Manager]

While File Manager can store compressed files, these files must be decompressed before they can be accessed as programs in Program Manager.

When you have identified the compressed file, go to the command prompt, type the keyword EXPAND, the path to the compressed file, and (where necessary) a file path for the file's destination.

This program or one of its components is compressed. Please uncompress it and try again.

[Task Manager]

Use the EXPAND command (in an MS-DOS window or by choosing Run from the File menu of File Manager) to expand this file. For more information, use the command expand /?

This replicant database is outdated; synchronization is required.

[Network] Net Message ID: 2249

The local server's security database is completely out of synchronization with that of the domain controller, so a complete synchronization is needed.

Use the Synchronize With Domain option in Server Manager to synchronize the local server's database with that of the domain controller.

This schedule date is invalid.

[Network] Net Message ID: 3802

You typed an invalid schedule date.

Specify either a day of the month represented by a number between 1 and 31, or a day of the week represented by one of the following abbreviations: M, T, W, Th, F, Sa, Su.

This screen saver has no options that you can set.

The Desktop Window's Screen Save option usually allows you to set a number of options, including such things as the length and width of the Screen Saver. These options differ, depending upon the type of Screen Saver that you select, and the one that you have currently selected has no options that you can set.

No action is needed.

This security ID may not be assigned as the owner of this object.

[Kernel32]

The owner of a new object must be one of the users or groups you have been given the right to assign as owner. Typically, this is your user account and, if you are an administrator, the administrator's local group.

Learn which users and groups you have the right to assign as owner. Then retry the operation with that knowledge.

This security ID may not be assigned as the primary group of an object.

[Kernel32]

Contact the supplier of the running application, or your technical support group or system administrator may know how to edit the security ID structure.

This selection contains open embedded objects that will be deleted.

[Write]

When you attempt to save a document containing embedded objects in a 3.0 Write or Word for MS-DOS format, embedded objects in the document disappear. If you need to preserve these objects, you may want to attempt to save them in a different format.

No action is needed.

This server's clock is not synchronized with the primary domain controller's clock.

[Network] Net Message ID: 2457

The internal clock for servers must be set to within 10 minutes of the domain controller's clock.

Use the Net Time command to synchronize the server's clock with the domain controller's clock.

This set contains an SMS data stream and cannot be viewed or restored.

[Backup]

Use the application with which the tape was written to view or restore the data.

This set is compressed and cannot be viewed or restored.

[Backup]

The data on the tape was compressed with another application. Backup cannot uncompress data.

Uncompress the data with the same application that was used to compress the data.

This set is not completely cataloged.

[Backup]

You have a set that crosses tapes, and you are not looking at all of the files and directories in the set.

No action is needed.

This set was written with a newer version of software and cannot be viewed or restored.

[Backup]

Use the application with which the tape was written to view or restore the data.

This share name or password is invalid.

[Network] Net Message ID: 2403

Either the share name or password you typed is incorrect.

Check the spelling of the share name or password. If you still have problems, ask your network administrator to verify the password and the share name. Your administrator should also verify that you have access to the resource. This problem can also be caused by duplicate computer names. Do not give computers on different networks identical computer names if there is any computer that is on both networks.

This shared resource does not exist.

[Network] Net Message ID: 2310

The share name you specified does not exist.

Check the spelling of the share name. To display a list of resources shared on the server, type NET SHARE.

This system has not been properly installed by Windows NT Setup. Although you may use the Domain Settings dialog, use of other configuration capabilities may have unpredictable results.

[Control Panel]

No action necessary; however, it would be best to reinstall Windows NT.

This system lacks a properly setup/installed Keyboard Layout entry for both the User and System default entries.

[Program Manager]

Two important entries are missing from your Registry. The Registry is probably corrupt.

Restart the computer, and press the spacebar immediately after selecting Windows NT at the Boot Loader prompt. Then choose Last Known Good.

This system lacks a properly setup/installed Keyboard Layout entry for both the User and System default entries.

[Program Manager]

In REGEDT32's HKEY_LOCAL_MACHINE\\SYSTEM\\CurrentControlSet\\Control KeyBoard Layout key, one of the value entries is missing or incorrect.

Run Maintenance Mode Setup or reinstall Windows NT.

This system lacks a properly setup/installed Locale entry for both the User and System default entries.

[Program Manager]

Two important entries are missing from your Registry. The Registry is probably corrupt.

Restart the computer, and press the spacebar immediately after selecting Windows NT at the Boot Loader prompt. Then choose Last Known Good.

This system lacks a properly setup/installed Locale entry for both the User and System default entries.

[Program Manager]

Two important entries are missing from your Registry Editor.

Run Maintenance Mode Setup or reinstall Windows NT.

This tape has been secured. You do not have the proper backup privileges.

[Backup]

You cannot write to this tape using your current logon name, because the security settings on the tape do not list you as having backup privileges.

Either log in with a user name that has backup privileges, or ask that the security settings be changed to give you backup privileges, or use a different tape.

This tape has been secured. You do not have the proper erase privileges.

[Backup]

You cannot erase this tape using your current logon name, because the security settings on the tape do not list you as having erase privileges.

Either log in with a user name that has erase privileges, or ask that the security settings be changed to give you erase privileges, or use a different tape.

This tape has been secured. You do not have the proper privileges.

[Backup]

You cannot perform the requested action on this tape using your current logon name, because the security settings on the tape do not list you as having the necessary privileges.

Either log in with a user name that has the necessary privileges, or ask that the security settings be changed to give you the necessary privileges.

This tape has been secured. You do not have the proper restore privileges.

[Backup]

You cannot read from this tape using your current logon name, because the security settings on the tape do not list you as having restore privileges.

Either log in with a user name that has restore privileges, or ask that the security settings be changed to give you restore privileges, or ask that someone with restore privileges restore the file or files for you.

This tape is of the same tape family. Insert a different tape in the drive.

[Backup]

The backup you are performing has filled the tape that is currently in the drive and needs to continue data onto an additional tape. It will not overwrite earlier tapes in this family.

Insert a blank tape or a tape that is not part of this family.

This tape was made with a newer version of software and cannot be read by this application.

[Backup]

Newer software has backward compatibility but earlier versions of the software do not have forward compatibility.

Use the version of the software with which the data was placed on the tape to read the data.

This tape was written with software ECC and cannot be read by this application.

[Backup]

Use the application with which the tape was written to view or restore the data.

This user account has expired.

[Network] Net Message ID: 2239

Only an administrator can access an expired account.

The administrator must reinstate this account before the action you specified can be taken.

This user account is undefined.

[Network] Net Message ID: 2238

This message should occur only on a down-level computer. Any action to correct the problem should be performed on that computer. A software error occurred.

Contact technical support.

This user is not cached in user accounts database session cache.

[Network] Net Message ID: 2235

This message should occur only on a down-level computer. Any action to correct the problem should be performed on that computer. A software error occurred.

Contact technical support.

This volume cannot be checked with this version of UHPFS.DLL.

[Chkdsk-HPFS]

To insure you are using the correct version of UHPFS.DLL, you might want to restore it from the distribution medium (you will have to decompress it), and then erase all other instances of UHPFS.DLL.

This volume cannot be checked with this version of UNTFS.DLL.

[Chkdsk-NTFS]

The file system version number on the NTFS volume indicates that it was created with a later release of Windows NT than this version of UNTFS.DLL.

Use the version of UNTFS.DLL that came with the later version of Windows NT.

This volume cannot be converted to *file system* **Possible causes are: 1.- Bad sectors in required areas of the volume. 2.-** *file system* **structures in areas required by** *file system*

[Convert]

The volume is still in its original (unconverted) state. However, there is nothing you can do to make this volume suitable for conversion.

This volume is not a valid HPFS volume; it cannot be converted.

[Convert]

Run the Chkdsk /f command and then try the conversion again.

This volume is not an Windows NT File System (NTFS) volume. You can only set permissions and auditing information on NTFS volumes and LAN Manager 2.x user-level servers.

[Security]

You attempted to set permissions on a directory or file on a FAT or an HPFS volume that is not a LAN Manager user-level server.

Move or copy the file or directory to an NTFS volume, then set permissions on it.

This volume is not an Windows NT File System (NTFS) volume. You can only set the owner on NTFS volumes.

[Security]

You attempted to set Permissions on a file on a FAT or an HPFS volume.

Move the resources on which you wish to set the owner to an NTFS volume, then set permissions on it.

This will cancel the current play operation, continue?

[CD Player]

You are playing a CD on a player with multiple drives, and you have opted to switch from one drive to another.

If you want to make the switch, choose Yes.

This will end mirroring and create two independent partitions. Are you sure you want to break the selected mirror?

[Disk Administrator]

When you choose to break a mirror relationship, the two partitions that mirror one another become independent partitions, and thus no longer reflect one another's contents.

If you are sure that you want to break the selected mirror, choose Yes. If not, choose No to return to Disk Administrator.

This will log off the current user. Any unsaved work will be lost.

[Workstation-Logon]

As the system administrator, you may force a user off of a workstation, and this is a standard confirmation message.

If you want to do this, continue.

This will terminate the entire installation process. Are you sure you wish to proceed?

[Control Panel]

You have selected an Exit or Cancel option at some point during an installation procedure.

If you want to terminate installation, choose Yes.

This Windows NT computer is configured as a member of a workgroup, not as a member of a domain. The Netlogon service does not need to run in this configuration.

[Network]

Do not start the Net Logon service, or set it for automatic startup unless you reconfigure this computer as a member of a domain.

This workstation is already logged on to the local-area network.

[Network] Net Message ID: 2200

This message should occur only on a down-level computer. Any action to correct the problem should be performed on that computer. A user is already logged on at this workstation.

To see who is currently logged on at the workstation, type NET CONFIG WORKSTATION.

This workstation is in use and has been locked. The workstation can only be unlocked by *name* **** *name* **(** *name* **) or an administrator.**

[Workstation-Logon]

The workstation onto which you are attempting to logon has been locked.

Contact your system administrator. If you are the system administrator, log onto your administrative account and press CTRL+ALT+DELETE to unlock the workstation.

This workstation is in use and has been locked. The workstation can only be unlocked by *name* **** *name* **or an administrator.**

[Workstation-Logon]

The workstation onto which you are attempting to logon has been locked.

Contact your system administrator. If you are the system administrator, log onto your administrative account and press CTRL+ALT+DELETE to unlock the workstation.

This workstation is locked. Only *computer name* **** *user name* **(***text***) or an administrator can unlock this workstation.**

[Workstation-Logon]

This message occurs when the delay time passes on a Screen Saver that is password-protected.

If you have an administrator's account on this workstation, type the user name and password for your administrator account in the Workstation Locked dialog box. If not, contact your system administrator.

This workstation is locked. Only *computer name* *****user name* **or an administrator can unlock this workstation.**

[Workstation-Logon]

This message occurs when the delay time passes on a Screen Saver that is password-protected.

If you have an administrator's account on this workstation, type the user name and password for your administrator account in the Workstation Locked dialog box. If not, contact your system administrator.

Thousand separator cannot contain digits.

[Program Manager]

In the Number Format dialog box, you entered a number in the 1000 Separator box empty.

Enter in the 1000 Separator box the mark that you want to see to the right of the 1000 column in numbers on your system.

Thread does not have a clipboard open.

[Kernel32]

An application, as part of its user interface, has tried to operate on the clipboard without first opening it.

Contact the supplier of the running application.

Time is invalid.

[WINS Service]

The time you entered is not valid, or is in an invalid format. Either it does not match the format specified in your International settings, or it is out of range (for example 25:00 or 13 p.m.) or it has characters that are not used to specify time.

Re-enter the time. If you are not sure what format is valid, choose the International icon in the Control Panel, and then select Time Format.

Time out error. From device: *name*

[QIC117]

The time-out interval elapsed without a response from the indicated device. The attempt to communicate with the device has been abandoned.

Reboot your computer. If you continue to get this message, contact the hardware vendor.

Time supplied is not exactly on the hour.

[Network] Net Message ID: 3764

Specifying minutes in your logon command is optional, but if included, the minutes must be in the format :00 (a colon and two zeros).

Retype the command, either omitting the minutes or using the correct format, :00.

Timeout (*number* **milliseconds) waiting for ReadFile.**

[Netevent]

The service controller could not communicate with the service within the specified time.

Ask your system administrator to start the service again using the Services option in Control Panel. If the service will not start, contact the service vendor.

Timeout (*number* **milliseconds) waiting for service to connect.**

[Netevent]

The service controller could not communicate with the service process within the specified time.

Ask your system administrator to start the service again using the Services option in Control Panel. If the service will not start, contact the service vendor.

Timeout (***number*** **milliseconds) waiting for transaction response.**

[Netevent]

A control message could not be sent to a service.

Retry the operation. If the problem persists, ask your system administrator to stop and then restart the service. It may be necessary to contact the vendor of the service.

Timeout before function completed

[Backup]

The driver expected the tape drive to respond in a certain amount of time. You may have a slower drive or the cabling may not be secure.

Check the Hardware Compatibility List for the compatible version of the tape drive. Also check the cabling.

Timeout occurred

[FTP Server] [TCP/IP]

The data connection, in use by a TCP/IP utility, was not properly closed down due to the loss of the ACK,FIN part of the TCP close-down sequence.

Retry the TCP/IP utility operation. If you still get this message, contact your network administrator.

Timer expired

The task could not be completed because there was no response within the timeout period.

Title setup error corrected; Please rerun Viewer.

[Disk Administrator]

Rerun Viewer to refresh your screen.

Tmm could not signal the client thread. This indicates something seriously wrong.

[WINS Service]

Contact Technical Support.

To change the Advanced I/O settings, you must be logged onto the Windows NT workstation as an Administrator.

[Program Manager]

Log onto the workstation as an administrator, then try again to change the workstation's Advanced I/O settings.

To join a workgroup, enter its name and click OK. To join a domain which already has an account for this computer, enter its name and click OK. If a computer account must be added for this computer, select the 'Administrator Name' option and enter the name and password of an administrative account on the domain.

[Control Panel]

You can join either a workgroup or a domain. No special permissions are needed to join a workgroup. To join a domain, there must be an account for this computer on that domain.

If you want to join a workgroup, enter the name of the workgroup in the Workgroup text box, and choose OK. If you want to join a domain, enter the name of the domain in the Domain text box, and choose OK. If you are logged are a domain administrator, you can also create an account for this computer on the domain at this time. Otherwise, make sure there is an account on the domain for this computer before you attempt to join it.

To seed this network, you must specify a default zone.

[Services for Macintosh (SFM)]

To specify a default zone, select a zone from the zone list and then choose Set to indicate a default zone.

To specify the size of the command history buffer under Window NT, use the /listsize switch which sets the number of commands to remember.

[Doskey]

The Windows NT version of Doskey does not recognize the /bufsize=size switch that was used in previous versions.

Use the /listsize switch instead. Note that the numeric value in the /listsize switch represents the maximum number of commands to remember, and not the size of the buffer in bytes.

Too little disk space for that catalog

[Disk Administrator]

Choose a smaller catalog, or delete some files from the disk and try again.

Too many arguments in command line

[More]

Make sure the syntax of the command line is correct, and that you only specify one process at a time. To check which arguments are valid for this command, type HELP at the command prompt followed by the command name (in this case, More).

Too many commands were outstanding; the application can retry the command later.

[Dynamic Data Exchange]

NetBIOS has as many commands waiting for processing as it can handle.

Wait and try again.

Too many directory windows are open. Close one or more windows, and then try again.

[File Manager]

To prevent users from accidentally opening an infinite number of windows, File Manager allows you to open no more than 27 windows at once. You either have 27 windows currently open, or you have opened so many windows that they are making demands upon your workstation's available memory.

Too many dynamic link modules are attached to this program or dynamic link module.

[Kernel32]

The system ran out of space for keeping track of dynamic-link modules that are attached to the module being executed or loaded.

Remove some dynamic-link library dependencies from the program or module. You may have to contact the supplier of the running application.

Too many errors occurred because of poor phone line quality.

[Remote Access Service]

Too many asynchronous errors occurred on your phone line during authentication.

Try to connect again. If the problem persists, lower your baud rate and disable any modem features that may be set. For more information, see "Setting Modem Features" and "Modem Idiosyncrasies" in the Remote Access Phone Book online Help.

Too many files opened for sharing.

[Kernel32]

The maximum number of files in the sharing buffer has temporarily been exceeded.

Retry the command when fewer programs are running.

Too many open files

[Xcopy]

Close some unneeded files, then retry the command.

Too many other files are currently in use.

[Program Manager] [Task Manager]

You are low on memory.

Close some of the files that you have open, then try again.

Too many parameters - *text*

[Command] [Utilities]

You typed too many parameters for this command. This message usually refers to parameters other than switches (which begin with a slash, such as /s) or keywords (which contain an equal sign, such as cols=80).

To determine which parameters are valid for this command, type HELP at the command prompt followed by the command name.

Too many posts were made to a semaphore.

[Kernel32]

There is a limited number of times that an event semaphore can be posted. You tried to post an event semaphore that has already been posted the maximum number of times.

Wait, and then retry the operation. If you still get this message, contact the supplier of the running application.

Too many recursive calls.

[Fonts (CP)]

There is a problem with the way one of the characters is constructed.

Contact the vendor of the font, and report this message.

Too many retries to "*name* " for xmit errors (*number*) ... closing connection

[Dynamic Data Exchange]

The connection is being closed because there was no response to data that was sent. There may be some data corruption.

Check any files that were being written to on the specified computer for corruption, and restore from a backup if necessary.

Too many security IDs have been specified.

[Kernel32]

Contact the supplier of the running application.

Too many string lists

[FINDSTR]

The regular expression you specified as a search string in the Findstr command is too complex.

Use a sequence of Findstr commands, so you can use simpler regular expressions. You can pipe the output of one Findstr command to the next, in order to achieve the regular expression you need.

Too many titles;displaying first 400.

[Help]

When you do a full text search, and your search references too many topics, this message appears.

Specify a more nearly unique keyword to reduce the range of topics found.

Too many transmit retries (*number*) for same packet to "*name* " ... closing connection

[Dynamic Data Exchange]

The connection is being closed because there was no response to data that was sent. There may be some data corruption.

Check any files that were being written to on the specified computer for corruption, and restore from a backup if necessary.

Too many xmit retries to "*name* " for memory errors (*number*) ... closing connection

[Dynamic Data Exchange]

The connection is being closed because there was no response to data that was sent. There may be some data corruption.

Check any files that were being written to on the specified computer for corruption, and restore from a backup if necessary.

Too much lost data to recover it all.

[Chkdsk-NTFS]

Run the Chkdsk command again, with the /f switch, to recover the rest of the data.

Topic name is invalid

[Dynamic Data Exchange]

A topic name can contain up to 255 characters. There can be no commas (,) in the name, and the vertical bar (|) cannot be the first or last character.

Enter a valid topic name.

Topic too long to edit copy selection and excess was trimmed. Use CTRL+INS while viewing to copy entire topic.

[Help]

When you attempt to copy a topic, and the topic is too long for the Copy dialog box, the topic is trimmed.

Perform the user action prescribed in the message.

Transmit buffer on port *address* **isn't drained!** (*code*)

[Digi]

Contact Digi technical support.

Try again later *code*

[FTP Server]

A new process, which is necessary for carrying out the Ftp command, could not be created.

Try the Ftp operation later. If you continue to get this message, contact your network administrator to interpret the error code displayed at the end of the message, and then take appropriate action.

Two ports, *number* **and** *number*, **on a single multiport card can't have two different interrupts.**

The IRQ value for one of these ports was entered incorrectly.

If the IRQ values were set by a setup program, contact the vendor of the application. Otherwise, use Regedit to correct the values.

Type a password which meets these requirements in both text boxes.

[Workstation-Logon]

This message is preceded by a message informing you of the Account Policy for passwords for this workstation.

Look at the specifications that precede this message, then type in a password that meets these requirements.

Type the password for *text* : *text*

[Network]

Enter the password for this resource, being sure to type the password correctly, including capitalization.

Unable load Windows Help application

[Solitaire]

This message occurs if (1) the file containing help for Solitaire is damaged, corrupted, or not in your Windows NT SYSTEM32 directory, or (2) your system is extremely low on memory.

If the file is not in the SYSTEM32 directory, find the file on your hard disk, then place it in the SYSTEM32 directory. If your system is low on memory, close one or more of the applications that you have running.

Unable open "Performance" key of RAS driver in registy. Status code is returned in data.

[Remote Access Service]

The Registry key should have been created when RAS was installed. There may be a problem with the configuration of RAS.

Check the Event Log in Event Viewer for messages related to this one. You might want to try using the Network option in Control Panel to remove and reinstall RAS. If you continue to see this message, contact technical support.

Unable the create helper thread.

[Services for Macintosh (SFM)]

This message is related to user security.

Contact technical support.

Unable to access device name *name*. Check current configuration.

[Digi]

DigiFep5 should not load if the specified component is not loaded.

Contact Digi technical support.

Unable to access netcard detection modules

[Control Panel]

The application could not detect the network adapter card because portions of the required .DLL files could not be accessed. It is possible that a needed file was accidentally deleted, or the file may be corrupt

The vendor of the network adapter card might be able to provide a new copy of the .DLL file. Or you can remove and reinstall the software for the card.

Unable to access Service Controller

[Control Panel]

The Network option is unable to access the service controller, the Windows NT component that loads and unloads drivers.

Try again. Or consult the event log in Event Viewer for details on the problem, and then contact your system administrator.

Unable to access the default control information for a new user account.

[Setup]

During initial installation of Windows NT, Setup was unable to access the default control information for a new user account in the security accounts manager.

Select Retry to retry the operation. If you get the same message, select Exit Setup and begin the initial installation again. If the message still occurs, contact your technical support group.

Unable to access the default control information for a new user account.

[Repair Disk]

During initial installation of Windows NT, Setup was unable to access the default control information for a new user account in the security accounts manager.

Select Retry to retry the operation. If you get the same message, select Exit Setup and begin the initial installation again. If the message still occurs, contact your technical support group.

Unable to access the local security accounts database.

[Setup]

Select Retry to retry the operation. If you get the same message, select Exit Setup and begin the initial installation again. If the message still occurs, contact your technical support group.

Unable to access the local security accounts database.

[Repair Disk]

Select Retry to retry the operation. If you get the same message, select Exit Setup and begin the initial installation again. If the message still occurs, contact your technical support group.

Unable to access the local security policy database.

[Setup]

During initial installation, Setup was trying to generate and set a unique security ID for the local domain, but the local security authority was unable to open the local security database.

Select Retry to retry the operation. If you get the same message, select Exit Setup and begin the initial installation again. If the message still occurs, contact your technical support group.

Unable to access the local security policy database.

[Repair Disk]

During initial installation, Setup was trying to generate and set a unique security ID for the local domain, but the local security authority was unable to open the local security database.

Select Retry to retry the operation. If you get the same message, select Exit Setup and begin the initial installation again. If the message still occurs, contact your technical support group.

Unable to acquire a node on adapter "*name* ".

[Services for Macintosh (SFM)]

The server may be running out of memory. Or, even though it is unlikely, the AppleTalk network might have too many computers in it. If this is the case, all the node addresses are in use by other computers.

Check the server's available disk space. If the server requires more memory, try stopping other running applications and services. You might also need to remove unused files and applications from the server's disk. If the disk has sufficient memory, try shutting down some other computers and then try starting the AppleTalk Protocol using the Devices option in Control Panel.

Unable to add accelerator.

[Help]

This error is from the Macro Language Editor for online help, and should not appear while using the Help file. Report this error to the provider of the Help file.

Unable to add button.

[Help]

This error is from the Macro Language Editor for online help, and should not appear while using the Help file. Report this error to the provider of the Help file.

Unable to add item *name* to the program group *name*.

[Setup]

Setup was unable to communicate with the Windows NT Program Manager through dynamic data exchange (DDE) to add an item to a program group.

Retry, and then if you get the same message, ignore it. You can add the item to the program group using Program Manager once Windows NT installation is complete.

Unable to add item *name* to the program group *name*.

[Repair Disk]

Setup was unable to communicate with the Windows NT Program Manager through dynamic data exchange (DDE) to add an item to a program group.

Retry, and then if you get the same message, ignore it. You can add the item to the program group using Program Manager once Windows NT installation is complete.

Unable to add menu item.

[Help]

This error is from the Macro Language Editor for online help, and should not appear while using the Help file. Report this error to the provider of the Help file.

Unable to add or change accounts on the domain controller. The account information entered does not grant sufficient privilege to create or change accounts.

[Control Panel]

You have to create or modify accounts on the domain controller, and you lack the permission to do so.

Contact the domain administrator. Or log on under an account that has permission to create and modify accounts.

Unable to add popup menu.

[Help]

This error is from the Macro Language Editor for online help, and should not appear while using the Help file. Report this error to the provider of the Help file.

Unable to add registry key and/or value to HARDWARE\\DEVICEMAP\\ *name*.

[Digi]

The driver is writing to the Registry where applications look for information about available serial ports. If the entries are not available, an application might be unable to access a port.

Contact Digi technical support.

Unable to add the user to the Administrator alias.

[Setup]

During initial installation of Windows NT, Setup was unable to add a user account alias to the Administrator account.

You can ignore this message and use Windows NT User Manager to do this after installation is complete.

Unable to add the user to the Administrator alias.

[Repair Disk]

During initial installation of Windows NT, Setup was unable to add a user account alias to the Administrator account.

You can ignore this message and use Windows NT User Manager to do this after installation is complete.

Unable to add to the security database session cache segment.

[Network] Net Message ID: 2233

The security database has reached its size limit. Nothing can be added to it.

Unable to add to the user accounts database.

[Network] Net Message ID: 2456

This message should occur only on a down-level computer. Any action to correct the problem should be performed on that computer. The user accounts database cannot be enlarged because the server's hard disk is full.

Check the server's disk and remove unnecessary and outdated files.

Unable to alloc conn block

[FTP Server] [TCP/IP]

The Tftp server cannot start up because there is not enough memory available to hold the control information about the remote connection, if one is made.

Wait a few seconds, then retry the operation. If you still get this message, quit some unneeded applications that are running, and then retry the operation.

Unable to allocate a *number* byte message to create the ARP cache.

[Netevent]

Memory allocation for the ARP cache entry failed.

Wait a few minutes and then retry the operation.

Unable to allocate a *number* byte message.

[Netevent]

The streams memory quota was exceeded or memory is unavailable for allocation.

No action is needed unless you see this message frequently. Then add more memory.

Unable to allocate a system resource required for the MacPrintService. (The data is the Win32 error code.)

[Services for Macintosh (SFM)]

No more print jobs will be accepted until resources are freed.

Try stopping other running applications. You might also need to remove unused files and applications from your disk.

Unable to allocate a timer. Please exit some of your applications and try again.

[Minesweeper]

Many applications require a timer, and you are running so many of these applications that a timer cannot be allocated to Minesweeper.

Close one or more of these applications.

Unable to allocate critical memory resources. The service could not be started.

[Netevent]

The system's memory is insufficient.

Stop other applications from running and retry the operation in a few minutes. If the problem persists, your system administrator may need to add more memory to your system.

Unable to allocate critical memory resources. The service failed to start.

[Netevent]

Stop other services from running and retry the operation in few minutes. If the problem persists, your system administrator may need to add more memory to your system.

Unable to allocate enough memory. Status codes returned in data.

[Remote Access Service]

The server may be running out of memory.

Try stopping other running applications and services. Also try restarting the server. If you continue to see this message, contact technical support.

Unable to allocate I/O request packet.

[Services for Macintosh (SFM)]

The server may be running out of memory.

Try stopping other running applications. You might also need to remove unused files and applications from the server's disk.

Unable to allocate Memory Descriptor Lists.

[Services for Macintosh (SFM)]

The server may be running out of memory.

Try stopping other running applications. You might also need to remove unused files and applications from the server's disk.

Unable to allocate memory.

[Services for Macintosh (SFM)]

The server may be running out of memory.

Try stopping other running applications. You might also need to remove unused files and applications from the server's disk. If possible, increase the server's memory.

Unable to allocate necessary system resource *code*

[TCP/IP]

The TCP/IP remote utility was unable to get the resources on the local computer it needed to send a command to the remote host.

This may be a temporary situation. Wait a few seconds and retry sending the remote command. If you still get this message, contact your system administrator to interpret the error code that is displayed at the end of the message, and take appropriate action.

Unable to allocate nonpaged memory resources.

[Services for Macintosh (SFM)]

The server may be running out of memory.

Try stopping other running applications. You might also need to remove unused files and applications from the server's disk.

Unable to allocate packet

[FTP Server] [TCP/IP]

The Tftp server was unable to start up, because it could not be served by the UPD protocol.

Contact your network administrator.

Unable to allocate paged memory resource.

[Services for Macintosh (SFM)]

The system is out of disk space.

Use the System option in Control Panel to increase the size of the paging file. Choose the Virtual Memory button. If the page file size cannot be increased, you will need to remove unused files and applications.

Unable to allocate resources from the NDIS wrapper.

[Services for Macintosh (SFM)]

The server may be running out of memory.

Try stopping other running applications. You might also need to remove unused files and applications from the server's disk. If possible, increase the server's memory.

Unable to allocate resources.

[Services for Macintosh (SFM)]

The server may be running out of memory.

Try stopping other running applications. You might also need to remove unused files and applications from the server's disk. If possible, increase the server's memory.

Unable to authenticate user.

[Services for Macintosh (SFM)]

The server may be running out of memory.

Try stopping other running applications. You might also need to remove unused files and applications from the server's disk.

Unable to bind to a adapter when in routing configuration.

[Services for Macintosh (SFM)]

Check the Even Log in Event Viewer for related errors from the installed adapters.

Unable to bind to interface *name*.**Error code** *code*.

[Netevent]

The TCP/IP protocol could not bind to the NDIS driver specified in the Registry. The Registry is either corrupted or was installed improperly.

Use the Network option in Control Panel to verify that the bindings of the TCP/IP match. If not, remove and reinstall the TCP/IP protocol.

Unable to browse the selected domain because the following error occurred: *text*

[Network]

You are temporarily unable to browse the selected domain, possibly because the domain controller is down.

See the event log in Event Viewer for details on the error. Or wait and try again later.

Unable to browse the selected domain because the following error occurred: *text*

[Security]

You are temporarily unable to browse the selected domain, possibly because the domain controller is down.

See the event log in Event Viewer for details on the error. Or wait and try again later.

Unable to change attribute - *filename*

[Attrib]

The Attrib command was unable to change an attribute (read-only, archive, system, or hidden) of the specified file.

Make sure the file exists and that you have access to it.

Unable to change menu item binding.

[Help]

This error is from the Macro Language Editor for online help, and should not appear while using the Help file. Report this error to the provider of the Help file.

Unable to close the adapter "*name* **".**

[Services for Macintosh (SFM)]

The AppleTalk protocol failed to unbind to an adapter. The protocol stack might fail to stop.

Use the Devices option in Control Panel to verify that the protocol stack has stopped. If not, restart the computer.

Unable to communicate with the NBT driver. Error code *code***.**

[Netevent]

Use the Network option in Control Panel to remove and then reinstall the driver. Select RFC NetBIOS, choose Remove, and then choose Add.

Unable to complete the requested operation because of either a catastrophic media failure or a data structure corruption on the disk.

[Kernel32]

The media that the security database is stored on failed, or a program error in the security software caused a corruption on disk.

First, restart your computer. Then, if the problem persists, restore your most recent backup.

Unable to configure NBT. Error code *code***. The service could not be started.**

[Netevent]

An internal error occurred in the NBTSVC service.

Reinstall the NBTSVC.DLL file and then retry the operation.

Unable to configure the addresses of the WINS servers.

[Netevent]

You will not be able to use the Windows Internet Name Service (WINS) because the addresses of the WINS servers could not be added to your configuration.

Unable to connect to the domain controller for this domain. Have your administrator check your computer account on the domain controller.

[Control Panel]

You have entered an invalid password. Or the domain controller has temporarily gone down.

Make sure that you have entered the correct password. If you have, wait and try at a later time.

Unable to connect to the local security accounts manager.

[Setup]

Select Retry to retry the operation. If you get the same message, and you are trying to add a user account or change a user password, you may choose Ignore and do the operations later on the installed system, using a built-in account (for example, the Administrator account). Otherwise, choose Exit Setup and reinstall Windows NT.

Unable to connect to the local security accounts manager.

[Repair Disk]

Select Retry to retry the operation. If you get the same message, and you are trying to add a user account or change a user password, you may choose Ignore and do the operations later on the installed system, using a built-in account (for example, the Administrator account). Otherwise, choose Exit Setup and reinstall Windows NT.

Unable to continue to use the local security authority (LSA).

[Setup]

During the initial installation of Windows NT, Setup sets up certain information for the local security authority (LSA) before signaling it to continue. Setup was unable to signal the LSA event.

Select Retry to retry the operation. If you get the same message, select Exit Setup and begin the initial installation again. If you still get this message, contact your technical support group.

Unable to continue to use the local security authority (LSA).

[Repair Disk]

During the initial installation of Windows NT, Setup sets up certain information for the local security authority (LSA) before signaling it to continue. Setup was unable to signal the LSA event.

Select Retry to retry the operation. If you get the same message, select Exit Setup and begin the initial installation again. If you still get this message, contact your technical support group.

Unable to copy ***filename***

[Program Manager]

You might not have permission to read the file you are trying to copy from. Or the shared directory you tried to copy from has become unavailable. Or you might not have Write permissions on the file or directory you are trying to copy to. Or the disk you are copying to might be full.

Make sure you have enough space on the disk you are copying to. Delete some files if necessary to make more room. Make sure the directory you are copying from is available. If it is not, contact the administrator of that share. Make sure that you have Write permissions on the directory and file you are copying to, and that you have Read permission on the directory and file you are copying from. If you do not have the necessary permissions, change them or ask an administrator to change them for you.

Unable to copy disk.

[File Manager]

The target disk may be write protected.

Make sure that the target disk is not write-protected, then try again.

Unable to create ***name*****, TrueType font not installed**

[Program Manager]

To install the font, choose Fonts from the Control Panel and then choose Add.

Unable to create ***filename*****, TrueType font not installed**

[Program Manager]

The font resource file for this TrueType font could not be created. You might not have permission to read the file you are trying to copy data from. Or the shared directory you tried to copy it from has become unavailable. Or you might not have Write permissions on the file or directory you are trying to copy the data to. Or the disk you are writing to might be full.

Make sure you have enough space on the disk you are writing to. Delete some files if necessary to make more room. Make sure the directory you are copying data from is available. If it is not, contact the administrator of that share. Make sure that you have Write permissions on the directory and file you are copying to, and that you have Read permission on the directory and file you are copying from. If you do not have the necessary permissions, change them or ask an administrator to change them for you.

Unable to create a device object.

[Services for Macintosh (SFM)]

The server is out of resources.

Close some running applications and optimize resources.

Unable to create a user account.

[Setup]

During the initial installation of Windows NT, Setup was trying to create a user account or an account for the computer name.

Select Retry to retry the operation. If you get the same message, you can select Ignore and log on to the Administrator account to add the user after Windows NT is installed. Or select the Exit Setup button and begin the initial installation again. If the message reappears, contact your technical support group.

Unable to create a user account.

[Repair Disk]

During the initial installation of Windows NT, Setup was trying to create a user account or an account for the computer name.

Select Retry to retry the operation. If you get the same message, you can select Ignore and log on to the Administrator account to add the user after Windows NT is installed. Or select the Exit Setup button and begin the initial installation again. If the message reappears, contact your technical support group.

Unable to create an initialization status event.

[Setup]

This is an informational message from Setup, which was unable to create the event that signals that the local security accounts manager is ready for use.

Select Retry in the message box to retry the operation. If you get the same message, select the Exit Setup button and begin the initial installation again. If the message still occurs, contact your technical support group.

Unable to create an initialization status event.

[Repair Disk]

This is an informational message from Setup, which was unable to create the event that signals that the local security accounts manager is ready for use.

Select Retry in the message box to retry the operation. If you get the same message, select the Exit Setup button and begin the initial installation again. If the message still occurs, contact your technical support group.

Unable to create directory - *name*

[Xcopy]

Xcopy could not create the target directory.

Make sure that you entered the target directory path correctly, and that you have permission to create that directory.

Unable to create file

[Program Manager]

The font resource file for this TrueType font could not be created. You might not have permission to read the file you are trying to copy data from. Or the shared directory you tried to copy it from has become unavailable. Or you might not have Write permissions on the file or directory you are trying to copy the data to. Or the disk you are writing to might be full.

Make sure you have enough space on the disk you are writing to. Delete some files if necessary to make more room. Make sure the directory you are copying data from is available. If it is not, contact the administrator of that share. Make sure that you have Write permissions on the directory and file you are copying to, and that you have Read permission on the directory and file you are copying from. If you do not have the necessary permissions, change them or ask an administrator to change them for you.

Unable to create file link.

[Backup]

The link to a previous file could not be created. This could be because the device you are restoring to does not support links.

Make sure you are restoring to an NTFS drive. Also make sure the file the application is trying to link to exists on the tape, and is restored.

Unable to create netcard detection dialog

[Control Panel]

An error occurred that prevented Windows NT from creating the dialog box you use to identify network adapter cards.

Contact your network administrator. It might be necessary to reinstall Window NT.

Unable to create new services with Service Controller

[Control Panel]

The service controller is a component that loads and unloads drivers. Either you lack the privilege to perform the current function or an internal software error has created problems with the service controller.

Restart your system and try again. If this fails, check the event log in Event Viewer to determine the nature of the problem, and then contact your system administrator.

Unable to create or allocate needed resource (err *number*). App will exit.

[CD Player]

The application needs to allocate some resource, such as memory; or it needs to create a resource such as a file. Because it could not do so, it will close.

Find out what resources this application requires, and make sure the resources are available to it. The resource must exist, and the user name from which the application is run must have permission to use the resource. If the application needs to create resources such as files or directories, make sure you are running it under a user name that has permissions to create these resources.

Unable to create or open system semaphore *name*.The error code is the data.

[Network] Net Message ID: 3109

This message should occur only on a down-level computer. Any action to correct the problem should be performed on that computer. A software error occurred.

Contact technical support.

Unable to create or open the file *filename*. (The data is the Win32 error code.)

[Services for Macintosh (SFM)]

The system might be out of disk space. Or, you may not have permission to write to the directory.

Remove unused files and applications from your disk. You might also want to contact your system administrator.

Unable to create port information table. Status codes returned in data.

[Remote Access Service]

The server may be running out of memory.

Try stopping other running applications and services. Also try restarting the server. If you continue to see this message, contact technical support.

Unable to create the "Network Trash Folder" on volume "*name* ".

[Services for Macintosh (SFM)]

Your system may be low on disk space or you may not have the necessary privilege to create the directory.

In either case, contact your system administrator to determine why the directory couldn't be created.

Unable to create the device "*name* ". AppleTalk protocol could not be started.

[Services for Macintosh (SFM)]

The driver could not create the AppleTalk device with the I/O system. This could happen if other drivers also create the same device before the AppleTalk protocol does.

Disable any unnecessary drivers. The device also may not have been created because the server is running out of memory.

Unable to create the device map entry for *name*.

Another serial port driver is already using this port name.

Unable to create the directory ***name*****.**

[Backup]

The named directory could not be created on the current drive, and therefore cannot be restored. Either you do not have Write privileges on the parent directory, or there is not room on the target disk.

Check to see that you have permission to write to the parent directory. If you do not, ask that permission be given to you, or log in as a user with the necessary permission. Check the available space on the disk. If the disk is full, delete some unneeded files to make room for the restored directory and its contents.

Unable to create the directory ***name*****.**

[Setup]

During the part of the Setup process that copies files from the distribution medium to the target computer, Setup was unable to create a directory on the target computer.

First, select Retry. If you get the same message, retry the Setup operation from the beginning. If you still get the same message, contact your technical support group.

Unable to create the directory ***name*****.**

[Repair Disk]

During the part of the Setup process that copies files from the distribution medium to the target computer, Setup was unable to create a directory on the target computer.

First, select Retry. If you get the same message, retry the Setup operation from the beginning. If you still get the same message, contact your technical support group.

Unable to create the file ***filename*****.**

[Backup]

The named file could not be created on the current drive, and therefore cannot be restored. Either you do not have Write privileges on the parent directory, or there is not room on the target disk.

Check to see that you have permission to write to the parent directory. If you do not, ask that permission be given to you, or log in as a user with the necessary permission. Check the available space on the disk. If the disk is full, delete some unneeded files to make room for the restored file.

Unable to create the Setup Window.

[Setup]

During initialization, Setup was unable to create the Windows NT Setup window through which to carry on a Setup dialog with the user.

Select OK to exit Setup. Then retry the Setup operation from the beginning. If you still get this message, contact your technical support group.

Unable to create the Setup Window.

[Repair Disk]

During initialization, Setup was unable to create the Windows NT Setup window through which to carry on a Setup dialog with the user.

Select OK to exit Setup. Then retry the Setup operation from the beginning. If you still get this message, contact your technical support group.

Unable to create the symbolic link for *name*.

Another serial port driver is already using this symbolic link.

Unable to create the symbolic link from <name> -> <name>.

[Digi]

User-mode programs will be unable to access ports because MS-DOS name space could not be created.

Contact Digi technical support.

Unable to delete a network connection because files were still open on the remote resource.

[Setup]

This can happen during maintenance Setup.

You can ignore this. Setup was attempting to delete a network connection, and the worst that can happen is that you will have an unneeded network connection. You can also retry the operation.

Unable to delete a network connection because files were still open on the remote resource.

[Repair Disk]

This can happen during maintenance Setup.

You can ignore this. Setup was attempting to delete a network connection, and the worst that can happen is that you will have an unneeded network connection. You can also retry the operation.

Unable to delete a network connection for the specified local device because it was not redirected over the network.

[Setup]

The device name specified to Setup was not currently redirected to a remote resource on the network.

You can ignore this. Setup was attempting to delete a network connection that was not redirected.

Unable to delete a network connection for the specified local device because it was not redirected over the network.

[Repair Disk]

The device name specified to Setup was not currently redirected to a remote resource on the network.

You can ignore this. Setup was attempting to delete a network connection that was not redirected.

Unable to delete button.

[Help]

This error is from the Macro Language Editor for online help, and should not appear while using the Help file. Report this error to the provider of the Help file.

Unable to delete menu item.

[Help]

This error is from the Macro Language Editor for online help, and should not appear while using the Help file. Report this error to the provider of the Help file.

Unable to delete services from Service Controller

[Control Panel]

The service controller is a component that loads and unloads drivers. Either you lack the privilege to perform the current function. Or an internal software error has created problems with the service controller.

Restart your system and try again. If this fails, check the event log in Event Viewer to determine the nature of the problem.

Unable to delete the "Network Trash Folder" from volume "*name* ".

[Services for Macintosh (SFM)]

There may be a sharing violation. The directory name may be selected in File Manager or some other application has the directory open.

Close other applications and then try the operation again.

Unable to deregister with the NDIS wrapper.

[Services for Macintosh (SFM)]

This message is for your information only.

No action is needed.

Unable to determine BACKACC revision of *filename*.

[Aclconv]

The data file you specified as input to the Aclconv utility was not produced by the BackAcc utility of LAN Manager version 2.0 or 2.1.

Retry the command, specifying a data file that was produced with the correct version of BackAcc.

Unable to determine how much available disk space is left. There may be a problem with your system. Contact your system administrator.

[MIDI Mapper (Control Panel)]

Exit the Control Panel, Shutdown Windows NT, then restart the system and try again.

Unable to determine local computer name.

[WINS Service]

Contact technical support.

Unable to display picture.

[Help]

Because you are low on memory, WinHelp cannot display the bitmap in a Help topic.

Close one or more of the applications that you have running, then try again.

Unable to do the specified file copy operation.

[Setup]

Select Retry to retry the operation. If you get the same message, select Exit Setup and begin the Setup operation again. Then, if you still get the same message, contact your technical support group.

Unable to do the specified file copy operation.

[Repair Disk]

Select Retry to retry the operation. If you get the same message, select Exit Setup and begin the Setup operation again. Then, if you still get the same message, contact your technical support group.

Unable to enable/disable button.

[Help]

This error is from the Macro Language Editor for online help, and should not appear while using the Help file. Report this error to the provider of the Help file.

Unable to enumerate Services from Service Controller

[Control Panel]

The service controller is a component that loads and unloads drivers. Either you lack the privilege to perform the current function or an internal software error has created problems with the service controller.

Restart your system and try again. If this fails, check the event log in Event Viewer to determine the nature of the problem.

Unable to execute DDE command '*name*' in Program Manager.

[Setup]

Setup uses dynamic data exchange (DDE) commands to communicate with Program Manager to create program groups, delete program groups, or add items to groups. A DDE link was established between Setup and Program Manager, but Program Manager did not carry out a command sent by Setup.

First, select Retry to retry the operation. If you get the same message, select Ignore. After Setup is finished, you can use Program Manager to do this work from the user interface.

Unable to execute DDE command '*name*' in Program Manager.

[Repair Disk]

Setup uses dynamic data exchange (DDE) commands to communicate with Program Manager to create program groups, delete program groups, or add items to groups. A DDE link was established between Setup and Program Manager, but Program Manager did not carry out a command sent by Setup.

First, select Retry to retry the operation. If you get the same message, select Ignore. After Setup is finished, you can use Program Manager to do this work from the user interface.

Unable to execute menu command.

[Help]

This error is from the Macro Language Editor for online help, and should not appear while using the Help file. Report this error to the provider of the Help file.

Unable to find DosDevices entry to name port.

[Digi]

The name by which the port is accessed in not in the configuration.

Use the Network option in Control Panel to check the configuration of the adapter.

Unable to find initialization file *filename*

The file of type .INI that is used by this application could not be found.

Re-install the application to create a new initialization file.

Unable to find registry value *name***.**

[Digi]

Use the Network option in Control Panel to check the configuration of the adapter. Also, contact Digi technical support.

Unable to find the .INF Source File. Check the /i switch on the Setup command line.

[Setup]

A required .INF file is either not in the current directory or not in the path specified in the /i switch on the Setup command line.

Correct the Setup command line and retry Setup. Note that if the /i switch is not used, then Setup is looking for the SETUP.INF file. Any other .INF file, such as INITIAL.INF or PRINTER.INF, has to be named in the /i switch. If, after changing the Setup command line, you get the same message, contact your technical support group.

Unable to find the .INF Source File. Check the /i switch on the Setup command line.

[Repair Disk]

A required .INF file is either not in the current directory or not in the path specified in the /i switch on the Setup command line.

Correct the Setup command line and retry Setup. Note that if the /i switch is not used, then Setup is looking for the SETUP.INF file. Any other .INF file, such as INITIAL.INF or PRINTER.INF, has to be named in the /i switch. If, after changing the Setup command line, you get the same message, contact your technical support group.

Unable to find the Setup Script Section in the INF file.

[Repair Disk]

Setup gets instructions from scripts in .INF files. Without a script, Setup cannot proceed.

Select OK to exit Setup. Then try to replace the .INF file with the .INF file from the distribution medium (you will have to decompress the file). Retry the Setup operation from the beginning. If you still get this message, contact your technical support group.

Unable to find the Setup Script. Check the /c switch on the Setup command line.

[Setup]

The .INF file is probably corrupted.

Select OK to exit Setup. Then restore the .INF file from the distribution medium (you will have to decompress the file). Retry the Setup operation. If you get this same message, contact your technical support group.

Unable to find the Setup Script. Check the /c switch on the Setup command line.

[Repair Disk]

The .INF file is probably corrupted.

Select OK to exit Setup. Then restore the .INF file from the distribution medium (you will have to decompress the file). Retry the Setup operation. If you get this same message, contact your technical support group.

Unable to find wallpaper. Please make sure a valid file name has been entered.

[Program Manager]

Make sure you have the correct file name for a wallpaper file that is on your computer. Then try again, being careful to type the name correctly.

Unable to find wallpaper. Please make sure a valid file name has been entered.

[Program Manager]

For a bitmap to appear in the Wallpaper menu of the Desktop option, the bitmap must be located in your Windows NT SYSTEM32 directory. In the Wallpaper menu box, you have entered the name of a bitmap that does not appear in this directory.

Exit or minimize Control Panel, open File Manager, and ensure that this bitmap appears in your SYSTEM32 directory.

Unable to finish operation on all files and directories.

[File Manager]

This message occurs when you attempt to copy, move, rename, or delete files without the appropriate permissions.

There is no user action for this message.

Unable to generate a unique security ID (SID).

[Setup]

Select Retry to retry the operation. If you get the same message, select Exit Setup and begin the initial installation again. If you still this message, contact your technical support group.

Unable to generate a unique security ID (SID).

[Repair Disk]

Select Retry to retry the operation. If you get the same message, select Exit Setup and begin the initial installation again. If you still this message, contact your technical support group.

Unable to impersonate via a named pipe until data has been read from that pipe.

[Kernel32]

Contact the supplier of the running application.

Unable to inform NBT of failure to link driver *name*. Error code *code*.

[Netevent]

The driver was not installed properly or has insufficient streams.

If the problem is with the driver, remove and then reinstall the NBT by selecting RFC NetBIOS in the Network option of Control Panel. If the system has insufficient streams, increase the limit of streams memory.

Unable to initialize ARP. Error code *code*. The service could not be started.

[Netevent]

The ARP IOCTL was installed incorrectly.

Remove the TCP/IP protocol and then reinstall it using the Network option in Control Panel.

Unable to initialize device *name***.**

[Print]

Either the device you specified in the Print command cannot be found or it cannot be initialized. (If you did not specify a device, PRN is used as the default).

Check your device specification in the Print command. You may have mistyped it. Also check that the device exists.

Unable to initialize IP. Error code *code***. The service could not be started.**

[Netevent]

The IP was installed incorrectly.

Remove the TCP/IP protocol and then reinstall it using the Network option in Control Panel.

Unable to initialize Registry

[Control Panel]

The Network option is unable to access the configuration information necessary for it to function properly.

See the event log in Event Viewer for details. Then contact your system administrator.

Unable to initiate DDE communication with the Program Manager.

[Setup]

Setup initiates dynamic data exchange (DDE) communication with the Program Manager in order to create program groups. This communication has not been established.

Select the Retry option several times; there is a good chance the link will be established on one of the retries. If you still get this message, select the Ignore option. You can create program groups after Setup is finished, by using Program Manager.

Unable to initiate DDE communication with the Program Manager.

[Repair Disk]

Setup initiates dynamic data exchange (DDE) communication with the Program Manager in order to create program groups. This communication has not been established.

Select the Retry option several times; there is a good chance the link will be established on one of the retries. If you still get this message, select the Ignore option. You can create program groups after Setup is finished, by using Program Manager.

Unable to install ***filename*****.**

[Program Manager]

The font resource for this TrueType font could not be add to the font resource file. You might not have permission to read the file you are trying to copy data from. Or the shared directory you tried to copy it from has become unavailable. Or you might not have Write permissions on the file or directory you are trying to copy the data to. Or the disk you are writing to might be full.

Make sure you have enough space on the disk you are writing to. Delete some files if necessary to make more room. Make sure the directory you are copying data from is available. If it is not, contact the administrator of that share. Make sure that you have Write permissions on the directory and file you are copying to, and that you have Read permission on the directory and file you are copying from. If you do not have the necessary permissions, change them or ask an administrator to change them for you. Rebooting your computer will solve this problem in some cases.

Unable to install the driver file. There may be a problem with your system. Check your system integrity or contact your system administrator.

[Drivers (CP)]

This is a general message that appears only under unusual circumstances: namely in the event of a General Protection fault.

Exit and restart Windows NT, then try again.

Unable to invoke the external program: *name*.

[Setup]

Select Retry to retry invocation of the external program. If you get the same message, select Exit Setup. Then retry the Setup operation from the beginning. If you still get this message, contact your technical support group.

Unable to invoke the external program: *name*.

[Repair Disk]

Select Retry to retry invocation of the external program. If you get the same message, select Exit Setup. Then retry the Setup operation from the beginning. If you still get this message, contact your technical support group.

Unable to link driver *name* **under driver** *name*. **Error code** *name*.

[Netevent]

A streams plumbing problem has occurred. The Registry may be corrupted or was installed improperly.

Remove the TCP/IP protocol and then reinstall it using the Network option in Control Panel.

Unable to link driver *name* under driver *name*. Error code *code*. The service could not be started.

[Netevent]

A streams plumbing problem has occurred. The Registry may be corrupted or was installed improperly.

Remove the TCP/IP protocol and then reinstall it using the Network option in Control Panel.

Unable to load a library required for this operation.

[File Manager] [Program Manager]

When you attempt to format a disk for the first time after installing Windows NT, you may receive this message.

Choose OK, then try again.

Unable to load catalog data from the tape.

[Backup]

The data in the catalog for the tape or backup set could not be copied to memory. This is probably caused by insufficient disk space.

Delete some files so backup can create its internal catalog file. If this is not the cause then there was a problem reading the data on the tape.

Unable to load library file *filename*.

[Setup]

Select Retry to retry loading the library file. If you get the same message, select Exit Setup. Retry the Setup operation from the beginning. If you still get the same message, contact your technical support group.

Unable to load library file *filename*.

[Repair Disk]

Select Retry to retry loading the library file. If you get the same message, select Exit Setup. Retry the Setup operation from the beginning. If you still get the same message, contact your technical support group.

Unable to load printer driver. Either there is insufficient memory or Windows is unable to find the printer-driver file. Use the Printers option in Control Panel to check the printer driver.

[Cardfile]

Every driver that you use, such as a mouse or a printer driver, must contain a corresponding .DRV file in File Manager. In addition, even if this .DRV file is present, the .DRV file cannot be loaded if you have too many applications running at once.

Use the Printers option in Control Panel to check the printer drivers. If the printer drivers are installed correctly, you probably have a number of applications running at once and they are making demands on your computer's memory. Close one or more applications to free up memory, then try again to print your Cardfile file.

Unable to load the Macintosh character set.

[Services for Macintosh (SFM)]

The Registry key or code page file might be missing from the Registry.

Check the key in the Registry. The path is HKEY_LOCAL_MACHINE\System|CurrentControl\Set|Control|Nls\CodePage\MACC P. Verify the value in this key. Then look for the value and a filename next to it. If a filename is there, verify that the file is in the <systemroot>\system32 directory.

Unable to load the MSV1_0 authentication package.

[Services for Macintosh (SFM)]

Users will be unable to log on.

Contact technical support.

Unable to locate ystemervices in Registry

[Control Panel]

The Network option was unable to locate one of the Registry keys critical to Network configuration.

See the event log in Event Viewer for details. Then contact your system administrator, or restart Windows NT.

Unable to lock configuration from Service Controller

[Control Panel]

You have requested information when someone else is working with that information. If you were permitted to lock the configuration, you and the other user could be working on the same information at the same time.

Wait until the other user is finished, and then try again.

Unable to lock the media eject mechanism.

[Kernel32]

An application may have attempted to lock the eject mechanism of a tape drive that is not designed to electronically eject a tape.

Lock the media eject mechanism manually. If that doesn't work, contact the supplier of the running application.

Unable to log you on because of an account restriction.

[Workstation-Logon]

The administrator of this workstation has configured your account so that you cannot presently log on.

Contact your system administrator. If you are the system administrator, log off, log on under your administrator account, then reconfigure permissions on the account on which you could not be logged on.

Unable to log you on because of insufficient disk space, please contact your administrator.

[Workstation-Logon]

Ask the administrator to delete some files from this computer so that you can log on.

Unable to log you on because of insufficient memory, please contact your administrator.

[Workstation-Logon]

Ask the administrator to add memory to this computer.

Unable to log you on because your mandatory profile is not available. Please contact your administrator.

[Workstation-Logon]

Your mandatory profile is temporarily unavailable.

Contact your system administrator. If you are the system administrator, logon under your administrative account, open User Manager and recreate the profile.

Unable to logon user "*user name* ".

[Services for Macintosh (SFM)]

The server may be running out of memory.

Try stopping other running applications. You might also need to remove unused files and applications from the server's disk.

Unable to map required address ranges for graphics card.

[Graphics]

Certain Mach-64 structures might have been changed in the software without various corresponding definitions being changed also. Or a few function calls might have failed.

Contact technical support.

Unable to modify button.

[Help]

This error is from the Macro Language Editor for online help, and should not appear while using the Help file. Report this error to the provider of the Help file.

Unable to modify the local security policy.

[Setup]

Select Retry to retry the operation. If you get the same message, select Exit Setup and begin the initial installation again. If you still get the same message, contact your technical support group.

Unable to modify the local security policy.

[Repair Disk]

Select Retry to retry the operation. If you get the same message, select Exit Setup and begin the initial installation again. If you still get the same message, contact your technical support group.

Unable to obtain configuration information for graphics card.

[Graphics]

There is a problem with the Mach 64 card.

Contact technical support.

Unable to obtain hardware bus info for this machine

[Control Panel]

Windows NT could not access information about the hardware connections within this computer. Either the bus type of this computer is not supported by Windows NT, or there is a defect in the computer.

Contact the vendor of the computer.

Unable to obtain RAS Statistics

[Remote Access Service]

A communication problem occurred between the RAS driver and Performance Monitor. Most likely, this is caused by a system error.

Restart the computer.

Unable to obtain security information.

[Services for Macintosh (SFM)]

The server may be running out of memory.

Check the server's available disk space. If you find that the server has sufficient memory, run Chkdsk to determine if there is a problem with the server's disk.

Unable to open a device that was sharing an interrupt request (IRQ)with other devices. At least one other device that uses that IRQ was already opened.

[Kernel32]

Windows NT allows more than one device to be assigned to an interrupt request (IRQ). But only one of the devices can be actively using the interrupt request at any one point in time.

Wait until the other device is finished and retry the operation, or stop using the other device and then retry the operation.

Unable to open a file.

[Setup]

Setup either could not find the specified file, or could not open a specified file. This can happen either during initial installation of Windows NT or during maintenance Setup.

Select Retry to retry the operation. If you get the same message, select Exit Setup and begin the initial installation or maintenance Setup operation again. If you still get the same message, contact your technical support group.

Unable to open a file.

[Repair Disk]

Setup either could not find the specified file, or could not open a specified file. This can happen either during initial installation of Windows NT or during maintenance Setup.

Select Retry to retry the operation. If you get the same message, select Exit Setup and begin the initial installation or maintenance Setup operation again. If you still get the same message, contact your technical support group.

Unable to open all the Registry keys that needed to be modified.

[Setup]

Setup was unable to open all the keys it anticipated using in HKEY_LOCAL_MACHINE and HKEY_CURRENT_USER. This can happen either at initial installation of Windows NT, or during maintenance use of Setup.

Select Retry to retry the operation. If you get the same message, select Exit Setup and begin the initial installation or maintenance Setup operation again. If the message still occurs, contact your technical support group.

Unable to open all the Registry keys that needed to be modified.

[Repair Disk]

Setup was unable to open all the keys it anticipated using in HKEY_LOCAL_MACHINE and HKEY_CURRENT_USER. This can happen either at initial installation of Windows NT, or during maintenance use of Setup.

Select Retry to retry the operation. If you get the same message, select Exit Setup and begin the initial installation or maintenance Setup operation again. If the message still occurs, contact your technical support group.

Unable to open an alias in the local security accounts manager.

[Setup]

During initial installation of the Windows NT system, Setup was unable to open the Administrator's alias in the local security accounts manager.

You can ignore this message and use Windows NT User Manager to do this after installation is complete.

Unable to open an alias in the local security accounts manager.

[Repair Disk]

During initial installation of the Windows NT system, Setup was unable to open the Administrator's alias in the local security accounts manager.

You can ignore this message and use Windows NT User Manager to do this after installation is complete.

Unable to open an object directory.

[Setup]

Setup was trying to open the object directory so it could search the object directory for symbolic link objects.

Select Retry to retry the operation. If you get the same message, select Exit Setup and begin the initial installation again. If the message still occurs, contact your technical support group.

Unable to open an object directory.

[Repair Disk]

Setup was trying to open the object directory so it could search the object directory for symbolic link objects.

Select Retry to retry the operation. If you get the same message, select Exit Setup and begin the initial installation again. If the message still occurs, contact your technical support group.

Unable to open ATK device for R access. Returning IO Status Block in Data.

[Services for Macintosh (SFM)]

The AppleTalk protocol is not installed or is not configured properly.

Use the Devices option in Control Panel to verify that the AppleTalk protocol is installed and started. You might also want to check for related errors in the Event Log in Event Viewer.

Unable to open device driver containing RAS performance data.

[Remote Access Service]

The device driver may not have loaded.

Check the Event Log in Event Viewer for errors related to this one. Also try removing and reinstalling RAS.

Unable to open driver *name*. Error code *code*. The service could not be started.

[Netevent]

The driver was installed incorrectly.

Remove the TCP/IP protocol and then reinstall it using the Network option in Control Panel.

Unable to open driver containing Appletalk performance data. To view the AppleTalk counters from Perfmon.exe, make sure the Appletalk driver has been started.

[Services for Macintosh (SFM)]

Use the Devices option in Control Panel to verify whether the driver has been started. The driver status should be Started. If not, select the driver and then choose Start.

Unable to open driver containing SFM file server performance data. To view the MacFile counters from Perfmon.exe, make sure the MacFile service has been started.

[Services for Macintosh (SFM)]

Use the Services option in Control Panel to verify that the status of File Server for Macintosh is started.

Unable to open RTMP/NBP/EP sockets on a node created on adapter "*name* ".

[Services for Macintosh (SFM)]

The AppleTalk protocol needs to open certain reserved sockets for operation. It was unable to do so in this case probably due to insufficient memory.

Stop and restart the stack. Also, try increasing memory.

Unable to open symbol file *filename*

This file could not be found in the expected directory or is corrupt.

Use the application's setup program to install this file.

Unable to open the adapter (bind to the mac) "*name* ".

[Services for Macintosh (SFM)]

The AppleTalk protocol failed to bind to an adapter.

Check the Event Log in Event Viewer for messages related to this one.

Unable to open the AFP Server's process token.

[Services for Macintosh (SFM)]

The server is out of resources.

Close some running applications and optimize resources.

Unable to open the AppleTalk key in the registry.

[Services for Macintosh (SFM)]

The AppleTalk Protocol was incorrectly configured by directly accessing the Registry instead of using the Network option in Control Panel.

Try removing and reinstalling Services for Macintosh.

Unable to open the file *filename* - skipped.

[Backup]

The named file could not be opened for backup.

Check your privilege to the parent directory. If you do not have Read access to this directory then log in as a user who does.

Unable to open the file *filename*.

[Setup]

Setup was unable to open a file required to complete the Setup process.

Select Retry to retry the operation. If you get the same message, contact your technical support group.

Unable to open the file *filename*.

[Repair Disk]

Setup was unable to open a file required to complete the Setup process.

Select Retry to retry the operation. If you get the same message, contact your technical support group.

Unable to open the local security accounts database.

[Setup]

Setup was trying to add a user account or change a user password, but was unable to do so.

Select Retry to retry the operation. If you get the same message, select Exit Setup and begin the initial installation again. If the message still occurs, contact your technical support group.

Unable to open the local security accounts database.

[Repair Disk]

Setup was trying to add a user account or change a user password, but was unable to do so.

Select Retry to retry the operation. If you get the same message, select Exit Setup and begin the initial installation again. If the message still occurs, contact your technical support group.

Unable to open the network connection profile.

[Kernel32]

An application was trying to make, cancel, or view a network connection. Windows NT cannot carry out the request because the file it uses to remember network connections cannot be opened.

Contact your technical support group.

Unable to open the specified symbolic link object.

[Setup]

Setup was trying to open a symbolic link object for query access.

Select Retry to retry the operation. If you get the same message, select Exit Setup and begin the initial installation again. If the message still occurs, contact your technical support group.

Unable to open the specified symbolic link object.

[Repair Disk]

Setup was trying to open a symbolic link object for query access.

Select Retry to retry the operation. If you get the same message, select Exit Setup and begin the initial installation again. If the message still occurs, contact your technical support group.

Unable to perform a security operation on an object which has no associated security.

[Kernel32]

Only objects that may be shared have security. You have tried to change security on an object that is not shared.

This operation is not supported. You may have to contact the supplier of the running application.

Unable to perform ioctl to device driver containing Appletalk performance data. To view the Appletalk counters from Perfmon.exe, make sure the Appletalk driver has been started.

[Services for Macintosh (SFM)]

Use the Devices option in Control Panel to verify whether the driver has been started. The driver status should be Started. If not, select the driver and then choose Start.

Unable to perform ioctl to device driver containing RAS performance data.

[Remote Access Service]

There was a problem with Performance Monitor's communication with the Remote Access Service driver using a device IOCTL.

Verify that the NDISWAN.SYS file is in your <systemroot>\system32\drivers directory. Also restart the server.

Unable to perform ioctl to device driver containing SFM performance data. To view the MacFile counters from Perfmon.exe, make sure the MacFile service has been started.

[Services for Macintosh (SFM)]

Use the Services option in Control Panel to verify that the status of File Server for Macintosh is started.

Unable to prime the NBT name cache from the LMHOSTS file. Error code *name*.

[Netevent]

Either the LMHOSTS service could not be started or the LMHOSTS file could not be read.

Verify that the LMHOSTS file is in the correct location and is not corrupted.

Unable to print.

[Help]

Because your system is low on memory, you cannot print the current Help topic.

Close one or more of the applications that you have running, then try again.

Unable to process requests due to insufficient resources.

[Services for Macintosh (SFM)]

The server may be running out of memory.

Try stopping other running applications. You might also need to remove unused files and applications from the server's disk.

Unable to process the Local Security Authority.

[Services for Macintosh (SFM)]

This is a critical error because no one is able to logon.

Contact technical support.

Unable to push module *name* onto a stream. Error code *code*. The service could not be started.

[Netevent]

The module was installed incorrectly.

Remove the TCP/IP protocol and then reinstall it using the Network option in Control Panel.

Unable to query an open symbolic link object.

[Setup]

During the initial installation of Windows NT, Setup was trying to query a symbolic link object that had been successfully opened for query access.

Select Retry to retry the operation. If you get the same message, select Exit Setup and begin the initial installation again. If the message still occurs, contact your technical support group.

Unable to query an open symbolic link object.

[Repair Disk]

During the initial installation of Windows NT, Setup was trying to query a symbolic link object that had been successfully opened for query access.

Select Retry to retry the operation. If you get the same message, select Exit Setup and begin the initial installation again. If the message still occurs, contact your technical support group.

Unable to query contents of directory "*name* ".

[Services for Macintosh (SFM)]

The volume might be corrupted, or the server may be running out of memory, or the permissions on the directory may be corrupted.

Run Chkdsk to determine if there is a problem with the server's disk.

Unable to query existing Registry node

[Control Panel]

The Network option was unable to access vital Registry information.

See the event log in Event Viewer for details. Then contact your system administrator.

Unable to query file information for "*filename* ".

[Services for Macintosh (SFM)]

Contact technical support.

Unable to query group membership for the user.

[Services for Macintosh (SFM)]

The server may be running out of memory.

Try stopping other running applications. You might also need to remove unused files and applications from the server's disk.

Unable to query service information from Service Controller

[Control Panel]

The service controller, an internal component that loads network drivers, is currently unable to provide necessary information.

Consult the event log in Event Viewer and contact your system administrator.

Unable to query size of "*filename* ".

[Services for Macintosh (SFM)]

Contact technical support.

Unable to query the file system type associated with "*filename* ".

[Services for Macintosh (SFM)]

The NTFS, FAT, or HPFS file system could not be searched for the specified directory.

Contact technical support.

Unable to read "*filename* ".

[Services for Macintosh (SFM)]

The file may be corrupt or missing.

The server will recover. No action is needed.

Unable to read entire directory. Only a partial listing will be displayed.

[File Manager]

The applications that you have running are making demands on your system's memory that make it temporarily impossible for File Manager to display the entire contents of the currently selected directory.

Close one or more applications, or use the System option in Control Panel to increase your virtual memory.

Unable to read from the file ***filename*****.**

[Setup]

There may be problems accessing the Windows NT distribution medium.

Select Retry to retry the operation. If you still get this message, contact your technical support group.

Unable to read from the file ***filename*****.**

[Repair Disk]

There may be problems accessing the Windows NT distribution medium.

Select Retry to retry the operation. If you still get this message, contact your technical support group.

Unable to read security information.

[Backup]

An error occurred while the application was reading security information for one or more files.

No action is needed. However, you might want to make sure the permissions are set correctly for this data.

Unable to read some object directory entries.

[Repair Disk] [Setup]

During the initial installation of Windows NT, Setup was searching the object directory tree for symbolic links, and was unable to read one or more object directory entries.

Select Retry to retry the operation. If you get the same message, select Exit Setup and begin the initial installation again. If the message still occurs, contact your technical support group.

Unable to read the "First Counter" value under the Remote Access\\Performance Key. Status codes retained in data.

[Remote Access Service]

The Registry key should have been created when RAS was installed. There may be a problem with the configuration of RAS.

Use the Network option in Control Panel to remove and reinstall RAS. If you continue to see this message, contact technical support.

Unable to read the "First Help" value under the Remote Access\\Performance Key. Status codes retained in data.

[Remote Access Service]

The Registry key should have been created when RAS was installed. There may be a problem with the configuration of RAS.

Use the Network option in Control Panel to remove and reinstall RAS. If you continue to see this message, contact technical support.

Unable to read the Alert names because the Services Control Database is locked by *user name* **for** *text*

[Server Manager]

Server Manager could not read the computer names to receive alerts because the Services Control Database is locked.

Try again later. Or contact the user who has locked the Services Control Database.

Unable to read the specified file.

[Setup]

Select Retry to retry the operation. If you get the same message, select Exit Setup and begin the initial installation again. If the message still occurs, contact your technical support group.

Unable to read the specified file.

[Repair Disk]

Select Retry to retry the operation. If you get the same message, select Exit Setup and begin the initial installation again. If the message still occurs, contact your technical support group.

Unable to read the tape in *drive letter*.

[Backup]

The tape that you have inserted is bad or represents an unrecognized format.

Insert another tape, then try again.

Unable to reconfigure services with Service Controller

[Control Panel]

The service controller, an internal component that loads network drivers, is currently unable to reconfigure services.

Wait and try again. Then contact your system administrator.

Unable to redirect the specified local device over the network because the local device name is invalid.

[Setup]

This may happen during maintenance Setup.

Select Retry to retry the operation. If you get the message again, select Exit Setup and begin the initial installation again. If the message still occurs, contact your technical support group.

Unable to redirect the specified local device over the network because the local device name is invalid.

[Repair Disk]

This may happen during maintenance Setup.

Select Retry to retry the operation. If you get the message again, select Exit Setup and begin the initial installation again. If the message still occurs, contact your technical support group.

Unable to redirect the specified local device over the network because the specified remote resource name was not acceptable to any provider.

[Setup]

This can only happen during maintenance Setup.

Select Retry to retry the operation. If you get the same message, you may want to select Ignore. Then, if you cannot continue with the Startup maintenance operation, restart the operation from the beginning. If the message still occurs, contact your technical support group.

Unable to redirect the specified local device over the network because the specified remote resource name was not acceptable to any provider.

[Repair Disk]

This can only happen during maintenance Setup.

Select Retry to retry the operation. If you get the same message, you may want to select Ignore. Then, if you cannot continue with the Startup maintenance operation, restart the operation from the beginning. If the message still occurs, contact your technical support group.

Unable to redirect the specified local device to a remote resource because the local device is already redirected.

[Setup]

Select Retry to retry the operation. If you get the same message, select Exit Setup and choose the Setup icon again to rerun the Setup maintenance task. If the message still occurs, contact your technical support group.

Unable to redirect the specified local device to a remote resource because the local device is already redirected.

[Repair Disk]

Select Retry to retry the operation. If you get the same message, select Exit Setup and choose the Setup icon again to rerun the Setup maintenance task. If the message still occurs, contact your technical support group.

Unable to redirect the specified local device to a remote resource because the specified password is unacceptable to the remote device.

[Setup]

Select Retry to retry the operation. If you get the same message, choose Exit Setup and begin the initial installation again. If the still get this message, contact your technical support group.

Unable to redirect the specified local device to a remote resource because the specified password is unacceptable to the remote device.

[Repair Disk]

Select Retry to retry the operation. If you get the same message, choose Exit Setup and begin the initial installation again. If the still get this message, contact your technical support group.

Unable to register name for node on adapter "*name* ". Either the name is already in use on the network or is longer than 32 characters long.

[Services for Macintosh (SFM)]

Duplicate node names are not allowed on the network.

Change the name of your node or shorten the name you are using.

Unable to register the server name with the network.

[Services for Macintosh (SFM)]

Change the name of one of the servers.

Unable to register with the NDIS wrapper.

[Services for Macintosh (SFM)]

The AppleTalk protocol was unable to establish communication with the NDIS layer. The server may be running out of memory.

Try increasing memory. Or try stopping other running applications and services.

Unable to register with the service controller. Error code *code*. The service could not be started.

[Netevent]

A call to WSAStartup or RegisterServiceCtrlHandler failed. The version number for the Windows NT sockets does not match the TCP/IP service or the TCP/IP service is not in the Registry.

Remove the TCP/IP protocol and then reinstall it using the Network option in Control Panel.

Unable to remove *filename.*

[Program Manager]

You cannot remove the specified font because another application is currently using it. Or, you do not have Delete permissions on the font file.

Make sure you have Delete permission on the font file and try again. If you still get this message, close applications that use this font and try again.

Unable to remove item *name* in the program group *name*.

[Setup]

Setup uses dynamic data exchange (DDE) commands to communicate with the Program Manager in order to delete an item from a program group. Program Manager was unable to carry out the request.

Select Retry to retry the operation. If you still get the same message, select Ignore. You can delete the item from the program group after the Setup operation is complete, using Windows NT Program Manager.

Unable to remove item *name* in the program group *name*.

[Repair Disk]

Setup uses dynamic data exchange (DDE) commands to communicate with the Program Manager in order to delete an item from a program group. Program Manager was unable to carry out the request.

Select Retry to retry the operation. If you still get the same message, select Ignore. You can delete the item from the program group after the Setup operation is complete, using Windows NT Program Manager.

Unable to restore the directory *name*.

[Backup]

The named directory could not be restored. An accompanying message provides more information.

Examine the accompanying message for information about the specific errors.

Unable to run more than one configuration operation at a time.

[Control Panel]

An application is already running that is changing the configuration.

Close the other application, or wait until it finishes. Then try again.

Unable to run the specified file.

[Help]

You have attempted to run a macro, and a necessary executable file is missing.

Reinstall the Help file.

Unable to send a ZIP packet on adapter "*name* ".

[Services for Macintosh (SFM)]

The server may be running out of resources.

Try increasing memory. Or try stopping other running applications and services. Also, check the Event Log in Event Viewer for messages related to the adapter.

Unable to set a Registry key value entry.

[Setup]

During initial installation of Windows NT, Setup attempted to write a value to a user or system environment key as part of registering a new user name or computer name.

Select Retry to retry the operation. If you get the same message, select Exit Setup and begin the initial installation again. If the message still occurs, contact your technical support group.

Unable to set a Registry key value entry.

[Repair Disk]

During initial installation of Windows NT, Setup attempted to write a value to a user or system environment key as part of registering a new user name or computer name.

Select Retry to retry the operation. If you get the same message, select Exit Setup and begin the initial installation again. If the message still occurs, contact your technical support group.

Unable to set security on service with Service Controller

[Control Panel]

The service controller, an internal component that loads network drivers, is currently unable to change the security settings on services.

Quit installing, then reinstall.

Unable to set size of "*filename* ".

[Services for Macintosh (SFM)]

Your system may be low on disk space.

Remove any unneeded files and directories from your disk.

Unable to set the control information for a new account.

[Setup]

During initial installation of Windows NT, Setup was unable to set the control information for the new account in the security accounts manager database.

You may choose to ignore this message and remove the incomplete account later using Windows NT User Manager, and then recreate the account. An alternative is to exit Setup now, and start the Windows NT installation process from the beginning.

Unable to set the control information for a new account.

[Repair Disk]

During initial installation of Windows NT, Setup was unable to set the control information for the new account in the security accounts manager database.

You may choose to ignore this message and remove the incomplete account later using Windows NT User Manager, and then recreate the account. An alternative is to exit Setup now, and start the Windows NT installation process from the beginning.

Unable to set the focus on your logged on domain *name* because the following error occurred: *text* Focus will be set to the local machine.

[Security]

The domain controller may not be available. Until a domain controller becomes available, the User Browser will be able to list users from the local computer only.

Wait a while, then try the operation again. If you continue to receive this message, contact technical support.

Unable to set the local computer name.

[Setup]

Select Retry to retry the operation. If you get the same message, select Exit Setup and begin the initial installation again. If the message still occurs, contact your technical support group.

Unable to set the local computer name.

[Repair Disk]

Select Retry to retry the operation. If you get the same message, select Exit Setup and begin the initial installation again. If the message still occurs, contact your technical support group.

Unable to set the lookahead size for adapter "*name* ".

[Services for Macintosh (SFM)]

The adapter does not support the minimum lookahead size the AppleTalk protocol requires. Also, the server may be running out of memory.

Try using a different adapter. Also, try increasing memory or stopping some running applications and services.

Unable to set the packet filter for adapter "*name* ".

[Services for Macintosh (SFM)]

The protocol was unable to let the adapter know that its ready to accept incoming packets. The protocol may not see any computers on the network on that adapter and vice versa.

Try stopping and restarting the AppleTalk protocol. Also try using another adapter if possible.

Unable to set the TimeZone

[Program Manager]

Log on as an administrator and try again.

Unable to set the user account password.

[Setup]

This can happen during the initial installation of Windows NT.

You can ignore this and change the password through the Windows NT interface after installation is complete.

Unable to set the user account password.

[Repair Disk]

This can happen during the initial installation of Windows NT.

You can ignore this and change the password through the Windows NT interface after installation is complete.

Unable to setup printer.

[Help]

Because your system is low on memory, you cannot complete Print Setup.

Close one or more of the applications that you have running, then try again.

Unable to show help information.

[Program Manager]

The file WINHELP.EXE is missing. Or, it failed to initialize due to insufficient memory.

Close some applications and try again. If you still get this message, restore WINHELP.EXE from a backup copy, or use Setup to reinstall the file.

Unable to show help information.

[User Profile Editor]

Either UPEDIT.HLP is not in your Windows NT SYSTEM32 directory, or the applications that you are running are making demands upon your system's memory that make it impossible for Windows NT do load Winhelp.

Make sure that UPEDIT.HLP is in your Windows NT SYSTEM 32 directory.

Unable to shutdown the system.

[Setup]

This can happen during initial installation of Windows NT.

Wait for a few seconds, and then manually restart the computer.

Unable to shutdown the system.

[Repair Disk]

This can happen during initial installation of Windows NT.

Wait for a few seconds, and then manually restart the computer.

Unable to start help.

[Network]

Either the Help files are not in your Windows NT SYSTEM 32 directory (or are corrupt), or you do not have enough available memory to start the Help program.

Look for files with the .HLP extension in the SYSTEM directory. If they are not there, use the setup program to install the Help files. If the files are present, close some applications and try again. If you still get this message, delete the files with the .HLP and reinstall them.

Unable to start help.

[Services for Macintosh (SFM)]

Contact technical support.

Unable to start packet reception on the adapter "*name* ".

[Services for Macintosh (SFM)]

The protocol was unable to let the adapter know that its ready to accept incoming packets. The protocol may not see any computers on the network on that adapter and vice versa.

Try stopping and restarting the AppleTalk protocol. Also try using another adapter if possible.

Unable to start services with Service Controller

[Control Panel]

The service controller performs such operations as loading and unloading drivers and starting critical network services. Currently, it is unable to start services.

See the event log in Event Viewer for details, then contact your system administrator.

Unable to start the File Server for Macintosh service.

[Services for Macintosh (SFM)]

Check the Event Log in Event Viewer for related errors. Be sure to make a note of this information to relay it to technical support.

Unable to start the router on adapter "*name* " because a node could not be acquired.

[Services for Macintosh (SFM)]

The server may be running out of memory. Or, even though it is unlikely, the AppleTalk network might have too many computers in it. If this is the case, all the node addresses are in use by other computers.

Check the server's available disk space. If the server requires more memory, try stopping other running applications and services. You might also need to remove unused files and applications from the server's disk. If the disk has sufficient memory, try shutting down some other computers and then try starting the AppleTalk Protocol using the Devices option in Control Panel.

Unable to stop the File Server for Macintosh service.

[Services for Macintosh (SFM)]

Contact technical support.

Unable to take ownership because the account "*name*" could not be accessed on the remote machine due to the following error: *text*

[Security]

An error occurred while trying to determine the owner of the selected file or directory. For example, you tried to take ownership of a resource on a remote computer, but your user account/primary group does not exist on the remote computer.

Contact the owner of the selected object, and make sure that the current owner has given you Full Control of the selected object.

Unable to translate ANSI to Unicode.

[Services for Macintosh (SFM)]

Contact technical support.

Unable to translate Unicode to ANSI.

[Services for Macintosh (SFM)]

Contact technical support.

Unable to unlink driver *name* **from under driver** *name*. **Error code** *name*.

[Netevent]

A streams plumbing problem has occurred. The Registry may be corrupted or was installed improperly.

Remove the TCP/IP protocol and then reinstall it using the Network option in Control Panel.

Unable to unload the media.

[Kernel32]

An application may have attempted to electronically eject a tape from a drive that does not support that.

Try manually ejecting the tape. If that does not work, contact the supplier of the running application.

Unable to unlock "*filename* ".

[Services for Macintosh (SFM)]

A range of bytes is an area that is in use. This is an internal error.

Contact technical support.

Unable to unlock configuration from Service Controller

[Control Panel]

The lock on the configuration could not be released. This may mean that your application is still working with the information.

Reboot and try again.

Unable to update local security in order to join domain.

[Control Panel]

In order for this computer to join a new domain, the application must make changes to the local security information. The application was unable to make these changes.

Make sure you have the necessary privileges to change local security. You might need to log on as a member of the Administrators group.

Unable to update the Desktop database for volume "*name* ".

[Services for Macintosh (SFM)]

Increase disk space by removing unneeded files and applications.

Unable to update the password because a password update rule has been violated.

[Kernel32]

Examples are: (1) the new password contains too many characters; (2) the administrator may have put limits on how often a password can be changed; or (3) the new password matches a password in the recent history log and the administrator does not want passwords to be reused.

Ask your administrator what the password update rules are, and then retry the operation.

Unable to update the password. The value provided as the current password is incorrect.

[Kernel32]

Try again with the correct value of the password.

Unable to update the password. The value provided for the new password contains values that are not allowed in passwords.

[Kernel32]

For instance, the new password may contain characters that cannot be entered from the keyboard.

Try again, retyping the new password.

Unable to use the network.

[Setup]

During maintenance Setup, either the network is not physically present (there is no network adapter installed or the network cable is disconnected from the network adapter), or one of the Setup support libraries could not be found.

Select Retry in the message box to retry the operation. If the message recurs, select the Exit Setup button and begin the initial installation again. If the message still occurs, contact your technical support group.

Unable to use the network.

[Repair Disk]

During maintenance Setup, either the network is not physically present (there is no network adapter installed or the network cable is disconnected from the network adapter), or one of the Setup support libraries could not be found.

Select Retry in the message box to retry the operation. If the message recurs, select the Exit Setup button and begin the initial installation again. If the message still occurs, contact your technical support group.

Unable to validate administrator's privilege. Access was denied.

[Services for Macintosh (SFM)]

Either you are not an administrator or you do not have administrator's privilege to administer Services for Macintosh.

Unable to write "*filename* ".

[Services for Macintosh (SFM)]

Your system may be low on disk space.

The server will recover. No action is needed.

Unable to write a line to INI file: *filename* **Section:** *name* **Key:** *name*.

[Setup]

During installation, Setup was unable to write the specified profile string to an .INI file.

Select Retry to retry the operation. If you get the same message, select Exit Setup. Then make sure there is enough room on the disk for the file. You may have to remove some unneeded files to make room. If that is not the problem, contact your technical support group.

Unable to write a line to INI file: *filename* **Section:** *name* **Key:** *name*.

[Repair Disk]

During installation, Setup was unable to write the specified profile string to an .INI file.

Select Retry to retry the operation. If you get the same message, select Exit Setup. Then make sure there is enough room on the disk for the file. You may have to remove some unneeded files to make room. If that is not the problem, contact your technical support group.

Unable to write security information.

[Backup]

An error occurred while the application was writing security information for one or more files.

No action is needed. However, you might want to make sure the permissions are set correctly for this data.

Unable to write the Alert names because the Services Control Database is locked by *user name* **for** *text*

[Server Manager]

Server Manager could not write the computer names to receive alerts because the Services Control Database is locked.

Try again later. Or contact the user who has locked the Services Control Database.

Unable to write to the file *filename***.**

[Setup]

Select Retry to retry the operation. If you get the same message, select Exit Setup. Then make sure there is enough room on the disk for the file. You may have to remove some unneeded files to make room. If that is not the problem, contact your technical support group.

Unable to write to the file *filename***.**

[Repair Disk]

Select Retry to retry the operation. If you get the same message, select Exit Setup. Then make sure there is enough room on the disk for the file. You may have to remove some unneeded files to make room. If that is not the problem, contact your technical support group.

Unable to write to the specified file.

[Setup]

Select Retry in the message box to retry the operation. If you get the same message, choose Exit Setup and begin the initial installation again. If the message still occurs, contact your technical support group.

Unable to write to the specified file.

[Repair Disk]

Select Retry in the message box to retry the operation. If you get the same message, choose Exit Setup and begin the initial installation again. If the message still occurs, contact your technical support group.

Unable to write to the tape in *drive letter***.**

[Backup]

You attempted to back up to a tape the format of which Backup does not recognize.

Insert a tape that Backup supports.

Unable to write to this file.

[Network]

This message should occur only on a down-level computer. Any action to correct the problem should be performed on that computer.

Undefined variable.

[Help]

This error is from the Macro Language Editor for online help, and should not appear while using the Help file. Report this error to the provider of the Help file.

Unexpected adapter close.

[Dynamic Data Exchange]

The network adapter card or the network adapter driver ended transmission unexpectedly.

Make sure the card is properly seated and that the cable is snug. Also make sure the driver is working properly. You might need to reinstall the driver.

Unexpected condition detected. Try operation again. From device: *name*

[QIC117]

A tape drive fault occurred.

Try again. If you continue to get this message, contact the hardware manufacturer.

Unexpected DOS error: *number***.**

[Program Manager] [Task Manager]

The application encountered an error for which it has no action.

Look up the indicated error and take appropriate action. Then try again. If you still get this message, call technical support.

Unexpected end of backup set encountered on *drive letter***.**

[Backup]

You aborted a restore operation while a file was being copied.

No action is needed.

Unexpected End of File

[File Compare]

The Comp command unexpectedly reached the end of one of the files being compared. If you see this message with the Comp command, most likely the file allocation table (FAT) entry for the file has been corrupted, causing part of the file to be lost.

The Chkdsk command with the /f switch may be able to recover all or part of the missing portions of a text file.

Unexpected product type *number.*

[PORTUAS]

The product type should be either a 1 or 2 for Windows NT and Windows NT Advanced Server, respectively.

Make sure you are running a version of PortUAS that is compatible with your operating system. If so, contact technical support because your Registry may be corrupted.

Unexpected return code *code* **from API** *name.*

[PORTUAS]

If the return code is 2100 or higher, type NET HELPMSG <code> at the command prompt. Otherwise, contact technical support.

Unknown error

[Backup]

Contact the supplier of the tape drive.

Unknown Error

[Registry Editor]

You attempted to print Registry data, the print job failed, and Regedt32 cannot determine specifically the nature of the problem.

Try again. Then, make sure that your printer connections are secure and that the printer is properly configured.

Unknown error

[Remote Access Service]

This is an internal error. The components may be out of synchronization.

Restart the system. If you continue to see this error message, check the Event Log in Event Viewer for information about related errors. Event Viewer is found in the Administrative Tools group.

Unknown Error Code returned by Lana number *number* while adding node name to network: *text*

[Dynamic Data Exchange]

An error was returned from the adapter card that is assigned the indicated LANA number.

Make sure the card is well seated and is working properly. Look in Event Viewer for related messages that appeared at about the same time as this one, and take appropriate action on those errors.

Unknown error.

[Print Manager]

An unknown error has been received from the system.

Contact technical support.

Unknown file type specified on line *number* in section *number*.

[Setup]

Contact the supplier for another copy of the installation media.

unknown host: *name*

[TCP/IP]

When using the TCP/IP Finger command, either you specified an invalid value for the host parameter; or the parameter was valid, but the host is not available to the network.

Check the host name parameter you typed. If it looks valid, ask your network administrator why that host is not available on the network. The host name you used is not in the HOSTS file on your computer or known to the Domain Name Service (DNS).

Unknown NetBIOS error

[Dynamic Data Exchange]

NetBIOS encountered an error for which it has no response.

Contact technical support. Report this message, and the number of the error as reported in the event log.

Unknown network card.

[Control Panel]

The installation of the TCP/IP protocol was terminated and the system was restarted.

Ask your system administrator to reinstall the operating system.

Unknown network card.

[TCP/IP]

The installation of the TCP/IP protocol was terminated and the system was restarted.

Ask your system administrator to reinstall TCP/IP. If you still get this message, remove and re-install the network card. If you still get this message after that, re-install Windows NT.

Unknown network card.

[IP]

The installation of the TCP/IP protocol was terminated and the system was restarted.

Re-install IPX. If you still get this message, re-install all network components.

Unknown printer driver. Please verify that a *computer name* **driver is installed on** *text*

[Common Dialog]

The application needs to use a printer driver that is not available.

Use Print Manager to make sure the indicated driver is available, and to install it if necessary.

Unknown registry value type specified on line *number* **!u! in section** *number***.**

[Setup]

Contact the supplier for another copy of the installation media.

Unknown state.

[Remote Access Service]

Use the Network option in Control Panel to remove and reinstall RAS.

Unreadable EA header. Cannot check EA log.

[Chkdsk]

The extended attribute file cannot be made readable. Unfortunately, some update information for extended attributes may be lost.

No action is needed.

Unreadable master file table. CHKDSK aborted.

[Chkdsk-NTFS]

Chkdsk could not read the master file table or its mirror on the NTFS volume.

Reformat the NTFS volume. Then restore the data from a backup.

Unrecognized error *number* **(** *number* **).**

[Print Manager]

Contact technical support.

Unrecognized message received in mailslot.

[Network] Net Message ID: 3215

A software error occurred.

Contact technical support.

Unrecognized Operating System on C:*text.*

[Setup]

Windows NT can detect the following operating systems: Windows NT; MS DOS; PC DOS; and OS/2.

Unrecognized response from the device.

[Remote Access Service]

Your modem (or other connecting device) has returned a message that is not listed in one or more of your Remote Access script files (PAD.INF, MODEM.INF, or SWITCH.INF).

If you are connecting through a supported modem, turn the modem off and back on. Then redial. If the problem persists, try connecting at a lower initial speed. For more information, see "Setting Modem Features" in the Remote Access Service online Help. If you are connecting through an unsupported modem, make sure that the indicated response is included in the appropriate script file. See "Modem Script File" in the Remote Access Service online Help. The Remote Access script files are located in the \SYSTEM32\RAS subdirectory of your Windows NT directory.

Unrecognized switch -*text***.**

[Command Prompt]

The switch that you used is inappropriate for the current command.

To determine which switches are appropriate for the command, type the command at the command prompt, then type /?.

Unrecoverable error in directory *name*

[Chkdsk]

The specified directory is too corrupt to repair.

As soon as possible, back up files from the specified directory. Chkdsk may also recover files from the affected directory and put them in the FOUND.xxx file.

Unrecoverable read error on drive *drive letter* **side** *number***, track** *number*

[Disk Copy]

The data could not be read from the specified disk on the indicated side and track.

Copy the files on this disk to another disk using the Copy or Xcopy command. Then use that floppy disk as the source disk for any more uses of the Diskcopy command. When you use Diskcopy, you want the source disk to be without bad sectors or flaws.

Unrecoverable write error on drive *drive letter* **side** *number*, **track** *number*

[Disk Copy]

The data could not be written to the disk in the specified drive on the indicated side and track.

Try again with a new disk.

Unsupported Adobe Type 1 file format.

[Fonts (CP)]

The font file is corrupt or does not conform to the Printer Font Binary (PFB) file format.

Restore the file from a backup, or obtain a new copy of the file.

Unsupported operator: ' *name* **'.**

[Fonts (CP)]

There is a problem with the font.

Call the vendor of the font and report this message.

Unsupported sector size. Cannot convert volume to *text*.

[Convert]

The sector size on this HPFS volume is not 512 bytes.

This volume cannot be converted. Back up all files, format the volume to NTFS, and then restore files.

Unused, unreadable, or unwritable portion of EA file removed.

[Chkdsk]

No data was lost.

No action is needed.

Use 'Configure' to customize any selected item.

[Control Panel]

Possibly, you attempted to activate another Setup application at the same time that you are using the Network option.

Wait until the other application that is using the process is complete, then try again.

User *user name* **at host** *computer name* **has timed-out after** *number* **seconds of inactivity.**

[FTP Server]

You may want to increase the Time Out limit of FTP Server with the Network option in Control Panel.

User *user name* denied access to the current directory *name* due to a security change.

[FTP Server]

A system administrator altered the read-access to the specified directory.

Contact your system administrator to request access to the specified directory.

User *user name* failed to log on, could not access the home directory *name*.

[FTP Server]

The specified user's logon was validated but the path for the user's home directory is invalid so the connection was terminated.

Check the path specified for the user's home directory.

User *user name* is already a member of group *group*.

[Network]

No action is needed.

User *user name* already exists. The security database is being updated...

[PORTUAS]

The security database is being updated with the current information for the specified user.

No action is needed.

user ' *user name* ' already exists as a global group name in the Windows NT security database *text*

[PORTUAS]

PortUAS will ask you for another name for the user, unless the Force Ignore option has been implemented.

user ' *user name* ' already exists as a local group name in the Windows NT security database.

[PORTUAS]

PortUAS will ask you for another name for the user, unless the Force Ignore option has been implemented.

User accounts can be unlocked but cannot be locked. Accounts are locked out by too many logon attempts with bad passwords.

[User Manager]

No action is needed. If you want, you can disable the account in the User Properties dialog box.

User configuration data for parameter *parameter* overriding firmware configuration data.

The settings you have specified are being used instead of the settings supplied by the manufacturer.

No action is needed.

User configuration data is overriding firmware configuration data.

Your settings, which are different from the settings supplied by the manufacturer, will be used to configure the device.

No action is needed.

User configuration for parameter *number* **must have** *text***.**

The indicated value entry is required but was not supplied.

Supply the required value.

Users have open files on *computer name***. Continuing the operation will force the files closed.**

[Network]

If the files are forced closed, the users might lose work or the files could be corrupted.

Contact the users and ask them to close files and programs they have open on this share or computer. Try again after the users have had a chance to close the files.

Using private DIALOG window words.

[Kernel32]

An application, as part of its user interface, has encountered this.

Contact the supplier of the running application.

Value name *name* **not found in Configuration Registry**

[Control Panel]

The Network option cannot complete the current operation because it is unable to locate an essential value entry.

See the event log in Event Viewer for details. Then contact your system administrator.

Value not found in Configuration Registry

[Control Panel]

The Network option cannot complete the current operation because it is unable to locate an essential value entry.

See the event log in Event Viewer for details. Then contact your system administrator.

Verbose output not supported by NTFS CHKDSK.

[Chkdsk-NTFS]

The Chkdsk command has a /v (verbose) option, which causes Chkdsk to display the full path and name of every file on the disk. However, the NTFS file system does not support this option. Large NTFS volumes can contain far too many files for such a display to be practical. Use File Manager to look at the paths and names of files on an NTFS volume.

This is an informational message. If you want to avoid this message in the future, do not use the /v option with the Chkdsk command when you are using Chkdsk on an NTFS volume.

Viewer Help file not found.

[Disk Administrator]

Make sure the file VIEWER.HLP is available. If it is not, install it from your application disk.

Virtual Device Driver format in the registry is invalid.

[Virtual DOS Machine (VDM)]

The name of the Registry key with the bad format is displayed in the message box.

Write down the name of the invalid Registry key and ask your system administrator to change that Registry key.

Volume label is not supported with /8 parameter.

[Format]

You cannot specify a volume label on a disk formatted with the /8 switch. This action is not permitted.

Volume sets cannot include partitions on removable media.

[Disk Administrator]

Because a volume set cannot maintain integrity if part of the set is removed, no part of the set can be on removable media.

Try again, specifying only permanent media.

Waiting for a process to open the other end of the pipe.

[Kernel32]

This is an informational message. No action is needed.

Warning! F parameter not specified. Running CHKDSK in read-only mode.

[Chkdsk-NTFS]

To fix errors on a disk volume, run Chkdsk with the /f switch.

WARNING! The *name* **file system is not enabled. Would you like to enable it (Y/N)?** *text*

[Utilities]

The I/O subsystem should automatically recognize and enable file systems.

Contact technical support.

WARNING! Diskette is out of sequence. Replace diskette or continue if OK *text*

[Repair Disk]

Restore the disks in the order that you backed them up.

WARNING! File *filename* **Is a read only file. Replace the file (Y/N)?** *text*

[Repair Disk]

Type Y if want to restore the read-only file from the backup disk. Type N if you do not want to restore this file.

Warning! File *filename* was changed after it was backed up. Replace the file (Y/N)? *text*

[Repair Disk]

The file you specified has changed since you created the backup. If you replace the file from the backup, you will lose any changes made since the backup was created.

Type Y if you want to replace the file, or type N if you do not.

WARNING! No files were found to restore

[Repair Disk]

The Restore command did not find the file that you specified on the backup disk.

Make sure you typed the filename correctly.

WARNING, ALL DATA ON NON-REMOVABLE DISKDRIVE *drive letter* : WILL BE LOST! Proceed with Format (Y/N)? *text*

[Format]

To format a hard disk, you must log on as an administrator or have administrator privileges.

To format the hard disk, choose Y. If you do not want to format the hard disk, choose N.

WARNING: Because of a lazy-write error, drive *drive letter* nowcontains some corrupted data. The cache is stopped.

[Network] Net Message ID: 3180

This message should occur only on a down-level computer. Any action to correct the problem should be performed on that computer. An error occurred when the lazy-write process tried to write to the specified hard disk.

Run CHKDSK on the specified drive to check for problems with the disk or the files affected by the lazy-write process.

Warning: Failed to notify library.

You attempted to save an object into the client application, and this attempt failed.

Try again. Then contact your system administrator.

WARNING: You have chosen to format this tape. All of the information on the tape will be destroyed!

[Backup]

If you are sure you want to format this tape, choose OK. If this tape has data that you do not want to lose, choose Cancel.

Warning: You will not be able to undo this action using the Undo command.

Most likely, you are low on system resources.

Close one or more of the windows or applications that you have running, then try again.

WARNING: "*filename*" is a corrupt file. This file cannot be verified.

[Backup]

The named file is corrupt.

No action is needed. However, you might want to restore the named file from a different backup set.

Warning: All data in the floppy disk will be erased.

[Repair Disk]

If this disk has data that you want to save, replace it with a blank disk or one that you want to overwrite before continuing.

WARNING: ALL of the data on the tape in *drive letter* will be replaced. Tape:*name* Tape #*number* Set #*number*:*name*. Do you want to replace this information?

[Backup]

If you continue this operation, the tape will be erased and then overwritten. All the data that is currently on the tape will be lost.

If you want to erase all the data on this tape and replace it with new data, choose Yes. Otherwise, choose No.

Warning: the attempted Domain change operation failed. This machine is currently not a member of any domain.

[Control Panel]

Try the operation again. If you continue to get this message, see the event log in Event Viewer for details. Then contact your network administrator.

Warning: the attempted Domain change operation failed. This machine is currently not a member of any domain. The error was: *text*

[Control Panel]

Because you are not a member of this domain, you may be unable to access any of the domain's resources.

Contact the domain administrator to determine the cause of the failure.

WARNING: The corrupt file *filename* was restored.

[Backup]

The named file was corrupt on the backup tape. This corrupt file has been restored to the target directory.

No action is needed. However, you might want to examine the file for missing or garbled data. You might also want to restore another version of the file from a different tape family.

WARNING: The CORRUPT.LST file was found. This file indicates that corrupt file(s) have been backed up.

[Backup]

CORRUPT.LST is created when a corrupt file is backed up. If CORRUPT.LST exists when files are being restored, this message appears to remind you to restore the files from another backup.

You should check this file before trying to backup, then delete it. If you do not, this message appears. Choose OK, then delete the CORRUPT.LST file. You might also want to restore the files in CORRUPT.LST from an earlier backup.

WARNING: The in-use file ***filename*** **was restored.**

[Backup]

The named file was in use when the backup version of that file was restored. The backup version was restored anyway.

No action is needed.

WARNING: This backup set contains Macintosh folders and files. To restore this information, filenames and directory names may need to be abbreviated from their original Macintosh format.

[Backup]

No action is needed. If necessary, the filenames will be abbreviated by the Backup application.

Warning: This operation will overwrite the data contained on this volume. Are you sure you wish to continue with this operation?

[Disk Administrator]

If you continue, all the data on this volume will be lost. You might want to have a backup copy of all data on the volume before completing this operation.

WARNING: This tape was created with the Transfer option. The data on this tape may have been permanently erased from your disk.

[Backup]

The transfer option moves data from the source to the target. The data that is about to overwritten may not exist anywhere else.

Be sure that you want to overwrite the data on this tape.

When accessing a new tape of a multivolume partition, the currentblocksize is incorrect.

[Kernel32]

Contact the supplier of the running application.

When focused on the remote computer *computer name*, you can only save the log in log file format on that computer.

[Event Viewer]

While focused on a remote computer, you have attempted to save a log file with an .EVT extension on a computer other than the one that you are focusing on.

Type a path for the file on the computer of focus.

While accessing the hard disk, a disk controller reset was needed, buteven that failed.

[Kernel32]

This is a hardware problem.

Contact the hard disk vendor and/or the disk controller vendor.

While accessing the hard disk, a disk operation failed even after retries.

[Kernel32]

Run the Chkdsk utility, with the /r switch, on the hard disk. After that, if you still get this message, run hardware diagnostics on the disk drive and it's controller. If the diagnostics do not detect a problem, contact the hardware and/or driver software suppliers. Before you contact the suppliers, note the information about the event that is in the Event Log. Information in both the Description and Data areas of the Event Detail window will be relevant to this problem.

While accessing the hard disk, a recalibrate operation failed, even after retries.

[Kernel32]

Run the Chkdsk utility, with the /r switch, on the hard disk. After that, if you still get this message, run hardware diagnostics on the disk drive and its controller. If the diagnostics do not detect a problem, contact the hardware and/or driver software suppliers. Before you contact the suppliers, note the information about the event that is in the Event Log. Information in both the Description and Data areas of the Event Detail window will be relevant to this problem.

While validating that *name* was really a serial port, a fifo was detected. The fifo will be used.

No action is needed.

While verifying the validity of old replicas, a name mismatch was noticed. The local record has the name *name* while the replica pulled in from the WINS that owns this record has the name *name*. This could mean that the remote WINS was brought down and then up again but its version counter value was set to its previous value before termination.

[WINS Service]

WINS will recover automatically.

Wildcard deletion of IP gateway table entries is not permitted.

[Netevent]

The IP received an invalid request from a route utility. The command is incorrect.

No action is needed because invalid requests are discarded.

Window creation failed!

[Volume Control]

You attempted to run Volume Control and the system was unable to generate the Volume Control window.

Contact your system administrator.

Windows did not make a copy of the font ' ***filename*** **'; do you want to delete the original font file?**

[Program Manager]

This font has not been copied to the \SYSTEM directory. If you delete this font file, you will not be able to use the font at a later time.

To save the file for use at another time, remove the font but leave the Delete Font File From Disk checkbox clear.

Windows did not make a copy of the font ' ***filename*** **'; do you want to delete the original font file?**

[Program Manager]

If you delete this file, you will not be able to use the font at a later time.

To save the file for use at another time, remove the font but leave the Delete Font File From Disk checkbox clear.

Windows NT could not be started as configured. A previous working configuration was used instead.

[Netevent]

The system detected an incorrect configuration so the system reverted to the last correct configuration.

Use Event Viewer to check the event log for details about the incorrect configuration.

Windows NT could not be started as configured. A previous working configuration was used instead.

[Network]

No action is needed. Be cautious about repeating changes that you made to your configuration the last time you started your computer.

Windows NT error 0x *number*

[Network]

Look up the specified message and take appropriate action.

Windows NT error 0x *code*

[Services for Macintosh (SFM)]

Contact technical support.

Windows NT error 0x *number* occurred.

[Network]

Look up the specified message and take appropriate action.

Windows NT error 0x *code* occurred.

[Services for Macintosh (SFM)]

Contact technical support.

Windows NT Networking is not installed. Install it now?

[Control Panel]

If you want to use the Windows NT networking feature, and want to install it now, choose Yes. Otherwise, choose No.

Wins adjusted a scavenging related time interval (*number*) so that it is compatible with the replication time intervals.

[WINS Service]

WINS regularly scavenges for names that are no longer in use, so that they can be registered to a requesting client. WINS assigns a time interval for scavenging. WINS also adjusts the time intervals set by the administrator so that they are suitable multiples of the maximum interval at which replications occur between push and pull partners.

No action is needed.

Wins adjusted a scavenging related time interval (*number*).

[WINS Service]

WINS regularly scavenges for names that are no longer in use, so that they can be registered to a requesting client. WINS assigns a time interval for scavenging.

No action is needed.

WINS Challenger thread encountered an exception.

[WINS Service]

Other activity on the computer has affected the activity of the specified thread. WINS will try to recover from the exception automatically.

No action is needed. If this error occurs often, stop and restart the WINS service.

WINS could not close an open key.

[WINS Service]

There is a shortage of some resource, such as memory, on the computer.

Reboot the computer.

WINS could not create a heap (a portion of memory reserved for the program's use) because of a resource shortage. Check if the computer is running short of virtual memory.

[WINS Service]

WINS could not reserve a portion of memory for itself because of a memory shortage on this computer.

Close some applications and try again. If you get this error often, you might want to add memory or change your pagefile size.

WINS could not create the TCP socket for listening to TCP connections. Make sure the TCP/IP driver is installed and running properly.

[WINS Service]

WINS was unable to perform a preliminary task. The task requires interaction with the TCP/IP driver.

Choose Network from the Control Panel and make sure the TCP/IP driver is installed and running. Then try again.

WINS could not create the TCP socket for making a TCP connection. Make sure the TCP/IP driver is installed and running properly.

[WINS Service]

WINS was unable to perform a preliminary task. The task requires interaction with the TCP/IP driver.

Choose Network from the Control Panel and make sure the TCP/IP driver is installed and running. Then try again.

WINS could not create the UDP socket for listening for connection notification messages sent by another thread (PULL thread) in the local WINS.

[WINS Service]

Make sure the TCP/IP driver is installed and running properly. Also, check the general health of this computer.

WINS could not create the UDP socket for listening for UDP packets. Make sure the TCP/IP driver is installed and running properly.

[WINS Service]

WINS was unable to perform a preliminary task. The task requires interaction with the TCP/IP driver.

Choose Network from the Control Panel and make sure the TCP/IP driver is installed and running. Then try again.

WINS could not do Static initialization

[WINS Service]

WINS attempted to initialize the database from a file, but was unable to do so.

Take the action recommended by the message that accompanied this one.

WINS could not get information about a key.

[WINS Service]

One or more keys in the WINS section of the Registry were deleted.

No action is needed. If you want, you can replace the keys using Regedit or by reinstalling WINS.

WINS could not get information about the DATAFILES key.

[WINS Service]

The indicated key in the WINS section of the Registry was deleted.

No action is needed. If you want, you can replace keys using Regedit or by reinstalling WINS.

WINS could not get information about the PULL key.

[WINS Service]

The indicated key in the WINS section of the Registry was deleted.

No action is needed. If you want, you can replace keys using Regedit or by reinstalling WINS.

WINS could not get information about the PUSH key.

[WINS Service]

The indicated key in the WINS section of the Registry was deleted.

No action is needed. If you want, you can replace keys using Regedit or by reinstalling WINS.

WINS could not get the time interval from a PULL record.

[WINS Service]

There will not be periodic pull replication with the Pull partner.

Use WINS Manager to specify a time interval for periodic replication.

WINS could not get the update count from a PUSH record.

[WINS Service]

The WINS server will not send notification messages to the WINS server listed under the Push key.

Use WINS Manager to specify an update count if you want notification messages to be sent.

Wins could not initialize because of some problem with the RPC service. Make sure that the RPC service is running.

[WINS Service]

In order for WINS to be monitored or administered, the RPC service must be running on the WINS server. The WINS service has started but could not initialize with the RPC service. Therefore WINS is running but cannot be monitored or administered.

Stop the WINS service. Then make sure that the RPC service is correctly configured and started before starting the WINS service again.

WINS could not open a subkey of the PULL key

[WINS Service]

The indicated key in the WINS section of the Registry was deleted.

No action is needed. If you want, you can replace keys using Regedit or by reinstalling WINS.

WINS could not open a subkey of the PUSH key.

[WINS Service]

The indicated key in the WINS section of the Registry was deleted.

No action is needed. If you want, you can replace keys using Regedit or by reinstalling WINS.

Wins could not open the file (*filename*) to be used for doing static initialization. Please check if the file is existent and readable.

[WINS Service]

The specified file must be opened by WINS in order for WINS to start.

Make sure the specified file is present and that its permissions allow the person who started WINS to read it.

WINS could not read the InitTimeReplication field of the PULL/PUSH key.

[WINS Service]

The indicated key in the WINS section of the Registry was deleted.

No action is needed. If you want, you can replace keys using Regedit or by reinstalling WINS.

WINS could not read the Refresh Interval from the registry

[WINS Service]

The indicated key in the WINS section of the Registry was deleted.

No action is needed. If you want, you can replace keys using Regedit or by reinstalling WINS.

WINS could not read the retry count for retrying communication with a remote WINS

[WINS Service]

The indicated key in the WINS section of the Registry was deleted.

No action is needed. If you want, you can replace keys using Regedit or by reinstalling WINS.

WINS could not read the Tombstone Interval from the registry

[WINS Service]

The indicated key in the WINS section of the Registry was deleted.

No action is needed. If you want, you can replace keys using Regedit or by reinstalling WINS.

WINS could not read the Tombstone Timeout from the registry

[WINS Service]

The indicated key in the WINS section of the Registry was deleted.

No action is needed. If you want, you can replace keys using Regedit or by reinstalling WINS.

WINS could not read the Verify Interval from the registry

[WINS Service]

The indicated key in the WINS section of the Registry was deleted.

No action is needed. If you want, you can replace keys using Regedit or by reinstalling WINS.

WINS could not set up the database properly.

[WINS Service]

Restore the WINS database from a backup copy, and restart the WINS service. If you still get this message, reinstall WINS.

WINS did not find any subkeys under the PULL key

[WINS Service]

This computer has no Pull partners.

No action is needed.

WINS did not find any subkeys under the PUSH key

[WINS Service]

This computer has no Push partners.

No action is needed.

WINS did not send a notification message to the WINS server whose address is given below, because it had a number of communications failures with that server in the past few minutes.

[WINS Service]

Normally each WINS server notifies its pull partner whenever there is a change in its address database, or when enough updates have occurred to trigger a notification. The specified WINS server was not notified of a recent change, because there have been several communication failures with this server in the past few minutes.

Check the specified server and correct any problems with its communication hardware or software. Check the network and routers, and correct any problems that would interfere with communication between these servers. If you still get this message, call Microsoft Product Support.

WINS does not support this functionality as yet.

[WINS Service]

No action is needed.

WINS encountered a memory error. Check to see if the system is running out of virtual memory.

[WINS Service]

You might need to close some applications and try again. Or, choose System from the Control Panel to change the Virtual Memory settings.

WINS encountered an error doing backup of the database to directory *name*. The error is given in the data section. The file where it occurred is *filename*.

[WINS Service]

Check to make sure the directory you specified exists, and make sure there is enough space on this disk for the backup file. Then try again. If you still get this message, call technical support.

WINS encountered an error while deleting the file *filename*. The error is given in the data section.

[WINS Service]

WINS creates a temporary file while importing a static mapping file. The file is then deleted. However, the permissions on the file were changed before the file could be deleted.

Delete this file explicitly. You might need to change the permissions on the file first.

WINS encountered an exception while processing a pull trigger.

[WINS Service]

A pull trigger became active because the conditions for pulling data were met. However, WINS was unable to implement the trigger.

You might want to manually pull data, using the Replication Partners dialog box.

WINS encountered an exception while retrieving data records

[WINS Service]

WINS retrieves records from the database as a result of a pull request from another WINS server or from an administrator. It also retrieves records while scavenging.

If this error appeared after you tried to manually pull records, try again. Otherwise, you need not do anything. WINS will try again after the appropriate time interval.

WINS got a Name Request with an invalid opcode. The request is being thrownaway

[WINS Service]

A delayed response was received, or a message was garbled in transit.

Ignore this message.

WINS got a packet that has the wrong format (for example, a label may be more than 63 octets).

[WINS Service]

Bad packets are being received by the WINS server.

If this message appears often, call technical support. Otherwise, ignore this message.

WINS got an exception while trying to release a record in the database. It is not known whether the exception occurred after or before the release was done

[WINS Service]

Use WINS Manager to see whether the record has been released, and release it explicitly if necessary.

WINS got an exception while trying to query a record in the database.

[WINS Service]

Check the general health of the WINS server. You might need to restore the WINS database from a backup copy.

WINS got an exception while trying to register a group entry. It is not known whether the exception occurred after or before the registration.

[WINS Service]

Use WINS Manager to see whether the record was registered, and register it explicitly if you wish. You might want to check the general health of the WINS server and then call technical support.

WINS got an exception while trying to register a replica. It is probably due to owner limit having been reached. Check the previous log entry

[WINS Service]

The maximum number of WINS servers is 25.

Use WINS Manager to see if there are already 25 WINS servers (for example, Push partners and Pull partners) listed in the database, delete some that are no longer active. Then try again.

WINS got an exception while trying to register a special group's replica. It is not known whether the exception occurred after or before the registration.

[WINS Service]

Use WINS Manager to see whether the record was registered, and register it explicitly if you wish.

WINS got an exception while trying to register a unique entry. It is not known whether the exception occurred after or before the registration.

[WINS Service]

Check the WINS server to see that it is generally healthy (enough memory, for example). You can use WINS Manager to see if the entry was registered, and register it explicitly; however if you register it explicitly it will be a static record. Call technical support if you get this message often.

WINS got an exception while trying to register a unique replica. It is not known whether the exception occurred after or before the registration.

[WINS Service]

Check the WINS server to see that it is generally healthy (enough memory, for example). You can use WINS Manager to see if the entry was registered, and register it explicitly; however if you register it explicitly it will be a static record. Call technical support if you get this message often.

WINS got an exception while trying to update the version number of a record in the database. It is not known whether the exception occurred after or before the update.

[WINS Service]

Check the WINS server to see that it is generally healthy (enough memory, for example). You can use WINS Manager to see if the entry was registered, and register it explicitly; however if you register it explicitly it will be a static record. Call technical support if you get this message often.

WINS has encountered an error that is causing it to shut down.

[WINS Service]

Check the Event log to find out what error caused WINS to shut down. Then take the appropriate action for that error.

WINS is being gracefully terminated by the administrator. The address of the administrator is *address*.

[WINS Service]

If you want, you can contact the administrator at the indicated network address to find out why the WINS service was stopped and when it will be available again.

WINS is has been asked to pull entries from its own self. Check all the subkeys of the PULL key for this WINS.

[WINS Service]

Use Regedit32 to make sure none of the entries under the PULL key list this computer's own address.

WINS Pull thread encountered an exception during the process of sending a push notification to another WINS. The exception code is given below in the data section.

[WINS Service]

The replication was not completed. There might have been a communication failure with the remote WINS server.

Make sure the remote WINS server and the router are up, and then use the Replication Partners dialog box to trigger immediate replication.

WINS Push thread encountered an exception. It will try to recover. The exception code is given in the data section below.

[WINS Service]

The replication was not completed, probably due to a communications failure.

Check if the WINS Push partners are up and running, and make sure all network connection between the WINS servers are working properly.

WINS received a replica whose state is incorrect. For example, it may have received a replica with state of RELEASED or it may have received the replica of a special (internet) group which does not have any members (i.e. all members are timed out) but state is not TOMBSTONE.

[WINS Service]

The information might have been corrupted in transit.

No action is needed.

WINS Rpl Pul Handler could not connect to a WINS server. All retries failed. WINS will try again after certain number of replication time intervals have elapsed.

[WINS Service]

WINS tried to pull address data from another WINS server, without success. It will try again later.

No action is needed. If this error happens frequently, there may be problems with the network that need to be identified and corrected.

WINS Scavenger thread could not scavenge a record. Will ignore this error and continue on to the next record if there.

[WINS Service]

No action is needed.

WINS Scavenger thread encountered an exception.

[WINS Service]

Other activity on the computer has affected the activity of the specified thread. WINS will try to recover from the exception automatically.

No action is needed. If this error occurs often, stop and restart the WINS service.

WINS sent a name query or a name release with a certain transaction id. It got back a response to its request which differed either in the name that it contained or in the opcode. WINS has thrown the response away.

[WINS Service]

A delayed response was received, or a corrupt packet was received.

Not action is necessary. WINS will recover automatically.

WINS TCP Listener thread encountered an exception.

[WINS Service]

Other activity on the computer has affected the activity of the specified thread. WINS will try to recover from the exception automatically.

No action is needed. If this error occurs often, stop and restart the WINS service.

WINS Timer thread encountered an exception.

[WINS Service]

Other activity on the computer has affected the activity of the specified thread. WINS will try to recover from the exception automatically.

No action is needed. If this error occurs often, stop and restart the WINS service.

WINS UDP Listener thread encountered an exception.

[WINS Service]

Other activity on the computer has affected the activity of the specified thread. WINS will try to recover from the exception automatically.

No action is needed. If this error occurs often, stop and restart the WINS service.

WINS was either provided a bad command code or else it got corrupted.

[WINS Service]

A packet might have been corrupted in transit.

No action is needed. If you see this message often, contact technical support.

WINS was terminated by the service controller. Wins will gracefully terminate.

[WINS Service]

No action is needed.

WINS was unable to propagate the push trigger.

[WINS Service]

There was a request to propagate a push trigger, but the trigger could not be propagated. The request either was made by the user or was sent from a push partner. The problem might be due to a communications failure.

Initiate a push using the Replication Partners dialog box.

Winsock Send could not send all the bytes. Connection could have been aborted by the remote client

[WINS Service]

This could be due to a communications failure.

Make sure the Push partners, Pull partners, and router are all running. Then try again.

WinSock send function returned with an unexpected error

[WINS Service]

This could be due to a communications failure.

Make sure the Push partners, Pull partners, and router are all running. Then try again.

Winsock startup routine failed. The NwSapAgent cannot continue.

[Netevent]

The application could not be started. You probably have an incompatible version of the WinSock interface.

Make sure you are running the current version of both Windows NT and the SAP Agent.

Workgroup name cannot be the same as the machine name.

[Control Panel]

You have attempted to join a workgroup that has the same name as your computer. This functionality is not permitted.

Rename your computer.

WOWExec Extremely Low on Memory

Close other applications or increase your pagefile, and try again.

Write error on local file ***filename*** **disk write error occurred** *text.*

[TFTP]

During the transfer of a file from a remote computer to your computer, the Tftp utility encountered an unrecoverable write error on your disk.

Retry the file transfer. If you still get this message, either run Chkdsk with the /r switch on your disk, or use a different disk as the destination of the file transfer. Then retry the Tftp command. You may need to contact your system administrator to diagnose your disk problems.

Write error.

[Recover-FAT/HPFS]

HPFS Recover encountered an error trying to write file data or file system structures.

Run Chkdsk /f and try the operation again.

Write protect error accessing drive.

[Xcopy]

You cannot format or write a file to a write-protected disk.

Either remove the write-protection, or use another disk.

Write to ConsoleOut error == *code*

[FTP Server]

The FTP service was unable to prompt for your password. The service cannot continue.

Reboot your computer and try again. If you still get this message, call technical support, and report this message and the error code displayed at the end of the message.

Wrong information specified.

[Remote Access Service]

The Remote Access Phone Book file and the current Remote Access configuration are probably inconsistent.

If you have changed your communications equipment (such as your serial port or modem), be sure to reconfigure Remote Access. Use the Network option in Control Panel to reconfigure Remote Access.

X.25 diagnostic indication.

[Remote Access Service]

Your X.25 connection has returned an error.

Ask your X.25 provider to interpret the diagnostic information provided.

You already have a connection to the domain. You must disconnect before joining the domain.

[Control Panel]

No action is needed. If you want to rejoin the domain with different user name or password, break the connection to the domain and then try again.

You are already using *application* to adjust your network connections. Choose the OK button to switch to the dialog you were using.

[Program Manager]

You cannot have two applications attempting to adjust network connections at the same time.

Choose OK. Then adjust the network connections from the resulting dialog box.

You are already using *application* to install or configure a printer. Choose the OK button to switch to the dialog you were using.

[Program Manager]

You cannot have two applications attempting to configure a printer at the same time.

Choose OK. Then configure the printer from the resulting dialog box.

You are inserting over a selection that contains open embedded objects. Close the open embedded objects by quitting the server application, and then try again.

[Write]

You used the Insert Object command to insert over a selection that contains an open embedded object.

Quit the server application (Paintbrush or Sound Recorder, for example), then perform the insert operation.

You are missing the necessary files to complete this operation. Make sure that OLECLI.DLL and OLESVR.DLL are in your Windows SYSTEM directory. If these files are missing, try reinstalling Windows.

[Cardfile]

In File Manager, search for OLECLI.DLL and OLESVR.DLL files, and move them to the SYSTEM32 directory.

You are not logged on. You must be logged as an admin to administer Remote Access servers.

[Remote Access Service]

Logon as an administrator or use an account with administrator privilege to administer the servers.

You are not logged onto the Windows NT workstation as a member of the user group that has the right to view the workstation's Recovery settings.

[Program Manager]

To view the Recovery settings in the Control Panel's System option, you must be logged onto the Windows NT workstation as an administrator or as a user who has been granted permission to read these settings.

Log on as an administrator or as a user who has the necessary permissions, and try again.

You are not logged onto the Windows NT workstation as a member of the user group that has the right to view the workstation's Recovery settings.

[Program Manager]

Log on as a different user and try again.

You are not logged onto the Windows NT workstation as a member of the user group that has the right to view the workstation's Virtual Memory settings.

[Program Manager]

Log on as a different user and try again.

You are not logged onto the Windows NT workstation as a member of the user group that has the right to view the workstation's Virtual Memory settings.

[Program Manager]

To view the Virtual Memory settings in the Control Panel's System option, you must be logged onto the Windows NT workstation as an administrator or as a user who has been granted permission to read these settings.

Log on as an administrator or as a user who has the necessary permissions, and try again.

You are still connected to a remote computer. Do you want to hang up and end your connection?

[Terminal]

When you are finished communicating with another computer, you must end the connection to that computer before you can establish a connection with another computer. Windows NT prompts you to do this.

To end your connection you must either type the exit command specified by the remote system (typically, "bye"), or choose the Hangup option from the Phone menu.

You are trying to paste into a card that already contains an open embedded object. Before you can complete this paste operation, you must close the object by closing the server application.

[Cardfile]

You have attempted to paste an embedded object into a card that already contains an open embedded object while the server application (the application in which the object was created) is still running.

To complete the operation, close the application in which the new embedded object was created, then try again.

You can only perform this operation on printers and communication devices.

[Network] Net Message ID: 3738

This command is valid only for device names of printers and communication devices.

No action is needed.

You can only specify a whole number between 1 and 32767.

[Write]

You used the Go To option, then specified a page number of 0, or a negative number.

Specify a valid number.

You can only type a positive number in the Height box.

[Paintbrush]

When you select the Image Attributes option in the Options menu, you must specify a positive number in the Image Attributes dialog box as the size of your image.

Double-check the height measurement specified in the Image Attributes dialog box to ensure that you have entered a positive number.

You can only type a positive number in the Width box.

[Paintbrush]

When you select the Image Attributes option in the Options menu, you must specify a positive number in the Image Attributes dialog box as the size of your image.

Double-check the height measurement specified in the Image Attributes dialog box to ensure that you have entered a positive number.

You can only type a positive number.

[Paintbrush]

Choosing the Page Setup option in the File menu, you designated a negative number as the margin for your Paintbrush image.

Change the negative margin that you entered in the Page Setup dialog box to a positive number.

You can view security information only for objects of the same type. Select only files or select only directories.

[Security]

You attempted to view permissions information on a mixed selection of files and directories. Because files and subdirectories often have different permissions than do their parent directory, this action is not permitted.

Follow the user action specified in the message.

You cannot check both User Must Change Password at Next Logon and User Cannot Change Password for the same user.

[User Manager]

You have selected both the Force Password Change at Next Logon, and the User Cannot Change Password options for the same user. Thus, the User Properties dialog box contains two contradictory properties.

Select OK, then choose either the User Must Change Password at Next Logon or User Cannot Change Password option.

You cannot delete *text* because it is referenced by *text*. Change the setup or patch map references, and then try again.

[MIDI Mapper (Control Panel)]

The word referenced in this message indicates that the listed patch/key map needs the listed setup/patch map to run. You cannot delete a key map that is used in a patch map or a patch map that is used in a MIDI setup.

Select OK, then change the setup or patch map references.

You cannot remove the default zone, unless it is the only zone in the zone list.

[Services for Macintosh (SFM)]

Make another zone in the list the default zone. Then remove the previous default zone from the list.

You cannot rename the root directory.

[File Manager]

You attempted to use the Rename option in the File menu to assign a new name to the root directory. File Manager does not permit you to rename the root directory.

Choose OK.

You cannot specify more than one zone for LocalTalk networks.

[Services for Macintosh (SFM)]

In LocalTalk networks, each physical network can be associated with only one zone. The Registry was edited to specify more than one zone for a network.

Use the Network option in Control Panel to reconfigure Services for Macintosh. Select Services for Macintosh and then choose Configure. Routing must be enabled. Remove the zone you don't want.

You do not have access to set UPS options.

[Control Panel]

You are not logged onto this workstation as a member of a local group that has the right to set UPS options.

Log onto this workstation under your administrative account. Or contact your system administrator.

You do not have administrator or supervisor privileges on *computer name.*

You attempted to perform an operation on the server that you don't have the privilege to perform.

Logon to the server as an administrator or supervisor or, contact your system administrator to perform the operation.

You do not have permission to access portions of *name*. **Please see the owner or administrator to get permission.**

[Backup]

The application cannot access portions of this directory in order to back it up or restore it, because your user account does not have permission to write to the directory.

Ask that permission be given to you, or log in as a user with the necessary permission.

You do not have permission to access portions of *name*. **Please see the owner or administrator to get permission.**

[Backup]

The application cannot access portions of this file in order to back it up or restore it, because your user account does not have permission to write to the file.

Ask that permission be given to you, or log in as a user with the necessary permission.

You do not have permission to access portions of *name*. Please see the owner or administrator to get permission.

[Backup]

The application cannot access portions of this directory or file in order to back it up or restore it, because your user account does not have permission to access the directory or file.

Ask that permission be given to you, or log in as a user with the necessary permission.

You do not have permission to access this directory.

[File Manager]

You attempted to open a directory that you do not have permission to open.

Contact the owner of the directory or the system administrator. If you are the owner of the directory, log off, then log onto the user account under which you assigned permission on the directory.

You do not have permission to access this file.

[File Manager]

You have attempted to access a file that you do not have permission to access.

Contact your system administrator or the owner of the file or directory. If you are the owner of the file, log on under the user account that you used to assign permissions on the file.

You do not have permission to change the security information on this printer.

[Print Manager]

You are not logged on as a member of the Administrators or Printer Operators local groups, and you have not been granted permission to perform the current operation.

Contact your system administrator. Or log onto this computer as a member of a local group that possesses the right to perform the current operation.

You do not have permission to change your password.

[Workstation-Logon]

The administrator of this workstation has not granted you the permission to change your password.

Consult your administrator. If you are the system administrator, log off, log on again under your administrative user account, and use the Properties option in User Manager to assign the right to change passwords to your other user account.

You do not have permission to shutdown this computer.

[Program Manager]

You are not logged on as a member of the Administrators or Printer Operators local groups, and you have not been granted permission to perform the current operation.

Contact your system administrator. Or log onto this computer as a member of a local group that possesses the right to perform the current operation.

You do not have permission to view the current owner but you may have permission to change it. Do you want to try overwriting the current owner?

[Security]

You have attempted to identify the owner of a file or directory to which you do not have Read access. However, you may be able to take ownership of the selected resource.

To attempt to overwrite the current owner, use the Ownership option on the Security menu.

You do not have permission to view the current security information for *name* but you may have permission to change it. Do you want to try overwriting the current security information?

[Security]

You do not have Read permissions on the currently selected resource, but may have permission to write to it.

To attempt to overwrite the current security information, choose Yes, then change the permissions. If you do not want to do this, choose No.

You do not have permission to view the security information for *name* but you may have permission to change it. Do you want to try overwriting the current security information for all of the selected items?

[Security]

You do not have Read permissions on the currently selected resource, but may have permission to write to it.

To attempt to overwrite the current security information, choose Yes, then change the permissions. If you do not want to do this, choose No.

You do not have sufficient permission to access the specified device, path or file.

[Program Manager]

You are logged on to a user account that lacks the level of permission required to access the specified device, path, or file.

Contact your system administrator. If you are the system administrator, log onto a user account that has permission to access the specified device, path, or file.

You do not have the proper privilege level to change the System Time.

[Program Manager]

Log on as a different user and try again.

You do not have the proper privilege level to change the System Time.

[Program Manager]

To change the System Time in the Control Panel's System option, you must be logged onto the Windows NT workstation as an administrator or as a user who has been granted permission to change this setting.

Log on as an administrator or as a user who has the necessary permissions, and try again.

You don't have enough disk space. Please remove some TCP/IP components.

[TCP/IP]

Delete enough files from the disk to make room for the TCP/IP components you want to install and try again. Or, install fewer components.

You entered an invalid value for the *command* option.

[Network]

To get a list of the options for the command, type net help <command> /options

You have either specified an invalid IP address or the end address is smaller than the start address.

[Remote Access Service]

Make sure you specify a valid IP address and make sure the end address is greater than the start address.

You have entered an invalid zone name.

[Services for Macintosh (SFM)]

The zone name you have entered contains invalid characters such as periods (.), at signs @, colons (:), apostrophes ('), or semicolons (;).

Enter a zone name that does not contain invalid characters.

You have exceeded the operating system's limit on the number of users and groups that can be in a security information structure. Remove some users or groups and try the operation again.

[Security]

You have added too many users or groups for this resource.

Remove some users or groups and retry the operation.

You have insufficient privilege to add or remove a driver

[Drivers (CP)]

The permission to install device drivers on Windows NT is reserved to users logged on either as an administrators or as a Power User.

Exit Windows NT and log on as either as an administrator or a Power User.

You have insufficient privilege to install or remove kernel driver file *filename*

[Drivers (CP)]

The permission to install or remove this driver file on Windows NT is reserved to users logged on either as an administrators or as a Power User.

Exit Windows NT and log on as either as an administrator or a Power User.

You have insufficient privilege to restart the system

[Drivers (CP)]

Exit Windows NT and log on as either as an administrator or a Power User.

You have not entered a valid selection.

[Network]

The name you entered while trying to set the focus is not a valid computername or domainname.

Make sure you have the correct name, and try again. If you are using a computername, be sure to precede the name with two backslashes (\\).

You have not selected a modem. Press OK to go back and make a selection that matches your modem.

[Remote Access Service]

The modem selection was set to none and you chose the OK button.

Select a valid modem entry and then choose OK.

You have not tried these new settings successfully. Please press the Test button to preview this new graphics mode.

[Display]

It is important that you test these settings while you are still in the Display Settings dialog box. Some settings are incompatible with some display drivers or monitors. This dialog allows you to recover from such problems.

Choose Test.

You have selected no password expiration. The user will not be required to change passwords at next logon.

[User Manager]

Only one of the two checkboxes, User Must Change Password at Next Logon and Password Never Expires, should be marked. Both were marked when you chose OK.

Clear one of the checkboxes and try again.

You have specified a value that is incompatible with servers with down-level software. Please specify a lower value.

[Network] Net Message ID: 3817

User account values cannot be replicated to down-level servers unless the account values are compatible with the down-level server's values.

No action is needed.

You have specified an IP End address that is less than the IP Start address. Please change the End address.

[Remote Access Service]

Use the Network option in Control Panel to specify an end address which is greater than or equal to the start address. For example, valid start and end addresses would be: 11.101.237.61 - 11.101.237.65. Choose Network. Then select Remote Access Service. Choose Configure and then choose Network. Change the IP end address.

You have the fastest time for beginner level. Please enter your name.

[Minesweeper]

When you perform very well on Minesweeper, you are presented with this message, and a dialog box in which to enter your name.

Enter your name, then choose OK.

You have the fastest time for expert level. Please enter your name.

[Minesweeper]

When you perform very well on Minesweeper, you are presented with this message, and a dialog box in which to enter your name.

Enter your name, then choose OK.

You have the fastest time for intermediate level. Please enter your name.

[Minesweeper]

When you perform very well on Minesweeper, you are presented with this message, and a dialog box in which to enter your name.

Enter your name, then choose OK.

You may not be able to browse all of the domains to which you have access because the following error occurred: *text*

[Network]

Most likely, the domain controller for one of the domains to which you have access is temporarily malfunctioning.

Look up the indicated error and take appropriate action. If one of the network resources that you need is unavailable, wait, and then try again.

You may not be able to browse all of the domains to which you have access because the following error occurred: *code*

[Security]

A problem occurred while you were attempting to enumerate the trusted domains of the server. Most likely, the domain controller for one of the domains to which you have access is temporarily malfunctioning.

If one of the network resources that you need is unavailable, wait, and then try again. If waiting does not eliminate the error, consult the event log in Event Viewer for details, and see your system administrator. Contact technical support and provide the details from the event log, as well as the number that appears in the error message.

You may not delete your own account.

[User Manager]

You have attempted to delete your own account, and User Manager does not permit this action.

No action is needed.

You may not remove the Local Logon right from the Administrators local group. Doing so would disable all local administration of this computer.

[User Manager]

In the User Rights Policy dialog box, you have attempted to remove the Local Logon right from the Administrator's local group. User Manager does not permit this option.

Select OK.

You may not specify paths for ADMIN$ and IPC$ shares.

[Network] Net Message ID: 3778

When you are creating the special shares IPC$ or ADMIN$, you may not specify a path.

Retype the command without a path. For example, type NET SHARE ADMIN$.

You must be an administrator or account operator to manage user accounts. The changes you made will leave you with insufficient privilege to administrate users in *group*. Do you want to continue?

[User Manager]

You have opted to remove your Administrative account from a server in your domain. When you make this selection, User Manager for Domains presents you with this confirmation message.

If you want to delete the account, choose Yes. If not, choose No.

You must be an administrator or account operator to manage user accounts. The changes you made will leave you with insufficient privilege to administrate users on *computer name*. Do you want to continue?

[User Manager]

You have opted to remove your Administrative account from a domain. When you select this option, User Manager for Domains presents you with this confirmation prompt.

If you are sure that you want to delete the account, choose Yes. If not, choose No.

You must be logged onto this system as an Administrator to change the Virtual Memory settings.

[Program Manager]

You attempted to change the Virtual Memory settings without sufficient privilege.

Log onto the workstation as an administrator, then try again to change the workstation's Virtual Memory settings.

You must be logged onto this system as an Administrator to change the Virtual Memory settings.

[Program Manager]

You attempted to change the Virtual Memory settings without sufficient privilege.

Log onto the workstation as an administrator, then try again to change the workstation's Virtual Memory settings.

You must be logged onto this system as an Administrator to install a new option on the system.

[Program Manager]

You attempted to install a new option, and you lack sufficient privilege.

Log onto the Windows NT workstation as an administrator, then try again to install a new option.

You must be logged onto this system as an Administrator to install a new option on the system.

[Program Manager]

You attempted to install a new option, and you lack sufficient privilege.

Log onto the Windows NT workstation as an administrator, then try again to install a new option.

You must be logged onto this workstation as an administrator to perform this operation on hard disks.

[File Manager]

Log on as an administrator, or ask an administrator to perform the operation.

You must insert tape 1 of the family to identify the tape.

[Backup]

The general information about the data on this tape is on the first tape in the sequence. (This message appears only if you start Backup while a Sytos Plus continuation tape is in the tape drive.)

Insert Tape 1 for this set of tapes.

You must re-boot this system for the VirtualMemory Paging file changes to take effect.

[Program Manager]

The Virtual Memory option in the System option box allows you to dictate the amount of memory that will be allocated to paging files. You have changed these settings, and now, you must restart your system for these changes to take effect.

From the File Menu in Program Manager, select the Shutdown option. When the Shutdown Computer dialog box appears, select the Restart when shutdown is complete option, then choose OK.

You must specify a name in the Domain Name Service (DNS) Search Order.

[Control Panel]

You must specify a name in the Domain Name Service (DNS) Search Order when you select any option except Hosts File Only.

Select Hosts File Only or add a DNS name.

You must specify a name in the Domain Name Service (DNS) Search Order.

[TCP/IP]

You must specify a name in the Domain Name Service (DNS) Search Order when you select any option except Hosts File Only.

Select Hosts File Only or add a DNS name.

You must specify a username and password if allowing anonymous connections.

[Control Panel]

You have left the Domain Name field blank.

Make an entry in this field.

You must specify the name of this computer's domain in the Domain Name field

[Control Panel]

You have left the Domain Name field blank.

Make an entry in this field.

You must supply a valid printer name.

[Print Manager]

You attempted to create a printer in Print Manager, but left the Printer Name option blank.

Assign a name of 20 characters or less to the printer that you are creating.

You must supply a valid printer name.

[Print Manager]

An error occurred when you attempted to add a port in Print Manager.

See the event log in Event Viewer for details on the error. Or contact your system administrator.

You must type a valid Group Name for the group.

[User Manager]

Global Group Names in User Manager for Domains can consist of no more than 20 characters, cannot be left blank, and cannot contain invalid characters (; : " < > * + = \\ | ? ,).

Specify a Global Group Name of twenty characters or less, containing only valid characters, then choose OK.

You must type a valid Group Name for the local group.

[User Manager]

In the New Group dialog box, you have specified a group name that exceeds the limit of 20 characters, have left the option blank, or have included invalid characters. The following are invalid characters for a group name: (; : " <> * + = \\ | ? ,).

Select OK to return to the User Manager window, then specify a valid group name.

You must type a valid Username for the user.

[User Manager]

In the New User dialog box, you have specified a user name that exceeds the limit of 20 characters, have left the option blank, or have included invalid characters. The following are invalid characters for a user name: (; : " <> * + = \\ | ? ,).

Select OK to return to the User Manager window, then specify a valid user name.

You only have permission to view the current security information on *name*.

[Security]

You have attempted to access an object on which read-only permissions have been set.

Choose OK. Then, if you want write permission, contact your system administrator, or contact the owner of the file.

You requested remote home directories for the selected user(s), but did not specify a remote home directory. Specify a remote home directory.

[User Manager]

In the Home Directory portion of the User Environment Profile, you chose the Connect radio button but did not specify a network path in the To box.

Specify a network path in the To box.

You specified an invalid file number.

[Network] Net Message ID: 3960

The file identification number you specified is either outside the valid range or is nonnumeric.

Retype the command with a valid file identification number. To see a list of the server's open files and their identification numbers, type NET FILE.

You specified an invalid print job number.

[Network] Net Message ID: 3961

The print job identification number you specified is either outside the valid range or is nonnumeric.

Retype the command with a valid print job identification number. To see a list of a server's print jobs, type NET PRINT \\\\<computer name>\\<share name>.

You specified an invalid remote home drive. Choose a drive letter or leave this field blank.

[User Manager]

In the User Environment Profile dialog box, you have requested a remote home directory, and have specified a drive path in the To option box, but have not specified the drive to which you want this home directory connected.

Select the Connect option in the Home Directory option box, then specify a drive name in the option box to the right of the Connect option.

You specified too many values for the *name* option.

[Network] Net Message ID: 3951

You specified too many values for the listed option.

Retype the command with the correct number of values. To see the syntax of this command, type NET HELP <command>.

You typed an invalid number. You must enter a valid number.

[Event Viewer]

In the Event ID option in the Find or Filter dialog box, you typed something besides a number.

Specify an event number, then try again.

You used an invalid option.

[Network] Net Message ID: 3501

You typed an invalid command option.

To see a list of options for this command, type NET HELP <command>. When typing commands, remember that most options must be preceded with a slash, as in /DELETE.

You used an option with an invalid value.

[Network] Net Message ID: 3505

You typed an incorrect value for a command option.

To see the syntax of this command and its options, type NET HELP <command>/OPTIONS.

You will not be able to use the Undo command to undo this action.

[Cardfile]

Because you computer is low on memory, you will not be able to undo the current action.

Select OK, close some of the applications that you have running, and then try again.

You will not receive network message popups.

[Remote Access Service]

Another computer already connected to the network is using your messaging name. Messages addressed to you will be sent to that computer.

If you want to receive messages at your remote workstation, you must remember to log off your office computer before you next dial in to the network.

Your account does not have permission to do this.

[PORTUAS]

PortUAS has stopped without making any updates to the Windows NT security database.

You must log on as an administrator to update the security database.

Your account has been disabled. Please see your system administrator.

[Workstation-Logon]

The administrator of this workstation has disabled this user account.

See your system administrator to have your account reenabled. Or, if you are the system administrator, log on to the workstation as the administrator, then use the Properties option in User Manager to reenable the disabled account.

Your account has expired. Please see your system administrator.

[Workstation-Logon]

The system administrator determines how long you have an account on a workstation, and yours has expired.

Contact the administrator. If you are the system administrator, and you wish to prolong the validity of this account, use User Manager for Domains to change the account's expiration date.

Your account has time restrictions that prevent you from logging on at this time. Please try again later.

[Workstation-Logon]

The administrator of a domain can determine the hours during which a user can log on to a workstation. You have attempted to work on a workstation during a time when you are not permitted to work.

Try logging on during your allotted hours. Or consult your administrator to set new logon hours. If you are an administrator, use User Manager for Domains to set logon hours.

Your account is configured to prevent you from using this workstation. Please try another workstation.

[Workstation-Logon]

You have been locked out of the workstation, probably by the system administrator.

Contact your system administrator. If you are the system administrator, log off, then log on under your administrator account.

Your central profile could not be updated with the local copy, write permission denied. Please contact your administrator.

[Workstation-Logon]

Ask the administrator to give you write protections on the profile file.

Your COM Port settings have changed.

[Program Manager]

You used the Ports option in Control Panel to change your COM Port settings.

No action is needed.

Your Crash Recovery system settings have changed.

[Program Manager]

No action is needed.

Your Crash Recovery system settings have changed.

[Program Manager]

You used the System option in Control Panel to change your Recovery settings.

No action is needed.

Your default gateway does not belong to one of the configured interfaces. Do you want to change it?

[TCP/IP]

The default gateway is not equal to one of the network identifiers (IP address or subnet mask).

Select No to ignore the dialog or Yes to change the default gateway.

Your file waiting to be printed was deleted.

[Kernel32]

The file you recently submitted for printing was deleted by another user on the server.

Contact the other user to find out why the file was deleted, or retry the command at a later time.

Your modem (or other connecting device) has reported an error.

[Remote Access Service]

Your modem (or other connecting device) has reported an error.

If you are using a supported modem, turn the modem off and then back on. Close and restart the Remote Access Service, and then redial. If your modem is not supported by Remote Access, contact your modem's manufacturer. For a list of supported modems, see the Windows NT Hardware Compatibility List. Make sure you have correctly configured your modem for Remote Access. For more information about checking your configuration, see "Reconfiguring Remote Access" in the Remote Access Service online Help.

Your modem (or other connecting device) is not functioning.

[Remote Access Service]

Your modem (or other connecting device) is not responding because the modem has been turned off, or the modem is not securely connected to your computer, or the serial cable does not have the correct specifications required by Remote Access, or the modem has experienced a hardware glitch.

Make sure your cable is securely fastened to both the modem and the computer. If so, verify that the serial cable has the correct specifications. For more information, see "Cabling Requirements" in the Remote Access Service online Help. If the modem has experienced a hardware glitch, turn off the modem, wait for 20 seconds, and then restart it.

Your new password does not meet the minimum length or password history requirements of the domain. Your password must be at least *number* characters long. Your new password cannot be the same as any of your previous *number* passwords.

[Workstation-Logon]

The options presented in this message have been set by the administrator of this workstation in the workstation's Account Policy.

If you want to change this policy, consult the administrator of this workstation. If you are the administrator of this workstation, and you want to redefine account policy, log on under your administrator account and choose the Account Policy option on the Policies menu in User Manager.

Your password cannot be changed until *date*.

[Network] Net Message ID: 3759

This message should occur only on a down-level computer. Any action to correct the problem should be performed on that computer. You cannot change your password until the listed date because of LAN Manager security restrictions.

Contact your network administrator if your password needs to be changed now. Otherwise, wait until the listed date to change your password.

Your password has expired and must be changed.

[Workstation-Logon]

Choose OK. When a dialog box appears prompting you for your new password, make sure that your entries in the Password and Confirm Password option boxes match, and then choose OK.

Your password is *number* days old, but it must be *number* days old before it can be changed.

[Workstation-Logon]

A user who logged onto this workstation as an administrator has determined in the Account Policy that a password must be a minimum age before it can be changed, and your password has not reached this age.

If you are the administrator of this workstation, log on as an administrator, open User Manager, then use the Account Policy option on the Policies menu to change the Minimum Password Age.

Your password will expire in *number* days. Do you want to change it now?

[Workstation-Logon]

The Account Policy on your workstation determines the minimum and maximum period of time that you can use the same password. Yours will expire in the specified number of days.

If you want to change your password now, select Yes and specify the same password in both the Password and Confirm Password options. Then choose OK.

Your persistent connections were not all restored.

[Network]

Loading of the profile stopped after an error occurred.

No action is needed.

Your system does not have any communication ports installed or the device driver for the communication port is not started.

[Remote Access Service]

Use the Ports option in Control Panel to verify installed ports. Use the Devices option in Control Panel to verify that the device driver is loaded and started.

Your system is running without a properly sized paging file. Please use the virtual memory option of the System applet in the Control Panel to create a paging file, or to increase the initial size of your paging file.

[Workstation-Logon]

A Paging File enables your system to make optimal use of memory.

To create such a file, choose the Virtual Memory option in the System option in Control Panel and specify the appropriate options.

Your TrueType system setting has changed.

[Program Manager]

No action is needed.

Your Virtual Memory and Crash Recovery system settings have changed.

[Program Manager]

No action is needed.

Your Virtual Memory and Crash Recovery system settings have changed.

[Program Manager]

You used the System option in Control Panel to change your Virtual Memory and Recovery settings.

No action is needed.

Your Virtual Memory system settings have changed.

[Program Manager]

No action is needed.

Your Virtual Memory system settings have changed.

[Program Manager]

You used the System option in Control Panel to change your Virtual Memory settings.

No action is needed.